Time Out

Milan

timeout.com/milan

Published by Time Out Guides Ltd, a wholly owned subsidiary of Time Out Group Ltd.
Time Out and the Time Out logo are trademarks of Time Out Group Ltd.

© Time Out Group Ltd 2005
Previous edition 2002

10 9 8 7 6 5 4 3 2 1

Milan 2nd edition (0-141-01617-5) first published in Great Britain in 2004 by the Penguin Group
This edition published in Great Britain in 2005 by Ebury Publishing
Ebury Publishing is a division of The Random House Group Ltd,
20 Vauxhall Bridge Road, London SW1V 2SA

Random House Australia Pty Limited 20 Alfred Street, Milsons Point, Sydney, New South Wales 2061, Australia
Random House New Zealand Limited 18 Poland Road, Glenfield, Auckland 10, New Zealand
Random House South Africa (Pty) Limited Endulini, 5A Jubilee Road, Parktown 2193, South Africa

Random House UK Limited Reg. No. 954009

Distributed in USA by Publishers Group West
1700 Fourth Street, Berkeley, California 94710

Distributed in Canada by Penguin Canada Ltd
10 Alcorn Avenue, Toronto, Ontario, Canada M4V 3B2

For further distribution details, see www.timeout.com

ISBN 1-904978-09-6

A CIP catalogue record for this book is available from the British Library

Colour reprographics by Icon, Crowne House, 56-58 Southwark Street, London SE1 1UN

Printed and bound in Germany by Appl
Papers used by Ebury Publishing are natural, recyclable products made from wood grown in sustainable forests

Edited and designed by
Time Out Guides Limited
Universal House
251 Tottenham Court Road
London W1T 7AB
Tel + 44 (0)20 7813 3000
Fax + 44 (0)20 7813 6001
Email guides@timeout.com
www.timeout.com

Editorial

Editor Sylvia Tombesi-Walton
Deputy Editor Nick Funnell
Consultants Roberta Kedzierski, Simone Muzza
Listings Researcher Simone Muzza
Proofreader Angela Jameson
Indexer Julie Hurrell

Editorial/Managing Director Peter Fiennes
Series Editor Ruth Jarvis
Deputy Series Editor Lesley McCave
Guides Co-ordinator Anna Norman
Accountant Sarah Bostock

Design

Art Director Mandy Martin
Acting Art Director Scott Moore
Acting Art Editor Tracey Ridgewell
Acting Senior Designer Astrid Kogler
Designer Sam Lands
Junior Designer Oliver Knight
Digital Imaging Dan Conway
Ad Make-up Charlotte Blythe

Picture Desk

Picture Editor Jael Marschner
Deputy Picture Editor Kit Burnet
Picture Researchers Ivy Lahon
Picture Desk Assistant Laura Lord

Advertising

Sales Director Mark Phillips
International Sales Manager Ross Canadé
International Sales Executive Simon Davies
Advertising Sales (Milan) MAD & Co International
Advertising Assistant Lucy Butler

Marketing

Marketing Manager Mandy Martinez
US Publicity & Marketing Associate Rosella Albanese

Production

Guides Production Director Mark Lamond
Production Controller Samantha Furniss

Time Out Group

Chairman Tony Elliott
Managing Director Mike Hardwick
Group Financial Director Richard Waterlow
Group Commercial Director Lesley Gill
Group Marketing Director Christine Cort
Group General Manager Nichola Coulthard
Group Art Director John Oakey
Online Managing Director David Pepper
Group Production Director Steve Proctor
Group IT Director Simon Chappell

Contributors

Introduction Monica Larner. **History** Gregory Dowling, Anne Hanley (*Coming to germs*; *Milan's heroines*; *Five alive* Roberta Kedzierski). **Milan Today** Mark Worden. **Art in Milan & Lombardy** Deborah Ball (*The dark side* Roberta Kedzierski). **Media Central** John Moretti. **Economic Powerhouse** Michael Thompson. **Where to Stay** Aaron Maines. **Sightseeing** Anne Hanley, Aaron Maines, Clarice Zdanski (*Novel approach* Gregory Dowling; *The woman on top*; *Brera's best-kept secret*; *The house Poldi Pezzoli built*; *Inside track*; *Battle royale*; *A family's fortunes* Aaron Maines). **Restaurants** Michael Thompson; *additional reviews* Simone Muzza, Sylvia Tombesi-Walton. **Cafés & Bars** Mark Worden; *additional reviews* Simone Muzza, Sylvia Tombesi-Walton. **Shops & Services** Valerie Waterhouse. **Festivals & Events** Gudrun Lake. **Children** Valerie Waterhouse. **Film** Aaron Maines. **Galleries** Roberta Kedzierski. **Gay & Lesbian** Jeremy Hayne, Francesco Lucchese. **Music** Mark Worden. **Nightlife** John Moretti; *additional reviews* Simone Muzza, Sylvia Tombesi-Walton. **Sport & Fitness** John Moretti. **Theatre & Dance** Roberta Kedzierski. **Lakes & Cities: Getting Started** Monica Larner. **Lago d'Orta** Valerie Waterhouse. **Lago Maggiore** Gudrun Lake. **Lago di Como** Roberta Kedzierski. **Lago di Garda** Gregory Dowling. **Bergamo & Around** Michael Thompson. **Brescia & Around** Gregory Dowling. **Mantova & Around** Michael Thompson. **Cremona, Crema & Lodi** Roberta Kedzierski. **Pavia & Around** Roberta Kedzierski. **The Mountains** Valerie Waterhouse. **Directory** Jeremy Hayne (*Further Reference* Anne Hanley, Nick Funnell; *Vocabulary* Anne Hanley).

Maps LS International Cartography, via Sanremo 17, 20133 Milan, Italy.
The Milan transport map is used by kind permission of ATM.

Photography Cesare Cicardini, except: page 6 Bridgeman Library; pages 10, 14, 35, 72, 248, 93 Corbis; pages 13, 16 AKG; page 18 Hulton Archive; page 19 Rex Features; page 24 The Art Archive; page 27 Archivio Iconografico, SA/Corbis; page 29 Giansanti Gianni/Corbis Sygma; page 32 courtesy of *TV Sorrisi & Canzoni*; page 153 Getty News; page 241 Massimo Listri/Corbis; page 255 Alamy Images. The following images were provided by the featured establishments/artists: pages 159, 183.

MAD & Co Advertising Advertising & Marketing Director: Margherita Tedone. Tel: +39 06 3550 9145. Fax: +39 06 3550 1775.

The Editor would like to thank: Marilisa Ambrosi, Alessandro Basta, Anne Hanley, Alissia Mancino, and all those who have contributed to the previous edition of this guide. Special thanks to Armando Tombesi, Luise Lorenz and David Tombesi-Walton.

Contents

Introduction   2

In Context   5

History   6
Milan Today   20
Art in Milan & Lombardy   24
Media Central   29
Economic Powerhouse   33

Where to Stay   37

Where to Stay   38

Sightseeing   51

Introduction   52
The Duomo & Central Milan   54
Castello Sforzesco, Brera
    & Northern Milan   66
San Babila & Eastern Milan   75
Porta Romana, the Navigli
    & Southern Milan   82
Sant'Ambrogio & Western Milan   91
Around Milan   99

Eat, Drink, Shop   109

Restaurants   110
Cafés & Bars   125
Shops & Services   131

Arts & Entertainment   151

Festivals & Events   152
Children   155
Film   158
Galleries   161
Gay & Lesbian   165
Music   170
Nightlife   175
Sport & Fitness   179
Theatre & Dance   182

Lakes & Cities   187

Getting Started   188
Lago d'Orta   190
Lago Maggiore   193
Lago di Como   200
Lago di Garda   212
Bergamo & Around   220
Brescia & Around   230

Mantova & Around   237
Cremona, Crema & Lodi   246
Pavia & Around   257
The Mountains   264

Directory   277

Getting Around   278
Resources A-Z   284
Vocabulary   295
Further Reference   296
Index   297
Advertisers' Index   302

Maps   303

Lombardy   304
Greater Milan   306
Milan Overview   307
Street Maps   308
Street Index   313
Milan Metro   316

Introduction

Milan is not an attractive city and perhaps it is not meant to be. Like many of the banality-defying garments that strut down its celebrated catwalks, Milan is about individuality, expression and possibility, about reading between the lines. Other cities, spanning the length of the Italian peninsula, have spent so many years looking up to this dizzying nucleus of frenetic innovation, they must suffer chronic neck spasms because of it. Milan merits admiration and envy because, no matter how you cut it, this city is to post-war Italy what Florence was to the Renaissance and what Rome was to the Baroque.

One of Milan's biggest appeals is that its urban genetics make London and New York first cousins. The Lombard capital is a pulsating metropolis, a melting pot of races, and a capital of media, design and fashion. Consequently, it is very wealthy and the *milanesi* claim they have as many banks as Rome has churches; its rival may have the Vatican, but Milan has the stock market. Wealth and worldliness put it a step ahead of the rest of Italy: urbanites will greet you with 'welcome to Europe, you just left Italy' and nothing could make them prouder.

But that's not to say that Milan is un-Italian. Chatty barmen serve cappuccinos with heart-shaped froth to pretty women, vegetable vendors hawk their goods on market day adding gossip and cooking tips into the bargain, and the city puts on a party in honour of its patron saint Sant'Ambrogio that rivals southern Italy's famous feasts. The saint's day, 7 December, is so important

it marks the opening of La Scala's opera season – the main event in the city's cluttered social calendar.

Milanesi are often depicted as an army of willingly servile, mobile-toting fashion victims. Yet this is a city that works hard, plays hard and knows how to separate the two. As soon as the banks and design studios call it a day, Milan's high-octane nightlife begins. First stop is happy hour. Here the *aperitivo* is more than a gastronomic preface – it's a cultural institution. Free finger foods are doled out with cocktails like bitter-sweet Campari, a Milan native, served in its trademark triangular bottle. And once your appetite has been *stuzzicato*, teased, Milan packs a powerful culinary punch. The city has Italy's highest concentration of gourmet restaurants. If a nightcap doesn't put you to bed, its afterhours activities will see you through to dawn. As a famous advertising campaign put it: This is *Milano da bere* (to be thirstily consumed). But oddly, Milan never seems to have a hangover the next morning.

Many visitors come to see Leonardo's *Last Supper* or to unleash their credit cards on the city's swanky shopping boulevards before moving on to the next city on the Italian Grand Tour. But those who look beyond the glitz and glamour will discover an introspective city with a gentle artistic heart. In this guide, we have done our best to explore Milan's biggest attractions – and uncover her hidden secrets.

And we hope to entice you to put down your bags and stay a while.

ABOUT THE TIME OUT CITY GUIDES

The *Time Out Milan Guide* is one of an expanding series of Time Out City Guides, now numbering over 45, produced by the people behind London and New York's successful listings magazines. Our guides are all written and updated by resident experts who have striven to provide you with all the most up-to-date information you'll need to explore the city or read up on its background, whether you're a local or a first-time visitor.

THE LOWDOWN ON THE LISTINGS

Above all, we've tried to make this guide as useful as possible. Addresses, telephone numbers, websites, transport information, opening times, admission prices and credit

card details are all included in our listings. And, as far as possible, we've given details of facilities, services and events, all checked and correct as we went to press. However, owners and managers can change their arrangements at any time. Also, in Milan, small shops and bars rarely keep precise opening hours, and may close earlier or later than stated. Similarly, arts programmes are often finalised very late. Before you go out of your way, we'd advise you whenever possible to phone and check opening times, ticket prices and other particulars.

While every effort has been made to ensure the accuracy of the information contained in this guide, the publishers cannot accept responsibility for any errors it may contain.

PRICES AND PAYMENT

We have noted where shops, restaurants, hotels and so on accept the following credit cards: American Express (AmEx), Diners Club (DC), MasterCard (MC) and Visa (V). Some shops, restaurants and attractions might also take major travellers' cheques.

THE LIE OF THE LAND

We have divided the city into five areas that do not necessarily reflect the local names; the sightseeing chapters and many others are arranged according to these areas. All other venues elsewhere have been listed with the relevant area name. Wherever possible, a map reference is provided for every venue listed, indicating the page and grid reference at which it can be found on the street maps (*see pp308-12*).

TELEPHONE NUMBERS

It is necessary to dial provincial area codes with all numbers in Italy, even for local calls. Therefore, all normal Milan numbers begin 02, whether you're calling from inside or outside the city. From abroad, you must dial 0039 (the international dialling code for Italy) followed by the number given in the book – which includes the initial 02. For more information on telephones and codes, *see p292*.

ESSENTIAL INFORMATION

For all the practical information you might need for visiting Milan, including emergency phone numbers, visa and customs information, advice on facilities for the disabled, useful websites and details of local transport, turn to the **Directory** chapter at the back of the guide. It starts on page 277.

MAPS

The map section at the back of this book includes a map of the Lombardy region, an overview map of the greater Milan area, detailed street maps of the centre, a transport map showing metro lines and a comprehensive street index. Many of the destinations featured in the Lakes & Cities section (*see pp187-275*) have detailed maps within the appropriate chapters. The maps begin on page 303.

LET US KNOW WHAT YOU THINK

We hope you enjoy the *Time Out Milan Guide*, and we'd like to know what you think of it. We welcome tips for places that you think we should include in future editions and take note of your criticism of our choices. There's a reader's reply card at the back of this book for your feedback, or you can email us at milanguide@timeout.com.

Advertisers

There is an online version of this book, along with guides to 45 other international cities, at **www.timeout.com**.

Italians do it better.

travelplan **it**
Done by Netplan, done by Italians.

www.travelplan.it

You're going to love the Italian portal **Travelplan.it** because it's just like having a guidebook at hand, free and always up to date.
That's why over 100,000 travelers like yourself log on every month and discover a passion for our country, along with absolutely everything needed to visit it.
Because there's only one way to see Italy: with those who really know it.

In Context

History	**6**
Milan Today	**20**
Art in Milan & Lombardy	**24**
Media Central	**29**
Economic Powerhouse	**33**

Features

St Misbehavin'	7
Coming to germs	11
Key events	12
Milan's heroines	15
Five alive	16
Milan's melting pot	23
The dark side	25
Boxing clever	32

History

From Celtic settlement to modern economic powerhouse, via Romans, Sforzas, Austrians and the fascists.

Strategically placed at the gateway to the Italian peninsula, Milan and the surrounding region of Lombardy have been the subject of constant disputes over the centuries. Celts, Romans, Goths, Lombards, Spaniards and Austrians have all ruled the city at some stage of its history, and that's not to mention the two powerful families who imposed their grandiose rule over Milan between the late 13th and early 16th centuries: the Viscontis and the Sforzas. For the most part, the city has capitalised on its position, weathering these changes – and even occasionally fighting back against foreign dominators – and has emerged today as the undisputed economic and cultural powerhouse of a united Italy.

PRE-ROMAN LOMBARDY

From prehistoric times right up to the Roman conquest of the zone, Lombardy's earliest inhabitants, the Camun people, had settlements in the Valcamonica area (*see p271*). Here they left a fascinating glimpse into their obsessions and skills in the thousands of 10,000-year-old picture carvings hacked into the rocks.

Down on the marshy plain of the Po river, other tribes, mostly from Liguria, dwelt in stilt-houses by the side of the region's many lakes. The rest of the Italian peninsula was populated by Italic peoples and Etruscans. Gallo-Celtic tribes moved across the Alps and into the fertile plains of the Po Valley

The **general strike** of 1898. *See p19.*

some time between the fifth and fourth centuries BC, spreading into territory occupied by Ligurians and Etruscans, and pitching camp in the vicinity of what are now Milan, Brescia, Bergamo, and Lombardy's other major cities.

These Celts – and particularly the Insubre tribe, whose settlement where Milan now stands had become large and dominant by this time – had their hearts set on further expansion southwards: in 390 BC only the cackling of geese on Rome's Capitol Hill tipped off sleeping Romans to the fact that the Celts were about to overrun their city. Ultimately, however, the tables turned and it was the Romans who pushed their borders northwards into what they termed Cisalpine Gaul ('Gaul this side of the Alps'). In the 280s they began their slow but unrelenting drive across the Po Valley from the east, founding colonies as they went and conquering the town of Mediolanum (Milan) in 222 BC.

ROMAN MEDIOLANUM
It was not all plain sailing for the Roman conquerors: during the Second Punic War (218-201 BC), for example, northern Italy's Celts and Ligurians rallied to the side of Hannibal, helping the great Carthaginian general's exhausted troops beat the Romans back across the Po.

It was a temporary hitch, though, and by 42 BC Rome had exerted its hold over Cisalpine Gaul sufficiently to make it officially part of its Italian territories. In his reorganisation of Italy in 15 BC, Emperor Augustus (30 BC-AD 14) made Milan the capital of the Transpadania region, which included the towns of Como, Bergamo, Pavia and Lodi, and extended as far west as Turin. No longer a mere military garrison, and with its own municipal and judicial structures, Mediolanum began to take on the importance expected of a city placed so strategically between the Italian peninsula and those areas beyond the Alps where Roman interests were widespread.

During the (relatively) peaceful times that extended from the reign of Augustus, the placid agricultural zone of northern Italy flourished: roads were built and rivers made navigable, to the benefit of both communications and trade. And though the area's elite still preferred their country villas over urban residences, towns were endowed with suitably imposing monuments; this was especially true of Mediolanum.

When barbarian tribes began baying at the Roman empire's northern borders in the third century AD, Diocletian (emperor 284-305) split the empire into two halves to streamline its military capacities. From AD 292 Mediolanum became the effective capital of the western emperor, Diocletian himself, while Byzantium was home to Maximian, his eastern counterpart, leaving Rome to languish.

As Milan's political and military star rose, so did its importance as a centre of Christianity, which – according to local lore – was brought to the city by St Barnabus, a friend of St Paul. Under Diocletian and his persecuting successors, Milan chalked up nearly as many top-notch martyrs as Rome. Constantine the Great (306-37), who reunified the two halves of the empire under his sole control and was only too aware of Mediolanum's strategic importance, diplomatically issued the Edict of Milan (313) putting an end to the persecution of Christians and paving the way for Christianity to become the religion of state. St Ambrose (*see below* **St Misbehavin'**) was elected bishop of Milan in 374, remaining in that office until his death in 397. His legendary piety and charity conferred untold prestige on the local Church, giving his successors in the region unrivalled spiritual and temporal clout for centuries to come.

St Misbehavin'

In a near-contemporary mosaic portrait in the church of Sant'Ambrogio, Milan's patron saint, Ambrose (c334-97), looks simple and humble. It's a misleading picture: this patrician Roman was a man of vast learning, a musician, a writer and an uncompromising weeder-out of heretics. And if his famously charitable works make his saintly status well deserved, his equally famous refusal to buckle under temporal authority gives some measure of the man who set the model for centuries of strong Church control in northern Italy.

Ambrose came to Milan as a public official but was proclaimed bishop by the locals in 374, then hastily ordained afterwards. He was an avid student of the (pagan) ancients, as is obvious from the quotations in and influences on his writings. It was he who imposed his Christian-Neoplatonic ideas on a doubting African convert called Augustine, who would go on to become one of the Church's greatest teachers and a saint.

With a crystal-clear vision of the need for the Church to emerge as a guiding beacon as the Roman Empire declined, Ambrose stood up to even the highest powers. Not only did he refuse to allow Empress Justina to build an Arian chapel in Milan, but also bundled Emperor Theodosius unceremoniously out of his church after news reached him of a massacre perpetrated under the emperor's orders.

RefrigiWear

THE ORIGINAL.
MADE IN AMERICA SINCE 1954

In 402, Emperor Honorius (395-423) moved the seat of the empire to Ravenna, an unfortunate decision that left Milan pretty much at the mercy of waves of attacking barbarian tribes.

After Attila the Hun left the city in 452, Milan was a smouldering wreck. It was partially rebuilt, only to be razed again by the Goths in 489 and 539. Most of the population had taken refuge in the countryside, and the clergy had fled to Genoa. However, by that time, the fate of the beleaguered city was of little interest to anyone. After the death in 476 of the last western emperor, Romulus Augustulus, and the collapse of the empire, Odoacer, the Latinised Goth who wielded the greatest power on the peninsula, had himself crowned king in what had become northern Italy's most important town: not Milan, but Pavia.

LOMBARDS AND FRANKS

For decades Goths and Byzantines alternately colluded and squabbled for control of the Italian peninsula, heedless of the threat swiftly mounting from across the Alps, where the bloodthirsty King Alboin was forging various antagonistic tribes of Germanic Lombard peoples into something like a unified front. In 568 the Lombards began their relatively challenge-free rampage through northern Italy, setting up their capital in Pavia, which fell to the invaders after a siege in 572. The region they overran was a shadow of its former self, its agriculture and infrastructure in tatters. This seemed to matter little to the ruling Lombards, who taxed and oppressed with glee, only becoming slightly less hostile after wily Pope Gregory the Great (590-604) persuaded the Lombard Queen Theodolinda to convert her people from Arianism (according to the Church, the heretical version of Christianity espoused by the Lombards) to Roman-style Christianity.

Later popes continued to clash with the ever-expanding Lombards, whose territory now extended from the myriad dukedoms of the Po Valley to the far south of mainland Italy. With the Normans of southern Italy also making life difficult for the occupant of the throne of St Peter's, outside help was sought, in the shape of the Franks. The head of this Germanic tribe in the second half of the eighth century was Charlemagne, a mighty warrior and impressive politician who, although illiterate, had established a glittering court at Aachen from where he had set out to conquer much of western Europe. In 774 Charlemagne turned his attention to Italy, where he crushed the Lombards – at the time under the leadership of King Desiderius, who was Charlemagne's own father-in-law – and added King of the Lombards to his long list of titles.

Pope Leo III (795-816) awarded him yet another title – *imperator augustus*, later known as Holy Roman Emperor – in 800. In the short term, it was a sound move on the part of the pontiff, forcing Charlemagne to uphold papal rights against encroaching foes. But after Charlemagne's death, no one could live up to his mighty reputation, and even before his direct family line had died out, his empire had fallen into the hands of bickering lordlings striving to be big fish in very small ponds.

Northern Italy was no exception to this. Already, under Lombard and Carolingian rule, religious orders had established control over large swathes of countryside, building monasteries in the midst of rich agricultural and pastoral holdings. With Magyar invaders harrying them through the ninth and tenth centuries, locals barricaded themselves into a series of fortified hamlets, each proclaiming its territorial rights over surrounding countryside and laying the foundations of an extensive feudal system that would later come into conflict with the religious oligarchy.

'The clergy effectively ruled Lombardy's increasingly wealthy cities from the start of the new millennium.'

Meanwhile, the region's rural poor were being reduced to the level of serfs, obliged to work for a living on lordly estates where ever-larger tracts of woodland – traditionally used for grazing by small-scale stock raisers – were being dug up and cultivated to provide crops to feed a growing population.

With the end of the Carolingian line in 888, northern Italy passed under the control of a series of Frankish *reucci* (literally 'little kings') of little worth, who occasionally found themselves in conflict with the questionable characters titled *imperator augustus* by popes kept firmly under the thumbs of Roman nobles.

It was the unwise attempt by kinglet Berengar II to force Adelaide, widow of his predecessor Lothar, to marry him (or possibly his son Adalbert; sources are divided) that upset this state of affairs. In 961 the eastern Frankish King Otto I responded to a plea for help from the beautiful Adelaide, who had been locked up in a tower overlooking Lake Garda (*see p212*) by her would-be spouse (or maybe father-in-law). Otto invaded Italy, carried Adelaide off (from Tuscany, where the feisty lady had already escaped under her own steam) and the following year was crowned Holy Roman Emperor in Rome, returning the title to a German.

Gian Galeazzo Visconti. *See p13.*

Under Ottos I, II and, in particular, the devout Otto III, Lombardy's clergy had a field day. Bishops and archbishops still exercised much influence – especially in major cities, which had declined but never died away, and bounced back strongly during any brief period of tranquillity and prosperity. The Church was given precedence over the landed nobility, whose uppitiness irked the emperors and whose power was consequently reduced. In Milan, a building boom gave the city a swathe of new Romanesque landmarks – including the basilica of Sant'Ambrogio (*see p91*). Allied with the *cives* – city-dwelling merchants or tradesmen – the clergy became the effective rulers of Lombardy's increasingly wealthy cities from around the start of the new millennium.

AGE OF THE *COMUNI*

By the end of the 11th century, the *cives* were demanding a greater degree of control: in Milan, a *consulatus civium* (town council meeting) was recorded in 1097. Bergamo, Brescia, Como, Cremona and Mantova followed suit in the second decade of the following century. The first of these meetings was held very much under the clergy's auspices, in the *brolo* (garden) of the bishop's palace – hence the abundance of later town halls around Lombardy called *palazzo del Broletto*.

But increasing civic feistiness also brought the various settlements of the Lombardy region into conflict with each other. Milan, the strongest and wealthiest, imposed its supremacy over Lodi, Cremona, Como and even Pavia, in spite of the latter's imperial connections.

> **'Lombardy was the doorway into Italy for a stream of northern invaders. But it was Milan's habit of wavering between outside powers that sealed its fate.'**

This was too much for the Holy Roman Emperor of the time, Frederick Barbarossa (1152-90), who marched across the Alps to bring Milan to heel. At the end of a seven-month siege in 1162, the emperor had the city's fortifications pulled down and the palaces of leading anti-imperial agitators destroyed. Hated as Milan was by many of its neighbours, Barbarossa's heavy-handed treatment of it failed to endear him particularly to any of the wary cities of Lombardy. In 1167, at a meeting of their representatives at Pontida, the *comuni* (towns run by the people) banded together in the Lega Lombarda (Lombard League). Its symbol was a large cart (*Carroccio*) with the Lombard standard flying atop it; popular lore has it that the forces of the Lombard League were rallied around this cart when they engaged with and beat back the imperial troops at the Battle of Legnano (*see p101* **Battle royale**) in 1176. Risorgimento (*see p18*) sentimentalists saw this battle – the subject of the eponymous opera by Giuseppe Verdi – as marking the beginning of Italian resistance to foreign tyrants; but if truth be told, it was the emperor as tax-imposer, rather than the emperor as foreign power, they were fighting against. The moment the Holy Roman Empire ceased to be a threat, the *comuni* returned to their self-interested squabbling. It is therefore eminently suitable that today's Northern League – the northern separatist party founded in 1984 by the irascible Umberto Bossi as a response to Roman political corruption – should have adopted the *Carroccio* as its symbol.

The Battle of Legnano was followed by further skirmishing against the emperor's forces, but in 1183 the Peace of Konstanz at last awarded Milan the privileges of independence and self-government that it had long considered itself more than worthy of. The city could now settle down happily to its own internal bickering. Most of the trouble arose from conflicts between the old aristocracy and the pushy ranks of merchants and tradesmen, conflicts that the city's institutions were powerless to resolve. Solutions were sought from outside, with the aristos lining up with the pro-empire Ghibelline party, and the parvenus joining the pro-papal Guelphs.

This was yet another indication of Milan's innate inability to free itself from outside interference. Admittedly, geography was against it: Lombardy was inevitably the doorway into Italy for a stream of northern invaders. But the city's habit of wavering between outside powers sealed its fate. In 1266, Pope Clement IV summoned Charles d'Anjou from France to deal with Barbarossa's heirs in Sicily. Forced into a decision, Milan's then-dominant Guelph (that is, pro-papacy) faction, led by the Torriani family, opted to back the anti-empire movement.

But if there was one thing you could be sure of at the time, it was that popes never continued backing winners – the plan was not to let anybody become too strong. Charles conquered the south and became king of Sicily, but then the pope switched allegiance, championed a German candidate for the title of emperor, and even backed anti-papal Ghibelline forces in the north.

THE VISCONTIS

Among these forces was one Ottone Visconti, an archbishop of Milan who had been ousted by the Torriani family. Ottone seized the initiative, scoring a major victory over the Torrianis in 1277. One year later he was declared *signore* (lord) of the city. The old *comune* system was over: Milan – like so many other northern Italian cities – was going the way of one-family rule.

Coming to germs

If it is true, as some people maintain, that the plague was transmitted by humans – and by armies in particular – it is surprising that anyone in Lombardy survived at all, given how many of the 'great unwashed' of various stripes rampaged back and forth over this region over the centuries.

The plague of 1630 is considered to have been provoked by a group of people called, in Italian, *lanzichenecchi*, a corruption of the Germanic word *landsknecht*. These mercenary pikemen and foot soldiers had a formidable reputation as fighters and, in the autumn of 1629, were helping to besiege Mantova. It's said that the plague was brought into the city on 22 October, when one Pietro Antonio Lovato, who had been recruited into the ranks of the *lanzichenecchi*, came to visit his *mamma*. By June 1630, infection was widespread, and people were looking for explanations.

That there might be someone going round deliberately smearing plague germs on walls, church pews and other places seemed as good an explanation as any. The hunt was on for these *untori* (anointers). On 21 June 1630, two women spotted what they claimed was a man in dark clothing, his hat pulled low, trailing his hand against the wall of a house. They called the local police chief, who confirmed that this was an oily smear. The 'culprit', Guglielmo Piazza, was actually a public health official whose duty it was to cart the diseased to the *lazzaretto* (hospital) and the dead to communal graves. He was promptly arrested and, under torture, he

named Giangiacomo Mora, his barber as a co-conspirator. Both men were later burned at the stake. Mora's house on Corso di Porta Ticinese was torn down and a column of infamy (*la colonna infame*) erected in its place. The column was destroyed by the Austrians in 1778.

The city's archbishop and spiritual leader at the time was Cardinal Federico Borromeo, the nephew of Carlo Borromeo, who was Archbishop of Milan between 1562 and 1584 and later sanctified. Federico's memoir of the plague, written in Latin, is in the Biblioteca Ambrosiana (*see p63*). Containing a vivid portrait of life during the epidemic, this memoir reveals that, although he was somewhat sceptical of some reports of *untori*, he apparently considered others credible. These included tales of anointers wiping prayer books so the clergy would be infected.

Many thousands of people died in the plague of 1630. Among these were the painter Daniele Crespi, whose final works were the frescoes in the Certosa di Garegnano (*see p67*).

Places in the city associated with the plague include the old *lazzaretto*, which lay in the area between what is now corso Buenos Aires, via Lazzaretto, via Vittorio Veneto and via San Gregorio. Built by Ludovico il Moro (*see p14*) in 1488 (another plague year), the *lazzaretto* was demolished in the 1880s. All that remains is the little church of San Nicola (via San Gregorio 5), now home to the city's Russian Orthodox community.

Key events

PRE-ROMAN LOMBARDY
5th-4th centuries BC Celtic tribes cross Alps from Gaul to Po Valley occupied by Ligurians.
280s BC Romans begin conquest of Po Valley.

ROMAN MEDIOLANUM
222 BC Romans conquer Mediolanum (Milan).
218-201 BC Second Punic War: Celts back Hannibal, beat Romans back across the Po.
42 BC Romans control Cisalpine Gaul.
15 BC Emperor Augustus makes Milan capital of 11th region, Transpadania.
1st & 2nd centuries AD Relatively peaceful times. Agricultural northern Italy flourishes.
3rd century Barbarians threaten; Diocletian splits the empire into two halves and makes Mediolanum capital of Western Empire (292).
4th century Empire reunited under control of Constantine the Great (306-37).
313 Edict of Milan legalises Christianity.
374-97 St Ambrose bishop of Milan.
452 Attila the Hun razes Milan.
476 Odoacer, a Goth, is crowned king in Pavia.

LOMBARDS AND FRANKS
568 Lombards begin rampage through Italy.
572 Lombards make Pavia capital.
774 Charlemagne defeats Lombards.
800 Charlemagne made Holy Roman Emperor; after his death (814) empire collapses.
9th-10th centuries *Reucci* (minor kings) bicker for control.
961 Frankish King Otto I invades; named Holy Roman Emperor in 962; clergy more powerful.

AGE OF THE *COMUNI*
Late 11th century *Consulatus civium* (town council meeting) held in Milan 1097.
Early 12th century Milan takes control over Lodi, Cremona, Como and Pavia.
1162 Holy Roman Emperor Frederick Barbarossa (1152-90) lays siege to Milan.
1167 Lombard *comuni* band together in the anti-imperial Lega Lombarda.
1176 Lega beats imperial forces at Legnano.
1183 Peace of Constance grants Milan independence; pro-Empire Ghibellines squabble with pro-pope Guelphs.

THE VISCONTIS
1277 Ottone Visconti's Ghibelline forces beat Guelphs; Ottone declared *signore* of Milan.
1294 Matteo Visconti controls all Milan area.
1330s Visconti take control of Bergamo and Novara (1332), Cremona (1334), Como and Lodi (1335), Brescia (1337).

1395 Gian Galeazzo Visconti (1378-1402) made Duke of Milan; Milan is Italy's largest city, population 250,000.
1402 Gian Galeazzo dies; cities break away.

THE SFORZAS
1447 Filippo Maria Visconti dies with no male heir; Milanese republic set up; Filippo Maria's son-in-law Francesco Sforza leads, then betrays, republicans.
1450 Francesco becomes Duke of Lombardy.
1476 Francesco's brother Ludovico il Moro becomes duke; court is centre of culture.
1499 France's King Louis XII invades Italy, takes il Moro prisoner.
1513 French expelled from Lombardy; Ludovico's son Massimiliano placed in power.

FOREIGN DOMINATION
1525 Francesco Sforza rules under tutelage of Holy Roman Emperor Charles V.
1535 Francesco dies, Charles V assumes power; 150 years of Spanish rule begins.
1560 Carlo Borromeo made archbishop of Milan; gives religious life new vigour.
1706 Milan is occupied by Austria.
1796 Napoleon invades, makes Milan capital of Cisalpine Republic; King of Italy (1805).
1814 Lombardy restored to Austria.
1848 Milanese rise up against Austrians in *Cinque Giornate* rebellion; revolt quashed.

A UNIFIED ITALY
1859 Second war of independence: Austrians cede Lombardy to Vittorio Emanuele II of Savoy, united Italy's first king.
1898 81 die, 502 injured in general strike protests in industrially booming Milan.
Post-1918 Fascist party emerges.
1943 Milanese workers strike, contributing to Mussolini's downfall.
April 1945 The Milanese liberate city from German control in three-day uprising.

POST-WAR YEARS
1960-70s Lombardy is the driving force behind Italy's 'economic miracle'.
1990s Separatist Lega Nord (Northern League) party gains support, representing widespread discontent with Rome.
1992 *Tangentopoli* scandal erupts in Milan; the investigation that follows becomes known as *Mani Pulite* (clean hands).
2001 Coalition led by controversial media magnate and Lombard lad Silvio Berlusconi wins general election.

In 1294, on payment of 50,000 florins to Holy Roman Emperor Henry VII, Ottone's great-nephew and designated successor, Matteo, was given the title of *vicario imperiale* (imperial delegate), a rank that also gave him a claim to authority over Milan's neighbours. He was driven out of Milan in 1302 by the Torriani family, but with the emperor's support he made a triumphant return in 1311. From then on, the Viscontis went from strength to strength. In 1330 Azzone Visconti was proclaimed *dominus generalis* (general ruler). Within the space of a generation, the surrounding cities all acknowledged Visconti rule – Bergamo and Novara in 1332, Cremona in 1334, Como and Lodi in 1335, Piacenza in 1336 and Brescia in 1337.

'Feudal lords who refused to recognise Gian Galeazzo Visconti's authority had their castles razed and were whipped off to prison.'

The family's splendour reached its zenith with the rule of Gian Galeazzo Visconti (1378-1402), who obtained the title of Duke of Milan in 1395 from Emperor Wenceslas. Two years later it was upped to Duke of Lombardy; Gian Galeazzo ruled over the second-largest *signoria* in Italy (only the kingdom of Naples was bigger), which included Milan, Pavia, Bergamo, Brescia, Como, Lodi, Cremona, Novara, Vercelli, Alessandria, Piacenza, Parma, Reggio, Verona, Vicenza and Belluno. Gian Galeazzo was a man of culture, whose greatest delight was to curl up with the classics. But there was nothing wimpish or velvet-gloved about his way of exerting command. Local feudal lords who refused to recognise his authority had their castles razed and were whipped off to prison. One chancellor, accused of treachery, was wrapped in an ox-skin and walled up alive.

It was under this cultured but ruthless despot that Milan became the largest city in Italy, with a population of around 250,000, at the turn of the 15th century. Major building projects were embarked upon in the region, including the Certosa (Charterhouse) in Pavia (*see p259*) – with Gian Galeazzo personally laying its first stone – and the Duomo (*see p54*) of Milan. When Visconti died of the plague in 1402, the great duchy was divided among his heirs, with his wife Caterina left as regent and tutoress.

Elsewhere in the duchy, Gian Galeazzo's death was the signal for other *signori* to raise their heads; Pandolfo III Malatesta declared himself *signore* of Bergamo and Brescia, while Facino Cane took over the territory in the west.

Cultured ruler **Ludovico il Moro**. *See p14.*

In Milan, meanwhile, Caterina died – perhaps poisoned – just two years after her husband; and their eldest son, Giovanni Maria, was killed on his way to church. It fell to the younger son, Filippo Maria, to try and regain control of things. He had inherited his father's ambitious spirit and intelligence, along with his bookish habits and suspicious, closed character. But Milan's further-flung neighbours proved more resilient than they had been in his father's day: despite a number of wars against Florence and Venice, Filippo Maria ruled over a much-reduced duchy, with Bergamo and Brescia ceding to Venice.

THE SFORZAS

When Filippo Maria died in 1447, leaving no male heirs, a group of noblemen attempted to re-establish republican life, setting up the *Aurea Repubblica Ambrosiana*. Never slow to take advantage of a neighbour's weakness, Venice attacked, grabbing Piacenza and Lodi. The new authorities of Milan (foolishly) entrusted its defence to Francesco Sforza, husband of Filippo Maria Visconti's illegitimate daughter Bianca Maria and the closest thing there was to a direct Visconti heir. Francesco won back the lost cities, but then did a secret deal with the Venetians, giving them Brescia and other territories in exchange for their recognition of him as the new duke of Lombardy.

Maria Teresa of Austria. *See p18.*

After a brief siege, Milan's republican forces capitulated in 1450. Francesco's rule was even more magnificent than that of Gian Galeazzo Visconti. He transformed the city into a powerful metropolis, building among other things the Castello Sforzesco (*see p66*) and the Ospedale Maggiore, now Ca' Granda (*see p82*). On his death in 1466 he was succeeded by his pleasure-loving son Galeazzo Maria, whose determination to transform the court into a brothel-cum-circus did not endear him to all his subjects. This was made clear in 1476, when he was stabbed to death in church by three young patricians.

As his son was only seven at the time, Galeazzo Maria's wife gave the regency to a trusty minister and to two of her husband's brothers. The younger, Ludovico Mauro, known as il Moro (the Moor) because of his dark complexion, was clearly the dominant figure and very soon he had the reins of power securely in his hands. He proved a good ruler, encouraging agricultural development and the silk industry. Under him, the court became one of Italy's great centres of art and culture, with architects like Donate Bramante and all-round geniuses such as Leonardo da Vinci (*see p92* **Guess who's coming to supper**) given free scope. Only the court of Mantova (*see p237*) could compete for brilliance: there, Ludovico's sister-in-law, the urbane Isabella d'Este, had married into the Gonzaga family (*see p240* **The Gonzaga saga**) and held sway over a centre of high culture. The Gonzagas may not have had Ludovico's military clout, but they could boast a truly great artist in Andrea Mantegna.

The life expectancy of these brilliant Renaissance courts as independent entities was, however, short. On a military plane, they hadn't a hope of vying with Europe's great powers. In a fatally flawed attempt to neutralise two birds with one cunningly launched stone (both Naples and France had a claim on the Duchy of Milan through complicated inter-dynastic marriages), Ludovico suggested that King Charles VIII of France might wish to regain the throne of Naples, which had been seized from the French Anjous by the Spaniards. Charles, who had dreams of becoming a second Charlemagne, was just waiting to be persuaded, and in 1494 descended into Italy, with encouragement also from Florence and the Pope.

However, after a fairly easy victory in the south, Charles embarked upon what was to become a French habit in Italy, and began looting the Kingdom of Naples. At this point he lost the support of the Neapolitan population and also learned how short-lived Papal support could be. Pope Alexander organised a Holy Alliance to drive him out, getting the backing of Ludovico as well. In 1495 Charles was defeated at Fornovo, near Parma, and returned to France.

But four years later, France's new king, Louis XII, took his revenge. When he invaded Italy – determined, among other things, to claim his rights over Milan – Ludovico appealed to the Holy Roman Emperor Maximilian. The ragged army of Swiss and German mercenaries that the emperor drummed up could not match French firepower, and with the help of Mantova's Gonzaga family, the French took il Moro prisoner in 1499; he died in France in 1508.

In the same year French-ruled Milan joined the League of Cambrai, which had been summoned by the great warrior – if not great pope – Julius II to counter the threat posed by the expansion of Venice on to the Italian mainland. The League scored a major victory against the Venetians at Agnadello (1509), after which the pope – surprise, surprise – changed allegiance, and started supporting the Venetians. In 1513 the papal armies, Venice and Spain all turned on the French, who were expelled from Lombardy, and Ludovico's son Massimiliano was put in power.

By this time, however, Lombardy's role as rugby ball in the endless scrimmages between the Great Powers – France, Austria and Spain – was firmly established: for the next three and a half centuries the region was trampled over by foreign armies and swapped about among the

Milan's heroines

You may have noticed that streets in Milan (indeed, all over Italy) are often named after famous people. Perhaps inevitably, most of these are men, but there are also some women worth remembering.

Gaetana Agnesi was one. Her street runs from via Giulio Romano to viale Sabotino, in the Porta Romana area (*see p82*). Born in Milan in 1718, Maria Gaetana Agnesi soon revealed her remarkable intellectual gifts, including a phenomenal aptitude for mathematics. She also wrote a discourse to show that liberal studies were not unsuited to her sex and showed. Indeed, her *Instituzioni Analitiche* was published in 1748 – when she was 30. Such was her reputation that, in 1750, she was appointed to replace her father as professor of mathematics in the University of Bologna after he became ill.

Two years later, when he died, she withdrew from academic circles, turning her attention to more local matters. She turned the family home in via Pantano (between the Duomo and the State University) into a hospice. Forced to move from there, she then opened a home for the mentally ill in nearby via della Signora. In 1771, she took over the women's section of the Trivulzio Hospice, which was run by the Blue Nuns. She held this post until her death in 1899, aged 81.

Luisa Battistotti Sassi is another person who has a street named after her. It's on the east side of the city, on the way to Linate airport. Born just outside Pavia, she came to Milan to marry an artisan. On the first day of the 1848 riots, when the uprising against the Austrians known as the Cinque Giornate (*see p16 **Five alive***) took place, she snatched one of the Austrian soldiers' pistols, and used it to force five others to surrender. Having changed into men's clothing, she then took to the first barricades, where she fought for the remaining five days. Recognised as an undisputed heroine of the *Cinque Giornate*, she was given a state pension. Her stature grew so much in the minds and hearts of the *milanesi* that her effigy was sold on the streets of the city. Luisa Battistotti Sassi spent her later years in the United States, where she died.

Beatrice d'Este was the duchess of Milan and has a viale named after her, again in the Porta Romana area. Born in Ferrara, Beatrice married Ludovico il Moro (*see p14*) in 1491,

when she was 16, and ably helped him fulfil his desire of bringing the best minds to the court in Milan, including Bramante and Leonardo da Vinci. She also acted as advisor to her husband, even if she did not get involved directly with his political intrigues. Beatrice had two sons: Ercole, later called Massimiliano, and Francesco. She died in childbirth in 1497 and her funeral was held n Santa Maria delle Grazie (*see p96*), which had been built by Ludovico, who wanted to be buried alongside her. Their funerary monument is housed in the church of the Certosa di Pavia (*see p259*).

While all these women could be dubbed high-flyers, Rosina Ferrario was one, literally. Born in Milan in 1888, she was the first Italian woman to get her pilot's licence – this in 1913, when there were only about ten other female pilots in the entire world. In the same year, she was invited to fly with one of Italian aviation's legendary figures, Achille Landini, to commemorate the centenary of Giuseppe Verdi's birth. Ms Ferrario was praised for her achievement, but several commentators implied that motherhood would have been a nobler calling. Via Rosina Ferrario is tucked away in Villapizzone, in the northern suburbs of the city, almost as a reluctant tribute to this proto-feminist (who did, however, later marry and have a family).

There is one last famous female figure in Milan's past worth mentioning, and although she has no street named after her, there is a chapel dedicated to her in the city's Duomo (*see p54*). Theodolinda was a gorgeous blonde Lombard queen whose beauty beguiled the inhabitants of the region in the late sixth and early seventh centuries AD. Daughter of Duke Garibaldo of Bavaria, she married Autari, king of the Lombards, in 589. Autari died the following year, but because Theodolinda was such a hit with the people – contrary to usual practice – they confirmed her as queen and invited her to take another husband. She chose Duke Agilulf of Turin, who dismayed many by allowing himself to be bought off by Pope Gregory the Great. Pope Gregory forged a friendship with Theodolinda; encouraged by him, she went on to convert her people from Arianism – the locally practised 'heretical' version of Christianity – and founded many churches and monasteries in the region.

Five alive

These days the Milanese, irritated by the way the government in Rome is running things, might call for secession from the rest of Italy, but the fire of patriotic pride has been known to burn even in these disillusioned hearts. To see a little frisson of *orgoglio italico* (Italian pride) in even the hardest of Milanese hearts, just mention the *Cinque Giornate*. These five memorable days in 1848 (18-22 March) truly changed the course of Italian history.

Fired by news that riots in Vienna had caused the Austrian Emperor to offer concessions to its inhabitants, the people of Milan – who had been under Austrian rule since the Treaty of Vienna in 1815 – decided to follow suit.

In less than a week, armed with little more than the materials to make barricades and a determination now only seen when they want to board an empty tram before everyone else, the *milanesi* succeeded in their plan. An initial demonstration on 18 March led to the capture of Palazzo del Governo (the building now known as Palazzo Reale, *see p54*). The

vice-governor, Heinrich Graf O'Donnell, was forced to allow the rebels to institute a civic guard and order the police force to stand down. The Palazzo del Governo was soon recaptured, but not before a provisional government had been set up. This was short-lived, but over the next four days, the *milanesi* managed to seize control of the city and of all its gates. Driven out at Porta Tosa – which since then has been known as Porta Vittoria – field-marshal Radetzky, his 16,000 troops and his 400 cannons retreated to Lodi.

great rulers. It was to become a pawn in the Thirty Years War that pitted Catholic leaders against Protestant, and the Habsburgs against just about everyone else around Europe.

> **'Under the Spanish, Milan became the neglected capital of a province: administered, guarded and taxed by foreigners.'**

FOREIGN DOMINATION

The region enjoyed a 14-year semblance of autonomy after France's King Francis I was defeated at Pavia in 1525, his efforts to assert French hereditary rights over Lombardy stymied by imperial forces. Massimiliano Sforza's brother

Francesco ruled under the tutelage of the Holy Roman Emperor Charles V (a Habsburg, and King Charles I of Spain); but when Francesco died in 1535, Charles assumed direct power. So began 170 years of Spanish domination. The once-proud independent Duchy of Milan became the neglected capital of a province: administered, guarded and taxed by foreigners. This is the wretched, humiliated Milan described in Manzoni's *I promessi sposi* (*see p64* **Novel approach**).

Milan's population fell from 130,000 to around 70,000; industry and agriculture wouldn't recover from the crisis until towards the end of the 17th century. Other Lombard cities were also in decline. Mantova was reduced to a mere buffer-state between Milan and Venice. When the last Gonzaga died in 1627, another convoluted war of succession ensued, bringing invading armies, famine and plague in its wake.

As the last Habsburg officials left the city, the *milanesi* formed a provisional government. Over the next few days, the revolt extended to other cities and within a short time, the Habsburgs could only count on what was known as the 'Quadrilateral', that is, the area delineated by Peschiera, Mantova, Legnano and Verona.

On 8 April, the provisional government of Milan became the provisional government of all Lombardy, replacing all the other ruling bodies established in the previous two weeks. On 8 June, a plebiscite (a change in the constitution brought about by public vote) resulted in Lombardy formally uniting with Sardinia. It was agreed that, until a constitutional assembly would be formed, the provisional government would continue. But on 27 July the tide started to turn in favour of the Austrians and Milan was recaptured on 7 August.

The five-day revolt was a landmark in the Italians' struggle for independence. But the road was to be a long one, with Italy only finally becoming a nation in 1870.

While the *Cinque Giornate di Milano* was an initial step on the long journey towards the creation of a united Italy, some of the uprising's other, more immediate, consequences are still visible – if you know where to look. For starters, there's Giuseppe Grandi's moving sculpture and obelisk commemorating the event and naming the fallen in the middle of piazza Cinque Giornate.

At number 13 corso Venezia, for example, we can see that there is a good-sized chunk missing from the hefty stone doorway of this handsome building. The explanation is provided on a brass plaque on the wall nearby. It reads 'Marzo 1848'. To someone who knows Milan, little more needs to be said. Evidence that the Austrian troops were not leaving quietly. Or maybe they just did not wanting to cart all those heavy cannonballs with them all the way to Lodi.

If you're visiting the Pinacoteca di Brera (*see p71*), you might also want to cast a glance at Palazzo Pisani Dossi at number 11 of via Brera. Two and a half cannonballs set into the wall in the courtyard testify to the passage of the Austrians as they left town. The building was hit, as the plaque tells us, on 19, 20 and 21 March. Ask the doorman to get access to the courtyard (open 9am-6pm Mon-Fri). Yet another cannonball from the Austrian retreat can be seen three metres above street level at via Sacchi 4.

To find out more on the *Cinque Giornate*, check out the Museo del Risorgimento (via Borgonuovo 23, 02 8846 4176). Here you can see the black hats with plumes worn by the leading member of the revolt, as well as a copy of the leaflets providing updates on the goings-on that were dropped from balloons in key areas outside the city centre.

One more thing: as you might imagine, Radetzky may be regarded as a great hero elsewhere, but not in Milan. Be warned.

In the second half of the 17th century, Milan's religious life was given fresh vigour – albeit of a rather dreary kind – by the imposing Cardinal (later Saint) Carlo Borromeo (*see p105* **A family's fortunes**). He was a leading figure in the Counter-Reformation – the movement that had arisen out of the Council of Trent (1545-63) – convened to clean up a hedonistic, corrupt Catholic Church whose authority and clout were being greatly undermined by the spread of militant northern Protestantism. There was no cheery bonhomie about the ascetic Carlo; but there can be no denying that he did a good deal to rid the Church of some of the abuses that got the Protestants protesting in the first place.

The 18th century began with the impossibly complicated War of Spanish Succession (1701-14), following upon attempts by the French king Louis XIV – who was married to a Habsburg – to grab for France all the various European possessions of Spain's last Habsburg monarch, Charles II. In 1706, in the course of this war, Milan was occupied by Eugenio von Savoy (whose Italian/German/French name indicates the complexity of his background) on behalf of Emperor Joseph I of Austria; the Peace of Utrecht (1713), and then the Treaty of Rastatt (1714), confirmed the new occupation.

Administratively, the Austrians were a step up from the Spaniards, who had made it their business to improve as little and tax as much as possible. They implemented various reforms, one of which was to draw up a land registry for tax purposes. Suddenly, aristocratic landowners faced an unprecedented need to make their land profitable. This instilled an unusual spirit of enterprise into the land-owning classes, which helped get the economy moving.

Benito Mussolini kept the Milanese under his spell – briefly. *See p19.*

The Austrians also did their best to alleviate some of the worst judicial abuses, abolishing ecclesiastic tribunals and the use of torture (to the dismay of some conservative Lombards). The intellectual climate brightened as well – a number of lively journals were published in Milan and Enlightenment ideas began to trickle down through the intellectual classes. Lombardy was undoubtedly the area of Italy most open to new ideas from the rest of Europe. Numerous learned institutions were founded, including the Accademia di Brera (*see p71*), instituted by Empress Maria Teresa in 1776. The Teatro alla Scala (*see p59*) was opened in 1778.

It was thanks to this climate of enlightenment that Napoleon, whom many optimists at the time saw as embodying the spirit of democratic reform, was received so enthusiastically by the Milanese when he marched into the city in May 1796. Milan became the capital of Napoleon's Cisalpine Republic. It was perhaps with rather less enthusiasm, in 1805, that the Milanese watched the French emperor assume the crown of Italy in the Duomo – the same iron crown (*see p100*) that had once sat on the heads of the old Lombard kings.

After Napoleon's fall in 1814, the Congress of Vienna restored Lombardy to Austria. Although the region thrived culturally and economically during the 19th century, the Milanese remained largely hostile to Austrian rule. This hostility found a musical outlet in some of Verdi's early operas, but finally exploded in the heroic *Cinque Giornate* (five days) of 1848 (*see p16* **Five alive**). Inspired by the spirit of the Risorgimento – the Italy-wide movement to create a united country – the Milanese, in an unprecedented display of unanimity, succeeded in throwing the Austrians out of the city after five days of street fighting. However, owing to the military incompetence of Carlo Emanuele of Piedmont, to whom the generally republican leaders of the insurrection had reluctantly turned for aid, the uprising eventually failed. Austrian forces re-entered the city, which, along with the whole Lombardy region, was placed under the iron-fisted control of their commander-in-chief Count Joseph Radetzky.

A UNIFIED ITALY

Liberation was postponed until the Second War of Independence in 1859. This time, under the pressure of combined military intervention by the French and the Piedmontese – and with the decisive action of Risorgimento hero Giuseppe Garibaldi and his guerrilla troops – the Austrians were forced to cede Lombardy to Vittorio Emanuele II of Savoy, the first king of a united Italy.

Lombardy was easily the most prosperous and dynamic region of the new united Italy. Though few doubted that the seat of government had to be Rome, Milan clearly considered itself the country's cultural and financial capital. In the years immediately after unification, the city celebrated its new free status by undertaking a number of grandiose building projects, including the construction of the great Galleria Vittorio Emanuele II (*see p54*).

On a more practical level, the opening of the San Gottardo tunnel through the Alps facilitated trade with northern Europe, and gave another boost, if one were needed, to Lombardy's industry. The flip side of this boom was suffering and unrest among the workers. Support for socialism grew; a general strike in 1898 was repressed with extreme brutality, leaving 81 'subversives' dead and 502 injured. Immediately after World War I there were 445 strikes within the space of a single year; it was in this tumultuous climate that the fascist party began its thuggish activities, with some of its earliest attacks being launched in Milan against the socialist newspaper *Avanti* (previously edited, curiously enough, by Mussolini himself).

'In April 1945 the Milanese rekindled the spirit of 1848, rising up against the Nazis.'

With fascism firmly established, demonstrations of proletarian discontent magically disappeared. It was not until 1943 that Milanese workers dared manifest their displeasure once again, bringing several factories in Milan and Turin to a halt; these protests contributed to the downfall of Mussolini's regime in July the same year. In April 1945 the population of Milan rekindled the old 1848 spirit, rising up against the occupying Nazi forces and liberating the city in just three days. If there is one thing that characterises the Milanese, it's their determination to improve on past records.

And it was in Milan that the fallen Mussolini made his grisly final public appearance. Having been captured in Dongo (*see p208*) and executed by Partisans in 1945, Mussolini and his mistress Claretta Petacci were strung up for all to behold in Milan's piazzale Loreto.

POST-WAR YEARS

At the end of World War II, Lombardy was instrumental in the boom that transformed Italy from a relatively backward, agricultural country to an industrial world leader. Following suit, the city of Milan became a major financial centre. The region's new-found wealth also attracted myriad workers from the south of Italy, in a wave of immigration that resulted in tensions and open racism towards the new arrivals. In the early 1990s, the federalist/separatist party, the Lega Nord (Northern League), capitalised on these feelings, finding fertile ground for its mix of xenophobia and grandiose secessionist plans.

A six-year (1992-98) investigation led by judge Antonio di Pietro into the massive bribes scandal dubbed *Tangentopoli* (bribesville) revealed that the spectacular wealth Milan had accumulated over the previous decade had been greased by floods of dirty money.

No rest for the righteous: **Antonio di Pietro**, leader of the *Tangentopoli* investigation.

Milan Today

Soccer, sex, transport and *i comunisti* are among the obsessions of modern-day Milan.

Ask a local to sum up the dominant themes of Milanese life today, and chances are they'll reduce it the crude binomial of *calcio e figa* (soccer and pussy). Though this might only be a semi-serious answer, it does give an indication of the obsessions in this city. Certainly, football is huge and for reasons that go beyond the game itself. According to psychologist Rosaria D'Amico: 'Soccer players have become the new sex symbols, along with *le veline* (the ever-younger TV showgirls; *see p32* **Boxing clever**). In the old days, the dream was to become an actor or actress, but now it is more to do with having a great body. Look at how much time and money people spend on going to the gym.'

In terms of football, the city's two teams, Milan and Inter, are two of the biggest, richest and most supported in Italy. Walk into any bar on a Monday morning and the barman and his customers will be engaged in a heated analysis of the previous day's matches (Sunday is soccer day). The conversation will feature gentle banter between Milan and Inter fans (Milan,

which was founded by English expats in 1899, traditionally had working-class, left-wing supporters; while Inter, founded in 1908 by Swiss expats who, legend has it, never got a game under the English, had more middle-class, right-wing fans – although these sociological distinctions have long since blurred). Great goals and bad mistakes will also feature in the conversation, as will dubious refereeing decisions invariably made in favour of the hated Fiat-owned Turin team, Juventus.

THE TRUTH BEHIND FOOTBALL

Such is the power of soccer in Milan that it also has considerable influence on business and politics. Owning a soccer club may be a great way for a multimillionaire to lose money, but the investment is invariably recouped in other fields, thanks to the knock-on public relations effect. In the 1980s, for example, Ernesto Pellegrini, the owner of a relatively unknown luncheon-voucher company, bought Inter and his turnover promptly quadrupled. For more cynical Italians, soccer is little more than a modern version of the gladiatorial games, which kept the plebs in their place with 'bread and circus'. In Turin, the Agnelli family has been able to get away with all sorts of cuts to the Fiat workforce by providing people with their regular dose of Sunday entertainment.

It is in Milan, however, where you will find the most dramatic example of football being used as a stepping stone to greater things. Silvio Berlusconi bought the AC Milan soccer club in 1986, saving it from bankruptcy, and the amazing results the team subsequently achieved on the pitch undoubtedly provided the basis for his dramatic rise to political power in the 1990s. Thanks to Berlusconi's money, the club went from a bunch of has-beens to European and world club champions; as a result, many voters believed he could do similar things for Italy as prime minister. Berlusconi has fervently exploited his soccer success: when he formed a new political party in 1993, after his sponsors in the Christian Democrats and Bettino Craxi's Socialist Party had been swept away by the anti-corruption *Tangentopoli* trials (which were held in Milan), he named it Forza Italia, or 'Come on, Italy', a phrase normally only heard at the soccer stadium.

MILAN'S PRODIGAL SON

The city's post-war industrial boom came to a halt in the 1970s, but whereas many British and American cities in a similar position were to decline, Milan bounced back, and almost overnight. It re-invented itself and started excelling in post-industrial fields such as fashion, design, advertising and television; indeed, private Italian TV, the other pinnacle of Berlusconi's political power, was born here (*see chapter* **Media Central**).

In many ways, Milan is something of a miniature New York. In addition to the afore-mentioned business activities, it is also the hub of Italian finance (the Italian Wall Street, piazza Affari, is here), publishing and the music industry. Milan even had its own miniscule version of 9/11, when in April 2002 a shady businessman, crippled by debts, crashed his two-seater plane into the Pirelli Building (the symbol of Milan's post-war boom and once Europe's tallest skyscraper; *see p73*), killing himself and two office workers.

The Milanese themselves have something of the New Yorker about them – they're hard-working, self-confident and self-obsessed. Berlusconi, a diminutive self-made man has these characteristics in abundance and, as a result, he is, like football and sex, another Milanese obsession.

Opinions about him are divided between love and hate, but people are seldom indifferent.

People on the right (and in Milan and the rest of Lombardy, these tend to be the majority: the city's mayor, Gabriele Albertini, is from Forza Italia) worship him. They see Berlusconi as embodying the virtues of the city, arguing that he has single-handedly built a successful empire and created jobs for people, despite the hindrances imposed by older Italian business and banking dynasties (Berlusconi's people despise the Agnellis), corrupt bureaucrats and politicians in Rome, prohibitive taxation and work-shy southerners.

A NEW ENEMY: *I COMUNISTI*

Most recently Berlusconi has identified a new potential nemesis for himself and every righteous Italian: *i comunisti*. As in McCarthy-era America, 'the communists' has become a blanket term for anyone who opposes Berlusconi.

'Leftists see Berlusconi as a dictator who hides his own interests behind a political movement voted for by semi-literate, TV-watching idiots.'

Leftists in Milan – and their numbers appear to be growing all the time – see Berlusconi as the architect, rather than the victim, of a conspiracy. For them he represents the worst, rather than the best of Italy – someone who's hijacked public resources for private gain. The leftists see Berlusconi as a freemason and a dictator who hides his own interests (namely, avoiding prison and holding on to his business empire) behind a political movement that is voted for by semi-literate, TV-watching idiots. They believe that civic virtue is a feature of the Italian left, rather than of the north, and that the Berlusconi coalition, with its mixture of racist *leghisti* (*see p23* **Milan's melting pot**), post-fascists and recycled Christian democrats and socialists, is the pits. As with the anti-communist paranoia of Berlusconi's admirers, hatred of him also borders on the obsessive: for many leftists, he is the root of all evil.

A REAL CONTENDER

Love him or hate him, the most important individual in Italy today is very much a Milan figure, and this is appropriate. Although the city has never been the capital of Italy and the hard-working inhabitants of this former outpost of the Austro-Hungarian empire see themselves as above the sordid wheeler-dealing of Rome's politicians, it has played a key role in modern Italian political history. Mussolini, even though he was from Emilia Romagna, lived and worked here and, after he had been shot by *partigiani* near Lake Como, his body was strung up in piazzale Loreto. Italy's student protests began in Milan (at the Cattolica university in 1968), as did terrorism (the first bomb attack was at a bank in piazza Fontana, behind the Duomo, in 1969), *Tangentopoli*, Forza Italia and, perhaps most significantly, the post-war economic miracle.

However, both the Milanese and Italian economies have been in poor shape of late and many people, including Silvio Berlusconi, have attributed this to the advent of the euro. In Berlusconi's case, however, there is the feeling that in so doing he's not only passing the buck in terms of his government's responsibilities, but also endeavouring to score points against his old left-leaning foe Romano Prodi, who – once he completes his term as president of the European Commission – is expected to return to Italian politics and challenge Berlusconi.

EURO STRIFE

That said, there is no denying that the euro has had an impact on the Italian, and more specifically, Milanese, economy. It has doubtless made it easier for foreigners to invest in the stock exchange, even though the Milan *borsa*, like other stock exchanges, has been going through a lean period. The famous Milan fashion business has also been in trouble over the last year or two. In the past, Italian governments were able to help exports by devaluing the lira, but this is no longer an option.

Although the euro isn't responsible for the economy's poor shape, it is undeniable that it has caused inflation, which has hit the consumer hard. Many businesses, such as shops, bars and restaurants, as well as their suppliers, have effected price hikes. The fact that one euro was worth nearly 2,000 lire meant that consumers took a long time to notice. Restaurant-goers, for example, would happily up a €50 restaurant bill shortly after the advent of the euro, on the grounds that it appeared cheap – all too many people interpreted the amount as 50,000 lire; only later did it sink in that they were in fact paying the equivalent of 100,000 lire.

One of the worst victims of the post-euro price hike has been Milan's public transport system. Ticket prices have doubled and the transport company, ATM, has got away with this by virtue of the fact it operates a monopoly. Yet public transport users have been less concerned about this than the all-round poor service. As in other Italian cities, public transport is limited – a popular conspiracy theory has it that this was a deliberate policy during the post-war boom to encourage people to buy Fiat cars – and things are getting worse. Bus and tram services in

particular are in decline, something brought home by a series of wildcat strikes in January 2004, which brought the city to a standstill. In the following weeks passengers vented their rage on the drivers, but the decay is more the fault of the corporation's new generation of managers, who, as in Britain, have considered profits more important than providing an acceptable level of service (ATM has been a publicly listed company since 2001). As with so many aspects of the economy, the advent of the euro happens to have coincided with a general decline, rather than being the actual cause of it.

NOT A PRETTY CITY

Milan is arguably Italy's most interesting and important city but, in physical terms, it leaves a lot to be desired. It was never a pretty place and the combination of heavy bombing by the British and Americans during the war (a flat city, its man-made hills were built out of war rubble) and rapid, poorly planned expansion in the post-war years has made it a mess today. The city has one of the lowest per capita quantities of park and green space in Europe, while its figures for the various toxic substances used to measure air pollution are among the highest in the world.

Many Milanese consider their city unlivable, but such is the awfulness of public transport and traffic that living outside and commuting is not a realistic option. The Milanese tend to look down on their neighbours in the surrounding Lombard towns; while Londoners dream of raising their kids in the country and sending them to better schools, the Milanese fear their kids would become subnormal out in the sticks. The Milanese do, however, love to get away at the weekend and the city's relative proximity to the mountains (for skiing in winter) and the sea (for sunbathing in summer) makes it ideal for this. As a result of the weekly exodus, the city's cultural life is poor, although the corruption trials of the early 1990s are another factor – the local government now has less money for all services, including the promotion of cultural events.

The desire to get way from Milan dogs its inhabitants throughout the week. Whenever there is nice weather, you hear people say, 'this is a great day to be in the mountains', or 'this is a great day to go to the beach'. You never hear them say, 'this is a great day to be in Milan'. It seems that everybody wants to get away, although people invariably come back. For Italians (and growing numbers of other nationalities) it really is like New York: it may be unbearable, but it's the place to be if you want to get ahead in life.

Milan's melting pot

Just like New York City, Milan has become a melting pot. In fact Milan was a city of immigration long before people from the Third World began to arrive. From Renaissance times onwards, the French, Spanish and Austrians took it in turns to invade the city, while the chaos of World War II saw yet more foreign armies appear.

In the post-war years, Milan, like Turin, was to absorb waves of southern immigrants, who came north to man the factories that powered Italy's boom. In many respects these economic migrants were like the cotton pickers from the Mississippi Delta who headed north to Chicago, and the reception they received was no less hostile. Many Milan landlords refused to rent accommodation to southerners, *meridionali* or, to use the offensive term, *terroni* ('earth people'), and anti-southern feeling is still a feature of Milan life, even if it is more marked in Lombardy's provincial communities. Umberto Bossi's Lega Lombarda, or Lega Nord, as it's now known, began as an anti-southern movement in the Varese area, but in recent years it has shifted its focus to Third World immigrants, whom it now sees as the cause of Italy's ills, along with Rome's politicians. And just as the sons of downtrodden Irish and Italian immigrants were to become the most racist in their treatment of black southerners in northern American cities, so it is the children of Italian southerners who are often the most vehemently anti-immigrant in northern Italy. Immigration has rocketed in recent years, thanks to the miles of coastline that make Italy an easy entry point into Europe, and

despite the recurrent horror stories on the news of boat people drowning off the Italian coast.

Milan's many South Americans are treated with a certain degree of caution, while the Filipinos, Indians and Sri Lankans are generally seen as hard-working, law-abiding citizens. The Chinese, meanwhile, have been in Milan for years. Chinatown, around Porta Volta, is worth a visit, even if tales of sweatshops, gang wars and SARS scares occasionally liven up the local news.

There are also a lot of immigrants from eastern Europe. The beggars on the Milan subway tend to be from the former Yugoslavia, while the gypsy musicians come from Romania. It's the Albanians, however, who cause significant fear among the natives – far more than, say, the friendly Senegalese street vendors, whose worst crime is considered to be the selling of pirate CDs (produced in the south by the mafia), or the North African Arabs (though anti-Muslim hatred post-9/11 has made life harder for them). Such is the hostility towards the Albanians that some years back, when a woman in the Brescia area and her lover murdered her husband and staged it to look like a break-in by Albanian burglars, the police initially believed their story.

Several eastern European women have, however, done rather better in the entertainment world. The current fad in Italian TV is for tall, beautiful Czech and Russian female presenters, who appear to have replaced blonde Americans as the average Italian male's favourite fantasy. They speak much better Italian too.

Caravaggio's **Supper at Emmaus**. *See p25.*

Art in Milan & Lombardy

With its commitment to contemporary art, Milan is striving to compensate for its less-than-splendid past.

Financial and industrial clout is something Milan has long had in abundance. When it comes to great art, however, the city has found it difficult to hold a candle to other Italian cities, such as Rome, Florence and Venice, which shamelessly display a much more grandiose artistic heritage.

Milan's shortage of classical features can be traced to a variety of factors. The city's long-standing position as underdog and also-ran is one. It's true that Milan was a capital under Diocletian (*see p7*) during the late Roman Empire, but Rome had already marked off its territory in terms of artistic and architectural style several centuries before, and Milan simply became a ready receptacle for Roman work, such as the portrait head of Maximinus or the torso of Hercules, both in the Civico Museo Archeologico (*see p96*).

In the 14th century, under its Visconti rulers (*see p11*), Milan was an important centre of the International Gothic. But art historians have

never been comfortable with the idea of the International Gothic as a high point of western art; and even Milan's most famous landmark, the Duomo (*see p54*), meant to be a celebration of this highly ornate style, took over 500 years to build, which meant that, by the time it was completed, its proposed architectural purity had been tainted by a variety of styles.

In the 15th century, Milanese ruler Ludovico il Moro Sforza (*see p14*) had the taste and the ambition to create a city as splendid as Renaissance Florence. He surrounded himself with the most renowned artists of the era, but his plans were nipped in the bud when he was taken prisoner by the French in 1499.

From the early 1500s until it became part of the Kingdom of Italy in the 19th century, Milan was ruled by foreigners. It's understandable, therefore, that indigenous qualities that could be held up as standards for posterity are hard to spot; the 'Lombard realism' recognised as a formative influence on the great baroque painter Caravaggio (*see p25* **The dark side**) is one. Like the city itself, Milan's art was under the sway of foreign imports and fashions. This is not to say that qualified local operators were absent, just that it takes a little extra effort to discover them.

Which is another problem in looking at art in Milan: us as viewers. Milan never had an artistic Golden Age like Florence in the 15th century, or Rome in the 16th. In the days of the Grand Tour it was largely left off travel itineraries and remains that way in the era of the package tour. Pieces that you are 'supposed to see' or 'can't miss' are generally not here. And when they are (for example, Leonardo's *Last Supper, see p92* **Guess who's coming to supper**), they've been reproduced so many times that you may find yourself at a loss trying to come to terms with the real thing.

The dearth of 'high' art can also be attributed to a tendency to turn greatness into something else. This is a truly Lombard characteristic: an exasperating urge not to create *ex novo*, but to add on, remodel or cover with whitewash. Little in Milan remained uninhabited or unused long enough to become 'artistic', 'charming' or 'quaint'. The city has always been all too glad to bury its past.

So it is not in its high art that the region's uniqueness lies. But forget your Grand Tour preconceptions, and you'll find there is a great deal to see in the city and beyond.

FROM CAVEMEN TO CHRISTIANITY

Lombardy's earliest artistic expression can be seen in the prehistoric caves and rock art in the Valcamonica (*see p271*). The Civiche Raccolte Archeologiche in the Castello Sforzesco (*see p66*) and the collections in the Musei Civici in the Villa Mirabello (*see p104*) in Varese also contain fine examples of prehistoric art.

The arrival of the Romans turned Milan – ancient Mediolanum – into the region's most important city. Yet only in the last century – with the construction of the *metropolitana* (the underground) – did its (very few) ruins emerge. When Mediolanum became the main city of Augustus's XI *regio* in 15 BC, it took the form of a Roman city with walls, *cardo* and *decumanus* and a forum where the church of San Sepolcro (*see p63*) now stands. Many great monuments were built at the end of the third century AD, when Diocletian made Milan the capital of the western half of the Empire, and again as the city emerged as a focal point of early Christianity.

When the charismatic Ambrose became bishop in 374, he embarked on a Christian building campaign that included five basilicas around the city walls and two cathedrals in the centre – among them, San Simpliciano (*see p71*). Though most of these were remodelled during the Romanesque period,

The dark side

In the same way that Leonardo da Vinci got his name because he came from a place called Vinci (*da* means 'from' in Italian), Michelangelo Merisi (1571-1610) came to be known as Caravaggio because he hailed from the village of that name near Bergamo. Actually, the young Merisi was probably born in Milan, but his family moved back to Caravaggio to escape the plague of 1577.

The artist's connection with Milan continued, however. In 1584, aged 13, he returned to the city and went to work with the painter Simone Peterzano. A pupil of Titian, Peterzano exposed Caravaggio to the Venetian Renaissance painting tradition, taking him to Venice several times, where the youngster was able to admire the work of Tintoretto.

These influences also came to bear on more local, Lombard developments. At this time in Milan, Bergamo, Brescia and Cremona, a number of artists (including

Lorenzo Lotto, Giovanni Battista Moroni, and Antonio and Vincenzo Campi) were experimenting with figurative art based on a faithful reproduction of reality. Caravaggio embraced naturalism wholeheartedly, creating paintings so lifelike, in both subject and rendition, they were unlike anything seen before.

Although Caravaggio left Milan for Rome when he was 20, the Lombard tradition left its mark on his work, various examples of which can be seen in Milan, including the *Basket of Fruit* in the Pinacoteca Ambrosiana (*see p63*) and *Supper at Emmaus* in Room XXIX of the Pinacoteca di Brera (*see p71*). Both these paintings perfectly capture the essence of Caravaggio's mature art, displaying the dramatic sense of naturalism he was renowned for and his mastery of the technique of *chiaroscuro*, which he achieved by placing his partially illuminated subjects against a dark background, thereby creating a dramatic contrast between light and dark.

the fifth-century chapel of Sant'Aquilino in San Lorenzo (see p85) still has mosaics that reveal the pictorial tastes of the age.

Modern historiography no longer looks upon the early medieval period as the Dark Ages; for Milan, however, it was as black as could be. Humbled and razed by successive waves of barbarian invaders, impoverished Milan was sidelined by flourishing neighbouring towns. The Germanic Lombards, who held sway from the sixth to the ninth centuries, favoured Monza and Pavia – the crown of Lombard Queen Theodolinda is in the treasury of Monza cathedral (see p100).

In the 1100s, however, bishops Angilbert II and Anspert ushered in a new age of monumental splendour for Milan with a burst of building activity and new city walls. Sant'Ambrogio (see p91) is home to the most important artistic works from this period: the ciborium (with recycled Roman porphyry columns and capitals), Angilbert II's gold altarpiece (depicting scenes from the life of Christ and St Ambrose), and the mosaics in the funerary chapel dedicated to San Vittore in Ciel d'Oro.

The reconstruction of Sant'Ambrogio in the 11th and 12th centuries inaugurated the great Romanesque period in Milan. The Byzantine, Islamic and Lombard influences on proto-Romanesque sculpture are clearly visible in the decoration on the capitals of the columns and the polychrome-and-gilt stucco of the canopy. Much of the work of the time was destroyed by later invaders, or subjected to heavy restoration at the end of the 19th century. But luckily, bits and pieces of many no-longer-extant buildings have been preserved in the sculpture museum of the Castello Sforzesco, including an early 'ideological' relief, St Ambrose Expelling the Arians, which is signed by Gerardo and Anselmo, two maestri campionesi – master stonecutters – from the Campione area, between the lakes of Lugano and Como.

Other signs of this period's prosperity are the great monastic complexes just outside Milan, such as the Cistercian abbey of Chiaravalle (see p106), founded by St Bernard in 1135 and consecrated in 1221. The religious Humiliati order – wiped out in the 16th century by the Counter-Reformation zeal of Carlo Borromeo – was also responsible for tremendous building activity, constructing the church of Santa Maria di Brera – now incorporated into the Pinacoteca di Brera (see p71) and abbeys at Viboldone (see p106) and Mirasole (see p107). On the portal of the church at Viboldone (begun in 1176) are sculptures of the Madonna with Child and Saints by another maestro campionese, the Maestro di Viboldone.

FAMILY INFLUENCE

By the 1330s, the powerful Visconti family had put an end to the free commune of Milan and seized power. Azzone Visconti ushered in a 150-year era of Gothic luxury that made Milan into a centre of art and culture – and, briefly, a rival to Florence. The wealth of artistic schools represented in the city at the time can be seen in the Pinacoteca di Brera. At Viboldone Abbey, the Last Judgment, attributed to Giusto de' Menabuoi, is considered one of the finest works of the era.

Azzone was responsible for importing another great Gothic master, Giovanni di Balduccio, who brought the imposing sculptural/architectural Pisan style of funerary monument to Milan. His masterpiece – the tomb of Stefano Visconti – is in the church of Sant'Eustorgio (see p85), while his sculptural decoration on the Porta Ticinese (see p85) is still in situ. Azzone's successor, Bernabò Visconti, favoured sculptor Bonino da Campione: his massive equestrian statue of Bernabò in the Castello Sforzesco matched his commissioner's ego.

> 'Ludovico Sforza strove to make Milan a true centre of Renaissance style by summoning the most highly acclaimed artists of the time, including Bramante and Leonardo, to his court.'

In painting, the International Gothic flourished in Milan under Bernabò's nephew Gian Galeazzo Visconti. His favourite artist was Giovannino de' Grassi, one of the many stonecutters and architects to work on the city's immense Duomo from 1386 onwards: his sculptures can be seen on the portals in the south sacristy and on St Catherine's altar in the left nave. Other examples of the refined Milanese culture of the period include Bonifacio Bembo's Tarocchi in the Pinacoteca Accademia Carrara in Bergamo (see p226), and the Zavattari brothers' frescoes in the chapel of Queen Theodolinda in Monza's Duomo.

The Viscontis' rule gave way to that of the Sforza dynasty, which aimed, at first, to conserve the city's International Gothic tradition. But both the first Sforza duke, Francesco, and his successor, Galeazzo Maria, were aware of the artistic goings-on in central Italy, which by then was on to its second generation of Renaissance painters (including Piero della Francesca, whose Montefeltro altarpiece is in the Brera). What emerged was a sort of Lombard-Tuscan pastiche, both in architecture and painting.

The leading artist of the age was **Vincenzo Foppa**, who blended Mantegnesque and Tuscan influences in his masterpiece *Scenes from the Life of St Peter the Martyr*, held in the Cappella Portinari, in Sant'Eustorgio (*see p85*).

Galeazzo Maria's half-brother Ludovico il Moro Sforza had very different ideas: while extending the territory under Milanese control well into present-day Switzerland, he strove to make the city a true centre of Renaissance style. To that end, he summoned the most highly acclaimed men of letters, musicians and artists of the time, including **Donato Bramante** and **Leonardo da Vinci** to his court.

Though Bramante is best known for his Milanese buildings (Santa Maria delle Grazie, *see p96*, and Santa Maria presso San Satiro, *see p63*), he also left his mark in frescoes: his *Portraits of Illustrious Men*, now in the Brera, show how extensively the humanistic culture of central Italy had penetrated Lombard territory.

Leonardo was commissioned to make a vast equestrian monument to Francesco Sforza, but the sculpture failed to get past the planning stage; the model for it was destroyed by French troops after Ludovico was ousted. (A reconstruction by sculptor Nina Akamu can be seen at the Ippodromo, piazzale dello Sport 15)

The most famous ducal commission, however, remains Leonardo's *Last Supper* (*Il Cenacolo, see p92* **Guess who's coming to supper**) in the refectory of Santa Maria delle Grazie, Ludovico's favourite church. In spite of being ravaged by time and by Leonardo's unfortunate experimental technique, the fresco still shows how far ahead of his time Leonardo was, especially in comparison with **Donato da Montorfano**'s fresco of the crucifixion on the opposite wall.

THE COUNTER-REFORMATION AND BAROQUE

Leonardo and Bramante had already left the city by the time Ludovico il Moro fell in 1499, but the Lombard tradition that had taken root there continued for two more decades. The prolific **Bernadino Bergognone** was its chief representative, leaving behind a prodigious amount of work at the Certosa di Pavia (*see p259*) and in Milan (*The Coronation of the Virgin* in the apsidal conch of San Simpliciano, and a series of Christ and the Apostles in the sacristy of Santa Maria della Passione, *see p79*). Great convent and monastery churches were built within the city walls, and decorated by the likes of **Giovanni Boltraffio** and **Bernardino Luini**.

The Kiss by Francesco Hayez.
See p28.

Holy Roman Emperor Charles V (*see p16*) had works by his Venetian favourite **Titian** (including *The Flagellation*, which was later carried off to Paris by Napoleon) installed in Milanese churches. Towards the middle of the century, another important Venetian work arrived in Milan: **Tintoretto**'s *Christ Disputing with the Elders in the Temple*, now in the Museo del Duomo (*see p54*).

The more austere spirit of the Counter-Reformation – personified in Milan by the all-powerful archbishop-cousins Carlo and Federico Borromeo – brought the first traces of the late Renaissance style, Mannerism. No area of artistic output in the region in the late 16th and early 17th centuries escaped the cousins' influence. Among their favourites was the Cremonese painter **Bernardino Campi**, whose work is cloyingly pious, while brothers **Vincenzo** and **Antonio Campi** from Cremona also found fertile terrain in Milan, as did **Simone Peterzano** from Bergamo. But the Lombard Mannerist artist *par excellence* was **Gaudenzio Ferrari** from Valsesia. He appeared on the scene in 1544-5, painting frescoes in Santa Maria della Pace (now in the Brera) and in Santa Maria delle Grazie.

Baroque hit Milan while Federico occupied the archbishop's throne (1595-1631) and a new generation of Milanese painters emerged: **Giovanni Battista Crespi** (aka **Il Cerano**), **Giulio Cesare Procaccini**, **Il Morazzone** and **Daniele Crespi**. A series of canvases with *Scenes from the Life of St Charles Borromeo* (1602-10) by Il Cerano and Procaccini is still exhibited in the Duomo from 4 November until 6 January each year. But the single greatest symbol of the cultural spirit of the age is the Pinacoteca Ambrosiana (*see p63*), founded in 1618 when Federico's own art collection was donated to the Biblioteca Ambrosiana.

ROMANTIC ROCOCO

During Milan's first stint under Austrian rule (1706-96), mature baroque and extravagant rococo flourished. The archetypal rococo dabbler, **Giambattista Tiepolo**, was called on to decorate many Milanese residences in the 1740s; the Venetian's paintings can be seen in Palazzo Clerici (*see p60*). Frescoes by a precursor of Tiepolo, **Sebastiano Ricci**, adorn the vault of San Bernardino alle Ossa (*see p82*).

The second period of Austrian rule (1815-59) brought Milan closer to the spirit of northern Europe; its open attitude towards liberal ideas made it a capital of the Romantic era, a role epitomised in **Francesco Hayez**'s *Il bacio* (*The Kiss*) in the Brera.

POST-UNIFICATION ENTHUSIASM

Milan's annexation into the Kingdom of Italy in 1805 magnified its twofold image as European city and Italian economic success story. Liberal-leaning private enterprise created great works such as the Cimitero Monumentale (*see p74*), and the Galleria Vittorio Emanuele (*see p54*).

In the arts, an eclectic movement of Lombard historicism sprang up, wandering from the Romanesque-Gothic to the Bramantesque styles of painting. Simultaneously, the avant-garde **Scapigliatura** school (comprising Federico Faruffini, Luigi Conconi and the sculptor Giuseppe Grandi) paved the way for the energetic celebration of modernism: **futurism**.

While **Filippo Tommaso Marinetti**, author of *The Futurist Manifesto*, held his famous salon in his home on corso Venezia (a plaque marks the spot), **Alessandro Mazzucotelli** and his **Società Umanitaria** were forging a socialist *arte nuova* in applied arts. Out of this came **Pelizza da Volpedo**'s *Fourth State*, now in the Galleria d'Arte Moderna (*see p81*), a symbol of artistic commitment to the forces of social change.

The Milan of the interwar years was a political and cultural contradiction. At the centre of humanitarian socialism, it was also the birthplace of fascism. The construction of the Palazzo dell'Arte (*see p67*) in 1932-3 as permanent headquarters for the Triennale exhibition demonstrated the city's connection with contemporary art at an early date.

The Palazzo d'Arte became a reference point for the first **Novecento** group, whose strongest exponents were the ex-futurists **Carlo Carrà** and **Mario Sironi**, as well as the **Chiaristi**, with their neo-impressionist painting, and the young expressionist painters of **Corrente**, such as **Aligi Sassu** and **Ernesto Treccani**. These last two organised their own gallery, Il Milione, where the first Italian abstract artists met. This period also saw the birth of great collections of contemporary art in Milan.

THE ARTISTIC SCENE TODAY

Milan has continued to be a centre for showing and producing art. Among the city's main post-war avant-garde movements are **Fronte Nuovo**; the abstract **MAC**; the 'spatial' and 'nuclear' groups of **Lucio Fontana**; urban-existential neo-realism gravitating around the **Centro dei Gesuiti di San Fedele**; **Piero Manzoni**'s conceptual and behavioural art; and the 'pop' art of **Valerio Adami** and **Emilio Tadini**. And examples of urban avant-garde sculpture are scattered around the city, including **Arnaldo Pomodoro**'s piece in piazza Meda.

Media Central

Berlusconi's far-reaching media empire was born in a small town just north of Milan.

Driving into Milan from its northern outskirts, the first thing to greet you is the blinking red eye of the Big Serpent – 'il Biscione', as the locals call it – the towering television antenna of private broadcaster Mediaset in the town of Cologno Monzese. It is a fitting monument for a city that broadcasts to the world an image of glamour, despite itself being, for the most part, a rather unglamorous-looking metropolis.

Mostly, though, the tower is a symbol of the man who built it: a man from these very streets, who used the profits and connections from property deals to create Italy's only alternative to state-owned TV. Along the way, he amassed an empire that now encompasses everything from insurance companies to Milan's oldest soccer team. His money and fame even helped him attain two stints as Italy's prime minister. Love him or hate him, Silvio Berlusconi is the most influential man in a land of powerful oligarchs, not only because he is the nation's wealthiest person and occasionally its prime minister, but also because most of what is written or said about him comes from journalists he employs.

His media empire includes Mondadori, the nation's largest publisher of books and magazines, and Einaudi, another respected publishing house. His brother Paolo runs Il Giornale, a conservative newspaper and mouthpiece for Silvio's party, Forza Italia. The high-brow Il Foglio, run by Giuliano Ferrara, is also under his thumb. He owns a film company called Medusa and a number of theatres. He is also the majority shareholder in video rental chain Blockbuster Italia. Many of these companies are based in the northern outskirts of Milan, just down the street from Berlusconi's palatial dacha in Arcore, and provide employment for a great deal of the area's residents.

But it's the tower in Cologno Monzese, standing defiant, that most dominates everyday life. It was never meant to be there. Before the arrival of Mediaset, legislation prohibited any company from creating a national television network to rival the state monopoly, RAI. Berlusconi attempted to get around this law by controlling a network of individual local stations and broadcasting the same programmes simultaneously. Officials in Rome weren't convinced this arrangement was any different from the national competition they were trying to prevent. Judges ordered the stations to shut down. But after just four days, Berlusconi's friend, then-prime minister Bettino Craxi, weighed in on the budding media baron's behalf by citing a technicality: the programmes were broadcast a split second out of sync across the different regions. In 1980 Mediaset was born.

BRUNCH AT THE HILTON MILAN
Sunday without rules

Fuel your imagination at the Hilton Milan. Treat yourself to a Sunday marked by goo(taste and relaxation, in the company of all your family and friends. Our brand-ne(brunch, created in collaboration with the exclusive Moët & Chandon, fuses breakfa(and lunch into a one-of-a-kind celebration of new and sophisticated flavours.

From 12:00
to 3:00 PM,
a warm and hospitable
atmosphere,
a luxurious selection
of hors d'oeuvres and
outstanding recipes,

awaits you in the
Pacific Milano
Restaurant,
with a play area
specially designed fo(the youngest membe(of the family

paired with the
effervescent elegance
of renowned
French champagnes,
accompanied by
pleasant
background music,

and the opportunity
to entertain yourself
online via our
state-of-the-art
wi-fi system.

29.90 Euros per adult
13.00 Euros per child up to 12 years of age

Hilton
Milan

This is the kind of behaviour that has made Berlusconi admired and loathed in equal measure, in Italy and abroad. Some beam at a businessman who managed to create an empire in the face of what they reckoned was an oppressive state, while others are critical of his rapport and dealings with Craxi. Milanese magistrates tend to fall into the second category.

One of Berlusconi's more famous dealings with Craxi was the so-called 'SME affair', the details of which emerged during an investigation that came to a head in 2003. The Milan magistrates brought charges against the media baron of obstructing justice in the state sale of food conglomerate SME to Berlusconi's arch nemesis, Carlo De Benedetti. The alleged offences took place in the late 1980s. The crackdown started in the 1990s, in a series of investigations earning the nickname *Mani Pulite* or 'Clean Hands'. Berlusconi, who was absolved in 2003, prefers to describe them as a left-wing conspiracy.

THE PRESS
The Clean Hands investigations resulted in the suicides of several high-profile executives, a great number of jail sentences, the exile of Craxi to Tunisia, where he died, and a self-conferred identity for Milan as the 'moral capital' of Italy.

The most tenacious reporting in the Milan courtrooms came from *Il Corriere della Sera*. The stodgy, greying paper, about as bland as they come in a country where most broadsheets, are drama-filled, is one of the few Italian papers that can justifiably call itself independent.

Indeed, the greatest fear of lovers of the free press is that Berlusconi will eventually snap up this prestigious publication as well. A shareholder pact of *Il Corriere*'s parent company Rizzoli – the largest shareholder is Fiat – declaring that the newspaper should never be separated from Rizzoli's less-profitable holdings has so far kept it from the reach of would-be raiders (you-know-who, especially). Even the blue-collar location of Rizzoli's headquarters lies squarely between Milano 2, the property development that launched Berlusconi, and the suburban sprawl that Mediaset now occupies. If *Il Corriere*, the number-one non-sports daily by circulation, were to be snatched up, it would leave the left-leaning, Rome-based *La Repubblica* (funded by, surprise, Carlo De Benedetti) as the only major news outlet outside Berlusconi's control.

Perhaps the most reliable and unbiased papers in Milan are the sports and financial ones. The pink pages of *La Gazzetta dello Sport*, the largest daily by circulation, are owned by Rizzoli. *La Gazzetta* shares its headquarters with *Il Corriere della Sera* in the Brera neighbourhood, on via Solferino. It is an Italian institution, begun at

the turn of the 20th century to follow cycling races and later dominated by stories on football, which took off in northern Italy a decade later when the teams of Genoa, AC Milan and Inter were born. Italian children, they say, are raised on *pane e Gazzetta* ('bread and the *Gazzetta*').

Milan's answer to the *Financial Times* is the peach-coloured *Il Sole 24 Ore*. Don't expect too many labour-friendly stories in this broadsheet, owned by the industrialist lobby Confindustria, but the reporting is very straightforward and the arts and culture section is very highly regarded.

TELEVISION
More worrisome for left-wing legislators than Berlusconi's control over the written word is his grip on television. As owner of Mediaset, he runs several of the most popular commercial TV stations; as prime minister, he oversees the three state channels of RAI, which means he has effective control over virtually 100 per cent of the airwaves. This conflict of interests led opposition legislators to request an assurance that political coverage would be fair and balanced. The result was a compromise known as *par condicio*, an agreement that both conservatives and liberals would receive equal airtime on TV.

'Both RAI and Mediaset serve up their share of junk because prime-time ratings matter to everybody.'

After all, Italians rely almost exclusively on television for news. Aside from the football games, it's about the only reason to turn the tube on at all. The division between public and private broadcasting might suggest that RAI would offer educational and family-oriented programming, while Mediaset, which relies on commercials for revenue, has the freedom to cater to the lowest common denominator. In reality, though, both serve up their share of junk because prime-time ratings matter to everybody. As anybody here will tell you, most of what you'll find on Italian TV is utterly unwatchable.

The bread-and-butter of prime-time programming has long been a line-up of quiz shows and 1950s-style variety shows, each with a generous helping of half-naked women (*see p32* **Boxing clever**) and comedy bordering on slapstick. Flip the channel and you are likely to find a B-grade American movie from the 1970s loaded with car chases and explosions.

On the bright side, Italian TV does run some outstanding documentaries and captivating shows on food and travel. The travel shows

Boxing clever

This time the TV producers had gone too far. The creators of the show *Libero* had stuck a 22-year-old half-naked blonde under a glass table, while the host went ahead with his routine of prank phone calls. The model, Flavia Vento, was asked only to look pretty. Most *veline* ('little sails' – the term for these scantily clad adolescent TV girls) are at least allowed to speak, the Vatican complained. Flavia, however, was meant to be seen and not heard.

When asked if she thought her role was demeaning, Flavia was nonplussed; 'a sculpture under glass that cannot be touched,' is how she described her character. 'If these priests are so shocked, they should see what else is on TV.'

This much is true. Channel-surfing would provide little relief to clerics or anyone else. *Veline* are ubiquitous on Italian TV. It all started in 1993, with a programme ominously called *Non è la RAI* (it's not RAI), shown on, natch, Berlusconi's Canale 5. The show consisted of songs, dance routines and more songs, all performed by a cast of 100 scantily clad girls. When *Non è la RAI* wrapped up, the most buxom of these young girls were hired to appear on the political comedy show *Striscia la Notizia* (literally 'crawling news') broadcast at prime time on Canale 5). The *veline* were born.

Ever since *Striscia la Notizia* unveiled their dancing girls to rave reviews, every other prime-time show has faced a choice: pony up some half-naked teens or watch the ratings go down. Enter the *postine* (little post-girls) of *C'è posta per te*, the *letterine* (little letters) of *Passaparola* and the *schedine* (little pool-girls) of *Quelli che il Calcio*. The format is always the same: the host does the talking while the goose-bumped starlets laugh on cue.

No problem, say the girls, who laugh all the way to fame and fortune, landing lucrative contracts and maybe even a soccer-playing

hubbie. *Veline* are the number-one role models for teenagers – after all, getting your face, and body, on TV is a dream come true for most Italian girls.

Occasionally *veline* end up on the commanding end of the microphone. Some of the best-recognised faces on Italian TV started off in hot pants and halter-neck tops. Simona Ventura began her career as a *velina* and now runs the show *Quelli che il Calcio*, with her own entourage of half-naked debutantes. True to form, she also bagged herself a footballer husband (Stefano Bettarini) in the process.

As for the majority of viewers, presumed to be housewives vacuuming in front of their TV sets, their long-buried aspirations were given a second chance in the form of *Velone* ('large *veline*'). The programme has the 65-and-up set shaking and shimmying, jealously vying for the fame once awarded to their granddaughters alone. Again, the Vatican cries foul play. This is not the alternative they had in mind.

are usually aired on Sunday mornings, and the documentaries late at night, crammed between ads for horoscope readers and, again, mountains of female flesh.

As sorry as the situation is, there are few alternatives. There is La Sette, a single-channel broadcaster that offers Italy's only independent political voice, and, of course, the videos of MTV. Both have their studios near the Martesana canal in the northern limits of the

Milan. For some truly base entertainment, there is local television. The two principal stations in Milan are Antenna 3, based in the northern suburb of Legnano, and Telelombardia, in the unflinchingly industrial district of Bovisa. Aside from the TV mystics and other paid programming that keep the fledgling stations alive, both offer some fun, off-the-wall sports commentaries, most notably those hosted by Maurizio Mosca on Antenna 3.

Economic Powerhouse

How Lombardy became known as the workhorse of Italy.

Milan makes the money and Rome spends it. Umberto Bossi's Northern League has been making political hay for years out of this widespread 'northern' *bon mot*, and stories about Milan (and Lombardy) being Italy's 'economic powerhouse' have become almost clichéd. Still, there's no disputing the numbers: the area around Milan accounts for close to 20 per cent of Italy's gross domestic product (GDP), and the Lombardy region boasts a GDP almost as large as Belgium's. In fact, given that Lombardy contributes more than three per cent of the GDP of the EU, it is probably more accurate to talk about Lombardy as a European, rather than an Italian, powerhouse.

The Milanese like to claim that Milan's history as a commercial centre dates back to Roman times, and the Lombards in general have long been known for their business prowess; 15th-century writer Matteo Bandello (whose version of *Romeo and Juliet* probably inspired Shakespeare's) bluntly said, 'In Bergamo and the surrounding countryside, men are in the habit of doing a lot of business.'

The habit of industriousness has allowed the Lombard economy to ride out Milan's numerous political misfortunes: Romans, Lombards, Sforzas, Holy Roman Emperors, Spanish, French and Austrians have all come and gone, but there has always been business to be done. After the Sforza family lost control to Spain, for instance, the cities of Lombardy languished, growing little economically or politically. The countryside, however, continued to trade and experiment with technological advances in agriculture. The increasing food supply meant that Lombardy could continue to grow, and the reliance on small-town artisans for tools planted the seeds of a deep-rooted manufacturing sector. These artisans grew accustomed to producing a limited range of high-quality goods (a skill that would stand Lombardy in good stead during the post-World War II boom), and to prospering outside of the big cities. Even today, some of Italy's most important exporters can be found in small provincial towns.

Milan not only weathered foreign occupation, but turned it to its economic advantage. As a result of Milan's intertwining relationships with Spain, France, Austria, not to mention Switzerland, the area became a European – not simply an Italian – centre of productivity.

By the time Lombardy joined the newly united Kingdom of Italy in 1859, it had a population of over three million, and was one of the most advanced regions in the country. Lombardy used the period between unification and the outbreak of World War I to industrialise and expand its horizons. Twenty-four-year-old Giovanni Battista Pirelli founded his rubber company in 1872, and by the 1880s, iron, steel and manufacturing plants could be seen throughout the Milan area. The opening

Armani is part of Milan's economic engine.

of the San Gottardo tunnel in 1882 plugged Lombardy directly into the commercial networks of northern Europe.

Despite labour strikes in the 1890s, Milan had reached a satisfying level of prosperity by the turn of last century. The good times were interrupted by World War I and the crippling inflation of the 1920s. The Milanese spent the fascist years persevering rather than prospering, and bombing raids during World War II severely damaged Lombardy's industrial plants.

Soon after the end of the war, however, Lombardy began to rebuild. Workers from the south headed to Milan to look for work at Alfa Romeo, Pirelli, Breda (railway construction) and the other big factories. This influx changed the face of Milan, as huge housing estates were built to accommodate the workers.

In the 19th century, Lombardy had managed the transition from an agricultural economy to an industrial one without crippling dislocations (even today Lombardy has more pigs and cows than any other region in Italy). By the 1960s, though, the region had become less competitive industrially, and jobs were – if not being lost – being created at a lower rate. This slide into post-industrialism spelled the need to transform the economy again. Service jobs – particularly in media and entertainment – began to replace manufacturing jobs. (Silvio Berlusconi caught this wave in the early 1970s when he founded TeleMilano; *see chapter* **Media Central**).

Despite the urban terrorism of the 1970s and early 1980s, Lombardy's new industries gained momentum. In 1975, trying to secure his place in the burgeoning fashion industry, Giorgio Armani sold his Volkswagen to finance his business. Gianni Versace started plying his trade in 1978.

Even while Milan was challenging Paris for designer dominance, it was facing threats to its economic development. Successive Italian governments had increased spending to the point that in 1992 national debt was 120 per cent of Italy's GDP. That sprawl of spending was matched by the amount of corruption companies faced doing business with the government. Since Lombardy was such a large contributor to the Italian economy, it was also a large contributor to the bribery scandal known as *Tangentopoli* (bribesville, *see p19*). In the 1990s, Milan got used to seeing its politicians and businessmen hauled into the halls of justice in corso Porta Vittoria (and being sent back out into the streets – very few people have served prison time because of the scandal).

Being nothing if not resilient, however, Lombardy was able to absorb the blow to its reputation, and recent years have seen an increase in industries such as financial services, IT, e-commerce and tourism.

SMALLER IS BETTER

More than in most other industrialised countries, Italy's businesses tend to be family-owned, and even in the case of industrial giants such as Fiat, members of the founding family usually remain in control. The real backbone of the economy, though, consists of the vast number of small to mid-sized firms. These firms, overwhelmingly family-owned and -run, are responsible for more than 70 per cent of jobs in Italy.

In Lombardy, medium-sized firms produce a stunning variety of goods: firearms (Beretta), brake pads (Brembo), silk (Ratti), sparkling wines (Berlucchi), synthetic foam (Crespi) and clothes (Armani). These companies can survive in a multinational world because they rely on Lombardy's time-honoured traditions of entrepreneurial spirit and niche marketing. Guido Berlucchi, for example, used the microclimate of Franciacorta (*see p236*) to develop the production of a world-class sparkling wine capable of challenging champagne. More remarkably, he did this at a time when the only Italian sparkling wine familiar to consumers was Asti Spumante.

Flexibility is the other key ingredient in the Lombard recipe for success. Italian manufacturers are famous for the ability to adapt – in stark contrast to the famously hide-bound public sector. Brembo, a brake-pad manufacturer near Bergamo that supplies brakes to Ferrari, will sometimes introduce more than 100 new products in a year. This flexibility allows the company to do well in the market for brake replacements, a classic example of a niche market.

Lombardy's manufacturers have relied on the region's traditions to produce their goods; they have also exploited Lombardy's connections to export their products: some 30 per cent of Italy's exports originate in the region.

MORE IS MORE

While the provinces continue to produce and export, Milan's economy has become primarily service-oriented. As Italy's financial capital, Milan hosts a vibrant stock market and more than 130 banks. It is the base of operations for many of the biggest designers in the world – not only fashion designers such as Armani, but furniture designers such as Kartell. The number of companies using Milan for their headquarters has created a formidable business services industry: secretaries, lawyers, accountants, photocopier repairmen all thrive in Milan. Just about half of Italy's television programming originates from Silvio Berlusconi's Mediaset, just across the city line in Cologno Monzese.

The provinces do not to limit themselves, either. Pavia, south of Milan, has developed into a high-tech area; it is also Europe's biggest rice producer. Cremona produces both chemicals and violins (Stradivarius). In the north, the province of Sondrio contributes tourism (Bormio is a big ski resort), engineering and apples to the region's industrial portfolio.

> **'Lombard families are faced with the choice of ceding control to outside managers, or risking the company on lacklustre internal direction.'**

This diversification is a major factor in the region's continued success. Not only can Lombardy withstand the loss of a particular industry, but the variety has allowed the area to develop an internal network of suppliers. The fashion designers of Milan, for instance, look to the textile firms of Bergamo to turn their designs into clothes.

WHAT'S NEXT?

Lombardy's business leaders talk with pride about how the region has managed the transition from a production to a service economy, but it is not complete. Indeed, Lombardy hasn't finished moving from an agricultural to an industrial economy yet, and towns in provinces on the plains, such as Cremona and Mantova, still lose their inhabitants to Milan. Unemployment may remain well below the national average, but events such as the closure of the Alfa Romeo plant in Arese are becoming more frequent. The question of how to handle displaced workers, and displaced older workers in particular, will vex the region for some time to come.

At the same time, workers continue to find jobs in Lombardy's factories. Increasingly, these workers are not immigrants from southern Italy (as they were after World War II), but immigrants from the Middle East, Eastern Europe and Africa. Lombardy is wrestling with how (and how much) to assimilate these new workers: on the one hand, the Northern League has a pronounced taste for running xenophobic ads to rally the faithful against the *clandestini* (illegal immigrants; though the Northern League tends to overlook details such as the possession of a work visa); on the other hand, manufacturing and agricultural companies point out that it is getting harder and harder to find Italians willing to do the jobs at the wages offered, and statisticians point out that without these new (younger) workers, Italy's dire pension situation would be even more dire.

Lombardy also has major problems with its infrastructure. The Lombard stretch of the A4, the motorway connecting Turin and Venice, is overburdened with trucks and commuters. Indeed, because so much of Italy's freight moves on wheels, and because so many of Italy's exports come from Lombardy, all of the region's motorways need help. There are two new motorways in the pipeline, one that will go from Milan to Bergamo, and on to Brescia, running parallel to the A4, and another that would pass north of Milan and link Malpensa Airport with the airport at Bergamo, Orio al Serio. But work has not yet begun on either, so it will be some time before there is any relief.

VICTIM OF ITS OWN SUCCESS

Ironically, one of the key strengths of Lombardy's economy is also cause for concern. Many of the family firms that powered the region's post-war success were founded in the 1950s and 1960s, and the founders have either retired or passed away. Because the business was so successful, many of the second (and third) generations have preferred to devote themselves to enjoying the fruits rather than learning the ropes. Now the families are faced with the choice of ceding control to outside managers, or risking the company on lacklustre internal direction. Then again, Lombard commerce has been able to withstand the vagaries of 2,000 years of history, so it should be able to withstand a few spoiled yuppie Italians with Porsches.

The region remains pro-entrepreneur, and the people remain pro-work. They may complain that the rest of Italy is riding the Lombard gravy train, but in quieter moments, they will concede that other northern regions such as Piedmont and the Veneto can pull their own weight. And in the quietest moments, they will even admit they like complaining about calling an office in Rome at 10am, only to find no one's arrived yet.

Where to Stay

Where to Stay   38

Features

The best Hotels   38
Milan's grande dame   47

Where to Stay

Milan's hotels are expensive, and often booked to the roof beams.
But look closer – there are also some affordable gems.

Unlike cities such as Rome, Florence or Venice, which cater largely to the tourist trade, Milan's hotels are (mostly) geared towards corporate travellers, who come here to attend fairs and exhibitions, and who demand a comfortable room fitted with all the gadgets to make life easier at the end of a long day at the stands.

Regular visitors to Milan tend to be people who have no time 'to stand and stare', which is just as well, since they'd have their work cut out looking for a room with a view in Milan – a window opening on to a brick wall is not unheard of, and the best one can expect is a long way from olive groves or charming piazzas: a quiet courtyard is more the norm. A room facing the inner courtyard is what you should ask for when booking your room – even double glazing cannot keep the noise of

Milan's traffic at bay, and the clank of trams on tracks can be unbearable for those trying to sleep past 5.30am.

Whether you choose a charming *locanda* in a 19th-century palazzo or the luxury, all-mod-cons hotel experience that few cities around the world can boast, you should come prepared to pay, if not through the nose, at least through gritted teeth. The country's business, financial, design and employment centre is not cheap. It's worth shopping around, especially while trade fairs are being held at the Fiera di Milano (*see chapter* **Festivals & Events**) and during the periods around March and October, when Milan's fashion machine cranks up to a fever pitch. The most convenient deals – for price and for location – are at the smaller downtown hotels. Call a few before making a decision; everyone will speak at least functional English, and some may offer special unadvertised rates or cash discounts.

Whenever possible, make your reservation well in advance. You will probably be asked to confirm your booking by fax or to leave a credit card number. If you cancel your reservation less than a day or two before your arrival, you may be required to pay for a night's lodging.

Milan suffers from a chronic shortage of parking space. Few hotels have their own car park or, if they do, they are pocket-handkerchief sized. To compensate, many have deals with local garages for overnight parking. The price of this service varies considerably, but can be as high as €50. Needless to say, don't come by car if you can help it – you won't need one anyway: Milan is a compact city that boasts an efficient and comprehensive public transport system.

The best Hotels

For throwing a room party
The Gray (*see p41*).

For stargazing
Grand Hotel et de Milan (*see p41*);
Park Hyatt Milan (*see p41*);
Sheraton Diana Majestic (*see p46*).

For design
Spadari al Duomo (*see p41*);
STRAF (*see p42*).

For pampering yourself
Four Seasons (*see p41*).

For chronic elegance
Grand Hotel et de Milan (*see p41*).

For absolute Milano
Antica Locanda dei Mercanti (*see p42*);
Antica Locanda Solferino (*see p45*).

For protecting your wallet
London (*see p45*);
Palazzo delle Stelline (*see p50*).

For protecting your planet
Ariston (*see p49*).

STANDARDS AND PRICES

Italian hotels are rated from one star to five-star deluxe. *Pensione*, although not an official term, is still used to describe one- and two-star hotels (€90-€130); these are usually family-run affairs where rooms tend to be functional and you may have to share a bathroom.

A *locanda* was traditionally a cheap place to eat and sleep: nowadays it usually signifies a fancy *pensione* with some olde worlde charm. Three- and four-star hotels have more facilities and the majority of rooms will have en suite bathrooms. There's a huge disparity in this category between the best and worst deals,

The highly stylised (and not very grey) **Gray**. *See p41.*

and higher prices do not guarantee cleanliness or better service. But this disparity can also work the other way, translating into value for money and some of the best hotels in this guide are the proof.

Five-star hotels in Milan are impressively luxurious and often breathtakingly expensive. The emphasis here is on opulence, but unless you're on your honeymoon or staying on a generous expense account, you're better off staying at the perfectly comfortable accommodation available in central locations for a fraction of the price.

When making a reservation, be sure that prices are quoted including *IVA* (sales tax): often this is not included in initial quotes, and an additional ten per cent on your bill can come as a nasty surprise.

Most hotel rates include breakfast (assume it's included unless otherwise stated in the listings): in the medium to high brackets, this is generally a buffet with hot and cold food; further down the scale you'll encounter the kind of dull-tasting coffee that foreign tourists are thought to enjoy with limp-looking *brioches* (croissants) or bread rolls, butter and jam. If you have a choice, pay for the room without breakfast and go to a local eaterie to enjoy the very Italian custom of knocking back an espresso standing at the bar. It'll cost less, the pastries will be fresh and the coffee real.

If you arrive at Malpensa or Linate airports with nowhere to stay, avoid the travel agency desks. They will book a hotel for you, but the choice is limited to the places that pay the agency a commission and the cost will be passed on to you. Instead, use the suggestions below or head to the APT office (via Marconi 1, 02 7252 4301, www.milanoinfotourist.com) in town near piazza Duomo, where staff will provide you with a free booklet on hotels that is wide-ranging and updated every six months.

Duomo & Centre

Expensive

De La Ville
Via Hoepli 6 (02 879 1311/fax 02 866 609/www. delavillemilano.com). Metro Duomo/bus 61/tram 1, 2, 20. **Rates** (+10% tax) €144-€282 single; €176-€320 double; €195-€381 triple; €485 junior suite; €710 suite. **Credit** AmEx, DC, MC, V. **Map** p311 A1/p312 B1.

An elegantly refined atmosphere pervades this traditional hotel near the Duomo and La Scala. The rooms are well appointed and the bathrooms have marble fittings. The adjoining Canova restaurant is open until late for returning theatre-goers; there's also a well-equipped fitness centre with sauna and Turkish bath, and conference rooms for business guests. The price reflects the prestigious location, but the quality and services are comparable with the far more expensive five-star hotels in the area.

Hotel services *Air-conditioning. Babysitting. Bar. Conference rooms. Disabled: lift, wide doors. Gym. Laundry. Limousine service. No-smoking rooms. Parking (€40 per day). Restaurant. Sauna.* **Room services** *Hairdryer. Internet access: dataport. Minibar. Room service (7am-midnight). Safe. TV: satellite.*

Four Seasons

Via Gesù 8 (02 77 088/fax 02 7708 5000/www.four seasons.com/milan). Metro Montenapoleone or San Babila/bus 61, 94/tram 1, 2, 20. **Rates** (+10% tax) €500 single; €570 double; €4,680 suite. **Credit** AmEx, DC, MC, V. **Map** p309 C1/p312 C1.

Housed in a 15th-century convent, with frescoes in some of the suites and an idyllic cloistered courtyard, the Four Seasons may be the most expensive hotel in Milan, but you get plenty of fabulous bang for your buck. The huge bedrooms feature Fortuny fabrics, pear and sycamore wood furniture, DVD players and opulent marble bathrooms big enough to sleep in, not to mention wonderfully plush, oversized towels and bathrobes. The Teatro restaurant is ranked among the top ten eateries in town. Beyond the means of most (guests typically include heads of state, wealthy industrialists and film stars), but very, very nice.

Hotel services *Bar. Conference rooms. Disabled: adapted rooms, ramp access. Gym. Laundry service. Limousine service. Parking (€50 per day). Restaurant.* **Room services** *Air-conditioning. Fax. Hairdryer. Internet access: dataport. Minibar. Room service (24hrs). Safe. TV: satellite, VCR, DVD.*

Grand Hotel et de Milan

Via Manzoni 29 (02 723 141/fax 02 864 6861/www. grandhoteletdemilan.it). Metro Montenapoleone/bus 61, 94/tram 1, 2, 20. **Rates** €418 single; €517 double (single occupancy); €517-€605 double; €699 junior suite; €968 superior suite; €1,210 deluxe suite. *Breakfast* €35. **Credit** AmEx, DC, MC, V. **Map** p309 C1/p312 B1.

The five-star Grand is an elegant 19th-century palazzo and is as sumptuous as it gets – all marble, flowers, draperies and antiques. The gorgeous suites are named after illustrious guests from the past, such as Giuseppe Verdi, Luchino Visconti and Maria Callas, and the efficient service is as discreet as it is friendly. Everybody should treat themselves to at least one day in the comfortable luxury of this hotel. Ask about weekend rates; you may be pleasantly surprised. *See also p47* **Milan's grande dame.**

Hotel services *Air-conditioning. Bars. Conference rooms. Disabled: adapted rooms, ramp access. Gym. Internet point. Laundry. Limousine service. Parking (€40 per day). Restaurants.* **Room services** *Hairdryer. Minibar. Room service (7am-1am). Safe. TV: satellite.*

The Gray

Via San Raffaele 6 (02 720 8951/fax 02 866 526/ www.hotelthegray.com). Metro Duomo. **Rates** (+10% tax) €300 single; €450-€900 double. *Breakfast* €25. **Credit** AmEx, DC, MC, V. **Map** p311 A1/p312 B1, B2.

The Gray, together with the STRAF (*see p42*), perfectly encapsulates the latest Milanese trend in high-end hostelry. It has a lounge-music-pulsing ambience, its own chic restaurant (Le Noir) and rooms that come equipped with everything from enormous plasma TVs to jacuzzis. Furniture and decor are all avant-garde and definitely not for those with an aversion to modern design; trendy party people, however, may find it difficult to leave their rooms.

Hotel services *Air-conditioning. Restaurant. Bar. Laundry. Limousine service. No-smoking rooms. Valet parking. Sauna. Wireless coverage.* **Room services** *Hairdryer. Internet access: dataport/ISDN. Minibar. Room service (24hrs). Safe. TV: satellite.*

Park Hyatt Milan

Via Tommaso Grossi 1 (02 8821 1234/fax 02 8821 1235/www.milan.park.hyatt.com). Metro Duomo/ bus 61. **Rates** €540-€590 single; €590-€740 double; €1,000-€5,380 suite. **Credit** AmEx, DC, MC, V. **Map** p310 A2/p312 B1.

Designed by Ed Tuttle, an American architect who made his bones creating luxurious hotels in Thailand, the Park Hyatt is an exercise in serenity. The warm, light-coloured rooms come equipped with bathrooms big enough to include their own solar system; amenities such as massage, steam room and spa are available around the clock. There is also free, unlimited high-speed internet access in each room. The hotel restaurant (entrance for non-guests in via Silvio Pellico 3) serves contemporary Mediterranean cuisine, while the hotel bar is swiftly becoming the latest spot for the Milanese see-and-be-seen crowd.

Hotel services *Air-conditioning. Babysitting. Bar. Conference rooms. Disabled: lift. Gym. Laundry. Limousine service. No-smoking rooms. Parking (€50 per day). Restaurant. Steam baths (male and female).* **Room services** *Hairdryer. Internet access: dataport. Minibar. Room service (24hrs) Safe. TV: satellite.*

Spadari al Duomo

Via Spadari 11 (02 7200 2371/fax 02 861 184/www. spadarihotel.com). Metro Cordusio or Duomo/bus 18/tram 2, 3, 14, 20, 27. **Rates** €198-€228 single; €208-€268 double; €288 junior suite; €308 suite. **Credit** AmEx, DC, MC, V. **Map** p310 A2/p312 B2.

Small, elegant and in the heart of Milan, the Spadari has been designed as a hotel-cum-exhibition space and a recent renovation project has turned the hotel into a work of art in its own right. During

Warm tones and flattering lighting at **Park Hyatt Milan**. *See p41.*

the restructuring, owner Marida Martegani and architect Urbano Perini commissioned well-known Italian artists to personalise the rooms. Sculptor Giò Pomodoro made a large wall sculpture and fireplace for the hall. But the most striking feature of the new decor is the soothing blue colour scheme that runs throughout the hotel. Great for art lovers; others might find it a bit pretentious.

Hotel services *Air-conditioning. Bar. Limousine service. Parking (€21 per day). Restaurant. Travel office.*
Room services *Minibar. No-smoking rooms. Room service (7am-11pm). Safe. TV: satellite.*

STRAF

Via San Raffaele 3 (02 805 081/fax 02 8909 5294/ www.straf.it). Metro Duomo. **Rates** €230-€240 single; €260 double. **Credit** AmEx, DC, MC, V. **Map** p311 A1/ p312 B1, B2.

The STRAF is a modern upscale hotel run by the same family that manages the Grand Hotel et de Milan (*see p41*). Sleek, minimalist rooms come equipped with every electronic and audio-visual amenity, and its utterly central location makes it ideal for downtown shopping. (And should the weight of all those designer bags get you down, every room on the hotel's fifth floor comes equipped with mini-spas that include electronic Japanese massage chairs and aromatherapy.) Despite its chichi overtones, the STRAF remains a remarkably good deal for its category.

Hotel Services *Air-conditioning. Bar (lounge). Gym.*
Room services *Internet access: dataport. Room service (7am-10pm). TV: satellite. Valet parking (€45 per day).*

Moderate

Antica Locanda dei Mercanti

Via San Tommaso 6 (02 805 4080/fax 02 805 4090/ www.locanda.it). Metro Cairoli or Cordusio/tram 1, 3, 4, 12, 14, 24, 27. **Rates** €118 single; €130-€255 double. **Credit** AmEx, MC, V. **Map** p310 A2/p312 A1.

Housed in a 19th-century palazzo just off via Dante, a pedestrian street in the centre of town, this is like something out of *A Room with a View* – with the occasional modern twist. The rooms are named after important merchants of the past, except for the four rooms on the top floor, which are blessed with a terrace and carry romantic monikers such as Pasha of Perfumes and Bamboo in the Wind. Fresh flowers and a range of books and magazines replace the standard TV set. To add a final touch of decadence, breakfast is served in bed.

Hotel services *Bar. Parking (€23 per day).*
Room services *Room service (7am-11pm).*

Gritti

Piazza Santa Maria Beltrade 4 (02 801 056/fax 02 8901 0999/www.hotelgritti.com). Metro Duomo/tram 2, 3, 12, 14, 27. **Rates** €90-€99 single; €129-€142 double; €181-€199 triple. **Credit** AmEx, DC, MC, V. **Map** p310 A2/p312 B2.

This hotel is just off via Torino, a busy shopping street near piazza Duomo that gets buzzing pretty early in the morning. In light of this, it might be wise to ask for a room overlooking the quiet inner courtyard. The rooms may not be the ultimate in modern design, but they are clean and comfortable, with modern fittings and a connection for your laptop.

Serenity now: the Zen tranquillity of the **STRAF**. *See p42.*

The three cheerful, charming, English-speaking concierges (Evandro, Mario and Bruno) will do anything in their power to ensure a pleasant stay.
Hotel services *Bar. Parking (€21 per day).*
Room services *Hairdryer. Internet access: dataport. Minibar. Room service (7am-midnight). TV: satellite.*

Manzoni

Via Santo Spirito 20 (02 7600 5700/fax 02 784 212/ www.hotelmanzoni.com). Metro Montenapoleone/bus 61, 94/tram 1, 2, 20. **Rates** €120-€140 single; €163-€178 double; €230 suite. *Breakfast* €15. **Credit** AmEx, DC, MC, V. **Map** p309 C1/p312 B1, C1.

The Manzoni is quite grand for a three-star, providing an impression of space that is usually lacking in this category (the bathrooms are especially roomy). The sombre brown carpet and sky-blue upholstered walls may not be to everyone's taste, but considering the hotel is right slap bang in the middle of the Golden Rectangle (*see p76*), Milan's chic fashion district, it's still a pretty good deal. Breakfast consists of a buffet brunch with hot and cold food, and there's also a garage – though both of these require a surcharge.
Hotel services *Air-conditioning. Bar. Conference room. Parking (€15-€33 per day).*
Room services *Room service (7.30am-3pm, 5-midnight). TV: satellite.*

Vecchia Milano

Via Borromei 4 (02 875 042/fax 02 8645 4292/ hotelvecchiamilano@tiscalinet.it). Metro Cordusio/bus 18/tram 2, 19, 20. **Rates** €55-€85 single; €90-€145 double; €130-€160 triple. **Credit** AmEx, DC, MC, V. **Map** p310 A2/p312 A2.

Friendly staff is just one reason why guests return again and again to this small, wood-panelled hotel. The central location and reasonable pricing are others. The rooms are a bit on the small side and simply furnished, but the building itself is an attractive old palazzo with an inn-like atmosphere. Parking in the very narrow streets around the hotel can be a problem, but fortunately there is a garage nearby.
Hotel services *Air-conditioning. Bar. Parking (€16.50 per day).*
Room services *Room service (7am-midnight). TV: satellite.*

Sforzesco & North

Expensive

UNA Hotel Century

Via F Filzi 25b (02 675 041/fax 02 6698 0602/ www.unahotels.it). Metro Centrale FS or Gioia/ bus 60/tram 2, 9, 20, 33. **Rates** €218-€452 single suite; €256-€452 double suite; €266-€452 executive suite. **Credit** AmEx, DC, MC, V. **Map** p309 B1.

A modern, nondescript tower-block hotel popular with visiting businessmen. The area around the railway station is not particularly inviting and can be downright unpleasant at night, but the hotel itself is set back from the main road. On the Executive Floor, the hotel's target audience is well catered for: all the suites have fax machines, trouser presses and linen bed sheets. The patio/garden is a welcome feature in the summer months.

A seamless blend of modern and olde worlde at the **Antica Locanda dei Mercanti**. See p42.

Hotel services *Air-conditioning. Bar. Conference rooms. Garden. Gym. Laundry. Parking (€20 per day). Restaurant.*
Room services *Coffee machine. Hairdryer. Internet access: dataport. Minibar. No-smoking rooms. Room service (6.30am-10.30pm). Safe. TV: satellite.*

Moderate

Antica Locanda Solferino

Via Castelfidardo 2 (02 657 0129/fax 02 657 1361/ www.anticalocandasolferino.it). Metro Moscova/bus 41, 43, 94. **Rates** €110-€140 single; €160-€190 double; €200-€230 triple; €160-€220 mini-apartments. **Credit** AmEx, MC, V. **Map** p309 B1.
This delightful hotel is located in a Napoleonic-era palazzo on the corner of via Solferino, in the heart of the bohemian Brera district. Each of the 11 charming rooms features floor-to-ceiling windows, beautiful cornicing, genuine antique furniture and Daumier lithographs on the walls, creating the feel that you've stepped into a corner of 19th-century Milan. The courteous, personable staff will help you make the most of the area by suggesting sightseeing itineraries and local amenities. Breakfast is served in the room, a nice pampering touch.
Hotel services *Garage (€25 per day). Laundry.*
Room services *Air-conditioning (some rooms). Jacuzzi (some rooms). Room service (7.30-10am). TV.*

Marconi

Via F Filzi 3 (02 6698 5561/fax 02 669 0738/www. marconihotel.it). Metro Centrale FS or Repubblica/ tram 2, 9, 33. **Rates** €70-€150 single; €130-€215 double; €150-€265 triple. **Credit** AmEx, DC, MC, V. **Map** p309 B1.
A three-star hotel conveniently located near Milan's Stazione Centrale. Some of the rooms look on to a delightful courtyard full of lemon trees and geraniums (closed for renovations at the time of writing, but due to re-open by the end of 2004); breakfast

is served out here in the summer. The rooms have standard fittings and tile floors, which keep them cool in hot weather, but can make them a bit chilly in winter, although central heating is fitted throughout the hotel (as is air-conditioning).
Hotel services *Air-conditioning. Bar. Conference room.*
Room services *Hairdryer. Minibar. Room service (24hrs). TV: satellite.*

Budget

London

Via Rovello 3 (02 7202 0166/fax 02 805 7037/www. hotel-london-milan.com). Metro Cairoli or Cordusio/ bus 18, 50, 58/tram 1, 3, 12, 14, 19, 20, 24. **Rates** €100 single; €150 double. *Breakfast* €8. **Credit** MC, V. **Map** p310 A2/p312 A1.
An excellent budget hotel close to both the Duomo and the Castello Sforzesco. The rooms are simply furnished and a bit poky, but the lobby and conversation area around the bar are welcoming and the staff are friendly and easy-going. Breakfast can be served in your room. There's a ten per cent discount if you pay cash. Considering its prime location, the London represents excellent value for money.
Hotel service *Air-conditioning. Bar. Parking (€25 per day).*
Room services *Hairdryer. Room service (7am-10.30pm). TV: satellite.*

Ostello Piero Rotta

Viale Salmoiraghi 1 (02 3926 7095/fax 02 330 0191/www.ostellionline.org). Metro Lotto or QT8/ bus 48, 68, 78, 90, 91. **Rates** €18.50 per person. **Credit** MC, V. **Map** off p308 A1.
The only youth hostel in Milan is out in the suburbs near the San Siro stadium, though the nearby Lotto metro station makes it easy to reach the centre. The price of a dormitory bed includes breakfast. The garden provides a welcome escape from city traffic. The

staff are not exactly falling over themselves to be helpful and friendly – but that doesn't stop the place being full most of the time.

San Babila & East

Expensive

Sheraton Diana Majestic

Viale Piave 42 (02 20 581/fax 02 2058 2058/www. sheraton.com/dianamajestic). Metro Porta Venezia/ tram 9, 29, 30. **Rates** €355-€418 double (single occupancy); €450 double; €620 junior suite; €1,170 deluxe suite. **Credit** AmEx, DC, MC, V. **Map** p309 C2.
This five-star art nouveau-style hotel is named after the first public swimming pool in Milan, which opened on this site in 1842. The pool has since been replaced with a small garden, dotted with tables spilling out from what is one of the city's trendiest bars. The large rooms are elegantly kitted out with antique furniture, while the bathrooms have attractive marble fittings. The hotel restaurant, Il Milanese, is popular with lunching businessmen. The tree-lined viale Piave is conveniently located close to the shops of corso Buenos Aires and the public gardens in corso Venezia.
Hotel services *Air-conditioning. Bars. Business centre. Conference rooms. Disabled: adapted rooms, ramp access. Garden. Gym. Laundry. Restaurants.* **Room services** *Hairdryer. Internet access: dataport. Minibar. Room service (7am-midnight). Safe. TV: satellite.*

Moderate

Etrusco

Via NA Porpora 56 (02 236 3852/fax 02 236 0553/ www.hoteletrusco.it). Metro Loreto/bus 55, 56, 62, 75, 92/tram 33. **Rates** €85-€103 single; €120-€155 double. **Credit** AmEx, DC, MC, V. **Map** off p309 B2.
The three-star Etrusco boasts a good price/quality ratio and a convenient location not far from the main railway station. The exceptionally clean rooms are sound-proofed (a major plus in this noisy city), and some have balconies overlooking a charming garden where breakfast is served in the summer. In the winter the heating in the rooms can be individually controlled – a welcome detail in a country where hotel rooms tend to be kept stifling.
Hotel services *Air-conditioning. Bar. Laundry. Parking (free).* **Room services** *Minibar. TV: satellite.*

Mazzini

Via Vitruvio 29 (02 2952 6600/fax 02 2951 0253/ www.hotelmazzini.com). Metro Centrale or Lima/bus 60/tram 5, 20, 33. **Rates** €70-€95 single; €90-€140 double; €140-€185 triple. **Credit** AmEx, DC, MC, V. **Map** p309 B2.
At this family-run hotel near the main railway station, the rooms are simply furnished, but clean and comfortable, with double-glazing, air-conditioning

and other features not always guaranteed in a hotel in this price range. Ask for a room overlooking the rear garden. Rates vary widely over the year, but prices are lowest in December, July and August. It's worth asking for the weekend rates too.
Hotel services *Air-conditioning. Bar. Internet access: dataport. Laundry service. Parking (€25 per day).* **Room services** *Hairdryer. Room service (7am-midnight). Safe. TV: satellite.*

Budget

Aspromonte

Piazza Aspromonte 12/14 (02 236 1119/fax 02 236 7621/www.venere.it/milano/aspromonte). Metro Loreto/bus 55, 56, 62, 90, 91/tram 33. **Rates** €45-€100 single; €55-€140 double; €84-€189 triple. **Credit** AmEx, DC, MC, V. **Map** off p309 B2.
The piazza from which the hotel takes its name is dotted with two-star hotels and there's not a lot to choose between them. But the Aspromonte can boast an added attraction in its pretty garden, which has a covered section where guests can take breakfast. The rooms look pretty much alike – they are decidedly basic, but come equipped with air-conditioning and the other simple amenities to which international travellers are accustomed. The playground in the piazza outside makes this a good bet for families travelling with children. The hotel can also arrange tickets for football matches.
Hotel services *Bar.* **Room services** *Hairdryer. Minibar. TV: satellite.*

Del Sole

Via G Spontini 6 (02 2951 2971/fax 02 2951 3689/ delsolehotel@tiscali.it). Metro Lima or Loreto/bus 55, 56, 91, 92/tram 33. **Rates** €60-€85 double; €95-€114 triple. *Breakfast* €4. **Credit** AmEx, DC, MC, V. **Map** p309 B2.
This family-owned and family-run hotel just off corso Buenos Aires features a spiral staircase leading from the lobby to a cosy bar/breakfast area. The rooms are clean, with tile floors and standard fittings, and there are two rooms with huge terraces overlooking the courtyard where you can sit outside and sip a glass of Prosecco – Italy's scrumptious bubbly – during the summer months.
Hotel services *Air-conditioning. Bar. Parking (€7-€15 per day).* **Room services** *TV.*

Nettuno

Via Tadino 27 (02 2940 4481/fax 02 2952 3819/ www.hotelnettuno.cjb.net). Metro Lima or Porta Venezia/bus 60/tram 1, 5, 11, 20, 33. **Rates** *Shared bathroom* €34-€40 single; €53-€68 double; €72-€87 triple. *En suite* €43-€50 single; €65-€95 double; €88-€125 triple; €115-€165 quad. **Credit** AmEx, DC, MC, V. **Map** p309 B2.
This cavernous and rather gloomy one-star hotel is located between the main station and the centre. Breakfast is not included, but there are hot and cold drinks dispensers in the lobby and loads of bars and

Milan's grande dame

The oldest and arguably most prestigious hotel in Milan (though no longer the most expensive), the Grand Hotel et de Milan is filled with history. From a marble statue in the lobby commemorating the abolition of slavery in Brazil – an act passed by the country's erstwhile emperor, Dom Pedro di Braganza, during his sojourn at the Grand Hotel – to the 300-400 AD Roman walls uncovered in the basement during a recent renovation, to the balcony from which an ailing Giuseppe Verdi saluted an adoring crowd of Milanese fans, the hotel has hosted illustrious people and important events for nearly 150 years.

The hotel was founded in 1863 following a design by the famous architect Andrea Pizzala. Originally much smaller than the current edifice, it expanded gradually, acquiring special importance at the end of the 1800s, when it was the only *albergo* in town to offer post and telegraph services, making it the unquestioned favourite for nobility, diplomats and businessmen.

A book on the hotel's history opens with a 1950s document that lists the 2,900-plus illustrious guests the hotel had hosted by then, including enough kings, queens, dukes, duchesses, lords and ladies to make even the most experienced tabloid reporter blush. (If you sojourn here, be sure to ask to see a copy; it provides a fascinating panorama of the people and events these walls have entertained over the years.)

The hotel has gone so far as to rename some rooms in honour of its most important guests. Room 105, the Giuseppe Verdi suite, has an ornate anteroom with a balcony on to which Verdi and lead tenor Tamagno were dragged by *vox populi* and showered with applause after the debut of Verdi's *Otello*. The composer called the hotel home when staying in the city, and even died here in 1901. In the months before his death, the streets around the hotel were strewn daily with straw to muffle the sounds of passing carts and horseshoes so as not to disturb the great maestro.

Other famous guests have included Enrico Caruso, Ernest Hemingway, Maria Callas and Rudolf Nureyev. In the 1970s, in accordance with a trend popular at that time, virtually every room in the hotel was rented out to fashion and furniture designers to serve as impromptu showrooms – even the elevator hosted an exhibition of accessories.

Extensive renovations carried out in 1993 and 1994 – the same renovations that revealed Roman walls below the building – returned many of the original decorations and details that had been destroyed by bombing during World War II.

Sitting in the skylit reading room, your feet nestled on a thick oriental carpet and verdant palms reaching over your shoulder as a white-gloved waiter brings your drink, you'll find it easy to feel quite noble yourself.

STRAF

IN THE HEART OF MILAN THERE IS A NEW DESIGN HOTEL: THE STRAF. AN INSPIRED FUSION OF ITALIAN FASHION, ORIGINAL DESIGN AND ELEGANCE, WITH THE LATEST TECHNOLOGY AND IMPECCABLE SERVICE. YOU COULD NOT WISH FOR A BETTER LOCATION: THE BUILDING IS SITUATED IN THE VERY HEART OF MILAN, ONLY FEW STEPS AWAY FROM THE DUOMO CATHEDRAL, THE GALLERIA, LA SCALA OPERA HOUSE, THE SHOPPING DISTRICT AND THE FASHIONABLE VIA MONTENAPOLEONE.

THE OLD FAÇADE DATED 1800, CONTRIBUTES TO CREATE AN UNUSUAL CONTRAST WITH A MINIMALIST DESIGN. ITS 64 ROOMS AND SUITES FUSE THE BEST OF DESIGN AND FUNCTIONALITY WITH A MAXIMUM COMFORT IN A RELAXED ATMOSPHERE MARKED OUT BY RARE MATERIALS. THE ARCHITECT, MR. VINCENZO DE COTIIS, ALSO FASHION DESIGNER OF 'HAUTE' COLLECTION, HAS FOLLOWED THIS PROJECT CHOOSING UNUSUAL MATERIALS, SUCH AS SCRATCHED MIRRORS, BURNISHED BRASS, IRON, BLACK STONE, CEMENT AND GAUZE PLACED BETWEEN PANES OF GLASS TO GIVE A TRANSPARENT EFFECT. THE LOUNGE BAR IS THE HANG OUT CHOICE FOR PEOPLE SEEKING A STYLISH YET RELAXED SETTING WITH AN UNCONVENTIONAL ATMOSPHERE. A GYM FEATURING STATE-OF-THE-ART-FITNESS EQUIPMENT IS OPEN TO HOTEL GUESTS 24 HOURS A DAY.

5 chromo and aromatherapy rooms equipped
with automassage Japanese armchair.

STRAF Hotel - Via San Raffaele, 3 - 20121 Milano
Tel. (+39) 02/805081 - Fax (+39) 02/89095294
E-mail: reservations@straf.it   Website: www.straf.it

restaurants nearby. The rooms are spartan, but spacious and clean, and the bathrooms have granite tiles. The reception is staffed around the clock.
Hotel services *Hot & cold drink dispensers.*
Room services *TV.*

San Francisco
Viale Lombardia 55 (02 236 1009/fax 02 2668 0377/www.hotel-sanfrancisco.it). Metro Piola/bus 62, 75, 90, 91/tram 33. **Rates** €52-€70 single; €85-€110 double. **Credit** AmEx, DC, MC, V. **Map** off p309 B2.
An attractive, modern two-star hotel with a small garden and patio. The rooms are well lit and very clean, with simple yet adequate furniture and fittings. There is also a small meeting room with fax service available. It's a bit off the beaten track, but La Matricola pub down the road has a friendly atmosphere if you fancy an evening drink.
Hotel services *Air-conditioning. Bar. Conference room. Fax. Internet access: dataport.*
Room services *TV: satellite.*

Porta Romana & South

Expensive

Liberty
Viale Bligny 56 (02 5831 8562/fax 02 5831 9061/www.hotelliberty-milano.it). Tram 9, 29, 30. **Rates** €106-€132 single; €132-€233 double; €232 suite. *Breakfast* €11. **Credit** AmEx, DC, MC, V. **Map** p310 B2.
A popular, though somewhat overrated and overpriced hotel. Breakfast is not included, but can be served in your bedroom – far better to get out and have a cappuccino and *brioche* (croissant) in a bar. The rooms have standard, modern-ish decor and fittings and four of the bathrooms are equipped with jacuzzis. What a shame that the effect of the pretty courtyard garden and gleaming lobby can be spoiled by some of the moodier members of staff.
Hotel services *Air-conditioning. Bar. Garden. Parking (€23-€28 per day).*
Room services *Hairdryer. Jacuzzi (4 rooms). Minibar. Room service (breakfast only). TV.*

Moderate

Ariston
Largo Carrobbio 2 (02 7200 0556/fax 02 7200 0914/www.brerahotels.com/ariston). Tram 2, 3, 14. **Rates** €106-€140 single; €155-€200 double; €190-€213 triple. **Credit** AmEx, DC, MC, V. **Map** p310 A2/p312 A2.
The Ariston is an extraordinary experiment in bio-architectural design: the lightbulbs are energy-efficient; the showers are designed to save water; all the fittings are made from natural or non-toxic materials. Even the water in your tea is purified, and organic products are served at breakfast. The hotel is conveniently located between the centre of town and the Navigli district, with trams stopping by the front entrance.

Hotel services *Air-conditioning. Bar. Conference room. No-smoking rooms. Parking (€13 per day).*
Room services *Room service (7am-11pm). TV: satellite.*

Mercure Milano Corso Genova
Via Conca del Naviglio 20 (02 5810 4141/fax 02 8940 1012/www.mercure.com). Metro Sant'Agostino/tram 2, 14. **Rates** €124-€158 single; €159-€176 double (single occupancy); €176-€194 double, €194-€216 triple and quad. **Credit** AmEx, DC, MC, V. **Map** p310 B2.
An excellent choice for both business travellers and families, this comfortable three-star hotel is located in a quiet and surprisingly green corner of Milan, close to the Navigli district, with its bars and restaurants. The centre of town is just ten minutes' walk in the opposite direction, and its friendly and helpful staff will be sure to point you in the right direction. The hotel was completely renovated in 1998 and joined the Mercure chain.
Hotel services *Air-conditioning. Bar (breakfast only). Beauty centre. Bicycles (free). Parking (€15.50 per day). Pizza delivery service.*
Room services *Hairdryer. Minibar. TV.*

Minerva
Corso C Colombo 15 (02 837 5745/fax 02 835 8229). Metro Porta Genova/bus 47, 59, 74/tram 2, 9, 14, 29, 30. **Rates** €55-€80 single; €80-€130 double; €120-€150 triple. Closed Aug. **Credit** AmEx, DC, MC, V. **Map** p310 B1.
Don't be put off by the lacklustre foyer and breakfast area. Or by the rooms, which, though clean, are drearily basic. The real advantage of this no-nonsense three-star hotel is that it's within walking distance of the bars and restaurants of the Navigli area and just across the road from the Porta Genova metro station. The 14 tram, which stops right by the front door, goes all the way to the Duomo. The free car park is another bonus if you're motoring.
Hotel services *Air-conditioning. Bar. Parking (free).*
Room services *Room service (breakfast only). TV.*

Sant'Ambrogio & West

Expensive

Antares Hotel Rubens
Via Rubens 21 (02 40 302/fax 02 4819 3114/www.antareshotels.com). Metro De Angeli or Gambara/bus 63, 72, 80/tram 24. **Rates** €99-€230 single; €120-€299 double; €160-€329 suites. **Credit** AmEx, DC, MC, V. **Map** off p308 C1.
A comfortable if rather dull four-star hotel, although the owners have made an effort to brighten things with individual decor in the rooms. It's much used by business travellers visiting the nearby Fiera complex (*see p97*), but it's not really near anywhere else of interest, unless you want to take in a football match at the San Siro stadium (*see p179*). The buffet breakfast is served on the top floor in the grandiosely named Sala delle Nuvole (Cloud

Room), which provides a panoramic view across this unexceptional part of the city. An entire floor is dedicated to non-smokers.

Hotel services *Air-conditioning. Bar. Parking (free). Restaurant.*
Room services *Internet access: dataport. Hairdryer. Minibar. Non-smoking floor. Room service (7am-1am). Safe. TV: satellite.*

Moderate

Antica Locanda Leonardo

Corso Magenta 78 (02 463 317/02 4801 4197/fax 02 4801 9012/www.leoloc.com). Metro Cadorna/ bus 18, 50, 58/tram 19, 20, 24. **Rates** €95 single; €150-€190 double, €195-€240 triple. **Credit** AmEx, DC, MC, V. **Map** p308 C1.

An immaculate little hotel set back from busy corso Magenta, within easy walking distance of Santa Maria delle Grazie and Leonardo's *Cenacolo* (*see p92* **Guess who's coming to supper**). The property (a late 19th-century palazzo) was fully renovated in 1997, and the rooms are all tastefully decorated with modern or antique wooden furniture and bathrooms with shower and bath tub. There is also a cosy breakfast/bar area, and the hotel has been managed by the same courteous and attentive family for more than 40 years. Ask for a room over-looking the flower-filled courtyard.

Hotel services *Air-conditioning. Bar. Parking (€25 per day). Safe.*
Room services *Safe. TV: satellite.*

Ariosto

Via Ariosto 22 (02 481 7844/fax 02 498 0516/ www.hotelariosto.com). Metro Conciliazione/bus 61, 68/tram 29, 30. **Rates** €145-€165 double (single occupancy); €205 double; €219 triple. **Credit** AmEx, DC, MC, V. **Map** p308 C1.

Via Ariosto is an elegant residential street, handy for both the central sights and the Fiera (*see p97*). The hotel is airy and well lit, with a beautiful art nouveau staircase. All the rooms have double-glazing, parquet flooring, and marble tiles in the bathrooms; a few also have walk-in wardrobes. The TV sets have a VCR incorporated and videos in different languages are available from reception. There is also a small, attractive patio garden. The bar and restaurant area resembles a cafeteria – so if you're after ambience, you might want to eat out.

Hotel services *Air-conditioning. Bar. Conference rooms. Parking (€25 per day). Restaurant. Video hire.*
Room services *Room service (7.30am-10pm). TV: satellite, VCR.*

King

Corso Magenta 19 (02 874 432/fax 02 8901 0798/ www.hotelkingmilano.com). Metro Cadorna/bus 18, 50, 58/tram 19, 20, 24. **Rates** €66-€148 single; €88-€215 double; €133-€290 triple. **Credit** AmEx, DC, MC, V. **Map** p308 C1.

Centrally located in a picturesque part of town, the King is just down the road from Bar Magenta (*see*

Charming **Antica Locanda Solferino**. *See p45.*

p129), a Milanese institution. The hotel was recently renovated, and the new decor in the public areas can be a little overwhelming to guests with simpler tastes. But the rooms are clean, tidy and quiet, with well-stocked minibars, and the buffet breakfast is generous. The atmosphere as you enter the lobby is warm and welcoming. Be aware that there is a sur-charge if you cancel a reservation.

Hotel services *Air-conditioning. Bar. Laundry service.*
Room services *Hairdryer. Minibar. Parking (€20 per day). Room service (7am-midnight). Safe. TV: cable.*

Palazzo delle Stelline

Corso Magenta 61 (02 481 8431/fax 02 4851 9097/ 02 4819 4281). Metro Cadorna/bus 18, 50, 58/tram 19, 20, 24. **Rates** €107 single; €127 single superior; €160 double; €190 suite. **Credit** AmEx, DC, MC, V. **Map** p308 C1.

This hotel and congress centre is housed in a beau-tiful 15th-century palazzo with arched cloisters over-looking a grass courtyard and a huge magnolia tree. The tastefully furnished rooms offer total privacy, a world apart from the hubbub of the city. Leonardo da Vinci is said to have grown vines here while painting *The Last Supper* (*see p92* **Guess who's coming to supper**) at the Santa Maria delle Grazie monastery across the road.

Hotel services *Air-conditioning. Bar. Conference rooms. Disabled: adapted suite.*
Room services *TV: satellite.*

Sightseeing

Introduction	52
The Duomo & Central Milan	54
Castello Sforzesco, Brera & Northern Milan	66
San Babila & Eastern Milan	75
Porta Romana, the Navigli & Southern Milan	82
Sant'Ambrogio & Western Milan	91
Around Milan	99

Features

Milan in a day… or two	53
The woman on top	56
Novel approach	64
Castello Sforzesco	68
Brera's best-kept secret	71
The road to Liberty	77
The house Poldi Pezzoli built	78
Canals plus	86
Guess who's coming to supper	92
Inside track	100
Battle royale	101
Parking spaces	102
A family's fortunes	105

Introduction

Dive into modern Milan; there is much that will surprise you.

Villa Reale. *See p100.*

Travellers often find it hard to reconcile Milan with their romantic visions of Italy. Gone are the quaint villas, gone are the verdant, rolling hills; in fact, gone is verdant altogether. Milan is a modern metropolis, and uncovering its charming attributes amid the honking crowds and big-city squalor requires some patience.

But there is beauty here, and in surprising abundance. Much of it is hidden behind the imposing granite façades of Milan's palazzi – the city is famous throughout Italy for its beautiful courtyards. Once a year, usually on the third weekend of March, the FAI (Fondo per l'Ambiente Italiano, or Italian Environmental Fund, 0141 72 08 50, www.fondoambiente.it) organises a grand 'open courtyard' day across Italy. For one weekend only, the courtyards of most of Milan's private palazzi are thrown open to the public. If you're lucky enough to be in the city during this spring celebration, take advantage of it – you'll enjoy a side of Milan usually only available to a select few.

MILAN ON FOOT

Large sections of the centre have been passed on to pedestrians. In addition to the principal shopping thoroughfare, corso Vittorio Emanuele II and piazza Duomo, via dei Mercanti and via Dante have been turned into car-free zones, creating a single pedestrian corridor that runs from the Castello Sforzesco all the way to San Babila. Via Garibaldi and corso Como have also been pedestrianised, and similar projects are underway in half a dozen other areas.

On many Sundays throughout the year, cars are banned in the city. Ostensibly determined by the level of pollution downtown, there is no way to predict when these *divieti* will take place; they are usually announced by local news services just a few days in advance. But if you happen to catch one of these car-free days you'll have all of downtown to roam through, accompanied only by taxis and Milanese families who set out on foot and by bike to enjoy their 'liberated' city.

MILAN BY THE BOOK

Paradoxically, the relative culture gap between Milan and other Italian cities – notably Rome, Florence and Venice – can work in your favour. You can probably visit all of Milan's major sights in well under a week (*see p53* **Milan in a day... or two**). Many of Milan's main attractions are grouped around the central piazza Duomo, home to the city's mammoth Duomo, and its elegant Galleria Vittorio Emanuele. From here you can reach the other main sites – Pinacoteca di Brera, Santa Maria delle Grazie (home to Leonardo's *Last Supper*), the Castello Sforzesco and the Poldi Pezzoli museum – in less than 20 minutes on foot.

MILAN'S CHURCHES

The more than 100 smaller churches dotting the cityscape provide pleasant surprises. Many of them are all but lost amid the bustle of downtown Milan, and are oases for the harried tourist. Almost without exception, these buildings are first and foremost active houses of worship. This means dress codes (bare shoulders and/or legs are prohibited) and variable visiting hours. Keep quiet inside the church; a raised voice could get you kicked out. Some churches have coin-operated lighting systems, audio-visual aids and computerised displays (usually in Italian, sometimes with English); bring loose change.

MILAN'S MUSEUMS AND GALLERIES

Milan's major museums and galleries generally stay open throughout the day, and some remain open until 10pm or later one night a week.

Admission to the city's collections was being transformed as this guide went to press. While many continue to offer free admission, some museums have begun to charge a small fee, and even the freebies warn they will start charging within the coming year (2004-05). Most offer discounts for students and over-60s, especially if they can demonstrate EU citizenship. Bring appropriate ID. Many galleries and museums stop issuing tickets 30 to 45 minutes before closing time.

TICKETS AND BOOKING

Booking is essential for Leonardo's *Last Supper* (*see p92* **Guess who's coming to supper**), though last-minute cancellations may allow you to get in without a reservation if you're prepared to wait. Many museums and galleries require reservations for groups of seven or more.

During the Settimana dei Beni Culturali (Cultural Heritage Week, *see p152*), which usually takes place in early spring, all publicly owned museums and sites have extended visiting hours and are free of charge.

Note the following combined tickets, which can be purchased at the sights themselves:
● Duomo roof (*see p54*) and Museo del Duomo (*see p59*), €7.
● *The Last Supper* (*see p96*), Museo del Teatro (*see p61*), Pinacoteca di Brera (*see p71*), €10 (plus €1.50 booking fee). Book on 02 8942 1146 and collect tickets from *The Last Supper*.
● Palazzo Reale (*see p59*) and Museo Poldi Pezzoli (*see p78* **The house Poldi Pezzoli built**), €9.

● Museo Diocesano (*see p85*), Cappella Portinari at Sant'Eustorgio (*see p89*) and Cappella di Sant'Aquilino at San Lorenzo (*see p89*), €12.

GUIDED TOURS

Milan's tourist office (APT, via Marconi 1, 02 7252 4301, www.milanoinfotourist.com) offers information on tours, as well as tickets for guided bus tours (depart 9.30am from the APT office Tue-Sun). In conjunction with Autostradale Milan, the APT runs a three-hour tour with stops at the Castello Sforzesco and Leonardo da Vinci's *Last Supper* (€40 including entry fees).

Several 1920s-era trams have been turned into tourist transport, complete with headphones and multiple-language commentaries. The 'hop-on, hop-off' trams are the most charming way to see the city (Ciao Milano Tourist Tram, 02 7200 2584; *see also p280*).

Other options include:
● Centro Guide Milano (via Marconi 1, 02 8645 0433, www.centroguidemilano.org), a non-profit association, offers tours in Milan and outside.
● Hello Milano (02 2952 0570) offers two-hour personalised tours of the city (€100).
● Sophisticated Italy (02 4819 6675/www. sophisticateditaly.com) has tours for small groups or individuals to experience Lombard food and wine, gardens and golf courses.
● Opera d'Arte (02 6900 0579/www.opera dartemilano.it) gives personalised guided tours of churches, museums, galleries and shops.
● Tempo Libero (02 607 1009) runs tours for children aged 5-12 (2pm & 4pm Sat; 10.30am, 2pm & 4pm Sun). Reservations obligatory.

Milan in a day... or two

Thanks to the rising importance of Malpensa airport as an international hub and Milan's prominence as a business and shopping metropolis, an increasing number of tourists hit the city for quick one- and two-day stopovers. Here are a few suggestions for what to do in under 48 hours.
● Check out the **Duomo** (*see p54*). If the weather is fine, pay the surcharge and go up on the roof; you'll enjoy an unbeatable view.
● The **Pinacoteca di Brera** (*see p71*) is a quick five-minute walk from piazza Duomo, and boasts the best art collection in the city.
● Walk from piazza Duomo up **via Dante** (*see p66*), a wide pedestrian boulevard packed with shops, bars and cafés. If you're hungry, try something from Garbagnati, a famous Milan bakery located halfway up the boulevard.

● Visit the **Castello Sforzesco** (*see p66*). This Renaissance jewel is the city's centrepiece, housing a number of eclectic museum collections, including rare musical instruments, drawings by Leonardo da Vinci and medieval arms. Entrance to several of the collections is free, so take a gander gratis.
● Visit **Santa Maria delle Grazie** (*see p96*). If you haven't already booked a ticket, your chances of getting in to see Leonardo's *Last Supper* are slim, but they do exist. No luck? Just check out the church and cloister instead.
● Take a break in the cafés in **Galleria Vittorio Emanuele II** (*see p54*) for a Milanese classic – the *aperitivo*. Your drinks will be overpriced, but will include a few nibbles – olives, potato chips, *bruschetta* – and a view providing some of the best people-watching in the city.

The Duomo & Central Milan

A (mostly) pedestrianised area where art, Christianity and high finance converge.

Around the Duomo

Downtown Milan is an exercise in contrast; a blend of ancient and ultra-modern, rich and poor, Italian and immigrant. The relatively few medieval buildings that survived heavy World War II bombing are tucked in – almost forgotten – between grey, modern office buildings and parking garages. Swanky, gleaming storefronts display the latest Bulgari jewellery behind a ragged Chinese man hawking lighters, counterfeit music tapes and foldable umbrellas. Perhaps nowhere else in Italy are the country's cultural crown jewels intermixed so completely with modern urban sprawl.

This is the heart of the city. Not for nothing do locals call the **Galleria Vittorio Emanuele II** – that enormous, glass-domed arcade connecting piazza del Duomo with piazza della Scala – *il salotto di Milano* (Milan's living room). Despite all the harried hustle and bustle, there remains something unmistakably Italian here. You'll find it at any one of the innumerable cafés and *gelaterie* around piazza del Duomo, or, if you happen to be visiting in the winter, in the smell of the fresh roasted chestnuts that street vendors extend to you in brown butcher's paper cones with a smile (which widens the second you reach for your wallet). You'll also see it in the elegant businesswomen and men, undoubtedly strapped for time between one meeting and the next, but nevertheless keen to walk down corso Vittorio Emanuele rather than stay on the much faster (but less scenic) subway.

This is the best Milan has to offer a pedestrian. Take advantage of it. Walk along via Dante, through the piazza del Duomo and up corso Vittorio Emanuele. Climb up to the top of the **Duomo** (a €7 cumulative ticket will give you access to both the roof and the **Museo del Duomo**). Treat yourself to a *gelato*, window-shop for an hour or two, then catch an exhibition at the **Palazzo Reale**.

The Milanese have made blending the modern with the traditional an art form, and both are here for you in abundance.

Duomo

Piazza del Duomo (02 8646 3456). Metro Duomo/ bus 50, 54/tram 1, 2, 3, 12, 14, 15, 20, 23, 24, 27. **Open** *Church 6.45am-6.45pm daily. Treasury & crypt of San Carlo Borromeo 9.30am-noon, 2.30-5pm daily. Baptistery San Giovanni alle Fonti & early Christian excavations 9.30am-5pm daily. Roof (Le Terrazze) Nov-Feb 9am-4.15pm daily. Mar-Oct 9am-5.45pm daily.* **Admission** *Church free. Treasury & crypt of San Carlo Borromeo €11. Baptistery & early Christian excavations €1.50. Roof (le terrazze) by lift €5; on foot €3.50 (groups of 15 or more €2). See also p53.* **Map** p311 A1/p312 B2.

This enormous marble marvel is the third-largest church in Christendom (topped only by St Peter's in Rome and the cathedral in Seville) and its towering, spiky Gothic façade dominates Milan's city centre. It took over 400 years to build, and art and architecture lovers will have a field day following the various styles that characterise both its interior and exterior.

Construction began in 1386 by order of Bishop Antonio da Saluzzo on a site that had already been associated with places of worship (a Roman temple to the goddess Minerva had previously stood here). As with most large medieval buildings, Milan's Duomo became a massive multi-cultural effort. It owes its northern Gothic appearance to French and German master masons called in to work alongside local Lombard stone-cutters and architects.

Originally designed in typical Lombard terra-cotta, the cathedral was ultimately clad in cream-coloured marble from Candoglia on Lake Maggiore (see *p194*), in accordance with the wishes of Gian Galeazzo Visconti, who then ruled the city. Gian Galeazzo envisaged a grandiose structure to equal northern Europe's international Gothic master-pieces. Marble for the church was shipped to Milan on the Ticino river, and then along a net-work of canals (*navigli, see p86* **Canals plus**) built especially for the purpose.

Although consecrated in 1418, the cathedral remained incomplete for centuries. Problems concerning money and politics, as well as downright indifference kept the project on permanent stand-by. Finally, early in the 19th century, the façade was put on the church by order of none other than Napoleon Bonaparte; he pushed the final construction through before crowning himself King of Italy here (see *p18*).

Piazza del Duomo.
See p54.

Take a spin for good luck in
Galleria Vittorio Emanuele II.
See p59.

The woman on top

O mia bella Madonina
Che te brillet de lontan,
Tutta d'òra e piscinina
Ti te dòminet Milan.
Sòtta a ti se viv la vita
Se sta mai coi man in man.
Canten tucc: 'Lontan de Napoli se moeur'
Ma poeu vegnen chì a Milan...

(Oh, my beautiful little Virgin Mary/Shining from afar/All golden and small/You dominate Milan./Under you we live out our lives/ We never waste our time./Everyone sings: 'Separated from Naples I die'/But then they move here to Milan.)

Outsiders may find it hard to grasp just what's so special about the golden lady perched almost 110 metres (360 feet) up on the summit of the Duomo, but for most *milanesi* the Madonnina (literally 'little Madonna', though there's nothing petite about this Virgin, which stands at four metres/13 feet tall) is the most heartfelt symbol the metropolis has.

Many songs have been written about her, including the popular paean above penned by Giuseppe D'Anzi in 1934 as a response to the southern Italian immigrants who had flocked to Milan to find work and who were soon filling the nightclubs where D'Anzi sang, clamouring to hear their Neapolitan favourites. D'Anzi claimed to have written the song in a single night, and since then every Milanese minstrel worth his salt has sung it.

The Madonnina is the culmination of the 400-plus years of work it took to build the Duomo. Construction of the church began in 1386 and continued into the early 1800s, giving rise to the popular Milanese saying that anything that takes forever to do is *come la fabbrica del Duomo* ('like constructing the Duomo').

Four centuries of labour created an enormous ongoing school and stoneworkers' workshop, the Veneranda Fabbrica del Duomo, a building alongside the Duomo that today functions as a museum (*see p59*) housing sculpture, documents and archives relating to its construction. The Fabbrica is still involved with the Duomo, overseeing the Sisyphean responsibility of cleaning and restoring the church's stonework.

In 1754 the directors of the Fabbrica hired sculptor Giuseppe Perego to participate in carving a section of the façade. Ten years later Perego produced the sketches for the Madonnina, and in 1774 the golden Madonna was placed atop the church's highest spire, her arms open and welcoming, her benevolent smile directed down to the industrious Milanese scampering about below.

When Mussolini was in power, he decreed that no other building in Milan should tower over the Madonnina. This rule was flouted in the late 1950s, with the erection of the Pirelli skyscraper (127m/416ft; *see p73*). The outraged cardinal of Milan strongly advised the city to keep the Madonnina as the highest point in the city; this resulted in an 85-cm-tall (33-in) replica of the Madonnina being placed on top of the Pirellone, where she became once more the highest point in Milan.

At night the statue on the Duomo is lit from below, crowning the piazza with a golden glow on Milan's many foggy evenings. In a richer, more ornate city, the high-flying Madonnina might be lost amid the church spires. But for the Milanese, she simply inspires, as the final verse of D'Anzi's song confirms:

...Si, vegnì senza paura
Num ve slongaremm la man
Tutt el mond a l'è paes, a s'emm d'accòrd,
Ma Milan, l'è on gran Milan.

The exterior

A staggering 3,500 statues adorn the Duomo, about two thirds of them on the exterior. The oldest are around the apse end, which was built from 1386 to 1447; those along the sides were added as the building work progressed, between the late 15th and early 18th centuries. The façade is baroque up to the first order of windows and neo-Gothic above. The five bronze doors that provide access to the Duomo were each sculpted by a different artist between 1840 and 1965 according to particular themes. Beginning from the left, they represent: *Constantine's Edict* (by Arrigo Minerbi, 1840); *The Life of St Ambrose* (by Giannino Castiglioni, 1950); *The Life of Mary* (by Lodovico Pogliaghi, 1908); *Important Events in Milan from Barbarossa to the Legnano Victory* (by Franco Lombardi and Virginio Pessina, 1950); and *The Golden Years of the Duomo up to St Carlo* (by Luciano Minguzzi, 1965).

To appreciate the stonework fully, take the lift to the roof from where, on clear days, you also get breathtaking views of the Alps. (In Milan, fog is the great enemy of visibility, so a slightly rainy day may offer you a clearer view than a sunny one.) A roof

(Yes, come without fear/we'll extend
our hands to you/life is the same
whever you go, we agree/but Milan,
she's a grand Milan.)

visit also brings you closer to the Madonnina (1774)
– the gilded copper figure of Mary on the church's
highest spire – which is the icon dearest to the hearts
of the Milanese (*see above* **The woman on top**).

The interior

The 52 pillars of the five-aisled Duomo correspond
to the weeks of the year. On their capitals, imposing
statues of saints stretch up into the cross vaults of
the ceiling, creating a vertiginous effect. On the floor
through the main entrance is a sundial installed in
1768 by astronomers from the Accademia di Brera

(*see p72*), placed so that it is struck by a ray of sun-
light breaking through a hole in the opposite wall.
On the summer solstice (21 June), the ray strikes the
tongue of bronze set in the floor; while on the winter
solstice (21 December), the ray of light stretches out
to reach the meridian. This sundial is so precise that
it was once used to regulate clocks throughout the city.

In the first chapel on the right is the 11th-century
sarcophagus of Bishop Ariberto d'Intimiano and a
17th-century plaque commemorating the founding of
the Duomo. The stained-glass windows in the next
three chapels date from the 15th and 16th centuries;
the oldest of all, with scenes from the life of Christ,
was made in 1470-75 and is in the fifth bay on the
right. In the seventh chapel, a window completed in
1988 provides a stark comparison of changing styles.

In the crossing of the transept, the presbytery floor
is shiny and worn by the passage of the many millions of pilgrims who have visited the Duomo over
the centuries; Cardinal-saint Carlo Borromeo (*see
p105* **A family's fortunes**) wanted the Duomo to
serve as his model Counter-Reformation church.

Flanking the 15th-century high altar are two gilded copper pulpits, both 16th-century works. The
organ is also here, its wooden shutters painted with
Bible scenes by Giovanni Ambrogio Figino, Camillo
Procaccini and Giuseppe Meda.

A nail allegedly from Jesus' Cross hangs at the
apex of the apse's vaulted roof. Once a year, on
the Saturday closest to 14 September (prior to the
beginning of vespers), the archbishop ascends to
the apex to retrieve the nail, moving slowly and
solemnly up through the air in the Duomo's decorated wooden *nivola* – an angel-studded basket
first constructed in 1577 under orders by Carlo
Borromeo and significantly renovated and redeco-
rated in 1701 (when the *putti*, or angels, were added).
The word *nivola* is a Milanese derivation of the
Italian word for cloud (*nuvola*), in reference to the
big basket's slow, floating ascent. The nail is then
exhibited at the altar until the following Monday
after vespers, when it is once again lifted up to its
lofty position below the church ceiling.

In the right transept, you'll find a funerary
monument to Gian Giacomo Medici that was long
attributed to Michelangelo, but is now recognised
as the work of sculptor and collector Leone Leoni
(1560-63).

On a pedestal in the wall opposite the Medici
monument stands an arresting and remarkably lifelike statue of a flayed St Bartholomew (note how
nonchalantly the martyr drapes his own skin
over his shoulder). This incredibly accurate study
of human anatomy was carved in 1562 by Marco
d'Agrate, a student of Leonardo da Vinci. Above
and to the right, the splendid stained glass showing
St Catherine of Alessandria – who died on the
original Catherine wheel – is the work of the
Arcimboldo brothers (1556).

Completed in 1614, the 17th-century sculpture that
closes the choir – designed by Pellegrino Tibaldi and
carved by Paolo de' Gazzi, Virgilio del Conte and the

**DOWN
TOWN**
P A L E S T R E

FITNESS DEPARTMENT
SALA FITNESS
CARDIO FITNESS

PERSONAL TRAINING
FITNESS
KICK & BOXE ACADEMY
FIGHT CLUB
WATER PERSONAL TRAINING
HOME PERSONAL TRAINING
FITNESS FOCUS

GROUP EXCERCISE

CYCLING

DAINAMI®
DAINAMI STUDIO
DAINAMI CORPO LIBERO
DAINAMI GRAVITY
DAINAMI PERSONAL TRAINING

GOLF INDOOR
DUE VIDEO POSTAZIONI

SQUASH

OASI - WATER SPACE
WATER GROUP EXCERCISE
ACQUATICITA' PER LA GRAVIDANZA
WATER PERSONAL TRAINING
JACUZZI
PERCORSO KNEIPP
RELAXATION
MASSAGGIO IN ACQUA - WATSU®

COMFORT ZONE
SAUNA
BAGNO TURCO
AROMARIUM
NEBBIA FREDDA
PIOGGIA TROPICALE
DOCCIA SCOZZESE
RELAXATION
VASCA DI REAZIONE
CASCATA DI GHIACCIO

SERVIZI ACCESSORI
GUARDAROBA
DEPOSITO BORSE
NOLEGGIO ARMADIETTI
DOWNTOWN SUN - UVA

SPA ⁰⁰ DOWNTOWN

DOWNTOWN HEALTHY FOO

DOWNTOWN STORE

DOWNTOWN MEETING ARE

P.zza Cavour, 2 20121 Milano
T 02 76011485   F 02 76394283
www.downtownpalestre.it   info@downtownpalestre.i

P.zza Diaz, 6 20123 Milano
T 02 8631181   F 02 86311850

Taurini brothers – is a masterpiece of its time. The three tiers of the sculpture represent (above) the life of St Ambrogio; (centre) the martyred saints venerated by the Milanese church; and (below) the Milanese bishops Anatalone and Galdino.

The ambulatory windows blaze with fabulous 19th-century stained glass by the Bertini brothers and depict scenes from both Testaments. From the ambulatory, stairs lead down to the crypt, where Carlo Borromeo is buried. Entrances to the treasury and the choir, with its 16th-century stucco decoration, are also in the ambulatory.

In the left transept, the fantastic monsters on the bronze Trivulzio Candelabra, an impressive example of medieval goldsmithing, are representations of the arts, professions and virtues and were created by the great 12th-century goldsmith Nicolas of Verdun. In the left aisle, the Cappella del Crocifisso (third past the transept) has stunning 16th-century stained glass.

The remains of the earlier churches of Santa Tecla and the Baptistery (where St Ambrose baptised St Augustine in 387) can be reached by descending the stairs just to the left of the entrance.

From 4 November until the Epiphany, the great *Quadroni di San Carlo*, a devotional pictorial cycle with scenes from the life of the saint, are displayed in the naves between the pillars. The works are a compendium of 17th-century Lombard painting.

Galleria Vittorio Emanuele II

Piazza del Duomo to piazza della Scala. Metro Duomo/bus 50, 54, 65/tram 2, 12, 15, 20, 23, 27. **Open** 24hrs daily. **Map** p311 A1/p312 B1.

The Galleria is, simply put, Milan's centrepiece. Stretching 47m (157ft) overhead, the two-winged glass-roofed arcade was designed to connect piazza del Duomo with piazza della Scala. Its main materials, glass and iron, hint at architect Giuseppe Mengoni's desire to take advantage of the technological developments of the time and to create a suitably monumental feature for the city. Mengoni, plunged tragically to his death from scaffolding just a few days before the Galleria's inauguration, carried out in 1867 by the king of the newly united Italy, Vittorio Emanuele II. Whatever the intentions of its creators, this arcade has now become Milan's de facto downtown. Home to touristy cafés – where you can spend as much as €10 on a coffee – shops, restaurants and mammoth media entertainment stores (*see chapter* **Shops & Services**), the Galleria pulses with life almost every hour of the day.

In the vaults are mosaics representing Asia, Africa, Europe and America. On the floor, at the point where each arm of the Galleria meets the central octagon, are more mosaics. You will find the coats of arms of Vittorio Emanuele's Savoia family, plus the symbols of Milan (a red cross on a white field), Turin (a bull), Rome (a she-wolf) and Florence (a lily). Join the queue and be a tourist (just this once) by spinning your heel once or twice on the bull's privates: it's a guarantee of good luck.

Museo del Duomo

Piazza del Duomo 14, at via dell'Arcivescovado 1 (02 860 358). Metro Duomo/bus 50, 54, 60, 65/ tram 15, 23, 27. **Open** 10am-1.15pm, 3-6pm daily. **Admission** €6; €3 concessions. *See also p53.* **No credit cards. Map** p311 A1/p312 B2.

The Museo del Duomo houses 14th-19th century sculpture, furniture and stained glass from the cathedral. Among its most precious works is Jacopo Tintoretto's *Christ in the Temple* (1530). A significant portion of the museum is dedicated to documenting the half a millennium it took to build the church, and includes a fascinating wooden model of the Duomo from 1519.

Palazzo Reale

Piazza del Duomo 12 (02 875 672/reservations 02 8439 580). Metro Duomo/bus 50, 54/tram 1, 2, 3, 12, 14, 15, 20, 23, 24, 27. **Open** for exhibitions only. **Admission** varies, depending on exhibition. *See also p53.* **No credit cards** (except for telephone bookings: AmEx, MC, DC, V). **Map** p311 A1/p312 B2.

This grand palazzo, organised around two opposing courtyards, was built in the 14th century by the Visconti family and revamped and expanded in the 16th by the Sforzas. The city's first theatre company performed on a makeshift stage here in 1598, and Mozart played here as a child. The old theatre was destroyed by fire in 1776, and replaced by the Teatro alla Scala (*see p61*). Giuseppe Piermarini gave the palazzo its neo-classical look in the 1770s, when he was commissioned to design a residence for Archduke Ferdinand of Austria. Its sumptuous stucco decoration, frescoes and inlaid furniture made it one of the most refined and stylistically consistent neo-classical palaces in Europe, though only a small part of the decor survived World War II bombardments.

The palazzo is now home to major exhibits, as well as the Museo del Duomo (*see p59*). If you are visiting in the late spring or summer, be sure to ask for a season programme, or check with the tourist office (*see p53*) or local press. On warm evenings, it usually hosts special film screenings, jazz concerts and offers aperitifs in its central courtyard. These events cost a small additional fee for entry, but are well worth the expense.

Around piazza della Scala: Manzoni's Milan

The northern end of Galleria Vittorio Emanuele II opens out on to piazza della Scala, the recently remodelled square that lies in front of the **Teatro alla Scala**, Italy's best-known and most prestigious opera house. On any given day you'll find the plaza filled with tourists, passers-by and flocks of well-dressed older gentlemen holding fort theatrically on a range of subjects. (Don't worry if you miss the gist – conversation tends more towards soccer scores than Socratic dialogue.)

Tiepolo's riot of colour on the vault of **Palazzo Clerici**.

Piazza della Scala forms the cornerstone for well-heeled Milan. **Palazzo Marino**, a building originally constructed by a wealthy Genoese banker and that has been the city government headquarters for almost a century and a half, stands opposite La Scala, and around the corner you'll find **San Fedele**, Milan's blatantly baroque 'church of the aristocracy'.

Further north, nearly lost in an unobtrusive side street, lies the striking façade of the **Casa degli Omenoni**. Follow the side street into a small piazza dominated by the **Casa del Manzoni**, where 19th-century novelist Alessandro Manzoni – one of Italy's greatest writers and curse of Italian schoolchildren – lived, worked and died.

Opposite, in a piazza by the same name, is **Palazzo Belgioioso** (No.2; closed to the public), designed by Giuseppe Piermarini in 1777-81 for Alberico XIII di Belgioioso d'Este – the family's heraldic symbols figure large in the façade's decoration. West of piazza della Scala, **Palazzo Clerici** houses frescoes by Giambattista Tiepolo.

Casa del Manzoni

Via Morone 1 (02 8646 0403/www.museidelcentro. mi.it). Metro Montenapoleone/bus 61/tram 1, 2, 20. **Open** 9am-noon, 2-4pm Tue-Fri. **Admission** free. **Map** p311 A1/p312 B1.

Writer Alessandro Manzoni (*see p64* **Novel approach**) lived here from 1814 to 1873, when he took a tumble on the steps of nearby San Fedele (*see p61*) and died. The ground floor of the house, including Manzoni's study, is perfectly preserved – as befits the home of a literary icon of this magnitude.

The house is also home to the Centro Nazionale di Studi Manzoniani, which includes a library of Manzoni's works and critiques of the author.

Casa degli Omenoni

Via Omenoni 3 (no phone). Metro Duomo or Montenapoleone/bus 61/tram 1, 2, 20. **Closed** to the public. **Map** p311 A1/p312 B1.

Eight muscle-bound Atlases, the work of Antonio Abbondio, dominate the ornate front of the studio-home that sculptor Leone Leoni built for himself in 1565. Beneath the cornice, a lion savaging Calumny reflects the creator's famously witty (and notoriously fiery) personality. Leoni's magnificent art collection was unfortunately broken up long ago, but it once included works by Titian and Correggio, as well as Leonardo da Vinci's *Codex Atlanticus* papers – now in the Biblioteca Ambrosiana (*see p63*).

Palazzo Clerici

Via Clerici 5 (02 878 266). Metro Cordusio/bus 61/ tram 2, 3, 4, 12, 14, 20, 24. **Open** by appointment only. **Admission** free. **Map** p308 C2/p312 B1.

Arguably the most luxurious 18th-century domicile in the city, Palazzo Clerici is the result of an enlargement of an earlier structure. Most of the work was carried out under the aegis of Giorgio Antonio Clerici, an ambassador at the court of Maria Teresa of Austria and a fine-art collector. The palazzo has marvellous rococo interiors, but the highlight is the vault of the reception room, which features a fresco by Giambattista Tiepolo (*The Course of the Chariot of the Sun*, 1740). A royal residence from 1773 until 1778, Palazzo Clerici was sold to the government in 1813 and used by the Appeals Court until 1940.

Palazzo Marino

Piazza della Scala 2. Metro Duomo/bus 61/tram 1, 2.
Closed to the public. **Map** p311 A1/p312 B1.
In 1558, Genoese banker Tommaso Marino entrusted architect Galeazzo Alessi with the construction of this palazzo. The building was meant to prove Marino worthy of the hand of a noble Venetian lady (it did, and he ended up marrying her). However, the patron's arrogant and tasteless flaunting of his wealth caused much resentment among the Milanese, who predicted that the palazzo, 'built by stealing, would either burn, fall into disrepair or be stolen by another thief'. Two of those prophecies have already come true, with Marino dying in poverty and the palazzo being confiscated by the Austrian army in 1814. The palazzo has been the city government headquarters since 1860. The Cortile d'Onore features a wealth of sculptural decoration. Quite inexplicably, local lore identifies this palazzo as the birthplace of the fictional nun of Monza, from Manzoni's novel *I promessi sposi* (*see p64* **Novel approach**).

San Fedele

Piazza San Fedele (02 7200 8027/www.gesuiti.it).
Metro Duomo/bus 61/tram 1, 2. **Open** 7.30am-2.30pm, 4-7pm daily. **Admission** free. **Map** p311 A1/p312 B1.
This imposing baroque church is the Milanese headquarters of the Jesuit order. It was designed by Pellegrino Tibaldi in 1569 as an exemplary Counter-Reformation church, following the architectural rules established by the Concilium of Trento (1545-63). Note its single nave, an invention that allowed the priest to keep his eye on the whole congregation. The cupola, crypt and choir were added by Francesco Maria Ricchini (1633-52). The carved wooden choir stalls in the apse were lifted from Santa Maria della Scala, the church demolished to make way for the Teatro alla Scala (*see below*).
The church is a who's who of Milanese baroque and mannerist painting. In the first chapel on the right is Il Cerano's *Vision of St Ignatius* (c1622); in a room leading to the sacristy beyond the second chapel on the right are a *Transfiguration* and *Virgin and Child* by Bernardino Campi (1565). The exuberant carvings on the wooden confessionals and the sacristy (designed by Ricchini and executed by Daniele Ferrari in 1569) help liven up the edifice's Counter-Reform sobriety.

Teatro alla Scala

Piazza della Scala (02 7200 3744/www.teatroallascala. org). Metro Duomo/bus 61/tram 1, 2. **Map** p311 A1.
Museo del Teatro *Corso Magenta 71 (02 4691 528/www.teatroallascala.org). Metro Cadorna/bus 18, 50, 58/tram 19, 20, 24.* **Open** 9am-6pm daily (last entry 5.15pm). **Admission** €5. *See also p53.*
Credit DC, MC, V. **Map** p308 C1, C2/p312 B1.
In 1776, when a fire in the Palazzo Reale (*see p59*) destroyed the city's main theatre, architect Giuseppe Piermarini was called upon to design a new one. His neo-classical masterpiece takes its name from Santa Maria della Scala, the church commissioned in 1381 by Regina della Scala, wife of Bernabò Visconti, and subsequently razed to make way for this opera house. It was inaugurated in 1778 with an opera by Antonio Salieri; many of the best-known works of Puccini, Verdi, Bellini and others premiered here.
La Scala is also a significant symbol of national pride. Destroyed by a heavy night of bombing during World War II, it was swiftly rebuilt after the war's close and reinaugurated in 1946 with an opera conducted by one of Milan's favourites, Arturo Toscanini. With its massive stage and seats for 2,015, La Scala is one of Europe's biggest theatres, and boasts some of the best acoustics in the world.
Every year on 7 December – the feast of Milan's patron saint, Sant'Ambrogio – a new season begins. The event is a perennial favourite for tabloids, gossip TV and even network news, and the cameras flash and reporters jostle to get a line from the furred and bejewelled glitterati.
Opening night is also a traditional opportunity for controversy and protest. Animal rights' activists show up regularly; they wreaked considerable havoc in the early 1990s, when they showered a crowd of mink-coated patrons with buckets of pigs' blood.
While this guide was being written, three-plus years of renovation were drawing to a close, and the merry media circus that surrounds events at this venerable theatre can be expected to roar back into action no later than December 2004.

Sightseeing

Casa degli Omenoni. *See p60.*

BLUE car
bus & limousine service srl

The Museo del Teatro, created in 1913, contains a collection of sculpture, autographs, paintings, costumes and other artefacts related to the theatre.

Around piazza Affari: financial Milan

The area immediately west of the Duomo was traditionally where Milan's craftsmen and artisans set up shop – attested to by the various street names describing activities that took place there: via Spadari (sword-makers), via Cappellari (milliners) and via Armorari (armourers), to name but a few. Some of these names remain appropriate today. For example, the area around via Orefici (goldsmiths) is packed with jewellery stores, most of which boast a small craftsman's shop in the back where some of the glimmering trinkets on display in their windows are created.

Parallel to via Orefici runs via dei Mercanti (Merchants' Street), where one of Milan's only remaining medieval edifices is located. Propped up on thick stone columns, the **Palazzo della Ragione** (Reason) once housed the city's court and judicial offices. Today it houses municipal offices and is closed to the public. Constructed in the early 1200s by Oldrado da Tresseno (then *podestà*, or city leader), it contains a large central courtroom where the lead magistrate once sat in judgment over his fellow Milanese. On either side of the magistrate sat two additional judges – the *cavallo* (horse), and the *gallo* (rooster). The former was charged with guaranteeing speedy hearings; the latter with providing extra vigilance.

Beneath the arches of this red-brick building Milan's medieval market once flourished, spilling out into the piazza Mercanti (aka piazza del Broletto Nuovo) on the other side. The coats of arms of patrician families who lived around the piazza are much in evidence (see, for example, the **Loggia degli Osii**, on the south-west side of the square, with Matteo Visconti's shield from 1316), as are portraits of classical scholars and church fathers (see the 1645 **Palazzo delle Scuole Palatine**, with statues of St Augustine and the Latin poet Ausonius). The well in the centre of this quaint medieval piazza dates from the 1500s, though it was moved here from its original location on the other side of the Palazzo della Ragione in 1879 when city planners extended via dei Mercanti through the area to connect piazza del Duomo with piazza Cordusio.

On the opposite side of via dei Mercanti is the Palazzo dei Giureconsulti (closed to the public), originally constructed in 1561 to house the new offices of Milan's magistrates.

West of this area you will find the church of **San Sepolcro**, as well as nearby 16th-century churches **San Sebastiano** and **Santa Maria presso San Satiro**, a Renaissance building constructed around an earlier ninth-century one. Situated behind San Sepolcro (the entrance is on the far side, in piazza Pio XI), the **Pinacoteca Ambrosiana** contains one of Milan's finest art collections. (It was from a balcony on the piazza San Sepolcro side of the **Biblioteca Ambrosiana** that Mussolini first explained the wonders of fascism to an attendant crowd.)

Further west you will reach piazza Affari (Business Square), built between 1928 and 1940 and home to the **Palazzo della Borsa**, Italy's main stock exchange and the economic pulse of the entire country.

Biblioteca & Pinacoteca Ambrosiana

Piazza Pio XI 2 (02 806 921/www.ambrosiana.it). Metro Cordusio or Duomo/bus 50/tram 2, 3, 4, 12, 14, 19, 24, 27. **Open** *Library* 9.30am-5pm Mon-Fri. *Pinacoteca* 10am-5.30pm Tue-Sun. **Admission** €7.50; €4.50 concessions. **Credit** (weekends only) AmEx, DC, MC, V. **Map** p310 A2/p312 A2.

In 1603 building began on Cardinal Federico Borromeo's (*see p105* **A family's fortunes**) Palazzo Ambrosiano, which was to be the venue for a sweeping cultural project that included a *biblioteca* ('library'; opened in 1609) and an art school (opened in 1629) to train artists in the new, more restrained spirit of the Counter-Reformation. Federico's private art collection was donated to this cultural centre in 1618, and formed the basis of a collection that would continue to grow over the centuries.

The 172 paintings donated by Federico are still together, housed in rooms 1 and 4-7 of the present-day Pinacoteca. These include Titian's *Adoration of the Magi* and a portrait of a man in armour in Room 1; Jacopo Bassano's *Rest on the Flight from Egypt*, Raphael's cartoon for *The School of Athens* and Caravaggio's *Basket of Fruit* in rooms 5 and 6; and works by Flemish masters including Jan Brueghel and Paul Brill in Room 7.

Renaissance masterpieces from outside the cardinal's collection are in rooms 2 and 3, including Sandro Botticelli's *Madonna del Padiglione* and Leonardo da Vinci's *Musician*. The rest of the Pinacoteca contains later works. A lachrymose *Penitent Magdalene* by Guido Reni – darling of the Victorians – is in Room 13 on the upper floor. There are two works by Giandomenico Tiepolo in Room 17. The De Pecis' donation of 19th-century works, including a self-portrait by sculptor Antonio Canova, can be found in rooms 18 and 19. The Galbiati wing houses objects such as a lock of Lucrezia Borgia's hair and the gloves Napoleon wore when he met his destiny at Waterloo, while the Museo Settala is a replica of a 17th-century *Wunderkammer* (chamber of wonders): a magnificent jumble of scientific instruments, fossils, semi-precious stones, paintings and books.

Novel approach

In the Italian literature stakes, Alessandro Manzoni (1785-1873) comes second only to Dante. Outside Italy, however, he trails way behind. It was not always so: when his great novel, *I promessi sposi* (*The Betrothed*), was first published in the 1820s, it was hailed as a masterpiece by the likes of Goethe and Stendhal. But Italy's first – and last – great 19th-century novel was soon overshadowed: composer Giuseppe Verdi became the cultural symbol of the age. However, Manzoni and his works remain relevant even today and can still help to understand the idiosyncracies of his native country.

Born into an Enlightenment background, Manzoni underwent a fervent religious conversion at the age of 25. His writing attempts to reconcile these strongly opposed influences, with his characters displaying a serenity of detachment that epitomises the Italian skill for compromise. In *I promessi sposi*, for example, the vow of virginity so fervently taken by Lucia is shrugged off at the end of the novel when she decides that she has no choice at the time but to adopt drastic strategies.

The novel is important also from a linguistic point of view: six centuries before, the writings of Dante had made Tuscan the language of the Italian peninsula's educated classes. Manzoni brought this language up to date, creating a vernacular novel, with forms not too far removed from everyday speech, and in a language comprehensible to any educated person in the dialect-divided Italian peninsula. A modern Italian literary language had been created.

However, none of this would count for anything had Manzoni not come up with a ripping yarn. Portrayed with memorable clarity, the characters and episodes of his novels are a part of every Italian's cultural DNA. Not many years ago, when someone rashly proposed removing *I promessi sposi* from the Italian school curriculum, the shocked outcry could hardly have been greater if they had suggested turning Milan's Duomo into a hamburger joint. For, despite its stultifying associations with plodding classroom study, this is the Italian novel *per eccellenza*.

At the heart of *I promessi sposi* is the classic theme of frustrated love: Renzo and Lucia – the betrothed of the title – are prevented from marrying by the machinations

of the wicked Don Rodrigo, who has other, more dastardly plans for the young lady. Thickening the plot are a wicked nun, a mysteriously nameless brigand leader and a pusillanimous priest; there's also an abduction to a mountain hideaway, street riots, scenes of famine and a bad bout of the plague. Despite the high drama, however, the tone throughout is of convincing historical and psychological realism.

Manzoni set the novel in Lombardy circa 1625, undoubtedly because events of that period would have been all too credible to his contemporaries in foreign-ruled Milan. Indeed, the helplessness of the humble against the arbitrary cruelty of those in power is a key theme in *I promessi sposi*. Some of the novel's finest moments revolve around string-pulling power play in the higher echelons of both court and Church. In one memorable scene, two minor characters arrange for the transferral of a meddlesome monk who has taken it upon himself to protect Lucia; any follower of contemporary Italian politics will recognise the tried-and-tested techniques described.

The Biblioteca is open to bona fide scholars with suitable letters of introduction only. Historical documents – including the collection of Leonardo's jottings known as the *Codex Atlanticus* – are kept firmly under lock and key, with facsimiles only available to library patrons.

Palazzo della Borsa

Piazza Affari 6, at via San Vittore al Teatro 14 (no phone). Metro Cordusio/bus 50, 58, 60/tram 19, 24, 27. **Closed** to the public. **Map** p310 A2/p312 A2.

Milan's stock exchange (*borsa*) was first founded in 1808. However, it led an unsettled, quasi-nomadic existence until 1931, when it found a permanent (and suitably large) home in the striking Palazzo della Borsa, designed by local architect Paolo Mezzanotte. The grandiose façade features four gigantic columns decorated with sculptures of allegorical figures. In the palazzo's cellar are the scant remains of a Roman theatre from the first century AD, destroyed during one of Holy Roman Emperor Frederick Barbarossa's (*see p10*) rampages in 1162. Tours of the theatre ruins, organised by the Chamber of Commerce, can be requested by calling 02 85 151, or by asking at the main desk inside the building's entrance.

Built according to the Rationalist style popular in the late 1920s and '30s, the façade of this palazzo, which reigns over piazza Affari, the heart of the financial district, provides an excellent example of the domineering, muscle-bound iconography common in fascist architecture.

Palazzo della Ragione

Piazza Mercanti (02 7200 3358). Metro Duomo/bus 50, 60/tram 1, 2, 3, 12, 14, 15, 24, 27. **Open** for exhibitions only. **Admission** varies, depending on exhibition. **No credit cards**. **Map** p310 A2/p312 B2.

The courtyard of the Palazzo della Ragione – also known as Broletto Nuovo (from *brolo*, an old word denoting a place where justice was administered) is one of the few quiet, sheltered corners of central Milan. The palazzo was erected in 1233 by order of Oldrado da Tresseno, the then *podestà* (mayor), to serve as law courts. Oldrado's portrait can be seen in relief on the façade facing piazza del Broletto Nuovo. Markets and public meetings were once held in the ground-floor porticos. People also flocked here to see executions (usually hangings).

Between the second and third arches on the via Mercanti side of the Palazzo della Ragione is a relief of the *scrofa semi-lanuta* ('semi-woolly sow'), a reference to the legend that the city of Mediolanum was founded on the site where a wild sow with hairy legs (*medio* means 'half', *lanum* is 'wool') was seen running about. (Milan's other foundation legends are equally unlikely: a theory that brothers Medio and Lano founded the city is too suspiciously reminiscent of Rome's Remus and Romulus tale, while the idea that the name derives from the German Mai – 'May', for a land where it's always spring – is extremely dubious given Milan's weather.)

San Sebastiano

Via Torino 28 (02 874 263). Metro Duomo/tram 2, 3, 12, 14, 12, 15, 24. **Open** 8am-noon, 3-6.30pm Mon-Sat; 9.30am-noon, 3.30-7pm Sun. **Admission** free. **Map** p310 A2/p312 A2.

When Milan emerged from a bout of the plague in 1576, residents heaved a sigh of relief and, to express their thanks, constructed this church on the site where the 14th-century church of San Quilino had once stood. Pellegrino Tibaldi designed the building, though he originally planned a much higher dome; if the heavenly vision of the *Evangelists and Church Fathers* (1832) by Agostino Comerio inside the cupola makes your head spin as it is now, just imagine the effect Tibaldi was originally aiming for. Most of the other – forgettable – works are by Andrea Lanzani (1490-1526) and Federico Bianchi (1635-1719).

San Sepolcro

Piazza San Sepolcro (no phone). Metro Cordusio or Duomo/tram 2, 3, 12, 14, 19, 24, 27. **Open** noon-2pm Mon-Fri. **Admission** free. **Map** p310 A2/p312 A2.

The forum of Roman Mediolanum occupied the area between piazza San Sepolcro and piazza Pio XI. It was here that a church dedicated to the Holy Trinity was built in 1030, only to be rebuilt in 1100 and rededicated to the Holy Sepulchre. The church underwent the usual Counter-Reformatory treatment in the early 1600s and an 18th-century façade was replaced by a neo-Romanesque one in 1894-97. The crypt, which runs the entire length of the church, is all that remains of the original Romanesque structure. A forest of slim columns divides its five aisles, and by the apse is a 14th-century sarcophagus with reliefs of the Resurrection.

Santa Maria presso San Satiro

Via Torino 17/19 (02 874 683). Metro Duomo/bus 54, 60, 65/tram 2, 3, 12, 14, 15, 24. **Open** 8.30-11.30am, 3.30-5.30 pm Mon-Sat; 9.30-10.30am, 4.30-5.30pm Sun. **Admission** free. **Map** p310 A2/p312 B2.

San Satiro (or Satirus) was St Ambrose's brother (*see p7* **St Misbehavin'**). It was to this little-known sibling that a certain Archbishop Anspert wanted a church dedicated and he left funds for the job when he died in 876.

All that remains of the early structure is the Greek-cross Cappella della Pietà. In 1478, Renaissance genius Donato Bramante was called in to remodel the whole church in order to provide a fitting home for a 13th-century image of the Virgin that was said to have bled when attacked by a knife-wielding maniac in 1242; the fresco concerned still sits on the high altar. Bramante's gift for creating a sense of power and mass – even in a space as limited as the one occupied by this church – emerges in the powerful, barrel-vaulted central nave that ends in a trick-perspective niche that manages to simulate a deep apse within a mere 97cm (38in).

The Cappella della Pietà contains fragments of early medieval fresco decoration and a terracotta sculptural group of the *Pietà* from 1482-3, a typically northern Italian devotional work.

Castello Sforzesco, Brera & Northern Milan

The city's colossal castle, gorgeous greenery and the most chic and up-and-coming *quartieri*.

Presiding over a large fountain that the Milanese none too affectionately refer to as the 'wedding cake', the Castello Sforzesco is a massive remnant of Milan's Renaissance leaders. With its imposing brick walls and distinctive tower, the castle gives a distinguished air to the already chic Brera neighbourhood – a warren of medieval streets, famous palazzi and wealthy inhabitants.

Brera is also a nexus for nightlife – the place to have your palms read or to pick up the latest Gucci handbag (fake, of course). In the evenings, especially in the warmer months, its narrow cobbled streets are dense with human traffic and it's not unusual, in one of the many outdoor cafés, to spot some famous soccer star sipping cocktails alongside a bunch of flushed, jolly German businessmen. This is Milan's hippest neighbourhood, a magnet for both the Milanese and the out-of-towners. Here you'll find the famous Pinacoteca di Brera and, behind the castle, the Triennale and the Torre Branca.

Still further north, the city extends into its up-and-coming fashion hub, including development-boom zones around the Porta Garibaldi train station and fervent Isola neighbourhood – once a left-leaning blue-collar stronghold, now a bohemian quarter and struggling artists' paradise.

In this broad area, you'll find remodelled Romanesque churches, the ethnic enclaves of via Canonica and via Bramante, museums, countless contemporary art galleries, the Piccolo group theatres and more.

Castello Sforzesco & Parco Sempione

Erected in the mid-1400s over the ruins of what had been a Visconti castle-cum-prison, the **Castello Sforzesco** (*see p68*) was designed by Francesco Sforza as both a defensive stronghold and a beautification exercise. The Castello was surrounded by woods, which were soon filled with deer, hares and pheasants imported from Varese and Como to indulge

Sforza's passion for hunting. Today the grand gardens live on in the form of Parco Sempione – it might be a mere fraction of what it once was, but it's still a welcome oasis of greenery within the city.

The Castello is part standing attraction and part museum, housing the eclectic collections of the Civici Musei. It also plays a central role in Milan's urban landscape, presiding over one end of a long pedestrian corridor that runs from the castle down **via Dante**, through piazza del Duomo, and all the way along via Vittorio Emanuele to piazza San Babila.

Started during Milan's brief spell under Napoleonic rule (1796-1814) and continued in the 19th century, the palazzi along via Dante were constructed to match the monumental feel of the new street. All, that is, except **Palazzo Carmagnola** (No.2), which, despite its neo-classical façade, dates back to the 14th century and still retains its original courtyard. It was here that Ludovico il Moro Sforza (*see p14*) lodged his mistress Cecilia Gallerani, as well as illustrious guests such as Bramante and Leonardo da Vinci. Next door is the original **Piccolo Teatro**, founded in 1947 by Italian contemporary theatre greats Paolo Grassi and Giorgio Strehler for their avant-garde company, and now called Teatro Grassi.

From largo Cairoli at the Castello end of via Dante, the semicircular foro Buonaparte sweeps left towards Cadorna metro and commuter station and right towards the **Teatro Strehler** (Nuovo Piccolo) (*see p185*). Architect Marco Zanuso began working on this theatre in the late 1970s, but it took 20 years, a sky-rocketing budget and many court cases before the lights went up in the Nuovo. Another Zanuso project is the nearby **Teatro Studio**, in corso Garibaldi. This is a highly controversial conversion of the charming old Teatro Fossati (1858-9) into a modern cylindrical space with traditional Milanese architectural motifs such as *ringhiera* (suspended balconies with railings). But while well intended, the historical touches failed to appease bemused locals.

Sightseeing

The Napoleonic grandeur of the **Arco della Pace**.

At the back of the Castello Sforzesco is **Parco Sempione**, with the **Palazzo dell'Arte** and the **Aquarium**. The former, a quintessential example of fascist architecture, is also known as the Triennale, after a famous art exhibition held within its halls. At the opposite end to the castle in Parco Sempione rises the **Arco della Pace**. Only Napoleonic urban planners could have come up with this pompous neo-classical arch standing at the head of corso Sempione, Milan's answer to the Champs Elysées. Designed as a link between Milan and Paris, corso Sempione also leads to the **Certosa di Garegnano** and, eventually, to Lake Maggiore (*see chapter* **Lago Maggiore**) on its way to France.

Certosa di Garegnano
Via Garegnano 28 (02 3800 6301). Bus 40/tram 14.
Open 7.30am-noon, 3-5pm daily. **Admission** free.
Map off p308 A1.
A gem of baroque architecture, pretty Carthusian monastery houses stunning frescoes created by 17th-century artist Daniele Crespi to thank the monks for granting him sanctuary after he had killed a man.

Civico Acquario e Stazione Idrobiologica (Aquarium)
Via Gadio 2, in Parco Sempione (02 8846 5750/ www.acquariocivico.mi.it). Metro Lanza/bus 43, 57, 70, 94/tram 3, 4, 12, 14. **Closed** until further notice.
Map p308 C2.
Designed by Sebastiano Locati in 1906, the aquarium's fantastic art nouveau decorative reliefs in polychrome majolica are some consolation for the

lack of hammerhead sharks and killer whales on display. The smattering of the world's marine life here consists of much smaller fry, starting with local fish and swamp life and ending up with uninspiring creatures of the deep from exotic climes. Visitors used to swankier institutions available in other big cities are likely to view it as something of a bottom-feeder. The aquarium is currently closed for restoration.

Museo del Collezionista d'Arte Fondazione Goffredo Matthaes
Via Quintino Sella 4 (02 7202 2488/www.museodel collezionista.com). Metro Cairoli or Lanza/bus 43, 57, 61, 70, 94/tram 1, 3, 4, 12, 14, 27. **Open** 10am-6pm Mon-Fri; 10am-2pm Sat. Closed 2wks Aug. **Admission** €6. **No credit cards. Map** p308 C2/p312 A1.
The fascinating world of art fakes is explored in this educational museum, which also contains a scientific research lab and art-certification office. The museum's declared goal is to help the collector distinguish works of true value from imitations. Twelve rooms house every kind of artwork and antique, from copies of the Old Masters to fabrics. There are explanations (in English) of how to test for authenticity.

Palazzo dell'Arte (Triennale)
Viale Alemagna 9, in Parco Sempione (02 724 341/ www.triennale.it). Metro Cadorna/bus 43, 61, 94/ tram 1, 19, 27. **Open** 10.30am-8.30pm Tue-Sun.
Admission €7; €5 concessions. **No credit cards.**
Map p308 C1, C2.
The Palazzo dell'Arte was constructed in 1932-3 by Giovanni Muzio to provide a permanent home for the Esposizione Internazionale di Arti Decorative,

Castello Sforzesco

The Castello Sforzesco is Milan's monolithic central monument, holding sway over the town centre and forming one pole of a pedestrian corridor that runs between Parco Sempione and piazza San Babila.

Begun in 1368 by Galeazzo II Visconti as part of the city's fortifications, the Castello continued to expand throughout the 14th century. Filippo Maria Visconti (*see p13*) transformed it into a sumptuous ducal residence. Partly demolished during uprisings in 1447, the castle was restored to its original splendour by Francesco Sforza in the 1450s.

The court gathered here by Francesco's son Ludovico il Moro included Bramante and Leonardo da Vinci, and was seen as one of Europe's most refined. But when Ludovico was captured by the French in 1499, the castle – like the court – fell into decline.

While Milan was under French rule in the early 19th century, the castle's star-shaped bulwarks were knocked down. By the late 1800s, there was talk of demolishing the rest, but luckily for the city, architect Luca Beltrami fought tooth and nail to preserve it, coming up with the idea of headquartering Milan's various art collections here. From 1893 until 1904, Beltrami oversaw the castle's restoration, rearranging and rebuilding unashamedly where it didn't quite fit in with contemporary ideas of what a 14th-century castle should look like. His unorthodox efforts saved the edifice from total oblivion.

Coming to a spindly point above the façade is a tower originally by the 15th-century architect Antonio Averlino (whose treatise on architecture contains a chapter on the ideal city of Sforzinda, a somewhat toady tribute to his Milanese patrons). The current tower is, in fact, a 1901-4 re-creation of the architect's original work, which collapsed in 1521.

Visitors enter the enormous piazza d'Armi through the gate at the base of the tower. This sweeping plaza, characterised by stone paths and islands of green, is a favourite hangout for lovers, teenagers skipping school and bookworms of all ages.

From the piazza d'Armi, gates lead into the Rocchetta (on the left) – the oldest part of the castle – and into the Cortile (courtyard) and Palazzo del Corte Ducale (on the right), in Renaissance style. The entrance to the Civici Musei is between the piazza d'Armi and the Cortile del Corte Ducale.

Civici Musei del Castello

The Castello's vast collections cover everything – from Renaissance masterpieces to mummies to musical instruments. If you have the time to wander through all the collections – and you'll need most of the day for such an undertaking – you'll find it worth the effort. Explanations of the works displayed are available (in English) in each room.

CIVICHE RACCOLTE D'ARTE ANTICA

The sculpture gallery begins on the ground floor with early Christian and medieval works, including a marble head of the Byzantine Empress Theodora. Dominating Room 2 is an equestrian statue (1363) of Bernabò Visconti by Bonino da Campione. Room 6 contains a bas-relief (1171) from the Porta Romana (*see p83*) showing Milanese scenes after one of Barbarossa's rampages. In Room 8, the Sala delle Asse, you'll find heavily restored frescoes attributed to Leonardo. There is a series of portraits of the Sforza family attributed to Bernardino Luini in rooms 9 and 10. The Cappella Ducale (duke's chapel, Room 12) was built by Galeazzo Maria Sforza in 1472 and decorated by the leading painters of the day under the direction of Bonifacio Bembo. Room 14 has a 15th-century portal from the Milan branch of the Medici bank and a collection of arms. Although the swords are forged with fierce inscriptions ('I love peace, but I bring war'), the small size of the suits of armour makes it difficult to believe their Lilliputian wearers constituted a major threat.

In Room 15, Bambaja's masterpiece, the monument to Gaston de Foix, is a tribute to the Lombard classical style of the early 16th century. (De Foix, Louis XII's nephew, was a French military commander who died heroically in Ravenna in 1512.) This journey through Gothic and early Renaissance works of art ends with an unfinished sculpture by Michelangelo: the *Rondanini Pietà*. First sculpted and subsequently partially destroyed and abandoned in the mid 1550s, Michelangelo returned to this sculpture only in the last year of his life, working to perfect it right up until his death in 1564. The piece is unfinished, with the remains (right arm and leg) of an earlier attempt at the Christ figure clearly visible alongside the incomplete sculpture, which manages to move in spite (or perhaps because) of its less-than-perfect state.

On the first floor, the Pinacoteca (picture gallery) begins with antique furniture borrowed from the Applied Arts Collection (*see below*). Highlights include the 15th-century *coretto* from the castle of Torchiara near Parma (Room 16): the box with a pyramid on top was designed to allow the castle's owner, Pier Maria Rossi, to hear mass with his lover Bianca Pellegrini da Como without falling prey to indiscreet glances from the congregation. In Room 17, frescoes depict an episode from Boccaccio's *Decameron* in which the Marquis of Saluzzo inflicts trials on his wife in order to test her virtue.

The gallery proper begins in Room 20 with a panorama of 15th-century Italian painting. The Veneto is represented by Giovanni Bellini's innocent *Madonna con Bambino* (1470s); Mantegna's majestic masterpiece *Madonna and Child with Saints and Angels in Glory* (1497), and Antonello da Messina's *St Benedict* (1470), with his penetrating, suspicious gaze. There are also works by the Florentines, including the *Madonna dell'Umiltà* (1430s) by Filippo Lippi. Room 21 is an extravaganza of Lombard painting from the early to late Renaissance, including Vincenzo Foppa's stoic *St Sebastian* (before 1490) and a *Noli Me Tangere* (c1508) by Bramantino. The 16th-century schools are represented by the languorous male nudes of Cesare da Sesto's *San Rocco* polyptych (1520s), the melting gaze of Correggio's *Madonna and Child with the Infant St John* (1517) and Moretto da Brescia's *St John the Baptist* (c1520); rooms 23-24, meanwhile, are full of the forced elegance and erudition of the Lombard mannerists. The Pinacoteca closes with 17th- to 18th-century works: Bernardo Strozzi's fleshy *Berenice* (1630) and the inevitable photo-realistic views of Venice by Canaletto and Guardi.

Civiche Raccolte d'Arte Applicata

This section runs the whole gamut of the so-called minor arts: wrought iron (Room 28); ceramics of the world from the 15th to the 19th centuries (Rooms 29-30; don't miss the eccentric pieces made by architect Giò Ponti (1920s) for Richard Ginori in Room 30); Italian and European porcelain (Room 31); liturgical objects, ivories and scientific instruments (Room 32); leather objects (Room 35); and goldsmith works, enamels, bronzes, textiles and wall coverings.

Civiche Raccolte Archeologiche e Numismatiche

Part of the city's prehistoric and ancient Egyptian collections is housed in the basement beneath the Cortile della Rocchetta (there's more in the Civico Museo Archeologico, *see p96*). Archaeological artefacts range from Paleolithic to Iron Age, with a fascinating section on the prehistoric people who lived in stilt-houses on Lombardy's lakes. The Egyptian collection is less complete, but contains sarcophagi, small pieces of sculpture and the usual mummies.

Museo degli Strumenti Musicali

The castle houses one of the largest collections of musical instruments in Europe (Rooms 36-37). In all, there are 640 instruments arranged in five sections: stringed, plucked, keyboard, wind and exotic. The exhibits range from the very rare – such as Giovanni Grancino's 1662 viol, one of the few stringed instruments in the world to conserve its original baroque neck; and violins by Stradivarius (*see p255* **Fiddling around**) – to the very bizarre. Among the latter are the pochette – pocket-sized violins used by dancing instructors – and combo guitar-mandolins. Even if antique instruments don't float your boat, take a peek into Room 37, the Sala della Balla, where lords and ladies used to play a sort of dancehall tennis. Hanging around this enormous hall are the Trivulzio tapestries, commissioned around 1504, which illustrate the labours of the months.

Castello Sforzesco

Piazza Castello (02 8846 3700). Metro Cairoli, Cadorna or Lanza/bus 43, 57, 61, 70, 94/ tram 1, 3, 4, 12, 14, 27. **Open** *Grounds* 8am-8pm daily. *Museums* 9.30am-5.30pm Tue-Sun. **Admission** free. **Map** p308 C2/p312 A1.

The **Pinacoteca di Brera** courtyard. *See p71.*

The Arena Civica, the mini-coliseum designed in 1806 by Luigi Canonica and located at the back of the park, is another addition from the city's Napoleonic period. The rulers of the Roman-inspired French Empire used it for open-air entertainment – chariot races and mock naval battles (for the latter, the Arena was flooded with water from nearby canals). Today it is used for international athletic events and occasional concerts.

A host of museums and galleries are nestled throughout the park, including the Civico Acquario and the Palazzo dell'Arte (Triennale). Be sure to visit the newly reopened Torre Branca, located next door to the Triennale. Besides incorporating one of the hippest café/restaurants in Milan (Just Cavalli Café, *see p117*), the tower offers visitors a sweeping, vertiginous 360⁰ view of the entire city.

The triumphal Arco della Pace, at the western end of the park, was begun in 1807 to a design by Luigi Cagnola to commemorate Napoleon's victories. Work proceeded too slowly, however, and came to an abrupt halt in 1808 after Napoleon fell from power. Construction resumed in 1826 – with a few essential changes to the faces in the reliefs – and the arch was eventually inaugurated on 10 September 1838 by Austrian Emperor Ferdinand I.

Brera

The narrow, winding streets of the Brera neighbourhood – characterised by low buildings, hidden courtyards and porphyry block paving stones – amount to all the olde Italy this city has left. Naturally, the neighbourhood's central location, small palazzi and genuine charm have combined to turn this ex-craftsmen's quarter into a hot spot for nightclubs, cafés, bars and people-watching.

From foro Buonaparte, via Cusani then via dell'Orso lead east towards Brera. Take a brief detour away from the heart of the district to visit the elegantly baroque church of **San Giuseppe**, on via Verdi, then trace your steps back to via Brera.

On the corner of via del Carmine is the 17th-century **Palazzo Cusani** (via Brera 15; not open to the public). It's said that the two Cusani brothers had irreconcilable ideas about how they wanted their individual private entrances to their common domicile to look, so they commissioned two architects to carry out the work in two different styles – one façade of the palazzo was modelled by Giovanni Ruggeri in 1719 in *barocchetto* style, with ornate windows and balconies, while the other was done in neo-classical style by Giuseppe Piermarini. Further along via del Carmine, in the square of the same name, is **Santa Maria del Carmine**, one of three (originally) Romanesque churches hidden in this web of roads that sadly fell prey to 19th-century restoration. Its companions in

held every three years. Since then, the Triennale has widened its scope to include exhibits on architecture, urban planning, industrial design, fashion and audiovisual communications. Even the new café on the first floor gets in on the action, treating patrons to a sitting exhibition of important designer chairs from the past century.

Parco Sempione

Metro Cadorna, Cairoli or Lanza/bus 43, 57, 61, 70, 94/tram 1, 3, 4, 12, 14, 27, 30. **Open** *Mar-Apr, Oct* 6.30am-9pm daily. *May* 6.30am-10pm daily. *June-Sept* 6.30am-11.30pm daily. *Nov-Feb* 6.30am-8pm daily. **Admission** free. **Map** p308 C1, C2.

The Sforzas' castle may face out on to some of Milan's most sought-after real estate, but behind it lies a treasure of a kind all too rare in this Italian metropolis: the great, green Parco Sempione.

Extending over 47 hectares (116 acres), this park is a 19th-century creation. The city's French rulers began carving it out of the remains of the ducal gardens – with their orchards, vegetable gardens and hunting reserve – in the early 1800s. The park was landscaped many years later, in 1893, by Emilio Alemagna. He opted for the then-popular 'English garden' fashion, with winding paths, lawns, copses and a lake.

art-history woe are **San Marco** (further north) and **San Simpliciano**, off via Solferino.

Back on via Brera is the Palazzo di Brera, which hosts the Biblioteca Braidense, a library with an intriguing collection of volumes as well as richly decorated interiors, an observatory, a botanical garden (*see p71* **Brera's best-kept secret**) and the **Pinacoteca di Brera**, one of Italy's most prestigious art collections.

The Franciscan church of **Sant'Angelo** stands north-east of here. From piazza Sant'Angelo, largo Donegani leads to via Turati and the **Palazzo della Permanente**, a venue for temporary exhibitions of modern art and a permanent collection of 20th-century Italian art.

Palazzo della Permanente

Via Turati 34 (02 655 1445/www.lapermanente-milano.it). Metro Turati/bus 43/tram 1, 2. **Open** Tue-Sun, hours vary. **Admission** varies according to exhibition. **No credit cards. Map** p309 B1, C1. A museum housing a permanent collection of Italian paintings, sculpture and graphics from the early 20th century onwards, including Giorgio De Chirico's *Prodigal Son* (1922), Amedeo Modigliani's *Portrait of Paul Guillaume* (1916) and Umberto

Boccioni's *Unique Forms of Continuity in Space* (1913). Other artists represented include Lucio Fontana, Mario Sironi, Carlo Carrà, Giacomo Balla, Giorgio Morandi and Massimo Campigli.

Pinacoteca di Brera

Via Brera 28 (02 722 631/reservations 02 8942 1146). Metro Lanza or Montenapoleone/bus 61/tram 1, 2, 3, 12, 14. **Open** 8.30am-7.30pm Tue-Sun (last entry 6.45pm). **Admission** €5; €2.50 concessions; free under-18s and over-65s. *See also p53.* **No credit cards. Map** p308 C2/p312 B1.
If you're only going to visit one museum while in Milan, this is it. The Pinacoteca (picture gallery) boasts an admirable, if relatively small, collection of masterpieces, and, while it cannot boast the breadth of exhibits on display at, say, the Louvre, it is accessible and easy to appreciate in a single afternoon.

With a collection that covers works by major Italian artists from the 13th to the 20th centuries, the Pinacoteca di Brera is a great place to learn the basics or improve on your existing knowledge of Italian painting. The collection includes important works of art, including the exercise in foreshortening that is *Dead Christ* by Andrea Mantegna; a mournful *Pietà* by Giovanni Bellini; Piero della Francesca's

Brera's best-kept secret

According to popular wisdom, the best bits of Milan are hidden from public view. Passing by monolithic palazzo façades in the city centre, you might be lucky enough to see the last thing any visitor to Milan expects – a glimpse of greenery. A big bronze door might open for a moment and the totally unexpected smell of cut grass fill your nostrils, or a glance down a dark, cavernous hallway might reveal grass, bushes, trees, flowerbeds, ivy… even the occasional fountain and trellis. These are the botanical wonders of Milan's many astonishingly beautiful private courtyards. Unfortunately, they're also exactly that – private.

However, here is at least one enclosed oasis that you can visit, and what's more, it's free. The Orto Botanico di Brera (Brera Botanical Garden) is a roughly 5,000 square-metre (54,000 square-foot) patch of park tucked away behind the Pinacoteca di Brera (*see p71*) and surrounded by large 17th- and 18th-century apartment buildings, many of which have now been converted into offices. The gardens were founded in 1774 by the abbot Fulgenzio Witman on orders from Maria Teresa of Austria. The empress aimed to provide a living, growing classroom to teach botany to students at the Brera school.

There are hundreds of different plant species in the gardens, including a giant Ginkgo biloba – rising over 30 metres (98 feet) tall – which was one of the first species the empress had planted in the gardens. Today, it is considered among the oldest of its kind in Europe.

Although the gardens reopened to the public in 1998, they remain relatively secret. Milan does little or nothing to promote them, and even those passing by on the other side of its walls seem to know nothing of their existence. (However, the gardens were being overhauled and restored with funding from a prominent local bank as this guide was being written, and may not be so secret for long.)

Officially, the gardens are open at set hours; in reality they can be accessed all day long through a back door on the ground floor corridor of the Accademia di Brera (downstairs from the Pinacoteca), although you'll have to wade through crowds of adolescent art students to get to it.

Orto Botanico di Brera

Via Brera 28 (02 8901 0419). Metro Lanza or Montenapoleone/bus 61/tram 1, 2, 3, 12, 14. **Open** 9am-noon, 1-4pm Mon-Fri. **Admission** free. **Map** p308 C2.

Sightseeing

Virgin and Child with Saints; the disturbingly realistic *Christ at the Column* by Donato Bramante, and Caravaggio's atmospheric *Supper at Emmaus.*

The palazzo was begun in 1651 by Francesco Maria Richini for the Jesuits, who wanted it to house their college, astronomical observatory and botanical garden. In 1776 part of the building was allocated to the Fine Arts Academy. The Pinacoteca was established as a study collection, with plaster casts and drawings for the students at the Academy. It was enlarged under Napoleon to house paintings from suppressed religious orders (check out the Canova statue of the notoriously diminutive French emperor in the guise of an ancient Greek athlete in the centre of the courtyard). Today, the 38 rooms are arranged in a circuit that begins and ends with 20th-century Italian painting. Another interesting sight is the ongoing restoration of Gerolamo Savoldo's *Pala di Pesaro*, an altarpiece so imposing that it's being worked on in situ (Room XIV). Visitors can look inside the glass laboratory built around the painting and watch the experts carefully bring this priceless piece of 16th-century art to mint condition.

Piero's **Virgin and Child with Saints**.

If you have time, wander into the botanical gardens behind the Pinacoteca (*see p71* **Brera's best-kept secret**), an attractive, relatively unknown green space tucked away in the heart of the city.

San Giuseppe
Via Verdi 11 (02 805 2320). Metro Cordusio or Duomo/bus 61/tram 1, 2, 20. **Open** 7am-6.30pm Mon-Fri; 9am-1pm Sat, Sun. **Admission** free. **Map** p309 C1/p312 B1.
A baroque façade with statues from the early 19th century hides the octagonal structure of this building, which is considered Francesco Maria Richini's greatest work. The interior is decorated with baroque works by locals Camillo Procaccini (1620-25) and Andrea Lanzani (1712).

San Marco
Piazza San Marco 2 (02 2900 2598). Metro Lanza/ bus 41, 43, 61/tram 3, 4, 12, 20. **Open** 7.30am-noon, 4-7pm daily. **Admission** free. **Map** p308 C2.
San Marco was built in 1254 by the Augustinian Lanfranco Settala on the site of a church that the Milanese had dedicated to Venice's patron, St Mark, as thanks to the Venetians for their intervention in the battle against Frederick Barbarossa (*see p10*). The façade was redone by Carlo Maciachini, a champion of neo-Gothic revival, while inside, nine chapels provide an overview of 16th- and 17th-century Lombard painting.

San Simpliciano
Piazza San Simpliciano 7 (02 862 274). Metro Lanza/bus 43, 57, 70/tram 3, 4, 12, 14. **Open** 7am-noon, 3-7pm Mon-Sat; 8am-noon, 4-7pm Sun. **Admission** free. **Map** p308 C2.
One of the oldest churches in the city, San Simpliciano was founded in the fourth century by St Ambrose and finished in 401. The original church was called the Basilica Virginum and had a porticoed structure where penitent parishioners and neophytes attended mass. The present façade was added in 1870 by Carlo Maciachini in the neo-Gothic style he favoured, while the central entrance dates from the 12th century. The apse decoration, the *Coronation of the Virgin*, is by Leonardo da Vinci's follower Bergognone.

Santa Maria del Carmine
Piazza del Carmine 2 (02 8646 3365). Bus 61/tram 1, 3, 4, 12, 14, 20, 27. **Open** 7.30-11.30am, 3.30-7pm daily. **Admission** free. **Map** p308 C2/p312 A1.
Built in 1250 and rebuilt in 1400, nothing much remains of the original Romanesque church of Santa Maria del Carmine. The present-day façade is the work of Carlo Maciachini (1880). The Carmine is full of Milanese history: the tomb (1472) of ducal councillor Angelo Simonetta stands in the right transept, while the body of finance minister Giuseppe Prina was brought to the sacristy after he had been massacred by the populace for raising the tax on salt in 1814. The wooden choir (1579-85) houses the plaster models that were used by the artists working in the Duomo during the 19th century.

Dead gorgeous: the **Cimitero Monumentale** is a shrine to art nouveau. *See p74.*

Sant'Angelo

Piazza Sant'Angelo 2 (02 632 481). Metro Moscova/bus 41, 43, 94. **Open** 8am-7.30pm daily. **Admission** free. **Map** p309 B1, C1.

Built in 1552 to take the place of a Franciscan church the Spanish had destroyed to build defence works, Sant'Angelo is a highly significant work of 16th-century Milanese architecture. The interior is full of paintings by noteworthy Milanese and Lombard artists from the 16th and 17th centuries, including Antonio Campi, Morazzone and Procaccini. There's also a copy of a work by Gaudenzio Ferrari.

Porta Garibaldi, Isola & beyond

A stroll down corso Garibaldi, an active commercial street that was recently turned into a partially pedestrianised thoroughfare, will take you past enticing speciality shops, intriguing boutiques and the church of **Santa Maria Incoronata**, a rare example of a double-fronted temple. As well as being architecturally unusual, this church boasts many artistic treasures, among them the 15th-century Biblioteca Umanistica (library of humanities).

The northern end of corso Garibaldi is crowned by the neo-classical **Porta Garibaldi** (1826). Known as Porta Comasina until 1860, this was the gate through which people from Como and the Brianza would pass on their way to find work in Milan's factories. The immigrant population grew so large that the urban fabric was extended to create the proletarian areas of Garibaldi and Isola. Much has changed since then, however, and these days this part of town is the nexus for a new Milanese financial/ convention area that is scheduled to include an enormous public park, although much of the development was still under construction when this guide was being written. Nearby is corso Como, a short, entirely pedestrianised boulevard with a host of excellent restaurants, popular bars and trendy boutiques, including Carla Sozzani's 10 Corso Como (*see p138*).

To the east of Porta Garibaldi, on a 1,000 square-metre (10,753 square-foot) site that was once occupied by Pirelli's tyre factory, rises the **Grattacielo Pirelli**, or Pirellone (Big Pirelli), as the locals call it. Erected between 1955 and 1960, the Pirellone is a tribute to post-World War II reconstruction, designed by a team of architects that included Giò Ponti, Pier Luigi

Nervi and Arturo Danusso. The Pirellone has notched up a handful of records in its 50-year life: it was the first building in Milan to dare rise higher than the Madonnina on top of the Duomo (*see p56* **The woman on top**); and, until the end of the 1960s, it was also the world's highest skyscraper in reinforced cement. On 18 April 2002 the Pirellone made the headlines again when a small plane flew into it, in a chilling, though apparently unintentional, repeat of 9/11.

Just to the right of the Pirellone is the massive bulk of **Stazione Centrale**, an overwhelming example of the heavy end of the Milanese Liberty style (*see p77* **The road to Liberty**), built between 1912 and 1931. The city's inter-war fascist leaders made it their own by applying the fascist bundle-of-sticks symbol wherever they could. On the façade, Anno IX refers to 1931, the ninth year of Mussolini's fascist regime, when the station was opened. A few blocks west of the station is the **Cimitero Monumentale**, a temple to Milanese art nouveau, aka Liberty.

The *quartiere* of **Isola** (island) is so named because of its isolation – it lies across the via Farini bridge along the east side of the cemetery, on what used to be the 'wrong' side of the railroad tracks. In the 19th century, this area was a gathering place for drunkards and petty criminals; slowly, however, its low property prices started to attract carpenters, blacksmiths and other artisans. These days, the area is the haunt of craftsmen of a more artistic calibre: jewellery makers, painters, sculptors have all opened pretty ateliers and workshops here. The word on the street is that Isola will soon rival Brera as the Milanese capital of cool.

From piazza Segrino in the heart of this area, via Thaon de Revel leads to the church of **Santa Maria alla Fontana**, which has a sanctuary that different experts attribute to both Leonardo da Vinci and Bramante.

West of here, the run-down industrial zone of **Bovisa** had been poised to undergo a minor renaissance linked to the creation of a university campus and the **Museo del Presente** in its decommissioned gasworks. However, several years after being OKed, neither project has yet taken off, so it remains to be seen whether the optimism was justified. To the north-east, on the other hand, a new university hub and the **Teatro degli Arcimboldi** (*see p174*) are injecting fresh cultural life into the Bicocca neighbourhood.

Cimitero Monumentale

Piazzale Cimitero Monumentale (02 8846 5600/ 02 659 9938). Bus 41, 43, 51, 70/tram 3, 4, 11, 12, 14, 29, 30, 33. **Open** 8.30am-5.15pm Tue-Sun. Closed pm during holidays. **Admission** free. **Map** p308 B2.

The cemetery was begun in 1866 by Carlo Maciachini (1866) and is 250,000sq m (2,688,000sq ft) of pure eclecticism. It's virtually an open-air museum of art nouveau, though later major Italian artists – including Giacomo Manzù, Adolfo Wildt and Lucio Fontana – were also commissioned to produce monuments. The whole complex centres on the 'Temple of Fame' (Famae Aedes), where famous *milanesi* and other illustrious 'guests' are buried, including Manzoni (author of *I Promessi sposi, see p64* **Novel approach**); Luca Beltrami (restorer of the Castello Sforzesco and champion of the neo-Gothic movement); conductor Arturo Toscanini; poet Salvatore Quasimodo, and singer, actor, comedian Giorgio Gaber. Non-Catholics are buried in separate sectors. A free map of the cemetery indicating the most noteworthy monuments is available at the entrance.

Santa Maria alla Fontana

Piazza Santa Maria alla Fontana 11 (02 688 7059). Metro Garibaldi or Zara/bus 82, 83/tram 4, 11. **Open** *Church* 7am-noon, 3-7pm Mon-Fri; 8am-1pm, 4-7pm Sat, Sun. *Sanctuary* 10am-noon, 3-5pm Sat; 9.30am-12.30, 4-5.30pm Sun. **Admission** free. **Map** p308 A2.

This church is essentially a modern structure in the neo-Renaissance style, with various nondescript additions. The presbytery, however, rests on a much older sanctuary, open during weekends. According to local tradition, French governor Charles d'Amboise was miraculously cured at a spring here, and so had an oratory built on the spot in 1506. The design for the building has variously been attributed to Leonardo da Vinci and Bramante, but more rigorous scholarship attributes it to Giovanni Antonio Amedeo, the genius behind the Certosa di Pavia (*see p259*) and much of Milan's Duomo (*see p54*). The original font is still inside the church.

Santa Maria Incoronata

Corso Garibaldi 116 (02 654 855/guided tours 02 607 1009/02 6900 0579). Metro Garibaldi or Moscova/bus 41, 43, 94. **Open** 7.30am-1.30pm, 4-7.30pm Mon-Fri; 7.30am-noon, 4-7.30pm Sat; 8am-12.30pm, 4-7.30 pm Sun and hols. **Admission** free. **Map** p308 B2, C2.

This basically Romanesque church is, in fact, made up of two buildings erected by Guiniforte Solari and subsequently united in 1468. The one on the left went up in 1451, coinciding with the arrival in Milan of Francesco Sforza. As a result, the Augustinian fathers dedicated it to the new duke. Nine years later, Francesco's wife Bianca Maria Visconti decided that another church should be erected next to and joined to the first one. She intended to show publicly the strength of their marital union. In the apse are frescoes from the 15th to 17th centuries. Frescos in the chapels in the left nave are attributed variously to the Leonardo-esque painter Zenale and da Vinci's *pupillo*, Bergognone. Guided tours held on Saturdays can be arranged by appointment.

San Babila & Eastern Milan

Public parks, belle époque architecture and designer shopping from A to Z.

Via della Spiga. *See p76*.

This end of town ranges from elite to everyday, with the aristocratic residences and glittering fashion houses that define the Quadrilatero della Moda (aka the Golden Rectangle) extending down via Veneto past the city's oldest public park, and petering out into the chaos of corso Buenos Aires – a wide boulevard that boasts the single highest density of shops per square metre in Europe, and bustles with activity 24/7.

On a clear day, staring straight down via Veneto, through Porta Venezia and off into the distance might earn you a sight of Italy's snowy Alps. Otherwise, you're probably better off window-shopping.

Via Manzoni & piazza Cavour

Formerly known as corsia del Giardino (garden thoroughfare) after the lush greenery that surrounded each of the wealthy villas along its length, via Manzoni was renamed in tribute to

one of the city's most famous residents (*see p64* **Novel approach**) after his death in 1873. Though the area had always been a popular choice in terms of real estate, in the late 19th century it became *the* street for Milan's elite, spelling doom for its verdure as plots were sold off to provide space for more palazzi.

Nestling between the impressive façades that line the street, is the entrance to the *casa-museo* (house-museum) **Poldi Pezzoli** (*see p78* **The house Poldi Pezzoli built**). This late 19th-century Milanese noble domicile holds one of the most prestigious European collections of art, furniture and decorative objects, assembled by the family over the course of several generations.

The eastern end of via Manzoni coincides with the arches of **Porta Nuova**, a city gate that was once part of the fortifications built to protect the city from the attacks of Frederick Barbarossa (*see p10*).

Though the gate was first erected in 1171, it was heavily restored in 1861, using white and black marble, and the more friable sandstone. The arches were then decorated with Roman funerary stones found in the area, including one depicting the Vettii, a family of textile merchants.

Beyond the gate is **piazza Cavour**, an attractive square dedicated to Camillo Benso, Conte di Cavour, the 19th-century statesman credited with bringing about the unification of Italy. His statue stands in the north-east corner of the square. The massive grey neo-classical hulk on the square's east side is the **Palazzo dell'Informazione**, designed by Giovanni Muzio in 1942 as the headquarters for the fascist newspaper *Il Popolo d'Italia*. Mussolini's daily only survived until July 1943, but thanks to its proximity to the most newsworthy area of the city (piazza Affari, *see p65*), the building has become the Milanese headquarters for many Italian and international press agencies, including Reuters and the Associated Press.

Quadrilatero della Moda

No other shopping area in Italy is as stylish, chic or positively dripping with wealth and self-indulgence as the Quadrilatero della Moda. And indeed, few places in the world have the same designer boutique density; they're all there, from A(rmani) to Z(egna) (*see p136* **After the fashion?**). This designer heaven is delineated by via Montenapoleone (or via Montenapo, as the locals refer to it), via Sant'Andrea, via Manzoni and the pedestrianised via della Spiga.

But even the visitor without a gold card will find this area worth a look, on both an anthropological level (it offers a fun insight into how the other half lives) and a cultural one: two eccentric but rewarding museums, the **Museo Bagatti Valsecchi** and the **Museo di Milano**, are located in the fashion zone, as is one of Milan's prettiest (and least visited) churches, **San Francesco di Paola**.

Museo Bagatti Valsecchi

Via Gesù 5 (02 7600 6132/www.museobagatti valsecchi.org). Metro Montenapoleone/bus 34, 61/tram 1, 2, 20. **Open** 1-5.45pm Tue-Sun. **Admission** €6; €3 Wed. **Credit** MC, V. **Map** p309 C1/p312 C1.
Opened in 1994, this neo-Renaissance palazzo – residence of the Bagatti Valsecchi brothers – is now a homage in museum form to the extraordinary tastes of these eclectic collectors from the late 19th century. Inside are innumerable works of Renaissance art – however, paintings are not the real reason to visit. Here, it's collecting itself that matters: the brothers shared a cultivated taste for all things Renaissance, and strove to reproduce 15th-century palazzo life right in their own home, from the paintings on the walls down to the toys their children played with.

Highlights include an extraordinary 16th-century bed carved with the Passion of Christ and scenes from the Old Testament, and a collection of children's furniture from the 15th to 18th centuries. If you don't feel one visit is enough, ask to have your ticket stamped when you enter – that way it will be good for two more visits over the following month.

Museo di Milano e Storia Contemporanea

Palazzo Morando Attendolo Bolognini, via Sant'Andrea 6 (02 7600 6245/www.museidelcentro.mi.it). Metro Montenapoleone/bus 61, 94/tram 1, 2, 20. **Open** *Museum* 2-5.30pm Tue-Sun. *Exhibitions* 9am-5.30pm Tue-Sun. **Admission** *Museum* free. *Exhibitions* (€2-€4). **No credit cards. Map** p309 C1/p312 C1.
Fully renovated in 2002, the Palazzo Morando Attendolo Bolognini is both a living museum exhibiting the former private apartments of the Countess Bolognini, and home to a section of the city's civic art collections. The bulk of the artwork exhibited here consists of Luigi Beretta's art collection, donated to the city of Milan in 1935. These paintings have helped historians create a thorough picture of Milan as it was during the Napoleonic era and under Austrian domination, as well as chart its urban development over the years. Of equal interest are the porcelains, sculptures, furniture and other decorative objects that belonged to the Countess; now on permanent display as integral parts of Palazzo Morando. The ground floor has been remodelled as open space for travelling exhibitions. Note that while entrance to the museum is free, you may have to pay a small €2-€4 charge to visit the travelling exhibition.

San Francesco di Paola

Via Manzoni 3 (no phone). Metro Montenapoleone/tram 2, 20. **Open** 9am-noon, 4-6.30pm daily. **Admission** free. **Map** p309 C1/p312 B1.
Displaying an almost divine sense of irony, this charming baroque church constructed by the Minimi fathers (a particularly ascetic Franciscan order founded in 1506) lies right in the heart of the wealthiest and most ostentatious part of Milan.

Its attractive baroque façade (completed in 1891) plays with concave and convex forms. Inside, in addition to the classic marble altars, gilded woodwork and detailed stucco, you'll find a painting in the vault by Carlo Maria Giudici figuring the glory of San Francesco di Paola, the church's patron saint.

The interior benefits from intensive renovation and restoration carried out during the 1990s and finished at the beginning of this century.

From San Babila to Porta Venezia

Corso Vittorio Emanuele II, one of Milan's main commercial arteries, links piazza Duomo (*see p54*) with piazza San Babila. Formerly known as corsia dei Servi (after a church erected by the fathers of the Serviti order), this large pedestrianised thoroughfare gets a special mention in Alessandro Manzoni's *I promessi sposi*, as the scene of the 1628 bread riots (*see p64* **Novel approach**).

Under the arcades near the neo-classical church of **San Carlo al Corso**, at No.13, is a third-century statue representing a Roman magistrate. With typical Milanese pragmatism, the sculpture has become known as the *Omm de preja* (man of stone) or *Scior Carera* (Mr Carera, after the first word of the Latin inscription, which reads, 'Those who criticise others should be free of any flaws themselves'). During the Austrian occupation, the hard-done-by Milanese would vent their spleen against their foreign rulers by attaching satirical notes of malcontent to the statue in the dead of night.

Unfortunately, the new (high) positioning of the statue doesn't allow the locals to affix any notes to protest against the current government.

The corso is capped at its far end by piazza San Babila, a frankly unattractive post-war revamp where eternally work-oriented *milanesi* bustle about. The brick faux-Romanesque façade of the church of **San Babila** stands meekly in the north-east corner of the square, dwarfed by the surrounding abundance of steel, stone and racing traffic.

Corso Venezia shoots straight as a die out of piazza San Babila and north-east to Porta Venezia. The thoroughfare is lined by elegant noble residences. Starting from piazza San Babila, the late 15th-century **Casa Fontana Silvestri** at No.10 is one of the few remaining examples of a Renaissance residence in the city,

The road to Liberty

At the end of the 19th century, as adventurous European gentry were opening up coffee plantations in South America and directing new-fangled flying dirigibles around Paris, belle époque artistry reigned supreme. The Liberty style, as the Italians call it, was quickly adopted by the Milanese, and nowhere is their love affair with this new architecture more evident than in the network of streets (vie Cappuccini, Barozzi, Vivaio, Mozart) around piazza Duse.

A short distance (north-east) from the quintessentially eclectic Civico Museo di Storia Naturale (*see p81*) on corso Venezia, a covered passageway leads (right) to via Salvini and piazza Duse. The architect Giulio Ulisse Arata is the genius behind three different palazzi built for the Berri Meregalli family in the area. One at **via Barozzi 1** (1910) is decorated with animal heads that brighten up the solid structure. Located on the corner of via Mozart, this palazzo butts up against the another at **via Mozart 21**, which has the same colour stone and rams' heads, plus floral capitals and grotesque masks to hide the gutters. Two nudes frescoed around the central balcony on the first floor heighten the grandiose tone of the architectural ornamentation. The third, at **via Cappuccini 8** (1911-14), is a curious mix of just about every artistic style imaginable, from Gothic

to Renaissance to Liberty. (Note the gloriously jungly garden nearby, with its curious mix of birds, including a flock of flamingos.)

Beyond traffic-packed Porta Venezia (*see p77*) is another little Liberty enclave. Across piazza Oberdan in via Malpighi are two gems of art nouveau architecture by Giovanni Battista Bossi, the **Casa Galimberti** (1905; No.3) and the **Casa Guazzoni** (1903-06; No.12), with their colourful, exuberantly decorated façades. The nearby **Sheraton Diana Majestic** (*see p46*) is another example of belle époque architecture; the hotel staff have done an admirable job of retaining the feel and presence of the building's exterior in the ground-floor bar and restaurant, which opens into a lovely garden in the summer.

possibly built to a design by Bramante; the terracotta decoration on the façade is typically Lombard. Across the street, at No.11, is the **Seminario Arcivescovile** (seminary of the archdiocese), commissioned by Carlo Borromeo (*see p17*) in 1565, to implement the Council of Trent's regulations concerning the education of the clergy. The monumental doorway, designed by Francesco Maria Richini and decorated with allegorical representations of Hope and Charity, was added in 1652. The neo-classical **Palazzo Serbelloni** (No.16), at the intersection with via San Damiano, was constructed in 1793; it hosted Napoleon in 1796, Metternich in 1838, and King Vittorio Emanuele II and Napoleon III in 1859. It is now home to the journalists' club, the Circolo della Stampa. Check the newspapers for presentations of books or cultural debates,

which are often held in the mirror-studded Salone degli Specchi. **Palazzo Rocca Saporiti** (No.40) was built to a plan by stage-designer Giovanni Perego in 1812; its imposing Ionic columns and cornice surmounted by statues of gods make it a perfect example of neo-Palladian architectural canons. The façade is decorated with a frieze displaying scenes from the history of Milan and was equipped with a *loggia* on the first floor from which its residents could watch parades. At No.47, **Palazzo Castiglioni**, with its imaginative bronze and wrought-iron art nouveau decoration, was built in 1904 by Giuseppe Sommaruga; the façade once contained statues of female nudes, which earned it the nickname *Ca' di Ciapp*, or 'Buns House'. (For more art nouveau extravaganzas in the area, *see p77* **The road to Liberty**.)

The house Poldi Pezzoli built

It's a classic fairy tale: a modest gentleman named Giuseppe, approaching his twilight years but still in possession of enough vigour to grab life and shake what he can out of it, inherits a fortune from a distant uncle. In a fit of passion (conditioned, of course, by the wisdom of his age), he weds a beautiful, wealthy and cultivated young noblewoman named Rosa.

The two are art fanatics and each amasses a considerable collection of masterpieces. Then two years after joining in matrimonial and artistic bliss, Giuseppe and Rosa are blessed with a son: Gian Giacomo.

When Giuseppe passes on, his wife and 11-year-old son retreat to the comfort of their home (one of the most beautiful palazzi in central Milan). Rosa, in the finest tradition of Italian motherhood, takes on full responsibility for young Gian Giacomo's education. At this point – let's face it – this tale could easily have degenerated from fairy to frightening. Rosa could have smothered Gian Giacomo and created yet another fortysomething *mammone* stuck at home, tied to his mother's apron strings. But she didn't, he wasn't, and our fairy tale continues.

Rather than stifle her son, Rosa instilled him with her own cultivated tastes and art-gathering aspirations, and as soon as the young man came into his own he started adding to his parents' collection. He began with armoured suits and weapons. But as maturity caught up with his inherited passion,

he travelled all over Europe gathering works of art – from precious medieval and Renaissance jewellery to tapestries, glasswork, porcelain, paintings and statuary. Botticelli, Mantegna, Lotto, Tiepolo and Bellini are just some of the artists whose works he snapped up.

Gian Giacomo turned his spacious Milan home into a sparkling, wondrously decorated domicile. He devoted each part of the house to objects of a certain period; so 18th-century porcelains found their place in the Stucco Room, Gothic golden jewels were placed in the Medieval Study, and baroque statues stand around the Antique Staircase.

But the erudite art collector's greatest stroke of genius came only in death. In 1881, two years after he had passed away and in strict accordance with his will, the Poldi Pezzoli house was opened to the public, becoming the first house-museum in the world.

Today, just as it has for over 100 years, the Poldi Pezzoli Museum fulfils Gian Giacomo's desire for his artwork to be 'of public use and benefit', introducing visitors to a collection that is as extraordinary as it is eccentric.

And the artwork lived happily ever after.

Museo Poldi Pezzoli

Via Manzoni 12 (02 794 889/www.museo poldipezzoli.it). Metro Montenapoleone/ bus 61, 94/tram 1, 2, 20. **Open** 10am-6pm Tue-Sun. Closed public holidays. **Admission** €9; €7 concessions. *See also p53.* **Credit** MC, V. **Map** p309 C1/p312 B1.

Who lives in a house like this? Renaissance-pretty **Casa Fontana-Silvestri**. *See p77*.

Corso Venezia ends in piazza Oberdan, where deafening, lung-challenging traffic screams around **Porta Venezia**, originally known as Porta Orientale. One of the eight main entrances in the 16th-century Spanish fortifications, it was the first to be redesigned by Giuseppe Piermarini (architect of La Scala) in 1782, when the city's Spanish walls were torn down to make way for tree-lined avenues. In 1828 Piermarini's original neo-classical gate was replaced by the two triumphal arches still standing today. Designed by Rodolfo Vantini, both elements have triple vantage points: towards the city, towards the country and towards the main thoroughfare viale Piave/bastioni di Porta Venezia.

Basilica di San Babila

Corso Monforte 1 (02 7600 2877). Metro San Babila/bus 54, 60, 61, 65, 73. **Open** 8am-noon, 3.30-6pm daily. **Admission** free. **Map** p309 C1/p312 C1. Standing out like a sore thumb in the midst of the post-war architecture and hectic traffic of piazza San Babila is the neo-Romanesque façade of the church that gives the square its name. The original fourth-century basilica was rebuilt in the 11th century, and further modified in the 16th century, only to have its Romanesque façade cack-handedly 'restored' in 1906 by Paolo Cesa Bianchi, who also did the main altar.

San Carlo al Corso

Piazza San Carlo, off corso Vittorio Emanuele II (02 773 302). Metro Duomo or San Babila/bus 51. **Open** 7am-12.20pm, 4-8pm Mon-Sat; 9am-1pm, 4-10pm Sun. **Admission** free. **Map** p311 A1/p312 B2.

This neo-classical building was begun in 1839 and completed in 1847. The church is essentially a cylinder covered with a dome, recalling pantheons in Rome and Paris.

South of corso Monforte

Via del Conservatorio connects busy corso Monforte to the Porta Vittoria zone and its law courts (*see p82*). Just past the political science department of the Università di Milano, located in the late baroque Palazzo Resta-Pallavicino at No.7, is a little piazza with its south-east corner enclosed by Milan's second-largest church, **Santa Maria della Passione**, and the **Conservatorio** (conservatory).

Directly opposite the church is via della Passione, opened in 1540 to create a panoramic view of Santa Maria della Passione and allow access from the church to the *navigli* (canals) that once ran there. Via del Conservatorio leads to via Corridoni and the church of **San Pietro in Gessate**. By taking a right at the end of via Corridoni and heading down viale Regina Margherita, you'll come to the elegant **Rotonda della Besana**, a structure built at the end of the 17th century to a design by Francesco Raffagno. Although originally conceived as a cemetery, the Rotonda's small central church and surrounding circular promenade of airy porticoes proved too beautiful to waste on corpses. Today it is used by the city to house important travelling exhibitions.

Branching out: **Villa Reale** is no longer reserved for emperors and aristocrats. *See p81.*

Conservatorio di Musica 'Giuseppe Verdi'
Via Conservatorio 12 (02 762 1101/www. conservatorio-milano.com). Metro San Babila/ bus 54, 61. **Open** 8am-8pm Mon-Fri. **Admission** free. **Map** p311 A1, A2/p312 C2.

The French dissolved religious orders when they ruled Milan in the early 19th century, freeing up prime real estate for ventures such as the Conservatorio, which was founded in 1808 in what had previously been the Lateran convent. Many key figures in Italian music studied in this prestigious institution – though the young Giuseppe Verdi, ironically, was rejected – and it still plays a fundamental role in Italian musical life today. There are two concert halls, one for chamber music and one for symphonic and choral music. The library houses over 35,000 volumes and 460,000 musical works, including manuscripts by Mozart, Donizetti, Bellini and Verdi. Rare string instruments are housed under glass cases along the corridor leading to the main concert hall, the Sala Verdi.

San Pietro in Gessate
Piazza San Pietro in Gessate, at corso di Porta Vittoria (02 5410 7424). Bus 60, 77, 84/tram 12, 20, 23, 27. **Open** 7.30am-6pm Mon-Sat; 8.30am-1pm, 4-8pm Sun. Closed pm summer and public holidays. **Admission** free. **Map** p311 A1/p312 C2.

This church was commissioned by Florentine banker Pigello Portinari and built between 1447 and 1475 to a design by Pietro Antonio and Guiniforte Solari. In 1862, frescoes were discovered hidden under a layer of plaster. During the 16th and 17th centuries, even artwork was affected by the mass paranoia at the time of the plague (*see p11* **Coming to germs**) – these frescoes were covered with fresh lime-based plaster in order to disinfect them. By all accounts, the artwork has remained healthy, and today, although heavily damaged during World War II, large parts of the pictorial decoration are still in place. The church's eight-stall choir is a reconstruction based on what was left of the one built in 1640 by Carlo Garavaglia: the original was used as firewood during World War II.

Santa Maria della Passione
Via Bellini 2 (02 7602 1370). Metro San Babila/bus 54, 61. **Open** *Church* 7am-noon, 3.30-6.15pm Mon-Fri; 9am-4pm Sat, Sun. *Museum* currently closed for restoration. **Admission** free. **Map** p311 A2/p312 C1.

Construction of the church of Santa Maria della Passione began in 1486 following a design by Giovanni Battagio. It was originally a Greek-cross church, but one arm was lengthened to form a nave and six semicircular side chapels were added in 1573, making it the second-largest in Milan after the Duomo (*see p54*). The façade and the adjacent monastery – now the seat of the Conservatorio (*see above*) – were added in 1692 by Giuseppe Rusnati, who kept the building low so as not to distract attention from the massive octagonal lantern of the dome (Cristoforo Lombardo, 1530).

The barrel vault of the church abounds with frescoes of the Evangelists, St Ambrose, St Augustine, angels and allegories of the virtues by Giuseppe Galbesio da Brescia (1583); more intriguing are the paintings lower down in the church's three-aisled interior, a veritable picture gallery of works by many of the leading 16th- and 17th-century Lombard artists, including Crespi, Procaccini and Bramantino. The 16th-century wooden choir stalls are inlaid with mother of pearl. In the niches of the choir are two fabulous organs with 16th- and 17th-century carvings, both of which are still used for concerts; the shutters were painted by Crespi with scenes from the Passion.

Giardini Pubblici & Villa Reale

Giardini Pubblici

Metro Palestro, Porta Venezia, Repubblica or Turati/ bus 94/tram 1, 9, 11, 29, 30. **Open** 6.30am-sunset daily. **Map** p309 C1.

Travelling down corso Venezia, you can't help but notice the park lining one side, especially as it's some of the only flora visible within city limits. The Giardini Pubblici were designed in the 'English' style by Giuseppe Piermarini in 1786, and enlarged in 1857 to include the Villa Reale and the Palazzo Dugnani. The park's present arrangement – complete with natural elements, such as waterfalls and rocky outcrops – was the work of Emilio Alemagna for the 1871 International Expo.

The park plays host to a number of minor attractions. On the western side, Palazzo Dugnani houses the Museo del Cinema. Further south-east, across via Palestra, are the Padiglione d'Arte Contemporanea (PAC) gallery and the Villa Reale, housing impressive modern-art collections and regular temporary exhibitions. North-east towards corso Venezia are the Civico Museo di Storia Naturale and the Planetario Ulrico Hoepli. Deep in the heart of the gardens, the Bar Bianco (02 2952 3354, open 8am-7pm daily), with its outdoor tables, is a pleasant place for a coffee break, even though it lacks the elegance of the former Padiglione del Caffè (1863), now a nursery school.

Civico Museo di Storia Naturale (Natural History Museum)

Corso Venezia 55 (02 8846 3280/guided tours 02 783 528). Metro Palestro. **Open** 9am-5.30pm Tue-Fri; 9am-6pm Sat, Sun. **Admission** unconfirmed at time of writing. **No credit cards. Map** p309 C1.

Giovanni Ceruti's neo-classical building was put up in 1838 to house collections left to the city by aristocratic collector Giuseppe de Cristoforis. The museum's collections cover palaeontology, botany, mineralogy, geology and zoology. The rooms dedicated to palaeontology have life-size reconstructions of a triceratops and allosaurus. The old-fashioned dioramas are a real treat.

Museo del Cinema

Via Manin 2b (02 655 4977). Metro Turati/ bus 41, 43, 94. **Open** 3-6pm Fri-Sun. **Admission** €3; €1.50 under-12s. **No credit cards. Map** p309 C1.

Palazzo Dugnani was constructed at the end of the 17th century and remodelled in the 18th. In 1846 it became city property, its large estate incorporated into the Giardini Pubblici. A monumental staircase sweeps up to the great hall where there's a musicians' gallery, plus frescoes (1731) by Giambattista Tiepolo: the *Allegory of the Dugnani Family* and *Episodes from the Lives of Scipione and Massinissa*. A Mafia bomb that exploded in nearby via Palestro in 1993 compounded damage from World War II bombardments; and the private apartments usually open to the public were closed for restoration as this guide went to press. However, the part of the palazzo housing the cinema museum remains open: 18th-century experiments in making moving pictures, the Lumière brothers' efforts, and cameras with sound-recording devices are all explained here. For information on film showings, *see p160*.

Planetario Ulrico Hoepli

Corso Venezia 57 (02 8846 3341/www.brera.mi. astro.it/planet). Metro Palestro. **Shows** 9pm Tue, Thur; 3pm, 4.30pm Sat, Sun. **Admission** €3; €1.50 concessions. **No credit cards. Map** p309 C1.

A gift to the city from publisher Ulrico Hoepli, the building was constructed in 1930 by Pietro Portaluppi in faux-classical style. Projections take place in a great domed room, last renovated in 1955.

Villa Reale & Galleria d'Arte Moderna

Via Palestro 16 (02 7600 2819). Metro Palestro/ bus 94. **Open** 9am-5.30pm Tue-Sun (guided tour 10am Thur). **Admission** free. **Map** p309 C1.

The neo-classical Villa Reale was built by Leopold Pollack in 1790 for Count Ludovico Barbiano di Belgioioso. Napoleon lived there in 1802, and after him Marshall Radetzky (*see p18*). After the unification of Italy, ownership passed to the Italian royal family, who gave the palazzo to the city of Milan in 1921. Many Milanese have spoken their marriage vows beneath Andrea Appiani's frescoes of Parnassus in the central hall.

The Galleria d'Arte Moderna is spread over 35 rooms in part of the central body and on the first and second floors of the west wing of this U-shaped building. The collections represent various currents in Italian painting in the 19th century from Francesco Hayez's historical Romanticism to the mostly Milan-based Scapigliatura movement and the branch of post-Impressionism known as Divisionism. The main part of the surprisingly rich collection is in the west wing, accessed by a rather inconspicuous entrance staircase in a sad state of disrepair. Here you'll find portraits of Arp, De Pisis, Carrà, Chagall and Stravinsky. The villa is also host to the Grassi Collection (second floor, west wing) and the Vismara collection (ground floor central core, accessible only when ceremonies are not being held), both of which include works by modern Italian and international masters such as Van Gogh, Gauguin, Cézanne, Matisse, Picasso and Morandi.

Sightseeing

Porta Romana, the Navigli & Southern Milan

A wealth of waterways, churches and historic palazzi, plus martyrs galore.

Southern Milan's single most prominent feature is the Navigli, a network of canals that once made this landlocked metropolis one of the principal ports in Italy. Underused and abandoned for years, the Navigli is currently enjoying something of a renaissance, with various clean-up projects in the works for both the canals and their surroundings.

Around this area is a host of small, out-of-the-way churches. Visiting some Milan sights can require effort, but these oft-forgotten gems prove it's worth it. Many of these churches house masterpieces by famous artists (including Bramantino and Tintoretto) – what's more, it's quite likely that you will find yourself enjoying them, plus a wealth of reliquaries, necropolises, martyred saints and exquisite stained glass, in total solitude.

The area around Porta Romana is also famous for its small shops and craftsmen's studios. Keep your eyes peeled as you walk along its streets: you never know where an unbelievable bargain might be waiting…

From the University to Porta Romana

The area stretching from the University of Milan to Porta Romana is largely student territory, and the shops, bars and cafés here reflect its youthful bent. This means eclectic shopping and, on the whole, more modest prices than in other central locations.

If you happen to have the misfortune (or fortune, depending on your point of view) of getting caught up in one of the countless student protests – and there seems to be a new one every week – step back and enjoy the show. Italian students love to protest, apparently as an excuse to play music, dance, spray graffiti and smoke. Stay upwind unless you want to get a whole new perspective on life…

In piazza Santo Stefano you'll find the churches of **San Bernardino alle Ossa**

and **Santo Stefano Maggiore**. The former is a sanctuary dating back to the 13th century that was originally erected to handle the burial of corpses for the nearby Ospedale del Brolo, Milan's most important hospital prior to the construction of the Ospedale Maggiore, now the Cà Granda (*see p83*). This way station for the dead is rendered even more macabre by its ossuary, a sanctum decorated with human bones that date back to an 18th-century reconstruction – the ossuary had been all but destroyed in 1642 when the tower of nearby Santo Stefano collapsed on it. Further east at Porta Vittoria 6, the city's library (*see p288*) is housed in the splendid 17th-century **Palazzo Sormani**, a building that was heavily restored after World War II and transformed for public use.

The nearby **Palazzo di Giustizia** is a heavy, travertine-clad building where many of the most important court cases in Italy are handled, including the one concerning the recent Parmalat scandal. This monstrous monument to justice was built between 1932 and 1940 by Marcello Piacentini in the then-popular fascist style as a replacement for the old Palazzo dei Tribunali in piazza Beccaria. It boasts well over 1,000 rooms and covers an area equivalent to more than three city blocks. Hopefully you won't have any reason to visit the building's interior (though its enormous atrium is decorated with mosaics by 20th-century artists, including Mario Sironi), but a long walk around the outside will give you an idea of its monolithic proportions – be sure to pack a lunch.

Nearby **Giardino della Guastalla**, Milan's oldest park, provides a welcome breather from the surrounding cement and concrete.

Across via Francesco Sforza, the large **Ca' Granda** (big house) was originally conceived in the 15th century to bring the city's 30-plus minor hospitals under one roof. The building now houses the arts faculties of the Università degli Studi di Milano.

All roads lead to Rome, especially the one through Milan's **Porta Romana**.

Rising up above the skyline to the north, you'll see the **Torre Velasca**. This oddly shaped 26-storey skyscraper (which the Milanese affectionately refer to as *il fungo*, the mushroom) was designed by Studio BBPR and inaugurated in 1958. Its top-heavy structure, a throwback to medieval architecture, is the studio's ingenious response to the need to create more office space than the available ground space would support. The tower takes its name from the piazza it faces. Ironically, this piazza was named after governor Juan Fernandez De Velasco in celebration of another piece of design ingenuity– widening the space between **Porta Romana** and via Larga, which facilitated the passage of the city's large carnival parades.

Ca' Granda
(Università degli Studi di Milano)

Via Festa del Perdono 7 (02 503 111/freephone 800 188 128). Metro Duomo or Missori/bus 54, 60, 65, 77/tram 12, 20, 23, 27. **Open** 9am-5pm Mon-Fri; 8am-11.30pm Sat. **Admission** free. **Map** p311 A1/ p312 B2, C2.

Now home to the arts faculties of Milan university, Ca' Granda began its life as a hospital and hospice. It was Francesco Sforza who set out to consolidate Milan's 30 hospitals into one *Casa Granda* or *Ospedale Maggiore* (main hospital) in 1456. His favourite architect, Il Filarete, incorporated the idea into his grandiose plan to transform Milan into an ideal Renaissance city. The building has one wing for men and another for women, each subdivided

into four inner courts and separated by the Cortile Maggiore (great court). Work continued on the project after Filarete's death (c1469), but ground to a halt with the fall of Ludovico il Moro (*see p14*), only to pick up again from time to time through the 17th and 18th centuries. In 1939 the hospital was moved to its new headquarters at Niguarda, in the northern suburbs. The university took up residence here in the 1950s.

The façade, with its typically Lombard terracotta decoration, is one of the few in the city to have been completed in the 15th century. The courtyards, also from the 15th century, were used for the women's baths and storing wood. The Cortile Maggiore, with its Renaissance portico and baroque loggia, is decorated with busts sculpted from the yellow, rose and grey stone from Angera on Lake Maggiore (*see p199*). The Cortile was reconstructed after sustaining heavy damage during World War II. The neoclassical Macchio wing – now home to university offices – once contained an art gallery. There's a canvas by Guercino (1639) in the 17th-century church of the **Annunciata** (02 583 074 65, open 7.30am-1.30pm Mon-Fri during university term) inside the courtyard.

San Bernardino alle Ossa

Piazza Santo Stefano (02 7602 3735). Metro Duomo or Missori/bus 54, 60, 65/tram 12, 20, 23, 27. **Open** 7.30am-noon, 2.30-6pm Mon-Fri; 7.30am-noon Sat, Sun. **Admission** free. **Map** p311 A1/p312 C2.

San Bernardino alle Ossa's ossuary chapel is decorated in delightfully macabre fashion with pictures and patterns picked out in human bones supplied

Ca' Granda. See p83.

by the nearby Ospedale del Brolo, and the occasional skull from decapitated criminals. Another, more colourful theory, states that these are the bones of the illegitimate children of Milanese noblewomen. The interior gloom is enlivened by the bright colours of the vault painting by Sebastiano Ricci (1659-1734), *Triumph of the Soul among the Angels*.

San Calimero

Via San Calimero 9/11 (02 5831 4028). Metro Crocetta/bus 65, 94/tram 4, 24. **Open** 8am-noon, 4-6pm daily. **Admission** free. **Map** p311 B1.

Said to have been built in the 5th century over the remains of a pre-existing pagan temple dedicated to Apollo, this church is dedicated to Saint Calimero, the fourth bishop of Milan, whose body it houses. The chapel was redone in Romanesque form in the 12th century, and then again in 1609 by Francesco Maria Richini. Disastrous restoration work by Angelo Colla in 1882 wiped out most traces of earlier architecture. The terracotta façade, with its porch resting on two stately lion bases, dates from Colla's renovation. The church is most notable for its rare portal of the Canonica – a double arch and circle of bricks over the main entrance that is one of the last examples left in Milan.

San Nazaro Maggiore

Piazza San Nazaro in Brolo 5 (02 5830 7719). Metro Missori/bus 65, 94/tram 4, 24. **Open** 7.30am-noon, 3-6.30pm daily. **Admission** free. **Map** p311 B1.

Situated on what was the ancient colonnaded corso di Porta Romana, San Nazaro was one of the four basilicas built during St Ambrose's evangelisation drive, between 382 and 386. Constructed to accom-

modate relics of the apostles Andrew, John and Thomas, and the first in the western world to be designed in the form of a cross, the church was given the name Basilica Apostolorum. When Ambrose brought the remains of local martyr St Nazarus (who died in 396) here, the church was rededicated: you can see the saintly remains in the two altars of the choir, but the silver vessel holding them is a copy – the one St Ambrose commissioned is in the Duomo treasury (*see p54*).

When it was built, the basilica stood outside the city walls in a Christian burial area, hence the sarcophagi behind the church. The church was destroyed by fire in 1075 and rebuilt using material from the original structure, including the pilasters holding up the central dome. The *basilichetta* of San Lino, to the right of the altar, dates from the 10th century. The octagonal Cappella Trivulzio, designed by Bramantino, was added to the church in 1512 as a mausoleum for the powerful Trivulzio family. Reworked in the late 16th century and given a neoclassical interior in the 1830s, the basilica suffered considerable damage during World War II. Between 1946 and 1963 the church was stripped of many of its post-fourth-century trappings to restore a sense of its early Christian austerity.

Santo Stefano Maggiore

Piazza Santo Stefano (no phone number). Metro Duomo or Missori/bus 54, 60, 65/tram 12, 20, 23, 27. **Map** p311 A1/p312 C2.

Santo Stefano was originally built in the fifth century, but what you see today is a 1584 reconstruction with a baroque bell tower added between 1643 and 1674 by Carlo Buzzi. The fragmentary pilaster just in front of the façade on the right is the only remnant of the medieval atrium where Galeazzo Maria Sforza (*see p14*) was assassinated on 26 December 1476. The church is currently closed to the public.

From via Torino to Porta Ticinese

Narrow and heavily trafficked, via Torino runs down from the south-west corner of piazza Duomo to largo Carrobbio (a name derived from the Latin *quadrivium*, a place where four roads meet), providing the intrepid pedestrian with a host of bargain shops, harried *milanesi* and inviting side streets.

South off via Torino, via Soncino leads to the **Palazzo Stampa**, a beautiful Renaissance building once home to a traitor. At the beginning of the 16th century, the building's owner Massimiliano Stampa was on excellent terms with the city's rulers, the Sforza family. But as the Sforza's star began to wane, Stampa sold his allegiance to Holy Roman Emperor Charles V. In return, he obtained the title of Count of the Soncino. Count Stampa was suddenly elevated to Renaissance star status, and the Palazzo Stampa was considered the most important salon in the city, attracting A-list nobility from across the region. But alas, Stampa's time in the sun was relatively brief, and the palazzo passed to the Casati family within the century. The new owners effected numerous changes on the building, opening, for example, a new entrance on to via Soncino. But they kept the Count's 15th-century tower, crowned with the golden globe, eagle, crown and cross escutcheon (still visible today) used by Charles V to express royal ownership. Of Count Massimiliano Stampa there remains no sign…

The corso di Porta Ticinese shoots south out of largo Carrobbio, passing by the church of **San Lorenzo Maggiore**. Facing the church are 16 massive Roman columns. They were recovered some time after the third century, most likely from a Roman spa or temple, and erected in commemoration of St Laurence, martyred in 258. Further down on the same street is the **Museo Diocesano**, a splendid treasure trove of religious art and artefacts.

At the corner of via de Amicis is the medieval **Porta Ticinese**, which in ancient times was the entry into the city for travellers coming from Ticinum (modern-day Pavia). Via E de Amicis leads west from here past the site of the **Roman amphitheatre** (at No.19, 02 2040 4175, www.mumi.it, scheduled to open in spring 2005 for visits by appointment only). First uncovered in 1936 but only brought fully to

light in the 1980s, the structure has suffered not so much the ravages of time as those of church-builders: much of it was dismantled and used to build San Lorenzo. Nearby, the little church of **San Vincenzo in Prato** stands in what was a pre-Christian necropolis.

A detour to the east of San Lorenzo along via Molino delle Armi and corso Italia leads to **piazza Vetra**, a name that probably derives from *castra vetera* (old barracks), an allusion to the fact that Roman soldiers defending the imperial palace camped here. During the Middle Ages, the piazza was often used as a point from which to defend the city; the Seveso and Nirone rivers converged here, and were redirected to feed defensive waterworks around the city walls.

All these military associations may have prepared piazza Vetra for an even bloodier vocation: as an execution ground. For a period of nearly 800 years, stretching from 1080 all the way to 1840, the piazza was the place where commoners condemned to death were decapitated. (Nobility got the more central, slightly more attractive piazza Broletto.) Cut through the pretty Parco delle Basiliche to the church of **Santa Maria dei Miracoli**, or head back westwards to **Sant'Eustorgio**, which stands on the spot where the first Milanese Christians are reputed to have been baptised by the apostle Barnabus.

Just west of here is the Darsena, the confluence of the two canals that connect Milan with the Ticino and Po rivers (*see p86* **Canals plus**). Built in 1603, the Darsena was Milan's main port, a hotbed of commercial activity for goods flowing in and out of the city. Today the waters have stilled, but every Saturday the *milanesi* continue to congregate here in droves to make the most of the great bargains, luscious foods and fresh produce at Milan's biggest open-air market (*see p142* **Market leaders**).

Just past the church of **San Gottardo al Corso** (corso San Gottardo 6, 02 8940 4432, open 7am-noon, 4-7pm daily), the street widens into largo Gustav Mahler. Here stands the **Auditorium di Milano** (*see p174*), Milan's new temple of music, unveiled in 1999.

Museo Diocesano

Corso di Porta Ticinese 95 (02 8940 4714/ bookings 02 8942 0019/www.museodiocesano.it). Metro Sant'Ambrogio/bus 94/tram 3, 20. **Open** 10am-6pm Tue, Wed, Fri-Sun; 10am-10pm Thur. **Admission** €6-€8.50. *See also p53.* **No credit cards. Map** p310 A2, B2.
The Museo Diocesano contains religious art treasures culled from churches and private collections throughout Lombardy – and what a splendid treasure trove it is. The new museum is a streamlined operation distributed over three floors of the former Dominican convent of Sant'Eustorgio.

Sightseeing

Canals plus

Although little is left of Milan's *navigli* (canals), the waterways were once the city's greatest asset, connecting it with the rest of Italy through an intricate network of locks and canals – many designed by Leonardo da Vinci himself.

Excavations for the Naviglio Grande – which carries the waters of the diverted Ticino river from Lake Maggiore (*see p193*) to the Darsena – were begun in 1177. Canals for Bereguardo, the Martesana and Paderno followed, thus boosting Milan's already considerable commercial clout. Barges floated in, carrying coal and salt (not to mention marble from Candoglia on Lake Maggiore used in the construction of the Duomo, *see p54*); they left laden with iron, grains, fabrics and other goods manufactured in the city.

However, the canals were too distant from the city centre and in 1359 a project was initiated to build the Naviglio Pavese. The waterway was initially conceived merely to irrigate Gian Galeazzo Visconti's hunting reserve near Pavia, but in the 15th century Ludovico il Moro Sforza called in Leonardo da Vinci to improve the system and create a canal network that extended into the heart of the city.

In 1597 a scheme to further improve the canal was initiated, but funds soon ran out, leaving what is still known as the *conca fallato* (failed sluice) in the southern suburbs. It wasn't until the French applied themselves to the task that the canal was finished. And not long after its inauguration in 1819, its traffic rates were outstripping those on the Naviglio Grande.

In the late 19th century the area along the *navigli* Grande and Pavese was a thriving port. The city retained its dense network of waterways through the first half of the 20th century, making landlocked Milan Italy's 13th-largest port by volume of trade. After World War II, materials for reconstructing the badly bombed city were transported by water.

Then work began to fill in the historic canals. By 1979 not a single working boat broke the surface of what remained of the waters.

Today Milan's Navigli neighbourhood begins at the Darsena between Porta Ticinese and Porta Genova and extends through a limited area to the south and west that is dominated by boutiques, artists' studios, antiques restorers, bookshops and a thriving nightlife (*see* chapters **Nightlife** *and* **Cafés & Bars**). On the north bank of the Naviglio Grande, the little church of **San Cristoforo** (open 7.30am-12pm, 4-7pm daily) is dedicated to the patron saint of boatmen. This is, in fact, two churches sandwiched together: the one on the left is the older of the two, and probably dates from the late 12th century. It was enlarged in 1398 when the adjacent Cappella Ducale was built to celebrate the end of a long famine; the portal and rose window on the older church were added at this time. The façade has traces of 15th-century fresco decoration and the bell tower also dates from the 15th century. Inside are frescoes by 15th- and 16th-century Lombard painters.

Nearby in via Neera, the deconsecrated church of **Santa Maria Annunciata** holds the last work of American artist Dan Flavin, the Progetto Chiesa Rossa (*see p164*).

The **Associazione del Naviglio Grande**, formed to protect the canal zone's cultural heritage, organises concerts, art exhibitions and antiques markets (*see p142* **Market leaders** *and chapter* **Festivals & Events**). Check the website (www.navigliogrande.mi.it) for further details of upcoming events.

The **Amici dei Navigli**, an institution dedicated to researching the *navigli* environment, organises round-trip boat tours of the canals from the Darsena.

Amici dei Navigli

www.navigamilano.it/www.amicideinavigli.org. **Boat trips** *Apr-mid Sept* by appointment daily. **Rates** *Tours* €18; €10 concessions (groups of more than 15 people). *Boat hire* (4hrs) €300 (morning), €360 (afternoon).

Incoming Partners

Via Felice Casati 32, East (02 6702 0280/ www.incomingpartners.it). Metro Porta Venezia or Repubblica/tram 1, 5, 11, 29, 30. **Open** 9.30am-1pm, 2-6.30pm Mon-Fri. **Credit** DC, MC, V. **Map** p309 B1, B2. Boat trips depart from the dock in piazza Cantore (map p310 B1) at the corner of viale G D'Annunzio.

Sightseeing

Hark! The herald angels blow the trumpets at **Santa Maria dei Miracoli**. *See p90.*

A slick entrance leads into a great hall; from here visitors can follow colour-coded ground plans on pamphlets, or simply read the explanatory placards and computer points scattered around (in Italian).

On the ground floor are select pieces from St Ambrose's time (coloured ochre on the plan), followed by the first part of an itinerary (blue-green) with works from the 14th to 19th centuries, a multimedia room, and a collection of 17th- and 18th-century Italian paintings. Liturgical furniture (reliquaries, crucifixes, chalices and the like) is housed in the basement.

The first floor contains a space for temporary exhibitions as well as the bulk of the collections. The (blue-green) itinerary that began downstairs – which includes some works from the closed museum at Santa Maria della Passione (*see p79*) – ends here with the collection's most recent pieces. This floor also houses the collections of several cardinals: Federico Visconti's collection (1617-93) is contained in one small room, with copies of famous drawings, including portraits of Raphael and Titian by an anonymous Lombard painter of the 17th century; Giuseppe Pozzobonelli's collection (1696-1783) has 17th-century Italian landscapes; Cesare Monti's (1593-1650) has Lombard and Venetian works of the 16th and 17th centuries (don't miss Tintoretto's *Christ and the Adulteress*, 1545-7). There is also a collection of 14th- and 15th-century altarpiece paintings with gold backgrounds, accompanied by a video (in Italian) explaining the gold-leafing process.

San Giorgio al Palazzo

Piazza San Giorgio 2 (02 860 831). Tram 2, 3, 14, 20. **Open** *7.30-noon, 3.30-6.30pm Mon-Fri; 9.30am-noon, 3.30-6.30pm Sat, Sun.* **Admission** *free.* **Map** p310 A2/p312 A2.

Founded in 750, San Giorgio was rebuilt in 1129 and heavily reworked in the 17th and early 19th centuries. Look hard amid the neo-classical trappings and you'll see a baptismal font fashioned out of a Romanesque capital and a couple of pilasters at the far end of the central nave from the original church. In the third chapel on the right don't miss the striking cycle of *Scenes from the Passion of Christ* by Bernardino Luini (1516).

San Lorenzo Maggiore (San Lorenzo alle Colonne)

Corso di Porta Ticinese 39 (02 8940 4129). Metro Sant'Ambrogio/bus 94/tram 3, 20. **Open** *Church and Cappella di Sant'Aquilino 7.30am-12.30pm, 2.30-6.30pm Mon-Sat; 7.30am-6pm Sun.* **Admission** €2; €1 concessions. *See also p53.* **No credit cards.** **Map** p310 A2, B2.

Built at the end of the fourth century, San Lorenzo may have been the chapel of the imperial Roman palace. It is certainly one of the oldest centrally planned churches anywhere. Fires all but destroyed it in the 11th and 12th centuries, but it was rebuilt to the original Roman model. When the cupola collapsed in 1573, the new dome – the tallest in Milan

– and a far cry from the original – outraged the local populace. Some traces of the original portals can be seen in the façade, heavily reworked in 1894.

On the backs of the two great arches that flank the main altar, columns were placed upside down to symbolise the Christian religion rising up from the ruins of paganism. To the right, the octagonal Cappella di Sant'Aquilino may have been an imperial mausoleum. On its walls are fragments of the late fourth-century mosaics that once covered the entire chapel. Behind the altar, a passage leads under the church, where stones from pre-existing Roman structures used in the construction of San Lorenzo can be seen, as well as a Byzantine sarcophagus.

Outside the church stand 16 Corinthian columns from the second and third centuries. They were moved here from some unidentified temple in the fourth century, and topped with pieces of architrave, only some of which date from the same period. The 17th-century wings flanking the entrance to San Lorenzo were designed to link the columns to the church in a sort of pseudo-ancient atrium. In the centre, a bronze statue of the Emperor Constantine is a copy of one in Rome; a reminder of Constantine's Edict of Milan (313), which put an end to the persecution of Christians.

Sant'Eustorgio

Piazza Sant'Eustorgio 1 (02 5810 1583/Cappella Portinari 02 8940 2671). Bus 59/tram 3, 9, 14, 15, 20, 29, 30. **Open** *Church 7.30am-noon, 3.15-6.30pm daily. Cappella Portinari 10am-6pm Tue-Sun.* **Admission** *Church free. Cappella Portinari €6; €1-€3 concessions. See also p53.* **No credit cards.** **Map** p310 B2.

The origins of this church are shrouded in legend – one has it that Sant'Eustorgio, when still a bishop in the fourth century, had the place built to house relics of the Three Kings; the site was chosen when animals pulling the relic-laden cart reached this spot and refused to budge. Frederick Barbarossa (*see p10*) supposedly absconded with the relics in 1164, but they were returned in 1903 and are venerated each Epiphany (6 January). The ceremony is timed to take place at the end of a mass to coincide with the arrival of a procession from piazza del Duomo led by the Three Kings.

Whatever its origins, the building has traces of seventh-century work, was rebuilt by the Dominican order in 1190 after being razed by Barbarossa, was restored and revamped on several occasions up to the 15th century, and had a new faux-Romanesque façade stuck on it in 1865. (The little pulpit on the façade is a 16th-century substitution of the original wooden one from which Dominican Inquisitor St Peter Martyr preached.) Sant'Eustorgio was the first of Milan's churches to have a clock put in its bell tower, in 1306.

Inside, the church is a treasure trove of works by Milanese and Lombard artists from the 13th to the 15th centuries: Giovannino di Grassi, Giovanni da Milano, Giovanni di Balduccio (see his Gothic

Heaven is a half pipe (or 16 Roman columns): **San Lorenzo Maggiore**. *See p89.*

funeral monument to Stefano Visconti, 1327, in the fourth chapel on the right), Bernardino Luini and the *maestri campionesi* all feature.

The main attraction, however, is the Cappella Portinari, built between 1462 and 1466 by Florentine banker Pigello Portinari for his own tomb, and as a repository for the body of St Peter Martyr, murdered when heretics sunk a knife into his skull 200 years earlier. Perhaps the earliest truly Renaissance work in the city, the chapel unites the classical forms championed by Brunelleschi in Tuscany with typical Lombard fresco decoration by Vincenzo Foppa. Foppa's scenes from the life of the Virgin and St Peter Martyr's miracles (1466-8) are perhaps the painter's greatest masterpieces. In the centre of the chapel, the Ark of St Peter Martyr, containing most of the saint's remains, is by Giovanni di Balduccio (1336-9). The rest of him (his skull) is in a silver urn in the little chapel to the left of the chapel. The former monastery is now home to the Museo Diocesano (*see p85*).

Santa Maria dei Miracoli & San Celso (Santa Maria presso San Celso)

Corso Italia 37 (02 5831 3187). Metro Missori/ bus 65, 94/tram 15. **Open** *Santa Maria* 7am-noon, 4-6.30pm daily. *San Celso* for exhibitions only. **Admission** free. **Map** p310 A2, B2.

Two little chapels once stood on this site where, according to legend, St Ambrose came across the bodies of martyrs Nazaro and Celso. The chapel of San Nazaro fell down long ago, but so great was the flow of pilgrims to the remaining chapel of San Celso – where, in the 15th century, the Virgin was said to be working miracles galore – that in 1493 construction began on something bigger: Santa Maria dei Miracoli. Preceded by a fine early 16th-century *quadriportico*, this church has a lively façade from the same era, animated by sculptures by Stoldo Lorenzi and Annibale Fontana. The interior was decorated by the usual cast of Lombard Renaissance, mannerist and baroque artists.

A separate entrance through a gate and across a garden will take you to what remains of San Celso. Founded in the ninth century and rebuilt in the 11th, this little Romanesque church is decorated with frescoes from the 11th to 15th centuries. The basilica is now also a venue for art exhibitions, theatrical performances and concerts. Entrance is free, but opening times vary.

San Vincenzo in Prato

Via Daniele Crespi 6 (02 835 7603). Metro Sant'Agostino/bus 94/tram 2, 14. **Open** 7.45-11.45am, 4.30-7pm daily. **Admission** free. **Map** p310 B1.

Once an expanse of *prati* (fields), the area around this little church was used first as a pagan, and subsequently Christian, necropolis. Benedictine monks occupied the adjacent monastery in the ninth century and remained there until 1520; it's uncertain whether the present church dates from the ninth or 11th century. French occupiers turned it into a storehouse and then barracks in 1798. Later, it became a chemical factory, belching fumes that earned it the nickname the Magician's House. It was restored and re-consecrated in the 1880s.

Sant'Ambrogio & Western Milan

See Roman relics, *The Last Supper* and San Siro before making an exhibition of yourself at the colossal Fiera.

As long as you spend as little time as possible on the narrow, fumy thoroughfare that is via Meravigli (which becomes corso Magenta further west from the centre), this part of town can be one of the most rewarding stomping grounds in Milan.

Characterised by antiques shops, rare-book dealers, charming hole-in-the-wall *trattorie* and a bustling street life (thanks to the nearby Università Cattolica), the neighbourhoods west of the Duomo have retained a little more olde worlde flavour than other parts of the city. Don't be afraid to turn up the random side streets; these obscure, narrow alleys are filled with tiny shops and eateries, often providing that elusive factor every well-travelled visitor craves: local flavour.

Around Sant'Ambrogio

Although the Duomo is unquestionably Milan's ecclesiastical claim to fame, **Sant'Ambrogio** is the city's 'true' church. Built outside the Roman city walls in an area of early Christian cemeteries and imperial buildings, this church takes its name from the city's patron saint (*see p7* **St Misbehavin'**). Nine Italian kings were crowned at its altar between the ninth and 15th centuries, and four of them are buried here. Even Napoleon (1805) and Ferdinand of Austria (1838) chose to respect this tradition, paying a dutiful visit immediately after their coronations in the Duomo.

Once a year the piazza outside and to the left of the church plays host to the 'Oh Bej! Oh Bej!' fair (*see p154*); the rest of the time you'll find it

Sant'Ambrogio. *See p94.*

Guess who's coming to supper

Leonardo da Vinci is the greatest artist-in-residence Milan has ever had. He arrived in 1482, aged 30 – just as he was reaching his artistic prime. He had been summoned by Ludovico il Moro Sforza to live and work in the budding northern city-state, which he would do for 17 years – before returning again in 1506 for another seven-year stint.

Leonardo was given the official position of *pictor et ingeniarius ducalis* (the duke's painter and engineer). It was the latter role that took up the lion's share of his time (reproductions of his sketches, as well as models constructed from them, can be seen in the Museo della Scienza e della Tecnologia; *see p93*). While in the city, Leonardo also beefed up Milan's fledgling network of *navigli* (canals), thus increasing its position as an important port and trade nexus – not bad for a city more than 150 kilometres (93 miles) from the sea.

As *pictor ducalis*, Leonardo produced fewer than ten works of art while in Milan. However, one of these was **The Last Supper** (1495-7), or *Il Cenacolo*, considered by many to be the greatest painting of the Renaissance, which must count at least double.

When Giorgio Vasari – painter, architect and biographer of Italian artists – saw *The Last Supper* in the 1550s, he called it a 'magnificent blur'. Following restorations through the ages, the mural is a little clearer today – but not much. The problem lies in the fact that for this piece Leonardo experimented with a new method of working on dry plaster. True frescoes were painted on wet plaster, guaranteeing the colours would impregnate the plaster and last longer, but denying the painter any real flexibility in tone or nuance. Leonardo aimed to get the same flexibility that oil paints allowed by painting directly on to dry plaster using a method similar to

tempera painting on panel and employing a layering effect. But while the immediate result was satisfying, it proved a fleeting success. Paint began peeling off almost at once, even within Leonardo's lifetime, resulting in what critics would come to call 'the most famous wreck in the history of art'.

Commentators noted as early as the beginning of the 16th century that *The Last Supper* was fading fast, and touch-ups were not infrequent. Historical events conspired to worsen the situation: under French rule in the early 19th century, the monastery refectory where the mural is located was used as a stable, and drunken soldiers used Leonardo's faulty masterpiece for target practice. Some nifty sandbagging during World War II, however, prevented its final destruction in air raids that wreaked serious havoc in the immediate area. On this occasion, the painting's salvation seemed like a divine act, since during the heaviest bombing all the other three walls of the refectory where *The Last Supper* is located were completely destroyed, leaving the fresco standing on its own under the open sky.

Though the mural has been more or less *in restauro* since it was made, the biggest, most definitive restoration got under way in 1977. This removed layers of paint and detritus accumulated over the centuries, which, when the fresco was finally unveiled again in 1995, allowed some of the Renaissance master's luminous colours to re-emerge.

The Last Supper captures the dramatic moment after Christ informed his disciples that one of them was about to betray him. The picture draws you in through the apostles' turbulent gestures and facial expressions, which radiate out from the central, serene figure of Christ. It's far more than a simple depiction of a Bible story; it's a study in human emotion. The expressions on the

filled with students from the nearby **Università Cattolica del Sacro Cuore**, an ex-monastic complex that now houses Milan's Catholic university.

Near the Sant'Ambrogio basilica, the **Pusterla di Sant'Ambrogio** is a 1939 imitation of the medieval gate that once stood here. Some older materials, including a 14th-century relief by the *maestri campionesi* showing saints Ambrose, Gervasius and Protasius, have been incorporated into it.

To the south, in via De Amicis, you'll find the crypt of **Santa Maria della Vittoria**, which houses artefacts from recent archaeological digs around Lombardy. Beyond the Pusterla, the **Museo Nazionale della Scienza e della Tecnologia** is a magician's cave of technological wonders from across the ages.

Next door, the church of **San Vittore al Corpo** stands on via degli Olivetani, where the prison of San Vittore – the temporary home of many of the businessmen and politicians

apostles' faces range from surprise and disbelief to shock and hostility – a clinical psychological probing that has earned the work a special place in art criticism.

The painting is also dear to mathematicians. The result of careful, deliberate planning, its spatial organisation revolves around trinities: the apostles are broken into four groups of three with Jesus in their middle (a technique also used to further isolate Judas, who sits slightly apart from his group, a bag of money trailing from one greyish hand); there are three windows behind Jesus, the central one boasting an arch that forms a symbolic halo over his head; the figure of Jesus himself, his arms outstretched in front of him in a gesture of forgiveness, is reminiscent of a triangle.

Note the rather clunky doorway at the centre of the painting, the top of which cuts off Jesus' feet. Although there is no hard evidence to support the theory, legend has it that a particularly tall priest, tired of banging his head on the bottom edge of the painting, ordered the doorway raised to accommodate passage underneath. An act of proto-feng shui that inflicted more damage on the painting than all the bombs and bullets.

On the opposite wall, Donato da Montorfano painted his *Crucifixion* in 1495. Leonardo added the portraits of Ludovico il Moro, his wife Beatrice and their children. Beyond *The Last Supper* and these portraits, however, there is little Leonardo left in Milan: in the Pinacoteca Ambrosiana there is his portrait of a musician, while the much-restored ceiling frescoes in the Sala delle Asse of the Castello Sforzesco (*see p68*) are also attributed to him. But perhaps the most bizarre tribute to the great man is the enormous bronze horse on display at the **Ippodromo** (piazzale dello Sport 15) in the San Siro district (*see p98*), gifted to the city in 1999 by an impassioned American who managed to find the funding to construct Leonardo's never-completed equestrian tribute to Ludovico Sforza (www.leonardoshorse.org).

The Last Supper (Il Cenacolo)

Piazza Santa Maria delle Grazie 2 (02 498 7588/reservations obligatory 02 8942 1146). Metro Cadorna or Conciliazione/ bus 18/tram 20, 24. **Open** *8.15am-6.45pm Tue-Sun.* **Admission** *€8. See also p53.* **No credit cards. Map** *p310 A1.*

caught up in the *Tangentopoli* scandal (*see p19*) and subsequent *Mani Pulite* investigations of the 1990s – looms threateningly.

Museo Nazionale della Scienza e della Tecnologia 'Leonardo da Vinci'

Via San Vittore 21 (02 485 551/www.museoscienza. org). Metro Sant'Ambrogio/bus 50, 54, 58, 94. **Open** *9.30am-5pm Tue-Fri; 9.30am-6.30pm Sat, Sun.* **Admission** *€7; €5 concessions.* **No credit cards. Map** *p310 A1.*

In what was formerly the convent of San Vittore, founded in the 11th century and rebuilt in the 16th, Milan has created a national museum of science and technology and dedicated it to one of its most famous residents: Leonardo da Vinci.

In the early 19th century the palazzo became a military hospital and then a barracks. Heavily damaged during World War II, it was restored and given over to its present role in 1947. The palazzo is built around two cloistered courtyards separated by an open portico. In the courtyards visitors can see the weathered remains of the octagonal mausoleum of Valentinian II and the Roman fort of San Vittore, both unearthed in excavations conducted after the World War II bombardments.

Few technical skills are overlooked in this all-encompassing, labyrinthine museum, with displays dedicated to printing, metallurgy, bell-casting, minting, engines, horology and time-keeping, as well as the sciences of physics, optics, acoustics and astronomy. An exhaustive computing section shows the evolution of calculating techniques from Pascal's abacus of 1642 to the first IBM processor.

Additional areas are devoted to the typewriter, cinema and photography, the history of television and the telephone, locomotion and aeronautics (in the via Olona pavilion). The long, first-floor Galleria di Leonardo da Vinci displays faithful reproductions of the Renaissance genius's scientific, archaeological and technical sketches, including designs for flying machines and impregnable city defences, accompanied by life-size models of some of his ideas.

On the mezzanine, the Civico Museo Navale Didattico has a vast collection of model boats and ships from all over the world. Its recently donated Mursia Collection includes figureheads, decorated shells, models of ships, compasses and whales' teeth, as well as an extensive library of texts that were still being catalogued as this guide went to press.

One final note: the Museo is in the process of updating its display and security systems; you may not be able to see all of the collections, and the museum floor plan available free at the entrance may correspond only roughly to reality.

Santa Maria della Vittoria

Via E De Amicis 11 (329 966 5460 mobile). Metro Sant'Ambrogio/bus 94/tram 2, 14. **Open** 10am-5pm Mon-Fri. **Admission** free. **Map** p310 A1, A2.
This new space, designed to house exhibits on recent archaeological research on prehistorical and Roman Lombardy, is located in a crypt built by Cardinal Luigi Omodeo in 1669 as a family mausoleum and now home to the Romanian Orthodox church (02 8940 7269, open for services only, 6.30-8pm Fri, 9.30am-1pm Sun).

Sant'Ambrogio

Piazza Sant'Ambrogio 15 (02 8645 0895). Metro Sant'Ambrogio/bus 50, 54, 94. **Open** *Church* 7am-noon, 2-7pm Mon-Sat; 7am-1.15pm, 3-7.45pm Sun. *San Vittore* 9.30-11.45am Mon; 9.30-11.45am, 3.45-5.45pm Tue-Sun. **Admission** *Church* free. *San Vittore* €2. **No credit cards. Map** p310 A2.
The charismatic Bishop Ambrose (Ambrogio) – who defended orthodox Christianity against Arianism and later became Milan's patron saint – had this Basilica Martyrum built between 379 and 386. It is located over a cemetery holding the bodies of local martyr-saints Gervasius and Protasius, whose remains still lie in the church's crypt.

The church was enlarged, with the Benedictines erecting the Campanile dei Monaci (monks' bell tower) to the right of the façade during the eighth

century. In the ninth century, under Archbishop Anspert, the atrium preceding the façade was added; it was here that the populace sought sanctuary in times of trouble. Anspert's atrium was remodelled in the 11th century, when a complete reconstruction of the church got under way. Its capitals have carved scenes from Bible stories and mythical beasts symbolising the struggle between Good and Evil.

The Torre dei Canonici (canons' tower) to the left of the façade was built in 1124. Further changes to the interior of the church were made in 1196 after the dome collapsed.

In 1492, Ludovico il Moro Sforza (*see p14*) called on Donato Bramante to remodel the eighth-century Benedictine monastery. The fall of il Moro in 1499 put an end to Bramante's makeover, which as a result was limited to one side of the old cloister (the Portico della Canonica, accessible from the left of the nave). The church had a lucky escape from a planned remodelling job in the 17th century, but suffered severe air-raid damage in 1943. The bombing destroyed Bramante's work, which was subsequently reconstructed using salvaged original materials.

The interior has the sober proportions of the austere Lombard Romanesque, with its three aisles covered with ribbed cross-vaults and fake women's galleries holding up the massive walls. Beneath the pre-Romanesque pulpit, reconstructed from the original pieces after the dome collapsed on it in 1196, lies what is known as the Stilicone sarcophagus, a fourth-century masterpiece traditionally believed to have been the burial place of the Roman general of that name who served the emperor Honorius and died in 408. Later research disproved this legend. The 12th-century golden altar illustrated with scenes from the life of Christ on the front and of St Ambrose on the back once covered the porphyry casket commissioned to house the remains of Ambrose, Protasius and Gervasius when they were dug up in the ninth century. The three saints now share an ornate glass coffin-for-three in the crypt. Suspended protectively above the altar, the tenth-century ciborium (canopy) is in the form of a little temple; its four porphyry columns decorated in stucco are recycled Roman artefacts.

To the right of the main altar, a series of chapels leads to the Sacello di San Vittore in Ciel d'Oro. Part of the church's original fourth-century structure, this chapel was clinically reworked in the 1930s, so that only its glorious, glowing golden fifth-century mosaics in the dome remain to remind us of its antique glory. They portray St Ambrose standing between Gervasius and Protasius, with a sprinkling of other minor local martyrs looking on. This part of the church has been converted into a small museum (entrance through the 18th-century Cappella di Sant'Ambrogio Morente), consisting of the mosaics and precious church furnishings, including the silver and gold cross that was carried by St Carlo Borromeo in 1576 in a procession giving thanks for the end of the plague.

There are more mosaics, from between the fourth and eighth centuries (though restored after extensive damage in 1943), in the apse of the main church. Christ sits enthroned between Gervasius and Protasius, while Ambrose performs miracles all around – including an interesting act of bi-location, where he's in Milan and at the funeral of St Martin in France at the same time .

The museum once housed in the cloisters has been split up and moved to the Museo Diocesano (*see p85*) and the San Vittore in Ciel d'Oro part of the basilica. The other remnant of the museum is an exhibition space opened in the Antico Oratorio della Passione (piazza Sant'Ambrogio 23a, opening times vary according to exhibition, admission free).

San Vittore al Corpo
Via San Vittore 25 (02 4800 5351). Metro Sant'Ambrogio/bus 50, 54, 58, 94. **Open** 7.30am-noon, 3.30-7pm daily. **Admission** free. **Map** p310 A1.
The church and former monastery of San Vittore al Corpo grew up around the mausoleum of emperor Valentinian II, who died in 392; parts of this ancient structure are now beneath the Museo Nazionale della Scienza e della Tecnologia (*see p92*). The complex was taken over in 1010 by Benedictine monks who got down to some serious rebuilding. It was given another overhaul in 1560, when it became one of Milan's most sumptuously decorated churches. Works by many local names of the late 16th and 17th centuries – Girolamo Quadrio, Camillo Procaccini, Giovanni Ambrogio Figino, Daniele Crespi – are still here. There are also choir stalls with wood-inlay intarsia work from the 1580s.

Università Cattolica del Sacro Cuore
Largo Gemelli 1 (02 72 341/freephone 800 209 902). Metro Sant'Ambrogio/bus 50, 58, 94. **Open** *Sept-May* 8am-9.30pm Mon-Fri; 8am-4.30pm Sat. **Admission** free. **Map** p310 A2.
In 1497 Ludovico il Moro called upon Donato Bramante to expand what had – before it was turned over to the Cistercine order in the late 15th century – been the most powerful and influential Benedictine monastery in northern Italy during the Middle Ages. Although Bramante was hired to add four grandiose cloisters, only two were completed (an Ionic one in

Palazzo Arese Litta. *See p96*.

1513 and a Doric one in 1630). In 1921 the ex-monastery became home to the Catholic university and throughout the 1930s and '40s architect Giovanni Muzio overhauled the complex in his usual dry, straightforward style (compare and contrast with the Palazzo dell'Informazione, *p76*, in piazza Cavour, or the Palazzo dell'Arte, *p67*, in Parco Sempione).

Around Santa Maria delle Grazie

Corso Magenta, a neighbourhood named after its most illustrious street, is a hodge-podge of new and antique, well-kept and run-down.

The corso itself is lined with important palazzi. The one at No.29 was given to Lorenzo de' Medici in 1486 by the Sforzas (though today there's nothing more remarkable about the edifice than that odd fact). At No.12 you'll find the **Casa Rossi**, a notable building designed by Giuseppe Pestagalli around 1860 to simulate the superimposed *logge* of Renaissance palazzi. The building boasts a peculiar octagonal courtyard that's worth a gander. At No.24, the **Palazzo Arese Litta**, now home to the Teatro Litta (*see p185*), has a rococo façade with two giant masks and two colossal *telamons* flanking the entrance. A monumental staircase built in the 18th century leads to the Sala Rossa, with its red brocaded walls, where a pearl embedded in the floor recalls a tear shed by the awestruck Duchess Litta when she met Napoleon.

On the opposite side of the street is the church of **San Maurizio**, and next door, the **Civico Museo Archeologico**.

Further down the street, you can have a drink in the **Bar Magenta** (*see p129*), a mainstay of the Milanese bar scene. At No.61 the **Palazzo delle Stelline** (little stars) has now been rather brutally remodelled, but continues to house Le Stelline, a charitable foundation named after the palazzo itself. Built upon the ashes of the original Santa Maria della Stella convent after it burned to the ground, the Palazzo delle Stelline was designated by Carlo Borromeo as an orphanage, and subsequently hospital, for young girls. It was given the name 'Stelline' in homage to the convent that once stood in its place. Palazzo delle Stelline continued to function as an orphanage until the 1970s, when it was shut down. Today, the Fondazione Stelline works to promote the cultural, social and economic development of the city.

Still further west down corso Magenta is **Santa Maria delle Grazie**, home to Leonardo's *Last Supper* (*see p92* **Guess who's coming to supper**). Pay a visit to the adjoining church and cloisters – a welcome break from the tourist chaos surrounding the master's masterpiece.

Civico Museo Archeologico

Corso Magenta 15 (02 8645 0011). Metro Cadorna/bus 18, 50, 58/tram 19, 20, 24, 27. **Open** *Museum* 9am-5.30pm Tue-Sun. *Monastero Maggiore di San Lorenzo* noon-2pm Tue-Sun. **Admission** free. **Map** p310 A1, A2.

The archaeological museum is conveniently situated over the only surviving stretch of Roman city walls, visible alongside the Etruscan, Pakistani and Greek exhibits in the basement beneath the second courtyard. In the first courtyard (once part of the Monastero Maggiore, home to the city's most influential order of nuns; *see also p96* San Maurizio) stands a Bronze Age-carved sacred stone from the Valcamonica (*see p271*). The itinerary starts on the ground floor, where a model gives an idea of how the ancient city of Mediolanum looked; the sculpture collection in the room on the right is further testimony to Milan's Roman heritage.

Highlights of the sculpture collection include the portrait of Maximian (second century AD) and the bust of Hercules from the baths built by Maximian (AD 286-305) in the area that is now corso Europa. Among the Roman artefacts, note the Parabiago plate, a gilded silver platter from the middle of the fourth century showing Cibele and her followers, and the Coppa Trivulzio, a master-piece of Roman glass-making from the late fourth century bearing the inviting inscription '*Bibe vivas multis annis*' (drink and you'll live long).

A divider separates the model of Roman Milan from a section dedicated to the art of the Lombards and other assorted 'barbarians'. The stretch of Roman wall in the courtyard incorporates a defence tower known as the Torre Ansperto.

San Maurizio

Corso Magenta 15 (02 866 660). Metro Cadorna/bus 50, 54, 58/tram 19, 20, 24, 27. **Open** 9am-noon, 2-5.30pm Tue-Sun. **Admission** free. **Map** p310 A1, A2.

San Maurizio was the church of the immense Monastero Maggiore (*see above* Civico Museo Archeologico), the headquarters of a powerful community of Benedictine nuns. Much of the monastery was demolished after 1864. The structure of the church – begun in 1503 – reflects the needs of the closed order for which it was built. The rectangular space is divided in half across the centre by a partition in the middle of which stands the high altar. On one side sat the congregation; on the other the nuns. To the right of the altar is the *comunichino*, the opening through which the nuns received communion. In the nuns' section is a rare 16th-century organ. Extensive fresco decoration by Bernardino Luini makes the church a gem of 16th-century Lombard art.

Santa Maria delle Grazie

Piazza Santa Maria delle Grazie (02 4801 4248). Metro Cadorna or Conciliazione/bus 18/tram 24. **Open** 7.30am-noon, 3-7pm daily. **Admission** free. **Map** p310 A1.

The delicate Bramantesque beauty of **Santa Maria delle Grazie**. *See p96.*

The church of Santa Maria delle Grazie was begun in 1463 to a plan by Guiniforte Solari. Just two years after it was finished in the 1480s, Ludovico il Moro Sforza (*see p14*) commissioned architect Donato Bramante to turn the church into a family mausoleum reflecting the new Renaissance styles. (Some experts, it should be said, reject this theory, either doubting Bramante's involvement in the project at all, or otherwise ascribing a minor, preliminary planning role to him.) So down came Solari's apse and up went a Renaissance tribune in its place. At the same time, the Chiostrino (small cloister) and a new sacristy were added to the adjoining Dominican monastery. The monks ran an active branch of the Inquisition in their monastery from 1553 to 1778, and continued to endow their church with decorative elements. The complex escaped meddling restoration until the late 19th century, when some faux-Renaissance elements were added. World War II bombing in 1943 destroyed the great cloister of the monastery but spared the Chiostrino and the refectory with Leonardo's *Last Supper* on its wall (*see p92* **Guess who's coming to supper**).

The terracotta façade of the church is in the best Lombard tradition; the portal is attributed to Bramante. Inside, Solari's Gothic leanings in the three-aisled nave clash with the fresco-covered arches and Bramante's more muscular, massive style. Standing out amid works by leading local artists from the 15th to 17th centuries is an altarpiece (in the sixth chapel on the left) showing the Holy Family with St Catherine by the 16th-century Venetian painter Paris Bordone. The carved wooden choir stalls in the apse date from 1470.

Entrance to the Bramantesque Chiostrino is just before the main altar, where a door on the left takes you through the Cappella di Santa Maria delle Grazie e del Santissimo Sacramento and the old sacristy/bookstore, with 15th-century frescoes (sometimes erroneously attributed to Leonardo) and huge cabinets with wooden inlay and painted Bible scenes. One cabinet used to hide a secret passage to the Castello Sforzesco (*see p66*), used by Ludovico. A door leads out into the Chiostrino, also known as the frog cloister after the four bronze amphibians continually spurting water from their mouths in the centre of the pool. Its gardens provide a welcome, relaxing atmosphere after the bustle and crowd in the piazza outside the church. During mass, the cloisters can be accessed through a door in via Caradosso 1 (same opening times as the church).

The Fiera & San Siro

Milan's extensive trade fair facilities occupy so much territory they're almost a city in themselves. (And, in fact, for years municipal development discussions have been monopolised by various proposals for moving the complex somewhere further away from downtown.) Stretching all the way from the post-war construction around largo Domodossola to piazzale Giulio Cesare and viale Scarampo, the thoroughfare that leads to the autostrada for Turin and the lakes, the **Fiera** sits smack dab in the middle of beautiful, tree-lined residential neighbourhoods. Unless

Football is Milan's modern religion and the **Stadio Giuseppe Meazza** is a temple of worship.

you've come to town for one of the Fiera's countless trade fairs (*see chapter* **Festivals & Events**), there's not much here.

The **Casa di Riposo per Musicisti**, final resting place of composer Giuseppe Verdi, is a short walk down tree-lined via Buonarroti from the piazzale Giulio Cesare side of the Fiera. Further south, corso Vercelli – a popular, expensive shopping street – heads east from piazza Piemonte.

West of the Fiera is the **San Siro** neighbourhood, an area characterised by modern apartment buildings, luxury cars and rooftop swimming pools. San Siro is a broad, verdant area that hosts numerous sports facilities, including the city's world-famous San Siro soccer stadium, or, to give it its proper name, **Stadio Giuseppe Meazza** (*see p179*). It is also home to several parks: **Monte Stella** (via Cimabue or via Terzaghi), an artificial hill created from World War II rubble; the **Parco del Trenno** (via Novara or via Cascina Bellaria); and nearby **Boscoincittà** (via Cascina Bellaria or SS11; *see also p156* **Good green fun**).

Casa di Riposo per Musicisti

Piazza Buonarroti 29 (02 4996 0001/02 499 6009). Metro Buonarroti/bus 61, 67. **Open** *Crypt* 10am-noon, 2.30pm-6pm daily. **Admission** free. **Map** off p310 A1.

A statue of composer Giuseppe Verdi presides over piazza Buonarroti, where a neo-Romanesque palazzo designed in 1899 by architect Camillo Boito (the top floor is a post-war addition) houses a retirement home for musicians. Across the courtyard – often filled with the sound of retired tenors or sopranos running through a few scales – stairs lead down to the crypt where Verdi and his wife Giuseppina are buried.

Fiera di Milano

Piazzale Giulio Cesare (freephone 800 820 029/02 499 71/information desk 02 4997 7703/www.fiera milano.it). Metro Amendola-Fiera/bus 48, 68/tram 19, 27/787 shuttle from Linate. **Open** times vary depending on exhibition. **Admission** prices vary depending on exhibition. **Map** off p310 A1.

Milan's original trade fair was set up near Porta Venezia (*see p79*) in 1920 in an effort to kick-start an economy that was proving slow to recover from World War I. As fair events grew, the structure was moved to its current location, expanding as permanent pavilions were added over the years. Of the original buildings, only the Palazzo dello Sport (1925) and a few art nouveau edifices near the beginning of via Domodossola survived wartime bombing. But reconstruction work was swift in the post-war period, and the Fiera is now among the largest trade structures in Europe. Its 375,000sq m (roughly 4 million sq ft) area hosts 26 exhibition pavilions and each year it plays host to 31,000 exhibitors and millions of visitors.

Around Milan

Grand buildings, grand parks and a Grand Prix make up Milan's suburbia.

In the interest of hanging on to its position as Italy's largest city, Rome has extended its boundaries all the way out to the foothills of its *colli romani*, making Romans of Italians who only set foot in the city once a year, if at all. Milan, by contrast, has had its statistical growth deliberately reined in. To hold back this expanding monster, city limits have been drawn where no obvious break in the urban sprawl exists, which has resulted in a ring of independent townlets around the northern metropolis that fail to provide a clear indication of where Milan ends and suburbia begins.

Towns like Cormano and Bollate to the north, Rho and Pero to the east, Buccinasco to the south, and Segrate and Peschiera Borromeo to the west conspire to make Milan seem never-ending. But the sprawl does not, cannot, extend for ever. And where it begins to break up, life becomes pretty, pleasant and plain – in the flattest, greenest sense.

In this no man's land between urban centre and open countryside are a number of attractive parks and reserves keeping it green (such as the Parco Naturale dell'Adda Nord and the Parco

delle Groane, *see p103*. See also *p102* **Parking spaces**). Rivers – the Lambro to the north, the Adda to the east, the Ticino to the west – and canals (the *navigli*, *see p86* **Canals plus**) add a picturesque watery element to the otherwise flat countryside.

Beyond the marshy Lombardy plains to the north, foothills rise up and lead to the Alps (*see also chapter* **The Mountains**), and present visitors with a host of beautiful abbeys, castles and *palazzi*.

Getting around

The easiest, most efficient way to visit the area around Milan is to hire a car (for car hire, *see p283*). But efficient public transport exists for most of the destinations covered in this chapter. See also *p283* **Getting around Lombardy**.

Monza & the Brianza

The rolling hills that begin north of Milan in the Brianza countryside have largely been given over to unattractive industry, but many elegant villas and *palazzi* remain.

Take me to the river: the **Naviglio Martesana** joins Milan to the River Adda. *See p102.*

The region's nature reserves (*see p102* **Parking spaces**) provide a welcome verdant escape for the city-weary.

Monza is undoubtedly the Brianza's biggest draw. Once a metropolitan centre that rivalled Milan in size and importance, the city still retains something of its medieval character in the 13th-century town hall, or **Arengario**, and the magnificent **Duomo**.

Lombard queen Theodolinda had a chapel dedicated to St John the Baptist built in the late sixth century where the Duomo now stands.

Inside track

In January 1922, a group of car enthusiasts gathered at the headquarters of the Milan Automobile Club and set about choosing an appropriate way to commemorate its 25-year anniversary. Several ideas were flung around, but ultimately these speed-loving gentlemen had only one thought on their minds: to create an Italian Grand Prix.

They wanted a modern racing circuit that was big, bad and (most important of all) better than the well-established Grand Prix that their rivals, the French Automobile Club, had set up near Le Mans, on a track called the Circuit de la Sarthe, in 1906.

The Villa Reale park in Monza was chosen as the best site for the Autodromo, and work began on 15 May that year. In just 110 days, a crew of 3,500 workers created the first ten-kilometre (6.2-mile) racetrack on an area of 3.4 square kilometres (1.3 square miles).

It was only the beginning. Over its 80-year-plus lifespan, the Autodromo has had more makeovers than a Hollywood star. The track has changed from macadam to concrete to high temperature-resistant asphalt over the decades, and at one point even included curves paved with porphyry stones. When not being used for racing, it is open to the public, and it's not unusual to see people speeding around the circuit on everything from roller skates to motorcycles.

Today the Autodromo is a year-round attraction. In addition to its F1 racing event (which usually takes place in September), which draws several hundred thousand spectators each year, the complex boasts camping facilities, an Olympic swimming pool, car museum and more, all set within a large verdant park.

Scant traces of this early Christian building still remain; the Duomo we see today is a mainly 14th-century structure with later additions. The lunettes above the door of the white marble Gothic façade show Theodolinda and her offspring presenting what is known as the Iron Crown to John the Baptist. In the **Cappella di Teodolinda**, located to the left of the high altar, you will see the fifth-century gem-encrusted crown – made of gold, though believed to contain an iron nail from Christ's cross – used to crown Italy's kings from the Middle Ages up to Napoleon. Around this chapel's walls are 15th-century paintings by Franceschino, Gregorio and Giovanni Zavattari depicting scenes from Theodolinda's life. Her remains are in a sarcophagus behind the altar.

A door off the left nave leads to the cemetery and the **Museo Serpero**, where treasures from the town's heyday are kept, including articles donated to the original chapel by Theodolinda and Pope Gregory the Great. Among the queen's gifts is a gilded, gem-studded missal. Theodolinda's crown – it looks a little like a bejewelled pillbox hat – is kept here, as is a gilded silver hen with seven chicks, made some time between the fourth and seventh centuries and said to represent the seven provinces of Lombardy.

North of the centre, the vast **Parco di Monza** (open 7.30am-6.30pm daily) contains the **Villa Reale** (built 1771-80) – originally the summer residence of the archduke of Austria – a golf course and the **Autodromo**, the renowned Formula One motor-racing track (*see p100* **Inside track**).

North of Monza is **Biassono**. Its town hall, Villa Verri, is a perfect example of the early 18th-century *barocchetto* style, while its **Museo Civico** (via San Martino 1, 039 220 1077, open 2.30-7pm Sat, admission free) has reconstructions of Brianza farm life through the ages. In **Carate Brianza**, the Villa Cusani Confalonieri (not open to the public) is a 17th-century remodelling of a late 16th-century castle. The church of **Santi Ambrogio e Simpliciano** (0362 900 164, closed noon-2pm daily) has outstanding canvases by Daniele Crespi and Francesco Hayez. In **Agliate,** the early 11th-century basilica of **Santi Pietro e Paolo** (036 29 871, open 8am-1pm, 4.30-7pm daily) is built in river stone set in a herringbone pattern, as is its baptistery, a rare nine-sided structure.

To the east of Monza, **Arcore** is now indelibly linked in the Italian psyche to prime minister Silvio Berlusconi, who resides in a high-gated villa here. But there is also the 18th-century **Villa Borromeo d'Adda** (039 601 2248, only the grounds are open to the public), just one of the magnificent properties owned by this

Battle royale

It was the early spring of 1176, and the Milanese were afraid for their lives. Emperor Frederick Barbarossa (*see p10*) was advancing (for the fifth time) on the city after wreaking havoc across northern Italy. Barbarossa had spent the previous year attacking Alessandria in Piedmont without success, and had now decided that conquering Milan was the key to dominating the region.

The Milanese had every reason to be afraid. Not only did Barbarossa's army significantly outnumber theirs, but the emperor could also count on support from German allies descending through the Alps. Many of the smaller outlying towns in northern Italy, terrified of Barbarossa's legendary cruelty and overwhelming military might, had already sworn allegiance to the invader.

But the intrepid Milanese had their own advantage: the *Carroccio*, a kind of medieval command centre and weapon of psychological warfare all rolled into one.

The *Carroccio* was an enormous wagon with four iron-sheathed wheels, draped in deep-blood-red cloth and drawn by six white bulls. It was a symbol of extreme religious and civic importance for the Milanese; in peace time it was kept in the city's main church, and before battle, mass was held from the wagon. It also carried several important religious artefacts, including the cross donated to Milan by Bishop Aribert as testament to the citizens' faith and unity.

The Milanese commanders used the wagon astutely to incite their outnumbered army. They surrounded the *Carroccio* with the Compagnia della Morte (Death Company), a group of some 900 hand-picked troops sworn to die protecting the city's mobile symbol.

The *Carroccio* also carried a special bell – the *Martinella* – which rang orders and encouragement from the commanders riding on the wagon's rooftop. This same bell was rung upon the *Carroccio*'s return to the city to announce a victory and commemorate the men who had fallen in battle. To this day, the word *martinit* is used in the Milanese dialect to refer to orphaned children.

Believing it was better to fight the battle outside the city, the Milanese army marched 30 kilometres (19 miles) north-west to Legnano. Here the two armies met and engaged. With cries of 'Sant'Ambrogio!' (Milan's patron saint; *see p7* **St Misbehavin'**), the Compagnia della Morte rallied around the *Carroccio* and threw themselves at Barbarossa's army.

Despite the odds, Barbarossa's army was defeated. The emperor's horse was killed underneath him, and Barbarossa managed to escape only by stripping off his royal armour and sneaking away in the heat of the fray.

The battle marked a turning point in the emperor's ambitions for Italy, forcing Barbarossa to abandon once and for all his plans to conquer the fractious peninsula. And the *Carroccio*, of course, kept right on rolling.

important Renaissance family (*see p105* **A family's fortunes**). The Borromeos also owned land in **Oreno**, three kilometres (two miles) to the east, where the **Villa Borromeo** estate (via Piave 12, 039 669 004, open by appointment only) boasts a hunting lodge with remarkable 15th-century frescoes of hunting scenes.

Despite being a thriving manufacturing centre, **Vimercate** has preserved much of its original charm. In the town hall (**Palazzo Trotti**), an 18th-century fresco cycle stretches over 11 rooms. The basilica of **Santo Stefano** (open 8am-noon, 5-7pm daily) was built between the 10th and 11th centuries on earlier foundations. Along via Cavour, off the central piazza Roma, are several 15th-century palazzi and the little Romanesque **Oratorio di Sant'Antonio**, with frescoes from 1450. At the end of the street, the **Ponte di San Rocco**, built from recycled Roman remains, was part of

the medieval fortifications. The local group Mirabilia (Villa Volonteri, via Velasca 22, 039 601 2697) organises tours of all Vimercate sights.

Autodromo di Monza

Parco di Monza (039 24 821/www.monzanet.it). **Open** (for driving) 9am-12.30pm, 2-5pm Sat, Sun. **Admission** *Driving* €30 per hr. **Credit** AmEx, DC, MC, V.
Check the website for racing fixtures and details of how to reach the track.

Duomo & Museo Serpero

Piazza Duomo (039 323 404). **Open** *Duomo* 9-11.30am, 3-5.30pm Tue-Sun. *Museum* 9-11.30am, 3-5.30pm Tue-Sat; 9am-12.30pm, 3-6.30pm Sun. **Admission** *Duomo* free. *Museum* €2.50. *Chapel of Theodolinda* €1. **No credit cards**.

Villa Reale

Viale Regina Margherita 2 (039 322 086). Closed for restoration. Call for up-to-date information.

Sightseeing

Parking spaces

Extending north from the Parco di Monza (*see p100*) through forests of oak, ash, chestnut and conifers, the **Parco Naturale della Valle del Lambro** covers 65 square kilometres (25 square miles) along the banks of the River Lambro. Stop in at the park headquarters at Triuggio (*see p102* **Getting there** for more information) for maps before starting out on an eight-kilometre (five-mile) hiking or bike circuit that cuts through the densely wooded valleys of the Lambro river – but be warned: the route is not always clearly marked. On a mix of dirt roads, trails and asphalt roads, you'll pass several 18th and 19th-century villas, as well as the sprawling Renaissance complex of the Jesuit-owned **Villa Sacro Cuore**, though none of it is open to the public.

North of Vimercate, the **Parco Regionale di Montevecchia e della Valle del Curone**, a weekend favourite with the Milanese, has a few short walks that wind through the hillside terraces planted with rosemary and sage. From the main square of the village of Montevecchia (the piazza is named after the mathematician Maria Gaetana Agnesi, 1718-99, whose villa is on its north-east side) a daunting stairway leads up to the village's 16th-century **Santuario della Beata Vergine del Carmelo** (open 3-7pm Sat & 8am-noon, 2-7pm Sun). From a landing halfway up, a *Via Crucis* (stations of the cross, open 2.30-6pm Sun) winds around the church on a lower terrace.

Back in the square, a stone path at the opposite end descends to several welcoming watering holes. The **Trattoria al Galeazzino** (via Galeazzino 4, 039 993 0850, closed Fri & Mon-Fri in Nov-Feb, average €16.50) serves simple food on a sunny terrace. The **Azienda Agricola Valcurone** (Cascina Casarigo, 039 993 0065, www.agriturismovalcurone.it, closed Mon & Tue, 3wks Jan, average €30) arranges food, wine and nature tours of the area (9am-noon, 3-7pm Tue-Sun). The wine producer **Vitivinicola Cattaneo** (viale Palazzetto 8, 039 993 0043) offers winery tours and meals by reservation only.

Parco Naturale della Valle del Lambro

Office: via V Veneto 19, Triuggio (0362 970 961/www.parcovallelambro.it). **Open** 8am-2pm Mon, Wed, Fri; 8am-noon, 1.30-6.30pm Tue, Thur.

Parco Regionale di Montevecchia e della Valle del Curone

Office: via Donzelli 9, Montevecchia, località Butto (039 993 0384). **Open** 9am-12.30pm Mon, Wed-Fri; 9am-noon Sat.
Call park volunteers (039 531 1275) on Friday (9-10pm) to arrange visits to the park museum or for information on excursions.

Getting there

By car
For Monza, take viale Zara out of Milan, which becomes viale Fulvio Testi. Journey time 15mins to 1hr, depending on traffic. From Monza, local roads are well signed for Biassono, Carate Brianza, Arcore, Oreno and Vimercate. Vimercate can also be reached via the A15 *autostrada*.

By train
Mainline trains for Monza leave Stazione Centrale or Porta Garibaldi about every 15mins. Trains also leave hourly (every half hour during rush hours) from both stations for Arcore, on the Milan–Sondrio line. Triuggio, headquarters for the Parco Lambro, is on the Sesto–Lecco line, with trains every hour.

By bus
ATM buses 723, 724 and 727 from Stazione Centrale or 721, 820 and 821 from Sesto FS metro station cover the short hop to Monza, Vimercate and other Brianza destinations.

Tourist information

Pro Monza (IAT)
Palazzo Comunale, piazza Carducci (039 323 222/ www.promonza.monza.net). **Open** 9am-noon, 3-6pm Mon-Fri; 9am-noon Sat.

Ufficio Cultura Arcore
Via Gorizia 20 (039 6013 263). **Open** 9.30am-12.30pm Mon, Wed, Fri, Sat.

The Valle dell'Adda

Work began on the **Naviglio Martesana** (*see p86 and p179*), which runs from Milan to the River Adda, in 1457. Its waters were – and still are – used to irrigate the surrounding countryside, as well as to provide a trade highway between Milan and the neighbouring Bergamo region.

The River Adda winds placidly through Lombardy, providing postcard-like scenes that have now been declared protected areas in the

Parco Naturale dell'Adda Nord. The
Martesana canal reaches the river near the town
of **Cassano d'Adda**, where the magnificent
Villa Borromeo (not open to the public) was
built in the first half of the 18th century and
redone in neo-classical style after 1781 by
Giuseppe Piermarini.

Further north in **Vaprio d'Adda**, the 1483
Villa Melzi d'Eril (reworked in the 17th
century and again in 1845; not open to the
public) has hosted such illustrious guests as
Leonardo da Vinci, Austrian empress Maria
Teresa and Napoleon.

Continuing upstream, picturesque **Trezzo
sull'Adda** is probably of Celtic origin. The
towering **Castello** that dominates the double
bend of the river here was built – according to
local lore – for Lombard queen Theodolinda.
What remains dates from the 13th and 14th
centuries and was erected by the Visconti family
(*see p11*); the castle was already in ruins in the
18th century (much of its masonry was recycled
to construct Milan's Arena Civica, *see p70*, and
the Villa Reale in Monza, *see p100*).

Il Castello

*Via Valverde 33, Trezzo sull'Adda (information
02 909 0146/guided tours 02 909 2569).* **Open**
Mar-Oct 2.30-6pm Sun. Also open by appointment.
Admission €4; €2 concessions. **No credit cards**.

Parco Naturale dell'Adda Nord

*Office: via B Calvi 3, Trezzo sull'Adda (029 091
229).* **Open** 9am-noon Mon-Sat.

Getting there

By car

Take via Palmanova out of Milan, which becomes the
SS11. This splits after 20km; take the SS525 branch
to Vaprio d'Adda. Journey time 30mins. From Vaprio
d'Adda local roads run north to Trezzo sull'Adda.

By metro & bus

You're almost there once you're at the end of the green
metro line, Gessate. Buses 920, 921 and 922 travel
regularly from Gessate to Cassano d'Adda and Trezzo
sull'Adda. SIA (030 44 061) operates four services
daily from piazza Castello on its Milano–Brescia
route that stop on the motorway at Trezzo.

Tourist information

Pro Loco Trezzo sull'Adda

*Via Carlo Biffi 4 (029 092 569/www.proloco
trezzo.com).* **Open** 9am-noon Mon, Wed, Thur-Sat.

North-west of Milan

In **Arese**, automobile enthusiasts will enjoy the
Museo Storico Alfa Romeo. The museum
collection includes more than 110 of the Italian
car manufacturer's most prestigious models
dating from 1910 to the present day.

In **Lainate**, the **Villa Borromeo Visconti
Litta** hosts special summertime events,
including open-air film screenings and tours by
guides in period costume. The villa's extensive
gardens include late 18th-century fountains
and water games designed as practical jokes
to be played on garden-party guests.

Occupying a vast 34-square-kilometre
(13-square-mile) spread between Bollate and
Saronno, the **Parco Regionale delle Groane**
was established in 1972 as a reserve for local
plants and wildlife. The park information office
is only open a few hours a day and visits are
best undertaken by independent and intrepid
travellers. That said, numerous scenic bike
tracks and dirt roads wind their way through
the park, providing backroad routes to Senago,
Garbagnate, Bollate and **Villa Arconati**, a
1730s villa located in **Castellazzo di Bollate**.
Every Sunday in July, the towns of Bollate,
Garbagnate and Arese organise summer

Sightseeing

Palazzo Estense. *See p104.*

festivals at the villa, opening its beautiful gardens, wooded groves, parterres, labyrinths and nymphaea to the public.

Saronno is the home of the world-famous Amaretto di Saronno almond liqueur and the sweet almond cookies (*amaretti*) served with dessert wines across Italy. Learn more about both at the local **Museo del Biscotto**. The **Santuario della Madonna dei Miracoli** (piazza Santuario 1, 02 960 3027, open 7am-noon, 3-7pm daily) was built in the early 16th century for the pilgrims who flooded to this spot after a miraculous cure reportedly took place here in 1447. Inside are works by the best Lombard masters of the 16th century, including Bernardino Luini and Gaudenzio Ferrari. Angelic musicians by the latter peer down from the cupola.

In **Legnano**, the 1176 defeat of Holy Roman Emperor Frederick Barbarossa at the hands of the local Lega Lombarda (*see p101* **Battle royale**) is celebrated on the last Sunday of May with the Sagra del Carroccio. In the town's main square, piazza San Magno, the basilica of **San Magno** (0331 547 856), built between 1504-13, has frescoes by Bernardino Luini and Bernardino Lanino. The **Museo Civico Guido Sutermeister** contains archaeological remains from the Bronze and Iron Ages, as well as Lombard-era artefacts and 15th-century architectural fragments.

Museo del Biscotto

c/o Museo delle Industrie e del Lavoro del Saronnese, via Don Griffanti 6, Saronno (029 607 459/for appointments 028 511 2216). **Open** 9-11pm Thur; 9am-noon, 3-6pm Sun. By appointment 9am-noon Thur. Closed Aug and public hols. **Admission** free.

Museo Civico Guido Sutermeister

Corso Garibaldi 225, Legnano (033 154 3005). **Open** 9am-12.30pm, 2.30-5pm Tue-Sat; 9am-12.30pm Sun. Closed Aug and public hols. **Admission** free.

Museo Storico Alfa Romeo

Viale Alfa Romeo, Arese (029 4442 9303). **Open** 9am-12.30pm, 2-4.30pm Mon-Fri. Closed Aug and public hols. **Admission** free.

Parco delle Groane

Office: via della Polveriera 2, Solaro (02 969 8141). **Open** 9am-noon Mon, Wed-Fri; 2.30-4.30pm Tue.

Villa Arconati

Via Fametta 1, Castellazzo di Bollate (festival info 02 3500 5575). **Open** *July* (gardens only) 9am-1pm, 3-7pm Sun. **Admission** €1.50; €3 guided tour. **No credit cards.**

Villa Borromeo Visconti Litta

Piazza Vittorio Emanuele, Lainate (339 394 2466 mobile/www.amicivillalitta.it). **Open** *May, Oct* 3-6pm Sun. *June, July, Sept* 9.15-10.30pm Sat; 3-6pm Sun. Closed Aug, Nov-Apr. **Admission** €6; €4 concessions. **No credit cards.**

Getting there

By car

For Legnano, take via Gallarate out of Milan and follow the SS33. Journey time 30mins. For Saronno, take viale Certosa, then the SS233, out of Milan. Journey time 20mins. Bollate, Arese and Lainate are all along the SS233. Journey time 10-30mins.

By train

Trains for Saronno leave Cadorna station every 10-15mins. Legnano is one (15min) stop along the Domodossola or Lago Maggiore lines, with trains leaving from Certosa or Garibaldi stations.

By bus

STIE (02 860 837) operates services for Saronno and Legnano that depart from via Paleocapa near Cadorna station. It also runs a service to Lainate, which departs from piazzale Lotto near Lotto metro station.

Tourist information

Ufficio Sagra del Carroccio

Piazza San Magno 6, Legnano (0331 471 258/ www.comune.legnano.com). **Open** 9am-12.30pm, 2.30-5.30pm Mon-Thur; 9am-12.30pm Fri.

Varese & around

Located halfway between lakes Como (*see p200*) and Maggiore (*see p193*), **Varese** stands out with its magnificent villas and extensive parks. **Palazzo Estense** (now a municipal complex including the town council offices and library; via Sacco, 0332 255 272, open 10am-noon, 2-6.30pm Mon-Sat) was built between 1766 and 1772 for regional governor Francesco III d'Este. Its beautiful Italian gardens are accessible from those of **Villa Mirabello**, a palazzo built in the 18th century and renovated in the English style in 1843. Villa Mirabello is now home to Varese's **Musei Civici**, which provides an insight into the lives of Lombardy's first inhabitants, including dioramas showing the stilt-houses they built on the area's lakes. At time of writing the museum was closed for restoration and due to reopen in November 2004.

Fortified medieval Varese lay between piazza del Podestà, corso Matteotti and via San Martino. The **Santuario della Madonnina in Prato** (piazza Madonnina, 0332 288 222, 8.30am-noon, 2.30-7pm Mon-Sat, 3.30-7pm Sun), at the end of via Dandolo, is a 17th-century reconstruction of a late Gothic building, with massive *telemons* (free-standing caryatids) shoring up its dramatic entrance. Charming via San Martino is lined with 16th- and 17th-century buildings boasting lively courtyards, porticoes and connecting passageways. In piazza San Vittore, the church of **San Vittore** (0332

A family's fortunes

Although Saint Carlo Borromeo usually gets all the attention, the entire Borromeo family has a rich, storied history with Milan and Lombardy that stretches back centuries and includes several dukes, counts and senators, seven cardinals, and countless lords and ladies of the Renaissance.

Originally from San Miniato al Tedesco, a small town outside Florence, the first Borromeos made a name for themselves halfway through the 1300s on either side of the bloody battles between the Guelphs and the Ghibellines. But the name might have passed quietly into the annals of history were it not for Giovanni Borromeo, who spent the latter half of the 14th century developing mercantile interests across Europe, founding a bank based in Venice with branch offices in Milan, Rome, Bruges, Barcelona and London.

Giovanni's wealth formed the foundations of a dynasty. Childless, he adopted a nephew, Vitaliano Borromeo, who would leverage the family's considerable economic muscle into noble titles and court appointments, culminating in 1432 when he gained the right to fortify his castle outside Milan (today's Peschiera Borromeo castle), and obtain the noble title of Count.

The Borromeo family had arrived, and now thrived. Successive generations added to the family's wealth and power, often through marrying into other prominent Italian families. Vitaliano's grandsons would purchase the island of San Vittore (today Isola Madre, *see p194*) and Isola

Bella (home to the extraordinary Castello Borromeo, *see p194*), which at that time was nothing more than a rocky peak jutting out of Lago Maggiore.

But the best of the Borromeos was still to come. In 1560 a 21-year-old Carlo Borromeo, the product of five generations of Borromeo dynasty, was studying in Rome to become a Catholic priest. Orphaned at a young age, his brother Federico then died suddenly, leaving Carlo as the only direct, living heir of the family.

Ordered by the Pope to leave the Church, marry and continue the family line, Carlo steadfastly refused. The sudden loss of his brother had affected him deeply, and he chose to continue his studies and dedicate his life to Christ.

There are few monuments in or around Milan that have remained untouched by Saint Carlo Borromeo. He donated his family possessions to the Church, and instituted a rigorous programme to renovate and renew every church, palazzo or charitable institution he could get his hands on, including the church of San Fedele (*see p61*), which the pious priest wanted to serve as a model Counter-Reformation church, and Milan's Duomo (*see p54*). Just outside Milan in Arcore, the Villa Borromeo d'Adda's attractive Renaissance gardens are still open for visits from the general public (*see p100*).

Following his death in 1584, Carlo Borromeo was buried in the Duomo in Milan. He was canonised by Pope Paolo V in 1610.

236 019, open 8am-noon, 2.30-7pm) was built between 1580 and 1615. Its neo-classical façade is flanked by a high-baroque bell tower (1617). Inside are works by 17th-century Milanese artists. Behind the bell tower, the **Battistero di San Giovanni** is the oldest building in the city. Its large seventh- to eighth-century baptism pool boasts a font decorated by a *maestro campionese* (*see p26*) in the 13th or 14th century.

North of Varese, the **Sacro Monte** in the **Parco Regionale Campo dei Fiori** is intended to provide a 3-D representation of the *Via Crucis* (stations of the cross); essentially, it's a sort of religious Disneyland. The first Sacro Monte was built in the late 15th century in the Piedmont region by a philanthropic monk called Fra Bernardino Caimi. He felt sorry for the poor and lame who would never make it to the Holy Land and so came up with a substitute. This

Lombard example is an admittedly garish attraction, with 14 highly coloured scenes of the Passion of Christ eerily frozen in tableaux-filled chapels leading to the piazza of the village of **Santa Maria del Monte**. If the chapels don't grab you, the road leading up to the Sacro Monte – lined with faux-medieval, neo-Renaissance and art nouveau villas – might.

Still further north on the SS394, the **Villa della Porta Bozzolo** in **Casalzuigno** is a splendid frescoed 18th-century villa with glorious baroque gardens.

To the west, the territory opens out into gentle, rolling hills and the lakes Varese, Monate, Comabbio and tiny Biandronno. A ferry (operated by the Ristorante Isolino Virginio, 0332 766 268, €3 round trip, operates year-round with more frequent services at weekends) plies between the village of

Biandronno and **Isola Virginia**, the area's most important prehistoric site. In the 1860s archaeological digs turned up neolithic and Bronze Age artefacts, many of which are displayed in the island's little museum. When the lake waters are very low, remains of the prehistoric pilings used to build stilt-houses are still visible in the mud.

South of Varese, **Castiglione Olona** is a little bit of Tuscany in the Lombard countryside. The exquisite village was the project of Lombardy-born Cardinal Branda Castiglioni, a papal legate who spent much of his career in Florence. At the beginning of the 15th century he returned to his home town – a village on the Olona river – with his head full of Renaissance ideas. He began his rebuilding campaign with a Lombard-Gothic look for the **Collegiata** church. Then he let rip, imposing new Brunelleschian models on the **Chiesa di Villa** and his family's **Palazzo Branda Castiglioni**. As the icing on the cake, he brought in Masolino da Panicale – teacher of Renaissance groundbreaker Masaccio – to paint frescoes in the palazzo and baptistery.

Chiesa di Villa
Piazza Garibaldi, Castiglione Olona (0331 858 048). **Open** 10am-noon, 2.30-5.30pm Tue-Sun. **Admission** free.

Collegiata della Beata Vergine e dei Santi Stefano e Lorenzo
Via Cardinale Branda Castiglioni 1, Castiglione Olona (0331 858 903). **Open** 10am-noon, 2.30-5.30pm Tue-Sun. **Admission** €5; €4 concessions. **No credit cards.**

Isola Virginia
Lago di Biandronno (0332 281 590). **Open** *Apr-Oct* 2-6pm Sat, Sun. **Admission** €2; €1 concessions. **No credit cards.**

Musei Civici
Villa Mirabello, piazza della Motta, Varese (0332 281 590). **Open** 9.30am-12.30pm, 2-5pm Tue-Sun. **Admission** *Museum* €2; €1 concessions. *Gardens of Palazzo Estense & Villa Mirabello* free. **No credit cards.**

Palazzo Branda Castiglioni
Piazza Garibaldi, Castiglione Olona (0331 858 301). **Open** *Oct-Mar* 9am-noon, 3-6pm Tue-Sat; 3-6pm Sun. *Apr-Sept* 9am-noon, 3-6pm Tue-Sat; 10.30am-12.30pm, 3-6pm Sun. **Admission** €2.50; €1.50 concessions. **No credit cards.**

Villa della Porta Bozzolo
Viale C Bozzolo 5, Casalzuigno (0332 624 136). **Open** *House* Oct-mid Dec 10am-1pm, 2-5pm Tue-Sun; Feb-Sept 10am-1pm, 2-6pm Tue-Sun. *Garden* 10am-5pm Tue-Sun. *Park* 10am-6pm Tue-Sun. Closed mid Dec-Jan. **Admission** €4.50. **No credit cards.**

Getting there

By car
For Varese, take viale Certosa out of Milan, which becomes the SS233. Journey time 40mins. Castiglione Olona is 8km (5 miles) south of Varese on the SS233.

By train
Services to Varese run from Milan's Cadorna station every 30mins and from Porta Garibaldi and Porta Venezia hourly. Journey time 25mins.

Getting around
GLC-Giuliani & Laudi (via Bainsizza 27, 033 228 1790) runs bus services to Castiglione Olona and Castelseprio from Varese.

Tourist information

APT Varese
Via Carrobbio 2 (0332 283 604/www.varesotto turismo.com). **Open** 9am-12.30pm, 2.30-4pm Mon-Fri; 9am-noon Sat.

Ufficio Informazioni Castiglione Olona
Palazzo Branda Castiglioni, piazza Garibaldi (0331 858 301). **Open** 9am-noon, 3-6pm Sat; 10.30am-12.30pm, 3-6pm Sun.

South of Milan

The area to the south of Milan is a web of *navigli* (canals) – once the city's main trade highways and still important sources of irrigation – and is home to some of northern Italy's most important religious foundations.

Many orders, including the powerful Cistercians and the Humiliati, built glorious structures from the 12th century onwards and managed to place the Church at the centre of everyday life. While winning over souls, the orders contributed greatly to farm technology by reclaiming land and improving water management in this wet river plain.

The extraordinarily beautiful Cistercian **Abbazia di Chiaravalle** was built in 1135 according to the specifications of the order's founder, St Bernard of Clairvaux. Many alterations were made before the abbey fell into disrepair after French rulers dissolved religious orders in the late 18th century; reconstruction began in 1894 and monks returned in 1952. Although on a heavily trafficked road, the abbey is one of the finest of its kind. If you can only visit one or two things outside Milan, come here.

The 13th-century **Abbazia di Viboldone** was built by the Humiliati, a local monastic order formed by Lombards defeated by Holy Roman Emperor Henry V in the early 12th century.

Despite their meek-sounding name, in the late 14th and early 15th centuries they became powerful enough to clash head on with the Catholic Church. On the pope's command, Cardinal Carlo Borromeo (*see p105* **A family's fortunes**) worked to suppress the Humiliati, but their fate wasn't fully sealed until they were dissolved by a papal bull in February 1571. Although only the church of the original complex remains, Viboldone abbey is one of the most important Gothic monuments in Lombardy. Inside you will find a *Last Judgment* by Giusto de' Menabuoi and frescoes by followers of Giotto.

The former **Abbazia di Mirasole** was another 13th-century Humiliati foundation, though it has been used as a hospital since the late 18th century. Beside the restored single-nave church is a pretty 15th-century cloister.

The two major *navigli* of the Milanese hinterland – the Pavese and the Grande – flow to the west of Mirasole. On the Naviglio Pavese is the town of **Binasco**, where the **Castello Visconteo** (via Matteo, 02 905 7811) is a much-restored building of 14th-century origins. A rectangular structure surrounded by a desiccated moat, this was where the jealous Filippo Maria Visconti had his hapless wife Beatrice di Tenda beheaded on suspicion of adultery. Today, rather more prosaically, the palazzo is home to the town council. Just off the piazza, the 1783 church of **Santi Stefano e Giovanni** (open 8am-noon, 4.30-7pm daily) has an altarpiece, *La Beata Veronica*, by Raphael's teacher Perugino.

The charming town of **Abbiategrasso** stands on the Naviglio Grande. Its church of **Santa Maria Nuova** (open 8.30am-1pm, 4.30-7pm daily) is thought to be the last work Donato Bramante completed in Lombardy before he left for Rome.

Six kilometres (3.5 miles) south, the Cistercian **Abbazia di Morimondo** was built from 1100 onwards. From the road it's difficult to imagine that anything could be behind that screen of humdrum residential buildings: but there lies the monastery church, dominating the farmhouse-dotted terrain that slopes down into the *rogge* (little inland channels) of the Ticino river.

Morimondo is in the heart of the vast **Parco Lombardo della Valle del Ticino**, a nature reserve instituted in 1974 that reaches over 900 square kilometres (347 square miles) across three provinces and through 46 municipal areas, from Sesto Calende in the north to Pavia (*see p257*) in the south. Designed to protect the abundance of aquatic flora and fauna sustained by the River Ticino, the park includes great woods in the north that are all that remains of the forests that once covered the Po Valley. Maps of the park's many trails can be obtained from the park office.

The Gothic **Abbazia di Viboldone**. *See p106.*

Abbazia di Chiaravalle

Via Sant'Arialdo 102, Chiaravalle Milanese (02 5740 3404). Metro Corvetto then bus 77. **Open** 9am-noon, 3-6pm Tue-Sun. **Admission** free.

Abbazia di Mirasole

Località Abbazia Mirasole, Comune di Opera (02 5503 8311). Tram 15, then a long walk. **Open** *June, July* 9am-12.30pm, 2.30-6pm daily. *Aug-May* 4-7pm Sun. **Admission** free.

Abbazia di Morimondo

Piazza San Bernardo 1 (02 9496 1919). Train from Porta Genova to Abbiategrasso then local bus. **Open** *Apr-Oct* 8.30am-noon, 2.30-6.30pm daily. *Nov-Mar* 8.30am-noon, 2.30-4.30pm daily. **Admission** free.

Abbazia di Viboldone

Via dell'Abbazia 6, San Giuliano Milanese (02 984 1203). Metro San Donato then bus San Giuliano/ train from Porta Garibaldi (Milano–Bologna line). **Open** 9-11.30am, 2.30-6pm daily. **Admission** free.

Parco Lombardo della Valle di Ticino

Office: via Isonzo 1, Pontevecchia di Magenta (02 972 101/www.comunic.it/parks.html). **Open** 9am-12.30pm, 2-5.30pm Mon-Thur; 9am-noon Fri. For guided tours, contact Centro Agrituristico Caremma (via Cascina Caremma 1, Besate, 02 905 0020) or TEA (via Bramante 29, Milan, 02 3453 4147). Ditta Michele Maggi (via Don Verzini 16/18, Ozzero, 02 940 7573) offers carriage tours. Call several days in advance (minimum four people, €16 per hour each).

Getting there

By car

For Chiaravalle, take corso Lodi outside Milan to San Donato Milanese, then follow signs. Journey time 15-45mins. For Abbiategrasso, take via Lorenteggio and the SS494. Journey time 25mins. For Binasco, take the A7. Journey time 20mins.

Sightseeing

Eat, Drink, Shop

Restaurants	**110**
Cafés & Bars	**125**
Shops & Services	**131**

Features

The best Restaurants	111
What's on the menu	115
Vinous delights	118
Food on the go	122
The pursuit of happiness	130
Via del Design	133
After the fashion?	136
Market leaders	142
Navigli newcomers	144
Chic for less	148

Restaurants

Fantastic cuisine from Milan, Lombardy, Italy and far beyond...

The **Bistrot Duomo** is the place for food with a view. *See p113.*

Restaurant-going Milanese have not been a happy lot in the past two years. Throughout Italy people have been bemoaning the rise in prices brought by the euro, but pockets in Milan seem to have been particularly badly hit. The quintessential week night out – a pizza and a beer *in compagnia* – has gone from 25,000 lire (about £8) to at least €20 (about £13), quite a steep hike. These days you'd be hard pushed to leave even a casual neighbourhood restaurant less than €30 poorer than when you went in. As far as just about everybody in Italy is concerned, €30 is equivalent to 60,000 *vecchie lire* (the exact exchange is 58,088), and that used to get you a lot more than a *primo* and a *secondo* in your local *trattoria*, even in Milan.

And the Milanese do like to eat in their neighbourhood trats. As the economic and financial capital of Italy, Milan has a need for (and no shortage of) serious restaurants where deals can be closed and clients wined and dined. But that's strictly business; off duty, starched white linen, tableware stretched as far as the eye can see and avant-garde cooking tend to make the natives restless.

The Milanese solution of choice has been to spend more time in the *osterie* along the Navigli and in the Porta Romana area. Some are regional places, offering nostalgia-repelling versions of classic recipes. Others are more upscale, offering refined takes on Italy's *cucina rustica* in a fashion not far removed from Paris's bistro scene. The atmosphere is casual, and the emphasis is on the ingredients – the chef is often as much purveyor as cook – and the beef may come from one particular breed found in one particular valley. It'll probably come served with polenta, though, and the sauce wouldn't be out of place in grandma's kitchen.

None of these places is as cheap as similar places in other Italian cities, but their honest values tend to take the sting out of the rise in prices. With their typical pragmatism, the Milanese have decided they might as well spend €35 and eat well.

The ever-rising cost of eating out might also be a contributory factor to the continuing success of ethnic eateries. Successive waves of immigration, first from the south of Italy, later from North Africa and the Far East, have made the Milanese more receptive than most Italians to *cucina esotica*. The fact that the average couple can often leave these restaurants with a full belly and some change from a €50 note has driven increasing numbers of traditional locals to try some foreign fare.

COURSES GALORE

On paper, the average Italian meal consists of an *antipasto* (starter), followed by a *primo* (usually pasta, risotto or soup) and *secondo* (the meat or fish course) accompanied by a *contorno* (vegetable side dish) and finally dessert, cheese, fruit, coffee and perhaps a *digestivo/amaro* or a grappa. However, the ever-hurried Milanese can no longer afford to spare two or three hours at the dinner table, so many either opt for just a starter and a *primo*, or a pasta course followed by a dessert, chopping and changing the standard menu sequence according to their taste and needs. Take their lead and don't feel pressured into eating more than you want.

Fixed-price meals are still seen as something for the tourists (indeed, you might want to steer clear of anywhere that offers a *menù turistico* written in several languages). Some of the more upscale/creative restaurants will offer a tasting menu (*menù degustazione*). This can be a good way of sampling a bit of everything if you're not going to be in town long enough to eat your way through the Milanese repertoire.

WHAT TO EAT

In much of Lombardy, rice tends to be more popular than pasta. Thick kernels of arborio or carnaroli rice are slowly simmered to absorb cheese, butter and broth, then vegetables, seafood or meat are mixed in. The result is divinely decadent and any leftovers are fried into crisp cakes (*risotto al salto*). Pasta is by no means ignored, however. *Tortelli di zucca*, or pumpkin-stuffed pasta, is a speciality of the Mantova province, while cooks from Valtellina, in the far north, adore *pizzoccheri*, buckwheat pasta with cheese, cabbage and potato.

Unlike other Italian soups, Lombard soups are so thick they easily constitute a main course. *Zuppa pavese* (broth with bread and eggs) and *zuppa di porri e bietole* (with leeks and Swiss chard) are found in rural eateries. *Casoeûla* is a soupy cabbage stew with polenta, pork and sausage. Polenta, topped with mushrooms or meat, is a common feature of menus in the Valtellina and, in winter, much of Lombardy.

When it comes to *secondo*, land-locked Lombardy is a surprisingly good place to eat fresh freshwater fish and seafood. Milan is Italy's biggest sea-fish distribution centre: the morning catch is flown in so quickly that it's as fresh here as on the coast. Lakes and rivers yield sturgeon and grey caviar in late November. Perch, trout, carp, salmon and eel are also used in the cuisine of the lake regions.

Succulent cuts of meat – veal in particular – are transformed into namesake specialities: *ossobuco alla milanese* (braised veal shanks) and *cotoletta alla milanese* (breaded and fried veal chop). Lombardy also produces cured meats: *bresaola* (paper-thin cuts of dried beef); *culatello* (the centre cut of ham); *salame milanese* (pork salami with garlic and spices); and *carpaccio* (thinly sliced raw beef).

From sharp gorgonzola to oozing taleggio and spreadable stracchino, Lombardy is a cheese heaven. Even the names of the towns – such as Cremona and Crema – remind you of dairy treats (*see also p252* **Say cheese**). In most Lombard dishes, olive oil is replaced by butter, and heavy cream is common.

The best Restaurants

For Milanese cooking
Da Abele (*see p119*); **Masuelli San Marco** (*see p119*); **Trattoria Madonnina** (*see p123*).

For rustic Italian cooking
L'Altra Pharmacia (*see p114*); **La Topaia** (*see p123*).

For regional Italian cuisine
Dongiò (*Calabrian, p122*); **Emilia & Carlo** (*Tuscan, p117*); **Giulio Pane e Ojo** (*Roman, p122*).

For being seen
Armani/Nobu (*see p117*); **Café Real** (*see p114*); **Da Giacomo** (*see p119*); **10 Corso Como Caffè** (*see p117*); **Just Cavalli Café** (*see p117*); **Shambala** (*see p124*).

For views
Bistrot Duomo (*see p113*); **La Terrazza di via Palestro** (*see p121*).

For value
Osteria delle Vigne (*see p122*); **Pastarito/Pizzarito** (*see p114*); **Warsa** (*see p121*).

For seafood
Ai Sabbioni (*see p121*); **Al Merluzzo Felice** (*see p121*); **Da Leo** (*see p124*).

For vegetarians
L'Ape Piera (*see p121*); **Joia** (*see p119*).

For exotic food
Serendib (*see p118*); **Tara** (*see p118*).

Eat, Drink, Shop

EXPLOIT

DRINKS&DINNER

Living

liqueurs & delights

MILANO

PIAZZA SEMPIONE 2

(Arco della Pace)

TEL.++39 02.33100824

www.livingmilano.com

WHERE TO EAT
In theory, an *osteria* is a place akin to a social club, where you can get a glass of wine and some nibbles; a *trattoria* is a cheap eaterie serving basic home cooking (*cucina casalinga*); and a *ristorante* is a more refined venue. In reality, though, the distinctions are quite blurred. Some of the most creative kitchens in Italy can be found in *osterie*, and many *trattorie* charge restaurant prices. Their decor might be all exposed brick and plain wood floors, but they're about as proletarian as Nobu, and, unless you're dining with Giorgio (Armani), you'll need to book well in advance. Authentic *trattorie* and *osterie* tend to have handwritten menus or even no menu at all; in the latter case, the day's fare is recited *a voce* (out loud).

Though McDonald's has made inroads, pizza remains the fast food of choice for most Italians. Most *pizzerie* worth their salt in Italy use wood-fired ovens. Toppings are manifold but, in general, traditional: you won't find pineapple on your pizza, for instance – though you may find gorgonzola cheese with pears.

For more Milanese fast-food options, *see p122* **Food on the go**.

LIQUID PLEASURES
Italian wine lists tend to offer a dazzling range of national wines, from local Nebbiolo to Nero d'Avola from Sicily, and a conspicuous dearth of anything foreign; even French, let alone Australian or Californian, wine is rarely found. The good news, however, is that Italy produces some first-class red and white wines. The DOC (*denominazione di origine controllata*) seal of quality on the bottle is a reliable pointer to a good wine, but there are also some equally wonderful *vini da tavola* (table wines) – sold under this humble guise because they do not conform to stringent DOC regulations. For more on Lombard wines, *see p118* **Vinous delights**.

Cheaper eateries also offer *vino sfuso*, which can be ordered in quarter-, half- or one-litre carafes. While the quality varies greatly, if you're lucky, you'll get a young, quaffable wine, particularly at the better *trattorie*. While drinking wine with your pizza is not a sin, the traditional accompaniment is beer or soft drinks.

If you've ordered a full meal, you might be offered a *digestivo* or a grappa on the house. The choice of *digestivi* is endless; Ramazzotti – a dark, syrupy liqueur made from herbs and spices – is a distinctly Milanese variant.

PRACTICALITIES
Most eating establishments charge *coperto* (cover charge) for providing a tablecloth and bread. This should never be more than €3.

Italians are not big on tips, and only tend to leave one if they feel the food or service was outstanding. Tourists, however, are generally expected to be more generous: anything between five and ten per cent will put a smile on your waiter's face, but bear in mind that you're under no obligation to leave anything, especially if you're dissatisfied with the service.

Do check your bill: most restaurateurs are scrupulously correct, but there are those who will try to pull a fast one on foreign visitors.

Italy is still predominantly a cash society and many establishments will try to dissuade you from using plastic. However, all but the smallest *trattorie* and *pizzerie* accept credit cards. By law you must be given an official receipt (*scontrino fiscale*) upon paying the bill. Hold on to this; in the unlikely event that a policeman catches you leaving a restaurant without one, you (and the restaurateur) could receive a nasty fine.

Italians like to eat at regular times and opening hours are fairly standard. The times listed in this guide refer to those when hot meals can be ordered, though the place may stay open much later. Normal eating hours are 12.30pm-2.30pm and 8-10pm.

VEGETARIANS
Exclusively vegetarian restaurants are few and far between in Milan; Joia (*see p119*), a temple to vegetarian haute cuisine, is an honourable exception. However, non-meat-eaters are by no means limited to salads and pizzas. Most Milanese restaurants offer a plethora of tasty vegetable dishes and pasta sauces; main courses can often be replaced by a *contorno* or a vegetable antipasto. Life will be harder for vegans (Lombard cuisine is heavily dairy-based), but again, there is never any shortage of fresh fruit and vegetables.

Average restaurant prices in the listings below are based on three courses (two for *pizzerie*) and do not include drinks.

Duomo & Centre
See also p141 **Peck**.

Italian

Bistrot Duomo
Via San Raffaele 2 (02 877 120/www.gmristorazione. it). Metro Duomo/bus 54, 60, 65/tram 2, 3, 14, 20, 27. **Meals served** 7-10pm Mon; noon-2.30pm, 7-10pm Tue-Sat. **Average** €40. **Credit** AmEx, DC, MC, V. **Map** p311 A1/p312 B1, B2.
Located on the top floor of the Rinascente building (*see p135*), this is the place to come if you simply have to dine right in the city centre and are willing

Emilia & Carlo puts art on the walls and good food on the table. *See p117.*

to pay over the odds for the privilege. Up here you're at the same level as the gargoyles atop the Duomo, and the view is certainly impressive – especially in summer, when the plexiglass roof is taken off. The pricey menu runs from traditional Italian to sushi; service is snootily efficient.

Pastarito/Pizzarito

Via Verdi 6 (02 862 210). Metro Cordusio or Duomo/bus 18/tram 2, 3, 12, 14, 19, 20, 24, 27. **Meals served** noon-2.30pm, 7.30-11.30pm Mon-Fri; noon-3pm, 7.30-11.30pm Sat, Sun. **Average** €15-€20. **Credit** AmEx, MC, V. **Map** p309 C1/p312 B1.
The place to come for a reviving pizza or plate of pasta when you're too tired from sightseeing to venture any further afield. Despite its prime location near La Scala, this restaurant (part of a growing chain of franchises) caters more to office workers than to fur-clad patrons of the arts. The staggering range of pizza toppings and pasta sauces ensures that there's something here for anyone.

Bar/restaurants

Café Real

Via Merlo 1 (02 7631 6505/www.cafereal.com). Metro Duomo/bus 50, 54, 60/tram 1, 2, 3, 12, 14, 15, 20, 23, 24. **Meals served** noon-3pm Mon-Fri, 8.30pm-midnight daily. Closed mid Jul-Aug. **Average** €40. **Credit** AmEx, DC, MC, V. **Map** p311 A1/p312 B2.
This lounge bar and restaurant takes its cue from late 19th-century Parisian venues – all red carpets, sumptuous drapes, sofas and low lighting. The divinely attired crowds busy themselves smoking,

chatting or just lazying in the comfortable armchairs to the incessant popping of champagne corks. The French-inspired menu changes daily, but most people come here for reasons other than foraging – impressing a date or simply seeing and being seen. After midnight, DJs take over and the place gets pumping to commercial dance and house sounds.

Sforzesco & North

Italian

L'Altra Pharmacia

Via Rosmini 3 (02 345 1300). Metro Moscova/bus 43, 57/tram 12, 14. **Meals served** noon-2.30pm, 7.30-11.30am Mon-Sat (in summer open Sun and closed Mon). Closed 2wks Aug. **Average** €35. **Credit** AmEx, MC, V. **Map** p308 B2.
This cosily rustic eaterie in Milan's Chinatown, with simple paper place mats and modern art copies on bare brick walls, attracts a varied clientele, from the regulars to the odd celeb. For a truly sublime culinary experience, try the delicious *risotto Milanese mantecato in forma di grana* – risotto with saffron served in the hollowed-out rind of a parmesan cheese, while those with a stronger stomach might want to tuck into a plate of tripe and beans.

Anema e Cozze

Via Palermo 15 (02 8646 1646). Metro Moscova/bus 41, 93, 94. **Meals served** noon-3pm, 7.30-midnight daily. **Average** €15-€20 (lunch €10). **Credit** AmEx, MC, V. **Map** p308 C2.

What's on the menu

Antipasti

Antipasto di mare: assorted fish. Common selections include *alici marinate* (marinated anchovies); *carpaccio* (very thin slices of raw fish, usually salmon [*salmone*], swordfish [*pesce spada*], or tuna [*tonno*]); *insalata di mare* (seafood salad, usually served at room temperature).

Affettati: cold cuts (often just called *antipasto misto*). Common selections include *bresaola* (cured, air-dried beef); *coppa* (cured pork meat from the neck and shoulder); *culatello* (similar to Parma ham); *lardo* (bacon fat, but otherworldly when prepared well and placed on warm bread); *pancetta* (the same cut as bacon, cured, not smoked); *prosciutto cotto* (boiled ham); *prosciutto crudo* (Parma ham); *salame* (salami); *salame di cinghiale* (wild boar); *salame d'asino* (donkey); *salame d'oca* (goose). Cold cuts will sometimes be served with polenta.

Bruschetta: toasted bread, usually served with good olive oil, and perhaps garlic and tomatoes.

Nervetti: salad of calf's foot, often served with beans and onions at room-temperature.

Sott'aceti: pickles. The most common types are *cipolle* (onions) and *cetrioli* (cucumbers).

Verdure ripiene: vegetables stuffed with garlicky breadcrumbs, and sometimes cheese. Common selections include: *carciofi* (artichokes); *melanzane* (aubergines); *peperoni* (green, red, or yellow bell peppers); *zucchine* (courgette).

Pasta

All'arrabbiata: with a spicy tomato sauce.
Al pomodoro: with a simple tomato sauce.
Al ragù: served with a meat sauce.
Alle vongole: with a clam sauce.
Casoncelli: meat-stuffed ravioli, often served with *burro sfuso* (brown butter with sage leaves) and *pancetta*.
Pizzoccheri: buckwheat noodles from the Valtellina area, cooked with potatoes, cabbage, and cheese.
Tortelli alla zucca: ravioli stuffed with pumpkin, speciality of Mantova.

Risotto

Alla certosina: prepared with frogs' legs and snails, a speciality of Pavia.
Alla milanese: prepared with saffron and, traditionally in the pre-BSE world, bone marrow.

Con radicchio: made with red *radicchio trevigiano* (other vegetables can also be used, most notably pumpkin).
Con valcalepio: made with red wine, sometimes served with beans or sausage.

Carne (meat)

Al forno: roast meat or poultry. Common selections include *agnello* (lamb); *coniglio* (rabbit); *faraona* (guinea hen); *pollo* (chicken); *tacchino* (turkey).
Alla griglia: grilled meat or poultry.
Arrosto: roast meat, most often beef (simply *arrosto*), pork (*maiale*) or veal (*vitello*).
Busecca: a stew of tripe, lard, butter, beef, tomatoes and beans.
Cotoletta milanese: breaded veal chop, served on the bone.
Cotechino: pork sausage.
Cassoeûla: a stew made from of pork cuts, sausage and cabbage.
Involtini: small rolls of beef or aubergine (*melanzane*) stuffed with ham and cheese.
Ossobuco: braised veal shanks.
Polpette: meatballs.
Polpettone: meat loaf.
Salsicce: sausages, often roasted or grilled.
Stufato: braised meat.

Pesce & frutti di mare (fish & seafood)

Fritto misto: mixed fried seafood, most often *calamari* (squid); *pesciolini* (sprats) and sometimes *gamberi* (prawns).
Lavarello: a freshwater fish from Lake Como.
Persico: a freshwater fish from Lake Como.
Seppie in umido: cuttlefish in a tomato casserole.

Contorni (side dishes)

Fagiolini: cooked green beans with garlic and lemon.
Funghi: mushrooms, often sautéed with olive oil, garlic and parsley.
Insalata: salad, either *mista* (mixed) or *verde* (green). Usually served with olive oil and vinegar.
Mostarda: candied fruit flavoured with mustard oil, often served with roasts.
Polenta: ubiquitous cornmeal mush, often served with roasts and *stufati*. It comes in a variety of forms, one of the most interesting (and filling) is *polenta taragna*, made with buckwheat flour, cornmeal, cheese and sometimes cream.

HUNGRY FOR NEW PLACES TO EAT?

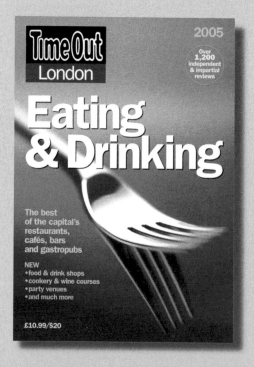

This Neapolitan-style chain of *pizzerie* (another location can be found just off piazza Cinque Giornate) garners rave reviews from homesick southerners. In addition to the full menu of pizzas, you can also find a good range of fresh fish (or simply put the two together and order a *pizza ai frutti di mare*, with shellfish).

Emilia & Carlo
Via Sacchi 10 (02 875 948). Metro Cairoli or Lanza/tram 3, 4, 12. **Meals served** 12.30-3pm, 8-11pm Mon-Fri; 8-11pm Sat. Closed Aug; 2wks Dec-Jan. **Average** €40. **Credit** AmEx, DC, MC, V. **Map** p308 C2/p312 A1.
The complimentary *stuzzichino* (appetiser) hints at the impeccable, attentive service at this creative Tuscan restaurant. Start your meal with a full tasting of cheese, *salumi* or olive oils, then move on to a main course: *pappardelle* with hare *ragù* and artichokes is especially delicious, as is the polenta with venison and truffles. A favourite of the acting set, the restaurant shamelessly flaunts its autograph collection (check out Monica Bellucci's signature, just by the ladies'). The extensive wine list completes the picture. Advance booking is advised.

Emporio Armani Café
Via dei Giardini 2 (02 723 18 680/www.giorgio armani.it). tram 1, 2, 20. **Meals served** noon-3pm, 7.30-11pm Mon-Sat. **Average** €40. **Credit** AmEx, DC, MC, V. **Map** p309 C1/p312 B1.
A bit more relaxed than Nobu (*see below*) in the Armani Superstore, this café is the perfect place for a revitalising lunch after a hard morning on the streets (and in the shops) of the Golden Rectangle. In the evening, you can buy an Armani-priced dinner (€50 plus) to go with your other Milan fashion purchases.

Innocenti Evasioni
Via Privata della Bindellina (02 3300 1882/www.innocentievasioni.it). Bus 57/tram 1, 14. **Meals served** 8-10pm Tue-Sat. Closed Aug. **Average** €30-€35. **Credit** AmEx, DC, MC, V. **Map** off p308 A1.
A delightful bolthole in an unlikely part of town (near piazzale Accursio, on a private road), with a young and adventurous chef-owner. The atmosphere is as understated as the waitresses' frumpy aprons. Unusual starters include *croccante di carciofi* (artichokes and mozzarella in a crispy pastry jacket); the *primi* include ravioli stuffed with polenta and toma cheese. There's a separate room with seating for couples and a lush garden with room for a few outside tables in summer. Despite its far-flung location, word is out, so it's best to book before making the trip out here.

La Latteria
Via San Marco 24 (02 659 7653). Metro Moscova/bus 41, 93, 94. **Meals served** 12.30-2.30pm, 7.30-10pm Mon-Fri. Closed Aug, Dec. **Average** €25. **No credit cards**. **Map** p308 C2.

It's worth the wait to get a table at this small *trattoria*, which was previously, as the name implies, a dairy. Not only does it offer clean, creative takes on Italian standards, but the closely packed tables allow you to eavesdrop on the hottest fashion designers and power brokers talking business over their plates of pasta.

Bar/restaurants

Armani/Nobu
Via Pisoni 1 (02 6231 2645/www.giorgioarmani.it). Metro Montenapoleone/tram 1, 2, 20. **Meals served** 7-11.30pm Mon; noon-2.30pm, 7-11.30pm Tue-Sat. **Average** €75. **Credit** AmEx, DC, MC, V. **Map** p309 C1/p312 B1.
Raw fish doesn't get any more chic than the sushi at the Milan outpost of Nobuyuki Matsuhisa's sushi empire. Purists will say the food isn't at the same level as his offerings in New York and London. That may be, but Nobu's happy hour is the place to be if you want to nibble on the bar eats and see Milan's fashion world unwind.

Just Cavalli Café
Viale Camoens (02 311 817). Metro Cadorna/bus 61/tram 29, 30. **Meals served** 8pm-2am daily. **Average** €50. **Credit** AmEx, DC, MC, V. **Map** p308 C1.
At the foot of Torre Branca, in Parco Sempione (*see p67*), designer Roberto Cavalli's first foray into the restaurant world is an impossibly stylish place (as if you expected otherwise). Steel beams, massive windows, leopard-print furnishings and the inevitable beautiful people contribute to the feeling of utter chic; the candles (and the huge but cuddly Argentinian mastiffs on the sofas) add a touch of homeliness. Excellent cocktails (if a little steep at €10), and international cuisine, from *maltagliati alla liquirizia* (pasta with a liquorice sauce) to *risotto di pernice* (with partridge) to the ubiquitous sushi.

10 Corso Como Caffè
Corso Como 10 (02 2901 3581/www.10corso como.it). Metro Garibaldi/tram 11, 25, 29, 30, 33. **Meals served** 8-11pm Mon; 12.30-3pm, 8pm-midnight Tue-Sun. *Brunch* 11am-5pm Sat, Sun. Closed 2wks Aug. **Average** €50. **Credit** AmEx, DC, MC, V. **Map** p308 B2.
This chic restaurant and designer store owned by fashion maven Carla Sozzani has become a beacon in Milan. A haven for everything that is stylish and fashionable, it is arranged around the courtyard of a former car repair workshop. The restaurant serves a fusion of Mediterranean and Japanese recipes in nouvelle cuisine portions and the prices verge on the outlandish, though the place is still popular with the post-theatre and pre-nightclub crowd (it's close to both the Teatro Smeraldo, *see p185*, and a host of nightlife venues). Great place for a quiet midday coffee break; think twice before forking out for a full meal.

Ethnic

Serendib
Via Pontida 2 (02 659 2139). Metro Moscova/bus 41, 93, 94. **Meals served** 7.30pm-midnight daily. Closed 10 days Aug. **Average** €25. **Credit** MC, V. **Map** p308 B2.
A Sri Lankan restaurant quietly offering some of the best value on Milan's growing ethnic scene. It's pleasantly low-lit with standard eastern decor, and there's a choice of set menus based on vegetable, meat or fish main dishes. Wash that curry down with Three Coins lager, and finish off with ginger tea. At weekends it's a good idea to book.

Tara
Via Cirillo 16 (02 345 1635/www.ristorantetara. com). Metro Cadorna/bus 57/tram 1, 29, 30. **Meals served** noon-2.30pm, 7-11.30pm Tue-Sun. **Average** €25. **Credit** AmEx, DC, MC, V. **Map** p308 B1.
When this thriving Indian restaurant just north of Parco Sempione opened up in 1997, its manager proclaimed that it would be more than just a curry house. Over the years it has developed quite a devoted clientele, which comes here to enjoy high-quality Indian food that wouldn't be out of place in London.

San Babila & East

Italian

Bottiglieria Da Pino
Via Cerva 14 (02 7600 0532). Metro San Babila, Duomo/bus 54, 60, 73/tram 12, 15, 23, 27. **Meals served** noon-3pm Mon-Sat. **Average** €17. **No credit cards. Map** p311 A1/p312 C2.
From the outside, this *trattoria* on a side street near Largo Augusto looks like any of the other myriad bars in the neighbourhood. In the dining room behind the bar, though, you'll find all the hustle, bustle and perpetual motion of an old-style workers' trat. You'll also find impeccably prepared food and plates of *formaggi artigianali* (artisanal cheeses).

Vinous delights

Lombardy has an odd relationship with wine. On the one hand, the Lombards have long been consumers of fine wine, eagerly importing the best from neighbouring Piedmont, Tuscany and even France. On the other hand, Lombard wines themselves have traditionally been something to quaff with lunch rather than something to cellar for that special dinner.

To a large extent, the wines of the Oltrepò Pavese (*see p263*) continue that tradition. The hills on the far side of the Po river are Italy's third-largest producer of wine after Chianti and Asti, yet Oltrepò wines are little known beyond the borders of Lombardy. For many producers, Milan is all the 'export' market they need, and since most Oltrepò wines don't scale new oenological heights, there isn't much incentive for other wine drinkers to seek them out.

But even if few of these wines are excellent, any number of them are delightfully pleasant; and quaffed *a là* milanese – with more singing than sniffing – they are a wonderful accompaniment to a meal with friends. The Oltrepò produces a variety of reds and whites. For the reds, the best bets are local types such as Bonarda, Barbera, Buttafuoco and Sangue di Giuda. The whites include Riesling and a sparkling wine made from Pinot Nero (which is – despite the fact that it is an ingredient in champagne – a red grape).

In the eastern part of the province, Franciacorta (*see p236*) long followed the tradition of producing undistinguished wines for Sunday lunches. That changed in the 1960s, when Guido Berlucchi realised that Franciacorta's microclimate could support the making of much better wines. Berlucchi decided to make a *spumante* – a sparkling wine – using the same techniques used to produce champagne. However, he used only two of the three principal champagne grapes, adding a third one of his choice. For the record, the three are Pinot Nero (Noir), Chardonnay and Pinot Meunier; in Franciacorta, the latter has been replaced by Pinot Bianco.

In the years since Mr Berlucchi set up shop, Franciacorta has become one of the world's great sparkling wines. Despite its reliance on French grapes and techniques, Franciacorta is not a champagne clone. For one thing, the blends are different. For another, its producers have been much more willing to experiment with techniques than tradition-bound champagne houses.

In addition to 'regular' Franciacorta, which is usually either brut or dry – you can also find *saten*, which is produced with less sugar than normal, and *non-dosato*, which is drier than brut. As well as Berlucchi, some of the best producers of Franciacorta are Ca' del Bosco, Uberti and Bellavista.

Armani/Nobu. *See p117.*

Da Abele

*Via Temperanza 5 (02 261 3855). Metro Pasteur/
bus 56.* **Meals served** 8pm-midnight Tue-Sun.
Closed Aug; 2wks Dec-Jan. **Average** €30. **Credit**
AmEx, DC, MC, V. **Map** off p309 A2.
Risotto is the only *primo* available at this restaurant,
but the choice of variations is endless: from the
classic *risotto milanese* (with saffron) to more imaginative concoctions such as *risotto cuneese* (with
bacon and potatoes) and *risotto con spinaci e
scamorza* (with spinach and smoked cheese). In
the summer there are lighter recipes, such as
risotto di fragoline (with tiny wild strawberries).
The service is friendly and informal, and reservations are made on a same-day basis; if you haven't
booked, make sure you get there early.

Da Giacomo

Via P Sottocorno 6 (02 7602 3313). Tram 29, 30.
Meals served 7.30-11pm Tue; 12.30-2.30pm, 7.30-
11pm Wed-Sun. Closed 3wks Aug; 2wks Dec-Jan.
Average €50. **Credit** AmEx, DC, MC, V.
Map p309 C2.
This place looks like nothing on the outside: an
anonymous suburban *trattoria* with frosted
windows in an anonymous suburban street. But
Da Giacomo is one of Milan's most exclusive
(though by no means most expensive) restaurants.
In a series of bright and chatty rooms decorated by
the late Renzo Mongiardino (interior designer to
the rich and famous), major players from Milan's
fashion and business worlds jostle for elbow
room. Service can be uncertain, and the competent
Mediterranean cuisine, with the emphasis on fish,
would not win any prizes. But this is just what
the city's captains of industry want: colour and
comfort food in a *trattoria* that is as difficult to
book as London's Ivy.

Joia

*Via P Castaldi 18 (02 2952 2124/www.joia.it).
Metro Porta Venezia or Repubblica/tram 29, 30.*
Meals served 12.30-2.30pm, 7.30-11pm Mon-Fri;
7.30-11pm Sat. Closed Aug. **Average** €50.
Credit AmEx, DC, MC, V. **Map** p309 B1, C2.
This sharp designer space near the Giardini
Pubblici (*see p81*) is the Prada of vegetarian
restaurants. Swiss chef Piero Leeman, who admits
to being heavily influenced by the Orient, exercises
his considerable culinary (and literary) talents in
dishes such as Discovery: Variations on the
Aubergine, or Asparagus Takes Form. Zen menu
pretensions aside, this is high-level meatless
cooking with plenty of hits and only a few misses.
Ingredients vary from the homegrown to the
exotic, and there's hardly a pasta dish in sight.
Book ahead, and don't ask for nut roast. Hurried
lunchers should try the €15 special.

Masuelli San Marco

*Viale Umbria 80 (02 5518 4138/www.masuelli-
trattoria.com). Metro Lodi/bus 84, 90, 91, 92.*
Meals served 8-10.30pm Mon; 12.30-2.30pm, 8-
10.30pm Tue-Sat. **Average** €35. **Credit** AmEx, DC,
MC, V. **Map** p311 B2.
Masuelli San Marco is a veritable Milanese institution,and one that never fails to live up to its scintil-
lating reputation. The atmosphere is warm, the
service attentive and the cuisine stretches from
Piedmont to Lombardy. Some of the dishes may
not be to everyone's taste – such as the *filetti di
aringhe* (herring fillets in milk), *bollito misto* (mixed
boiled meats) or even tripe – but you won't find
better versions of these classics anywhere else in
Milan. Start with the excellent choice of cured
hams and salami, and order a good bottle of Barbera
to wash it all down.

Eat, Drink, Shop

THE
ITALIAN JOB

Time Out
'The best city guides in print' The Independent
Florence
& the best of Tuscany

Time Out
'The best city guides in print' The Independent
Milan
The Lakes & Lombardy

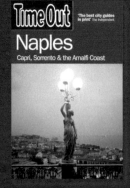

Time Out
'The best city guides in print' The Independent
Naples
Capri, Sorrento & the Amalfi Coast

Time Out
'The best city guides in print' The Independent
Rome

Time Out
'The best city guides in print' The Independent
Turin

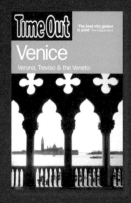

Time Out
'The best city guides in print' The Independent
Venice
Verona, Treviso & the Veneto

Available from all good bookshops
and £2 off at www.timeout.com/shop

Time Out

Osteria Grand Hotel
Via Cardinale A Sforza 75 (02 8951 6153). Bus 59, 91. **Meals served** 8-10.30pm Tue-Sun; noon-2pm Sun. Closed 3wks Aug; 2wks Dec-Jan. **Average** €30. **Credit** DC, V. **Map** p310 B2, C2.
The cuisine is solidly Mediterranean, with fine salami or hams to start, followed by meat or vegetable main courses such as the baked potato and artichoke *timballo*; portions, though, can be tiny. Unusually for Italy, the extensive wine list ventures outside the country, with labels from all around the world. The bower outside is a welcome attraction in warm weather, as is the live jazz at weekends. Parking, on the other hand, is a nightmare.

La Terrazza di via Palestro
4th floor, via Palestro 2 (02 7600 2277/www.gm ristorazione.it). Metro Palestro or Turati/bus 61, 94. **Meals served** 12.30-2.30pm, 7.30-10pm Mon-Fri. Closed 3wks Aug; 2wks Dec-Jan. **Average** €45. **Credit** AmEx, DC, MC, V. **Map** p309 C1.
On the top floor of an office block just outside Porta Nuova, this panoramic restaurant with summer terrace overlooking the gardens of via Palestro is one of the few with a sense of design to match Milan's reputation. The look is *Wallpaper** 1950s retro, with cherry-wood consoles and chrome globe lights. Light, modern seafood dishes dominate the menu, beginning with the house speciality (Mediterranean sushi), a surprisingly successful attempt to use Italian fish, rice and pasta to re-create the spirit of Japan's top food export.

Ethnic

Warsa
Via Melzo 16 (02 201 673). Metro Porta Venezia/ tram 5, 9, 11, 30. **Meals served** noon-3pm, 7-10.30pm Mon, Tue, Thur-Sun. **Average** €15. **Credit** MC, V. **Map** p309 C2.
In the Porta Venezia area, home to much of Milan's large African community, this welcoming family-run place offers good and filling Eritrean cooking at a price that won't damage your purse. The menu includes dishes with veal, beef and chicken, plus a wealth of vegetarian options – all eaten with your fingers. Try the *miès*, an aromatic wine.

Pizza & snacks

Pizzeria 40
Via P Castaldi 40 (02 2940 0061). Metro Porta Venezia or Repubblica/tram 29, 30. **Meals served** noon-2.45pm, 6-10.45pm Mon, Thur-Sun; noon-2.30pm Tue. **Average** €10. **Credit** MC, V. **Map** p309 B1, C2.
If you've been shopping in corso Buenos Aires, this is an ideal place to stop for a quick lunch or snack. Although there are some pasta dishes on the menu, the house speciality is *pizza al trancio* – deep-pan pizza served in whopping big slices (real men ask for it *abbondante* – in an extra-large portion).

Porta Romana & South

Italian

Ai Sabbioni
Viale G d'Annunzio 7/9 (02 8942 0252). Metro Porta Genova or Sant'Agostino/bus 47, 59, 71, 74/tram 2, 3, 14, 15, 20, 29, 30. **Meals served** 12.30-2.30pm, 7.30-11pm Mon-Fri; 7.30-11pm Sat. Closed 1wk Aug. **Average** €30. **Credit** DC. **Map** p310 B2.
Housed in a 19th-century palazzo, Ai Sabbioni offers excellent (mostly) fish dishes in an area where it's all too easy to stumble into sub-quality fixed-price *menù turistici*. The *misto crudo* is easily on a par with the sushi found at many Japanese restaurants; the *risotto vongole e bottarga* (with cockles and mullet roe) is to die for, as is the *branzino all'aceto balsamico* (sea bass with balsamic vinegar).

Al Merluzzo Felice
Via L Papi 6 (02 545 4711). Metro Lodi, Porta Romana/bus 62, 77/tram 9. **Meals served** 8-11pm Mon; 12.30-2pm, 8-11pm Tue-Sat. **Average** €40. **Credit** AmEx, DC, MC, V. **Map** p311 B2.
At the Michelin-starred 'Happy Cod', the fish-only menu includes shellfish risotto, fried codfish, smoked tuna, octopus and deep-fried breaded sardines. But the speciality is swordfish, which is prepared in a bewildering variety of ways. The atmosphere is warm and welcoming, the service friendly and attentive, and the cellar is chock-full of good Sicilian wines. This small restaurant is always packed to the rafters, so book ahead.

L'Ape Piera
Via Lodovico il Moro 11 (02 8912 6060/www.ape piera.com). Bus 47/tram 2. **Meals served** noon-2pm Mon; noon-2pm, 8-10.30pm Tue-Fri; 8-10.30pm Sat. Closed 3wks Aug; 1wk Jan. **Average** €45. **Credit** AmEx, MC, V. **Map** off p310 C1.
This *osteria* is spread over two floors, each with their own attractions, whether it be the view over the Navigli (upstairs), or the original beams, massive fireplace and cobbled paving (downstairs). The menu changes according to what is in season and ranges from pumpkin soup with prawns to potato-stuffed pasta with courgette flowers and clams. Also available is a vegetarian menu, and an embarrassing choice of cheeses and mustards. The wine list is select. Finish off with one of the home-made desserts or a refreshing herbal concoction to aid digestion.

Da Teresa
Via Pavia 3 (02 5811 1126). Bus 50, 91/tram 3, 15. **Meals served** noon-2.15pm, 8-10.15pm Mon-Sat. **Average** €18. **Credit** AmEx, MC, V. **Map** p310 C2.
Half social club, half ambassador for Pugliese cooking, this simple *trattoria*, with its Formica tables and accents from the south, is just a step or two above visiting your Italian aunt's house for dinner. There are no frills, and the same waiter that drops your food in front of you may well ask you later why you haven't cleared your plate.

Dongiò

*Via Corio 3 (02 551 1372). Metro Porta Romana/
bus 9, 62, 77/tram 9.* **Meals served** noon-2pm,
8-11pm Mon-Fri; 8-11pm Sat. Closed 3wks Aug.
Average €35. **Credit** AmEx, DC, MC, V.
Map p311 B2.

A favourite stand-by for Milanese craving solid
home cooking, this Calabrian trat serves up well-
spiced *primi* such as *fusilli con 'nduja* (Calabrian
sausage), plus some of the best steaks in town.

Giulio Pane e Ojo

*Via L Muratori 10 (02 545 6189). Metro Porta
Romana/bus 62, 77/tram 9.* **Meals served** 12.30-
2pm, 8-12.30pm Mon-Sat. Closed 2wks Aug.
Average €25. **Credit** AmEx, MC, V. **Map** p311 B2.

A comfortable *osteria* offering a taste of Rome.
Favourites include the Roman classic *spaghetti*

cacio e pepe and *abbacchio scottadito*, perhaps the
best lamb chops you'll ever have.

Osteria delle Vigne

*Ripa di Porta Ticinese 61 (02 837 5617). Metro Porta
Genova/bus 47, 74/tram 2.* **Meals served** noon-
2.30pm, 8-11.30 m Mon-Sat. Closed Aug. **Average**
€30 (lunch €11). **Credit** AmEx, MC, V. **Map** p310 B1.

This cosy, inexpensive *osteria* offers a surprisingly
good wine list and a highly varied menu. And if
that's not enough to tempt you, the ambience is
decidedly laid-back – a plus in a district where the
eating places tend to be noisy and overcrowded. The
caramelle di ricotta e spinaci (sweet-shaped ravioli
stuffed with spinach and ricotta cheese) are a
delight. The tables are large, and it's a good place to
relax and chat. The lunchtime menu is one of the
best bargains in Milan.

Food on the go

Elsewhere in Italy, the myth of the
leisurely lunch remains. People may
not sit down to a three-hour meal
followed by a nap as often as they used
to, but they still think this is the way it's
supposed to be done. The Milanese, on
the other hand, gave up the ghost long
ago. For the typical Milan worker, a lunch
hour means exactly that, and most
restaurants are adept at getting people
back to work before the boss gets angry.

Bars, too, are attuned to Milan's
prandial needs. The Milanese have
raised the *panino* (sandwich) to an art
form, and even the humblest bar will
offer a decent selection. The menu at
better-stocked bars can seem quite baroque.
Many bars also offer a *tavola calda* (hot
buffet), which means you can enjoy hot
pastas or simple main courses (usually
made earlier that day, and reheated in
the microwave) there.

Milan has a wide array of shops offering
pizza by the slice (*al trancio*), slabs of
focaccia, and *panzerotti* (fried or baked
turnover similar to a *calzone*). Many
bakeries (*panifici*) also offer quick bites
to go. *Rosticcerie* are a type of delicatessen
serving spit-roast chicken, chips, stuffed
vegetables and pasta dishes, either to
eat in or take away.

Panzerotti Luini

*Via S Radegonda 16, Centre (02 8646
1917). Metro Duomo/bus 54, 60, 65/tram 2,
3, 14, 20, 27.* **Open** 10am-3pm Mon; 10am-
8pm Tue-Sat. **Map** p311 A1.

This Milan institution located behind the
Rinascente department store in piazza
Duomo has been dishing up *panzerotti* and
focaccia since 1940. Indeed, its *panzerotti*
are such a draw that people queuing at the
counter don't even need to say the word –
just muttering '*uno*' (one) gets them a
steamy *panzerotto* in a paper bag.

Princi

*Via Speronari 6, Centre (02 874 797). Metro
Duomo/bus 54, 60, 65/tram 2, 3, 14, 20,
27.* **Open** 7am-8pm Mon-Sat. **Map** p310 A2.
*Via Ponte Vetero 10, North (02 7201 6067).
Metro Lanza, Cairoli/bus 18, 50, 58, 61/
tram 1, 3, 4, 12, 20, 27.* **Open** 7am-8pm
Mon-Sat. **Map** p308 C2.

This chain of well-stocked bakeries has two
central locations: one up the block from La
Scala, the other a few steps from the Duomo.
Both offer mouthwatering slabs of *focaccia*
and pizza, and the via Ponte Vetero shop
also dishes up hot food in the afternoon.

Compagnia Generale dei
Viaggiatori Naviganti e Sognatori.

La Topaia

*Via F Argelati 40 (02 837 3469). Metro Porta
Genova or Romolo/bus 47, 90, 91.* **Meals served**
noon-2.30pm, 8-11.30pm Mon-Fri; 8-11.30pm Sat.
Closed Aug. **Average** €25. **Credit** AmEx, DC, MC,
V. **Map** p310 B1.
This delightful old-style restaurant, complete with
candlelight and guitar-strumming crooners, is a
short distance from the overcrowded, noisy dives of
the Naviglio Grande. The menu is solidly traditional,
with hearty dishes such as *minestrone d'orzo* (bar-
ley soup) and *stinco arrosto* (roast shin of pork).
Home-made desserts and a friendly atmosphere
more than make up for the indifferent wine list.

Trattoria Madonnina

*Via Gentilino 6 (02 8940 9089). Bus 59/tram 3,
15.* **Meals served** noon-2.30pm Mon-Wed; noon-
2.30pm, 8-11.30pm Thur-Sat. Closed Aug. **Average**
€25. **Credit** MC, V. **Map** p310 B2.
As the name suggests (the *Madonnina* is the gold-
en statue on top of the Duomo, *see p56* **The woman
on top**), the menu at this 1817-established *trattoria*
is typically Milanese, simple and filling. Try the cod
with polenta, or the *vitello tonnato* (veal in a delicate
tuna sauce). The place also offers an informal, cosy
atmosphere, wooden tables, a picturesque garden
and a rich history – throughout the 1950s and '60s,
the La Scala choir would put in regular appearances
and even soprano Maria Callas ate here.

Bar/restaurants

Tuberi Americani

Via Vetere 9 (02 8324 1152). Tram 2, 14. **Meals
served** noon-3pm, 7.45pm-midnight Tue-Sat; noon-
3pm Mon. Closed 1wk Aug. **Average** €25. **Credit**
DC, MC, V. **Map** p310 B2.

This bar/restaurant is wholly dedicated to the
humble potato; you'll find the versatile tuber
included in everything, from the cocktail buffet to
the main courses. All the à la carte menu and cheaper set menu dishes are cooked to order, so be prepared to wait for your potato concoction (a potato
timbale takes about 20 minutes). Marble and steel
surfaces provide a suitably stylish setting for
design-conscious Milanese diners.

Ethnic

Compagnia Generale dei Viaggiatori Naviganti e Sognatori

*Via Cuccagna 4 (02 551 6154). Metro Porta
Romana/bus 62, 77/tram 9.* **Meals served** 8pm-
midnight Tue-Sat; 8-11.30pm Sun. Closed 3wks Aug;
2wks Dec-Jan. **Average** €40-€45. **Credit** DC, MC, V.
Map p311 B2.
This Japanese bar and restaurant has a delightful
name, the 'General Company of Travellers, Navigators
and Dreamers', which it inherited from the previous
occupier of this property in a late 18th-century farmhouse. The food is also remarkable: sushi,
teppanyaki, soba, udon and sashimi dishes are all
excellent. The decor is upbeat, all the more so when
the restaurant stages one of its regular art shows.

Feijào Com Arroz

Via Corrado il Salico 10 (02 8951 2722). Tram 24.
Meals served 8pm-11am Tue-Thur, Sun; 8pm-1am
Fri, Sat. Closed 2wks Aug. **Average** €25-€30. **No
credit cards. Map** p311 C1.
A fair hike from the centre, in the suburbs south-
west of Porta Romana, this Brazilian diner provides
a touch of Latin-American colour in fog-bound
Milan – not least because it's popular with the city's
South American transvestite community. The

portions are generous and the Italo-Brazilian staff very friendly. Try the *frango a passarinho* (lemon-fried chicken pieces), followed by *picanha* (grilled beef with bean paste) and *bobo de camaràο* (shrimps in broth with cassava).

Shambala

Via Ripamonti 337 (02 552 0194). Tram 24.
Meals served 8pm-1am Tue-Sun. Closed 3wks Aug; 2wks Dec-Jan. **Average** €45. **Credit** AmEx, DC, MC, V. **Map** p311 B1, C1.
Milanese in the know just can't stop raving about this place. The service is efficient and discreet, the atmosphere soothing – thanks to cool background music, incense and perfumed candles. However, the main reason behind Shambala's continuing success is the excellent Vietnamese/Thai/Japanese cuisine: duck breast with tamarind sauce, stir-fry prawns with oyster sauce, or *kaeng kung* – steamed shrimps in coconut milk. There's also an enormous terrace for open-air dining in the summer. A little pricey, undoubtedly, but very nice.

Sushi-Kòboo

Viale Col di Lana 1 (02 837 2608). Bus 65, 79/ tram 15, 29, 30. **Meals served** 12.30-2.30pm, 7.30-11.30pm Tue-Sun. Closed 2wks Aug.
Average €30. **Credit** DC, MC, V. **Map** p310 B2.
A Japanese restaurant with a wide choice of fresh sushi and surprisingly reasonable prices. In the bright, clean interior, you can eat seated around the conveyor belt, or at a table.

Pizza & snacks

Be Bop

Viale Col di Lana 4 (02 837 6972). Bus 65, 79/ tram 15, 29, 30. **Meals served** 12.30-2.30pm, 7.30-11pm daily. **Average** €20. **Credit** AmEx, MC, V. **Map** p310 B2.
A short walk from the Darsena, this art deco-ish *pizzeria* offers up large, thin-crusted pizzas and a delightful assortment of *primi*. It will also prepare gluten-free pizza for people with allergies.

Premiata Pizzeria

Via Alzaia Naviglio Grande 2 (02 8940 0648). Metro Porta Genova/bus 47/tram 2. **Meals served** 12.30-2.30pm, 7.30pm-1am daily. **Average** €20. **Credit** AmEx, MC, V. **Map** p310 B1.
Whenever Milanese argue about the best pizza in town, the Premiata Pizzeria – at the beginning of the Naviglio Grande – invariably pops up. With chewy, Neapolitan-style pizzas (cooked in a wood-fired oven, of course) and a satisfying selection of *primi* and *secondi*, the comfortable dining rooms (and outside garden) are a great place to be after a stroll along the Navigli.

Super Pizza

Viale Sabotino 4 (02 5832 0410). Metro Porta Romana/tram 9, 29, 30. **Meals served** noon-2pm, 7-10pm Tue-Sat; 7-10pm Sun. Closed Aug. **Average** €10. **No credit cards. Map** p311 B1.

Famous throughout the city for its wafer-thin, Roman-style pizzas, this no-nonsense pizzeria packs 'em in and moves 'em out (you're not encouraged to linger here). Besides the standard pizzas, there are also some more inventive toppings, such as salmon, and gorgonzola and bacon. No reservations accepted: just join the queue.

Sant'Ambrogio & West

Italian

Da Leo

Via Trivulzio 26 (02 4007 1445). Metro De Angeli or Gambara/bus 18, 63, 72, 80. **Meals served** 12.30-2.30pm, 7.30-10.30pm Tue-Sat; 12.30-2.30 Sun. Closed 3wks Aug; 2wks Dec. **Average** €35.
No credit cards. Map off p310 A1.
Puglia-born Giuseppe Leo has been going to Milan's fish market at the crack of dawn for the past 30 years to source and select the freshest produce for his fish-only restaurant. The food he serves is simple and wholesome: *spaghetti in bianco* (spaghetti – the only pasta on offer here, by the way – without tomatoes) with tuna, clams, king prawns or calamari and main course fish dishes that vary according to the catch of the day. The interior could do with a little renovating touches, but the service is friendly and efficient, and the wine list extensive. It's best to book ahead for dinner.

Jacaranda

Piazza VI Febbraio 26 (02 3459 2152). Tram 12, 15, 19, 20, 23, 27. **Meals served** 8-11pm Mon; noon-3pm, 8-11pm Tue-Sat. Closed Aug. **Average** €30. **Credit** MC, V. **Map** p308 B1.
An intimate restaurant, with just ten or so tables in a long, thin room decorated with hundreds of cookery books and luxuriant bamboo plants. The creative Mediterranean cuisine changes on a daily basis and includes a wealth of options for everybody, irrespective of their dietary requirements. Start your meal with one of Jacaranda's excellent soups, and don't forget to *fare scarpetta* (mop up) with the delicious handmade walnut bread. The wine list is extensive.

Il Luogo di Aimo e Nadia

Via Montecuccoli 6 (02 416 886/www.aimoenadia. com). Metro Primaticcio/bus 63, 64. **Meals served** 12.30-2pm, 8-10pm Mon-Fri; 8-10pm Sat. Closed 1wk Jan, Aug. **Average** €100. **Credit** AmEx, DC, MC, V. **Map** off p310 A1.
Aimo and Nadia are obsessive about finding the freshest ingredients for their dishes, and are still very much present in the dining room (despite the fact they've recently opened another place, L'Altro Luogo di Aimo e Nadia, piazza della Repubblica 13, 02 2901 7039) to see that you get the most from your out-of-the-way dining experience. *See also p189* **Lombard gourmands**.

Cafés & Bars

Caffeine fixes and happy-hour feeding frenzies.

For Italians coffee has the same, almost mystical status that tea and beer have for the British. As a result, you won't have to walk too far in this city to find a decent cup of the stuff. During the day *il caffè* (by which Italians mean espresso) is consumed rapidly, usually while standing at the bar, and it is only in the evening that people actually begin to sit down and unwind, usually over less stimulating substances. If, however, you want to drink coffee, or anything else, at a more leisurely pace, then you might want to try some of Milan's classy *pasticcerie* (pastry shops), such as Biffi (*see p129*), which is like an elegant Old-World tea room, even if cake and pastries are its official raison d'être.

In actual fact, the assorted definitions – cafés, bars, pubs, *pasticcerie*, restaurants and even ice-cream parlours (*gelaterie*) – are often vague. To add to the confusion, some bakeries have taken to serving coffee and alcohol, thus becoming, to all intents and purposes, bars. Of particular interest are the four shops in the Princi chain. The flagship store at via Ponte Vetero 10, on the edge of the Brera area, is worth checking out, not least because it offers both bread and life on a Sunday.

Duomo & Centre

Caffè Miani (aka Zucca) △¹
Galleria Vittorio Emanuele (02 8646 4435). Metro Duomo/bus 54, 60, 65/tram 12, 20, 23, 27. **Open** 7.30am-8.30pm Tue-Sun. **Credit** AmEx, MC, V. **Map** p311 A1/p312 B1.
Most bars in the Galleria Vittorio Emanuele are tourist traps, but this establishment, which opened along with the Galleria in 1867, is a veritable institution. It has changed hands and name many times, and was once owned by the Campari dynasty – as a result, that's the drink to order. The interior is spectacular, with a high ceiling and walls that feature splendid mosaics. You might want to stand and drink at the bar – prices increase dramatically once you sit down and have a waiter come to your table.

Caffè Verdi
Via Giuseppe Verdi 6 (02 863 880). Metro Cordusio or Duomo/bus 61/tram 1, 2, 20. **Open** *Mar-Oct* 7am-8pm Mon-Sat. *Nov-Feb* 7am-8pm daily. Closed mid Jul-Aug. **Credit** AmEx, DC, MC, V. **Map** p309 C1/p312 B1.
This quietly dignified *caffè* may not be a swinging nightspot, but it's a must for opera fans. Situated across the road from La Scala, it's where company

Plenty of waiting room at **ATM**. *See p126*.

members go for their coffee breaks during the day… or where they would go, if La Scala was open. Still, even if you don't run into Placido Domingo, you can soak up the atmosphere, surrounded by busts and photos of composers, while unobtrusive classical music plays in the background. The €6-a-shot cocktails have names like Callas, Verdiano and Mozart. At lunchtime Caffè Verdi is a favourite haunt for the banking community; it serves *panini* at €4, pasta dishes at €5 and *secondi* at €8.

Victoria Café
Via Clerici 1 (02 805 3598/02 8646 2088). Metro Cordusio or Duomo/bus 61/tram 1, 3, 4, 12, 14, 20. **Open** 7.30am-2am Mon-Fri; 5pm-2am Sat, Sun. Closed 3wks Aug. **Credit** AmEx, MC, V. **Map** p308 C2/p312 B1.
Named after a coffee machine, not Great Britain's own dear queen, this is one of the few decent watering holes within walking distance of the Duomo. Housed in a former bank building tucked away behind La Scala and done out in an intriguing Liberty style, it caters to business types during

the day and bright young things at night. It is also popular with expats and visitors, doubtless attracted to its on-tap Guinness, Kilkenny and Tennents (€5 a pint), cocktails (€7; €5 at happy hour, which runs 6-8.30pm) and music. You can also get food (sandwiches €4, pasta dishes €6-€7, desserts €3.50).

Sforzesco & North

ATM
Bastioni di Porta Volta 15 (02 655 2365). Metro Moscova/bus 51, 57/tram 3, 12, 14. **Open** 11am-3pm, 6pm-2am Mon-Sat. **Credit** (only at lunchtime) AmEx, MC, V. **Map** p308 B2.
Named after the Milan public transport company (it is housed in a converted passenger waiting room), this was one of Milan's coolest drinking places in the 1990s. It may have lost a bit of its shine, but it is still a lively hangout for a younger, left-of-centre crowd who likes to forage here during happy hour. It is also a favourite for designers when they come to town for the Salone del Mobile (furniture fair, *see p152*) in spring.

Bhangrabar
Corso Sempione 1 (02 3493 4469). Tram 1, 29, 30. **Open** 7am-3pm, 6.30pm-2am Mon, Wed-Sun; 7am-3pm Tue. **Credit** MC, V. **Map** p308 B1.
This lounge bar and restaurant is a celebration of everything Indian. The decorative features – from the handmade screens that create privacy, to the bar itself (a huge counter formerly used in a textile store) – were shipped directly from Asia. During happy hour the assuredly prepared cocktails are a snip at €5.50; the price of a drink also includes as many trips as you like to the varied Indian buffet. After dinner, live DJ music shakes the joint.

Caffè Letterario
Via Solferino 27 (02 2901 5119). Metro Moscova/ bus 41, 43, 94. **Open** 8am-1am Mon-Sat. Closed 2wks Aug. **Credit** AmEx, DC, MC, V. **Map** p308 B2.
This small but charming *ristorante,* bar and *galleria* opened in 1997, but recently changed management and underwent extensive renovation. The new owners plan to introduce live music (jazz and classical) here, as well as arty and literary events, in order to make it Milan's *salotto* (drawing room), in keeping with the Literary Café name. There's also a fun variation on the happy hour theme: here they do 'spoon hour', with mini portions of salmon and other goodies. Champagne cocktails cost €6 (as opposed to the usual €5) during this time.

Cajun Louisiana Bistro
Via Fiori Chiari 17 (02 8646 5315/www.louisiana bistro.it). Metro Lanza/bus 61/tram 3, 4, 12, 14, 27. **Open** noon-3pm, 6pm-2am Tue-Sat; 11.30am-3.30pm (brunch), 6pm-2am Sun. **Credit** AmEx, DC, MC, V. **Map** p308 C2.
This three-floor establishment is popular with models and young Americans. Even though it is technically a restaurant, that's way up on the third

floor, and its ground-floor bar is the place to go. Its massive TV screens are particularly enticing if you're a long way from home at the time of the Super Bowl or FA Cup final.

Da Claudio Pescheria dei Milanesi
Via Ponte Vetero 16 (02 8056 857). Metro Cairoli or Lanza/bus 18, 50, 58, 61/tram 1, 3, 4, 12, 20, 27. **Open** for *aperitivi* noon-2.30pm, 5-9pm Tue-Sat. **Credit** MC, V. **Map** p308 C2/p312 A1.
Claudio, already established as the fishmonger of the wealthy and the beautiful in Milan, has expanded into the world of *aperitivi* with a formula that suits the locals down to the ground. During *aperitivo* hour, at the counter you can help yourself to a *misto crudo* (raw fish selection) including tuna, salmon, swordfish and prawns, while sipping a glass of chilled Chardonnay (€8). Still hungry? Move on to the oysters and the seafood platter… One of the best spots in town, and the ideal starting point for an evening in the trendy Brera district.

10 Corso Como
Corso Como 10 (02 2901 3581/www.10corsocomo. com). Metro Garibaldi/tram 11, 25, 29, 30, 33. **Open** 11am-3pm, 6pm-2am daily. **Credit** AmEx, MC, V. **Map** p308 B2.
To catch a glimpse of why Milan is the fashion and design capital, away from the shops of via Montenapoleone, head to 10 Corso Como, a multifunctional arts centre that consists of a bar, restaurant (*see p117*), art gallery (*see p163*) and fashion boutique (*see p138*). Owned by the formidable Carla Sozzani, and frequented by the in crowd (Giorgio Armani is said to be a regular, while the whole place was closed off, like a city hosting a G8 summit, when Madonna paid a visit), it is located in an old *casa a ringhiera*, a working-class apartment building. Outside, the street itself has been successfully transformed into a pedestrian precinct.

Dynamo
Piazza Greco 5 (02 670 4353/02 669 2124). Bus 43, 81. **Open** 6pm-2am (happy hour 6-9pm) Tue-Sun. *Brunch* noon-4pm Sun. **Credit** AmEx, DC, MC, V. **Map** off p309 A1.
Away from the super-trendy (and super-crowded) *locali* in the city centre is Dynamo, a cocktail bar built over three floors: a raised chill-out, catch-up area; a lounge bar-cum-restaurant on the ground floor; and the basement, with comfy seating and a dance floor. Dynamo hosts poetry readings, themed parties and book and record launches. The most recent addition is the *cantina*, a cellar gathering a wide selection of fine wines from all over Italy; wine tastings are also available.

Good Fellas
Via Cusani 4 (02 869 0142). Metro Cairoli or Lanza/bus 61/tram 1, 3, 4, 12, 14, 27. **Open** 8am-2am Mon-Sat. **Credit** MC, V. **Map** p308 C2/p312 A1.
A small bar with a glass front (you could be forgiven for thinking it was a shop when walking by), this is a good place to go for morning coffee and evening

Working-class environment Italian-style at **10 Corso Como**. *See p126.*

aperitivi. In the summer you can sit outside on the street and enjoy the view of the massive Emporio Armani billboard, the ultimate fashion statement, in the adjoining *piazzetta* (little square).

Jamaica
Via Brera 32 (02 876 723/www.jamaicabar.it).
Metro Lanza or Montenapoleone/bus 61, 94/tram
3, 4, 12, 20. **Open** *June-Sept* 9am-2am Mon-Sat.
Oct-May 9am-2am Mon-Sat, 9am-8.30pm Sun.
Credit AmEx, DC, MC, V. **Map** p308 C2/p312 B1.
This bar opened in 1921 and, according to lore, Benito Mussolini still owed it money for a series of unpaid *cappuccini* when he became prime minister the following year. The bar changed its name to Jamaica after the war and was the favourite hangout of artists and writers in the 1950s; it is still very much a Milan institution. The Jamaica started doing its own in-house art and photography shows (*see p130* **The pursuit of happiness**) long before everybody else. If you want to move on after a drink here (cocktails €5.50), the three bars across the road (Bar Brera, Art Café and El Beverin) are also pretty good.

Nordest Caffè
Via Borsieri 35 (02 6900 1910/www.nordestcaffe.it).
Metro Garibaldi or Zara/bus 82, 83/tram 4, 11.
Open 8am-1am Mon-Fri; 8.30am-8.30pm Sun.
No credit cards. Map p309A1.
The North-East Café is one of several lively bars in the Isola neighbourhood, to the north of the Porta Garibaldi railway station. The recent opening of the Blue Note Jazz Club has doubtless boosted business in this street, even though the Nord Est does its own live jazz music, featuring admittedly less famous names. Via Borsieri is worth checking out: it's developing into one of Milan's nightlife hubs.

Radetzky
Corso Garibaldi 105 (02 657 2645). Metro Moscova/
bus 41, 43, 94. **Open** 8am-1.30am daily. Closed
2wks Aug. **Credit** AmEx, MC, V. **Map** p308 B2.

Named, somewhat bizarrely, after the despised Austrian field marshal who suppressed the 1848 uprising (legend has it that La Scala's orchestra never plays Strauss's *Radetzky March*; *see p16* **Five alive**) – this is a hip hangout throughout the week, but is particularly recommended on Sundays, when Milan is pretty lifeless. Famous for its brunches, Radetzky also prides itself on its *cotoletta alla milanese* (Wiener schnitzel, another reminder that Milan was once a province of the Austro-Hungarian Empire), which is served at all hours.

Roialto
Via Piero della Francesca 55 (02 3493 6616). Bus
43, 57, 78/tram 1, 29, 33. **Open** 6pm-2am Tue-Sat;
12.30-3.30pm (brunch), 6pm-2am Sun (*aperitivo*
6-9pm). **Credit** AmEx, DC, MC, V. **Map** p308 B1.
The Roialto has established itself as one of the hippest joints in town since taking over a spacious warehouse in 1999. The decor, which is genuine 1940s to '60s, includes comfortable armchairs, large overhead fans and an enormous bar, where Cuban rum bottles and cigars are prominent. It could be Key Largo and you almost expect Humphrey Bogart to walk in. The Roialto's location, near piazza Firenze, at the north end of corso Sempione, used to be out of the way geographically, but it's beginning to feel like the centre of the universe, with an increasing number of clubs and bars opening up.

San Babila & East

Art Deco Café
Via Lambro 7 (02 2952 4760/www.artdecocafe.it).
Metro Porta Venezia/tram 5, 11. **Open** 6pm-2am
daily. Closed 3wks Aug. **Credit** AmEx, DC, MC, V.
Map p309 C2.
This place is worth a visit for its Miami Beach interior, with revolving lights that create 256 different pastel colours, and the massive TV screen that broadcasts (appropriately enough) the Fashion

TV channel – quite a change for a location that used to house a snooker hall. Some people find it a bit too cool, but hey, this is Milan. The owners are planning to export the franchise: Warsaw has already said yes and London is thinking about it, apparently.

Bar Basso

Via Plinio 39 (02 2940 0580). Metro Lima or Piola/bus 60. **Open** *9am-1.15am Mon, Wed-Sun.* **Credit** AmEx, MC, V. **Map** p309 B2.

This bar became fashionable after current owner Mirko Stocchetto took it over in 1967 and introduced cocktails to Milan; until then they had only really been available in hotels. Stocchetto and his son Maurizio still enjoy inventing cocktails and designing cocktail glasses (which are on sale here for €20) and thus Negronis and other classics are a must at €5.50 (no happy hour here). Its €6.50 ice-creams are another Milanese institution.

Diana Garden

Viale Piave 42 (02 205 8081). Metro Porta Venezia/ tram 9, 29, 30. **Open** *June-Sept* 10am-1am daily. *Oct-May* 10am-midnight daily. **Credit** AmEx, DC, MC, V. **Map** p309 C2.

Housed in the Sheraton Diana Majestic (*see p46*), this has been a happening place at happy hour since it first opened in 2000. In the summer months you can sit in the fabulous garden, but the place is also lively in the winter season. Once you've tired of staring at the gorgeous, impeccably attired clientele, check out the semi-circular interior, a fin de siècle throwback. Cocktails range from €8 to €12. There's an adjoining restaurant, but with prices around €50 a head, you might prefer to eat elsewhere.

L'Elephante

Via Melzo 22 (02 2951 8768). Metro Porta Venezia/tram 5, 9, 11, 30. **Open** 6.30pm-2am Tue-Sun. **No credit cards**. **Map** p309 C2.

Although a gay and lesbian bar first and foremost, this establishment caters to all groups. Cocktail prices drop from €6-€7 to €5 during happy hour, which runs 6.30-9.30pm. L'Elephante is across the road from Art Deco (*see p127*), in spite of having a different street address, and within walking distance of the Diana Garden (*see above*), should you want to see three different places in one evening.

Porta Romana & South

Le Biciclette

Via Torti, at Conca del Naviglio (02 839 4177/ 02 5810 43259/www.lebiciclette.com). Metro Sant'Ambrogio/bus 94/tram 3, 14, 20. **Open** 6pm-2am Mon-Sat; 12.30-4pm, 6pm-2am Sun. Closed 3wks Aug. **Credit** AmEx, DC, MC, V. **Map** p310 B2.

Formerly a bike shop, The Bicycles is a vibrant bar and restaurant, and part of a growing nightlife hub – the establishments on via de Amicis are close by, which is worth knowing when any one of these places get too crowded. Le Biciclette opened for business in 1998 and prides itself on its art shows, its 'personalised buffet' (served during happy hour, 6-9pm, when cocktails cost €6, instead of the usual €7) and its Sunday brunch (€18, excluding drinks).

Caffè della Pusterla

Via de Amicis 24 (02 8940 2146). Metro Sant'Ambrogio/bus 94/tram 2, 3, 14, 20. **Open** 7am-2am Mon-Sat; 9am-2am Sun. **Credit** AmEx, MC, V. **Map** p310 B2.

Here wine cocktails (such as red with lemon sorbet) are the thing and have even been the subject of magazine features. This establishment caters to an assorted clientele throughout the day, with families and locals giving way to a younger crowd around happy hour (6-9pm). Cocktails cost €6 (€5 in happy hour) and food is also served: €6.50 for a first course and €7.50 for a *secondo*.

Cuore. *See p129.*

Cuore △5

Via G Mora 3 (02 5810 5126/www.cuore.it).
Metro Sant'Ambrogio/bus 94/tram 2, 3, 14, 20.
Open 6pm-2am daily. Closed 2wks Aug.
No credit cards. Map p310 A2, B2.

Tucked away in a quiet little street near San Lorenzo alle Colonne (*see p85*), this place is hard to find (look out for the letter 'C'), but well worth the effort. Cuore (heart) features ever-changing decor and an eclectic entertainment programme, which includes DJs, bands and even Elvis impersonators, who make surprise, unannounced appearances. The atmosphere is fun and friendly: many gay people enjoy coming here, even if it isn't a gay bar as such.

Fresco Art

Viale Monte Nero 23 (02 5412 4675). Metro Porta Romana/tram 9, 29, 30. **Open** 7.30am-2am Tue-Sun.
Credit MC, V. **Map** p311 B2.

Fresco Art is run by the same organisation that owns ATM (*see p126*). The place evolves through the day, being genteel in the morning, busy at lunch and enjoyable in the evening. Lawyers who work at the nearby Palazzo di Giustizia (an incredible piece of fascist-era architecture, *see p82*) like to unwind here. 'In that respect,' says the manager, 'we're a bit like a swimming pool for sharks.'

Ragno D'Oro

Piazza Medaglie d'Oro 2 (02 5405 0004/www.ragno doro.it). Metro Porta Romana/tram 9, 29, 30. **Open** 6.30pm-2am Tue-Sun. **Credit** V. **Map** p311 B1.

This place is at its best between April and September, when you can sit outside and admire its impressive location, within the battlements of the old city walls (*bastioni*), which were built by the Spanish. Like ATM, this place has a public transport link: it used to be the recreational centre for tram and bus drivers who would bring their wives and girlfriends for a twirl on the dance floor. The

name (golden spider) refers to the cumbersome microphone used on the bandstand in those halcyon days. Try the signature cocktail, the Spider Fresh (apple, cranberry, vodka, lime, mint and sugar). The venue is often used for musical and other events.

Sant'Ambrogio & West

Baci e Abbracci △6 ♡

Via de Amicis 44 (02 8901 3605/www.bacieabbracci. it). Metro Sant'Ambrogio/bus 94/tram 2, 3, 14, 20. **Open** 12.30-2.30pm, 6.30pm-2am Mon-Fri; 6.30pm-2am Sat, Sun. **Credit** AmEx, DC, MC, V. **Map** p310 A2.

Kisses 'n' Cuddles is frequented by soccer players (mainly Inter's Christian Vieri and AC's Gennaro Gattuso) and the showgirls who often decorate their arms. It prides itself on the quality of its cocktail ingredients, especially the vodka, as well as its happy hour buffet spread – its pizza has won awards and the desserts are made by an in-house pastry chef. Food is served at both lunchtime and in the evening, but your best bet is to tuck in at happy hour (6.30-9pm), when cocktails are €6 instead of €7.

Bar Magenta

Via Carducci 13 (02 805 3808). Metro Cadorna/bus 18, 58, 70, 94/tram 1, 19, 20, 24, 27. **Open** 5pm-3am Mon; 8am-3am Tue-Sun. Closed 2wks Aug.
No credit cards. Map p308 C2/p312 A1.

Not exactly the most stylish of places, but a Milan institution and much loved by the expat community, probably because it's more a pub than a fancy bar. The wooden interior, which wouldn't look out of place in a film about Edwardian London, is fun, but it's in the summer months, when the young customers sit at outdoor tables and generally crowd the pavement, that this place comes into its own.

Biffi

Corso Magenta 87 (02 4800 6702). Metro Conciliazione/bus 18/tram 20, 24. **Open** 7.30am-8.30pm Mon, Wed-Sun. Closed 1wk Aug.
No credit cards. Map p308 C1, C2.

One of Milan's historic cafés, Biffi is located on the edge of one of the city's most affluent neighbourhoods. The counter is cosy but never overcrowded and the tea room has a handful of tables for chatting and resting. The tri-chocolate, tri-layered cake will impress even the most seasoned chocoholic.

Colonial Fashion Café

Via de Amicis 12 (02 8942 0401). Metro Sant'Ambrogio/bus 94/tram 2, 3, 14, 20. **Open** 6.30pm-2am Mon-Thur, Sun; 6.30pm-3am Fri-Sat. **Credit** AmEx, MC, V. **Map** p310 A2.

Both the name and the business card (which features a model as its motif) are designed to attract the fashion crowd, while the bright outdoor lights are also pretty cool. The place seems to have achieved its objective – indeed, its success is such that the owners recently opened another establishment, Siddharta in via Elvezia 4. Cocktails at the Colonial Fashion Café cost €7.

Lounge Paradise

*Via Montevideo 20 (no phone/loungeparadise@
tiscali.it). Metro Sant'Agostino/bus 50/tram 20, 29,
33.* **Open** *mid Apr-mid Aug 2004* 6pm-midnight
daily. **No credit cards. Map** p310 B1.
Next to Milan's main public pool (*see p181*), this bar
is the ultimate destination during the hot Milanese
summer. Run by the people behind Cuore (*see p129*),
Lounge Paradise combines South Pacific atmos-
pheres (cue the chaises longues, bamboo sofas and
exotic-looking drinks) and 1930s Chicago (the elegant bar counter) without jarring. Get there after dinner, order yourself a cocktail and look cool
wandering through the place, entertained by the DJ
set and the art installations often organised here.

Morgan's

*Via Novati 2 (02 867 694). Metro Sant'Ambrogio/
bus 50, 58, 94/tram 2, 14.* **Open** 6pm-2am Mon-Sat.
Closed Aug. **Credit** AmEx, DC, MC, V. **Map** p310
A2/p312 A2.
This is a small, friendly bar for thirtysomethings,
who are attracted by its warm, pub-on-a-winter's-
evening interior and general lack of pretence.
Morgan's has the advantage of being located in
one of the more agreeable areas of the city: the quiet,
residential (and very affluent) backstreets that lie
to the south of piazza Sant'Ambrogio. In addition to
speaking fluent English, Jimmy, the Sri Lankan
barman, mixes many a mean cocktail, the prices of
which range from €5.50 to €6.50.

The pursuit of happiness

If cocktails took off in Milan bars in the
1960s (courtesy of Bar Basso, *see p128*)
and US-style brunch was all the rage in the
1980s, then it was the turn of another import
in the 1990s: happy hour.

But while cocktails
and brunch remained
faithful to their original
meaning, in Milan
happy hour (which
typically lasts three
hours, 6-9pm, as
opposed to one) has
undergone a strange
linguistic and physical
evolution. Your
average Milanese
happy hour does see
a token drop in the
price of drinks, but the
most important thing,
and what ensured its
popularity in this no-
nonsense city, is that
access to a self-service buffet is usually
thrown into the bargain, such as at
Bhangrabar (*see p126*), Le Biciclette
(*see p128*) and Baci e Abbracci (*see p129*).
Indeed many young people use happy hour
as a way of getting a relatively inexpensive
evening meal, since very few places impose
a limit on how much you can eat. You can
keep piling up your plate and, as the manager
of the fashion industry hangout Art Deco
(*see p127*) puts it: 'Happy hour customers
can keep eating until they're sick and we
won't say anything.'

Of course, happy hour isn't to everyone's
liking: more traditional establishments such

as Jamaica and Bar Basso have never gone
in for it, and the appeal is wearing off for
many customers: after all, being charged
€5 for a drink makes sense if you're going
to stuff your face; it doesn't if you just want
a glass of mineral
water before heading
elsewhere for dinner.

So, now that even
the prospect of free
food is no longer
guaranteed to entice
customers, bars are
also going in for art
and photography
exhibitions – another
marked Milan bar
trend. Bars in the arty
Brera area have been
doing this for decades,
but plenty of others
have recently followed
suit. Fresco Art near
Porta Romana, for
example, now displays work by students at
the Italian Photography Institute. It's a smart
idea: prospective couples can always discuss
the pictures on the wall if conversation proves
difficult on their first date.

The other tactic for luring the punters is
a thing called public relations, which, like
happy hour, has undergone a subtle change
in meaning: in Milan, it often means paying
famous people to frequent an establishment
in order to create a celeb buzz. Yet in a
country where expensive lawsuits have
replaced duelling as the main way of
expressing offence, we'll refrain from
suggesting which bars might be doing this.

Shops & Services

Do it till you drop, then get up and do it some more.

If you're under the impression that Milan's greatest attraction is Leonardo's *Last Supper*, think again. As every self-respecting fashionista knows, the city's number-one asset is its shops. For proof, put on your best togs and take a glance at the lobby of the Four Seasons hotel (the international fashion crowd's favourite lodgings) any day of the week. There may be a couple of cultural mags on the concierge's desk, but they'll be more or less invisible behind the array of designer shopping bags delivered from the nearby boutiques (Prada, Gucci, Armani et al) to hotel guests.

SO MANY SHOPS, SO LITTLE TIME...

When it comes to shopping in Italy, there are several reasons why Milan is the hands-down winner. First of all, Milan is the home of dozens of top designers, including Giorgio Armani, Miuccia Prada, Donatella Versace, (Domenico) Dolce & (Stefano) Gabbana, Mariuccia Mandelli (Krizia) and Gianfranco Ferré. Because there's always the risk that the designers might set foot in their own stores, shop managers are keen to *fare bella figura* (look the part) by having up-to-the-minute interiors, jaw-droppingly handsome sales assistants and the very best stock.

What's more, many of the stores have special features that you won't find anywhere but Milan: Armani's megastore in via Manzoni is the largest in the world; the Prada store in Galleria Vittorio Emanuele (est 1913) is the globe's oldest; while Gianfranco Ferré's boutique on via Sant'Andrea boasts an attached spa. Other designer 'specials' include the Dolce & Gabbana men's boutique on corso Venezia, with a barber, a health spa and super-smooth cocktail bar, and the Krizia store on via della Spiga, which also has a small bar. For ideas on where to pick up your designer gear, *see p136* **After the fashion?**

Those who are allergic to big brands should head to the smaller, more alternative stores on corso di Porta Ticinese (*see p144* **Navigli newcomers**) or in the Brera area. Other zones worth a trawl include the upcoming corso Vercelli, and the art nouveau-lined roads in the Isola area, behind Stazione Garibaldi. For the Italian version of Bridget Jones-style high-street shopping, try corso Buenos Aires, via Torino or corso Vittorio Emanuele. Though most of the shoppers on these lesser streets still look intimidatingly smart, head-to-toe Prada is not obligatory here.

But those whose budget has boundaries will find plenty of reasons to shop here, too. The city's dense concentration of fashion houses means that it's one of the best places to pick up bargain designer stock. Shops selling end-of-season returns, catwalk cast-offs and seconds abound, as do boutiques selling second-hand and vintage clothing handed down by wealthy *signoras* (not surprisingly, it seems there are a lot of well-dressed people in this city whose wardrobes are just too full). You'll also find heart-stopping bargains on the markets – from Gucci shoes to cashmere sweaters, all at prices that even the lowest-budget traveller can afford. (*see p148* **Chic for less** *and p142* **Market leaders**).

DESIGN CENTRAL

A second reason for shopping in Milan is that it is the undisputed world capital of furniture and household design. Each April, around 200,000 design types flock here for the Salone Internazionale del Mobile, one of Europe's main furniture fairs (*see p152*), and companies located around and about Milan include Cappellini, B&B Italia, Kartell and Alessi; Brianza, an area just outside the city, is a major furniture production zone. All have showrooms and stores in Milan; you'll find a good number of them along via Durini (*see p133* **Via del Design**). Here, you can pick up anything, from a designer toilet brush to a carving knife by Philippe Starck.

EAT YOUR HEART OUT

Close behind 'fashion' and 'furniture' is the third 'F' on any serious shopper's list: 'food'. Foodies' paradise Peck (*see p141*) is the sort of shop that sends even the most self-denying health freak into a gluttony-fuelled shopping spin, while the piles of mouthwatering goodies at the Mercato Comunale at piazza Wagner (*see p142* **Market leaders**) will have those from less food-centric cultures reeling in disbelief.

OPENING HOURS

Generally speaking, Tuesday to Saturday retail hours are 9.30am-12.30pm and 3.30-7.30pm, with a half day on Monday (3.30-7.30pm), though increasingly clothing boutiques in the 'Golden Rectangle' (between via della Spiga and via Montenapoleone, via Manzoni and corso Venezia) open on Monday mornings. The rule that everything is closed on Sundays still holds true for many shops, though fashion stores stay open during the major fashion fairs. Throughout the year, most shops in downtown Milan no longer close for lunch.

If you're travelling in December, you'll find almost all of the city's stores open for pre-Christmas shopping all day, every day. Not so in August, when most of Milan shuts down for the summer holidays.

TAX REFUNDS

Non-EU residents can claim back the value added tax (*IVA* in Italian) on purchases totalling over €154.94 from a single store that displays a 'Tax-Free Shopping' sign. To do so, ask for a 'VAT back' form at the moment of purchase, keep your receipts, and pack your unworn, newly acquired stuff at the top of your suitcase (you may have to show it). Then have the receipts for your goods stamped at customs when you leave Italy and submit your 'VAT back' paperwork.

There are refund centres at Malpensa and Linate airports (open 7am-11pm daily). There's also a tax free centre on the seventh floor of La Rinascente department store (open 9am-10pm Mon-Sat; 10am-8pm Sun; for address, *see p135*), where you can get your cash back before leaving the country. However, you'll still have to queue to clear documents at the airport upon leaving. For more information, check the www.globalrefund.com website or phone 800 018 415 (free, from inside Italy only).

Antiques

Via Pisacane (metro Porta Venezia) is home to over 30 antique shops, selling everything from ceramics, to prints and antique timepieces. Otherwise, shops dealing in furnishings from the 16th to the 19th centuries are located along the ancient vie Lanzone, Caminadella, San Giovanni sul Muro and Santa Marta. Many of the shops here are decidedly knick-knacky and deal in odds and ends that can easily be carried home, such as frames, vases and jewellery. The pocket guide *Milano Cultura & Shopping*, available free in any of the neighbourhood's antique shops, gives a brief history of the area that will enhance your walk through Milan's oldest quarter.

Antik Arte e Scienza

Via San Giovanni sul Muro 10, Centre (02 8646 1448/www.antik.it). Metro Cadorna or Cairoli/bus 18, 50, 58/tram 1, 18, 20. **Open** 3.30-7.30pm Mon; 10am-1pm, 3.30-7.30pm Tue-Sat. Closed Aug. **Credit** AmEx, DC, MC, V. **Map** p310 A2/p312 A1.
Run by the extremely knowledgeable Daniela Giorgi, Antik specialises in scientific (especially astronomical and medical) objects, tools, compasses, globes and brass measuring devices.

La Biscaglina

Via Lanzone 27, West (02 805 7272). Metro Sant'Ambrogio/bus 94. **Open** 3.30-7.30pm Mon; 9.30am-12.30pm, 3.30-7.30pm Tue-Sat. Closed Aug. **No credit cards**. **Map** p310 A2/p312 A2, B1.
La Biscaglina is run by a trained architect with an eye for collecting pieces with rustic charm from throughout Italy. Painted cabinets are a speciality.

Pit, 21

Via Santa Marta 21, Centre (02 8901 3169). Metro Cordusio or Missori/bus 54, 65/tram 2, 3, 14, 19. **Open** 2-7pm Mon; 10am-7pm Tue-Sat. Closed 3wks Aug. **Credit** DC, MC, V. **Map** p310 A2/p312 A2.
Contemporary design sits alongside period pieces in this well-curated, unusually large antiques store. Pit, 21 seamlessly blends the old with the new, East with West, humour and elegance into a coherent entity.

Understate/Raimondo Garau

Via Varese 20 (enter from viale Crispi), North (02 6269 0435). Metro Moscova/bus 41, 49/tram 3, 4. **Open** 10am-1pm, 3-7.30pm Tue-Sat. **Credit** MC, V. **Map** p308 B2.
On one side of the shop are 'really old' antiques; on the other, reproductions and originals of the greatest furniture hits from the 20th century. Understate has a lovely spacious showroom, but the real action takes place in the overstuffed basement. Ask to see it.

Artists' supplies & stationery

Fabriano

Via Verri 3, East (02 7631 8754). Metro Montenapoleone or San Babila/bus 54, 64, 91. **Open** 3-7.30pm Mon; 10am-7.30pm Tue-Sat. Closed 3wks Aug. **Credit** AmEx, DC, MC, V. **Map** p309 C1/p312 B1, C1.
This quality papermaker dates back to 1264, but its products are totally up to date, and include writing paper in contemporary colours, as well as art, photocopying and security paper. Even Italy's euros are printed on the company's paper.

F Pettinaroli

Piazza San Fedele 2 (entrance in via Marino), Centre (02 8646 4642/www.fpettinaroli.it). Metro Duomo/bus 61/tram 1, 2, 20. **Open** 3-7pm Mon; 9am-1pm, 3-7pm Tue-Sat. Closed Aug. **Credit** AmEx, MC, V. **Map** p311 A1/p312 B1.
Staff wearing green surgical uniforms serve from behind wooden cabinets at this delightfully old-fashioned stationer and printer. On sale: paper with traditional designs, old prints and maps, plus more banal items such as Filofax pages, diaries and pens.

Mastri Cartai e Dintorni

Corso Garibaldi 26/34, North (02 805 2311/www.mastricartai.com). Metro Lanza/bus 57, 70/tram 3, 4. **Open** 3.30-7.30pm Mon; 11am-7.30pm Tue-Sat. Closed 3wks Aug. **Credit** AmEx, DC, MC, V. **Map** p308 B2, C2.

Via del Design

Milan's number-one slot on the world household-design rankings is well deserved. The city is stuffed to the brim with sleek stores and showrooms, many of which are unique. Until recently, however, there was no 'Design Quarter' in Milan, and design aficionados had to flit from zone to zone, wielding maps and guidebooks, to track down the spots they couldn't miss. Now, though, several design companies have taken over spaces on via Durini, in the centre of Milan.

Where else would Giorgio Armani locate his largest **Armani Casa** (No.24, 02 7600 3030) store? Drop in for bronze bowls, streamlined cutlery and little candles, all in Giorgio's fave tones of grey, beige, cream and black.

The list of doyennes who have designed for minimalist kings **B&B Italia** (No.14, 02 764 441) reads like a who's who of international design. You'll find geometric vases by Ettore Sottsass, salad bowls by Arne Jacobsen and kitchen utensils by Milanese design hero Antonio Citterio – all displayed on museum-like plinths in this massive store.

When Milanese design starts to feel just a bit too slick, head to **Gervasoni** (No.7, 02 780 414) for a spot of ethno-chic relief. Thinking of snapping up a holiday home in warmer climes? This is the place to pick up a rattan pouffe or a wicker-wrapped electric fan.

If your suitcases still aren't stuffed, check out **Alessi** (corso Matteotti 9, 02 795 726), no more than a couple of hops, skips and jumps away. Here you'll find everything the company has ever done in fluorescent plastic and shiny polished steel – from toothpick holders to the famous Merdolino toilet brush. See also p192 **Aladdin's cave**.

Along the street from Alessi is **De Padova** (corso Venezia 14, 02 777 201), one of Milan's loveliest designer stores. In and among the serious designer stuff, you'll find witty little bits and bobs, like designer dishcloths and repro vintage toy cars.

Just five minutes from piazza San Babila is **Sawaya & Moroni** (via Manzoni 11, 02 874 549). Serious designers come here to check out the wave-backed armchairs by William Sawaya, and the landscape-inspired furniture by Iraqi-British architect Zaha Hadid. If these are a little too bulky, invest in a lime-green crocodile-skin tray, or in Hadid's solid silver tea and coffee set, displaying her trademark, how-on-earth-will-that-stay-upright? sloping sides.

The texturally rich, handmade paper sold at Mastri Cartai sparks the imagination and begs the question of where paper stops and fine art begins. Products here run the gamut from thick, brightly coloured card up to fine jute netting. You'll be hard-pushed to leave the shop without one of the store's delightful signature *sculture luminose* (paper lampshades).

Pellegrini
Via Brera 16, North (02 805 7119). Metro Lanza/ bus 61/tram 3, 4, 12, 20. **Open** 8.30am-7pm Mon-Fri; 8.30am-1pm, 2.30-7pm Sat. Closed 2wks Aug. **Credit** AmEx, DC, MC, V. **Map** p308 C2/p312 B2.
Any international artist worth their salt will want to make an obligatory stop at this venerable shop to peruse its vast assortment and unique selection of fine art products. Prices are competitive, and the service competent and courteous. To make things even more enticing, Pellegrini is strategically located near the Pinacoteca di Brera (*see p71*).

Bookshops

La Feltrinelli
Via Ugo Foscolo 1/3 (enter from piazza Duomo, through Autogrill), Centre (02 8699 6903/www. lafeltrinelli.it). Metro Duomo/bus 54, 60, 65/tram 12, 20, 23, 27. **Open** 10am-11pm Mon-Sat; 10am-8pm Sun. **Credit** AmEx, DC, MC, V. **Map** p311 A1.
One of Italy's leading book chains, this central store has lots of titles in English, including one of the city's best selection of English-language travel books.

La Feltrinelli International
Piazza Cavour 1, North (02 6595 644/www.la feltrinelli.it). Metro Turati/bus 61, 94/tram 12, 29, 30. **Open** 9am-7.30pm Mon-Sat; 10am-1.30pm, 3.30-7pm Sun. **Credit** AmEx, DC, MC, V. **Map** p309 C1.
This recently opened branch of La Feltrinelli has an excellent choice of books in English, Spanish, French, German, Portuguese, Romanian, Albanian

www.urushi.it

CA-DO

E S S E N T I A L   L I V I N G

LINEAR, MINIMAL, ESSENTIAL.
The beds manufactured by URUSHI
mingle together your wish to sleep
naturally with the need to decorate
your private spaces with first-class furniture.
URUSHI's style talks to your soul,
whispering to it. URUSHI's style.

FU-CI

SHIMA

and Russian. There are also well-stocked travel and cookery sections, plus a large range of international magazines and DVDs.

Fnac
Via Torino, at via della Palla 2, Centre (02 869 541). Metro Duomo/tram 2, 3, 4. **Open** 9am-8pm Mon-Sat; 10am-8pm Sun. **Credit** AmEx, DC, MC, V. **Map** p310 A2/p312 A2.
Part of the French chain, Fnac has books (some in English), CDs, a photo-developing service, electronic gadgets, a café, an exhibition space and an internet point. It also sells tickets for concerts, theatre and sporting events (*see p150*).

Libreria Internazionale Ulrico Hoepli
Via Ulrico Hoepli 5, Centre (02 864 871/www. hoepli.it). Metro Duomo/bus 54, 60, 65/tram 12, 20, 23, 27. **Open** 10am-7.30pm Mon-Sat. **Credit** AmEx, DC, MC, V. **Map** p311 A1/p312 B1.
Swiss-born publisher Ulrico Hoepli established this bookstore in 1870, originally specialising in scientific and technical books. Today it is the most complete source in Milan for books in any language, on any subject. There's even an extensive selection of English-language books on a variety of topics within each subject heading.

Messaggerie Musicali
Corso Vittorio Emanuele, Centre (02 760 551). Metro Duomo/bus 54, 60, 65/tram 12, 20, 23, 27. **Open** 1-8.30pm Mon; 10am-11pm Tue-Sun. **Credit** AmEx, DC, MC, V. **Map** p311 A1/p312 B2, C1.
This large book and music store has a vast selection of English-language books on the first floor, plus the best selection of Italian-language learning textbooks in Milan. There's also a ticket counter for concerts and other events (*see p150*).

Panton's English Bookshop
Via Mascheroni 12 (entrance in via Ariosto), West (02 469 4468/4549 7568/www.english bookshop.it). Metro Conciliazione/bus 68/tram 29. **Open** 9.30am-7.30pm Mon-Sat. Closed 10 days Aug. **Credit** AmEx, DC, MC, V. **Map** p308 C1.
Founded in 1979, this shop boasts the most varied and comprehensive English-language selection of both fiction and non-fiction in the city. There are also English-language DVDs, audio books, rare antiquarian history and travel books and an extensive children's section, plus a noticeboard with expat community postings.

Department stores

Coin
Piazza Cinque Giornate 1a, East (02 5519 2083). Bus 60/tram 12, 20, 23, 27. **Open** 10am-8.30pm Mon-Sat; 10am-8pm Sun. **Credit** AmEx, DC, MC, V. **Map** p311 A2.
A retail focal point on the mid-priced shopping street of corso di Porta Vittoria, this multi-storey department store caters to the refined Milanese

taste for classic, high-quality, good-value clothing and accessories for men, women and children. It also sells homeware, cosmetics and shoes, plus there's a restaurant and two bars.
Other locations: corso Vercelli 30/32, West (02 4399 0001); piazzale Cantore 12, South (02 8940 9550).

La Rinascente
Piazza Duomo, Centre (02 88 521). Metro Duomo/ bus 54, 60, 65/tram 12, 20, 23, 27. **Open** 9am-10pm Mon-Sat; 10am-8pm Sun. **Credit** AmEx, DC, MC, V. **Map** p311 A1/p312 B2.
This eight-floor colossus is distinguished by a sporty actionwear department at the back of the first and second floors, reached by a well-hidden indoor bridge. But the store sells everything you can think of – from lingerie to colourful ceramics. On the top floor there is a tax-free shopping information point, a glass-roofed branch of chic hairdresser's Aldo Coppola, an Estée Lauder spa, plus an indoor and outdoor café where you will be at roughly the same height as the visitors walking the Duomo's roof.

Fashion: accessories

Most designer brands and fashion boutiques offer a selection of accessories in their shops, and are sometimes the best source for fashionable bits and pieces, including bags, belts, jewellery, shoes and underwear (*see p136* **After the fashion?**). For lower-priced alternatives, *see p148* **Chic for less**, or take a hike around the markets (*see p142* **Market leaders**).

Jewellery & watches

Donatella Pellini
Via Manzoni 20, East (02 7600 8084). Metro Montenapoleone/tram 12, 20. **Open** 3.30-7.30pm Mon; 9.30am-7.30pm Tue-Sat. Closed Aug. **Credit** AmEx, DC, MC, V. **Map** p309 C1/p312 B1.
Ms Pellini augments her own signature synthetic-resin jewellery designs with baubles and bangles that she collects during her worldwide travels. Not a shy piece among them.

Era L'Ora
Corso Magenta 22, West (02 8645 0965). Metro Cadorna/bus 18, 58 /tram 20, 24, 29, 30. **Open** 10am-7pm Tue-Sat. Closed Aug. **Credit** AmEx, DC, MC, V. **Map** p308 C1, C2.
This time-oriented shop (the name means 'about time') specialises in rare vintage wrist and pocket watches, as well as clocks. Sales, repairs and restoration of the utmost quality are all done in-house.

La Gioielleria del Corso Vercelli
Corso Vercelli 2, West (02 469 4169). Metro Conciliazione/bus 18/tram 24. **Open** 9.30am-1pm, 3-7pm Tue-Sat. Closed 3wks Aug. **Credit** AmEx, DC, MC, V. **Map** p308 C1.

After the fashion?

No place on earth makes designer devotees happier than the famed Golden Rectangle (*see p76*) between via Spiga, via Montenapoleone, via Manzoni and via Sant'Andrea. You'll find more designer stores per square inch here than just about anywhere else in the world, so if hunting out hard-to-find catwalk pieces is your thing, you can do no better than head here.

The area is best reached from metro Montenapoleone or San Babila, by bus 15 or tram 2. Once upon a time, label-hunters were disappointed on Monday mornings, as most of the stores were closed. In these harder times, however, most hawk their wares all day, every day Monday to Saturday; many even stay open on Sundays in December and during the major fashion fairs. Exceptions to these rules are given below. All will accept any kind of plastic you flash at them.

Here's a list of the principal ones:

Giorgio Armani

Superstore: *Via Manzoni 31 (02 7231 8600)*. **Open** 10.30am-7.30pm Mon-Sat.
Giorgio Armani: *Via Sant'Andrea 9 (02 7600 3234)*. **Open** 10.30am-7.30pm Mon-Sat.
Accessories: *Via della Spiga 19 (02 783 511)*. **Open** 10am-7pm Mon-Sat.
Armani Collezioni: *Via Montenapoleone 2 (02 7639 0068)*. **Open** 10.30am-7.30pm Mon-Sat.
Armani Casa: *Via Durini 24 (02 7600 3030)*. **Open** 3-7.30pm Mon; 10.30am-7.30pm Tue-Sat.
Armani Junior: *Via Montenapoleone 10 (in arcade) (02 783 196)*. **Open** 3-7pm Mon; 10am-7pm Tue-Sat.

Cacharel

Via San Paolo 1 (02 8901 1127). **Open** 3.30-7.30pm Mon; 10am-7.30pm Tue-Sat.

Roberto Cavalli

Via della Spiga 42 (02 7602 0900). **Open** 3-7pm Mon; 10am-7pm Tue-Sat.

Chanel

Via Sant'Andrea 10a (02 782 514). **Open** 10am-7pm Mon-Sat.

Dolce & Gabbana

Womenswear: *Via della Spiga 2 (02 7600 1155)*.
Accessories: *Via della Spiga 26 (02 795 747)*.
Menswear: *Corso Venezia 15 (02 7602 8485)*.
D&G: *Corso Venezia 7 (02 7600 4091)*.
Vintage: *Via della Spiga 26 (02 799 950)*.
Open (all shops) 10am-7pm Mon-Sat.

Etro

Via Montenapoleone 5 (02 7600 5049). **Open** 10am-7pm Mon-Sat.
Perfumes: *Via Verri, at via Bigli 2 (02 7600 5450)*. **Open** 3-7pm Mon; 10am-1.30pm, 2.30-7pm Tue-Sat.
Made-to-measure: *Via Montenapoleone 5 (02 7639 4216)*. **Open** 10am-1.30pm, 2.30-7pm Mon-Sat.

Exté

Via della Spiga 6 (02 783 050). **Open** 3-7pm Mon; 10am-7pm Tue-Sat.

Fendi

Via Sant'Andrea 16 (02 7602 1617). **Open** 10am-7pm Mon-Sat.

Gianfranco Ferré

Via Sant'Andrea 15 (02 794 864). **Open** 10am-7pm Mon-Sat.

Alberta Ferretti

Via Montenapoleone 21a (02 7602 2780). **Open** 10am-7pm Mon-Sat.

Romeo Gigli

Via della Spiga 30 (02 7601 1983). **Open** 10am-7pm Mon-Sat.

Gucci

Via Montenapoleone 5-7 (02 771 271). **Open** 10am-7pm Mon-Sat.

Hermès

Via Sant'Andrea 21 (02 7600 3495). **Open** 3-7pm Mon; 10am-7pm Tue-Sat.

Hugo Boss

Corso Matteotti 11 (02 7639 4667). **Open** 3-7pm Mon; 10am-7pm Tue-Sat.

Helmut Lang

Via della Spiga 11 (02 7639 0255). **Open** 10am-7.30pm Mon-Sat.

Eat, Drink, Shop

Menswear, men's accessories, women's shoes, men's and women's sportswear: *Via Sant'Andrea 21 (02 7600 1426)*. Accessories: *Via della Spiga 1 (02 7600 2019)*. **Open** (all shops) 10am-7.30pm Mon-Sat. Lingerie: *Via della Spiga 5 (02 7601 4448)*. **Open** 10am-2pm, 3-7.30pm Mon-Sat.

Paul Smith
Via Manzoni 30 (02 7631 9181).
Open 10am-7pm Mon-Sat.

Trussardi
Accessories and home collection: *Piazza della Scala 5 (02 806 8821)*. Womenswear and menswear: *Via Sant'Andrea 3-7 (02 7602 0380)*. **Open** (both shops) 10am-7pm Mon-Sat. T-Store (casualwear): *Galleria Strasburgo 3 (02 7601 1313)*. **Open** 3-7pm Mon; 10am-2pm, 3-7pm Tue-Sat.

Bruno Magli
Corso Vittorio Emanuele, at via San Paolo (02 865 695).
Open 10am-7pm Mon-Sat.
Via Manzoni 14 (02 7631 7478).
Open 10am-1pm, 2-7pm Mon-Sat.

MaxMara
Piazza del Liberty 4 (02 7600 8849).
Open 10am-7.30pm Mon-Sat.

Miu Miu
Corso Venezia 3 (02 7600 1799).
Open 10am-7.30pm Mon-Sat.

Moschino
Via della Spiga 30 (02 7600 4320).
Via Sant'Andrea 12 (02 7600 0832).
Open (both shops) 10am-7pm Mon-Sat.

Philosophy by Alberta Ferretti
Via Montenapoleone 19 (02 796 034).
Open 10am-7pm Mon-Sat.

Prada
Womenswear, menswear, sportswear, shoes, bags, eyewear: *Galleria Vittorio Emanuele II 63/65 (02 876 979)*. Menswear, men's accessories: *Via Montenapoleone 6 (02 7602 0273)*. Womenswear, women's accessories, men's bags: *Via Montenapoleone 8 (02 777 1771)*.

Valentino
Uomo: *Via Montenapoleone 20 (02 7602 0285)*
Donna: *Via Santo Spirito 3 (02 7600 6478)*
Open (both) 10am-7pm Mon-Sat.

Gianni Versace
Via Montenapoleone 11 (02 7600 8528).
Versus: *Via San Pietro all'Orto 10 (02 7601 4722)*.
Home collection: *Via San Pietro all'Orto 11 (02 7601 4544)*.
Open (all shops) 10am-7pm Mon-Sat.

Louis Vuitton
Via Montenapoleone 2 (02 777 1711).
Open 9.30am-7.30pm Mon-Sat; 11am-7.30pm Sun.
The new Vuitton store is scheduled to open in Galleria Vittorio Emanuele II, opposite Prada, in spring 2004.

Ermenegildo Zegna
Via Pietro Verri 3 (02 7600 6437).
Open 10am-7pm Mon-Sat.

Authorised dealer of trendy watchmakers Locman, Gucci, Emporio Armani, Tissot and Baume & Mercier, with a fine jewellery range from Damiani, Pomellato, DoDo, Visconti, Gavello, Talento and others. The atmosphere is relaxed but professional.

Shoes

Les Amis
Corso Garibaldi 127, North (02 653 061). *Metro Moscova/bus 41, 43, 94/tram 3, 4, 12, 14.* **Open** 3.30-7.30pm Mon; 10am-7.30pm Tue-Sat. Closed 3wks Aug. **Credit** AmEx, DC, MC, V. **Map** p308 B2, C2.

This is a tiny women's shoe shop that packs a real punch. There's always something out of the ordinary at Les Amis, but it also offers enough jazzed-up basics to keep the bills paid. Boots are its strong suit. A sister store selling last season's stock and lower-priced items recently opened a couple of doors away.

Pollini
Piazza Duomo 31, Centre (02 875 187). Metro *Duomo/bus 54, 60, 65/tram 12, 20, 23, 27.* **Open** 2.30-7.30pm Mon; 10am-7.30pm Tue-Sat; 10am-1pm, 2-7pm Sun. **Credit** AmEx, DC, MC, V. **Map** p311 A1/p312 B2.

Pollini is a leading name in sombre yet razor-sharp footwear for men and women. Nobody will doubt that these shoes were made in Italy; add a matching belt and bag and you almost qualify for national citizenship. They also do a nice line in leather and fabric jackets, cardigans and trousers.

Le Solferine
Via Solferino 2, North (02 655 5352). Metro *Moscova/bus 41, 43, 94/tram 3, 4, 12, 14.* **Open** 3-7.30pm Mon; 10am-7.30pm Tue-Sat. **Credit** AmEx, DC, MC, V. **Map** p308 B2, C2.

Le Solferine has a choice selection of shoes for men and women that's slightly left of offbeat. Silver glitter winkle-pickers set the standard… no plain Janes here.

Fashion: boutiques

At the following multi-label boutiques, the buyers have cherry-picked items from the designer collections to create their own edited version of the fashion world for you to enjoy.

Antonioli
Via Pasquale Paoli 1, at Porta Ticinese, South (02 3656 6494/www.antoniolishop.com). Metro Porta Genova/bus 47, 74/tram 2, 9. **Open** 3-8pm Mon; 11am-8pm Tue-Sat, last Sun of each month, every Sun during fashion weeks. Closed 3wks August. **Credit** AmEx, DC, MC, V. **Map** p310 B1.

A hit with the crowds of fashion types that periodically swamp Milan. Most of the clothes are dark and conceptual – and the decor (which includes an electro-coloured steel ramp and scraped-down walls)

is designed to match. The labels on sale are mostly small and quirky, and include Alexander McQueen, Helmut Lang, Rick Owens and Haute.

Biffi
Corso Genova 6, South (02 831 1601/www.biffi.com). Metro Sant'Ambrogio/bus 94/tram 2, 14. **Open** 3-7.30pm Mon; 9.30am-1.30pm, 3-7.30pm Tue-Sat. Closed 2wks Aug. **Credit** AmEx, DC, MC, V. **Map** p310 B2.

A Milanese institution for men's and women's classic designer choices, Biffi also stocks the mildly wild trend pieces of the season. Among the designers showcased here are Yohji Yamamoto, Marc Jacobs and John Galliano.

Bipa
Via Ponte Vetero 10, North (02 878 168). Metro Cairoli/bus 18, 50, 58, 61/tram 1, 3, 4, 12, 14. **Open** 3-7pm Mon; 10am-7pm Tue-Sat. Closed 3wks Aug. **Credit** AmEx, DC, MC, V. **Map** p308 C2/p312 A1.

Bipa offers fashion forward-picks of the daring designers. It-girls will delight in the fashion lunacy, but be warned: most of the garments at this boutique will not outlive their sell-by date.

Love Therapy by Elio Fiorucci
Largo Toscanini 1, at corso Europa, East (02 7609 1237). Metro San Babila/bus 54, 60, 65/tram 12, 20, 27. **Open** 10am-8pm Mon-Sat; 1-8pm Sun. **Credit** AmEx, DC, MC, V. **Map** p311 A1/p312 C1.

When Milan's famed Fiorucci store closed down in 2003, the city's fashionistas suffered withdrawal symptoms. But those who can't get through a trip to Milan without a Fiorucci fix should head for this tiny new store. Snap up a couple of the designer's kitschy cool pieces (including T-shirts, heart-splattered bags, fuchsia feather lamps… or furry handcuffs) – and you might start to feel a little better.

No Season
Corso di Porta Ticinese 77, South (02 8942 3332). Metro Porta Genova/tram 3, 2, 14. **Open** 3-7.30pm Mon; 10am-1pm, 3-7.30pm Tue-Sat. Closed 2wks Aug. **Credit** AmEx, DC, MC, V. **Map** p310 A2, B2/p312 A2.

Men's, women's and children's fashions and shoes, along with all the necessary music, books and gadgets to fill in the spaces of modern urban living. Labels include: Givenchy, Costume National, Victor & Rolf. An oasis of cool and calm in a happily chaotic shopping street.

Plus
Piazza Missori 2, Centre (02 8646 1820). Metro Missori/bus 54, 63/tram 4, 15, 24. **Open** 3-7pm Mon; 10am-7pm Tue-Fri; 10am-1.30pm, 2.30-7pm Sat. Closed 3wks Aug. **Credit** AmEx, DC, MC, V. **Map** p310 A2/p312 B2.

Clothes, shoes and accessories to enhance your own unique personality without being overtly unique themselves. An intelligent, wearable mix of modern classics and contemporary lines, for women only. On the racks: Jean Paul Gaultier, Philosophy by Alberta Ferretti, Marithè + François Girbaud, Chine.

La Perla is one of the many gems in via Montenapoleone's crown. *See p141.*

10 Corso Como

Corso Como 10, North (02 2900 2674). Metro Garibaldi/tram 11, 29, 30, 33. **Open** 3-7.30pm Mon; 10.30am-7.30pm Tue, Fri-Sun; 10.30am-9pm Wed, Thur. **Credit** AmEx, DC, MC, V. **Map** p308 B2.

This emporium is owned by former *Italian Vogue* editor Carla Sozzani. Prices are not for the faint-hearted, but this place is a must-see for neophyte and seasoned fashionistas alike. The merchandise mix includes men's and women's fashions, accessories, shoes, bags, housewares, books and CDs; the common denominator throughout is the doyenne's unmistakable penchant for the thoroughly modern with a hint of the rough-hewn.

Bargain hunters will be relieved to learn that 10 Corso Como now has an outlet selling last season's stock at cut prices (via Tazzoli 3, North; 02 2901 5130. Open 1-7pm Wed-Fri; 11am-7pm Sat, Sun).

2Link Black Label

Via Solferino 46 (02 8907 6833). Metro Moscova/ bus 41, 43, 94. **Open** 3-8pm Mon, Sun; 10.30am-8pm Tue-Sat. Closed 3wks Aug. **Credit** AmEx, DC, MC, V. **Map** p308 B2.

A decidedly avant-garde selection of men's and women's clothing, plus accessories with a deconstructionist essence. The experimental style flows into related merchandise such as vases, jewellery and pasta sauces by trendy food company Dress Italian.

Zap!

Galleria Passarella 2, Centre (02 7606 7501). Metro San Babila/bus 54, 60, 65/tram 12, 20, 27. **Open** 10-7pm Mon-Sat. Closed 2wks Aug. **Credit** AmEx, DC, MC, V. **Map** p311 A1.

This small department store offers a constantly evolving merchandise mix. There are around 40 women's labels, including Blumarine, Laltramoda

and Roberto Cavalli lingerie. There is also a tiny second-hand section in the basement, a selection of collector's Barbie dolls, jewellery by Tarina Tarantino (of Hello Kitty fame), shoes and accessories. An Aldo Coppola hair salon crowns the top floor.

Fashion: designer boutiques

Anybody who is a fashion anybody has an outlet in Milan: just slink around the chic alleyways of high fashion along via Montenapoleone and via Spiga (*see p136* **After the fashion?**) and you'll see what we mean. Big-name stars aside, the following are Italian designers who may not have a global marketing team placing their products in the suburbs of Tokyo, but still have their own following of fashion insiders.

Lorella Braglia

Via Solferino, at via Ancona, North (02 2901 4514). Metro Moscova or Moscova/bus 43, 61/tram 20. **Open** 3-7pm Mon; 10am-2pm, 3.30-7.30pm Tue-Sat. Closed 3wks Aug. **Credit** AmEx, DC, MC, V. **Map** p308 C2.

Perfectly balanced lines, luxurious fabrics and a young quirky attitude sum up this very feminine, modern line of women's clothing, in which fashion acumen is expressed with sufficient subtlety to allow the wearer's own personality to shine through.

Luisa Beccaria

Via Formentini 1, North (02 863 807). Metro Lanza/bus 57, 70/tram 3, 4, 12, 14. **Open** 3-7.30pm Mon; 10am-7.30pm Tue-Sat, third Sun of the month. Closed 1wk Aug. **Credit** AmEx, DC, MC, V. **Map** p308 C2.

With a gentle nod to the classic ladylike lines of yesteryear and a couture sensibility, Ms Beccaria offers impeccable suits and feminine dresses that would make Audrey Hepburn swoon. A selection of children's clothing is also available in the same, finely executed style. At a price, of course…

Martino Midali
Via Ponte Vetero 9, North (02 8646 2707). Metro Cairoli/bus 18, 50, 58, 61/tram 1, 3, 4, 12, 14. **Open** 3-7.30pm Mon; 10am-2pm, 3-7.30pm Tue-Sat. Closed 3wks Aug. **Credit** AmEx, DC, MC, V. **Map** p308 C2/p312 A1.
Martino Midali's fashion is characterised by its use of rich colours, and by texturally interesting knits. It's popular with modern, stylish women who've discovered the comfort and ease of knitwear and will never turn back.

Fashion: leatherwear
Cut
Corso di Porta Ticinese 58, South (02 839 4135). Metro Porta Genova/tram 2, 3, 14. **Open** 3-7.30pm Mon; 10.30am-1.30pm, 3-7.30pm Tue-Sat. Closed Aug. **Credit** AmEx, DC, MC, V. **Map** p310 A2, B2/p312 A2.
Cut is certainly not stocked with the ubiquitous Brad Pitt leather blazers. Instead, you'll find a range of artisan-made and designed, high-quality leather garments for both men and women.

Fashion: lingerie
Christies
Corso Vercelli 51, West (02 4802 2152). Metro Conciliazione or Pagano/bus 18, 67/tram 20, 24, 30. **Open** 3-7pm Mon; 10am-2pm, 3-7pm Tue-Sat. Closed 3wks Aug. **Credit** AmEx, DC, MC, V. **Map** p308 B2.
Christies stocks clean, unfussy but supersexy lingerie, swimwear and a small selection of ready-to-wear pieces. The smooth Tatto ('touch') line comprises bras and knickers with absolutely no stitching. Extra-large sizes too.

Kristina Ti
Via Solferino 18, North (02 653 379). Metro Moscova/bus 41, 43, 94/tram 3, 4, 12, 14. **Open** 3-7pm Mon; 10am-7pm Tue-Sat. Closed 3wks Aug. **Credit** AmEx, DC, MC, V. **Map** p308 B2, C2.
The best thing to come out of Turin since the Fiat Cinquecento, Kristina Ti's lingerie is so delicate, it's almost fragile. Also available is a complete line of super-feminine ready-to-wear.

La Perla
Via Montenapoleone 1, East (02 7600 0460). Metro Montenapoleone or San Babila/bus 54, 61/tram 1, 12, 20. **Open** 3-7pm Mon; 10am-7pm Tue-Sat. Closed 2wks Aug. **Credit** AmEx, DC, MC, V. **Map** p309 C1/p312 B1, C1.
The words sultry, sophisticated and sexy made manifest in lingerie, swimwear and ready-to-wear

gear. How can something so small cost so much? Well, La Perla's delicate garments are of outstanding quality, manufactured in Bologna using only the finest fabrics.

Fashion: mid-range
Avant
Corso Buenos Aires 39, East (02 2951 1115). Metro Lima/bus 60/tram 5, 11, 33. **Open** 2.30-7.30pm Mon; 10.30am-7.30pm Tue-Fri; 10am-7.30pm Sat. **Credit** AmEx, DC, MC, V. **Map** p309 B2.
An enormous shop for women where the merchandise is so close to being ugly that it's fabulous. Dress like a rock star in clothing that screams 'I'm unique' – but is also cheap.

Nadine
Corso Vittorio Emanuele 34, Centre (02 7600 9028/www.nadinefashiongroup.com). Metro Duomo or San Babila/bus 54, 60, 65/tram 12, 20, 27. **Open** 10am-8pm daily. **Credit** AmEx, DC, MC, V. **Map** p311 A1/p312 B2, C1.
Savvy city gals know they can head to Nadine to pick up sexed-up basics at commodity prices as well as the odd directional piece able to update a tired wardrobe instantly. The company is particularly strong on colourful knits. Visit the website for other locations.

PromMod
Via Mazzini 2, at via Torino, Centre (02 7208 0009). Metro Duomo/tram 2, 3, 14, 19, 20, 24. **Open** 10am-8pm daily. **Credit** AmEx, MC, V. **Map** p310 A2/p312 B2.
PromMod has cornered the cute and affordable casualwear market for young women. Clothing and accessories are styled with a French sensibility for colour, pattern and cut that is *très* chic.

Zara
Corso Vittorio Emanuele II 11, Centre (02 7639 8177). Metro Duomo or San Babila/bus 54, 60, 65/tram 12, 20, 27. **Open** 10am-10pm Mon-Sat; 10am-8pm Sun. **Credit** AmEx, DC, MC, V. **Map** p311 A1/p312 B1, C1.
Rumoured to be the Spanish chain's most profitable store worldwide, this branch had Milan's harder-up fashion hounds screaming with relief when it finally opened in the city. Head here to check out the customers: no one knows how to mix Gucci, Prada and Zara better than the Milanese.
Other locations: corso Buenos Aires 54, East (02 2953 3238).

Food & drink
See also p142 **Market leaders**.
Peck
Via Spadari 9, Centre (02 802 3161). Metro Duomo/bus 54, 60, 65/tram 12, 20, 27. **Open** 3-7.30pm Mon; 8.45am-7.30pm Tue-Sat, Sun (in Dec). **Credit** AmEx, DC, MC, V. **Map** p310 A2/p312 B2.

Market leaders

As any seasoned traveller knows, if you want to know how a city's people really live, head to its markets. And since most of Milan's markets aren't exactly tourist hotspots, they offer a particularly rich insight into what the thousands who wouldn't dream of shopping on via Montenapoleone actually eat and wear. They also offer an unparalleled array of bargains for anyone with a sharp eye. Note that no credit cards are accepted at any of the markets listed below.

Antiquariato sul Naviglio Grande

Strada Alzaia Naviglio Grande/Ripa di Porta Ticinese, South (02 8940 9971/www.naviglio grande.mi.it). Metro Porta Genova/bus 59/ tram 3, 9, 15, 20, 29, 30. **Open** *9am-5pm last Sun of every month.* **Map** *p310 B1.*
Four hundred antique dealers display their wares at this picturesque market alongside the canal. Hunt between the furniture stalls for souvenirs to squeeze into your suitcase, from silverware to antique watches to postcards and prints. Local bars and restaurants stay open all day when the market is in full swing.

Fauché

Via Fauché, North. Bus 43, 57/tram 1, 12, 14, 19, 33. **Open** *8.30am-1pm Tue; 8.30am-5pm Sat.* **Map** *p310 B1.*
The fashionistas' favourite market for cut-price designer shoes. You'll find discounted footwear by Gucci and Prada, as well as smaller, more interesting brands like Alessandro dell'Acqua and Les Tropeziennes.

Fiera di Sinigaglia

Darsena Naviglio, South. Metro Porta Genova/bus 59/tram 3, 9, 15, 20, 29, 30. **Open** *8.30am-5pm Sat.* **Map** *p310 B2.*

A flea market, mixing ethnic products, Italian knick-knacks, second-hand military gear, and undisguised junk. A good place to locate your stolen bicycle – or pick up spare parts for next to nothing.

Isola

Piazzale Lagosta/via Garigliano, North. Metro Garibaldi or Zara/bus 43, 82, 83/ tram 2, 4, 11. **Open** *8.30am-1pm Tue; 8.30am-5pm Sat.* **Map** *p309 A1.*
This underrated market is a bargain hunter's delight. Look out for cut-price Tuscan ceramics, end-of-season clothes by Miss Sixty and other labels, offcuts of brightly coloured printed Como silks. Also good for food products and ultra-cheap, wear-once-then-chuck-'em clothes.

Mercato Comunale

Piazza Wagner, West. Metro Wagner/bus 18, 61, 67/tram 20, 24. **Open** *8.30am-1pm Mon; 8.30am-1pm, 4-7.30pm Tue-Sat.* **Map** *off p310 A1.*
Disaster struck this smart, covered market, when subsidence was discovered beneath the building in 2003. Luckily, it has now reopened after a major overhaul. Fruit and flower sellers, fishmongers, butchers and cheese sellers are all here… and the Mercato Comunale remains one of the best places to shop for gourmet food.

Papiniano

Viale Papiniano, West. Metro Sant'Agostino/ bus 50/tram 20, 29, 30. **Open** *8.30am-1pm Tue; 8.30am-5pm Sat.* **Map** *p310 A1, B1.*
The city's most popular open-air market, with food, plants, clothing, shoes, homeware and textiles. Walk past the junk and keep your eyes peeled for designer bargains on the prettier-looking stalls.

A temple of fine food and wine for more than 120 years, Peck was founded in 1883 by a humble pork butcher from Prague, Franz Peck. These days, the main action is in the three-floor flagship shop on via Spadari, where there is a butcher, bakery, dazzling delicatessen, a vast selection of wines (over 1,800 labels from all over the world), prepared foods, oils and bottled sauces, plus a delightful tearoom.

But that's definitely not the whole story, as most of a city block has now become Peck-land. Around the corner at via Victor Hugo 4 is the sit-down restaurant Cracco-Peck (02 76 774, closed

Sat lunch and all Sun, average €100) which has confirmed Carlo Cracco, who honed his craft working with Gualtiero Marchesi (*see p189* **Lombard gourmands**), as one of Italy's most promising young chefs, and which is now considered among the top restaurants in the city. At via Cantù 3, you'll find another of the Peck empire's outposts: a restaurant and bar named Peck Italian Bar.

If your budget doesn't stretch to such gourmet excesses, you can always grab a take-away from the hot food counter in the main store. Peck is the first and last word on bacchanalian and gastronomic delights in Milan.

Confectionery & cakes

Cherubini
*Via Trincea delle Frasche 2, South (02 5410 7486).
Metro Porta Genova/tram 3.* **Open** *Bar* 7am-3pm
Mon-Fri; 7pm-2am Sat, Sun. *Winebar & restaurant*
7pm-2am Mon-Sat. **Credit** AmEx, DC, MC, V.
Map p310 B2.
Although this is a full-service bar and café, it is best
known for its delicious home-made pastries and
brioche breakfast rolls, all made fresh daily on
the premises. Polite service in an old world atmosphere. Located on a tiny street on the south-east side
of piazza XXIV Maggio.

Ethnic food

OK Superpolo
*Largo La Foppa 1, North (02 657 1760). Metro
Moscova/bus 41, 43, 94.* **Open** 9am-8pm Mon-Sat.
Credit MC, V. **Map** p308 B2.
This international food market has a little bit of
everything from many countries around the world,
as well as the basics. A large selection of frozen
goods, dry goods, fresh organic produce, kosher
food, plus dairy and soya-based products.

Health food

Centro Botanico
*Piazza San Marco 1, North (02 2901 3254/www.
centrobotanico.it). Metro Lanza/bus 57, 61, 70/
tram 20.* **Open** 10am-2.30pm, 3.30-8pm Mon-Fri;
10am-8pm Sat; 3-7.30pm Sun. Closed 3wks Aug.
Credit AmEx, DC, MC, V. **Map** p308 C2.
Founded in 1975, this place is a true centre for health
and natural products. It stocks organically grown
produce, macrobiotic groceries, vitamin capsules,
pure fibre clothing, baked goods and more. There's
also a juice bar and café on site. Open for lunch.

Ice-cream

Gelateria Marghera
*Via Marghera 33, West (02 468 641). Metro De
Angeli/tram 24, 63.* **Open** *Oct-Feb* 10am-midnight
daily. *Mar-Sept* 10am-1am daily. **No credit cards.**
Map off 308 C1.
One of Milan's best parlours, Gelateria Marghera
offers a mind-boggling array of flavours, including
a range of chocolate-based ice creams (the rum
chocolate is to die for). The high quality of the
product on sale ensures there are always queues
and that the staff are too harassed to have time for
friendliness. Be prepared.

Viel
*Via Paolo da Cannobio 9, at via Baracchini, Centre
(02 805 5508/www.fruttetoviel.it). Metro Missori/
bus 65/tram 12, 20, 27.* **Open** 9am-12.30am
Mon-Sat. Closed 3wks Aug. **No credit cards.**
Map p311 A1/p312 B2.

An all-time Milanese favourite, Viel serves up some
tasty, straightforward *gelato*, not to mention an
utterly tempting range of excellent fresh-fruit
frullati (smoothies).

Supermarkets

Esselunga
*Viale Papiniano 27, West (02 498 7674/www.
esselunga.it). Metro Sant'Agostino/bus 50/tram
29, 30.* **Open** 8am-9pm Mon-Sat; 9am-8pm Sun.
Credit AmEx, DC, MC, V. **Map** p310 A1, B1.
A large, modern supermarket stocking all major
food brands, plus an extensive line of biologically
pure products and organically grown produce.
There's also a wide-ranging deli counter offering
catering services and some takeaway choices.
Other locations: viale Piave 38 (02 204 7871);
viale Certosa 59 (02 3300 3711) and 26 other stores
throughout the city.

Wine

For a real treat, don't miss the wonderful wines
at **Peck** (*see p141*).

L'Altro Vino
*Viale Piave 9, East (02 780 147). Metro Porta
Venezia/bus 54, 61/tram 9, 20, 29, 30.* **Open**
11.30am-7.45pm Tue-Sat. Closed Aug.
Credit AmEx, DC, MC, V. **Map** p309 C2.

The extremely knowledgeable and approachable proprietors make this a pleasant shop that you can wander around without feeling intimidated. L'Altro Vino offers a vast selection of national and international bottles, with regular tastings organised on the first and third Thursdays of the month.

Health & beauty

As well as boasting state-of-the-art gym facilities, **Downtown Palestre** (see p168 and p180) offers beauty treatments for men and women.

Univers Beauté

Via Conca del Naviglio 18, South (02 8940 0850). Metro Porta Genova/bus 94/tram 2, 9, 14. **Open** 9.30am-6.30pm Tue-Sat. Closed 3wks Aug. **Credit** MC, V. **Map** p310 B2.
If, after shopping yourself silly, you're feeling stressed out and tired, or just in need of a little pampering, head to this all-encompassing beauty store by the Navigli. Facials, body treatments, massage, waxing and more beauty services *pour femme*, from a team of caring professionals. Indulge in the glorious *pedicure estetico e curativo*, which includes rose petals floating in the foot bath.

Navigli newcomers

Located near the hip Navigli area, corso di Porta Ticinese has always offered a more individualist version of fashion than the super-slick streets in the centre of Milan. But over the past couple of years, the street has been in ferment. Artisans have been moving out, and young, urban streetwear brands have been moving in. Fortunately, many artisans are determined not to be pushed around – and most of the global newcomers have adapted to the street's character, stocking one-of-a-kind or vintage pieces that can only be bought here. There are also a number of free-standing fashion boutiques offering an intriguing mix of offbeat clothing, plus several second-hand clothing stores.

Diesel's eccentric owner Renzo Rosso practically staged a takeover when he opened not one, but three boutiques dedicated to the Italian brand along the street. The best is the unmarked **Diesel Store** (No.44, 02 8942 0916), selling one-off prototype jeans and the hard-to-find denim line by Karl Lagerfeld in a homely space filled with vintage memorabilia and antiques. **DieselStyleLab** (No.60, 02 8320 0500) sells the higher-priced, experimental fashion line, while **55DSL** (courtyard of No.75, 02 8324 1649) concentrates on snow, skate and surfboard wear. Not new, but worth checking out, is **B-Fly** (No.46, 02 8942 3178), with remakes of vintage Levi's styles. The models' favourite, **Custo** (No.58, no telephone yet) of Barcelona, is scheduled to open in spring 2004, hawking one-of-a-kind apparel fashioned from vintage bits and bobs picked up around the world. Maverick design team **Marithé + François Girbaud** will also be opening a shop in 2004.

The street's best multibrand fashion boutique is **No Season** (see p138), a temple of designer delights, but the most original finds are to be had at the plethora of stores belonging to artisans and small, Milan-based designers that you won't find anywhere but here. For original, artisan-made leather apparel, go to **Cut** (see p141), or dive into **Anna Fabiano** (No.40, 02 5811 2348) for beautifully tailored jackets and skirts, with patchwork inserts on the collar turn-ups or in the pleats. Another original designer line by Le Petit Bruno is on show at **PP 458** (No.87, 02 8940 2675), a former dry cleaner's. For mid-priced shoes made by artisans in the footwear-producing town of Parabiago, near Milan, don't miss **Panca's** (No.96, 02 839 4543). And for second-hand clothes from a company that has been around since before 'vintage' was a twinkle in the most forward-thinking fashionistas' eye, try **Lo Specchio di Alice** (No.64, 02 5810 3481).

After all this, give your fashion feelers a rest and get some aural pleasure at CD shop **Supporti Fonografici** (see p147), or check out the vintage and contemporary design objects at **Studio 1950** (No.68, 02 836 0304). Each piece has such a strong personality, it is sure to bring a friend or loved one to mind. Finally, the grand merchant of stuff you didn't know you needed (but is so cheap you can't live without) is **Paradiso delle Sorprese** (No.62, 02 835 7187). However, the golden rule on this street is to follow your nose; there are numerous equally worthy boutiques not mentioned here.

Shops on corso di Porta Ticinese generally follow regular trading hours (3.30-7.30pm Mon, 9.30am-12.30pm, 3.30-7.30pm Tue-Sat) and accept, at the very least, MasterCard and Visa. Map p310 A2, B2.

Make-up-mad gals should head to **Madina**.

Body art

GP

Via Ciro Menotti 6, East (338 351 3391 mobile).
Metro Dateo/bus 54, 60, 61, 62/tram 2, 3, 5, 11.
Open 11am-1pm, 3-7pm Tue-Sat. **No credit cards.**
Map p309 C2.
GP stands for Gianpaolo, the friendly owner and
piercer of this tiny and spotlessly clean studio that
is a member of APTI, the Italian tattooists and
piercers' professional union. Prices start from €50
(eyebrows, nose and ear) and rise to €80 for a surface piercing. It's a good idea to call before your visit.

Stigmata Tatuaggi

*Via Arcimboldi 5, Centre (02 860 354). Metro
Duomo/bus 54, 60, 65/tram 2, 3, 14, 27, 20.* **Open**
10.30am-1pm, 2.30-7pm Tue-Sat. **No credit cards.**
Map p311 A1/p312 B2.
Run by Raffaella and Brunella, two sisters who specialise in tribal and figurative tattoos respectively,
Stigmata has been trading since 1996. The reception
area offers photo albums of the girls' work, which
you can look through for inspiration (though they'll
also do custom work from your own design); the ink-
ing action takes place in the downstairs studio,
where all the latest hygiene regulations are followed.

Cosmetics & perfumes

Madina

*Via Meravigli 17, Centre (02 8691 5438). Metro
Cairoli or Cordusio/bus 18/tram 12, 19, 20, 24.*
Open 3.30-7.30pm Mon; 10am-7.30pm Tue-Sat.
Closed 3wks Aug. **Credit** AmEx, DC, MC, V.
Map p308 C2.

Products carrying the name Madina Milano become
coveted souvenirs not only for their high quality, but
also for their international cachet. The line has a
strong following in the beauty trade, as well as
colours galore: 400 lipstick shades, 250 eyeshadows
and 300 foundation, blusher, bronzer and face pow-
der tones.
Other locations: via Tivoli 8, North (02 860 746);
corso Venezia 23, East (02 7601 1692).

Pharmacies

See also p287.

Antica Farmacia di Brera

*Via Fiori Oscuri 13, North (02 8646 1949). Metro
Lanza/bus 57, 61, 70/tram 20.* **Open** 8.30am-1pm,
3.30-7pm Mon-Fri; 9.30am-12.30pm Sat. Closed 3wks
Aug. **Credit** AmEx, MC, V. **Map** p309 C1.
Founded in 1699, this is the oldest pharmacy in
Milan. It stocks everything you'd expect from a mod-
ern pharmacist, but you'll also find homeopathic
products and natural cosmetics.

Farmacia Santa Teresa

*Corso Magenta 96, West (02 4800 6772). Metro
Conciliazione/bus 18, 58/tram 20, 24, 29, 30.*
Open 8.30am-12.30pm, 3.30-7.30pm Mon, Tue,
Thur, Fri; 8.30am-12.30pm Sat; 8.30am-1pm, 3.30-
8pm Sun. **Credit** DC, MC, V. **Map** p308 C1, C2.
The art nouveau interior alone warrants a visit to
this well-run, modern pharmacy, where you'll also
find traditional and homeopathic cures. Another
bonus: you can still get your medicine after closing
time – ring the bell and someone will pass it
through a little hole in the shutter. This service is
available every night of the year, from 8pm to
8.30am the following morning.

Home design & accessories

High-Tech

*Piazza XXV Aprile 12, North (02 624 1101/www.
high-techmilano.com). Metro Garibaldi or Moscova/
tram 11, 30, 33.* **Open** 10.30am-7.30pm Tue-Sun.
Credit AmEx, DC, MC, V. **Map** p308 B2.
A labyrinth packed to the rafters with every imaginable item and gadget for the design-conscious
home-owner. Goodies range from homeware and
office accessories to beauty and bath products.
Hours and hours can evaporate wandering in a daze
from room to room – or simply trying to locate the
exit. Cargo High-Tech, an offshoot on via Meucci,
sells cut-price merchandise. There's also a bar and
a bakery on site.
Other locations: Cargo High-Tech, via Meucci 39,
East (02 2722 1301).

Penelopi 3

*Via Palermo 1, North (02 7200 0652/www.
penelopi3.it). Metro Moscova/bus 41, 43, 94/tram 3,
4.* **Open** 3-7.30pm Mon; 10.30am-7.30pm Tue-Sat.
Closed 2wks Aug. **Credit** AmEx, DC, MC, V.
Map p308 C2.

Desirable small furnishings, tempting design objects and eclectic decorative pieces with a faintly exotic, international flavour are all up for grabs here.

360°
Via Tortona 12, South (02 835 6706). Metro Porta Genova/bus 68/tram 14. **Open** 11am-7pm Tue-Sat; 8pm-midnight Thur, Fri; 11am-5pm Sun. Closed Aug. **Credit** MC, V. **Map** p310 B1.
This multifaceted design space is dedicated to well-being and soothing the senses with simple treatments. It deals in an odd mix of exotic plants, food, young designer furniture and oriental-style massage to create a unique shopping environment. A small kitchen turns out a mainly vegetarian buffet lunch, weekend brunch and dinner on some evenings.

Fabric

Le Mercerie
Via San Vittore 2, West (02 8645 4338). Metro Conciliazione or Sant'Ambrogio/bus 50, 58, 94. **Open** 3-7pm Mon; 9.30am-1.30pm, 3-7pm Tue-Fri; 9.30am-1pm, 3-7pm Sat. Closed 3wks Aug. **Credit** AmEx, MC, V. **Map** p310 A1.
Le Mercerie is a treasure trove for all sorts of textiles and accessories. A system of sliding cupboards reveals buttons, ribbons and *passementerie* three shelves deep, and fabrics in virtually every colour or pattern, plus cross-stitch and embroidery kits.

Silva
Via Olona 25, West (02 8940 0788). Metro Sant'Agostino or Sant'Ambrogio/bus 94/tram 20, 29. **Open** 10.30am-7pm Mon-Fri. Closed 3wks Aug. **Credit** MC, V. **Map** p310 A1.
Silva has an insane selection of curtain and upholstery fabrics, rugs and groovy wallpaper, plus a range of vintage 1960s and '70s fabrics and wallpaper. It's located in the building's courtyard, where you can also park.

Music: CDs, records & instruments

Ricordi Media Store
Galleria Vittorio Emanuele, Centre (02 8646 0272). Metro Duomo/bus 54, 60, 65/tram 12, 20, 23, 27. **Open** 10am-11pm Mon-Sat; 10am-8pm Sun. **Credit** AmEx, DC, MC, V. **Map** p311 A1.
A subterranean media emporium beneath the glass-covered Galleria. Ricordi stocks a varied selection of CDs of all genres, plus instruments, sheet music, games and concert/theatre tickets. The connecting La Feltrinelli bookstore (*see p133*) can be accessed from inside here.

Supporti Fonografici
Corso di Porta Ticinese 100, South (02 8940 0420/ www.supportifono.com). Metro Porta Genova/tram 3, 12, 14, 19. **Open** 3-7.30pm Mon; 9am-7.30pm Tue-Sat. **Credit** AmEx, DC, MC, V. **Map** p310 A2, B2/p312 A2.

Oi! Listen up at **Ricordi Media Store**.

Some customers never set foot in the store but buy only on the shop's website. Listening samples and recommendations are provided by a staff of genuine enthusiasts well versed in the likes of indie, new wave, Britpop and electronica.

Services

Dry-cleaning/laundry

Ondablu
Via Savona, opposite No 1, South (no phone/www. ondablu.com). Metro Porta Genova/tram 14, 29. **Open** 8am-10pm daily. **No credit cards**. **Map** p310 B1.
Coin-operated launderette with washers and dryers. **Other locations**: see website for other locations.

Hairdressers & beauticians

Antica Barbieria Colla
Via Gerolamo Morone 3, Centre (02 874 312). Metro Montenapoleone/tram 1, 2, 20. **Open** 8.30am-12.30pm, 2.30-7pm Tue-Sat. Closed 3wks Aug. **No credit cards**. **Map** p311 A1/p312 B1.
Going for that groovy Giacomo Puccini look? The barbers in this shop have been shearing since 1904 and proudly display the scissors used to keep the composer's locks properly coiffed. Call for an appointment. Men only.

Intrecci
Via Larga 2, Centre (02 7202 2316). Metro Duomo or Missori/bus 54, 60, 65/tram 12, 20, 23, 27. **Open** 11am-8pm Mon; 10am-11pm Tue-Fri; 10am-9pm Sat. **Credit** MC, V. **Map** p311 A1/p312 B2.
The stylists here blur the line between male and female, making this a unisex salon in more ways than one. Music blares and impromptu dances are

Eat, Drink, Shop

Chic for less

Ever wondered how just about everyone in Milan – from the humblest shop assistant to the oldest granny – manages to look so smart? Surely they can't all have limitless budgets to spend on clothes? The truth is that the city is awash with boutiques and bargain basements, selling designer returns, cast-offs and vintage pieces at prices almost anyone can afford. For some of the best, read on...

Stock houses

Many stock houses are treasure troves of designer goods, with racks of end-of-season shop and warehouse returns, stock from boutiques that have closed down, and some factory seconds. Among the best is **Il Salvagente** (lifebelt), which garners most of the top stuff, simply because it's been around for ever. Pick through an ever-changing kaleidoscope of designer goods for men and women; for children there's a separate location called **Salvagente Bimbi**.

With a sneaky name and a cryptic location (just off corso Vittorio Emanuele), **Diffusione Tessile** (textile warehouse) requires some sleuthing, but it rewards you in full. This shop deals exclusively in the womenswear brands under the MaxMara umbrella, including Sport Max, Marina Rinaldi and Marella. There is a vast selection of clothing and shoes, tidy racks, plus friendly and helpful staff.

For last season's shoes by less obvious fashion brands such as René Caovilla and Alessandro dell'Acqua, head to **Le Vintage**, in the increasingly trendy Isola area, behind Garibaldi station. The shop also has a small but well-chosen selection of vintage clothes.

Fashion slaves on a budget shouldn't miss the **10 Corso Como** outlet (*see p138*).

Diffusione Tessile
Galleria San Carlo 6, Centre (02 7600 0829). Metro Duomo/bus 54, 60, 61, 65/tram 12, 20, 23, 27. **Open** *3.30-7.30pm Mon; 10am-7.30pm Tue-Sat.* **Credit** *AmEx, DC, MC, V.* **Map** *p311 A1.*

Salvagente
Via Fratelli Bronzetti 16, East (02 7611 0328). Metro Porta Venezia/bus 54, 60, 61, 62/tram 12, 27. **Open** *3-7pm Mon; 10am-12.30pm, 3-7pm Tue, Thur, Fri; 10am-7pm Wed, Sat. Closed Aug.* **Credit** *V (non-Italians only).* **Map** *p311 A2.*

Salvagente Bimbi
Via Balzaretti 28, East (02 2668 0764). Metro Piola/bus 62, 90, 91/tram 11, 23. **Open** *3-7pm Mon; 10am-1pm, 3-7pm Tue, Thur, Fri; 10am-7pm Wed, Sat. Closed Aug.* **No credit cards.** **Map** *off p309 C2.*

Le Vintage
Via Garigliano 4, North (02 6931 1885). Metro Garibaldi or Zara/bus 23, 43, 82/tram 2, 4, 11. **Open** *3.30-8pm Mon-Tue; 11am-2.30pm, 3.30-8pm Wed-Fri; noon-7.30pm Sun. Closed 3wks Aug.* **Credit** *AmEx, DC, MC, V.* **Map** *p309 A1.*

Clothing previously worn by...

Many Milanese women offload last season's clothes to make space in their wardrobes (and their budgets) for the latest designer looks, so second-hand shops are a big thing here. **Il Nuovo Guardaroba** has well-organised racks of classic women's used clothing and accessories, with a small selection of men's items too; a separate shop nearby called **Il Guardarobino** has children's clothing and baby hardware, such as strollers and highchairs.

High-end designer duds swiped from the closets of socialites and TV personalities who wouldn't be caught dead in the same outfit twice are regular stock at **Tè con Le Amiche** (tea with the girls). Although the name suggests an easy-going oasis, the atmosphere is a bit chilly and the owner is strictly business.

At **L'Armadio di Laura** there's good reason for the sign reading 'please don't ask for further discounts' – the prices in this thriftstore-like shop are low enough already.

For vintage clothing from old hands in the business, try **Cavalli e Nastri**. Each piece in this tidy collection is in mint condition and selected with a razor-sharp eye that weeds out obvious and dowdy 'period' pieces, leaving only the crème de la crème of vintage chic. If you're looking for an authentic Victorian gown or a 19th-century smoking jacket, try their other, larger location, at via de Amicis.

But passionate vintage fans should head straight for **Franco Jacassi**, a treasure trove of antique clothing, bags, shoes, hats, buttons, trimmings and rare fashion publications. This is where Milan's big-name designers come for inspiration.

Fashion looks that were pioneered in the 1960s, '70s and '80s can be bought in their original retro form or in reinterpreted, brand-new versions at **Docks Dora**. Merchandise here includes a well-tended selection of vintage coats and jackets, plus skirts made from swirly curtain fabrics. Sanderson circa 1970, anyone?

L'Armadio di Laura
*Via Voghera 25, South (02 836 0606).
Metro Porta Genova/bus 68/tram 11, 29.*
Open *Spring/summer* 10am-6pm Tue-Sat.
Autumn/winter 10am-6pm Mon-Sat. Closed
20 July-8 Sept. **Credit** MC, V. **Map** p310 B1.

Cavalli e Nastri
*Via Brera 2, North (02 7200 0449). Metro
Cairoli or Lanza/bus 61/tram 3, 4, 12, 20.*
Open 3.30-7pm Mon; 10.30am-7pm Tue-Sat.
Closed Aug. **Credit** AmEx, DC, MC, V. **Map**
p308 C2.
Other locations: via de Amicis 9 (entrance in
via Arena), South (02 8940 9452).

Docks Dora
*Viale Crispi 7, North (02 2900 6950).
Metro Moscova/bus 41, 43, 94/tram 3, 4,
11.* **Open** 3-8pm Mon; 11am-8pm Tue-Sat;
3-7.30pm Sun. **Credit** AmEx, DC, MC, V.
Map p308 B2.

Franco Jacassi
*Via Sacchi 3, North (02 8646 2076). Metro
Lanza/bus 61/tram 1, 3, 4, 12, 20, 27.*
Open 9.30am-1pm, 2-6.30pm Mon-Fri. Closed
Aug. **Credit** AmEx, MC, V. **Map** p308 C2.

Il Guardarobino
*Via Washington 5, West (02 4801 5802).
Metro Wagner/bus 61, 67/tram 24.* **Open**
10am-1pm, 3-7pm Tue-Sat. Closed 2wks July,
4wks Aug. **No credit cards**. **Map** off p310 A1.

Il Nuovo Guardaroba
*Via Privata Asti 5a, West (02 4800 1678).
Metro Wagner/bus 61, 67/tram 24.* **Open**
10am-6pm Tue-Sat. Closed 3wks Aug.
No credit cards. **Map** off p310 A1.

Tè con Le Amiche
*Via Visconti di Modrone 33, East (02 7733
1506). Metro San Babila/bus 54, 60, 61,
65/tram 12, 20, 27.* **Open** 3-6.30pm Mon;
10am-12.30pm, 3-6.30pm Tue-Fri. Closed
July-Aug. **Credit** AmEx, DC, MC, V.
Map p311 A1.

Outlet malls

Forget the high prices of downtown, but don't forget your passport. The originator of factory outlet shopping is the recently expanded **FoxTown Factory Stores**, just over the northern Italian border, in Switzerland. There are 130 international shops housed inside a four-storey mall with three restaurants, a café and snack bar, free parking, a kids' playground, currency exchange and one of Switzerland's most frequented casinos.

The other main outlet mall is the exceptionally popular **Serravalle Outlets**, located between Milan and Genoa, in the town of Serravalle Scrivia. With more than 150 shops carrying international brands for clothing, sport and housewares, plus six food areas and 3,000 free parking spaces, it aims to become the largest shopping centre in Europe.

Both FoxTown Factory and Serravalle Outlets are open Sundays.

FoxTown Factory Stores
*Via A Maspoli 18, Mendrisio, Switzerland
(0041 848 828 888/www.foxtown.ch).* **Open**
11am-7pm daily. **Credit** AmEx, DC, MC, V.
From Milan, take the A9 motorway; 7km
(4.5 miles) after the border take the
Mendrisio exit and turn left.

If you are travelling by train, go from Milan's Stazione Centrale to Chiasso. A bus departs from the station every hour to go to FoxTown, which is 7km away.

Serravalle Outlet
*Via della Moda 1 (Strada Statale 35 bis),
Serravalle Scrivia (0143 609 000/www.
mcarthurglen.it).* **Open** 10am-7pm Mon-Fri;
10am-8pm Sat, Sun. **Credit** MC, V.
From Milan, take the A7 Milan–Genoa
motorway; exit at Serravalle Scrivia and
at the roundabout take the road towards
Novi Ligure. The mall is 1km (half a mile)
from the motorway exit.

If you are travelling by train, go from Milan's Stazione Centrale to Arquata Scrivia. The mall is a 10km (6-mile) taxi-ride from the train station at a fixed fee of 13. More adventurous types can wait for one of the fairly frequent buses, then hike from the stop down the road from the mall. Don't try this on Sundays as buses are scarce.

performed, while the receptionist makes your bill out from behind a haze of smoke. Its hair and make-up services (the latter by appointment only) will get you club-ready.

Marchina
2nd floor, corso Venezia 3, East (02 799 636). Metro San Babila/bus 54, 60, 65/tram 12, 20, 27. **Open** 9am-6.30pm Tue-Sat; 9am-10pm Thur. **Credit** DC, MC, V. **Map** p309 C1.
Expert haircutter Pino Marchina lords it over a busy staff of master colourists, cutters and beauticians in this clean, modern salon near San Babila. It's a full-service salon for hair, nails and body for men and women, and everybody sails out looking far better than when they walked in. Mary speaks perfect English and all the staff are efficient and friendly.

Opticians

Salmoiraghi & Viganò
Corso Matteotti 22, East (02 7600 0100). Metro San Babila/bus 54, 60, 65/tram 12, 20, 27. **Open** 3-7pm Mon; 10am-7pm Tue-Sat. **Credit** AmEx, DC, MC, V. **Map** p309 C1/p312 C1.
A solid optician well known throughout Italy for its professionalism, expertise and selection of frames. **Other locations**: throughout the city.

Pet services

For Pets Only Beauty & Spa
Via San Pietro all'Orto 3, Centre (02 795 694). Metro San Babila/bus 54, 60, 73/tram 12, 20, 27. **Open** 10am-8pm Tue-Sat, 1pm-8pm Mon, Sun. **Credit** AmEx, DC, V. **Map** p309 C1/p312 C1.
Wanna tell your pooch back home that you missed him? Try with a diamanté-studded collar, or a chichi fake-fur coat from this colourful store. It also offers beauty treatments for four-legged friends in a sooth-ing environment, with chill-out music, perfumed candles and a no-rush policy.

Photocopy/fax/photo developers

Almost any stationery store (*cartoleria*) offer a fax and photocopy service; just ask. If you've got 24 hours, Esselunga supermarket (*see p143*) does traditional photo processing, and its rates are much cheaper than the 30-minute specialist photo places.

Mail Boxes Etc
Via del Torchio 4, South (02 7200 2932). Metro Duomo/bus 54, 60, 65/tram 2, 3, 14, 20, 27. **Open** 9am-6.30pm Mon-Fri. Closed 3wks Aug. **Credit** AmEx, DC, MC, V. **Map** p310 A2/p312 A2.
Provides photocopying and fax facilities, UPS couri-er pick-up, business card printing, Western Union point, internet access, document laminating, post-box rental, packaging and office supplies sales. **Other locations**: around 30 throughout the city.

NE.CA Fiera
Via Giovanni da Procida 29, West (02 317 465). Tram 1, 19, 33. **Open** 8.30am-7.30pm Mon-Fri; 9am-7pm Sat. Closed 2wks Aug. **Credit** AmEx, DC, MC, V. **Map** p308 B1.
This store develops any kind of film in 30 minutes and specialises in digital printing and image manip-ulation. Top-name cameras for sale as well.

Ticket agencies

There is no single source for concert and event tickets and information in Milan. However, if one ticket agency is sold out, another may still have tickets available. Tickets for Teatro alla Scala must be purchased through the theatre (*see p174*). You can also get many tickets for classical music concerts through the APT on via Marconi 1/piazza Duomo (*see p294*). Otherwise, try the various record shops: Messaggerie Musicali (ticket counter 02 795 502; *see p135*), Fnac (ticket counter 02 8695 95; *see p135*), or Ricordi (ticket counter 02 869 0683; *see p147*).

Travel agencies

CIT (Compagnia Italiana Turismo)
Via Dante 6, Centre (02 8637 0226/www.cit italia.net). Metro Cordusio/tram 12, 19, 20, 24. **Open** 9am-7.30pm Mon-Fri; 10am-1pm, 2-7pm Sat. **Credit** AmEx, DC, MC, V. **Map** p311 A1/p312 A1.
CIT is a full-service agency for most travel needs (except rail travel). Package holidays, air and ferry tickets on the spot, plus a bureau de change are all available here.

Video & DVD rental

Blockbuster
Via Mario Pagano 31a, West (02 4801 3664/ www.blockbuster.it). Metro Pagano/bus 61/tram 19, 27, 29, 30. **Open** 11am-11pm Mon-Thur; 11am-midnight Fri-Sun. **Credit** MC, V. **Map** p308 C1.
Multiple city branches and a selection of English-language titles (on DVD only) make this interna-tional conglomerate hard to ignore. **Other locations**: throughout the city.

Bloodbuster (sesso, sangue & risate)
Via P Castaldi 30, East (02 2940 4304). Metro Porta Venezia/tram 1, 11, 29, 30. **Open** 3-7pm Mon; 10am-1pm, 3-7pm Tue-Sat. **Credit** DC, MC, V. **Map** p309 B1, C2.
Original-language videos and DVDs for hardcore film buffs. Bloodbuster (tag line: 'sex, blood and laughs') specialises in Chinese action movies, horror and mondo movies. If it was made on a shoestring and/or you saw it on cable TV at 3am, chances are it'll be here. Also books, music and memorabilia.

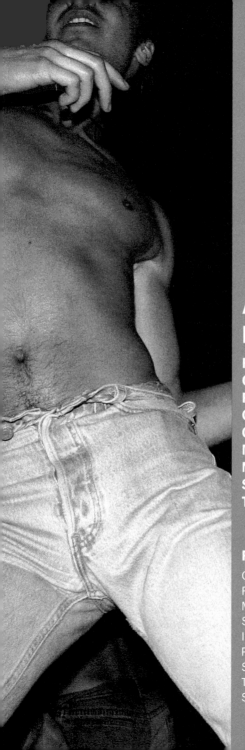

Arts & Entertainment

Festivals & Events	152
Children	155
Film	158
Galleries	161
Gay & Lesbian	165
Music	170
Nightlife	175
Sport & Fitness	179
Theatre & Dance	182

Features

Good green fun	156
Renaissance man	159
Make it snappy	163
Stonewall in Milan?	167
I heart Milan	171
Power stations	172
Star gazing	177
True colours	180
Smile-high club	184

Festivals & Events

Sleek business exhibitions jostle with street parties and cultural events to keep the *milanesi* entertained.

Milan's full calendar of religious and cultural events neatly illustrates two contrasting aspects of the city. The usually reserved Milanese take to the streets in a riot of noise and colour for their traditional celebrations, including Oh Bej! Oh Bej! and Carnevale, both festivals with religious origins. Just as colourful in their own way are the more recently established events, such as Fashion Week and the Furniture Fair, both of which highlight the slick, commercial face of the city.

The traditional festivals tend to be located around Milan's prominent churches, particularly the Duomo, or in residential neighbourhoods, while the commercial events are focused on the Fiera di Milano exhibition centre (*see p97*), one of the largest trade-fair grounds in Europe. Not all events are open to the public. Telephone 02 49 971 (freephone 800 820 029) or check out the Fiera's website (www.fieramilano.it) for a list of what's coming up.

It's well worth being aware of what events are taking place in Milan during your stay. Not only does the buzz surrounding some of them pervade the whole city, adding another dimension to your experience of the place, but in practical terms, the influx of visitors for the larger exhibitions at the Fiera can mean hotels are booked up months in advance and taxis are scarcer than usual.

For further information about what's on, contact the APT tourist office (02 7252 4301/02/03, www.milanoinfotourist.com, *see also p294*), which also publishes *Milano Mese*, a monthly guide to events throughout the city.

Spring

Settimana dei Beni Culturali
Various locations throughout the city. Information www.beniculturali.it. **Date** Usually early spring.
During the Cultural Heritage Week, all of Italy's publicly owned museums and galleries are free.

Giornata FAI di Primavera
Various locations throughout the city. Information 02 467 6151/www.fondoambiente.it. **Date** Third weekend of Mar.
Many of Milan's historic palazzi and monuments, most of which are closed for the rest of the year, are opened to the public thanks to this initiative sponsored by the Fondo Ambiente Italiano.

Salone Internazionale del Mobile (Furniture Fair)
Fiera di Milano, largo Domodossola 1 & piazzale Giulio Cesare (freephone 800 820 029/02 499 771/information 02 4997 7703/www.fieramilano.it). Metro Amendola-Fiera or Lotto/bus 48, 68, 78/tram 19, 27. **Map** off p310 A1. **Date** Mid April.
Milan goes into party mode for one of the world's largest exhibitions of furniture and fittings from cutting-edge designers from all over the world. Although the event traditionally centres on the Fiera, over the years collections have also increasingly been shown at smaller venues around the city, particularly in the warehouses around via Tortona, behind Porta Genova station.

During the fair, Milan's design and furniture emporia fling open their doors freely to all-comers – a great opportunity for an unself-conscious snoop around some of the more intimidating establishments.

Pick up a copy of *Interni* magazine for a list of what's on where (or visit www.internimagazine.it), or look out for signs on buildings around town. Many venues allow free entry to their opening parties.

Stramilano
www.stramilano.it. **Date** Mid April.
Central Milan is closed to traffic as locals and athletes from all over the world take to the streets for Milan's own fun mini-marathon (15km/9.5 miles). Stramilano sets off from piazza Duomo and goes through some of the main arteries in the city, including corso Vittorio Emanuele, corso Venezia and corso Buenos Aires, to finish in Parco Sempione (*see p67*).

Mercato dei Fiori
Along the Naviglio Grande, South (02 8940 9971/www.navigliogrande.mi.it). Metro Porta Genova/bus 47, 59, 71, 74/tram 3, 4, 15, 29, 30. **Map** p310 B1.
Date Third Sun of Apr.
The Naviglio Grande takes on a Dutch flavour as this flower fair creates a spectacular splash of colour and fragrance along the canal. Nurseries and horticultural schools from all around Italy take part in the exhibition of plants, flowers and garden equipment.

Pittori del Naviglio Grande
Along the Naviglio Grande, South (02 8940 9971/www.navigliogrande.mi.it). Metro Porta Genova/bus 47, 59, 71, 74/tram 2, 3, 15, 29, 30. **Map** p310 B1.
Date Second weekend of May.
This open-air art exhibition along the Naviglio Grande showcases work by more than 300 artists from all over Italy.

Kenya's John Birgen wins the 2003 **Milano Marathon**. *See p154.*

International Antiques Fair (Milano Internazionale Antiquariato)

Fiera di Milano, largo Domodossola 1 & piazzale Giulio Cesare, West (freephone 800 820 029/ 02 499 771/information 02 4997 7703/www. fieramilano.it/www.expocts.it/mia). Metro Amendola-Fiera or Lotto/bus 48, 68, 78/ tram 19, 27. **Map** off p310 A1. **Date** Mid May.
One of the highlights of the international art trade's calendar, this bi-annual event (held in even years) is attended by numerous galleries from Italy and overseas and provides a good guide to the Italian antiques market.

Cortili Aperti

Various venues around the city (02 7631 8634/www. italiamultimedia.com/cortiliaperti). **Date** Late May.
Private residences open their splendid courtyards to the public for one Sunday for the Cortili Aperti initiative. In previous years, many of the art nouveau buildings along corso Venezia (*see p77* **The road to Liberty**), including Casa Fontana Silvestri, Palazzo Serbelloni and Palazzo Castiglioni, have taken part in this annual event.

Summer at Idroscalo

Idropark Fila, Circonvallazione Idroscalo Est 51, Segrate (02 7720 0902/www.provincia.milano.it/ idroparkfila). **Map** p306 **Greater Milan**. **Date** Late May-Sept.

The summer season of sporting events, concerts and nightlife (as well as mass family picnics) gets under way at the Idroscalo Park, near Linate Airport, on the eastern outskirts of town.

Summer

Milano Moda Uomo Primavera/Estate

Information www.cameramoda.it. **Date** June.
Men's Fashion Week for spring and summer might not be the most important event in Milan's fashion calendar, but it is responsible for bringing some of the world's best-looking men to the city for a couple of weeks.

Notturni in Villa

Information 02 8912 2383/www.amicidellamusica milano.it. **Date** mid June-Aug.
A series of jazz and classical music concerts is held in patrician villas around the city, notably Villa Litta, near Parco Sempione (*see p67*), and Villa Simonetta, near the Cimitero Monumentale (*see p74*). The performances start at 10pm and entry is free.

Festa del Naviglio

Along the Navigli, South. Metro Porta Genova/ bus 47, 59, 71, 74/tram 2, 3, 15, 29, 30. **Map** p310 B1. **Date** First two weeks of June.
Street artists, concerts, sporting events, antique markets, regional cooking and other events take place along the Navigli canals.

Milano d'Estate

Castello Sforzesco, Piazza Castello, North. Information APT 02 7252 4301/www.milano infotourist.com. Metro Cadorna, Cairoli or Lanza/ bus 43, 57, 61, 70, 94/tram 1, 3, 4, 12, 14, 27. **Map** p308 C2. **Date** June-Aug.
Open-air concerts and performances are organised to entertain those unfortunate *milanesi* who can't leave the city in the heat of the summer. The action takes place behind the Castello Sforzesco.

Sagra di San Cristoforo

In front of the church of San Cristoforo, Navigli, South. Information APT 02 7252 4301/www. milanoinfotourist.com. Metro Porta Genova/bus 47, 59, 71, 74/tram 2, 3, 15, 29, 30. **Map** p310 B1. **Date** Third Sun of June.
The feast of the patron saint of drivers takes place in the square in front of the little church of San Cristoforo (*see p86* **Canals plus**). Decorated boats float down the Naviglio.

Navigli Summer Jamboree

Navigli area, South. Metro Porta Genova/ bus 47, 59, 71, 74/tram 2, 3, 15, 29, 30. **Map** p310 B1. **Date** June-Sept.
The usually traffic-choked streets around the Navigli close for an annual summer jamboree, allowing bars and restaurants to spill out into the roads from 8pm-2am every day for three months.

Festival Latino Americando

FilaForum, Via D Vittorio 6, Assago (199 128 800/ www.latinoamericando.it). Metro Famagosta then bus 'Assago'. **Map** p306 **Greater Milan.** **Date** Late June-early Aug.

Milan celebrates all things Latino during the summer months with this festival in Assago, on the outskirts of the city. Over 60 concerts, events and exhibitions celebrate aspects of the continent's culture, including music, arts, dance, food, handicrafts and cinema. Many top-name Latin musicians fly in to give performances.

Autumn

Milano Moda Donna Primavera/Estate

Information www.cameramoda.it. **Date** Early Oct.

Yet another Fashion Week. On this occasion leading Italian designers present their womenswear collections for spring/summer.

SMAU Technology Fair

Fiera di Milano, largo Domodossola 1 & piazzale Giulio Cesare, West (freephone 800 820 029/02 499 771/information 02 4997 7703/www.fieramilano.it/ www.smau.it). Metro Amendola-Fiera or Lotto/bus 48, 68, 78/tram 19, 27. **Map** off p310 A1. **Date** Late Oct.

Watch Italy's telecom operators battle it out with blaring sound systems and saucy dancing girls at this technology fair, which runs for a week in the Fiera. The exhibition wows thousands of visitors each day with the latest gadgets, from personal computers to mobile phones. As well as consumer goods, it showcases e-government and e-business technologies.

Expo dei Sapori

Fiera di Milano, largo Domodossola 1& piazzale Giulio Cesare, West (freephone 800 820 029/02 499 771/information 02 4997 7703/www.fieramilano.it). Metro Amendola-Fiera or Lotto/bus 48, 68, 78/ tram 19, 27. **Map** off p310 A1. **Date** Mid Nov.

A delicious fusion of flavours is cooked up as Italy's regions congregate at the Fiera to offer the best local gourmet specialities.

Winter

Milano Marathon

www.milanomarathon.it. **Date** one Sun, late Nov-early Dec.

Nearly 5,000 competitors take part in Milan's annual marathon. The starting point is at Stazione Centrale and the race finishes in piazza del Duomo.

L'Artigiano in Fiera (Milan Crafts Fair)

Fiera di Milano, largo Domodossola 1& piazzale Giulio Cesare, West (freephone 800 820 029/02 499 771/information 02 4997 7703/www.fieramilano.it). Metro Amendola-Fiera or Lotto/bus 48, 68, 78/ tram 19, 27. **Map** off p310 A1. **Date** Early Dec.

The world's biggest trade fair dedicated to arts and crafts includes ceramics, wood, textiles, glass, silver, jewellery, furnishings and fittings.

Oh Bej! Oh Bej!

Piazza Sant'Ambrogio, West. Metro Sant'Ambrogio/ bus 50, 58, 94. **Map** p310 A2. **Date** 7 Dec.

This street market is one of Milan's most important festivals and is held on the feast of Milan's patron saint Sant'Ambrogio (*see p7* **St Misbehavin'**). The streets around piazza Sant'Ambrogio throng with crowds sampling traditional food including fried pancakes, pastries, roasted meats, chestnuts and mulled wine. Stalls sell everything from handicrafts and antiques to CDs and African sculptures.

Epiphany

Various locations throughout the city. **Date** 6 Jan.

Epiphany is also known as *La Befana*, after a kind-hearted witch who is said to bring presents to well-behaved children and coal to the naughty ones. Crowds turn out for the morning procession of the Three Wise Men from the Duomo (*see p54*) to the church of Sant'Eustorgio (*see p85*).

Milano Moda Uomo Autunno/Inverno

Information www.cameramoda.it. **Date** Mid Jan.

Men's Fashion Week for autumn and winter is a bit of a side-show to the women's event (*see below*). Still, the talent it attracts is first rate.

Carnevale

Various locations throughout the city. **Date** Feb.

Milan's Carnevale takes place in the days following Shrove Tuesday, later than in the rest of Italy. The celebrations are essentially for children, who roam the streets in fancy dress chucking handfuls of confetti. A fancy-dress parade takes place around the Duomo (*see p54*) on the first Saturday of Lent.

Milano Moda Donna Autunno/Inverno

Information www.cameramoda.it. **Date** Late Feb.

Milan's moment in the fashion spotlight, as 80-odd designers unveil their autumn/winter collections. The global economic downturn of recent years has perhaps made Fashion Week less glitzy than it once was, but it is still a highlight of the city's calendar.

Catwalks are assembled at venues around the city, but entry to the shows is strictly by invitation only. The smaller houses show at the Fiera (*see p97*), but a growing number are setting up in the former industrial sites in the south of the city. Prada's lovely old renovated warehouse puts on art displays when it's not Fashion Week (02 546 70515, www.fondazione prada.org, *see p164*), while Armani holds his shows at a former Nestlé factory transformed into a theatre (via Bergognone 59, www.giorgioarmani.com).

Visitors are not able to participate directly, but it is still possible to enjoy the atmosphere of Milan at its most fashionable, and follow the events on the catwalks through the local press.

Children

There's more for kids in Milan than you might imagine.

At first glance, Milan may not look like the most child-friendly city on the map. But those brave souls who do arrive with kids in tow will be well-rewarded. Much of the centre is pedestrianised, making sightseeing with families far easier than in some other Italian cities. What's more, many of Milan's museums and monuments now organise activities for children and the city's parks (*see p156* **Good green fun**) have been cleaned up, allowing lively little ones to let off steam in relative safety.

GETTING AROUND

If your kids have never ridden a tram, there's no better amusement than a trip on one of the ancient orange or whizzy green wonders that shuttle around Milan. You might want to splash out on the hour-and-a-half-long ride on the **Ciao Milano Tourist Tram**, which dates from the 1920s and does a scenic tour of the main sights. You'll be given headphones providing English commentary, which may amuse the smaller members of the family for a minute or two. If restlessness kicks in, get off at an appointed stop, walk about and then take the next tram (start off early to make the most of this). If your budget is limited, get on one of the old, orange trams – complete with wooden benches and little lampshades – that still ply some routes.

On trips where getting from A to B is the main purpose, be prepared to face occasional hassles. There's no space to store pushchairs on trams, buses and metro trains, and some underground stations have no escalators. On the upside, Italian kid-worship means you'll never be short of people willing to help you clamber on or off or give up their seats.

Tourist Tram

From piazza Castello at No.1 tram stop (02 3391 0794). **Open** *Apr-Oct* 11am, 1pm, 3pm daily. *Nov-Mar* 11am, 1pm Sat-Sun. **Tickets** €20 adults; free to under-12s. Buy tickets on board. **Map** p308 C2/p312 A1.

Sightseeing

The best bet for kids under 12 is a sprint around the fun sights in the extensive central pedestrianised area. Parents can walk from piazza San Babila, east of the Duomo, to Parco Sempione, north of Castello Sforzesco without ever (well, hardly ever) having to keep an eye out for Italian drivers. That said, one or two well-trafficked thoroughfares do still cut through this pedestrian paradise, so watch out.

A sure-fire first port of call for anyone unencumbered by prams is the Duomo roof (*see p54*). The 150-odd steps leading to the top are climbable for anyone in good health over

Nano Gigante.
See p157.

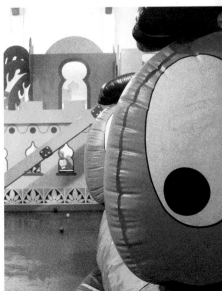

the age of four; others can take the lift. Once up on the well-barricaded roof, kids can clamber along little parapets, pick out the weirdest of the 3,500 sculptures, or simply pretend they're drifting around on a pink marble wedding cake.

From the Duomo, head west towards the Castello Sforzesco (see p66). Ignore the sterile displays on the top floors (no need to feel guilty – admission is free) and make for the armoury hall (Room XIV), where kids can gawp at a knight on horseback and some vicious-looking swords.

On Sundays, there's a tour for kids aged eight and over, but be warned that it contains a lot of Italian chat. Those who risk it should come with a torch to pick out the details of the secret underground passages (02 659 6937, 3.30pm Sun, reservations obligatory by the preceding Friday).

MUSEUMS AND OTHER ATTRACTIONS

Beyond the pedestrianised zone, Milanese families at a loose end trail past the stuffed animals and dinosaur skeletons at the **Civico Museo di Storia Naturale** on the fringe of the Giardini Pubblici (see p81); an alternative is to check out Leonardo's inventions at the **Museo Nazionale della Scienza e della Tecnologia** (see p92). Kids may also appreciate the **Museo del Giocattolo e del Bambino**, which houses antique toys and a mock-up of a 19th-century classroom in a scruffy ex-orphanage. All these museums host workshops and guided tours, some of them in English. Call for details.

If all this culture is more than your juniors can stand, take football enthusiasts for a trip around the San Siro stadium (see p179), home to both the Inter and AC Milan squads.

Museo del Giocattolo e del Bambino

Via Pitteri 56, East (02 2641 1585/www.museo delgiocattolo.it). Metro Lambrate/bus 54. **Open** 9.30am-12.30pm, 3-6pm Tue-Sun. **Admission** €5; €3 concessions; free under-14s Sun. **No credit cards**. **Map** off p309 B2.

Eating out

Most eateries in Milan welcome children. It's not unheard of for waiters to whisk baby off for a tour of the kitchen and even the most terrifying table manners will be met with indulgent smiles from fellow diners. Many restaurants will drag out high chairs on request and some even offer kids' menus, though changing facilities are still almost non-existent.

Recently, brunch has become an excuse for weekend outings in Milan. The child-friendly **Dulcis in Fundo** serves home-made, health-

Good green fun

Milan will never be famous for its parks and gardens, but over the past few years, the city's green spaces have undergone a major overhaul, making several of them rather more pleasant than you might expect.

Among the best and most central places for your kids to let off steam is **Parco Sempione** (see p67). Offspring aged three to ten can burn off excess energy on the bumper cars or mini-train, then romp around the small but well-appointed play area, while parents sink gratefully on to a park bench.

The other largish green area in the centre is the **Giardini Pubblici** (see p81), where the main attractions are a playground, mini-train and small lake. The park is also home to the **Civico Museo di Storia Naturale** (see p81) and the **Planetarium** (see p81), both of which may be worth a peek inside.

There can't be many parks that adults aren't allowed into unless accompanied by a child under 12, but the small and attractive **Giardini della Villa Comunale** (via Palestro) is one of them. Napoleon's former villa – in the grounds – is currently closed. If you're lucky, your offspring may be mesmerised by the lake and the tinkling waterfall. If not, head for the slides and swings.

Explorer-types might have the energy to head out to the **Boscoincittà**, an 800-square-kilometre (300-square-mile) woodland on the fringes of Milan (via Novara 340, 02 4522 401, metro De Angeli then 72 bus). This wildish park has walking and bicycle tracks, picnic zones and a barbecue area near the ancient Cascina San Romano farmhouse that lies at its heart.

Finally, when it's just too hot, head out for the **Idropark Fila**, formerly the Idroscalo (via Circonvallazione Est, Segrate, 02 7020 0902), near Linate airport. This park, with its two-and-a-half-kilometre-long (1.75 mile) lake, was originally built as a waterplane runway. These days it's used for watersports and swimming, while the artificial beach provides a spot for sunbathing. Around the lake are a running track, play areas for kids, funfair-type rides and a host of bars. In the winter, you can go ice-skating there.

conscious savouries and irresistible cakes. There's also a play area and designer chairs (this is Milan after all). Saturday brunch here is a high spot on the Milanese kiddie social scene.

Ventaglio Caffè offers children's entertainment (magicians, make-up artists, clowns in a separate play area) for three- to eight-year-olds, while Tex Mex restaurant **Dixieland** has a free babysitting service (artwork and games in a play area) that allows parents to enjoy their food in peace.

Finally, chic kids will love acting grown-up at the **Diana Garden** (*see also p46*), a trendy restaurant with one of the most beautiful gardens in town (open in warm weather only). Family brunchtime is on Sundays, when you can pile up your plates from a 15-metre-long (48-foot) buffet table.

Reservations are obligatory at several of these venues, and it is always advisable to book ahead.

Diana Garden
Sheraton Diana Majestic, viale Piave 42, East (02 20 581). Metro Porta Venezia. **Brunch** 12.30-2.30pm daily (€29-€35 adults, around €15 children). **Credit** AmEx, DC, MC, V. **Map** p309 C2.

Dixieland
Piazzale Aquileia 12, West (02 436 915) Metro Sant'Agostino. **Brunch** noon-3.30pm Sun (€14 adults, €3 children). **Credit** AmEx, MC, V. **Map** p310 A1.

Dulcis in Fundo
Via Zuretti 55, North (02 6671 2503). Metro Centrale FS. **Brunch** noon-3pm Sat (€15.50). **Credit** MC, V. **Map** p309 A2.

Ventaglio Caffè
Piazza Piemonte 12, West (02 4544 0500). Metro Wagner. **Brunch** noon-5pm Sun (€20 adults, €10 children). **Credit** MC, V. **Map** off p310 A1.

Entertainment & babysitting

Nano Gigante
Via Lambrate 18, East (02 2682 6650). Metro Loreto or Pasteur/bus 55, 62/tram 33. **Open** 9am-7pm Mon-Fri; 10am-7pm Sat, Sun. **Admission** Membership fee €15.50 (includes 1 free entry); then €8-€10.50 per visit. **Credit** MC, V. **Map** off p309 A2. A play centre with the usual ball pools, bouncy castles and the like. Book in advance for the 'parking' service for children aged three to ten (9am-1.30pm Mon-Fri, €3.60-€7.70 per hour).

Pottery Café
Via Solferino 3, North (02 8901 3660). Metro Lanza/bus 41, 43, 61. **Open** 9am-8pm Tue-Thur; 10am-midnight Fri, Sat; 11am-8pm Sun. Closed 1wk Aug. **Ceramic fee** €10 minimum. **Credit** DC, MC, V. **Map** p308 C2. Kids aged four and over can create colourful and cheerful ceramics in this café-cum-art lab while mum and dad relax over cappuccino.

ProntoBaby
Via Lario 16, North (02 6900 2201/www.infanzia. com). Metro Zara/bus 82, 83/tram 4, 90, 91. **Rates** €7.30 per hour. **No credit cards. Map** p309 A1. Desperate for a night out? Book a babysitter through ProntoBaby, organised by Infanzia, a school for childcare professionals in the north of Milan. Some are English-speaking.

Teatro del Buratto al Pime
Via Mosè Bianchi 94, West (02 2700 2476/www. teatrodelburatto.it). Metro Amendola-Fiera or Lotto/bus 48, 49, 90, 91. **Tickets** €6. **No credit cards. Map** off p308 B1. This 30-year-old puppets and actors' theatre recently transferred to new premises. Family events are held on Sunday afternoons.

Shopping

Milan is a paradise for design-conscious families on a budget. For listings of 20 bargain clothing outlets for kids, pick up *La Guida Agli Spacci* by Marina Martorana (Sperling & Kupfer, 2001). It's in Italian, but you don't need to be a linguistic genius to read the addresses. Top outlets include **Salvagente Bimbi** (*see p148*), which stocks designer returns by top labels, and **Il Guardarobino** (*see p148*), selling barely worn designer cast-offs. If your brood includes children under 6, you may want to dive into **Chicco** (piazza Diaz 2, 02 8699 8597) for a spot of pint-sized clothes shopping, while your kids are entertained in the large basement play area (complete with tricycles and bouncy castle).

Via Dante offers plentiful opportunities for more kids' clothes shopping. Splash out on designer outfits at French favourite **Petit Bateau** (No.12, 02 8699 8098) and **L'Angelo** (No.18, 02 866 151); or fight with Milan's mums over the cheap and chic outfits at French chain **Du Pareil au Même** (No.5, 02 7209 4971).

Publications

The **Libreria dei Ragazzi** has a wide range of (mostly Italian) fun kids' guides. Children's events are listed in the *ViviMilano* supplement (Wednesday) of the *Corriere della Sera*, in the *Tutto Milano* supplement (Thursday) of *La Repubblica*, and in *Milano7*, a city guide available at newsstands.

Libreria dei Ragazzi
Via Tadino 53, East (02 2953 3555). Metro Lima/bus 60/tram 1, 5, 20. **Open** 3-7pm Mon; 9.30am-7pm Tue-Sat. **Credit** AmEx, DC, MC, V. **Map** p309 B2. As well as imaginative Italian books (look for the series purported to be written by the journalist mouse Geronimo Stilton), this children's bookstore offers a small selection of more familiar, English-language editions, plus kids' guides to Milan.

Arts & Entertainment

Film

With 113 cinemas, a fistful of festivals and plenty of original-language fare, Milan's a fine spot for catching flicks.

Cinema has traditionally taken a backseat to cabaret and theatre in Milan – witness the incredible success of *Zelig* (*see p184* **Smile-high club**), which has even made waves on TV, becoming one of the three most-watched television shows in Italy in 2002 and 2003. But as Hollywood's influence has grown, public demand for live theatre has begun to wane, and many big downtown theatres are being turned into movie houses. There are 113 cinemas in Milan, the biggest of which are concentrated in the centre, along corso Vittorio Emanuele.

In Milan, as everywhere else in Italy, foreign films are dubbed. Italy has a powerful dubbing union that employs top-notch professional actors to cover foreign voices. Italians are proud of their dubbing and some displays startling artistry. Now however, thanks in large measure to its burgeoning immigrant population, Milan cinemas are offering an increasing number of films in their original language.

The Sound & Motion Pictures Group presents original-language film screenings that take place in a different cinema three days a week – the Anteo on Mondays, the Arcobaleno on Tuesdays and the Mexico on Wednesdays. These three cinemas keep a thick sheaf of leaflets detailing the forthcoming schedule.

For information about what flicks are playing where and when, consult the *Corriere della Sera*'s *Milano* section. Original-language films are advertised as *film* (or *versione*) *in lingua originale* (sometimes simply abbreviated to *Lingua orig*).

At most cinemas, tickets cost between €4 and €5.20 for the early afternoon shows, and from €6 to €7.50 for later performances. Show times vary considerably, though in most cinemas the last show begins at around 10.30pm.

For more details, see the websites www.milanoalcinema.com/soundmot.htm and www.anteospaziocinema.com.

First-run cinemas

Arcobaleno Film Center
Viale Tunisia 11, East (02 2940 6054/reservations 199 199 166/info 02 2953 7621/www.milanoal cinema.com). Metro Porta Venezia/tram 1, 5, 11, 29, 30. **Tickets** €4-€6; €4.50 under-18s. *Ten films* €35; €30 foreign students. **No credit cards.** **Map** p309 B1, B2.

This recently remodelled cinema takes part in the increasingly popular Sound & Motion scheme, which brings the best foreign-language films to the city. Arcobaleno shows the latest releases in their original languages on Tuesday evenings (mostly without intrusive subtitles).

Ariosto
Via L Ariosto 16, West (02 4800 3901). Metro Conciliazione/bus 61, 66, 67/tram 24, 29, 30. **Tickets** €6; €4 over-60s. **No credit cards.** **Map** p308 C1.

This is the place to catch first- or second-run Spanish and French films. Recent international and independent films are screened here in Italian at 5pm, 7.30pm and 10pm Tuesday to Sunday, and in *lingua originale* on Monday.

Odeon
Via Santa Radegonda 8, Centre (199 757 757). Metro Duomo/bus 50, 54, 60/tram 1, 2, 12, 14, 27, 24. **Tickets** €4.50-€7.50. **Credit** MC, V. **Map** p311 A1/p312 B1.

Once a bustling production house, the Odeon is now a cineplex with ten screens. It often shows mainstream films in the original language, occasionally dedicating an entire week to a screening, but there is no set schedule. Call for information.

Art-house cinemas

Anteospazio Cinema
Via Milazzo 9, North (02 659 7732/www.anteo spaziocinema.com). Metro Moscova/bus 41, 43, 94/tram 11, 29, 30, 33. **Tickets** €3.50-€7. **Credit** (shop & restaurants only) MC, V. **Map** p308 B2.

With its restaurant, bookshop, exhibition space, film courses and conferences – not to mention three screens showing everything from classics to avant-garde films to independent contemporary flicks – the Anteo offers something for just about everyone. Original-language films are shown on Monday as part of the Sound & Motion scheme.

Centro Sociale Barrio's – Cineclub Simone Signoret
Corner via Barona & via Boffalora, South (02 8915 9255/www.barrios.it). Metro Famagosta, then bus 74/bus 71, 74, 76. **Tickets** €4.50. **Film shows** 9pm Thur. **Map** off p310 C1.

The Centro Sociale Barrio's is a makeshift social centre, providing computers for email and the internet, as well as accommodating a film club that holds screenings on Thursday evenings.

Renaissance man

International film lovers will recognise him as the gruff, lovable sergeant in *Mediterraneo* (which won the 1992 Oscar for Best Foreign Language Film), but to the Milanese Diego Abatantuono is nothing short of a home-grown hero. Born in Milan's poor Giambellino neighbourhood, Abatantuono came from a family with a foot in the performing arts. His uncle owned Il Derby, the first cabaret club in Italy, where his mother worked as a cloakroom attendant. A young, energetic Diego first found work there as a lighting technician. Soon, he earned a spotlight on its stage as *il Terrunciello*, a southern Italian immigrant who insisted he was *milanese al ciento pe' ciento* (100 per cent Milanese) despite obvious proof to the contrary. (Though an ardent fan of the AC Milan football team, the *Terrunciello* had a Pugliese accent thick enough to cut with a knife and sported an afro to rival most '70s blaxploitation stars.) Poking fun at 'ultra' soccer fans, southern Italian stereotypes and the Milanese all at the same time, the character was an instant hit. The *Terrunciello* had such resonance that Abatantuono was quickly tapped to star in several hit films, including *Il Pap'occhio* (In the Pope's Eye, 1980) and *Eccezzziunale... veramente* (Truly Exceptional, 1982), playing variations on the theme.

Abatantuono said farewell to these lowest common denominator comedies in 1986, with a role in Pupi Avati's *Regalo di Natale* (The Christmas Present). His strong performance won him more dramatic roles and Abatantuono soon became an art-house darling, working for some of Italy's most respected film-makers, such as Carlo Mazzacurati (*Il Toro*, 1994), Simona Izzo (*Camere da Letto*, 1997)

and Ettore Scola (*Concorrenza Sleale*, 2001). But it is with Gabriele Salvatores that Diego Abatantuono has found a Scorsese to his De Niro. The two men have collaborated on seven projects (and counting), from *Marrakech Express* (1989) to the recent *Io Non Ho Paura* (I Am not Scared, 2003)

In 2004 Abatantuono opened his own cabaret theatre in Milan, the Colorado Café (*see p183*), which has its own weekly show broadcast on national television (Italia 1) throughout the year.

Cinema Mexico
(The Rocky Horror House)

Via Savona 57, South (02 4895 1802/www.cinema mexico.it). Metro Porta Genova or Sant'Agostino/bus 61, 68, 90, 91/tram 14. **Tickets** €4-€6. **No credit cards.** **Map** p310 B1.

During the cold winter months, Cinema Mexico keeps Milanese movie buffs warm with the often-riotous Revolution Music Film Festival. During this series (organised by the cinema itself) anything from *A Hard Day's Night* (1964) to *Pink Floyd Live at Pompeii* (1971) makes its way on to the big screen. New-release original-language films are shown all day Thursday (as part of the Sound & Motion scheme, *see p158*), while the 10pm show on

Friday is that Jim Sharman favourite that gave this cinema its nickname. Cinema Mexico also runs workshops on a variety of film-related subjects.

Cineteatro San Lorenzo
alle Colonne

Corso di Porta Ticinese 45, South (02 5811 3161). Bus 94/tram 3. **Tickets** €4. **No credit cards.** **Map** p310 A2, B2/p312 A2.

As well as its usual roster of independent film showings, this art-house cinema runs special weekend double-bill sessions in which two films by the same international director are screened each evening in their original language. Note that Cineteatro San Lorenzo charges a one-off member-ship fee of €1.

Anteospazio Cinema. See p158.

Cineteca Italiana

Spazio Oberdan, viale Vittorio Veneto 2, East (02 7740 6300/www.cinetecamilano.it). Metro Porta Venezia/ tram 29, 30. **Tickets** €5; membership fee €3. *Eight shows* €32. **No credit cards. Map** p309 B1, B2.

The Cineteca has been a member of the Fédération Internationale des Archives du Film (FIAF) since 1948. Its mission: restoring, lending and promoting films, and its archive now runs to 15,000 titles. It is also responsible for the Museo del Cinema (*see below* and *p81*). Film screenings take place in the Spazio Oberdan, a 193-seat space revamped by architect Gae Aulenti in 1999. The programme includes seminars, debates and screenings on themes as far-ranging as the origins of pornography in film and cinematic shorts. The website has details of events.

Museo del Cinema

Palazzo Dugnani, via D Manin 2b, North (office 02 2900 5659/info 02 655 4977/www.cinetecamilano. it). Metro Turati/bus 43/tram 1, 2. **Open** 3-6pm Fri-Sun. **Admission** *Museum* (includes film ticket) €3; €1.50 under-12s. **No credit cards. Map** p309 C1.

Besides cabinets full of cinematographic curios, the Museo del Cinema offers screenings of obscure Italian titles at 4pm and 5pm. *See also p81.*

Festivals

Festival del Cinema Africano a Milano

Via G Lazzaroni 8, North (02 6671 2077/02 669 6258/www.festivalcinemaafricano.org). Metro Centrale FS/bus 42, 60, 81, 82/tram 2, 5, 9. **Dates** end Mar. **Tickets** prices vary. **Map** p309 B1.

This seven-day festival of works by African filmmakers has been going for 14 years and has grown to include movies from Asia and Latin America. The competing films and videos are screened in six cinemas around the city, such as the Arcobaleno (*see p158*) and Spazio Oberdan (*see above*).

Festival Internazionale di Cinema Gaylesbico

Cinema Pasquirolo, corso Vittorio Emanuele II 28 (02 7602 0757/www.cinemagaylesbico.com). Metro Duomo or San Babila. **Dates** late May-early June. **Tickets** prices vary. **Map** p311 A1/p312 B2, C1.

Now in its 17th year (2004), this festival is a celebration of films on gay themes by directors from countries as diverse as Canada, Israel, Haiti and Ghana. Previous winners include *Two Minutes after Midnight*, an Australian feature film about gay life seen through an adolescent's eyes, and an Argentinian love story (*Tan de Repente*).

Film Festival Internazionale di Milano

Various venues (02 8918 1179/www.miffmilano festival.com). **Dates** late Oct/early Nov. **Tickets** prices vary. **No credit cards.**

This festival, established in 2000, has been hailed as the European Sundance. It promotes film as art and provides an international platform for experimental and independent filmmakers to strut their celluloid stuff.

Milano Film Festival (MFF)

Teatro Strehler (Nuovo Piccolo), largo Greppi, North (02 7233 3222/www.milanofilmfestival.it). Metro Lanza/bus 43, 57, 70/tram 3, 4, 12, 14. **Dates** mid-late Sept. **Tickets** *Daily pass* €6. *Weekly pass* €20. **No credit cards. Map** p308 C2.

Started in 1996 as a festival to showcase shorts by young Milanese film-makers, MFF was opened to international contributors and feature films in 2000. It's a brilliant chance to see contemporary developments in international cinematography from over 30 countries. The Festival is a superbly organised, interdisciplinary affair that includes art exhibitions, live music, performances and workshops. Take your pillow along for the movie marathon, in which some 300 Italian short films are screened.

Sport Movies & TV International Festival

Via E de Amicis 17, South (02 8940 9076/fax 02 837 5973/www.ficts.com). Metro Sant'Ambrogio/ bus 94/tram 3. **Dates** end Oct-early Nov. **Admission** free. **Map** p310 A2.

Into its 21st year in 2004, this is one of the most important festivals dedicated to sports films, documentaries and television programmes. It's organised by the International Federation of Sport in Cinema and Television and recognised by the IOC.

Galleries

The galleries may be small, but their number and scope are anything but.

Stark white walls are a perfect foil to Technicolor art at **Galleria Carla Sozzani**. *See p163*.

The handsome Castello di Rivoli near Turin may have the most beautiful setting, and Bologna may have ArteFiera, the leading annual exhibition; but Milan surely has the best selection of small private galleries for contemporary art.

The lack of one overriding Milan-based art movement, such as Arte Povera in Turin or Transavanguardia in Rome, has made the city a free-for-all, contemporary art-wise. That said, the Milanese tendency to look beyond its borders in many areas has led many galleries to devote themselves to work by British, American, German, Japanese – in a word, anything but Italian – artists. As one Milan-based artist says: 'A gallery that offers a 1:2 ratio Italian to non-Italian can be considered a gallery that showcases Italian artists.'

Nevertheless, most of the time – except for in August, when much of the city shuts down for holidays – there are plenty of shows to attend. For a list, pick up a copy of the *Artshow* booklet (www.artshow.it) from the APT tourist office near the Duomo (*see p53*) or from any

of the galleries listed here. The booklet contains information on some 100 Milanese galleries.

The longest-established galleries tend to be along via Manzoni and in the Brera area, and right the way up to Foro Buonaparte, but many other areas are starting to figure large on the art scene. These include recently gentrified parts of town such as via Farini and via Maroncelli, in the Porta Garibaldi (for both, map p308 B2). You'll find some galleries are housed in apartment buildings: ring the bell and you'll be buzzed in.

Private galleries

Antonio Colombo
Arte Contemporanea

Via Solferino 44, North (02 2906 0171/www.colombo arte.com). Metro Moscova/bus 4, 43, 94/tram 11, 30, 33. **Open** 4-7.30pm Tue-Sat. Closed Aug, 2wks Dec-Jan. **No credit cards**. **Map** p308 B2, C2.
Established in 1996, Antonio Colombo's gallery focuses on young Italian artists. The emphasis is on figurative art and media, including painting,

sculpture, photography and installations. Artists who have exhibited here include Annalisa Sonzogni, Gabriele Di Matteo, Carlo Benvenuto, Andrea Aquilanti and Sergia Avveduti.

B&D Studio Contemporanea

Via Calvi 18, East (02 5412 2563/www.bnd.it). Bus 60, 73/tram 12, 27. **Open** 10am-6pm Mon; 10am-7.30pm Tue-Fri; 11.30am-7.30pm Sat. Closed Aug, 24 Dec-6 Jan. **No credit cards. Map** p311 A2.
This very cool space provides a backdrop for works in a variety of technological media, including digital photography, video and light. Prices from €500.

Ca' di Fra'

Via Farini 2, North (02 2900 2108). Metro Garibaldi/tram 3, 4, 11, 29, 30, 33. **Open** *Sept-June* 10am-1pm, 3-7pm Mon-Sat. *July* By appointment only. Closed Aug, 24 Dec-7 Jan. **No credit cards. Map** p308 B2.
Discover the work of young Italian and international artists in this charming, cosy space. Recent exhibitions have featured Danilo Buccella and Joseph Kosuth. The library is open 10am-1pm Tue-Fri, by appointment.

Galleria Blu

Via Senato 18, East (02 7602 2404/www.galleriablu. com). Metro Montenapoleone or Turati/bus 61, 94. **Open** 10am-12.30pm, 3.30-7pm Mon-Fri; 3.30-7.30pm Sat. Closed Aug, 2wks Dec-Jan. **No credit cards. Map** p309 C1/p312 C1.
Milan's oldest and arguably most prestigious venue was founded in 1957 to promote post-war avant-garde artists. This was the first gallery to showcase the likes of Lucio Fontana, Alberto Burri and Emilio Vedova. Others on show have included Braque, Basquiat, Chagall, Giacometti, Kandinsky and Klee. Two out of three exhibitions feature Italian artists.

Galleria Emi Fontana

Viale Bligny 42, South (02 5832 2237). Metro Porta Romana, then tram 9, 29, 30/bus 79. **Open** 11am-7.30pm Tue-Sat. **No credit cards. Map** p310 B1/p311 B2.
Galleria Emi Fontana has been showing the hottest international contemporary artists working in all media – including Turner Prize-winner Gillian Wearing – since 1992.

Galleria Pack

Foro Buonaparte 60, North (02 8699 6395/www. galleriapack.com). Metro Cairoli or Lanza/bus 18, 50, 58, 94/tram 1, 3, 4, 12, 20, 27. **Open** 1pm-7.30pm Tue-Sat; mornings by appointment. Closed Aug, 24 Dec-6 Jan. **Map** p308 C2/p312 A1.
Not to be confused with the PAC, the Padiglione di Arte Contemporanea (*see p164*), this astoundingly handsome venue showcases artists such as MM Campos Pons, Pietro Finelli, Robert Gligorov, Miriam Cabessa and Ofri Cnaani. A word of advice: the street numbering in Foro Buonaparte is misleading – number 60 is in fact closest to the corso Garibaldi end.

Galleria Salvatore + Caroline Ala

Via Monte di Pietà 1, Centre (02 890 0901). Metro Montenapoleone/bus 61/tram 1, 2, 20. **Open** 10am-7pm Tue-Sat. Closed Aug. **No credit cards. Map** p309 C1/p312 B1.
The Alas provide exhibition space for young artists, Italian or otherwise, in solo or group shows.

Giò Marconi

Via Tadino 15, East (02 2940 4373/www.gio marconi.com). Metro Lima or Porta Venezia/bus 60/tram 5, 20, 33. **Open** 11am-7pm Tue-Sat. Closed August, 23 Dec-8 Jan. **No credit cards. Map** p309 B2.
Giovanni Marconi's three-level space caters to all tastes, exhibiting everything from Italian post-war art to the latest in video. On average two out of three artists on show are Italian.

Lia Rumma

Via Solferino 44, North (02 2900 0101/www.galleria liarumma.com). Metro Moscova/bus 41, 43, 94. **Open** 11am-1pm, 3-7pm Tue-Sat. **No credit cards. Map** p308 B2, C2.
Both established and emerging international artists are displayed in this long, narrow, corridor-like gallery, the sister-space of the renowned Lia Rumma gallery in Naples.

Spazio Erasmus Brera

Via Formentini 10, North (02 8646 5075). Metro Cairoli or Lanza/tram 3, 4, 12, 20. **Open** 11.30am-1pm, 4-7.30pm Tue-Sat. **No credit cards. Map** p308 C2.
This relatively small space is hidden away in the maze of cobbled streets off via Fiori Chiari, in the Brera neighbourhood. Spazio Erasmus is worth checking out for its interesting young artists, both from Italy and abroad, as well as its contemporary photography exhibitions.

Spaziotemporaneo

Via Solferino 56, North (02 659 8056/www.gospark. com/spaziotemporaneo). Metro Moscova/bus 41, 43, 94. **Open** 4-7.30pm Tue-Sat. Closed mid Jul-Aug, Christmas. **No credit cards. Map** p308 B2, C2.
Established by Patrizia Serra in 1983, this gallery features younger artists – Italian, Italian-based and otherwise, all linked by a common thread: dealing with visual arts in the post-conceptual era. Among them are Carlo Bernardini, Paolo Borrelli, Rebecca Forster, Daniela Nenciulescu, Alessandro Traina and Irma Blank.

Studio Guenzani

Via Eustachi 10, East (02 2940 9251). Bus 60, 62/tram 5, 11, 23. **Open** *Sept-July* 3-7.30pm Tue-Sat. Closed Aug. **No credit cards. Map** p309 B2, C2.
Under the direction of distinguished art collector Claudio Guenzani, Studio Guenzani has shown Cindy Sherman, Hiroshi Sugimoto and Joseph Kosuth. It also has a strong link with Milanese artists, including painter Margherita Manzelli and photographer Gabriele Basìlico.

Make it snappy

Milan has a good selection of galleries dedicated to contemporary photography. As well as the spaces listed below, keep an eye out for photography shows at Spazio Erasmus Brera (*see p162*), Studio Guenzani (*see p162*) and Zonca & Zonca (*see p164*). The foyer area of the Anteo Cinema (*see p158*) also provides a venue for photography shows; your ticket includes entrance to the exhibition.

Galleria Carla Sozzani

Corso Como 10, North (02 653 531/www.galleriacarlasozzani.org). Metro Garibaldi/tram 11, 29, 30, 33. **Open** 3.30-7.30pm Mon; 10.30am-7.30pm Tue; 10.30am-9pm Wed, Thur, Fri-Sun. **Credit** AmEx, MC, V. **Map** p308 B2.

Part of the 10 Corso Como boutique (*see p138*), this gallery specialises in photographic shows. The artists on show are mostly non-Italians, and include Manuel Alvarez Bravo, Bruce Weber, Edward S Curtis, Rodman Wanamaker, Herb Ritts and Mary Ellen Marks. Print prices average €1,000-€3,000. During Milan Fashion Week and the Milan Furniture Fair (*see chapter* **Festivals & Events**) the gallery is also open Monday mornings.

Galleria Officina Fotografica

Via Farini 6, North (02 657 1015). Metro Garibaldi, then tram 11, 33. **Open** 3-6pm Mon-Thur, or by appointment. Closed July, Aug, 25 Dec-6 Jan. **No credit cards**. **Map** p308 B2.

Galleria Officina Fotografica opened in 2000. Most of the artists it exhibits are Italian and include Sergio Tori, Costantino Liquori, Alberto Magrin and Paola Rizza. The gallery holds shows throughout the year, except for July and August. Prices start at about €150.

Museo di Fotografia Contemporanea

Villa Ghirlanda, via Frova 10, Cinisello Balsamo (02 6602 3550/www.museo fotografiacontemporanea.com). Bus 727 from Stazione Centrale. **No credit cards**. **Map** p306.

If you're an avid photography fan, have a car, or do not mind a 40-minute bus ride, then this museum – housed in the 17th-century Villa Ghirlanda and due to open by the end of 2004 – will probably be worth a visit. In the meantime, check out the website, and see some of the photos in the extensive archives.

Photology

Via della Moscova 25, North (02 659 5285/ www.photology.com). Metro Moscova/bus 94. **Open** 11am-7pm Tue-Sat, or by appointment. Closed Aug, 26 Dec-6 Jan. **No credit cards**. **Map** p308 B2.

Photology has been around since 1992 and holds shows throughout the year, except, of course, in August. Shows at Photology tend to be split 50/50 between Italian and other artists. Among the artists Photology represents are Mario Giacomelli, Ettore Sottsass and Gian Paolo Barbieri. Other photographers whose work has been shown include Luigi Ghirri and Giacomo Costa.

Studio di Fotografia Italiana

Corso Venezia 22, East (02 784 100/www. fotografiaitaliana.com). Metro Porta Venezia/ tram 9, 29, 30. **Open** 4-7pm Tue-Sat, or by appointment. Closed Aug, 26 Dec-6 Jan. **No credit cards**. **Map** p309 C1/p312 C1.

Established by Nicoletta Rusconi in May 2003, with Fabio Castelli as artistic director, the Studio di Fotografia Italiana is the only gallery in Italy dedicated solely to local talent. Among those who have exhibited here are Francesco Pignatelli, Manuela Carrano and Silvio Wolf, as well as Luigi Ghirri, Franco Fontana, Davide Tranchina and Mario Cresci.

Arts & Entertainment

Zonca & Zonca

*Via Ciovasso 4, North (02 7200 3377/www.zoncae
zonca.com). Metro Cairoli or Lanza/bus 61/tram 3, 4,
12, 20.* **Open** *3.30-7.30pm Mon; 10am-1pm, 3.30-
7.30pm Tue-Sat.* **No credit cards. Map** p308 C2.

A father-and-daughter-run space merging Italian
modernism with the super-contemporary in six
annual exhibitions. Selections by Gianfranco Zonca,
which have included work by Lucio Fontana and
Mimmo Rotella, are offset by Elena Zonca's predilec-
tion for cutting-edge installation and photography.

Public spaces

C/O (Care Of)

*Fabbrica del Vapore, via Luigi Nono 7, North (02
331 5800/www.careof.org). Bus 41, 43/tram 12, 14,
29, 30, 33.* **Open** *3-7pm Tue-Sat. Closed Aug, 24
Dec-6 Jan.* **Map** p308 B2.

Run by Viafarini (*see below*), this non-profit gallery,
whose aim it is to increase public knowledge of
contemporary art, features monthly exhibitions, conferences, workshops and external projects.

Galleria L'Affiche

*Via Unione 6, Centre (02 8645 0124/www.affiche.it)
Metro Duomo or Missori/tram 2, 3, 4, 12, 14, 15,
20, 24, 27.* **Open** *4-7pm Tue-Sat. Closed Jan-mid
Feb, July, Aug.* **Map** p310 A2/p312 B2.

As well as exhibitions at the gallery in via Unione,
L'Affiche has a store that sells posters from the early
20th century to the present in via Nirone 11.

Nuages

*Via del Lauro 10, North (02 7200 4482/www.
nuages.net) Metro Cairoli or Lanza/tram 3, 4, 20,
12.* **Open** *2-7pm Tue-Fri; 10am-1pm, 2-7pm Sat.
Closed Aug.* **Map** p308 C2.

Lorenzo Mattotti, Tullio Pericoli and Gianluigi
Toccafondo are among the Italian artists exhibited
here; international stars have included Milton Glaser,
Sempé, Folon, and Art Spiegelman. Nuages also
has a publishing branch that produces gorgeously
illustrated classics (from *Alice in Wonderland* to
Les Fleurs du Mal) as well as artists' anthologies.

PAC (Padiglione d'Arte Contemporanea)

*Via Palestro 14, East (02 7600 9085/www.pac-
milano.org). Metro Palestro or Turati/bus 61, 94.*
Open 9.30am-7pm Tue, Wed, Fri-Sun; 9.30am-10pm
Thur. **Admission** €5.20; €2.60 concessions. **Credit**
MC, V. **Map** p309 C1.

The work of Ignazio Gardella (1905-99), the
Padiglione di Arte Contemporanea (PAC) opened in
1979, and so far has put on over 200 exhibitions.
This despite the fact that it was closed for three
years, having been almost completely destroyed in
a bomb explosion that killed five people on the night
of 27 July 1993. The PAC was rebuilt, with enhancements, and reopened in 1996. Among the artists
whose work has been shown here are Andy Warhol,
Michelangelo Pistoletto and Laurie Anderson.

La Triennale di Milano

*Viale Alemagna 6, West (02 724 341/www.
triennale.it). Metro Cadorna/bus 43, 61, 94/
tram 1, 19, 27.* **Open** 10.30am-8.30pm Tue-Sun.
Admission varies. **No credit cards. Map** p308 C1.

For fans of architecture and design, the Triennale is
the place to go. It's located in Parco Sempione in the
Palazzo d'Arte (*see p67*), a building worth seeing for
its own sake.

Viafarini

*Via Farini 35, North (02 6680 4473/www.viafarini.
org). Metro Porta Garibaldi/bus 51, 70, 41/tram 3,
4, 7, 11, 29, 30.* **Open** *Sept-July* 3-7pm Tue-Sat.
Admission free. **No credit cards. Map** p308 B2.

More than just a gallery, this space – run in conjunction with the city council – provides facilities for
researching contemporary art in Milan. There's an
art library and an archive on young working artists.

Private foundations

Fondazione Nicola Trussardi

*Palazzo Marino alla Scala, piazza della Scala 5,
Centre (02 806 8821/www.fondazionenicola
trussardi.com). Metro Duomo/bus 61/tram 1, 2, 20.*
Map p311 A1/p312 B1.

If you recall the exhibition space on the second floor
of this handsome building, you may be disappointed to hear that it is no longer. However, the
Fondazione Nicola Trussardi is still sponsoring contemporary art in venues around the city. If you're in
town in May and November, look out for its eye-
catching site-specific installations.

Fondazione Prada

*Via Fogazzaro 36, at via Cadore, East (02 5467
0515/www.fondazioneprada.org). Bus 62, 84/tram 3,
4, 9.* **Open** *Mar-May, Oct-Dec* 10am-8pm Tue-Sun.
Admission free. **Map** p311 B2.

Situated in a former bank archive, this massive
space is worth seeing in its own right. The vast
majority of artists showing here are non-Italian,
and have included Thomas Friedman, Anish
Kapoor, Marc Quinn and Carsten Höller. The 62 bus
is the only one that stops virtually outside, but
other buses – such as the 60 and 73, as well as trams
12 and 27 – will take you as far as via Cadore; it's
a ten-minute walk from there.

Progetto Chiesa Rossa, Dan Flavin, Untitled 1996

*Via Neera 24, South (02 5467 0216/www.
fondazioneprada.org). Tram 3, 15/bus 79.* **Open** 4-
7pm daily. **Admission** free. **Map** off p310 C2.

Site-specific art at its best. This fluorescent light
installation by American minimalist Flavin was
created for the Chiesa Rossa, on the eastern bank
of the Naviglio Pavese, in conjunction with the
Fondazione Prada (*see above*). Flavin's last work,
completed two days before his death in 1996, it is
best seen after dark. Try to avoid arriving during
mass (4.30-5pm daily).

Gay & Lesbian

High levels of tolerance (nurtured largely by the rag trade) help to make Milan a mecca for the gay community.

Gay Teadance. *See p167.*

With its mind-your-own-business, workaholic attitude, Milan offers both advantages and disadvantages to gay and lesbian tourists. On one hand, it is certainly the out-est Italy gets: by being both the country's economic engine room and the world's design and fashion capital, this stylish, progressive city attracts flocks of gay Italians from all over the country, be they besuited businessmen or dedicated followers (or creators) of fashion. The flipside of the coin is that, with so many locals flaunting the trademark 'Milanese cool' attitude and keeping themselves to themselves, finding out where to go when you arrive can be a bit of an enterprise.

There is no obviously gay area, except perhaps for via Sammartini, but bars and clubs abound – though they need some winkling out. Garibaldi, on the other hand, has more than its fair share of transsexuals and transvestites.

The gay community faces problems in Milan just like everywhere, and recent police raids on the more open pubs (*see p167* **Stonewall in Milan?**) have made owners even less willing to flaunt their activities. Yet behind the grey-stoned palazzi the scene is hopping, and regular clubs like Nuova Idea as well as one-nighters such as Join the Gap and Billy are bursting at the seams. There is a gay film festival (*see p160*) as well as art exhibitions for culture vultures, but there are also plenty of pink

and proud parades for extroverts. Don't be surprised about having to make taxi trips to the suburbs to reach some venues, but do expect to feast your eyes on a lot of cute locals when you get there. Happy hunting!

PRACTICALITIES

More and more of Milan's gay clubs require clients to have an ArciUno Club Card, issued by Arcigay, Italy's leading gay and lesbian organisation (*see p168*); you'll need it to get into certain saunas, discos and bars – we've indicated which ones in listings below. The card can be bought at any club that requires it. Annual membership costs €13.

Another indispensable tool for clubbing in Milan is the free map found at most clubs and at Milan's leading gay and lesbian bookstore, Libreria Babele Galleria (*see p168*). The map has a comprehensive list of clubs, shops, saunas and cruising areas with contact details.

Like just about everything else in the city, most gay and lesbian venues close for a good part of July and/or August, as well as for up to two weeks around Christmas. Annual closure dates can vary from year to year; it pays to call ahead to check that venues are open. Many predominantly straight clubs have gay nights (*see chapter* **Nightlife**). These can change from time to time; again, phone ahead to make sure you're going to the right place on the right night.

Arts & Entertainment

Forever blowing bubbles at **Metro Centrale**. *See p168.*

Gay Milan

Milan's gay venues offer something for everyone. Obviously, there are the fashionista locales where you go to see and be seen – good looks, a hot body and the fanciest of clothes are essential for these places. But there's plenty of scope for mere mortals too, including those with a penchant for leather and/or dark rooms.

Bars & clubs

Flexo Club
Via Oropa 3, East (02 2682 6709/www.flexoclub.it). Metro Cimiano. **Open** 10pm-4am Tue-Thur; 10pm-7am Fri; 10pm-midnight Sat. **Admission** *With ArciUno Club Card* €5 before midnight; €10 after midnight (inc drink and cloakroom). **Credit** AmEx, DC, MC, V. **Map** off p311 A2.
This bar attracts old and young looking for close encounters. Privacy is guaranteed by relaxation cabins and dark rooms. It also has a XXX cinema, a large cocktail bar and a leather section. Men only.

G Lounge
Via Larga 8, Centre (02 8053 042/www.glounge.it). Metro Duomo or Missori/bus 54, 60, 65/tram 12, 20, 23, 27. **Open** 7am-6pm Mon; 7am-2am Tue-Sat; 7-10pm Sun. Closed 3wks in August. **Admission** free. **No credit cards. Map** p311 A1/p312 B2.
This venue has a rich history as a former *bocciodromo* (boules alley) and fascist headquarters. During the day it is crowded with professionals from nearby offices, but after dark G Lounge switches up a gear

with its friendly gay evenings, which attract a hip, trend-setting clientele. On Thursdays the joint is jumping to electronica, while Sundays are quieter and more sedate, with a fun *aperitivo* hour.

Nuova Idea
Via De Castillia 30, North (02 690 07859). Metro Garibaldi or Gioia/bus 42, 82, 83/tram 30, 33. **Open** 10.30pm-3am Thur, Fri; 10pm-4am Sat. **Admission** €10-€16. **No credit cards. Map** p309 B1.
Milan's first gay club has been going for over 20 years. One of its two dancefloors has commercial music, the other is reserved for ballroom dancing and a live orchestra at weekends. Serving a mixed crowd, it is also a hangout for the zone's famous transvestites.

Ricci Bar
Piazza della Repubblica 27, North (02 6698 2536). Metro Repubblica/bus 2, 11/tram 2, 9, 20, 33. **Open** 8pm-2am Tue-Sun. Closed 3wks Aug, 2wks Dec-Jan. **Admission** free. **No credit cards. Map** p309 B1.
This is one of Milan's most famous gay clubs, but you'd never know it if you passed by during the day, when office workers flock to it – in its guise of local café – for their shots of caffeine. Only after dark does it blossom into a trendy bar and Milan's fashion set and beautiful people replace the hassled workers.

Discos

Billy Club
Amnesia, via Gatto, corner of viale Forlanini, East (335 832 7777 mobile/www.billyclub.it). Bus 38. **Open** noon-5am Sat. Closed Aug. **Admission** €16-€18 (inc drink). **Credit** AmEx, MC, V. **Map** off p311 A2.

Billy Club hosts international DJs, making the music one of its strongest points. The clientele is not exclusively gay, but gorgeous looks, cool and cutting-edge designs are the norm here. Check out the website for info on guest DJs and the monthly programme. In June and July, Billy Club moves to Spider Disco (02 7020 8264), near the Idroscalo.

Gay Teadance

Gasoline, via Bonnet 11, North (02 2901 3245/ www.teadance.it). Metro Garibaldi/bus 94/tram 29, 30. **Open** *Sept-May* 5-10pm Sun. **Admission** before 5.30pm (with flyer from www.teadance.it); €8 after 5.30pm (inc drink). **No credit cards.** **Map** p308 B2.

This Sunday afternoon club is housed in Gasoline (*see p176*) and caters to a good-looking crowd of 16- to 30-year-olds. Cube dancers provide entertainment for the largely male crowd, with happy hours and a sushi bar for sustenance. On the colourful Teadance website you can sign up for updates on special theme parties, or send messages to someone you spotted on the dancefloor.

Glitter

Cafè Dalì, largo Schuster 3, Centre (02 8699 7277). Metro Duomo/bus 54, 60, 65/tram 12, 20, 23, 27. **Open** 12pm-4am Sat. Closed Aug. **Admission** €10 (inc drink). **No credit cards.** **Map** p311 A1/p312 B2.

This tiny, hot, colourful club has been competing with the largest venues on the queer scene for the past six years, often coming up trumps. Gays and lesbians mix with straight folks to dance to '80s sounds, electronica, Britpop and trash. The staff keep things lively by entertaining the crowds with shows and impromptu performances.

Join the Gap

Borgo del Tempo Perso, via Fabio Massimo 36, South (339 441 8441 mobile). Metro Porto di Mare/ bus 84, 93, 95. **Open** 8pm-1am Sun. **Admission** €10 (inc drink). **Credit** AmEx, DC, MC, V. **Map** off p311 C2.

This out-of-the-way club night is a magnet for those who like dancing but have to get up early for work on Monday. A richly baroque interior (where else can you find a buffet by the light of a silver candelabra?) contrasts with the down-to-earth clientele who make this place crackle. Get there early... as the evening progresses, the buffet gives way to a floor show and classic tracks and you can still be home by midnight.

Sodoma/Pervert

Hollywood, corso Como 15, North (02 6598 9967/ www.discotecahollywood.com). Metro Garibaldi/ tram 11, 29, 30, 33. **Open** *Sept-May* 10.30pm-4am Wed. **Admission** €20 (inc drink). **Credit** AmEx, DC, MC, V. **Map** p308 B2.

Stonewall in Milan?

Throughout 2003 there was a series of police raids in via Sammartini, Milan's only official 'queer street'. On one occasion the police arrested Frank Semenzi, editor of the gay monthly *Pride*, confiscated property and forced the patrons to surrender their ID cards.

The protests that ensued resembled a smaller version of New York's Stonewall, with gay Milanese making their concerns heard outside the gay locales that had been targeted by the police. However, the police raids continued.

To the vast majority of the Milanese gay community, such events are clearly the expression of the present government's right-wing attitudes. While prime minister Silvio Berlusconi has never declared himself or his party to be anti-gay, some of the members of his coalition, notably Gianfranco Fini of Alleanza Nazionale, have not been so shy about expressing their homophobic views. One of the early fruits of such open discrimination is a new law stating that sexual orientation is reason enough to dismiss an employee. 'Not even Mussolini managed to pass a law discriminating

against homosexuals, but trust Berlusconi's government to succeed in that,' lamented Franco Grillini, president of Arcigay.

If this government continues to have its way, the queer community will be increasingly pushed to the sidelines. As well as police raids on their venues, gays are suffering from the shrinkage of available cruising space as the authorities place fences and street lighting around favoured spots to discourage illicit activity. In the eastern suburbs of Lambrate, the flowering bushes in piazza Leonardo da Vinci that used to provide gay *milanesi* with a good spot for close encounters, have been removed and bright illumination put in place. Not far from here, at the Orto Mercato and along via Cimino in particular, cruising is done mostly by car, but police checks are frequent. Further east and outside the city's boundaries, the Idroscalo, once the busiest spot for motorised cruising has been fenced off and is no longer accessible. Outdoor lovers look forward to the new elections, hoping that they will bring an end to Berlusconi's right-wing rule.

Every Wednesday the Hollywood (see p177), which usually welcomes footballers and models, hosts one of Milan's most transgressive events. At the entrance half-clad beautiful girls behind glass panes move to impossibly loud house music, setting the scene for what goes on inside… gay-oriented clientele, along with transvestites and hard-core clubbers.

Saunas

Metro Centrale
Via Schiapparelli 1, North (02 6671 9089/www.metroclub.it). Metro Centrale FS/bus 42, 53, 60, 90, 91/tram 2, 5, 20, 33. **Open** noon-2am Mon-Fri, Sun; noon-3am Sat. **Admission** *With ArciUno Club Card* €14 (€11.50 after 8.30pm); Sun €16.50 (€14 after 8.30pm). **Credit** MC, V. **Map** p309 A2.
Metro Centrale is spread out over two floors, with jacuzzis, a steam bath, a massage room and a Finnish sauna. For your private viewing pleasure, there are videos in the chill-out rooms, as well as an internet hook-up. Free condoms are handed out at the door. There are discounts for under-26s.

Royal Hammam
Via Plezzo 16, East (02 2641 2189). Metro Lambrate, bus 72. **Open** 2pm-2am Mon-Fri, Sun; noon-3pm Fri-Sat. **Admission** €14; €16 Sat, Sun. **Credit** MC, V. **Map** off p309 B2.
The superb facilities at Milan's most recent sauna include a large pool, jacuzzis and massage rooms. Its young and trendy clientele find it an elegant venue in which to relax and socialise.

Sauna Cimiano
Via Oropa 3, East (02 285 10528/www.metroclub.it). Metro Cimiano. **Open** 2pm-2am Tue-Thur; 2pm-7am Fri-Sat. **Admission** €13 before 8pm; €10 after 8pm. **Credit** AmEx, DC, MC, V. **Map** off p309 A2.
In the same building of Flexo Club Bar, Cimiano is a smaller version of sister Metro Centrale (see p167). It offers the same facilities and is located off via Palmanova, one of Milan's main access routes.

Thermas
Via Bezzecca 9, East (02 545 0355). Bus 60/tram 27, 29, 30, 84. **Open** noon-midnight daily. Closed 2wks Aug. **Admission** €11-€14; €11 after 8pm daily. **Credit** AmEx, DC, MC, V. **Map** p311 A2.
Spartan but clean, Thermas serves a diverse crowd of all ages, ranging from corporate executives to designers. There's a steam bath, a very small body-building room, TV, a cooling-off area, a jacuzzi and red leather beds in the changing rooms.

Miscellaneous

American Contourella
Piazza della Repubblica 1a, North (02 655 2728/www.contourella.it). Metro Repubblica/tram 11, 29, 30. **Open** 7am-10.30pm Mon-Fri; 8am-8pm Sat; 10am-6pm Sun. **Admission** €15. **Credit** AmEx, DC, MC, V. **Map** p309 B1.

Though not exclusively gay, this gym is a well-known meeting place for gay men (who tend to be less flash here than at Downtown Palestre, *see below*). The gym offers all the standard physical fitness services, from free weights to an 18m pool.

Company Club
Via Benadir 14, East (02 282 9481). Metro Cimiano/bus 53, 56. **Open** 10pm-3am Tue-Thur, Sun; 10pm-9am Fri, Sat. **Admission** free with ArciUno card. **No credit cards.** **Map** off p309 A2.
A fair hike from the centre, near the Parco Lambro in the north-eastern suburbs, this leather club is the place for anyone looking for a quick hook-up. There's a dark room and a video room.

Cruising Canyon
Via Paisiello 4, East (02 2040 4201). Metro Loreto/bus 90, 91, 92. **Open** 24hrs daily. **Admission** €8-€10 (inc cloakroom). **No credit cards.** **Map** off p309 B2.
This enormous venue is a sex club, pure and simple. A one-stop shop with indoor reproductions of cruising areas, the Canyon has a mock-up park, a cinema and a labyrinth. Definitely for those looking for a quick but close encounter.

Downtown Palestre
Piazza Cavour 2, North (02 7601 1485/www.downtownpalestre.it). Metro Turati/bus 61, 94/tram 1, 2, 20. **Open** 7am-midnight Mon-Fri; 10am-9pm Sat, Sun. **Admission** €50 per day; €170 per mth. **Credit** AmEx, MC, V. **Map** p309 C1.
This (by no means exclusively gay) gym is one of the trendiest in Milan and is a well-known magnet for some of the best-looking gay men in the city. The crowd is a mix of fashion types, managers and executives, some of whom spend as much time checking out their prospects as toning their pecs. Its restaurant is great for scoping out new prospects.

Organisations & shops

The best source of information on gay events, clubs and publications throughout Italy is the www.gay.it website, which also offers a wealth of links to other organisations, chatrooms and venues, as well as updates on special events.
    Newsstands that stock gay pornography include the one in piazza Oberdan at the corner of via Tadino, as well as the one on corso Buenos Aires, close to Porta Venezia. Some steamy stuff can also be found at the newsstands in and around Stazione Centrale. Libreria Babele Galleria (*see below*) is your best bet for queer lit.

Arcigay
Via Bezzecca 3, East (02 5412 2225/helpline 02 5412 2227/www.arcigaymilano.org). Bus 45, 66, 73/tram 27. **Open** 3-8pm Mon-Fri; 3-7pm Sun. Closed 1wk Aug; 1wk Dec. **Map** p311 A2.
The Bologna-based Arcigay and Arcilesbica (*see p169*), Italy's main gay and lesbian associations, are important sources of information on gay and

lesbian life. The Arcigay website is excellent and the association runs a telephone service for those looking for services or in need of help. It also issues the ArciUno card (*see p165*), which is becoming ever more essential for getting into Milan's gay venues. The Milan office of Arcigay is open on Sunday afternoons to welcome new members and answer questions. The group also hosts occasional members' dinners (call for times and dates), while the cultural office organises film festivals and debates. There is a small library stocked with gay-related books, magazines and videos.

Libreria Babele Galleria
Via San Nicolao 10, West (02 8691 5597/www. libreriababele.it). Metro Cadorna/bus 50, 58, 94/ tram 1, 19, 24. **Open** 2-7pm Mon; 10am-7pm Tue-Sun. Closed 2wks Aug. **Credit** AmEx, MC, V. **Map** p310 A2.
Milan's main bookstore for gays and lesbians. In addition to its 7,000 books, it sells foreign and Italian magazines, videos, posters, postcards and a variety of gadgets. It also hosts cultural events and exhibitions and houses a gay and lesbian travel agency, Arcoturismo. Many of its products are also on sale over the internet.

Sex Sade
Via Secchi, at corso Buenos Aires, East (02 2024 1193/www.sexsade.it). Metro Porta Venezia/tram 9, 20, 23, 30. **Open** 3-7.30pm Mon; 10am-1pm, 2.30-7.30pm Tue-Sat. **Credit** AmEx, MC, V. **Map** p309 B2.
If you're into S&M, this is the place for you. Latex and leather clothing, accessories and underwear are here in abundance.

Lesbian Milan

While gay clubs are relatively plentiful in Milan, the city offers much less for lesbians, with just a handful of long-standing bars and discos geared towards women seeking women. The bimonthly magazine *Towanda!* (in Italian) has information on lesbian life in Milan. A highbrow publication with book reviews, political commentary and art critiques, it also contains ads for lesbian-only vacation spots and news on events organised by Italy's main lesbian group, Arcilesbica (*see below*). Libreria Babele Galleria (*see above*), also has updated information on clubs, events and film series. Finally, a good resource for events, chatrooms and even job listings is the Lista Lesbica portal at www.listalesbica.it.

Bars & clubs

Mokò
Via Calabria 5, North (02 376 1531/www. associazionemoko.it). Bus 90, 91, 92. **Open** 9pm-1am Wed, Thur; 9pm-2am Fri, Sat; 5pm-1am Sun. Closed Aug. **Admission** €2.50; annual membership €12. **No credit cards**. **Map** p308 A1.

A bit out of the way, and with ultra-simple decor, Mokò is a lively joint, with cabaret, live music or a DJ, depending on the evening, as well as the odd cultural event such as a book presentation or lesbian film festival. The clientele – from the city and the hinterland – is friendly. There's a wide age range, though Fridays tend to draw a slightly younger crowd. Friday, Saturday and Sunday evenings are women-only.

Oca Dipinta
17.3km along Statale Paullese, Zelo Buon Persico, near Lodi (02 906 5027/www.ocadipinta.it). Tram 12 or 27 to viale Umbria, then bus Q8 or 12B from via Cena. **Open** 8pm-3am Thur, Sat. Closed 2wks Aug. **Admission** €8-€15. **Credit** AmEx, MC, V. **Map** p306.
The Oca Dipinta is 15km (9.5 miles) outside the city, but it's worth the trip. A disco and eaterie are housed in a renovated farmhouse, and the place is open throughout the summer, when the action moves out to the garden. Thursday night is lesbian night.

Sottomarino Giallo
Via Donatello 2, East (339 545 4127 mobile/www. sottomarinogiallo.it). Metro Loreto or Piola/tram 11, 33/bus 55, 56, 90, 91. **Open** 11pm-3am Wed, Sun; 11pm-4am Fri; 11pm-5am Sat. Closed 3wks Aug. **Admission** €10 (inc drink). **No credit cards**. **Map** off p309 B2.
One of Milan's long-established lesbian clubs, the Yellow Submarine has a cosy lounge-like bar upstairs and a disco downstairs, which features mainstream dance music. The place is popular with a range of age groups, though most of those who come here are in the thirtysomething band. Saturday nights are women-only; gay men or male friends of regulars are admitted on other nights.

Organisations

Arcilesbica
Corso Garibaldi 91, North (02 6311 8654/www.arci lesbica.it). Metro Moscova/bus 41, 43, 94/tram 3, 4, 12, 14. **Open** for events only. **Map** p308 B2.
While Arcilesbica is much less active than its brother group Arcigay (*see p168*), it is nevertheless Italy's main political organisation for lesbians. Its website contains a calendar of activities, which range from long weekend trips to political workshops and film screenings. The group also runs a helpline at the number given above, open 7-9pm on Thursdays.

Collettivo Donne Milanesi
Corso Garibaldi 91, North (02 2901 4027/cdm@ women.it). Metro Moscova/bus 41, 43, 94/tram 3, 4, 12, 14. **Open** for events only. **Map** p308 B2.
CDM is one of the most active lesbian associations in Milan and works in close association with Arcilesbica (*see above*). It organises everything from brunches to lesbian-themed film screenings to political debates. Some events are held at the Libreria Babele Galleria (*see above*), where calendars of the group's activities can also be found.

Arts & Entertainment

Music

La Scala might be closed, but Milan is still buzzing with all sorts of sounds.

Milan is without doubt the hub of Italy's music industry and most of the major record labels (and many indies) have their headquarters here. The reasons are historical: the presence of La Scala (see p174) meant that sheet music publishing companies such as Ricordi were already up and running in operatic days, while in the 1940s and '50s, La Galleria del Corso, an elegant gallery off corso Vittorio Emanuele, behind the Messaggerie Musicali retail store (see p135), became the city's equivalent of New York's Tin Pan Alley.

Milan's importance is such that most leading artists have homes in the city, even if few of them were born here. Laura Pausini, a singer who has sold well abroad, lives in Milan, though she is from a small town in Emilia Romagna, while Eros Ramazzotti, who has fans all over the world, moved here from Rome.

Milan has, however, produced plenty of artists of its own over the years. Adriano Celentano, a veteran whose albums sell well in an increasingly mature market, was born and raised here, as was Giorgio Gaber, a singer-songwriter who died in early 2003. Gaber's widow, Ombretta Colli, is president of the province of Milan, but the fact that several leading politicians attended his funeral (Gaber is buried at the Cimitero Monumentale, see p74) has more to do with the high standing accorded to cultural figures in Italy. In the late 1950s the young Gaber (on guitar) and Celentano (vocals) played together in the same band, The Rock Boys, as did two other future stars, Luigi Tenco (on sax; he committed suicide after being eliminated from the 1967 Sanremo Festival, which he had entered as a singer) and Enzo Jannacci (keyboards). The latter also wrote songs with Dario Fo, who in 1997 went on to win the Nobel Prize for

Literature. Even though Jannacci became famous, he never gave up his day job as a doctor at a Milan hospital and you occasionally still see him around town.

Milan's younger generation has also had its fair share of success stories. Current sensation Le Vibrazioni, a band whose music and laid-back approach to life have shades of the early Beatles, are from here, as are the hilarious Elio e le Storie Tese. Assorted Milanese locations provide the backdrop for the latter's splendid video, *Se fossi figo* (literally, 'if I were sexy'), which shows Elio, the band's far-from-handsome lead singer, and 1960s singing legend Gianni Morandi jogging together and sipping coffee in bars, while the subtitles reveal that they are having an intense, detailed conversation about facial creams and other beauty products. It represents Italian humour – and music – at its best.

Rock & pop

Milan, by virtue of its large population, is an important concert venue, both for international and Italian artists. Obtaining tickets for cultural events can be a complicated and frustrating process, though, and the idea of calling up a venue's box office and leaving a credit card number never really caught on here. For this reason, one of the less stressful ways to buy tickets is to head to one of the special booking centres in the large record/book stores in the centre of Milan, such as Fnac (see p135), Messaggerie Musicali (see p135) and Ricordi (see p147).

For information about concerts, pick up copies of the two weekly supplements published by the daily papers *Il Corriere della Sera* and *La Repubblica*. Every Wednesday *Il Corriere*

Elio e le Storie Tese

I heart Milan

Whereas songs about Naples and Rome tend to praise the cities' beauty, songs about Milan usually concentrate on other aspects of life, such as the love-hate relationship most of its inhabitants have with it. A good example would be *Milano Milano*, a loud rap number recorded by the group Articolo 31 in 2002. The lyrics tell us: 'Whenever I go away, I want to come back, but as soon as I come back, I want to escape,' but we learn that 'you're too beautiful to make me to want to say farewell.' The song also highlights the haves and the have-nots – fashion models and Brera bar yuppies on the one hand and drug addicts and immigrants on the other – and the heavy traffic.

That Milan had problems was also evident to an earlier generation. Adriano Celentano was born here in 1938, the son of immigrants from Puglia. His 1968 song *Il Ragazzo della via Gluck* (The Lad from via Gluck) tells of a young man (presumably himself) who grew up in a house surrounded by fields on the edge of town. He moves to the city, makes some money and thinks how nice it would be to go back to the scene of his childhood. Yet so much building has taken place in the meantime ('where there used to be grass, now there's a city') that he can't recognise it. Celentano continued to complain that rapid expansion was destroying Milan and the Milanese in his 1972 song, *Un Albero di 30 Piani* (A Tree with 30 Floors), and he clearly thinks things have only got worse in the last 30 years. When the song was recently re-released in a greatest hits compilation,

Celentano dedicated it to the city's mayor, Gabriele Albertini of Silvio Berlusconi's Forza Italia party.

Alex Britti, a young singer and accomplished blues guitarist from Rome, came to Milan after getting a record deal, and his song *Milano* (2001) conveys the sense of loneliness and melancholy that can afflict immigrants of every type when they first move here. It describes long, pointless Sunday walks, ultra-violet lamp sun tans, American bars, the fashion industry and traffic: modern Milan in a nutshell.

The city described in Roberto Vecchioni's song *Luci a San Siro* (Lights at San Siro, 1971) is also not such a nice place. The chorus, about the famous soccer stadium (and its fog) may be nice to sing along to, but the lyrics in the verses tell us about the compromises you have to make to get ahead in the music industry, which is based in Milan.

Older songs about Milan tend to take a more romantic view. The city's unofficial anthem is Giovanni D'Anzi's *O mia bella Madonina*. It was written in 1937 and nowadays even Romanian buskers can be heard singing it on trams. 'Oh my beautiful little Virgin Mary' is a tribute to the city's main symbol, the gold statue that stands on top of the Duomo (*see p56*). Yet even this more nostalgic view of Milan has its down side: the song has often been criticised for its racist comments about the Neapolitans who moved to Milan. Clearly, southern immigration was already an issue in Milanese life in the 1930s.

publishes the *ViviMilano* supplement, while on Thursdays *La Repubblica* prints *Tutto Milano* in handy booklet form. The city's three free dailies, *Leggo*, *City* and *Metro*, which are distributed at subway stops in the morning, also contain music and other listings. *City* is the most detailed and informative. There is also a monthly arts magazine, *Carnet*, with extensive listings in every field.

Mega venues

Filaforum

Via D Vittorio 6, Assago, South (199 128 800/ www.forumnet.it). Metro Famagosta, then bus to Assago. **Open** hours vary. **Tickets** €22-€100. **No credit cards. Map** off p310 C1.

The location of this sports and concert centre, out to the south of the city in Assago, leaves a lot to be desired. You can get there with a special bus service from Famagosta metro station, but most Milanese concert-goers prefer to sit in a traffic jam, both going there and coming back. The acoustics are pretty poor, too, but it's an important venue nonetheless. Typical performers include Eros Ramazzotti, Laura Pausini and Coldplay.

Mazda Palace

Via Sant'Elia 33 (02 3340 0551/www.mazda palace.it). Metro Lampugnano. **Open** hours vary. **Tickets** free-€87. **No credit cards. Map** p306.

The Mazda Palace changes name – and sponsor – with alarming regularity. Over the years it has been known as PalaTrussardi (after the fashion dynasty whose founding father was killed in a car crash),

Arts & Entertainment

PalaVobis and even PalaTucker. Its acoustics aren't great but, to give you an idea of its significance as a venue, two great late Italian-Americans – Frank Zappa and Frank Sinatra – played here.

Stadio Meazza (San Siro)
Viale Piccolomini 5, West (02 4870 7123). Metro Lotto/tram 16. **Concerts** in June & July. **Open** hours vary. **Tickets** €22-€81. **No credit cards.** **Map** off p308 B2.
The city-owned soccer stadium occasionally plays host to really big acts, such as Bruce Springsteen and the Rolling Stones. It is also filled by Italian artists with large followings, such as Luciano Ligabue (who could be described as the thinking woman's sex symbol) and veteran rocker Vasco Rossi.

Medium to large

Alcatraz
Via Valtellina 25, North (02 6901 6352). Bus 82, 90, 91, 92/tram 3. **Concerts** occasionally Mon, Thur. **Open** hours vary. **Tickets** €22-€37.50. **No credit cards.** **Map** p308 A2.
Alcatraz is a disco at the weekend and an important concert venue during the week. Housed in a large converted industrial space (3,000sq m/32,290 sq ft)

in the northern – but reasonably central – part of town (not too far from Porta Garibaldi), it is a respected location for both Italian and international acts, as well as a favourite for music industry awards shows.

C-Side
Via Castelbarco 11, South (02 5831 0682). Bus 70, 79, 91. **Concerts** occasionally Mon, Tue. **Open** hours vary. **Tickets** €15 €24. **No credit cards.** **Map** p310 C2.
Like Mazda Palace, this place changes name pretty regularly. Previously known as City Square and Propaganda, it was calling itself C-Side when we went to print. Finnish sensation Rasmus recently played there.

Leoncavallo
Via Watteau 7, North (02 670 5185). Bus 43/ tram 1. **Open** hours vary. **Admission** usually €6. **No credit cards.** **Map** off p309 A2.
This *centro sociale* was public enemy number one when the city had a mayor from the Northern League, Marco Formentini, in the early 1990s, but he was unable to get rid of it. The Leonka is a haven for radical left-wing culture, which, for example, was the breeding ground for Italian rap and hip hop. Artists with claims to street cred, such as 99 Posse, play here when they come to town.

Power stations

Italian radio, like Italian TV, tends to be chaotic, not only in terms of its content, but also in terms of the vast number of unregulated stations. The general standard is not great. Most of the commercial stations are brash and noisy; the three state-owned networks (RAI Radio 1, 2 and 3) are, at best, dull: think BBC World Service, circa 1953.

Milan does, however, have two stations that have managed to break the mould. One is Radio Popolare, a left-leaning news and music station (born in the 1970s in reaction to RAI's awful reporting); the other is the relaxing LifeGate Radio (FM 105.1), which has been playing soothing world music, without the interruptions of DJ chatter and advertising, since 2001. It rapidly acquired a cult following in Milan and it isn't hard to see why: stressed-out office workers and their bosses just love it.

LifeGate is broadcast from Merone, in the hills of nearby Brianza, towards Como, and the story of its owners, the Roveda family, is unusual. Now in his early 50s, Marco Roveda made his money as a young man in the construction business, but soon realised that

financial success didn't necessarily mean happiness. He decided to drop out and use his money to buy a farm, la Fattoria Scaldasole, where he specialised in the production of organic food, and, thanks to the explosion of the health food boom in Italy, it became massively successful.

Roveda and his wife Simona sold the Fattoria Scaldasole company to the Plasmon corporation in 1998 and, along with their son Enea, set up LifeGate with the proceeds. The radio is in fact part of a larger LifeGate project that includes a web portal, an ethical insurance company and bank, a holistic clinic and a health food restaurant, which opened in Milan in December 2003. The Rovedas also have plans for a TV station, although they admit this would be even more costly and ambitious. They believe it is possible to protect the environment, promote spiritual and physical wellbeing and make money all at the same time, saying: 'Our philosophy is: people, planet, profits.'

LifeGate Restaurant
Via Orti 10, South (02 5411 6754/www. lifegaterestaurant.it). Metro Porta Romana/ tram 29, 30. **Map** p311 B1.

And all that jazz: head to the **Blue Note** for Milan's smoothest sounds. *See p174.*

Magazzini Generali

Via Pietrasanta 14, South (02 5521 1313). Bus 90, 91/tram 24. **Open** for concerts, usually Mon. Closed July, Aug. **Tickets** free-€18. **No credit cards.** **Map** p311 C1.

Magazzini is many things – a concert venue, disco, party space and/or art gallery – and has been one of the places to be seen in Milan since it opened in 1995. It hosts musical acts of every genre – from Pavement to the Black Crowes to Wyclef Jean.

Rolling Stone

Corso XXII Marzo 32, East (02 733 172/www.rolling stone.it). Bus 45, 73/tram 12, 27. **Concerts** occasionally Mon, Tue, Wed. **Tickets** free-€22. **No credit cards.** **Map** p311 A2.

A classic venue for rock concerts in Milan, this functions as a disco most of the time.

More intimate

La Feltrinelli

Piazza Piemonte 2, West (02 433 541/www.la feltrinelli.it). Metro Wagner/tram 24. **Admission** free. **Map** off p308 C1.

La Feltrinelli (*see also p133*) regularly offers live music free of charge, via promotional 'showcases', in which record labels present their artists to the public. Thanks to the open-plan layout of the store, if the music isn't to your liking, you can always go and browse the CDs and books (the English section, on the first floor, is rather good). British and American writers also present their work here from time to time. Check the press for listings.

Fnac

Via Palla 2, at via Torino, Centre (02 869 541/www.fnac.it). Metro Duomo/tram 2, 3, 12, 15, 24. **Admission** free. **Map** p310 A2/p312 A2.

The French-owned megastore (*see also p135*) also hosts showcases, even though they are held in a special room, which makes it harder to wander out if you don't like what's on offer. Check the press for listings.

La Salumeria della Musica

Via Pasinetti 2, South (02 5680 7350/www.la salumeriadellamusica.com). Bus 34, 95, 99/tram 24. **Open** 9pm-1am Mon-Sat. **Admission** €5-€20. **Credit** MC, V. **Map** off p311 C1.

This place is a little out of town, lying to the south, but is accessible by tram. Nevertheless it's a popular venue for concerts and indeed showcases. Jazz is dominant, but other musical genres are also on offer. Norah Jones made her first Milan appearance here.

Jazz

Italian jazz enjoys a good reputation and Umbria Jazz, an international event held every July in Perugia, is considered a key calendar date. If international artists have always enjoyed playing in Italy, then Italian artists often had to emigrate (commonly to Paris) in order to find an appreciative audience. Yet today they are finally gaining recognition at home. The older generation of Italian *jazzisti* would include names such as Enrico Rava,

Arts & Entertainment

Romano Mussolini (the son of Il Duce) and suave pianist and singer Paolo Conte, but there are plenty of successful younger artists such as trumpeter Paolo Fresu and pianist Stefano Bollani.

Blue Note

Via Borsieri 37, North (02 6901 6888/www.blue notemilano.com). Metro Porta Garibaldi or Zara/bus 82, 83/tram 4, 7, 11. **Open** 7.30pm-1.30am Mon-Sat; noon-3.30pm (brunch), 6-11pm Sun. **Tickets** €10-€30. **Credit** AmEx, DC, MC, V. **Map** p309 A1.
The opening of the Blue Note Jazz Club Restaurant & Bar in Milan in March 2003 (the original Blue Note is in New York's Greenwich Village) was interpreted as a sign of Italian jazz's good health. Ray Carter, Billy Cobham, Tuck and Patti are just some of the names who have played here of late. The club's artistic director is Nick the Nightfly, a Scotsman famous in Italy for hosting the laid-back, late-night radio show, *Monte Carlo Nights*.

Caffè Letterario

Via Solferino 27, North (02 2901 5119). Metro Moscova/bus 41, 43, 94. **Open** 8am-1am Mon-Sat. Closed 2wks Aug. **Admission** free. **Map** p308 B2.
Jazz is also on the rich cultural entertainment programme at the Caffè Letterario, where the new managers are hoping to get touring musicians to play on their days off.

Nordest Caffè

Via Borsieri 35, North (02 6900 1910/www.nord estcaffe.it). Metro Porta Garibaldi or Zara/tram 4, 11. **Open** 8am-1am Mon-Fri; 8.30am-8.30pm Sun. **Admission** free. **Map** p309 A1.
In the same street as the Blue Note, this offers free, but quality live jazz (mainly on Wednesdays) as a way of attracting eaters and drinkers.

Scimmie

Via Cardinale A Sforza 49, South (02 8940 2874/ www.scimmie.it). Metro Porta Genova/bus 59/tram 3, 15. **Open** 7pm-3am daily (restaurant closed Mon). **Admission** €5-€10. **Credit** AmEx, DC, MC, V. **Map** p310 B2, C2.
Located in the lively Navigli area, Scimmie (Italian for 'monkeys') is a well-known jazz spot, but is not above hosting blues, rock and even reggae acts, not to mention private parties. Its smallish size also makes it a popular choice for record label showcases (John Mayer being a fairly recent example). It consists of a bar and a restaurant, with the strange boat moored outside on the canal taking care of the overflow.

Opera & classical

Auditorium di Milano

Largo Mahler 1, South (02 8338 9201/www. auditoriumdimilano.org/www.orchestrasinfonica. milano.it). Tram 3, 15. **Open** Box office 10am-7pm daily. *Performances* times vary. **Tickets** €7-€50. **No credit cards**. **Map** p310 B2.

A key venue for classical music, this has been home to the city's Verdi orchestra and choir since 1999. The acoustics in this 1,400-seat auditorium (a former cinema) are excellent and it is also used for some jazz events. The venue has a good reputation, even though its website lists concerts that took place more than a year ago.

Conservatorio di Musica 'Giuseppe Verdi'

Via Conservatorio 12, East (02 762 1101/www. conservatorio-milano.com). Metro San Babila/ bus 54, 61. **Open** Box office 8am-8pm Mon-Fri. *Performances* 9pm Mon-Fri. **Tickets** €5-€13. **No credit cards**. **Map** p311 A2/p312 C2.
Listen to Conservatorio students and travelling ensembles play favourites such as symphonies by Mozart and violin concertos by Bach and Paganini.

Teatro Alla Scala

Piazza della Scala (02 7200 3744/www.teatro allascala.org). Metro Duomo/bus 61/tram 1, 2. **Map** p311 A1/p312 B1.
This world-famous opera house needs no introduction, but since 2001 it has been shut while a controversial renovation project is carried out – this is designed to improve security and to renovate the ageing fixtures and fittings. It remains to be seen whether it will be completed by December 2004, but you can be sure of one thing: getting opera tickets to the new La Scala will be just as impossible as getting them for the old. Obtaining concert tickets, on the other hand, isn't quite so tricky.

Teatro Dal Verme

Via San Giovanni sul Muro 2, North (02 8790 5201/box office 02 87 905/www.dalverme.org). Metro Cairoli/tram 1, 27. **Open** Box office 11am-9pm Tue-Sun. *Performances* 9pm Thur; 5pm Sat. **Tickets** €8-€35. **Credit** AmEx, DC, MC, V (not valid for Ticketone events). **Map** p308 C2.
Inaugurated in 1872, the Dal Verme was transformed from a theatre to a cinema after World War II. In April 2001 it reopened its doors as a concert hall after 20 years behind scaffolding. As well as a varied evening programme by visiting orchestras, this spacious wood-floored venue offers classical music from the Orchestra I Pomeriggi Musicali on weekends at 5pm.

Teatro degli Arcimboldi

Viale dell'Innovazione, North (02 7200 3744/www. teatroallascala.org). Metro Precotto, then shuttle bus 44. **Open** Box office noon-6pm; noon-8pm performance days. *Performances* times vary. **Tickets** €10-€90. **Credit cards** AmEx, DC, MC, V. **Map** off p309 A2.
Its turn as a temporary home for La Scala should come to an end in late 2004, which will be a relief to opera purists. The Arcimboldi is an impressive modern auditorium (designed by Vittorio Gregotti) with good acoustics, but its location, out in the northern suburbs, is decidedly remote. What will become of it after La Scala goes home remains to be seen.

Nightlife

If your idea of an Italian holiday includes a lively club scene, you've come to the right place.

Everybody is a star at the celebrity-owned **Hollywood**. *See p176.*

Milan is one of the few cities in Italy where nightlife means more than a drawn-out dinner. Dozens of clubs here cater to every walk of life, from young to not-so-young, swanky to funky, navy-blue blazers to studded leather and chains. There are also lots of places where you don't need to be trendy to fit in. In fact, despite Milan's reputation, first-time fashionistas will find it hard to find places that can go toe-to-toe on the hip scale with clubs in London, New York or Paris. Even when the fashion shows are on (*see chapter* **Festivals & Events**) most of the movers and shakers can be found at private parties or having a nightcap back at the hotel. The fashion infantry and their adolescent entourage, meanwhile, grind it out at clubs on corso Como.

Whatever your style, the whole point of going out in Milan is to look your best, which helps explain why few patrons get totally out of control. Also, Italians don't tend to have the same nocturnal thirst for alcohol as their European neighbours. This is just as well, as the cocktail-price-to-income ratio is high. You can expect to pay up to €7 for a drink,

whether it's a beer or a measure of spirits, and even designated drivers should budget a few euros for each soft drink or mineral water.

Several clubs have introduced a pay-as-you-leave system. Where this is the case, you'll be given a ticket (*tessera*) at the door; this will be punched when you use the cloakroom, buy drinks, food, and so on. Hang on to that card: the fine for losing it is exorbitant. Most clubs serve dinner before the business of the night begins in earnest: food is unlikely to be great, but it will certainly be more than palatable, and there is often live jazz music during dinner. Taking a table usually ensures access to the *privé* (a fancy term for a restricted chill-out room).

INFORMATION

ZeroDue is a free mini-sized fortnightly magazine that is indispensable for finding out what's going on where and when. Look for it in the little orange racks with the free advertising postcards in cafés and bars that cater to the hip crowd. The **www.milanoin.it** website has events listings; only in Italian.

Eyeing up at **Tocqueville 13**. *See p177.*

ON THE TOWN

For loud and smoky late-night bars (*locali*), the **Brera**, **corso Como**, **Porta Ticinese** and **Navigli** districts are hopping: head for one of these neighbourhoods in the evening and you're guaranteed to find a place with good drinks, a good crowd and good music. Closing time for most bars is around 2am; clubs usually stay open until at least 4am.

Duomo & Centre

Try also **Cafè Real** (*see p114*).

La Banque

Via B Porrone 6 (02 8699 6565/www.labanque.it). Metro Cordusio/bus 20, 50, 58/tram 1, 3, 12, 19, 24. **Open** 6pm-4am daily. Closed Aug. **Admission** €12-€16 (inc drink). **Credit** AmEx, MC, V. **Map** p310 A2/p312 B1.

Staid and central, La Banque is the kind of place that attracts guys who go out in suits. On weekdays La Banque opens for *aperitivi* at 6pm, and serves an elegant dinner from 8pm to midnight every night. No trainers, please – you'll be turned away if you're not turned out appropriately.

Sforzesco & North

Alcatraz

Via Valtellina 25 (02 6901 6352). Bus 82, 90, 91, 92/tram 3. **Open** 10pm-3.30am Fri, Sat. Closed Jul-Aug. **Admission** *Club* €15 (inc drink). **Credit** MC, V. **Map** p308 A2.

During the week this ex-industrial building hosts live music; on weekends, it turns into a dance club. Friday nights feature house and 'revival' music; Saturdays are all rock 'n' roll.

Casablanca Café

Corso Como 14 (02 6269 0186/www.casablanca cafe.it). Metro Garibaldi/tram 11, 29, 30, 33. **Open** 6.30pm-3am Tue-Sun. Closed Aug. **Admission** €10-€15 (inc drink). **Credit** AmEx, MC, V. **Map** p308 B2.

This disco-bar and restaurant has an impossibly strict door policy, so get ready to be scrutinised. The DJ plays commercial house and there's some dancing, but that's not what the Casablanca is about. *Milanesi* come here to enjoy a spot of people-watching in the Moroccan-flavoured back room before hitting more serious clubs.

De Sade

Via Piazzi 4 (02 688 8898/www.desade.it). Bus 82, 90, 91, 92/tram 3. **Open** 9.30pm-3am Thur-Sun. Closed June-Aug. **Admission** €16-€20 (inc drink). **Credit** MC, V. **Map** p308 A2.

The name says it all: dress as wildly as you dare and don't be surprised if the most glamorous women head for the men's loo. But different nights cater to different clientele, so check the website for events.

Gasoline

Via Bonnet 11a (02 2901 3245/www.discogasoline.it). Metro Garibaldi/bus 94/tram 29, 30. **Open** 10.30pm-4am Thur-Sat; 5-10pm Sun. Closed Aug. **Admission** €8-€16 (inc drink). **Credit** MC, V. **Map** p308 B2.

Situated in the Bermuda Triangle of nightlife around hip corso Como, this small club features everything from 1980s pop to deep house. Those who are after something a little different should try the Gasoline's Sunday afternoon gay tea dance (*see p166*).

Hollywood

Corso Como 15 (02 659 8996/www.discoteca hollywood.com). Metro Garibaldi/tram 11, 29, 30, 33. **Open** 10.30pm-4am Tue-Sun. Closed July, Aug. **Admission** €15-€20 (inc drink). **Credit** AmEx, DC, MC, V. **Map** p308 B2.

Arts & Entertainment

There's a high model-to-mortal ratio in this locale, especially on Friday nights: suck in your cheeks and look bored if you want to fit in. The music is definitely commercial: this is not a cutting-edge place. It's somewhere you go just to say you've been there.

Leoncavallo

Via Watteau 7 (02 670 5185/www.leoncavallo.org). Bus 43/tram 1. **Open** 8.30pm-1am Mon-Thur, Sun; 8.30pm-4am Fri, Sat. **Admission** *With membership card (available at the door)* €5-€6. **No credit cards. Map** off p309 A2.

The Leonka (as locals call it) is an institution for the city's left-wing youth. A very active *centro sociale*, it hosts talking shops and protest meetings in the afternoon and more underground entertainment at night, with DJs playing sets until the wee hours. Drinks are cheap, as is the late-serving cafeteria.

Old Fashion Café

Viale E Alemagna 6 (02 8056 231/www.oldfashion.it). Metro Cadorna/bus 61/tram 1, 27. **Open** 8.30pm-4am Wed-Sat. *Brunch* noon-4pm Sun. **Admission** €8-€20 (inc drink). **Credit** AmEx, MC, V. **Map** p308 C1.

Central and hip, the Old Fashion Café draws a good crowd throughout the week. Wednesday is student night, so steer clear unless that's your cup of tea. If beautiful people are what you're after, Mondays and Saturdays are best. It also opens for a nice Sunday brunch (€18).

Soul To Soul

Via San Marco 33a (02 2900 6350). Metro Moscova/bus 41, 43. **Open** 9.30pm-4am Wed-Sun. **Admission** free with €20 annual membership. **No credit cards. Map** p308 B2.

Playing hip hop and R&B, this small basement disco is a refreshing antidote to Milan's homogenous dancing scene. Soul To Soul gets pretty hot and sweaty and it's definitely a long way from chic, but if commercial house is wearing you down, give it a go.

Tocqueville 13

Via Tocqueville 13 (02 2900 2973). Metro Garibaldi/tram 11, 29, 30, 33. **Open** 10pm-3am daily. Closed July, Aug. **Admission** €10-€19 (inc drink). **Credit** AmEx, MC, V. **Map** p308 B2.

At this classic night-time venue, with 1970s-inspired decor, the emphasis is on commercial house music and some Latino grooves. Tocqueville attracts footballers, models and local VIPs on Sunday nights (they're likely to be tucked away in the *privé*, however); Mondays and Thursdays are popular with a more sophisticated, well-dressed crowd. Dinner is served from 9.30pm until midnight (average €35), and if you eat, you too can be privy to the *privé*.

San Babila & East

Plastic

Viale Umbria 120 (02 733 996/www.clubplastic.biz). Bus 92/tram 12. **Open** midnight-5am Thur-Sat; 8pm-2am Sun. Closed July, Aug. **Admission** €15-€20 (inc drink). **No credit cards. Map** p311 B2.

At this enduringly trendy spot (be sure to dress to impress or you'll never make it past the bouncers) you can dance 'til late to an agreeable mix of house and hip hop. It's a popular gay destination and a prime place to spot some of the city's loveliest drag queens. The atmosphere is a touch mellower in the Juke Box Hero Room, where you can play billiards as you down your drinks.

Star gazing

For some *milanesi*, a good night out is one where they brush up against greatness, which means sighting a football star. For the truly *sfigati* (losers) a night without at least one celeb sighting is reason enough to change clubs.

Frankly, it's not too difficult to find the athletes, since they regularly lurk around nocturnal venues and Milan is not a huge city. The stars come out just after dark, and a good spot for an early-evening sighting is in the neighbourhoods most frequented for *aperitivi*: Brera and the Navigli. Just look for the table for two surrounded by empty ones and the crowd of standing gawkers trying to be polite.

Fortunately for us mere mortals, football players have made it much easier for us to pick them out by opening their very own venues.

Go for an *aperitivo* at **Baci e Abbracci** (*see p129*), owned by Inter superstar Christian Vieri and AC Milan's Cristian Brocchi, or for a pizza at **Osteria del Pallone**, opened by the former national team coach Cesare Maldini. After dinner, Brocchi and team-mates Gennaro Gattuso and Christian Abbiati reserve at least a little time in their schedule for their newly opened club, **C-Side** (*see p178*). Located near Milan's business school, Bocconi, it attracts a late-twenty- to thirtysomething crowd. If you go, don't feel the need to look hip. The dress can be described as managerial-sporty at best. Besides, all eyes will be on someone more famous than yourself.

Other *re del pallone* (football royalty) can be caught working off the carbs on the dancefloor (or smooching the showgirl of the moment in the *privé*) of places like **Casablanca Café** (*see p176*), **Tocqueville 13** (*see above*), **Gasoline** (*see p176*) and **Hollywood** (*see p176*; one of the owners here is Paolo Maldini, Cesare's son and former captain of the Italy football team).

Rolling Stone

*Corso XXII Marzo 32 (02 733 172/www.rolling
stone.it). Bus 45,73/tram 12, 27.* **Open** 11pm-4am
Thur-Sun. **Admission** *Club* €8-€13 (inc drink).
Credit AmEx, MC, V. **Map** p311 A2.
Milan's leading rock venue spreads over three floors
and offers gigs during the week and dancing on
Fridays and Saturdays. The sounds vary from floor to
floor and include hip hop, ragga and Latin music.

Porta Romana & South

Café Atlantique

*Viale Umbria 42 (02 5519 3925/www.cafe
atlantique.com). Bus 90, 91, 92.* **Open** 9pm-4am
Tue, Wed, Fri, Sat; 7.30pm-4am Thur, Sun. Closed
July, Aug. **Admission** €10-€25 (inc drink). **Credit**
MC, V. **Map** p311 B2.
If you don't seriously dress up, you'll never get
through the door. Positioned beneath an enormous
and truly incredible modern chandelier, the circular
bar in the centre of the main room is one of the best
places in the city to watch Milan's 'I'm too cool'
crowd, notoriously known as *fighetti*.

C-Side

Via Castelbarco 11 (02 5831 0682). Bus 79, 90, 91.
Open 11pm-4am Wed-Sat. Closed July, Aug.
Admission €10-€15 (inc drink) Wed, Fri, Sat.
Free to all Thur. **Map** p310 C2.
This club seems to suffer from a personality disorder:
not only is it a venue for live music, it also opens its
doors to students (on Wednesdays, commercial music)
and private parties. If you're looking for cutting-
edge music, you might want to go elsewhere, but
there's no denying that the celebrity ownership
(including Gattuso of AC Milan) is a crowd magnet.

Divina

*Via Molino delle Armi, at via della Chiusa (02 5843
1823/www.divina.biz). Metro Crocetta or Missori/bus
65, 94/tram 3, 15.* **Open** 11pm-4am Sat. Closed June-
Aug. **Admission** €15-€18 (inc drink). **Map** p310 B2.
This elegant venue offers one of the few truly fun
Saturday nights in town. Carefully organised entertainment (including dance instructors), house music
spun by famous Italian DJs and a fun, up-for-it
crowd all contribute to making this an ideal place to
make new friends. Shame about the expensive cocktails served in plastic cups.

Magazzini Generali

*Via Pietrasanta 14 (02 5521 1313). Bus 90, 91/
tram 24.* **Open** *Sept-June* 11.30pm-4am Wed, Fri,
Sat. Closed July, Aug. **Admission** €18 Fri; €16 Sat.
Free to all Wed. **No credit cards. Map** p311 C1.
With a capacity of about 1,000, Magazzini hosts
musical acts of every genre as well as popular club
nights. Avoid Wednesdays unless you're after a
student crowd. Jet Lag on Friday is a Milanese
classic: heavily gay but not exclusively so, with
muscular go-go dancers and house music. Saturday
is more commercial and attracts a younger set.

Rocket

*Via Pezzotti 52 (02 8950 3509/www.therocket.it).
Metro Famagosta/bus 65, 90, 91, 95/tram 3, 15.*
Open 9pm-3am daily. Closed Aug. **Admission** free.
No credit cards. Map p310 C2.
This club is popular thanks to a simple (yet rare, in
Milan) formula: the entry is free of charge, the sounds
are excellent (from rock to electro to 80s music) and
the bartender creates out-of-this-world cocktails.
Fight your way through the *über*-crowded entrance
and lose yourself on the purple-walled dancefloor.

Summer venues

Most of the action on summer nights is at the
Idroscalo – a huge man-made lake near Linate
airport. Because the Idroscalo is not the easiest
place to reach by public transport, you might
want to make friends with some four-wheeled
locals, or start saving now for taxi fare. At the
southern entrance, gate seven, **Café Solaire** is
one of the most popular summer party places,
where tanned, sweaty flesh is exposed to hordes
of nasty mosquitos. Other clubs worth checking
out here are **Dieci 57** and **Punta dell'Est**.
South-east of the centre, **Borgo del Tempo
Perso** is another summer hangout, with DJs,
drinks and dancing in its two gardens and
inside. Once there, head for **Karma**, a newer
club that attracts an in-the-know crowd.

In summer, the Navigli area is closed to
traffic after 8.30pm, and canal-side bars and cafés
stay open until late. The neighbourhoods of
Brera, corso Como and Porta Ticinese come
out of their shells and on to the pavement with
the arrival of warm weather, giving scope for
curbside table-hopping seven nights a week.

Borgo del Tempo Perso/Karma

*Via Fabio Massimo 36, East (02 569 4755/www.
borgodeltempoperso.com). Metro Corvetto or Porto di
Mare.* **Open** *May-Sept* 11.30pm-4am Thur (Borgo),
Tue, Fri-Sun (Karma). *Oct-Apr* 11.30pm-4am Fri-Sat.
Admission €15 (inc drink). **Credit** AmEx, DC, MC,
V. **Map** off p311 C2.

Café Solaire

*Idroscalo, Segrate, East, southern entrance, gate 7
(02 5530 5169/www.cafesolaire.it).* **Open** *May-Sept*
9.30pm-4am Thur-Sat; 6pm-2am Sun. **Admission**
€10-€18 (inc drink). **Credit** MC, V. **Map** off p311 A2.

Dieci 57

*Idroscalo, Segrate, East, c/o Idropark Fila,
Circonvallazione Idroscalo Est 51 (02 7020 8357).*
Open 11pm-4am Fri-Sat; 6pm-2am Sun. **Admission**
€13-€18. **No credit cards. Map** off p311 A2.

Punta dell'Est

*Idroscalo, Segrate, East, Circonvallazione Idroscalo
Est 21 (02 6071 253).* **Open** *June* 11pm-4am,
Wed-Sun. *Oct-May* 11pm-4am Fri, Sat. **Admission**
€10-€25. **No credit cards. Map** off p311 A2.

Sport & Fitness

How to be a perfect fit in Slim City.

With its smoggy and congested roads, Milan isn't much of a jogger's city, so when workaholic Milanese need to blow off steam, they head straight for the city's fitness centres. Swimming, squash, tennis and martial arts are perennial favourites in Milan, though aerobics, yoga and dance lessons have also taken off in recent years.

Staying in shape is essential in what must be one of Europe's slimmest cities, and there is no shortage of ideas in Milan on how to get fit efficiently. TV infomercials promise women a trimmer figure by wearing tight-fitting lycra shorts, or attaching electrodes to the neediest areas. Subways are plastered with promotions for slimming centres such as Figurella (www.figurella.it) and Linea Snella (www.lineasnella.com), which employ some very serious-looking technology and have their own patented methods. Linea Snella, for example, has women perform arduous exercise in sweltering temperatures and then take a bath in ionised oxygen. It may sound a bit esoteric, but many women swear by it.

Cycling

There are three main cycle paths in Milan, each passing historic sites and patches of natural beauty. The longest path crosses the whole city, from the waterfalls of the Martesana canal in the north-east, along much of the canal's length, through Parco Sempione (*see p67*) and Brera (*see p70*) to Porta Genova in the south-west.

The paths along the Naviglio Pavese and the Naviglio Grande lead to the towns of Pavia (*see p257*) and Abbiategrasso. The former track passes locks designed by Leonardo da Vinci, but is rough riding: you'll need a mountain bike to handle the bumps. The latter track is a dream, often consisting of finished jogging surfaces and populated mostly by fellow cyclists. Abbiategrasso, just an hour away at racing speed, is quite bland, but the path continues up past verdant stretches with views of the Alps and a further 15 kilometres (9.5 miles) down the road is the medieval town of Vigevano (*see p261*).

For bike hire, *see p283*.

Football

Stadio Giuseppe Meazza, aka **San Siro** – after its neighbourhood – is perhaps the most renowned stadium in Italy (*see also p98*).

Third-ring seats are pretty far away from the pitch, but unlike Rome's Stadio Olimpico, for example, the field is not surrounded by an athletics track, which means the stands are closer to the action. San Siro's other attraction is ease of exit: it is said that no stadium in the world can fill up or empty out as quickly.

Most importantly, the San Siro is home to two of Italy's top teams, AC Milan and Inter Milan. The former was founded in 1899 by a group of British expats, who found themselves with few outlets for English sports in a cycling-mad city. So successful was AC Milan that in 1908 the Italian Football Federation harshly decided to exclude foreign players from the championship. The internationals on AC's roster formed their own club and called it Football Club Internazionale, or Inter. Eventually, they won the right to compete in the championship and a rivalry was born (*see p180* **True colours**).

The names of the players who have passed through the two clubs' ranks over the decades – Rivera, Mazzola, Facchetti, Baresi, Gullit, Maldini, Ronaldo and so on – provide enough fodder for an entire football Hall of Fame. So the teams built one: the **Museo Inter e Milan**, located at the stadium. Here you can sort through memorabilia, brush up on your Italian football trivia and take a tour of the stadium. On match days, a ticket for the game allows entrance to the museum until 30 minutes before kick-off.

Museo Inter e Milan

Gate 21, Stadio Giuseppe Meazza, via Piccolomini 5, West (02 404 2432/02 4879 8253/www.sansirotour.com). Metro Lotto/tram 24. **Open** 10am-5pm Mon-Sat; 10am-30 mins before kick-off on match days (usually Sun). **Admission** €12.50; €10 concessions. **Credit** AmEx, DC, MC, V. **Map** off p308 B2.

Tickets

AC Milan vs Inter matches generally sell out far in advance; but if you're determined to get in, the ticket touts around the stadium before the game will be happy to help you… at a price.

Milan Point

Via San Gottardo 2 (entrance in piazza XXIV Maggio), South (02 8942 2711). Metro Porta Genova/bus 59/tram 3, 20, 29. **Open** 10am-7.30pm Mon-Sat. **Tickets** €11-€270. **No credit cards**. **Map** p310 B2.
The sales point for tickets to AC Milan home games.

Ticket One/Spazio Oberdan
Viale Vittorio Veneto 2, East (02 2953 6577/www. ticketone.it). Metro Porta Venezia/tram 9, 20, 29. **Open** 10am-10pm Tue-Sun. **Tickets** €11-€250. **No credit cards** (AmEx, MC, V are accepted for online transactions). **Map** p309 C2.
The place to come for tickets to Inter home games.

Golf

The countryside around Milan has some of the most beautiful golf courses in Italy. However, almost all require membership. The one exception is Golf Le Rovedine: the only public course in Lombardy. It is situated, appropriately enough, on via Karl Marx.

Golf Le Rovedine
Via Karl Marx 18, Noverasco di Opera, South (02 5760 6420/www.rovedine.com). Metro Porta Romana, then tram 24. **Open** *Summer* 8am-8pm daily. *Winter* 8am-6pm. **Rates** €35 Mon-Fri; €59 Sat, Sun & hols. **Credit** AmEx, DC, MC, V. **Map** off p311 C1.
This basic, par-72 course is 7km (4.5 miles) outside the city. Le Rovedine can draw a crowd in good weather, especially at weekends, so booking is always advisable.

Gyms

Much of Milanese fitness revolves around gyms, or *centri di benessere* (health and fitness centres). Facilities at these temples of body worship commonly include dance studios, sunbeds, nutritionists, pools, hairdressers, saunas, squash courts, boxing rings, climbing walls and sports equipment stores, not to mention the ubiquitous relaxation rooms.

Downtown Palestre
Piazza Cavour 2, North (02 7601 1485/www.down townpalestre.it). Metro Turati/bus 61, 94/tram 1, 2, 20. **Open** 7am-midnight Mon-Fri; 10am-9pm Sat, Sun. **Rates** €50 per day; €170 per month. **Credit** AmEx, MC, V. **Map** p309 C1.
Downtown's clientele consists of the rich, the famous and the very beautiful, including models keeping catwalk-trim for the spring and autumn fashion shows. There are postmodern workout services such as Watsu and water massage, Tantsu Thai treatments, kick-boxing, yoga and all sorts of classes, plus two floors of gym equipment, including treadmills and stair-climbers. The spa and beauty centre, at the same address (02 7631 7233), offers all kinds of pampering treatments.

True colours

Even if you aren't passionate about football, you shouldn't miss the chance to see Italy's oldest rivals – AC Milan and Inter – square off against each other in their shared stadium, the San Siro. The derby comes around but twice a year, once in the autumn and once in late winter or early spring, but during the week-long build-up to the match people talk about little else.

Once upon a time, team affiliations cleaved fairly neatly down political lines. From the 1950s up until Silvio Berlusconi bought a nearly bankrupt AC in 1986, *milanisti* were known as *cacciavite* (screwdrivers), a reference to the club's blue-collar fan base. In the tumultuous 1970s, the club represented the hard left, and the red of their red-and-black strip signalled their communist leanings. Inter, on the other hand – with regal blue-and-black stripes – has always been associated with the bourgeoisie. The Moratti family of oil barons presided over the club for most of the 20th century.

These days, the socioeconomic lines have blurred, but the colours remain the same. The greatest difference between the two fan bases now seems to be that *milanisti* think of the game as an important step to another trophy, while an Inter fan's greatest joy is simply to watch AC lose. Inter regularly finishes near the top, but has been jinxed in recent years by last-minute collapses.

On derby day, though, anything can happen. Though AC seems to have taken the upper hand in the last few match-ups – it recently set a new record for a derby trouncing, hammering Inter 6-0 – overall, it is one of the tightest rivalries in the world. Since the first derby in 1908, each team has won about 100 games, and nearly as many have ended in a draw.

It goes without saying that for a match this big you will need to buy tickets a few weeks, or even months in advance. Be sure to get to the game a good hour ahead of time to secure your spot. If you're going as a family or are squeamish about rowdy fans, the tamest areas are in the grandstands along the sidelines. Each team's *curva*, or end zone, is the most raucous. Crowds aren't quite as violent as in other football-mad parts of the world, but there's no guarantee you won't be hit by a flying orange or beer can. Ironically the safest places are far away from the riot-geared police, as they are the most common target for projectiles.

Pitching in at **San Siro**.
See p179.

Skorpion Club

Corso Vittorio Emanuele 24, East (02 781 424).
Metro San Babila/bus 54, 60, 65/tram 12, 20, 27.
Open 7am-10pm Mon-Fri; 10am-9pm Sat, Sun.
Rates €60 per day; €130 per week. **Credit** AmEx,
MC, V. **Map** p311 A1/p312 B2, C1.

Skorpion is the most central gym in Milan and is
consequently pricey. It offers a full range of activities,
including Turkish baths for men and women. The
11th-floor solarium has a sweeping view of the city.

Pools

While most private gyms have their own pools,
many Milanese opt for a pay-as-you-go plan.
Public pools are much cheaper, though the
open-access swimming schedules can be
ridiculously complicated. Remember your
bathing cap: you will not be allowed in the
water without one. Times given below are
for open-access swimming: at other times,
pools are usually used for swimming classes.

Parco Solari

Via Montevideo 20, West (02 469 5278). Metro
Sant'Agostino/bus 50/tram 14, 20, 29, 30. **Open**
7.15-9am, noon-2.30pm Mon, Thur; 7.15-9am, noon-
2.30pm, 6.30-10.30pm Tue; 7.15-9am, noon-2.30pm,
7.30-10.30pm Wed; 7.15-9am, noon-2pm, 6.30-9.30pm
Fri; 1am-6pm Sat; 10am-7pm Sun. **Rates** €4 Mon-Fri;
€5 Sat, Sun. **Credit** AmEx, DC, MC, V. **Map** p310 A1.

One of the city's more modern-looking public pools
is housed in a saddle-shaped building with floor-
to-roof windows looking out on to the park, but there
are few frills and the staff can be surly. Swimming,
water aerobics and scuba courses are available.

Piscina Cozzi

Viale Tunisia 35, East (02 659 9703). Metro Porta
Venezia or Repubblica/tram 2, 11, 29, 30. **Open** noon-
10.30pm Mon; 7.30am-1.30pm Tue, Thur; 8.30am-4pm,
6-9pm Wed; 8.30am-4pm Fri; 10am-5pm Sat, Sun.
Rates €4 Mon-Fri; €5 Sat, Sun. €40 per 11 visits.
€250 annual pass. **No credit cards. Map** p310 B1, B2.

Built in 1934, with a typically grandiose fascist
exterior and a Soviet interior, this is one of Milan's
most popular and populist pools. It's Olympic-size,
but often crowded. Opening hours are extended
during the hottest months.

Squash

Although old-school *milanesi* still opt for tennis
in clubs that require year-long memberships,
squash is becoming increasingly popular in
rainy, workaholic Milan: it's quick, played
indoors and has a northern European feel.
Slower outdoor sports, Milan's *squashisti*
believe, are best left to the Romans.

Tonic Club

Via Mestre 7, East (02 2641 0158/www.tonicnet.it).
Metro Udine/bus 55, 75. **Open** 7am-midnight
Mon-Fri; 9am-7.30pm Sat, Sun. **Rates** €25 per day;
€160 for 10 sessions. **Credit** AmEx, MC, V.
Map off p309 B2.

Tonic is large, industrial and generally devoid of
the glamour of the clubs closer to the centre. In
2001 the management attempted to turn it into an
all-purpose health and fitness centre; the clientele
remains the same, however. It has four squash
courts and racket rental. Most members go in for
the dance lessons, climbing wall and martial arts
training. Day passes and multiple entries are valid
for all equipment.

Vico Squash

Via GB Vico 38, West (02 4800 2762/02 4801 0890).
Metro Sant'Agostino/bus 50, 94/tram 2, 14, 20.
Open 7am-11pm Mon, Wed; 8.30am-11pm Tue, Thur,
Fri; 10am-9pm Sat, Sun. **Rates** €50 per day; €300 per
3mths; €840 per year. **Credit** MC, V. **Map** p310 A1.

With a dozen squash courts, this is the place to
practice Milan's favourite New Economy sport.
Ironically, Squash Vico is located opposite an Old
Economy monument: the San Vittore prison, where
many of the city's former elite did time after the
Tangentopoli (bribesville) scandal (*see p19*).

Theatre & Dance

Italy's theatre capital offers an eclectic and exciting roster.

Many would say Milan has Italy's liveliest theatre scene by far. This is true, but it is not saying much. Although the Italians have excelled at opera – and indeed this is often what they mean when they talk of *andare a teatro* – prose theatre has lagged behind.

The reason has to do with language. Until 1870, Italy was a group of city states, each with its own dialect. One of the challenges faced by Italian-language playwrights was how to present people speaking Italian in everyday situations when, in fact, people did not speak Italian in everyday situations. Carlo Goldoni was one such playwright and his fame rests in part on the fact that he was able to create a 'naturalistic' Italian idiom. It is not surprising, therefore, that there is relatively little in the way of Italian-language theatre. However, Milan has between 30 and 40 small theatre companies that put on plays *in milanese*. Most of the plays revolve around the past, domestic matters – the trauma of the Milanese family whose daughter wants to marry someone from the south – and so on. These drama groups – all amateur – are usually linked to the parish churches, which often have a small theatre attached.

THEATRE

The more than 35 theatres in Milan offer foreign visitors quite an intriguing experience. How does Shakespeare sound in Italian? How do you translate Woody Allen's one-liners? How does a performance of a Bertolt Brecht play here differ from one performed in London, New York or, indeed, Germany? These are just some of the options you can check out over the average season and they testify to an immensely open-minded cultural approach.

Getting to see a play can be a technical struggle, though. As well as the seasons being short (usually October-late May), the runs are often limited to ten or so performances. Getting tickets is no easy feat, either. In most cases, you have to go direct to the box office, and many theatres do not accept credit cards. The venues themselves are not huge – just a handful have more than 500 seats (this in a city of 1.2 million inhabitants). Many also sell season tickets, which means that most of the seats are block-booked.

There are other factors concerning Milan's theatre scene. The city's theatre companies are, for the most part, doing their best about not making a drama out of a crisis. Their energy and enthusiasm are commendable in the face of very straitened conditions. State and local subsidies are provided for drama in Italy, but these sums have been reduced over the years, and even when funds are available, bureaucracy makes delays common. Ambitious refurbishment projects have also been taken in hand, but similarly, many of these have been delayed for lack of ready money – it's there somewhere, but the appropriate person has not signed the appropriate piece of paper.

DANCE

The **Centro di Ricerca per il Teatro** (CRT) is Milan's main purveyor of contemporary dance. The **Teatro Carcano** and **Teatro Out Off** also occasionally schedule international choreographers into their programme, while **La Scala** (at the Teatro degli Arcimboldi until December 2004, *see p174*) is the city's main classical ballet venue. The 2003/04 programme included Kenneth Macmillan's *L'histoire de Manon*; Roland Petit's *The Bat* and *Commedia*; and *Swan Lake*. There were eight performances of each piece over the season.

INFORMATION AND TICKETS

You can purchase tickets in person at individual theatre box offices. If you speak Italian and have plastic, take advantage of the fact that some venues accept credit-card bookings over the phone. Tickets should be picked up an hour before curtain up.

For the majority of theatres listed below you can check programmes and buy tickets online through www.ticketweb.it, www.ticketone.it, www.ticketitalia.it and www.prenofacile.it. They all accept major credit cards.

Discounts on theatre tickets are offered at the discretion of the management, usually to the under-25s and the over-60s. If you wish to benefit from such discounts, ask if the theatre you're planning to go to operates such a scheme when you buy your tickets. Have your passport handy to prove your age.

Should you be staying in Milan for a while, you might be interested in the **Invito a Teatro** scheme. For €68, you can choose eight shows to see over a single season at 15 city theatres. You can get the pass from participating theatres (labelled with an asterisk (*) in the listings

The performers at the **Colorado Café** colour Milan with fun and laughter.

below), from Ticket One in the Spazio Oberdan centre on viale Vittorio Veneto 2 (02 2953 6577), or from the online box offices mentioned above.

Venues & companies

Colorado Café
Salumeria della Musica, via Pasinetti 2, South (02 5680 7350). Tram 24, 95, 99. **Open** *Box office* 6-9pm Wed. *Performances* 10pm Mon, Tue. **Tickets** €10. **No credit cards. Map** off p311 C1.
Twice a week the intimate, post-industrial Salumeria della Musica (music charcuterie), complete with hanging *prosciutti* and cold-cut dinners, offers its stage to actor Diego Abatantuono's (*see p159* **Renaissance man**) baby. Colorado Café is one of Milan's most popular cabaret nights and has been quickly snapped up by TV (the show is broadcast on Italia 1 on Tuesdays).

*CRT Teatro dell'Arte
Viale Alemagna 6, West (02 8901 1644/www.teatro crt.org). Metro Cadorna/bus 61/tram 1, 19, 27, 29, 30. **Season** Oct-May. **Open** *Box office* 11.30am-7pm Mon-Fri; 3-7pm Sat. *Performances* 8.30pm Tue-Sat; 4pm Sun. **Tickets** €15; €10 under-25s; €7.50 over-65s. **Credit** AmEx, MC, V. **Map** p308 C1, C2.
Established in 1974, the Centro di Ricerca per il Teatro (CRT) is Italy's leading forum for theatrical experimentation. Along with contemporary drama, opera and classical theatre, the CRT also features contemporary dance. One of the highlights of the dance season is the Short Formats Dance Festival (mid to late May), which features 14 European companies focusing on the latest trends in contemporary

dance. Performances are held at the Teatro dell'Arte, in the centre of town, and also at the smaller CRT Salone (via Dini 7, South, 02 8901 1644).

*Teatridithalia Elfo
Teatro dell'Elfo, via Ciro Menotti 11, East (02 716 791/www.elfo.org). Bus 54, 61/tram 5, 11. Teatro Leonardo da Vinci, via Ampere 1, at piazza Leonardo da Vinci, East (02 2668 1166/www.elfo. org). Metro Piola/bus 62, 90, 91. **Season** Oct-end May. **Open** *Box office* 10am-6.30pm Tue-Fri. *Performances* 8.45pm Tue-Sat; 4pm Sun. **Tickets** €18-€19; €9-€12 concessions. €12 to all Tue. **No credit cards. Map** p309 C2.
The brainchild of Gabriele Salvatores (the director of the film *Mediterraneo*) and Ferdinando Bruni, the Teatro dell'Elfo came into being in 1973. One of the least traditional theatre companies in Milan, it still focuses on radical, hard-hitting drama by the likes of Fassbinder, Rimbaud, Mishima, Camus, Berkoff and Pasolini. The theatre company has expanded to occupy two theatres, the Elfo and the Leonardo.

*Teatro Arsenale
Via C Correnti 11, South (02 832 1999/www.teatro arsenale.org). Bus 94/tram 2, 3, 14, 20. **Season** Oct-June. **Open** *Box office* 6-8pm Tue-Sat; 30mins before performances. *Performances* 9.15pm Tue-Sat; 4.30pm Sun. **Tickets** €15; €11 under-26s, over-60s. €11 to all Tue, Sun. **No credit cards. Map** p310 A2.
Housed in a deconsecrated 13th-century church, this 150-seat theatre is located in the extension of via Torino. Throughout the 2003/04 season, Dante's *Divine Comedy* was being read (two cantos at a time) and discussed. As well as some Ionesco, Pirandello

Arts & Entertainment

and Bukowski, TS Eliot is part of the repertoire. *La terra desolata*, anyone? There's also poetry, plus some chamber music concerts.

*Teatro Carcano

Corso di Porta Romana 63, South (02 5518 1377/ www.teatrocarcano.com). Metro Crocetta/bus 77, 94/ tram 4, 24. **Season** Oct-May. **Open** *Box office* 10am-6.30pm Mon; 10am-8pm Tue-Sat; 1-6.30pm Sun. *Performances* 8.45pm Tue-Sat; 3.30pm Sun. **Tickets** €27-€20.50. **No credit cards. Map** p311 A1, B1.

Designed by Luigi Canonica (1762-1844), the Carcano opened its doors in 1803, and was the setting for debut performances of operas by both Vincenzo Bellini and Gaetano Donizetti. When the theatre was threatened with closure in 1998, it was bought out by its artistic director, the 73-year-old Bergamo-born actor Giulio Bosetti, and seven of his friends. The programme ranges from plays by Goldoni and Pirandello to puppetry, dance performances and operetta.

Smile-high club

Zelig has been the place to go for live Italian-language comedy acts since 1986. Originally a cooperative, it has become a launching-pad for an extraordinary number of Italian comics, including Aldo, Giovanni and Giacomo; Gioele Dix; Gene Gnocchi and Elio e le Storie Tese.

Humour is, of course, subjective and rarely crosses cultural boundaries. Italian humour is no exception. However, if you want to find out what makes the Italians laugh, or if you want to savour a live comedy show Italian-style, you can't do better than head for Zelig. It's hard to pinpoint its style, but visual gags and zany stuff perhaps best describe what's on offer. Each of the comics has his/her own quirky trademark 'character', such as the neurotic one or the one with the funny way of speaking.

Many entertainment spots in Milan close in August, when most of the potential audience are at the beach. Zelig is no exception. However, in 2003, it took the show on the road during the *ferie*, hitting the most popular tourist spots. Although this was the first official excursion beyond Milan, Zelig has been a nationwide phenomenon since 1995, when it was picked up by Berlusconi's Italia Uno TV station. It regularly scored viewing figures over nine million viewers in its late-evening slot, and has now been moved to Canale 5.

Should you be in Milan on a Monday or a Tuesday between February and May, you could try to get tickets for the recordings. For details, see the Zelig site: www.areazelig.it.

And in case you were wondering, Zelig is named after the 1983 Woody Allen movie – though for no particular reason.

Finally, if you are after English-language entertainment, you need not despair. Thanks to Laughing Matters, English-language stand-up comedy has been part of the Milan entertainment scene since early 2003. At time of writing, the programme features one

act for three nights every month at **Scimmie** (*see p174*), in the Navigli area. Performers have included the UK's Ross Noble, Greg Proops from Canada and Ardal O'Hanlon from Ireland. For more details, see www.anythingmatters.com/italia.

Zelig

Viale Monza 140, East (02 25 70 73 01/ www.areazelig.it). Metro Gorla or Turro. **Season** Sept-mid July. **Open** *Box office* after 6pm. *Performances* 9pm. **Tickets** €18-13 (includes one drink). **Credit** AmEx, V. **Map** off p311 A2.

Teatro Ciak
*Via Sangallo 33, East (02 7611 0093/www.teatro
ciak.com). Bus 38, 54, 93/tram 5.* **Season** Oct-mid
May. **Open** *Box office* 11am-6.30pm Mon-Sat;
4-6.30pm Sun. *Performances* 9pm Tue-Sun.
Tickets €23.50-€18. €12 Sun. Tickets also sold
at Teatro Smeraldo (*see below*). **No credit cards.**
Map off p311 A2.
'Ciak' is an onomatopoeic word describing the
sound made by a clapperboard. This theatre was
converted from a cinema in 1977 by Leo Wachter
(whose other claim to fame is that he organised
the Beatles' first performance in Italy). Currently the
temporary home of the Franco Parenti company
(*see below*), the Ciak also features comedy acts.
Worth exploring if you're into Italian humour, or
are fascinated by the idea of an Alan Ayckbourn
play in Italian.

*Teatro Franco Parenti
*Via Vasari 15, South (02 599 951/www.teatro
francoparenti.com). Metro Porta Romana/bus 62/
tram 4, 9, 29, 30.* **Season** Oct-late May. **Open**
Box office 10am-6.30pm Mon-Sat; 11am-12.30pm
Sun. *Performances* 8.30pm Tue-Sat; 4pm Sun.
Tickets €25; €13.50 under-26s, over-60s.
Credit DC, MC, V. **Map** p311 B2.
Since refurbishment work started in early 2004,
Franco Parenti's programme is being accommo-
dated at the Teatro Ciak (*see above*). Director Andrée
Ruth Shammah is to be applauded for both her tire-
less fund-raising efforts and interesting program-
ming – it's surely one of the only companies in
the country to offer Sarah Kane and Arnold Wesker
to the Italian public. In Italian, of course.

*Teatro Litta
*Corso Magenta 24, West (02 8645 4545/www.
teatrolitta.it). Metro Cadorna/bus 18, 50, 54/tram
19, 20, 24.* **Season** mid Oct-mid June. **Open** *Box
office* 2.30-7pm Mon-Sat. *Performances* 9pm Tue-Sat;
4.30pm Sun. **Tickets** *Tue, Wed* €16; €8 under-26s,
over-60s. *Thur-Sun* €16; €11 under-26s; €8 over-60s.
€1 booking fee. **Credit** MC, V. **Map** p308 C1, C2.
Located in the sumptuous Palazzo Arese Litta (*see
p96*), the Teatro Litta is a stunning baroque palazzo.
It reopened after extensive refurbishment in late
2003, with eight shows, most of which were drama-
tisations of 20th-century novels, such as Henry
James's *Turn of the Screw* or Manuel Puig's *Kiss of
the Spider-Woman*.

Teatro Manzoni
*Via Manzoni 42, Centre (02 763 6901/www.teatro
manzoni.it). Metro Montenapoleone/bus 61, 94/tram 1,
2, 20.* **Season** Nov-mid June. **Open** *Box office* 10am-
7pm Mon-Sat; 11am-5pm Sun. *Performances* 8.45pm
Tue-Sat; 11am, 3.30pm Sun. **Tickets** €28 + 10%
(booking fee). **Credit** MC, V. **Map** p309 C1/p312 B1.
As well as theatre productions, you might be interested in the Manzoni's Sunday-morning jazz concerts
(Aperitivi in Concerto). The performance starts at
11am and the seats are not numbered. So, having
bought tickets, you stand in the ticket-holders

line from about 10am; when the doors open it's
everyone for themselves. Be prepared to be elbowed
out of the way by the bejewelled and be-furred.

Teatro Nuovo
*Piazza San Babila, East (02 7600 0086/www.teatro
nuovo.it). Metro San Babila/bus 37, 54, 60/tram 2,
3, 14, 27.* **Season** Oct-end May. **Open** *Box office*
11am-6pm Tue-Sat; 11am-1pm, 4.30-6pm Sun.
Performances 8.45pm Tue-Sat; 4pm Sun. **Tickets**
prices vary. **Credit** MC, V. **Map** p309 C1.
Located inside a shopping arcade and downstairs to
boot, the Teatro Nuovo is hard to spot. If you are in
piazza San Babila, facing towards the Duomo, locate
the illuminated noticeboard on your right. The
entrance is just underneath. The theatre features
musicals, as well as names from Italian TV, such as
Giorgio Panariello, who turned an excellent performance as Molière's *Bourgeois Gentleman*.

*Teatro Out Off
*Via Dupré 4, North (02 3926 2282/www.teatroout
off.it). Metro Bovisa/bus 90, 91/tram 1, 2.* **Season**
Nov-late June. **Open** *Box office* 9am-6pm Mon-Fri.
Performances 9pm Tue-Sat; 4pm Sun. **Tickets** €12;
€8.40 under-25s; €6 over-60s. **Credit** AmEx, MC, V.
Map off p308 A1.
Because it is poised to move to a new location, Out
Off has a limited programme for the 2003/04 season,
with just five productions scheduled. It also holds
an annual poetry festival, Contrasti Poetici, from
mid May to mid June.

Teatro Smeraldo
*Piazza XXV Aprile 10, North (02 2900 6767/www.
smeraldo.it). Metro Garibaldi or Moscova/bus 43/
tram 11, 29, 30, 33.* **Season** Sept-July. **Open**
Box office 11am-6.30pm Mon-Sat; 11am-1pm Sun.
Performances 8.45pm Tue-Sat; 4pm Sun. **Tickets**
prices vary. **No credit cards. Map** p308 B2.
With nearly 2,000 seats, this is the largest of the city's
theatres. It features many big-name musicals and has
played host to performers such as David Bowie, Paolo
Conte and Miles Davis. The programme changes little year on year, an advantage to visitors: you can be
sure that, say, the *Rocky Horror Show* will be here for
a couple of weeks in May, if you want to catch it.

Teatro Strehler (Nuovo Piccolo)
*Largo Greppi, North (02 7233 3222/www.piccolo
teatro.org). Metro Lanza/bus 43, 57, 61, 70/tram 1,
3, 4, 12, 14.* **Season** Sept-late June. **Open** *Box office*
10am-6.45pm Mon-Sat; 1-6.30pm Sun. *Performances*
8.45pm daily. **Tickets** €29.50-€15. **Credit** AmEx,
MC, V. **Map** p308 C2.
This theatre is named after Giorgio Strehler (1921-
97), the most influential Italian theatre director of
the second half of the 20th century, as well as the
man responsible for introducing the rest of the world
(and many Italians) to the prolific 18th-century
Venetian playwright Goldoni. It offers an interesting programme of theatre and dance, including the
chance to catch interesting international names
such as Peter Brook and Lev Dodin.

Arts & Entertainment

EVERYTHING YOU NEED
FOR THE
PERFECT BREAK

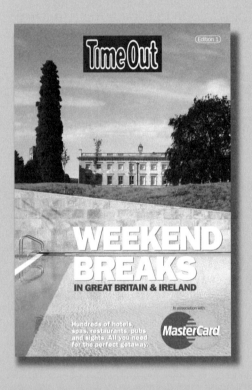

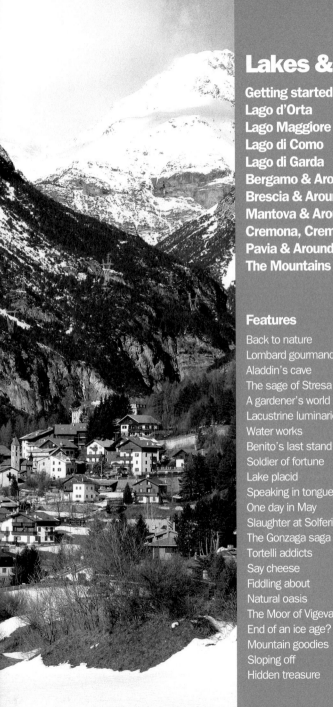

Lakes & Cities

Getting started   188
Lago d'Orta   190
Lago Maggiore   193
Lago di Como   200
Lago di Garda   212
Bergamo & Around   220
Brescia & Around   230
Mantova & Around   237
Cremona, Crema & Lodi   246
Pavia & Around   257
The Mountains   264

Features

Back to nature   188
Lombard gourmands   189
Aladdin's cave   192
The sage of Stresa   198
A gardener's world   202
Lacustrine luminaries   206
Water works   215
Benito's last stand   218
Soldier of fortune   222
Lake placid   224
Speaking in tongues   226
One day in May   232
Slaughter at Solferino   239
The Gonzaga saga   240
Tortelli addicts   243
Say cheese   252
Fiddling about   255
Natural oasis   259
The Moor of Vigevano   261
End of an ice age?   267
Mountain goodies   268
Sloping off   272
Hidden treasure   274

Getting Started

Leave Milan's hive of activity behind and embrace some well-deserved R&R.

After the bright lights of Milan, the rest of Lombardy comes across like a soothing lullaby. The Italian Alps butt up against the Swiss border like a carpet pressed too close to a wall, and hidden within the folds of the landscape is an infinity of panoramic combinations, microclimates and villages. To the south, the region flattens out to the valley of the River Po and its tributaries, and spans across some of Italy's most important agricultural plains where fog and clover blanket a land that sustains long dairy and rice-growing traditions.

The highlight is the lake region – Lombardy's most visited attraction. Italy at its most romantic takes the form of lakes Maggiore, Como and Garda (and the smallish Lake Orta, which is big in beauty and cannot be omitted from this guide even though it's located in neighbouring Piedmont). What moves the soul is the presence of two converging perspectives: the perfectly horizontal line of the lakes'

Peaceful and picturesque: the villages around **Lake Maggiore**. See p193.

Back to nature

Some 5,000 square kilometres (1,900 square miles) of Lombardy – over 20 per cent of the region's territory – are protected in national, regional and local parks and reserves. For more information, consult **www.parks.it** or the WWF's Italian site (**www.wwf.it**). Parks covered in this guide include:
Parco delle Incisioni Rupestri (Grosio). See p268.
Parco Lombardo della Valle del Ticino. See p107.
Parco Naturale dell'Adamello. See p271.
Parco Naturale dell'Adda Nord. See p103.
Parco Naturale della Valle del Lambro. See p102.
Parco Nazionale delle Incisioni Rupestri. See p274.
Parco Nazionale dello Stelvio. See p270.
Parco Regionale delle Groane. See p103.
Parco Regionale delle Orobie Valtellinesi. See p265.
Parco Regionale di Montevecchia e della Valle del Curone. See p102.
Riserva Piramidi di Zone. See p224.

surfaces and the sudden vertical rise of the mountains that flank them like corridor walls. Each lake is detailed in a separate chapter with itineraries that begin at the southern point and continue clockwise around the shores.

Lombardy is also home to a collection of picturesque towns that make ideal day-trip destinations from Milan. Majestically built high on a hill, Bergamo prides itself as a world apart. Brescia is flanked by Franciacorta, Italy's best-known sparkling wine region, while Mantova, in the south-eastern corner of the region, is encased on three sides by freshwater lakes. Other cities, like Cremona and Crema, are named after the dairy treats that put them on the culinary map, while Pavia is nestled between rice paddies. In all of these towns, pushbikes outpace motorised transport, *pensionati* meet each afternoon in the main square and locals seem to have perfected the art of living life in the slow lane.

Each chapter in this section contains information on travelling from Milan to its associated area – both by car and by public transport – and on getting around within it.

Lakes & Cities

Lombard gourmands

Lombardy is the geographic equivalent of a reduction sauce. Culinary traditions from the rest of the nation and beyond have been scrupulously simmered down and blended to appease the most sophisticated and demanding palates. Whereas in much of the rest of Italy, a restaurateur need only serve hearty fare at decent prices, in Lombardy *cucina italiana* is a craft reserved for an elite group of artists. Every attention is paid to preparation, presentation and to polishing the celebrity chef's ego. The following is a bite-sized selection of the best eating experiences the region has to offer.

Milan

Il Luogo di Aimo e Nadia
Via Montecuccoli 6, Milan (02 416 886/www. aimoenadia.com). **Meals served** 12.30-2pm, 8-11pm Mon-Sat. Closed 1wk Jan, all Aug. **Average** €90. **Credit** AmEx, DC, MC, V.
The final stop for Italy's best ingredients. Black truffle from Norcia, chestnuts from Piedmont and oversized prawns from San Remo are deftly transformed here. Conversation-prone waiters and a colourful collection of contemporary art mean the menu is not the restaurant's only charm.

Lake Como

Vecchia Varenna
Contrada Scoscesa 10, Varenna (0341 830 793/www.vecchiavarenna.it). **Meals served** 12.30-2pm, 8-10pm Tue-Sun. Closed Jan. **Average** €50. **Credit** AmEx, DC, MC, V.
The excitement here is twofold: knockout food and knockout views of the lake (which is so close you can almost drape your arm into the water). The speciality is freshwater fish, including roasted pink trout with garlic. Refreshingly informal and with enough scenery to contemplate over a very long lunch.

Bergamo

L'Osteria di via Solata
Via Solata 8, Bergamo Città Alta (035 271 993/www.osteriaviasolata.it). **Meals served** 12.30-2pm, 7.30-10pm Mon, Wed-Sat; 12.30-2pm Sun. Closed 3wks Aug. **Average** €75. **Credit** AmEx, DC, MC, V.

Traditional recipes are interpreted with a contemporary twist by chef and sommelier Ezio Gritti here. The menu features *gnocchetti* with pigeon *ragù*; spaghetti with oysters, pine nuts and basil; and pheasant served in a pool of port, pear and coffee-essence sauce. White chocolate mousse or *semifreddo* with rose petals bring up the rear. Extra marks for food presentation and the intimate dining room.

Near Brescia

Castello Malvezzi
Via Colle San Giuseppe 1, Mompiano Brescia (030 200 4224/www.castellomalvezzi.it). **Meals served** 12.30-2pm, 7.30-10pm Wed-Sun. Closed 3wks Jan, 2wks Aug. **Average** €50. **Credit** AmEx, DC, MC, V.
This gorgeous castle with sumptuously elegant interiors hosts wine-and-food pairing events and theme-food nights. A Franco-Italo cooking team proposes escargot in white wine and spaghetti with prawns and a basil sauce.

Gualtiero Marchesi
Via Vittorio Emanuele 11, Erbusco (030 776 0562/www.marchesi.it). **Meals served** 12.30-2pm, 7.30-10pm daily. Closed 4wks Jan-Feb. **Average** €90. **Credit** AmEx, DC, MC, V.
Chef Gualtiero looms large in Lombardy's epicurean diary and still nabs top scores for his tried and true classic: *riso oro e zafferano* (risotto with saffron and gold leaf). Watch out: the romantic dining room in this enchanting villa has squeezed marriage proposals out of the most adamant bachelors.

Near Mantova

Dal Pescatore Santini
Località Runate, Canneto sull'Oglio (0376 723 001/www.dalpescatore.com). **Meals served** 8-10.30pm Thur-Sun; noon-2.30pm, 8-10.30pm Mon-Wed. Closed 2wks Jan, all Aug. **Average** €130. **Credit** AmEx, DC, MC, V.
Located in an idyllic country home, Nadia and Antonio Santini's gastronomic wonderland always features prominently on lists of Italy's best restaurants. But some things have changed since you last read about it. For example, recipes now call for fewer calories. Even flagship *tortelli di zucca* (with pumpkin filling) are made with less butter – although you'd probably never notice.

Lago d'Orta

A picture-perfect lake experience for those with little time in their schedule.

For a waterside weekend away from Milan, you can't do better than Lake Orta. Located west of Lake Maggiore (*see p193*), in the Piedmont region, this smallish stretch of water (measuring just 18.2 square kilometres/seven square miles) is the only northern lake you can take in at a single glance. Most of its attractions – from the romantic, medieval town of Orta San Giulio, to its picture-postcard-sized island and lakeside museums – can be seen in a couple of days. People come here to steep themselves in the area's natural beauties and well-preserved history, but that's not to say the locals are stuck in their ways. The lakeside town of Omegna is the unlikely home of Alessi, whose factory regularly churns out icons of Italian design (*see p192* **Aladdin's cave**).

Getting there

By car

Take the motorway for the lakes (Ai Laghi). When it divides, head for Malpensa/Varese/Sesto Callende, then join the A26 in the direction of Gravellona Toce. Exit at Borgomanero, then follow signs to Gozzano and Lago d'Orta.

By train

Mainline service from Stazione Centrale or Porta Garibaldi to Novara, then local service stopping at Orta/Miasino, Pettenasco and Omegna. Note: all stations except Omegna are located up steep hills above the towns, 15-20mins walk from the lake. You can pre-book a taxi through Lago D'Orta Autonoleggio (338 986 4839 mobile).

Getting around

By car

The two-lane road surrounding the lake is 33km (21 miles) long, with a smooth surface. A car is essential for visiting the towns above the lake shore. Orta San Giulio's town centre is closed to traffic; cars must be left in the pay parking lots at the edge of town.

By boat

Navigazione Lago d'Orta (0322 844 862) operates a boat service around the lake, stopping at Orta, Isola San Giulio, Pettenasco, Gozzano and elsewhere (daily Easter-mid Oct; Sat, Sun in Oct-Nov; Sun only in Jan). The best departure points are Pella, where there's ample parking, and Omegna. A full day's ticket is €6.50. No credit cards. Another option is to book a tour in a motor taxi from the Servizio Pubblico Motoscafi (333 605 0288 mobile) at Orta San Giulio.

By bike

Lago d'Orta Autonoleggio (338 986 4839 mobile) rents mountain bikes with pick-up in Orta San Giulio: €4.50 per hour, €10 per half-day, €15 per day. No credit cards.

Orta San Giulio

Visitors to the medieval lakeside town of Orta San Giulio could be forgiven for thinking they have stumbled on to the set of a romantic film. A dramatic pathway sweeps from the main waterside square (piazza Motta) to the yellow-stained church of **Santa Maria Assunta** (1485); crumbling villas flank the shorelines stretching out from the town; and, back in the café-lined main square, models are often found posing for photoshoots beneath the *loggia*-stilts of the 16th-century **Palazzo della Comunità** (the former town hall). It's no wonder that Orta is a popular spot for weddings (if you get the urge to tie the knot, there's even a resident British wedding organiser: Philippa Lane on 338 461 0665 mobile).

Perched above the town, in the wooded **Sacro Monte** nature reserve, are 20 small chapels (1591-1770) containing remarkably lifelike terracotta tableaux depicting scenes from the life of St Francis. A pleasant pilgrims' path (30 minutes) winds uphill from piazza Motta, leading to the 17th-century **Chiesa di San Nicolao** and the Sacro Monte. Alternatively, you can drive to the top.

Where to stay, eat & shop

The luxurious **Villa Crespi** (via Fava 18, 0322 911 902, closed Jan-mid Feb, doubles €165-€230) is an over-the-top, Moorish villa on the road from the station. The villa's restaurant (average €72) – under young Neapolitan chef Antonino Cannavacciuolo – is ranked as one of Italy's best, so it is wise to book ahead.

The historic four-star **Hotel San Rocco** (via Gippini 11, 0322 911 977, www.hotelsanrocco.it, doubles €159-€221) offers lakeside rooms and dining (average €49), as does the three-star **Leon d'Oro** (piazza Motta 43, 0322 911 991, closed Jan, doubles €96), where tables are spread over an outdoor terrace (average €30).

The 500-year-old wine bar **Osteria al Boeuc** (via Bersani 28, 0322 915 854, closed Tue Apr-Dec & Mon-Wed Jan-Mar, average

Charming **Lago d'Orta**.

snakes and dragons. These days you can reach the enchanting island and its basilica (founded in AD 4 or 5) by taxi boat from piazza Motta at Orta San Giulio (333 605 0288 mobile, €3 round trip). From here you can also book a 20- or 30-minute tour of the lake (€6-€8), or if you're feeling sporty, row yourself across (boat hire €10 per hour). Once on the lake you might notice a curious phenomenon: unlike all the other pre-Alpine lakes and rivers, Orta's waters flow north.

Inside the **basilica**, a black marble pulpit has rare Saxon-influenced carvings, while frescoes from many centuries battle for space around its walls. A circular pathway (via del Silenziao) runs around the island, past the cloistered Benedictine convent and many romantic villas.

If you are here for St Julius's feast day (31 January), rap on the convent door to get a bag of *pane San Giulio* (dried fruit, nut and chocolate bread) for a small donation. (This treat is for sale in mainland bakeries all year round.) There is no hotel on the island, but there is an eaterie (**Ristorante San Giulio**, via Basilica 4, 0322 90 234, www.orta.net/sangiulio, closed Mon Apr-Oct, Mon-Sat Jan-Mar, all Nov-Dec, average €28), though atmosphere outstrips quality here.

Around the lake

Perched on the hill above Orta San Giulio, **Vacciago di Ameno** houses the **Collezione Calderara di Arte Contemporanea**. This museum was transformed from a late 17th-century home by Antonio Calderara (1903-78) and of the 327 paintings and sculptures inside, 56 are by Calderara himself. The impressive collection documents the international avant-garde from the 1950s and '60s, with an emphasis on kinetic art, geometric abstractionism and visual poetry.

Pettenasco stands on the lake shore north of Orta. Its Romanesque church tower started life attached to the church of Sant'Audenzio, a pal of San Giulio, as well as Pettenasco's town prefect in AD 300. The intricate woodwork for which the town was once famous is commemorated at the **Museo dell'Arte della Tornitura del Legno**, which displays tools, wooden objects and machines collected from the town's old factories.

Named after the battle cry uttered by Julius Caesar (*Heu moenia!* – 'Woe to you, walls!') before he ploughed through the defences of the city, **Omegna** was the site of tremendous battles during World War II. Today the town – the biggest on the lake – manufactures metal kitchenware products. In the **Forum di Omegna** cultural centre a museum documents

€10) serves bruschetta, cheese, cold cuts, *salsiccia ubriaca* ('drunken' sausage) and over 350 wines. If what's on the menu particularly titillates your taste buds, drop into the Boeuc's food store next door, **La Dispensa**.

The intimate **Taverna Antico Agnello** (via Olina 18, 0322 90 259, closed Tue & Dec-Jan, average €40) serves creative regional food in a cosy dining room.

Finally, lovers of local crafts shouldn't miss **Penelope** (piazza Motta 26, 0322 905 600) for hand-woven kitchen linens printed with antique wooden stamps and natural dyes.

Tourist information

Distretto dei Laghi
Via Panoramica, Orta San Giulio (0322 905 614/ www.distrettolaghi.it). **Open** usually 9am-1pm, 2-6pm Mon-Fri, but times vary.

Isola San Giulio

Legend has it that St Julius (San Giulio) drifted over to this island using his cloak, then got down to banishing its thriving population of

Lakes & Cities

the area's industrial history. A gift shop sells discounted items from local manufacturers Alessi (*see below* **Aladdin's cave**), Bialetti (the inventor of the espresso coffee maker), Calderoni (cutlery), Lagostina (pans) and others.

Seven kilometres (4.5 miles) west and up from Omegna, **Quarna Sotto** offers great views of the lake, plus one of the area's wildest museums. Around the late 1800s, the town was famous around the world for its wood and metal wind instruments. The **Museo Etnografico** honours this tradition with graphic explanations of manufacturing methods. But this lovingly curated gem also has displays on housing design, local costume and domestic arts as well as a water mill.

Aladdin's cave

Lake Orta isn't all about mystical monasteries and romantic alleyways. Tucked away at the end of the lake, at Crusinallo, are the factory, offices, museum and outlet store of Alessi, the company whose slick household objects crop up in stylish kitchens and bathrooms across the planet. Known for its glistening steam kettles and Philippe Starck-designed spindly legged juice squeezers, the company began life in 1921 as a humble producer of homewares in brass, nickel and silver. During the 1960s and '70s, the big designers were drafted in and the company morphed into a global brand. Today, visitors can't miss the aqua-and-orange factory with a giant sculpture of Alessi's archetypal, squat 1940s teapot outside.

Understandably, the company is a little reluctant to let all and sundry through its gates. Although the museum is jam-packed with over 22,000 design objects, only industry specialists (designers, students and professionals by appointment only) are allowed a glimpse inside this Aladdin's Cave. Fortunately, there is rather more chance of being let loose in the factory outlet. Head here for Alessi pieces at knock-down prices and join the legions of style hounds who can't survive for another minute without one more Alessi gewgaw shimmering in their homes.

Alessi Outlet Store
Via Privata Alessi, Crusinallo (0323 868 611). **Open** 2.30-6pm Mon, 9.30am-6pm Tue-Sat. **Credit** AmEx, DC, MC, V.

From **Pella**, on the lake's western shore, a signposted road climbs uphill for ten kilometres (six miles) to the church of Madonna del Sasso. En route, the hamlet of **Artò** has antique wash-houses, sundials and a building adorned with a 16th-century fresco, and **Boleto** is a picture with its cobbled lanes and church. At the top, the **Madonna del Sasso** church (0323 896 229, open irregular hours daily), built between 1730 and 1748, sits 638 metres (2,127 feet) above the lake on a granite outcrop. In thanks for some miracle, a successful local cobbler arranged for the bones of San Donato to be transferred here from the San Callisto catacombs in Rome. The holy skeleton, resting oddly on its side, lies in a transparent casket to the left of the altar. Most of the frescoes are the work of local artist Lorenzo Peracino, while the painting above the pink, grey and black marble altar is the *Pietà* (1547) by Fermo Stella da Caravaggio.

Collezione Calderara di Arte Contemporanea
Via Bardelli 9, Vacciago di Ameno (0323 89 622). **Open** *Mid May-mid Oct* 10am-noon, 3-6pm Tue-Sun. *Mid Oct-mid May* by appointment. **Admission** free.

Forum Omegna
Parco Maulini 1, Omegna (0323 866 141/www. forumomegna.org). **Open** 10.30am-12.30pm, 3-6.30pm Tue-Sat; 3-6.30pm Sun. **Admission** €2.50; €1.50 concessions. **Credit** MC, V.

Museo dell'Arte della Tornitura del Legno
Via Vittorio Veneto, Pettenasco (0323 89 622). **Open** *June-Sept* 10am-noon, 2-6pm Tue-Sun. **Admission** free.

Museo Etnografico e dello Strumento Musicale a Fiato
Via Roma, Quarna Sotto (0323 89 622). **Open** *Mid June-Sept* 10am-noon, 2-6pm Tue-Sun. *Oct-mid June* by appointment. **Admission** €2.60; €1.60 concessions. **No credit cards.**

Where to eat & stay

The **Hotel Panoramico Ristorante** in Boleto (via Frua 31, 0322 981 312, www.hotel panoramico.it, closed Nov and mid Jan-Mar, doubles €70-€85) has plain but comfortable rooms and a restaurant (average €28) with two outdoor terraces and wonderful lake views.

Tourist information

Pro Loco di Omegna
Piazza XXIV Aprile 17 (0323 61 930). **Open** *Apr-Sept* 9am-noon, 2.30-5.30pm Mon-Fri; 9am-noon Sat.

Lago Maggiore

A picturesque oasis in the midst of Italy's industrial core.

Garda may be larger and Como more celebrated, but Lake Maggiore, with its open vistas, whimsical landmarks, intriguing islands and historic towns set against the crags of the high Alps, can easily match either for charm.

Maggiore is 65 kilometres (40 miles) long and picturesque from almost any angle. The quiet reed banks and gentle undulations of its southern reaches give way to choppier waters and wider expanses more suggestive of the sea in the middle stretch. Further north, towards Switzerland, the lake narrows and the landscape becomes more dramatic as higher, sheerer mountains plunge into the water.

The towns around Maggiore started life as fishing villages, but by the Middle Ages were under the control of families of loftier extraction. The powerful Viscontis and later the Borromeos made Maggiore their fief and created some of its most celebrated landmarks, including the island gardens, fortresses and the looming statue of celebrated son Carlo (*see below*). It later became a stop-off point on the grand tours of the 18th and 19th centuries, with its mild climate and enchanting position attracting Italian nobility, the budding industrial bourgeoisie and wealthy foreigners, who built the sumptuous villas and gardens that characterise the lakefront.

Maggiore today has a life beyond the tourist trade – factories, workshops and industrial estates have sprung up over the surrounding country, while the mountains around some of its most famous towns have been blasted to extract the renowned local granite and marble.

But these modern blights give a sense of life and purpose to the lake beyond the historical and picturesque – and it's still easy enough to immerse yourself in Maggiore's tranquillity and escape the 21st century.

Getting there

By car
From Milan, take the A8 motorway and then the A26 towards Gravellona Toce for towns on the lake's western shore. For Luino, take the A8 to Varese and local roads for the remaining 25km (15 miles) to Luino. For Locarno, take the A9 and exit at Bellinzona.

By train
Trains run from Milan's Stazione Centrale and Porta Garibaldi for the Piedmont shore (journey time 45mins-1hr 30mins) and Locarno (2hrs 30 mins);

services for Luino depart from Stazione Garibaldi (1hr 30mins); services for Laveno leave from Cadorna station (1hr 30mins-2hrs).

By bus
Autoservizi Nerini (0323 552 172, www.safduemila. com) provides a twice-daily bus service for the Piedmont shore (8.30am & 5.50pm Mon-Sat, tickets Milano–Verbania €7.20, Milano–Arona €5.50, Milano–Stresa €6.35); Baldioli (0332 530 271) also runs services (5.15pm Mon-Fri, 2.15pm Sat, 9.15am & 7.30pm Sun, tickets Milano–Luino €5.50) to the Lombard shore. All leave from Porta Garibaldi.

The Piedmont shore

Lake Maggiore's tourist trade centres on the western shore. From Arona to Cannobio, small towns alternate with majestic villas and gardens. Most of these are in private hands and best visible from the boats that criss-cross the lake.

At the southern tip of Lake Maggiore is **Arona**, a lively commercial town with a pretty, historic centre. San Carlo, the celebrated son of the powerful Borromeo family (*see p105*) was born here and a 17th-century, 35-metre (117-foot) tall copper **statue** of the saintly local hero, built using the same technique employed to construct the (later) Statue of Liberty, stands high on a hill above the town. Those with steely nerves can climb a narrow internal spiral staircase and 10-metre (32-foot) vertical ladder to the statue's head to peer at the lake through the saint's eyes.

A few kilometres north, the smaller town of **Meina** has some attractive private residences, although derelict hotels and villas give the place a somewhat dilapidated air. A dark chapter of Italian history mars the town's apparent serenity. In September 1943, Nazi troops shot 16 Jewish guests at a local hotel.

Further north, **Lesa** is home to the **Museo Manzoniano**, with a collection of mementoes of author Alessandro Manzoni's stay.

Above **Belgirate**'s tiny historic centre is the so-called **Chiesa Vecchia** (Santa Maria del Suffragio, open Sun), lavishly adorned with frescoes by the school of Bernardino Luini, the local 16th-century artist.

Stresa stands on the Golfo Borromeo, which, with its islands, is the heart of the lake. The town became famous after Dickens and Byron gave it rave reviews; Hemingway also set chapters of *A Farewell to Arms* here. During

Lakes & Cities

the belle époque, Stresa's grandiose hotels, refined attractions and casino rivalled those of Monte Carlo and the Venice Lido.

Villa Ducale, former home to controversial religious philosopher Antonio Rosmini (*see p198* **The sage of Stresa**) and now the International Centre of Rosminian Studies, stands on the lakefront. It contains a small museum displaying documents and artefacts and the spartan bedroom where he died. **Villa Pallavicino** has a vast English-style garden where kids can enjoy close encounters with llamas, zebras, deer and exotic birds.

The 1,491-metre-high (4,970-feet) summit of **Mottarone** mountain can be reached by cable car or a five-hour hike from Stresa. It becomes a ski resort in winter and, on a clear day, you can enjoy a stunning view of the Alps. The cable car also stops at the **Giardino Alpinia**, which has hundreds of alpine plant species.

A flotilla of boats ferry tourists from Stresa to the captivating **Isole Borromee**, which can become unpleasantly crowded in high season. The Borromeo feudal lords took possession of the islands in the 16th century. **Isola Bella**, or **Isola Inferiore**, was named in honour of Isabella d'Adda, whose husband Carlo Borromeo III began transforming the island in 1632. The island's grandiose baroque **Palazzo Borromeo** (where Napoleon and Josephine slept after his conquest of northern Italy) has a stately Italian-style garden with albino peacocks. The **Isola Superiore**, or **Isola dei Pescatori**, is a strip of narrow lanes and whitewashed houses, ending in a park with benches and shady trees. The 16th-century **Palazzo Borromeo** on **Isola Madre** (the largest of the three Isole Borromee) has an 18th-century puppet theatre and is surrounded by an English-style garden.

Beyond Stresa, **Baveno** is home to the tenth-century church of **Santi Gervasio e Protasio** (open daily, hours vary). The octagonal baptistery dates back to the fifth century. The town's famous pink granite is quarried locally and exported worldwide.

The reed thickets in **Fondotoce**'s **Riserva Naturale** (0322 240 239), at the mouth of the Toce river, is a nesting ground for many birds. Some of the hiking and bike trails here lead to the smaller **Lago di Mergozzo**. Marble used in the construction of Milan's Duomo (*see p54*) was extracted nearby at **Candoglia**.

Verbania, the provincial capital, is made up of several towns unified in 1939. **Pallanza** is renowned for its gardens and has an attractive lakeside promenade abundant with flowers. The gardens of **Villa Giulia** at the end of the promenade have views over the privately owned islet San Giovanni Battista, where composer Arturo Toscanini spent his holidays.

The **Museo del Paesaggio** houses a rich collection of Piedmontese and Lombard art. One branch of the museum has paintings, sculptures and archaeological finds. The other, devoted to popular piety, gives a unique perspective of centuries of home-grown religious art with its collection of 5,000 votive offerings.

The famous garden at **Villa Taranto**, between Pallanza and Intra, was laid out by Scottish captain Neil McEacharn, who bought the property in 1931, and contains over 20,000 species of plants. **Intra** was an industrial centre in the 19th century, with a booming trade in textile manufacturing. More recently it has seen a proliferation of boutiques and speciality stores, and fills up on Saturdays for a large market.

You may dip your toes in the lake at **Verbania** and Cannobio, further north, since both have received the European blue flag for the quality of their water and beach facilities.

One of Europe's largest wilderness areas, the **Parco Nazionale della Val Grande** stretches behind Verbania and is reached from the town of **Cicogna** in the hills above. Dozens of hiking and bike trails lead to meadows, gorges, and peaks where chamois goats far outnumber hikers.

Heading towards Switzerland, the stretch of road from Intra to Cannobio is perhaps one of the loveliest on the lake. Bordered by weathered stone walls, it winds round the shoreline passing through quiet, genteel towns, offering views of ruined castles on tiny islands and the sheer mountainsides of the sparsely inhabited eastern shore.

The **Riserva Naturale Sacro Monte della Santa Trinità**, extending behind **Ghiffa**, has well-marked hiking trails. Ghiffa has a museum commemorating its once-thriving trade in felt hat manufacture, the **Museo dell'Arte del Cappello**.

Emerging from the waters off the shores of **Cannero Riviera** are the romantic medieval ruins of the Malpaga castles, built on two rocky islets between the 13th and 15th centuries. At one time they were inhabited by the Mazzarditi brothers, pirates and brigands who plundered and pillaged the local towns.

Cannobio is a handsome town with a pleasant promenade, lined with cafés and restaurants. It was once an important centre of transit and commerce and is the last major stop before the Swiss border. Nearby, the **Orrido di Sant'Anna** is a dramatic gorge plunging into dark depths and crossed by stone bridges. The 17th-century church of **Sant'Anna** (open in summer only, hours vary) totters over one edge.

Giardino Alpinia

Montagna Mottarone, Località Alpino (0323 20 163). **Open** *Apr-mid Oct* 9am-6pm Tue-Sun. **Admission** free.

Museo Manzoniano

Villa Stampa, via la Fontana, Lesa (0322 76 421). **Open** *July & Aug* Sat, Sun, hours vary. **Admission** €2. **No credit cards**.

Museo dell'Arte del Cappello

Corso Belvedere 279, Ghiffa (0323 59 174/0323 59 209). **Open** *Apr-Oct* 3.30-5.30pm Sat, Sun. At other times (winter also) groups only, by appointment. **Admission** free.

Museo del Paesaggio, Sezione Archeologia, Scultura, Pittura

Palazzo Viani Duniani, via Ruga 44, Pallanza (0323 556 621). **Open** *Apr-Oct* 10am-noon, 3.30-6.30pm Tue-Sun. **Admission** €2.50; €1.25 concessions. **No credit cards**.

Museo del Paesaggio, Sezione Religiosità, Arte e Cultura Popolare

Palazzo Biumi Innocenti, Salita Biumi 6, Pallanza (0323 556 621). **Open** *Mar-Dec* 10am-noon, 3.30-6.30pm Tue-Sun. **Admission** €2.50. **No credit cards**.

Palazzo Borromeo

Isola Bella (0323 30 556). **Open** *End Mar-Oct* 9am-5.30pm daily. **Admission** €9; €4-€7 concessions. **No credit cards**.

Palazzo Borromeo

Isola Madre (summer 0323 31 261/winter 0323 305 56). **Open** *Mar-Oct* 9am-noon, 1.30-5.30pm daily. **Admission** €8.50; €4-€7 concessions. **No credit cards**.

Parco Nazionale della Val Grande

Via Sanremigio 19, Verbania (0323 557 960/ www.parcovalgrande.it). **Open** *Office* 8.30am-1pm, 2.30-4.30pm Tue-Thur; 2.30-4.30pm Mon, Fri. **Admission** free.

Riserva Naturale

Ente Gestione Parchi Lago Maggiore, via Canale 48, Verbania Fondotoce (0322 240 239/www.parchilago maggiore.it). **Open** *Office* 10am-noon Mon-Fri; 5.15-6.15pm Tue-Thur. **Admission** free.

Riserva Naturale Sacro Monte della Santa Trinita'

Via Santissima Trinita' 48, Ghiffa (0323 59 870/ www.sacromonteghiffa.it). **Open** *Office* 8.30am-1pm, 1.30-6pm Mon, Wed; 8.30am-2pm Tue, Thur, Fri. **Admission** free.

Lakes & Cities

Isola Madre. *See p194.*

Statua San Carlo
Piazzale San Carlo, Arona (no phone). **Open**
Apr-Oct 9am-12.30pm, 2.30-6pm daily. *Nov-Mar*
9am-12.30pm, 2.30-5pm Sat, Sun. **Admission** €2.50.
No credit cards.

Villa Ducale
Corso Umberto I 15, Stresa (0323 30091). **Open**
Museo Romagnano 9am-noon, 3-6pm Mon-Fri.
Admission free.

Villa Giulia
Corso Sanitello 10, Pallanza (0323 503 249).
Open *Apr-Oct* 9am-12.30pm, 3-6.30pm.
Dec-Jan Exhibitions only. **Admission** free.

Villa Pallavicino
*Strada Statale 33, Località Stresa (0323 31 533/
www.parcozoopallavicino.it).* **Open** *Mar-Oct*
9am-6pm daily. **Admission** €6.70; €4.20-€5.70
concessions. **No credit cards.**

Villa Taranto
*Via V Veneto 111, Pallanza (0323 556 667/0323
404 555/www.villataranto.it).* **Open** *Apr-Oct*
8.30am-6.30pm daily. **Admission** €8; €4.30-€6.50
concessions. **No credit cards.**

Where to eat

In Arona, the stylish **Caffè della Sera**
(lungolago Marconi, 85, 0322 241 567, closed
2wks Jan-Feb, average €30) serves a simple
menu that includes excellent grilled vegetables
with smoked cheese. Four kilometres (2.5 miles)
away is **Trattoria Campagna** (via Vergante
12, San Carlo, frazione Campagna, Arona, 0322
57 294, closed dinner Mon Sept-June, all Tue,
2wks June & 2wks Nov, average €30), which
serves *pasta e fagioli* (bean soup).

In a villa just outside Lesa is the elegant fish
restaurant **Antico Maniero** (via alla Campagna
1, 0322 7411, reservation only, closed lunch,

Mon and Nov, average €65); the fish ravioli at
the **Triangolo** in Stresa (via Roma 61, 0323 32
736, closed Tue Sept-July, average €35) is superb
and compensates for the lack of a view.

In Verbania-Suna, the lively **Osteria Boccon
Di Vino** (via Troubetzkoy 86, 0323 504 039,
closed lunch Wed, all Tue and Jan, average €28)
serves local fare and fine wine, while the cuisine
at the elegant **Monastero** (via Castelfidardo 5/7,
0323 502 544, closed Mon, Tue and 2wks Aug,
average €46) draws diners from miles around.

At Mergozzo, the **Ristorante Vecchio
Olmo** in the main square on the lakefront
(piazza Cavour 2, 0323 80 335, closed Thur from
Sept to July, all June) serves a good-value set
menu and excellent fish and home-made pasta.

In Pallanza, **Milano** (corso Zanitello 2, 0323
556 816, closed dinner Mon, all Tue and mid Nov-
mid Feb, average €60) serves classic dishes and
excellent fish on its lakeside terrace. In Intra, the
Osteria del Castello (piazza Castello 9, 0323
516 579, closed Sun, 1wk Oct & 1wk Feb, average
€23) has homely fare: cold cuts and local cheeses.

In the village of Bee in the hills behind
Verbania, the **Chi Ghinn – Locanda e
Ristoro** (via Maggiore 21, 0323 56 430/0323
56 326, closed lunch Wed, all Tue and 7
Jan-Feb, average €30) has a terrace where
local delicacies such as crayfish are served.

In Cannobio, **Lo Scalo** (piazza Vittorio
Emanuele III 32, 0323 71 480, closed lunch Tue,
all Mon and 5wks Jan-Feb, average €45) serves
fresh market produce and home-baked bread.

Where to stay

At the pleasant **Hotel Giardino** (corso della
Repubblica 1, Arona, 0322 45 994, www.
giardinoarona.com, doubles €83-€90) half of the
rooms have lake views, and some have jacuzzis.

In Lesa, **Villa Lidia** (via Giuseppe Ferrari 7/9, 0322 7095, 02 5810 3076, doubles €70) is a charming three-room B&B.

Among Stresa's most sumptuous five-star belle époque hotels are the **Grand Hotel des Iles Borromees** (corso Umberto I 67, 0323 938 938, www.stresa.net/hotel/borromees, closed mid Dec-mid Jan, doubles €308-€374) and the **Hotel Regina Palace** (corso Umberto I 33, 0323 936 936, closed 2wks Dec-Jan, doubles €250-€330).

The **Lido Palace Hotel Baveno** (SS Sempione 30, 0323 924 444, www.lidopalace. com, closed Oct-Apr, doubles €160-€340) has an enviable view over the Borromeo islands. All rooms have en suite bathrooms, but the luxury suites also feature jacuzzis.

In Pallanza, the **Hotel Villa Azalea** (salita San Remigio 4, 0323 556 692, www.albergo villaazalea.com, closed Nov-mid Mar, doubles €61 or €70 with breakfast) is small and high in the hills. On the waterfront, the **Hotel Pace** (via Cietti 1, 0323 557 207, closed Nov-Apr, doubles €85-€100) has ten comfortable rooms.

In Intra, the **Hotel Ancora** (corso Mameli 65, 0323 53 951, www.hotelancora.it, doubles €146-€166) and the **Hotel Intra** (corso Mameli 133, 0323 581 393, www.verbaniahotel.it, doubles €68 or €114) are both delightful.

In Cannobio, the **Hotel Pironi** (via Marconi 35, 0323 70 624, www.pironihotel.it, closed mid Nov-mid Mar, doubles €105-€140) offers modern comforts in a former 15th-century monastery with frescoed ceilings. Two kilometres south, the **Hotel Del Lago** (via Nazionale 2, Carmine, 0323 70 595, www. enotecalago.com, closed Nov-Mar, doubles €105-€120) has ten rooms (most of them with a view over the lake), a private beach and a restaurant serving classic cuisine (average €65). In Cannero Riviera, **La Rondinella** (via Sacchetti 50, 0323 788 098, www.hotel-la-rondinella.it, doubles €73-€86) offers 13 rooms in a 1930s villa furnished with antiques.

Getting there & around

By car

The S33 winds along the Piedmont shore to Fondotoce, where it becomes the S34 to Cannobio.

By train

Most trains from Milan's Stazione Centrale and Porta Garibaldi for Domodossola, Paris or Geneva stop in Arona (journey time 1hr), Stresa (1hr) and Verbania (1hr 30mins). Local services stop at all towns in between.

By bus

Trasporti Nerini (0323 552 172) runs buses between Arona and Verbania. VCO Trasporti (0323 518 711) takes over from Verbania to Brissago in Switzerland.

By boat

Navigazione Lago Maggiore (0322 46 651/www. navigazionelaghi.it/www.navlaghi.it) operates boats, from paddlewheels to hydrofoils, to most of the towns around the lake. Schedules are seasonal.

Tourist information

For full, regularly updated information on lake sights and events, see www.lagomaggiore.it.

APT Arona

Piazza Duca d'Aosta (0322 243 601). **Open** *Apr-Sept* 9am-12.30pm, 3-6pm Mon-Sat. *Oct-Mar* 9am-noon, 3-6pm Mon-Fri.

IAT Stresa

Piazza Marconi 16 (0323 30 150). **Open** *Nov-Feb* 10am-12.30pm, 3-6.30pm Mon-Sat. *Mar-Oct* 10am-12.30pm, 3-6.30pm daily.

IAT Verbania

Corso Zanitello 6/8 (0323 503 249). **Open** *Apr-Sept* 9am-12.30pm, 3-6pm Mon-Sat. *Oct-Mar* 9am-12.30pm, 3-6.30pm Mon-Fri.

Pro Loco IAT Cannobio

Viale Vittorio Veneto 4 (0323 71 212). **Open** *Apr-Sept* 9am-noon, 4-7pm Mon-Sat; 9am-noon Sun. *Oct-Mar* 9am-noon, 4.30-7pm Mon-Wed, Fri, Sat; 9am-noon Sun.

The Swiss shore

Mellowed stone, elegant villas and a certain shabby gentility give way to modern buildings and an air of efficiency over on the Swiss side. But what it gains in steel-and-glass modernity, it loses in charm – though its bustling towns and smart boutiques make it worth a visit.

Brissago's reputation rests on its production of fine cigars. During the summer, small boats operated by Navigazione Lago Maggiore (*see above*) leave **Porto Ronco** for the **Isola di San Pancrazio**, with its **Parco Botanico**.

An ancient fishing village, **Ascona** is now a fashionable resort with chi-chi boutiques and art galleries. The town hosts an important European jazz festival (end June-early July, www.jazzascona.ch) and, from August to October, classical music events (www. settimane-musicali.ch).

Locarno, at the lake's northern tip, hosts a prestigious film festival (www.pardo.ch) each August. The remains of a 14th-century tower are a reminder that the Viscontis once ruled here, while in the jumble of streets of the old centre, churches and noble palazzi alternate with more plebeian dwellings. The city has a **Pinacoteca** (art gallery) in the 17th-century Casa Rusca, and a **Museo Archeologico** inside the largely rebuilt 14th-century **Castello Visconteo**. The art-filled Madonna del Sasso

The sage of Stresa

Priest and philosopher Antonio Rosmini (1797-1855) was born in Trentino-Alto Adige, but moved to Stresa in 1839. A brilliant scholar, he wrote prolifically and founded a religious community, the Institute of Charity (Rosminians), and its sister organisation, the Sisters of Providence, which today have missions all over the world.

He quickly rose within the ranks of the Church and, as a committed nationalist, entreated both Pope Pius IX and King Carlo Alberto di Savoia to find a way to create a unified Italian state. However, the controversy surrounding one of Rosmini's books, *The Five Wounds of the Church* (in which he criticised the Church for being obsessed with its

wealth), put an end to his blossoming diplomatic career. The publication of his *Constitution According to Social Justice* was the final straw for the Church: in 1849 it accused him of promoting heretical ideas and banned his writings.

Rosmini ended his days living among his religious brothers in a villa in Stresa, where he was visited by a stream of eminent guests and was known for his wisdom and humility. In 1887 the Vatican formally denounced some of his theories. Rosmini has since been rehabilitated, although Pope John Paul II, while acknowledging him as one of the Church's most influential thinkers, claims not to support the full body of his work.

---

church (open 7am-6pm daily) can be reached by funicular or by walking up a steep hill flanked by the Stations of the Cross.
Note: to dial a Swiss number from outside Switzerland, prefix it with the code 0041.

Museo Archeologico
Castello Visconteo, via al Castello, Locarno (0041 91 756 3170). **Open** *Apr-Oct* 10am-noon, 2am-5pm Tue-Sun. **Admission** SF7. **No credit cards.**

Parco Botanico del Canton Ticino
Isola di San Pancrazio (0041 91 791 4361). **Open** *21 Mar-Oct* 9am-6pm daily. **Admission** SF7; SF3 concessions. **No credit cards.**

Pinacoteca
Casa Rusca, piazza Sant'Antonio/via Collegiata 1, Locarno (0041 91 756 3185). **Open** 10am-noon, 2pm-5pm Tue-Sun. Closed 2wks Jan. **Admission** SF7 or €5; SF5 or €3.50 concessions. **No credit cards.**

Where to eat, drink & stay

In Brissago, there is a pleasant feel to the family-run **Hotel Eden** (via Vamara 26, 0041 91 793 1255, www.hotel-eden-brissago.ch, closed Nov-mid Mar, doubles SF156-SF204).

In Ascona, a 13th-century castle houses the **Romantik Castello-Seeschloss** (piazza Motta, 0041 91 791 0161, www.castello-seeschloss.ch, doubles SF248-SF548, closed Nov-Mar).

In Locarno, the lakefront **Treff Hotel Beau Rivage** (viale Verbano 31, 0041 91 743 1355, closed Nov-begin Mar, doubles SF140-SF240) is modern and attractive. For a more historic stay, the **Schlosshotel** (via Rusca 9, 0041 91 751 2361, closed Dec-mid Mar, doubles SF154-SF208) occupies part of the Visconti castle (*see p197*).

Centenario (lungolago Motta 17, 0041 91 743 8222, closed Mon & Sun, 3wks Jan & 3wks July, average SF80) is an elegant eaterie in Locarno. In the Valle Maggia, 11km (7 miles) north of Locarno, **Uno Più** (Gordevio, 0041 91 753 1012, closed Dec-Mar, average SF30) serves local seasonal delicacies; it also rents out six rooms (doubles SF110-SF168).

Getting there & around

By car
The road that meanders along the lake starts as the via Cantonale 13, becoming 22 on the eastern side.

By train
Trains run from Locarno (towards Domodossola) along the northern shore, and all along the eastern shore (from Domodossola).

By bus
FART Viaggi (0041 91 751 8731) runs a regular service between Brissago and Locarno.

By boat
Navigazione Lago Maggiore (0041 91 751 6140/ www.navigazionelaghi.it) also operates services on the Swiss side of the lake.

Tourist information

Ente Turistico Lago Maggiore
Via B Luini 3, Locarno (0041 91 791 0091/www. maggiore.ch). **Open** *Apr-Oct* 9am-5.30pm Mon-Fri; 10am-5pm Sat; 10am-noon, 1-3pm Sun. *Nov-Mar* 9.30am-12.30pm, 2-5.30pm Mon-Fri; 9.30-11.30am, 12.30-3.30pm Sat.
The tourist office includes a bureau de change.

The Lombardy shore

Despite a couple of unmissable sights, the lake's eastern (Lombard) shore is less of a draw for tourists and has a decidedly low-key feel.

In **Luino** the church of San Pietro (open daily, hours vary) has frescoes attributed to local artist Bernardino Luini and a Romanesque bell tower.

Laveno is a busy port, with ferries to Intra. In 1856 the Richard Ginori ceramics company was founded here; the 16th-century Palazzo Perabo houses the **Museo di Design Ceramico-Civica Raccolta di Terraglia**.

Perched precipitously on a lip in the rockface 18 metres (60 feet) above the water is the exquisite 12th-century **Sanctuary of Santa Caterina del Sasso Ballaro** near Leggiuno. Home to Dominican monks and lavishly adorned with frescoes dating from the 14th century, it has heart-stopping views across the lake. It can be reached by boat or by steep descent down 250-odd steps from the car park.

Angera's **Rocca**, a towered and crenellated fortress built in the 11th century and expanded and fortified until the 17th, dominates the lake's southern stretches from its clifftop position. In Visconti hands from the 13th century, it became Borromeo property in 1449. One wing has a rare cycle of 14th-century frescoes by local Lombard artists; another houses a collection of 17th-century dolls and children's toys. The Borromeo wing has frescoes taken from their Milan palazzo.

Sesto Calende's good **Museo Archeologico** at the lake's southern tip, is usually bypassed for the nearby ninth- to 12th-century abbey of San Donato (0331 924 692, open 8am-noon, 5-6.30pm daily), or the Iron Age tombs at Golasecca, which are accessible from the Sesto–Golasecca road.

Museo di Design Ceramico-Civica Raccolta di Terraglia
Frazione Cerro, Laveno (0332 666 530). **Open** *Sept-June* 2.30-5.30pm Tue-Thur; 10am-noon, 2.30-5.30pm Fri-Sun. *Jul & Aug* 2.30-5.30pm Fri-Sun. Closed public holidays. **Admission** €2; €1 concessions. **No credit cards.**

Rocca Borromeo di Angera – Amministrazione Isole Borromeo
Via alla Rocca 10, Angera (0331 931 300). **Open** *Mid Mar-end Oct* 9am-5.30pm Mon-Sat; 9am-6pm Sun & holidays. **Admission** €7; €4.50 concessions. **No credit cards.**

Santa Caterina del Sasso Ballaro
Via Santa Caterina 5, Leggiuno (0332 647 172). **Open** *Nov-Feb* 9am-noon, 2-5pm Sat, Sun. *Mar* 9am-noon, 2-5pm daily. *Apr-Oct* 8.30am-noon, 2.30-6pm daily. *23 Dec-6 Jan* 9am-noon, 2-5pm daily. **Admission** free.

Where to eat & stay

Don't miss the fish at **Il Sole di Ranco** (piazza Venezia 5, Ranco, 0331 976 507, closed Tue, Dec-mid Feb, average €70).

In Luino, the **Camin Hotel Luino** (viale Dante 35, 0332 530 118, www.caminhotelluino.com, closed 5wks Dec-Jan, doubles €115-€150) is a 19th-century villa with a garden, decorated with art deco furniture. **Giardinetto** restaurant (via Rossini 6, 0332 537 882, average €25) serves simple, traditional fare.

South of Laveno in Mombello, the **Hotel Porticciolo** (via Fortino 40, 0332 667 257, www.ilporticciolo.com, closed 1wk Nov & 2wks Jan-Feb, doubles €92-€144) is a charming hotel and good restaurant (average €45, closed Tue). A less expensive option is the lakefront **Hotel Moderno** (via Garibaldi 15, Laveno, 0332 668 373, closed Jan & Feb, doubles €63-€73), which has simple, clean rooms.

In Angera, the pleasant **Hotel Dei Tigli** (via Paletta 20, 0331 930 836, www.hoteldeitigli.com, closed 4wks Dec-Jan, doubles €100) has period furniture. In Sesto Calende, the seven-room **Locanda Sole** (via Ruga del Porto Vecchio 1, 0331 914 273, doubles €87.47) is in a central 18th-century house, and has a restaurant.

Getting there & around

By car
From Milan leave the A8 at Sesto Calende and follow the signs to the lake's eastern shore.

By train
From Milan's Porta Garibaldi station, go to Sesto Calende, Novara or Gallarate and change. Journey time 1hr 30mins-2hrs. Local trains stop at most towns on the eastern shore.

By bus
Autolinee Nicora e Baratelli (0332 668 056, www.sila.it) runs regular services between Luino and Laveno.

By boat
See p197.

Tourist information

IAT Luino
Via Piero Chiara 1 (0332 530 019/www.luino-online.it). **Open** 9am-noon, 3-6.45pm Mon-Sat.

IAT Laveno-Mombello
Via de Angeli 18 (0332 666 666/www.laveno-online.it). **Open** *Apr-Sept* 9am-noon Mon-Sat. *May-Aug* 9am-noon, 3-6pm Mon-Sat.

Lakes & Cities

Lago di Como

One of the world's great beauty spots, Lake Como has attracted poets, politicians and Hollywood stars.

Extending in an inverted Y-shape from the Alpine peaks in the north to the plain just 70 kilometres (42 miles) from Milan in the south, Lake Como – or the Lario, as it has been known since Roman times – is made up of three sections. At each southern end are the cities of Como and Lecco. The northernmost point is Gera Lario, some 50 kilometres (30 miles) from Como. The three 'arms' come together to form the promontory of Bellagio.

Formed during the Ice Age, the lake is 198 metres (660 feet) above sea level. Going down to 410 metres (1,367 feet) between Argegno and Nesso, it is Europe's deepest lake. Although it measures 145 square kilometres (56 square miles), its maximum width is only 4.4 kilometres (3 miles) – between Menaggio and Varenna – which creates a sense of intimacy, despite the fact that the lake has a 178-kilometre (106-mile) perimeter. Not only does each kilometre bring new and delightful views in all directions, the gentle mist enhancing rather than detracting from the beauty, but each of the lake's arms is different.

While the Como section is relatively narrow and the mountains behind are somewhat uniform, with plenty of little towns and grand villas along the shoreline, the Lecco branch is more rugged and rocky, the jagged edges of the Grigne range providing a strong contrast. The northern part features deep valleys and tall mountains, and is the most dramatic.

The central section of the lake (*centro lago*), based around the triangle of Bellagio, Menaggio and Varenna (*il triangolo lariano*), is where the scenery is at its most spectacular.

The northern lake – known as the Lago di Colico or Alto Lario – is quieter, the sharp edges of the central section dissolving into reed beds in places. The mountain backdrop, and the fact that Colico is the point where the roads to the Alpine passes of the Splügen and the Stelvio converge, remind us that this is where many invaders have entered Italy over the centuries.

Others have invaded more peaceably, and continue to do so. The poet Percy Bysshe Shelley said that Lake Como 'surpasses in beauty everything I have ever seen hitherto',

A sea of tranquillity: glorious **Lake Como**.

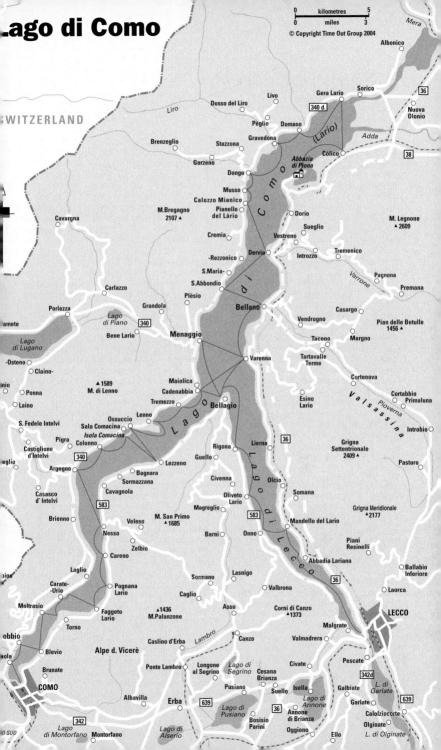

A gardener's world

The balmy microclimate of Lake Como has afforded splendid opportunities to gardeners and garden-lovers over the centuries. One of the finest examples is the garden of **Villa del Balbianello**, located just south of Lenno. Built on a headland that protrudes into the lake, a space that offered no scope for a formal Italian garden, nor for what the Italians call *un giardino all'inglese*, the gardens are what one might call site-specific. They interact with the lake and shoreline rather than follow any set design or concept. That they are approached by water only adds to the impact: visitors can feel what it was like to arrive as a guest of the original owners – the Cardinal Durini, the families of Porro Lambertenghi and Arconati Visconti, as well as the Butler Ames family from the United States, and count Guido Monzino, a famous explorer. The latter bequeathed Balbianello to the FAI (Fondo Ambiente Italiano), Italy's equivalent of Britain's National Trust.

Renowned for its plane trees clipped into candle shapes, the garden follows a steep slope, where statues alternate with wisteria, and azaleas and rhododendrons provide exhilarating bursts of colour throughout the spring and early summer. Built in the 16th century and extended in the 18th, the villa can be visited by appointment only.

Rhododendrons are also very much in evidence among the 500-plus species that can be seen in the 80,000 square metres (861,000 square feet) of garden at **Villa Carlotta** in Tremezzo. Named after princess Charlotte, who received it as a wedding present from her mother princess Marianna of Nassau in 1843, the villa was built in neo-classical style in the early 18th century for the marquis Giorgio Clerici.

Leading to the villa are five terraces, with stairs to either side; the geometric lines are softened by vines, climbing roses and trailing geraniums. See the pergola on the second terrace and note that the lemon and orange trees are planted directly into the ground, not into pots, as is usually the case. This is because Como's climate is so mild that there's no need for a *limonaia* (a special shed in which citrus plants are placed in the winter). The house contains many sculptures, including Antonio Canova's *Cupid and Psyche*.

Villa Melzi and Villa Serbelloni are two extra attractions for visitors to Bellagio. While neither of the houses is open to the public, the gardens are more than worth seeing. **Villa Melzi** boasts a pretty Japanese garden, some splendid water lilies and a Moorish-looking, lapis lazuli-blue coffee house.

Open for guided tours twice a day, the 17th-century **Villa Serbelloni** – which is owned by the Rockefeller foundation – stands high on the point above Bellagio's town centre. It may be on the site of Pliny the Younger's villa Tragedia (he had another villa called

but he was just one in a long line of writers, composers, artists, lovers and other visitors who have come here from early spring to late autumn. It is a common belief in Italy that lakes in general, not just Como, are *tristi* (sad) during the rest of the year. Make up your own mind, but bear in mind that some hotels and restaurants may well be closed during the winter months.

HISTORY

Although human life has been documented in the area from at least the 11th century BC, things really started to get going around Lake Como when the Celts made their way through the Splügen (or possibly the San Bernardino) pass, decided they liked it, and stayed. According to Livy, this occurred in about 520 BC. In 196 BC, the Romans took over, setting up a *castrum* (settlement) in what is now downtown Como. The area was considered of considerable commercial and strategic importance – the link between central Europe and the Mediterranean – and the Romans reinforced their position in the area over the years. In 89 BC Como became a *colonia* and 30 years later Julius Caesar made it a *municipium*, which meant that the inhabitants of the Lario area became Roman citizens. At the same time, JC brought in several thousand new settlers, including 500 Greeks.

The Lombards conquered Como in AD 569 and took residence within the walled town. In the 11th century, Como expanded its hold over the surrounding area. In 1117, it and Milan became involved in what came to be known as the Ten Years War, and by 1127 the city had been destroyed. After being rebuilt by Frederick Barbarossa (*see p10*), the city signed a peace treaty in 1186 and from then on, Como followed the fortunes of Milan.

Commedia at Lenno, see p208). The trees in the gardens of Villa Serbelloni, added in the 19th century, are worth noting. Although they seem to blend effortlessly into the landscape, these were, in fact, among the first examples of magnolias, oleanders, palms and cedars ever planted in Italy.

Villa del Balbianello
Via Comoedia 8 (0344 56 110/www.fondo ambiente.it). **Open** *Early Mar-Oct* 10am-1pm, 2-6pm Tue, Thur & Fri; 10am-6pm Sat, Sun. Last admission 30mins before closing. **Admission** €5. **No credit cards**.
Boats depart every half hour from the jetty at Lenno (*see p208*) 9.45am-3.45pm. On Tue, Sat, Sun and public holidays, a footpath provides access to the gardens from Lenno.

Villa Carlotta
Via Regina 2 (0344 40 405/www.villa carlotta.it). **Open** *Apr-Sept* 9am-6pm daily. *Mar & Oct* 9-11.30am, 2-6.30pm daily. **Admission** €7. **No credit cards**.

Villa Melzi
Lungolario Marconi (031 950 318/031 950 204). **Open** *Mid Mar-Oct* 9am-6pm daily. **Admission** €5. **No credit cards**.

Villa Serbelloni
Piazza della Chiesa (031 950 204). **Open** *Apr-Oct* 11am & 4pm Tue-Sun. **Admission** €6.50. **No credit cards**.
Only guided tours of the garden are available. You can book tickets at the IAT Bellagio (*see p211*), also located on piazza della Chiesa.

Defeated militarily, Como succeeded brilliantly on an artistic level. All through the Middle Ages, the skills of its itinerant stonemasons – the *maestri comacini* – were in demand far and wide. Their exquisite carvings embellished brick- and stone-faced walls and façades throughout the region, the rest of northern Italy and beyond.

As elsewhere, crippling taxes impoverished the area when the Spanish took over in 1535. Como gradually built a reputation as a centre for silk-weaving and by 1769, when Emperor Joseph II of Austria visited, some 155 looms were licensed. The city is still famed for its silk, even if the silkworms are no longer raised on the lake and raw thread is now imported from the Far East.

Lake Como has long been famed as a great place to live. Como-born Pliny the Younger (AD 62-112) wrote ecstatically of the 'several villas'

he possessed on the lake, singling out two (which he called Comedy and Tragedy) as his special favourites. One was on a hill, the other by a shore, presumably in the vicinity of Bellagio. From the latter, 'you can quite simply cast your line out of the window without getting out of bed'. For more on people who came, saw and lingered a while, see *p206* **Lacustrine luminaries**.

Getting there

By car
For Como, take the A8 motorway west out of Milan and fork on to the A9 after Lainate. Alternatively, the SS35 takes you to Como, and the SS36 to Lecco.

By train
Two railway companies serve Como. The state railways (Ferrovie dello Stato, aka Trenitalia) offer hourly services from Milan's Stazione Centrale on

Lakes & Cities

the Chiasso–Lugano route. This takes 30mins and comes into San Giovanni station at Como. There is also an hourly service from Porta Garibaldi station.

The Ferrovie Nord service departs every 30mins from Cadorna station for the Como Nord Lago station. Journey time 1hr.

For Lecco, there is an hourly service from Porta Garibaldi (journey time 1hr), and one train every two hours (journey time 45mins) from Stazione Centrale.

By bus

Autostradale (information 02 63 79 01/www. autostradale.it) runs infrequent services from Milan to Como's lakeside towns.

Getting around

By car

The SS340 and SS583 around the lake's shores are very scenic, but traffic is heavy, especially in summer and at weekends. Progress is quicker, if less picturesque, on the SS36, which follows the eastern shore of the lake. Bear in mind that minor roads up into the surrounding hill villages can be challenging, to say the least.

By bus

Società Pubblica Trasporti (031 247 247, www. sptcomo.it, open 8am-6pm Mon-Thur, 8am-5pm Fri) runs services from piazza Matteotti in Como to towns around the lake and throughout the area.

By boat

Navigazione Lago di Como (via per Cernobbio 18, Como, 031 579 211, www.navigazionelaghi.it, office open 8am-noon, 1-5pm daily) operates ferry and hydrofoil services year-round. Timetables change often. The boats run very frequently and there are services to Tavernola, Cernobbio, Moltrasio, Torno, Urio and Pognana Lario at the southern end of the lake; Colico at the lake's northern tip; and to intermediate towns such as Bellagio, Varenna, Cadenabbia, and Menaggio. There are also some car-ferry services. Special tourist cruises are also on offer, but the point-to-point commuter services are perfect for visiting the lakeside towns.

Como

Como is busy, industrialised and, outside the pretty pedestrianised area, very traffic-ridden. If you enjoy open-air markets, come here on a Saturday. Several piazze in the centre, as well as the entire area around the city walls, fill up with stalls. Offerings range from fruit and veg, to clothes, shoes and antiques, along with a section given over to rocks and minerals.

On the lakeside by the ferry jetty, piazza Cavour is a bustling meeting point. The neo-classical **Mausoleo Voltiano**, aka Tempio Voltiano (viale Marconi, 031 574 705, open Apr-Oct 10am-noon, 3-6pm Tue-Sun, Nov-Mar 10am-noon, 2-4pm Tue-Sun, admission €3) in the **Giardini Pubblici** west of the square was

erected in 1927 to mark the centenary of the death of Alessandro Volta, the Como-born physicist who invented the battery and gave his name to the volt.

Arcaded via Plinio leads south from piazza Cavour to piazza del Duomo, home to the **Duomo**. This is late-Gothic, with spectacular Renaissance additions. To the right as you exit the Duomo is the **Broletto**, the 13th-century town hall. Having also done service as a theatre and a record office, it's now used for exhibitions.

At the apse end of the Duomo, in piazza Verdi, stands the 19th-century **Teatro Sociale** (via Bellini 3, 031 270 170, www. teatrosocialecomo.it, open 1-6pm Mon-Fri, 10am-1pm Sat), its neo-classical façade adorned with six mighty Corinthian pillars. The theatre had its moment of glory at the end of World War II when its opera season outshone Milan's, if only because La Scala (*see p61*) had been badly damaged in bombings.

Further east, in piazza del Popolo, is Giuseppe Terragni's visionary ex-**Casa del Fascio** (1932-6), also known as Palazzo Terragni. The building is currently used by the Guardia di Finanza, the Italian customs and excise police. Visits are possible, though (after 4.30pm Mon-Thur, after 1pm Fri, 10am-1pm Sat, Sun), subject to someone being available to accompany you. Ask at the porters' lodge (*portineria*) and be prepared to leave an ID document for the duration of the visit. Fans of the work of Terragni (1904-1943) might also like to see the **Asilo Sant'Elia** (1936-37). The building, which is on the corner of piazza San Rocco and via dei Mille, is used as a nursery school, so visits are only possible after 5pm, when the children have gone home. Contact Signor Bianchi at the town hall (031 252 602, 9am-noon Mon-Fri) for more information.

Still further west, in via Sinigaglia, Terragni's **Novocomum** apartment block (1927-9) is a prime example of Italian rationalist architecture.

Via Vittorio Emanuele leads southwards out of piazza del Duomo. At the far end, on the piazza of the same name, is the church of San Fedele, Como's former cathedral. Viale Battisti leads south-west along one of the few remaining stretches of Como's 12th-century walls to the imposing **Porta Torre** gate (1192). Continue south-west into the areas of town that sprang up around the old walls in the Middle Ages, through a heavily traffic-laden area to reach the breathtaking Romanesque **Basilica di Sant'Abbondio**.

Heading east, viale Battisti becomes via Grossi. Here is the start of a steep path leading up to **Brunate**, a village high – 720 metres (2,400 feet) to be precise – above Como. The

Lakes & Cities

Follow in the footsteps of Pliny, Shelley and Clooney and take a stroll around **Lake Como**.

funicular railway will take you up there in just under seven minutes. However, if this seems like the easy way out, by all means walk it – it will take about one and a half hours to cover the five kilometres (3 miles). On the way up, stop at the **Sagrario degli Sports Nautici** (031 305 958, open 2.30-6pm Sun), a parish priest's slightly dotty tribute to the lake's strapping young water-sportsmen, in a dinghy-shaped chapel.

The point of going to Brunate? To enjoy the view of the lake and to stroll around and see some of the villas (from outside the perimeter walls only) built in the 19th and early 20th centuries, when Brunate became a resort for the well-heeled, thanks to the construction of the aforementioned funicular. The **Grand Hotel Brunate** and the **Grand Hotel Milano**, both of which have now been diverted to other functions, attest to that past glory.

Back down in Como, the **Museo Didattico della Seta** (silk museum) in Como's southern suburbs, is a little off the beaten track, but the effort is well worth it. A ten-minute walk from the Como Borghi railway station on the Ferrovie Nord line, it is probably best reached by number 7 bus from the San Giovanni train station (FS line) or from behind the Duomo. The stop is Scuola di Setificio.

Basilica di Sant'Abbondio

Via Sant'Abbondio (no phone). **Open** 8am-6pm daily. **Admission** free.
Visiting monks from northern Europe are perhaps responsible for the innovative design of this Benedictine abbey church – including the twin bell towers, a Norman touch – built to replace an earlier structure in the 11th century. Wherever the inspira-

tion came from, this remains one of the greatest jewels of Lombard Romanesque, its five aisles separated by slim columns of granite, and its starkly simple walls broken by bands of intricate carving around the windows of the apse, which contains 13th-century frescoes.

Duomo

Piazza del Duomo (031 265 244). **Open** 8am-noon, 3-7pm daily. **Admission** free.
A brilliant fusion of Romanesque, Gothic, Renaissance and baroque, Como's cathedral is unique – as well as spectacularly beautiful. It was begun in 1396 on the site of the Romanesque basilica of Santa Maria Maggiore, growing in fits and starts, and eating into the adjacent buildings. The Broletto next door sacrificed a wing to the nave, while the Palazzo del Pretorio was eventually demolished altogether. The late-Gothic façade (1455-86) is striking enough, with its host of sculptures, but the fact that pride of place is given to two renowned pagans – the Plinies, Older and Younger – makes it even more remarkable. Much of the carving was done by the Rodari family of stonemasons – Giovanni and his sons Bernardino, Jacopo, and Tommaso – during the late 15th and early 16th centuries. They originated from Maroggia in the Canton Ticino but are considered, nonetheless, local. Note also Tommaso Rodari's intricate Frog Door (Porta della Rana) leading into the left side of the nave.

In the Latin-cross interior, the three-aisled nave is Gothic, the transept Renaissance, while the great octagonal dome was designed by Filippo Juvarra in 1744. The lions holding up holy-water bowls by the main portal came from the original basilica of Santa Maria Maggiore, while the tapestries lining the central nave date from the 16th century. More sculptural extravaganzas from local masters, including the Rodari family, mingle with mostly Renaissance

Lakes & Cities

Lacustrine luminaries

Word is that, following **George Clooney**'s purchase of **Villa Oleandra** at Laglio, a few miles north of Moltrasio, local estate agents have been inundated with calls from Hollywood stars also wanting a house on Lake Como. The immediate thought is: what took them so long? The Lombardy area offers at least seven lakes to choose from, each different from the other, but Como surely ranks as one of the must-see – and perhaps must-stay – places in the world.

In fact, Georgey-boy was not the first big name to take up residence. If we discount people like Pliny *père et fils*, who settled here in the first century AD, there's always the late **Gianni Versace**, who purchased **Villa Le Fontanelle** in Moltrasio in 1977.

There are other important villas in Moltrasio, small though the town might be. Indeed, next door (in a manner of speaking) is **Villa Le Rose**, which has a handsome garden.

Its other claim to fame is that **Winston Churchill** stayed here in 1945. The town's most significant property, though, is **Villa Passalacqua**. Originally commissioned by the Odescalchi family, it was bought by Andrea Passalacqua in 1787, who had it extensively redesigned by Felice Soave – and presumably changed its name. Whereas Versace had Elton John stay at his villa, Passalacqua offered hospitality to the opera composer **Vincenzo Bellini** between 1829 and 1833; and it was here that Bellini wrote *La sonnambula*.

Just across the water from Moltrasio is the village of Torno. Here too have come famous visitors. In the 19th century, Shelley, Stendhal and Rossini all stayed at the **Villa Pliniana**. As is typical with many of these dream residences, the villa can only be reached by a footpath or by water – privacy guaranteed.

---

paintings of varying quality by lake artists, plus a lovely *Holy Family* by Bernardino Luini over the fourth altar on the right, and several other works by the same artist elsewhere. By the second altar on the right is the sarcophagus of Bishop Bonifacio of Modena (1347), another relic from Santa Maria Maggiore, as is the relief of *Mary Enthroned* (1317) on the pulpit in the apse.

Funicolare Como–Brunate

Piazza de Gaspari 4 (no phone/www.geocities.com/ funicolarecomobrunate). **Open** 6am-10.30pm daily. **Tickets** €2.50. **No credit cards.**
Located adjacent to the Como Nord Lago railway station, and built in 1894, the funicular takes six and a half minutes to cover 1,084m (3,500ft) at gradients of up to 55%. An experience.

Museo Didattico della Seta

Via Valleggio 3 (031 303 180/www.museoseta como.com). **Open** 9am-noon, 3-6pm Tue-Fri; by appointment Sat. **Admission** €8; €2.60 students. **No credit cards.**
Take the number 7 city bus from behind the Duomo to get to this lovingly curated museum, which brings the city's main industry – silk – to life. Housed inside Como's silk-making school, its displays range from the life cycle of the silkworm to the earliest and more modern silk looms, printing equipment, dyeing processes and numerous examples of the luxurious end-product.

San Fedele

Piazza San Fedele (no phone). **Open** 8am-noon, 3-7pm daily. **Admission** free.

This basilica – built some time between the tenth and 12th centuries – is named after the saint who brought Christianity to Como in the fourth century, and was Como's cathedral until the Duomo was built. It was erected over the sixth-century church of Sant'Eufemia; an eighth-century lion from the portal of that earlier church holds up the holy-water stoop in the left-hand bulge of the oddly shaped transept. Also odd are the five-sided apse and the 13th-century rear door, with its presiding monsters. The rose window over the reconstructed main entrance is from the 16th century; the majority of the decorations inside are baroque.

Where to eat & drink

Good pizza at **Le Colonne Ristorante Pizzeria** (piazza Mazzini 12, 031 266 166, average pizza €15, menu €25). **Breeze Inn Ristorante** (via Natta 29, 031 242 320, www.breeze-inn.com, closed lunch Mon, all Sun, 2wks Aug & 1wk Dec, average €45) serves local specialities in a pleasant setting. Housed in a converted barn, **Il Solito Posto** (via Lambertenghi 9, 031 271 352, closed Mon, 1wk Aug & 1wk Jan, average €40) does creative things with local dishes.

Where to stay

The **Barchetta Excelsior** (piazza Cavour 1, 031 3221, www.hotelbarchetta.com, doubles €190-€230) is located right on the lakeside.

In the same square, the **Metropole & Suisse** (piazza Cavour 19, 031 269 444, www.hotel metropolesuisse.com, closed 3wks Dec-Jan, doubles €166-€196) has been going strong since 1892; its restaurant, **L'Imbarcadero** (*menu del giorno* €25, à la carte €50), is highly regarded. **Le Due Corti** (piazza Vittoria 12/13, 031 328 111, doubles €130-€190) is a romantic spot with beauty treatments available, while **Posta** (via Garibaldi 2, 031 266 012, www.hotelposta.net, doubles €70-€90) is comfortable and central.

Where to shop

Although Como's reputation as a centre of excellence for silk textile manufacturing and printing lives on, there are no silkworms here now – the raw thread is imported from the Far East. Factories with retail outlets include **Martinetti** (via Torriani 41, 031 269 053, www.martinetti.it, open 2.30-6pm Mon, 9am-noon, 2.30-6pm Tue-Sat) which can be reached on foot from piazza Cavour. Take via Garibaldi and then viale Varese.

Check out the collection called La Tessitura by Mantero, one of Italy's, and therefore the world's, top names in luxury silk design and production. These women's, men's and home accessories have been designed by Mantero's in-house team of young international designers using remnants of luxury silk that have been re-dyed, re-textured, re-woven, reprinted or taken from one-off colour samples. See them at the **Mantero HQ** (viale Roosevelt 2a, 031 321 666, www.latessitura.com, open 9.30am-7.30pm Mon-Sat, 10am-7pm Sun, prices €7.50-€1,500).

Tourist information

IAT

Piazza Cavour 17 (031 269 712/www.lakecomo.com). **Open** *June-Sept* 9am-1pm, 2.30-6pm Mon-Sat; 9am-1pm Sun. *Oct-May* 9am-1pm, 2.30-6pm Mon-Sat.

The western shore

Via Regina heads along the western shore of the lake out of Como town. The first stop on the commuter-boat service from Como is **Cernobbio**. This town of magnificent villas and private boat jetties is dominated by the **Villa d'Este**. Originally called Villa Garrovo, it was one of three villas built for Tolomeo Gallio, when he was made a cardinal in 1565, by architect Tolomeo Pellegrino Tibaldi (1527-96). In 1814, the villa became the home of Princess Caroline of Brunswick, the estranged wife of Britain's Prince Regent. It was she who decided to remodel the house and gardens, and to call it Villa d'Este. There is, in fact, no connection

with the famous d'Este family from Ferrara. In 1873, Villa d'Este started its life as a luxury hotel (*see p209*). Although much of the magnificent 16th-century Italian garden has been lost, the double water staircase survives – walk up its grass-covered steps and experience the sight and sound of falling water on either side. Framing the staircase are theatrical shell- and pebble-mosaic wings topped with obelisks.

Villa Bernasconi (via Regina 7, 031 334 7209, open for exhibitions only) is a stunning example of Liberty (art nouveau) style, complete with colourful ceramics and beautiful wrought iron.

Back on the boat, head straight for **Moltrasio**, from which the local building stone with its distinctive bluish-grey streaks takes its name. Popular with sculptors and church builders, this is quarried locally. A **gorge** that splits the small town in two and fills with a rapidly flowing torrent in spring as the snow above melts and the 11th-century church of **Santa Agata**, with its fine campanile, are reasons to stop here a while. Next to Santa Agata is the 18th-century **Villa Passalacqua**, which has a stunning Italian garden (open 9am-noon, 3-6pm Thur, *see also p206* **Lacustrine luminaries**).

Just north of Moltrasio in **Laglio** is the **Grotta del Buco dell'Orso**. Discovered in 1841, it was found to contain the fossilised remains of *Ursus spaeleus*. While the bear is now in the Civico Museo di Storia Naturale (Natural History Museum) in Milan (*see p81*), the cave is still worth seeing for its fast-running stream that forms a lake. Since 1896, this stream has provided drinking water for Laglio, as well as Carate Urio and Brienno.

Back in Moltrasio, take the fast ferry for Colico and get off at the first stop, the little resort of **Argegno**. From here, a cable car operates all year (031 821 344, open Apr-June 8am-noon, 2-6pm daily, July & Aug 8am-noon, 2-7pm daily, Sept-Mar 8am-noon, 2-5pm daily, single €1.95, return €3) up to **Pigra**, a lofty hamlet with superb views across the lake to Isola Comacina and the Bellagio promontory. Argegno is on the bus route from Como to Menaggio.

Boats depart from **Sala Comacina** (031 821 955, 335 707 4122, www.boatservices.it, operates Mar-Oct 9am-midnight daily) for **Isola Comacina**, the only island on the lake. Just 600 metres long (1,970 feet), 200 wide (650 feet), and two kilometres (1.25 miles) round, it has plenty of history to boast about. Used by the Romans and the Byzantines as a fortified settlement, it was seized in AD 590 by the Lombard king Autari. In what was probably not their smartest move, the islanders struck an alliance with the Milanese and, thus,

Lakes & Cities

Gorge-ous: the **Orrido di Bellano**. *See p209*.

against Como (which also had Frederick
Barbarossa on its side) in the early 12th
century. As a result, the *comaschi* razed it,
forcing the inhabitants to flee to Varenna (*see
p209*) on the eastern shore. The island was
bought in 1918 by the king of Belgium, who
later donated it to Milan's fine arts academy.
Today, it is home to a restaurant, a handful
of ancient ruined churches and the baroque
oratory of **San Giovanni** (St John), the patron
saint. This is also why the island is sometimes
referred to as the Isola San Giovanni. The
festival of Saint John (24 June) provides the
occasion for a spectacular firework display.

LA TREMEZZINA

The stretch of shore from Lenno to Menaggio –
known as La Tremezzina, or the Riviera delle
Azalee – is lakeland *per eccellenza*, awash with
the camelias and azaleas for which the lake,
with its balmy microclimate, is famed, and
home to any number of villas. It also has a
few faded reminders of an age when British
dowagers came to winter (and summer) here:
an Anglican church (in Cadenabbia), a Victorian
tea room and even a crazy-golf course.

    Lenno may have been the site of Commedia,
one of Pliny the Younger's villas (*see p203*) –
the baths of a sumptuous Roman villa were
unearthed in the crypt of the town's 11th-
century parish church of **Santo Stefano** (open
8am-noon, 3-6pm daily), which has an octagonal
baptistery. Just south of the church of Santo
Stefano, a path leads to the 12th-century abbey
of **Acquafredda** (0344 55 208, open 9am-
4.30pm daily), built by Cistercian monks but
now home to some Capuchins. The remains
of an earlier pre-Romanesque chapel are still
visible below the campanile. Lenno's jetty is

the departure point for boats to the picture-
postcard **Villa del Balbianello** (*see p202*
A gardener's world).

    In **Tremezzo**, the neo-classical **Villa
Carlotta** (*see p202* **A gardener's world**)
boasts statues by Antonio Canova and a
massive, spectacular garden.

    At **Cadenabbia**, the lake is at its widest.
A foot and car ferry plies between here and
Bellagio, while another car ferry goes to
Varenna. Giuseppe Verdi composed much of
La Traviata in the **Villa Margherita Ricordi**
(not open to the public), which is in the nearby
hamlet of **Maiolica**.

    Long a bustling commercial town and now
an equally bustling resort, pretty pink- and
ochre-tinted **Menaggio** has a ruined castle
and lovely views across to Bellagio and the
eastern shore. Menaggio is 12 kilometres
(eight miles) from Lake Lugano; keen walkers
(with the emphasis on keen), might want to
consider the hike up to **Monte Bregagno**
from which, on a very clear day, it is possible
to see both lakes. A car ferry links Menaggio
and Varenna.

THE NORTHERN REACHES

Continuing north towards the towering
heights of the Valchiavenna (*see p264*), we
reach the **Tre Pievi** (three parishes) of
Dongo, Gravedona and Sòrico. These formed
an independent community in the Middle Ages,
and were powerful enough to wrest a special
deal at the Treaty of Constance (1183), which
put an end to the wars between Frederick
Barbarossa and the Italian city-states.

    Remembered as the place where Mussolini
and his lover Claretta Petacci were captured
on 27 April 1945 as they headed for the Swiss
border, **Dongo** was also the scene of violence
in 1252, when St Peter Martyr was finished
off with a hatchet through the head by
Cathar heretics; the subject is a favourite
one in the devotional iconography of his
order, the Dominicans.

    A manufacturing town and popular water
sports centre, **Gravedona** was the most
important of the Tre Pievi and a key ally of
medieval Milan – hence it was razed by Como
in the 12th century. The Romanesque church
Santa Maria del Tiglio (via Roma, open
3-5pm Mon-Fri, 10am-6pm Sat, Sun) is simple,
severe and stunning. **Palazzo Gallio**, also
known as Palazzo Del Pero, was the second
of the three houses commissioned by Tolomeo
Gallio from Pellegrino Tibaldi.

    The fishing village of **Domaso** still produces
a white wine mentioned by Pliny the Elder.
It is also Lake Como's recognised windsurfing
centre. In fortified **Sòrico**, tolls were extracted

Lakes & Cities

from travellers arriving on the lake's shores from the Valchiavenna (*see p264*) and the Valtellina (*see p265*).

Where to eat

In Moltrasio, the **Crotto Valdurino** (via Besana 37, 031 290 101, closed Tue, average €20) and the **Imperialino** (via Antica Regina 26, 031 346 600, closed Mon, 5wks Jan-Feb and Oct-Mar, average €55) are both reliable.

In Sala Comacina, the **Alessio** (via Statale 14, 0344 55 035, closed Mon and Nov, average €25) offers filling, hearty pasta dishes, while **La Tirlindana** (0344 056 637, piazza Matteotti 5, closed Mon in Mar-Oct and Mon-Fri in Nov-Feb, average €45) is renowned for its delicious home-made ravioli stuffed with lemon-flavoured cheese. In Lenno, the family-run **Santo Stefano** (piazza XI Febbraio 3, 0344 55 434, closed Mon, mid Jan-mid Feb, average €25) serves the hard-to-find local delicacy *missoltini* (called 'shad' in English, but don't let that put you off) and other lake fish. Tremezzo has various restaurants linked to the **Grand Hotel** (*see below*). But, for a change of pace (and price), try the **Trattoria del Rana** (via Monte Grappa 27, 0344 40 602, closed Tue and 3wks Oct, average €20), a laid-back *trattoria*.

Where to stay

For unbeatably elegant luxury, and if you are happy to dress for dinner, the **Villa d'Este** (via Regina 40, Cernobbio, 031 3481, www.villadeste.it, closed mid Nov-Feb, doubles €595-€675) is the place. More realistically, stay somewhere else but, for the price of a drink at the bar (€10), pay a visit to the gardens (*see p207*). Get a ticket at the entrance.

In Tremezzo, the splendid art nouveau **Grand Hotel Tremezzo** (via Regina 8, 0344 42 491, www.grandhoteltremezzo.com, closed end Nov-end Feb, doubles €200-€594) is another luxury option, with spectacular lake views.

In Moltrasio, the **Albergo Posta** (piazza San Rocco 5, 031 290 444, www.hotel-posta.it, closed Jan & Feb, doubles €100-€125) is a reliable bet, while Lenno's **San Giorgio** (via Regina 81, 0344 40 415, closed Oct-Mar, doubles €110-€120, breakfast €10.50) is modest but pleasant, in a modern building with a garden.

Menaggio's **Grand Hotel Victoria** (lungolago Castelli 9, 0344 32 003, www.palacehotel.it, doubles €180-€230) was built in 1806 and retains much of its old world charm; what's more, its private beach is a great base for windsurfing from.

Tourist information

APT Cernobbio
Piazza Cavour 17 (031 510 198/www.lakecomo.org). **Open** *May-Sept* 9am-1pm, 2.30-6pm Mon-Sat; 9am-12.30pm Sun.

IAT Menaggio
Piazza Garibaldi 3 (0344 32 924/www.menaggio.com). **Open** 9am-noon, 3-6pm Mon-Sat.

Pro Loco Tremezzo
Via Regina 3 (0344 40 493). **Open** *May-Sept* 9am-noon, 3.30-6.30pm Mon-Wed, Fri, Sat.

The eastern shore

Mountains plunge precipitously into the lake waters along much of Como's eastern shore, making for considerably lower-density tourist development than across the water.

At the far north-eastern end of the lake, **Colico** is an unprepossessing port town that was prone to flooding from the River Adda until the 19th century when the banks were reinforced. From Colico, by road, the SS36 plunges through tunnels on its swift way south towards Lecco (*see p211*) and Milan. Opt for the slower lakeside road if you want to see the sights, or take a boat excursion to the nearby **Abbazia di Piona** (0341 940 331, www.cistercensi.info/piona/capitolo.htm, open 8.30am-12.30pm, 1.30-6.30pm daily). This is on a small promontory separating Lake Como proper from the oddly green Laghetto di Piona. Consecrated as a Cluniac house in 1138, the very striking abbey is now home to Cistercians. The complex has a 13th-century cloister with Romanesque and Gothic columns and fragments of earlier frescoes lining its walls, as well as the abbey-church of San Nicolao, which contains 13th-century frescoes and a couple of marble lions that used to hold up the raised pulpit. Groups seeking to meditate in peace can rent rooms in the monastery.

The Pioverna river thunders down the **Orrido** (gorge) **di Bellano**, providing the driving force for the hydroelectricity that has long powered the area's textile industry. You can feel the force for yourself by braving the **bridge** suspended above the torrent (0341 821 124, www.comune.bellano.lc.it, open Oct-May 10am-1pm, 3-6pm Mon-Sat, 10am-6pm Sun, June-Sept 10am-10.30pm daily, admission €2.60).

There's something magical about **Varenna**, an ancient fishing village and the most sedately elegant of the lake's resorts. The **Villa Monastero** (0341 295 450, http://villa monastero.org, gardens open end Mar-Oct 9am-7pm daily, admission €2-€1.30) began life as a 13th-century convent, whose rather too worldly nuns were evicted in the 16th century. Adjacent to Villa Monastero, is **Villa Cipressi** (0341 295 450, 0341 830 113, gardens open Apr-Oct 9am-7pm daily, admission €2). It was built for the Serpenti family who were merely following current fashion when, in the late-16th century, they constructed a home on the lake shore in a particularly panoramic position, and complemented it with beautiful gardens.

A path leads from Varenna, past the village cemetery, to the **Fiumelatte** (river of milk). This is Italy's shortest, most mysterious, and most predictable, river. Its frothy milk-white water rushes for all of 250 metres (833 feet), down the rockface and crashes into the lake from the end of March to the end of October each year – and then stops. Leonardo da Vinci climbed down to find out what happened to it the rest of the year, but neither he nor anyone else has ever discovered the secret. (He made reference to it in the *Codex Atlanticus*, which is in the Biblioteca Ambrosiana in Milan, *see p63*.) A 20-minute walk from what Mr da V called the Fiumelaccio leads to the ruined **Castello di Vezio** (open Feb, Mar, Oct at weekends, Apr-Sept daily, Nov & Dec Sun), which offers a splendid view of the lake. Then you can take the relatively short – but rather steep – set of steps (it takes about 20 minutes) back down to the centre of the town, and have a well-deserved drink in the piazza.

Passenger ferries connect Varenna with Menaggio (*see p208*), while a car ferry links it to Cadenabbia (*see p208*) and Bellagio (*see p211*).

Bikers may want to stop off in **Mandello del Lario**, a sprawling town that cowers beneath the wild and woody Grigna mountain range. Once a silk centre, the town began producing Moto Guzzi motorbikes in 1919, as lovingly documented in its **Museo del Motociclo**.

Museo del Motociclo

Via Parodi 57, Mandello del Lario (0341 709 111/www.motoguzzi.it). **Open** 3-4pm Mon-Fri. **Admission** free.

Where to stay & eat

In Varenna, romantic **Vecchia Varenna** (contrada Scoscesa 10, 0341 830 793, www.vecchiavarenna.it, closed Mon in May-Oct, Mon & Tue in Nov-Mar, all Jan, average €40) serves excellent fish fresh from the lake on a lovely terrace in summer or in its cosy interior when temperatures drop. Equally romantic, the 19-room **Hotel Du Lac** (via del Pristino 4, 0341 830 238, www.albergodulac.com, closed mid Nov-mid Mar, doubles €140-€210) is a 19th-century palazzo. The **Royal Victoria** (piazza San Giorgio 5, 0341 815 111, www.royal victoria.com, doubles €150-€210) has period furniture in its public rooms. In addition to its main restaurant (average €30), known for its good-value delicate cuisine, the hotel also has the **Victoria Grill** pizzeria (closed Mon except in summer, average €15).

Tourist information

Pro Loco Varenna

Piazza Venini 1 (0341 830 367/www.varenna italy.com). **Open** *Apr-Sept* 10am-12.30pm, 3-6pm Tue-Sat; 10am-12.30pm Sun & public hols. *Oct-Mar* 10am-4pm Sat.

Varenna. *See p209.*

Lecco, Bellagio & the southern shore

Stunningly located but grimly overshadowed by its iron and steel industry, the city of **Lecco** signifies just one thing to the vast majority of Italians: *I promessi sposi*. For this was the birthplace of Alessandro Manzoni (1785-1873), author of that seminal novel, and this was the background against which he set the adventures of Renzo and Lucia. *See also p64* **Novel approach**.

Settled from prehistoric times, Lecco and its tribes were brought to order by the Romans in 195 BC. The town stood on key trading routes, and was an important link in the defences of Milan's Visconti family (*see p11*). Azzone Visconti had an eight-arch bridge (three more arches were added later) built over the River Adda in 1336; it survives today and still bears his name. Central piazza Manzoni boasts an impressive statue of the town's most famous son, while piazza Cermenati is the site of the basilica of **San Niccolò**, the city's cathedral. Local lore attributes the original church to the Lombards of the seventh century. The current building owes more to 19th-century makeovers, though there are remnants of a 12th-century church in the Cappella del Battistero.

To find out more about the author Italian schoolchildren love to hate, visit Alessandro's birthplace, the **Villa Manzoni** (via Don Guanella 1, 0341 481 247, open 9.30am-5.30pm Tue-Sun, admission €4; €2.50 groups of eight or more people), which houses a collection of memorabilia and manuscripts, as well as a small collection of works by local artists.

Perched at the tip of the southern promontory, **Bellagio** is simply glorious. Narrow streets zigzag up the hill from a port lined with impressive reminders of a more elegant age of tourism. Among those who came and were enchanted were Franz Liszt, Stendhal, and Flaubert who wrote that: 'One could live and die here. The outlook seems designed as a balm to the eyes… the horizon is outlined with snow and the foreground alternates between the graceful and the rugged – a truly Shakespearean landscape, all the forces of nature are brought together, with an overwhelming sense of vastness.'

Two villas provide the icing on the cake: the **Villa Serbelloni** – crowning the hill where one of Pliny the Younger's villas may have stood – and the **Villa Melzi**, a Napoleonic pile surrounded by lush gardens. These are especially worth seeing between late-April and mid-May when the azaleas and rhododendrons are in flower (*see p202* **A gardener's world**).

Where to eat

For a dinner or Sunday lunch of first-rate fish (at top prices) in Lecco, head for **Al Porticciolo** (via Valsecchi 5/7, 0341 498 103, closed Mon, Tue, 2wks Jan & all Aug, average €60). **Nicolin** (via Ponchielli 54, 0341 422 122, closed Tue and 4-25 Aug, average €40) is a lively father-and-son operation offering meaty Lombard specialities for those fed up with lake fish.

In Bellagio's outskirts, heading towards Como, the family-run **Silvio**, which is both a hotel and restaurant (via Carcano 12, 031 950 322, www.bellagiosilvio.com, closed mid Nov-mid Feb), offers lake fish (average €30) and beautiful views; it also has 21 good-value rooms available (doubles €80-€90).

In Bellagio itself, **Barchetta** (salita Mella 13, 031 951 389, closed Dec-Feb, average €40) is a romantic location for an intimate dinner under a pergola; the desserts are out of this world.

Where to stay

In Bellagio the well-appointed **Hotel Du Lac** (piazza Mazzini 32, 031 950 320, www.bellagiohoteldulac.com, closed Nov-end Mar, doubles €110-€206) has been welcoming travellers for 150 years. Located in an 18th-century palazzo, the **Florence** (piazza Mazzini 46, 031 950 342, www.bellagiolakecomo.com/florence, closed end Oct-Easter, doubles €135-€180) has charming rooms; book well in advance.

For real luxury, follow in the footsteps of Winston Churchill and John F Kennedy and make for the **Grand Hotel Villa Serbelloni** (via Roma 1, 031 950 216, www.villaserbelloni.it, closed Nov-Mar, doubles €310-€800) where facilities include indoor and outdoor pools, a gym, sauna, Turkish bath, day spa and a beauty farm, not to mention spectacular views over the lake.

Tourist information

APT Lecco
Via Nazario Sauro 6 (0341 362 360/www.aptlecco.com). **Open** 9am-12.30pm, 2.30-7pm daily.

IAT Bellagio
Piazza della Chiesa (031 950 204). **Open** *Apr-Oct* 9am-noon, 3-6pm daily. *Nov-Mar* 9am-noon, 3-6pm Mon, Wed-Sat.

Lago di Garda

The former home of a washed-up Mussolini is now a magnet for tourists.

Lago di Garda, the largest Italian lake, lies on the map like an elephant head with its trunk raised in triumph to the skies. The broad southern basin – the elephant's head and ears – is 18 kilometres (11 miles) across at its widest point and is flanked by gentle hills that rise into sheer mountains on either side of the north-eastward-pointing trunk. In the north at Torbole (a full 53 kilometres/33 miles from the opposite extremity) the trunk's nostrils imbibe the River Sarca; at the bottom tip of the ear, by Peschiera, the River Mincio spills out southwards.

The lake is one of the main tourist attractions in northern Italy, drawing great crowds from beyond the Alps. But although German may seem the dominant language in summer, Lake Garda is also used by the inhabitants of Brescia and Verona, the two cities to the lake's west and east, as a handy substitute for the sea. There may be no sand or crashing breakers, but the water is clean and mountain breezes provide ideal conditions for windsurfing. With an average depth of 135 metres (443 feet), the lake remains cool even in the hottest months.

If you're planning on long, lonely walks by the waterside, you had better choose a different lake, though. The southern shores are hemmed in by an endless sprawl of campsites, hotels, amusement parks and discos, while to the north the mountains rise so sheerly out of the water that there are no long lakeside paths for the rambler. Whether you go north or south, however, the resorts on the lake are all extremely picturesque – they have medieval centres and are often guarded by miniature castles. There are several fine Romanesque churches, while Desenzano and Sirmione also contain important Roman remains. The lake may not offer much in the way of romantic solitude, but it has a range of attractions, both cultural and sporting, to satisfy most visitors.

Getting there

By car
The Milan–Venice A4 motorway has exits at Desenzano, Sirmione and Peschiera.

By train
Many trains on the Milan–Venice line from Stazione Centrale stop at Desenzano and Peschiera. Journey time around 1hr 30mins.

By bus
SAIA (030 230 8811/www.infopoint.it) operates hourly Brescia–Verona services, calling at Desenzano (journey time 1hr, €2.75), Sirmione (journey time 1hr 20mins, €3.25) and Peschiera (journey time 1hr 30mins, €4.10).

Getting around

By car
The lake itself is encircled by the Gardesana road, an amazing feat of engineering completed in 1931; on the north-western shore, the road bores its way through many miles of solid mountain, with nearly 80 tunnels helping connect a number of villages that were previously accessible only by boat. Their economies and gene pools have undoubtedly benefited; their charm and tranquillity less so. In summer expect heavy traffic, particularly around the Gardaland amusement park (*see p213*).

By bus
The southern shore (Desenzano, Sirmione, Peschiera) is served by buses from both Brescia and Verona (*see above* **Getting there**). SAIA (030 230 8811/www.infopoint.it) runs buses from Desenzano to Riva along the western shore; Verona's APT (045 805 7911/www.apt.vr.it) operates services from Peschiera to Riva along the eastern shore.

By boat
Hydrofoil and steamer services are frequent in the summer, connecting the most important points on the lake. Throughout the year there is a regular car ferry service (roughly every 40mins) between Toscolano Maderno and Torri del Benaco. All boat services are operated by Navigazione sul Lago di Garda (030 914 9511/www.navigazionelaghi.it).

The southern shore

Nestling in Garda's south-western corner, **Desenzano del Garda** is the largest of the lakeside towns, with a thriving tourist industry. Behind the quaint old port is the arcaded piazza Malvezzi, with its statue of St Angela, and the church of **Santa Maria Maddalena** (open 9am-noon, 4-6pm daily). Inside the church is a striking *Last Supper* signed by Giambattista Tiepolo, although it is painted in a style more reminiscent of his son, Giandomenico, who may have restored *papà*'s work extensively. To the west, along via Crocefisso, is the **Villa Romana**. The remains of this large third-century Roman

Lakes & Cities

villa were dug up in 1921. Note the lively fishing and hunting scenes in the splendid mosaic floors.

Six kilometres (3.5 miles) east, perched at the end of a three-kilometre (two-mile) lizard-tongue promontory, the medieval spa town of **Sirmione** is the lake's main tourist magnet, protected by the supremely picturesque 13th-century **Rocca Scaligera**. This moat-girdled castle contains little of major interest, but there are wonderful views of the lake from its battlements.

Sirmione's other attraction is the **Grotte di Catullo**, the extensive ruins of a colossal first-century villa, which is in fact unlikely to have belonged to a mere poet like Catullus (*see p215* **Water works**). There is a good museum at the entrance, but the main pleasure of the site is its magnificent setting amid sloping olive groves at the tip of the peninsula.

Peschiera, at the south-eastern corner of the lake, has a decidedly military feel to it. Fortified since Roman times, in the 19th century the Austrians rebuilt and strengthened its 16th-century Venetian defences. The town now provides an equally important environmental defence, in the form of a huge purifying plant.

Just to the north of the town is **Gardaland** – Italy's answer to Disneyland – which draws more than three million visitors each year.

Opened in 1975, it has grown steadily over the years – its Dinosaur Islands, Dolphinariums and Jungle Rapids engulfing ever more of the lakeside and its traffic queues strangling the road system. In high season expect a one-to-three ratio of active fun to passive queuing.

Gardaland
SS 249 Gardesana Orientale, Castelnuovo del Garda, Località Ronchi (045 644 9777/045 644 9555/ www.gardaland.it). **Open** *Late Mar-late June, last 3wks Sept* 9.30am-6pm daily. *Late June-early Sept* 9am-midnight daily. *Oct* 10am-6pm Sat, Sun. *7 Dec-24 Dec* 10am-6pm Sat, Sun. *25 Dec-6 Jan* 10am-6pm daily. *During winter school holidays* 10am-6pm daily. Closed Nov-late Mar. **Admission** €23; €19.50 children over 1m & under 10; free children under 1m. **Credit** AmEx, DC, MC, V.

Grotte di Catullo
Piazza Orti Manara, Sirmione (030 916 157). **Open** *Museum* Mar-Oct 8.30am-7pm Tue-Sun. *Grounds* Mar-Oct 8.30am-7pm Tue-Sun; Nov-Feb 8.30am-5pm Tue-Sun. **Admission** €4; free-€2 concessions. **No credit cards**.

Rocca Scaligera
Piazza Castello, Sirmione (030 916 468). **Open** *Oct-July* 8.30am-7pm Tue-Sun. *Aug-Sept* 8.30am-7pm daily. **Admission** €4; free-€2 concessions. **No credit cards**.

Lakes & Cities

No wonder Catullus and Tennyson were inspired by **Sirmione**. *See p213*.

Villa Romana

Via del Crocefisso 22, Desenzano (030 914 3547).
Open *Mar-mid Oct* 8.30am-7pm Tue-Sun. *Mid Oct-Feb* 8.30am-5pm Tue-Sun. **Admission** €2; free-€1 concessions. **No credit cards**.

Where to stay & eat

In Desenzano, the **Hotel Tripoli** (piazza Matteotti 18, 030 914 1305, doubles €100-€110, closed 20 Dec-20 Jan) has lake views and comfortable, if anonymous, rooms. For ice-creams and cocktails, head to **Bar Agorà** (piazza Malvezzi 10, 030 999 1010, closed Wed), with its Gaudí-inspired interior.

In Sirmione, luxury is available at non-luxury rates at **Hotel Fonte Boiola** (viale Marconi 11, 030 990 4922, closed 2wks Dec, doubles €54-€110 per person, half board). It has a spa, a restaurant and a wonderful garden on the lake. The **Osteria Torcol** (via San Salvatore 30, 030 990 4605, closed Wed, average €25) serves home-made pasta and hot and cold snacks. Four kilometres (2.5 miles) from the centre of Sirmione, at Lugana di Sirmione, **Trattoria Vecchia Lugana** (piazzale Vecchia Lugana 1, 030 919 012, closed Mon & Tue, early Jan-mid Feb, average €60) serves an outstanding seasonal menu in an elegant, cosy locale.

Tourist information

IAT Desenzano

*Via Porto Vecchio 34 (030 9141 510/www.apt.
brescia.it)*. **Open** 9am-12:30pm, 3-6pm Mon-Fri; 9am-12.30pm Sat.

IAT Peschiera

Piazzale Betteloni 15 (045 755 1673). **Open** *Nov-Feb* 8am-1pm Tue, Thur, Fri; 8am-1pm Wed, Sat. *Mar-Oct* 8am-1pm, 3-6pm Mon-Sat; 8am-1pm Sun.

IAT Sirmione

Viale Marconi 2 (030 916 114/www.apt.brescia.it).
Open *Apr-Oct* 9am-12.30pm, 3-6pm daily. *Nov-Mar* 9am-12.30pm, 3-6pm Mon-Fri; 9am-12.30pm Sat.

The western shore

Garda's western shore is more magnificently rugged than the eastern one (*see p218*), particularly in its northern reaches. It was here that lakeside tourism really began: splendid villas built from the 18th century onwards dot its shores. Two of these were home to a pair of major actors on the 20th-century world stage: the poet Gabriele D'Annunzio and Benito Mussolini.

The lakeside road leads north from Desenzano to **Salò** (known in Roman times as Salodium), set in a deep bay. The town's name is irrevocably linked with the puppet republic set up here by the Nazis in 1943 for Mussolini (*see p218* **Benito's last stand**). But Salò's other, happier, claim to fame is as the birthplace of Gasparo da Salò (1540-1609), generally agreed hereabouts to have invented the violin.

The fine art nouveau hotels along the lakefront were built after an earthquake in 1901. The many medieval and Renaissance palazzi in the centre, however, show that the town was important well before then. In piazza del Duomo, the cathedral of the **Annunziata** (open 8.30am-noon, 3.30-6.30pm daily) has a Renaissance portal in its unfinished façade and a splendid Venetian-Gothic interior. It also has a Gothic altarpiece with gilded statues of saints, while the walls and chapels of the left aisle contain two paintings by Romanino and a polyptych by Paolo Veneziano. Around the cathedral is the oldest part of the town, with fine palazzi from the 15th to the 18th centuries lining the main street parallel to the lake.

Four kilometres (2.5 miles) further north is **Gardone Riviera**. It was here, in the 1880s, that German tourists began their occupation of the lake after scientist Ludovic Rohden noted the mildness of the climate. The town dates from that period – cosmopolitan hotels were set up and holiday villas constructed, including **Villa Alba**, a large neo-classical building created as a mini-replica of the Parthenon for the Austrian emperor (he never used it). The villa looks on to the Gardesana and is now a conference centre.

Gardone's main attraction is the **Giardino Botanico Hruska**. Laid out from 1910-71 by Arturo Hruska, a dentist and naturalist, it contains a host of plants from every continent and climate, including magnolias, reeds and ferns. The *giardino* is mainly notable for its rock gardens and Alpine flora.

From Gardone there is a good view of **Isola del Garda**. In the ninth century, Charlemagne gave this island to Verona's archbishop, later saint, Zeno. It remained in ecclesiastical hands until 1798. The present extraordinary villa – in Venetian Gothic style – was built by the noble Borghese family in 1900-03 and is still privately owned (not open to the public).

On the hill above Gardone Riviera is the old town of **Gardone di Sopra**, notable mostly as the site of the grandiose **Vittoriale degli Italiani**. This presumptuously named villa was the residence of poet, novelist, dramatist, man of action and grand poseur Gabriele D'Annunzio. Mussolini himself authorised the poet to turn his own house into a national monument; it was one way for him to exert some kind of control over the only Italian capable of upstaging him. 'If you have a rotten tooth,' said Il Duce of the popular poet and hero, 'either you have it pulled out or you cover it with gold.'

The gold was laid on lavishly; despite the patriotic name, Il Vittoriale is essentially an extravagant monument to its owner, in which no aspect of his character or achievements is uncelebrated. The villa's interior, with its claustrophobia-inducing clutter, reveals D'Annunzio's numerous rampant enthusiasms: music, literature, art, the Orient and – most rampant of all – sex. Highlights include the spare bedroom with the coffin in which D'Annunzio would meditate Bela Lugosi-style, and the dining room, which is complete with a bronze-embalmed pet tortoise that died from overeating. The grounds celebrate his more extrovert passions, from theatre (his most celebrated love affair was with actress Eleonora Duse) to bellicose heroics: where other people might have garden gnomes, D'Annunzio erected the prow of the battleship Puglia to

Water works

The most euphonious description of Sirmione in the English language is in the poem 'Frater Ave atque Vale' (1880) by Alfred Lord Tennyson: 'Sweet Catullus's all-but-island, olive-silvery Sirmio!'

Tennyson's poem, written on Lake Garda while mourning his brother's death, pays homage to Catullus's elegy for his own brother, in which the Latin poet recounts his joy at returning to Sirmione after travels in Asia Minor. Tennyson transfers the joy to the lake itself, with an effective sparkling image: 'the Lydian laughter of the Garda Lake below'.

Few definite facts are known about Catullus's life. One of them is that he came from a prosperous family of Verona, who probably also owned a villa at Sirmione. The magnificent villa that now bears his name was almost certainly not it, although the family were wealthy enough to entertain Julius Caesar. Like many young people with cultural ambitions, Catullus made his way to the capital city and most of his poems were written in and about life in Rome.

Tennyson's homage to Catullus was no novelty. The Latin poet has always managed to strike new generations of artists as particularly relevant to them. This is partly because of the range of his compositions: he wrote love poems, elegies, bawdy verse and satirical epigrams with equal skill. Thus each new generation could pick the facet of his work that most appealed to them.

In the 20th century, Catullus's reputation was mostly based on his love poems to his mistress. Many 20th-century poets, from Yeats onwards, were particularly struck by the way he gave expression to excruciatingly contradictory feelings, most famously in the two-line poem beginning with the words: *Odi et amo* ('I hate and I love'). These love poems' lyrical intensity place them among the greatest of all time, but they only make up one eighth of Catullus's total output. He was a supremely conscious artist, for whom wit and emotion went hand in hand, which is why it is limiting to see him only as the author of the Lesbia poems.

commemorate his Quixotic attempt to 'liberate' the city of Fiume (Rijeka) from Yugoslav rule. Lastly, don't miss (you can't) his monstrous wedding-cake mausoleum. The grounds also contain the **Museo della Guerra** (War Museum, guided tour), celebrating his more aggressive adventures: from the ceiling hangs the plane D'Annunzio used to fly over Vienna in 1918.

Continuing north, **Toscolano-Maderno** is a resort with a good beach. Maderno – the more touristy of the two connected villages – was once Benacum, the most important Roman town on the lake, which sank under water after an earthquake around AD 243. Roman and Byzantine traces can be found in the 12th-century Romanesque church of **Sant'Andrea** (piazza San Marco, open 8.30am-noon, 2.30-7pm daily), particularly in the pillar-capitals; the church is a miniature version of Verona's San Zeno Maggiore.

Bogliaco, the next village, is home to the grandiose 18th-century **Villa Bettoni** (closed to the public), the largest villa on the lake after the one on Isola del Garda, and where the ministers of the Salò republic (*see p218* **Benito's last stand**) would meet. The villa was damaged during over-enthusiastic celebrations after the Liberation, while the Gardesana road has severed it from its magnificent formal gardens (also closed).

DH Lawrence lived in nearby **Gargnano** from 1912-13; his *Twilight in Italy* contains – amid reflections on Italian phallocentricity – some of the finest descriptions of the lake ever written. Gargnano's fine 13th-century church of **San Francesco** (open 9am-noon daily) has Gothic cloisters; note the pillar-capitals with carved lemon leaves. Looking on to the lake by the jetty is **Palazzo Feltrinelli**, built in 1894 for a wealthy industrialist family; during the Republic of Salò, this was Mussolini's administrative headquarters. It is now a conference centre for Milan University. Il Duce's private residence was in the larger **Villa Feltrinelli**, set in an expansive garden to the north of the town. This has recently been restored as a luxury hotel (www.villafeltrinelli.com).

Beyond Gargnano, the lake narrows and the mountains rise sheer out of the water. The Gardesana continues as a series of tunnels driven through solid rock; the road rises steeply, offering occasional stunning views of the lake. During World War II, the tunnels were used as bombproof factories for weapons (Breda and Beretta), car engines (Fiat) and aeroplane engines (the Luftwaffe).

Larger than most of the northern villages, **Limone sul Garda** has a small port and an attractive medieval centre with steep, narrow streets and staircases. There's also a two-mile beach. It's unclear whether the town's name derives from the Latin *limen* (border) or from its extensive lemon plantations, said to have been the first in Europe. After Italian unification in the 1870s, the Garda citrus industry couldn't compete with that of Sicily. The bare pillars that used to support protective greenhouse cover during the winter months now stand, as DH Lawrence fancifully put it, like 'ruined temples… forlorn in their colonnades and squares… as if they remained from some great race that had once worshipped here'.

The parish **church** (open 9am-6pm daily) in the main square has pretty patterns picked out in cobbles and contains a fine, late 16th-century wooden crucifix. At the northern end of the village, at the top of a steep staircase and amid the lemon groves, is tiny 14th-century **San Rocco** (often closed but viewable through the window), with a frescoed altarpiece inside a trompe-l'oeil frescoed frame.

Through yet more tunnels, the Gardesana leads to **Riva del Garda**, the largest town in the northern half of the lake. It stands between Monte Brione to the east and the sheer cliffs of Monte Rocchetta to the west, which bring early dusk to the town. Once a major port, from 1813 until 1918 it lay in Austrian territory, and saw fighting during World War I. Though it's now a prosperous tourist resort, Riva still has some of the feel of a lively trading centre. The centre of the town is piazza III Novembre, with the imposing 13th-century **Torre Apponale**, the 14th-century **Palazzo Pretorio** (not open to the public) and picturesque medieval porticoes. An archway beneath the Palazzo Pretorio leads to tiny piazza San Rocco, where the surviving apse of a church, destroyed in World War I, has been converted into an open-air chapel. Eastwards from piazza III Novembre is the moat-encircled **rocca** (castle), containing a **Museo Civico** with collections of archaeology and armour. North, through porta San Michele, viale Roma leads to the **Chiesa dell'Inviolata** (open 8.30am-noon, 4-6pm daily), an octagonal 17th-century church designed by a Portuguese architect whose name local history has failed to record; he saw no reason to stint on stucco and gilt, covering every square inch with decoration. Paintings by the prolific Palma il Giovane adorn the chapels.

More baroque splendour can be found in the Madonna chapel of the **Chiesa dell'Assunta** in via Mazzini (open 8.30am-noon, 3-6.30pm daily), with cavorting putti and lavish carved marble drapery. The energetic can follow a zigzag path up to

Grotte di Catullo.
See p213.

the **Bastione**, a cylindrical tower built by the
Venetians in 1508, commanding a splendid
view (212 metres, 707 feet) over the town.

Giardino Botanico Hruska

Via Roma 2, Gardone Riviera (336 410 877 mobile).
Open *Mid Mar-mid Oct* 9am-7pm daily. Closed
Nov-Feb. **Admission** €7; €3-€6 concessions.
No credit cards.

Rocca & Museo Civico

Piazza Battisti 3, Riva del Garda (0464 573 869).
Open *Mid Mar-mid June, mid Sept-Oct* 9.30am-
12.45pm, 2.15-5.30pm Tue-Sun. *Mid June-mid Sept*
9.30am-6pm daily. Closed Nov-mid Mar (except for
exhibitions). **Admission** €3. **No credit cards.**

Vittoriale degli Italiani &
Museo della Guerra

Via Vittoriale, Gardone di Sopra (036 529 6511/
www.vittoriale.it). **Open** *Garden* Apr-Sept 8.30am-
8pm daily; Oct-Mar 9am-5pm daily. *House and
Museo della Guerra* Apr-Sept 9.30am-7pm Tue-Sun;
Oct-Mar 9am-1pm, 2-5pm Tue-Sun. **Admission**
Garden €7. *Garden & house* €11. *Garden, house
& Museo della Guerra* €16. **No credit cards.**

Where to stay & eat

In Salò, the **Gallo Rosso** (vicolo Tomacelli 4,
0365 520 757, closed Tue & Wed lunch, 1wk Jan
& 1wk June, average €25) offers good fish-based
meals. Five kilometres (3 miles) from Salò, in
località San Carlo–Gavardo, **San Carlo** (0365
371 850, closed Mon-Thur, Jan, July, average
€30) offers rustic fare based on home-grown
products. Near the cathedral is the **Hotel
Duomo** (lungolago Zanardelli 91, 036 521 026,
www.hotelduomosalo.it, doubles €95-€220),
with rooms looking either on to the cathedral
or the lake. **Pignino Sera** (via Panoramica 13,

036 522 071, www.contiterzi.it, rates €30-€35
per person) is a farm situated about a kilometre
(half a mile) from the centre of Salò in olive
groves, with a splendid lake view, offering
basic accommodation for groups of six people.

In Gardone di Sopra, **Agli Angeli** (piazza
Garibaldi 2, 036 520 832, closed Mon mid Feb-
Easter, mid Nov-mid Feb, average €40) was
the restaurant Gabriele D'Annunzio advised
his friends to try, although he himself always
ate at home. The home-made pasta is good.

In Limone, the **Hotel Bellavista** (via
Marconi 20, 0365 954 001, www.gardalake.it/
hotelbellavista, closed Nov-mid Mar, doubles
€96) is by the lake and has a pretty garden.
The same family has run it for nearly a century.

In Riva the **Ristorante Al Volt** (via Fiume
73, 0464 552 570, closed Mon and mid Feb-mid
Mar, average €30) offers excellent meals with
fish from the lake; try the varied *menù
degustazione* (sample meal) at €32. The **Grand
Hotel Riva** (piazza Garibaldi 10, 0464 521 800,
www.gardaresort.it, doubles €82-€140) is a
large and comfortable hotel in a fine central
position by the castle. It has a dining room on
the top floor with panoramic views of the lake.

Tourist information

APT Garda Trentino

Giardini di Porta Orientale 8 (046 455 4444/
www.gardatrentino.com). **Open** *Apr-Oct* 9am-noon,
3-6.30pm Mon-Sat; 10am-noon, 2pm-6.30pm Sun.
Nov-Mar 9am-noon, 2.30-5.15pm Mon-Fri.

IAT Gardone Riviera

Corso Repubblica 8 (036 520 347). **Open** *Apr-Sept*
9am-12.30pm, 3-6.30pm Mon-Sat; 9am-12.30pm Sun.
Oct-Mar 9am-12.30pm, 3-6pm Mon-Wed, Fri, Sat;
9am-12.30pm Thur.

Benito's last stand

By the time northern Italy's Nazi occupiers installed Mussolini in Villa Feltrinelli in Gargnano (see p216), the fascist leader had been humbled by history. Most of his Grand Council had voted to remove him from power on 25 July 1943, by which time Anglo-American forces were firmly installed in Sicily and inflicting crushing blows up the boot of Italy. The king had defected to the Allied side and had Mussolini imprisoned in a mountain fastness in Abruzzo; it had taken an SS commando team to get him out and whisk him off to the north.

Il Duce's comeback took the vicious, squalid form of the Repubblica di Salò. Mussolini did not choose the place from which he was to 'govern' northern Italy for the next 18 months – he would have preferred to return to Rome for a bloody settling of accounts, but the more pragmatic Germans put their jack-booted feet down and kept him in the more easily controllable north. Just to make sure he was under no illusions that he was running anything other than a puppet administration, the Germans spread ministries haphazardly around lakeside towns and made it clear that everything – including Mussolini's letters to

his lover Clara Petacci, who had been housed in an ex-convent in Gargnano – was checked over by the SS.

Holed up in Villa Feltrinelli, Mussolini was a pathetic parody of his former self. He drew up futile plans for the war effort, refusing to face the fact that it was now the Nazis running the show.

The Salò Republic's one memorable act was the trial and subsequent execution of five members of the Grand Council who had voted Mussolini out of office, including his son-in-law, Galeazzo Ciano. Mussolini went to great lengths to pretend that malevolence of others had prevented him from signing a pardon. When his daughter refused to believe him, he whinged that it was his 'destiny to be betrayed by everyone, including my own daughter'.

The beauty of the setting in which these sordid events took place was of little consolation to Mussolini. 'Lakes are a compromise between river and sea,' he moaned, 'and I don't like compromises.' As it turned out, it was beside another lake – Como – that he was to be executed by partisans.

IAT Gargnano

Piazza Feltrinelli (036 571 222/www.proloco gargnano.it). **Open** 3.30-6.30pm Mon; 9am-noon, 3.30-6.30pm Tue-Sat; 9am-noon Sun.

IAT Salò

Palazzo Municipale, Lungolago Zanardelli (036 521 423/www.comune.salo.bs.it/www.apt.brescia.it). **Open** *Apr-June* 9am-12.30pm, 3-6pm Mon, Tue, Thur-Sat; 9am-12.30pm Wed. *July-Sept* 9am-12.30pm, 3-6pm Mon-Sat; 9am-12.30pm Sun. *Oct* 9am-12.30pm, 3-6pm Mon, Tue, Thur, Fri; 9am-12.30pm Wed. *Nov-Mar* 9am-12.30pm, 3-6pm Mon-Fri; 9am-12.30pm Sat.

IAT Toscolano-Maderno

Via Lungolago 18 (036 564 1330). **Open** *Apr-Sept* 9am-12.30pm, 3-6.30pm Mon-Sat; 9am-12.30pm Sun. *Oct-Mar* 9am-12.30pm, 2.30-6pm Mon, Tue, Thur-Sat; 9am-12.30pm Wed.

The eastern shore

Steep shores and magnificent views on the stretch from Torbole in the north give way to relentless campsites and amusement parks further south, with only the occasional small medieval town to provide aesthetic relief.

A short tunnel beneath the massive wedge of Monte Brione joins the town of Riva (see p216) to **Torbole** on the lake's north-eastern corner. It is here that the River Sarca, the lake's main feeder, flows in. Torbole's port is extensive. In 1439 it witnessed the launching of a fleet of 26 Venetian ships that had been dragged, Fitzcarraldo-style, over the mountains for a surprise attack on the Milanese rulers, the Visconti.

Malcesine (15 kilometres/9.5 miles south) is arguably the eastern shore's most delightful town, with the fine **Castello Scaligero** on a craggy headland looming over the medieval quarter. The castle has a small museum with sketches done by Goethe in 1786. While making the sketches, the poet was nabbed by a suspicious local and arrested for spying – an auspicious start to German tourism. There are fine views from the castle tower.

Close to the Gardesana road is the church of **Santo Stefano** (open 8am-noon, 3-6pm daily), with its impressive altar (1771) and *Via Crucis* (stations of the Cross). In via Capitanata del Lago, alongside the lake, the **Palazzo dei Capitani del Lago** (not open to the public) has a fine frescoed lion of St Mark on the ceiling of the entrance hall and frescoed coats of arms of the Captains of the Lake (local administrators from the 16th to the 18th century) upstairs. There is also a garden courtyard overlooking the lake.

From Malcesine it is possible to take a 15-minute cable-car ride to the top of **Monte Baldo** (€14 return, closed Mar, Nov), a popular ski-resort in winter. The new cableway, with rotating cabins, was inaugurated in July 2002.

In **Torri del Benaco** are a few remnants of the ancient town walls and the 14th-century **Castello Scaligero**, built, like many in the region, by Verona's ruling Della Scala family (the adjective of which is *scaligero*). Inside is a small museum with worthy but not exactly thrilling displays on local crafts. In the eponymous square the church of **Santissima Trinità** (open 9am-noon, 4-6pm daily) contains 15th-century frescoes, including a splendid Christ Pantocrator in gleaming hippie-style flowered garb.

The town of **Garda** lies on a deep bay with Monte Garda behind. It was in a no-longer-extant castle on this hill that Queen Adelaide was imprisoned by Berengar II, after he had murdered her husband and she had refused to marry his son Adalbert (*see p9*). The centre of Garda has several notable Renaissance palazzi. For more, take the magnificent (but unshaded) path north along the curving shore towards **Punta San Vigilio**, lined with villas, hotels, and gardens rolling down to the lake.

At the tip of the headland is a harbour, with a tiny chapel dedicated to **San Vigilio** (erratic opening times, no phone); a path leads up to the 16th-century **Villa Guarienti**; it's privately owned but a glimpse can be caught of its splendid formal gardens, much loved by Winston Churchill and Laurence Olivier, among others. Nearby is **Locanda San Verolo**, modest in appearance but offering luxury hotel service (045 720 0930/ www.sanverolo.it). On the other side of the promontory is the tiny **Baia delle Sirene**, which has a beach.

South of Garda, the waterside footpath is a pleasant and mostly pine-shaded walk as far as **Bardolino**, a small town famed for its wine. Bardolino has two fascinating churches. The tiny **San Zeno** (open 9am-6pm daily) can be reached by turning eastwards off the Gardesana road along the suburban-looking via San Zeno. Standing in a rustic courtyard, it is a ninth-century building with faint traces of frescoes. **San Severo** (open 9am-6pm daily), a well-preserved 12th-century building with a good campanile, contains notable 12th- and 14th-century frescoes. The town is flanked by fine gardens giving on to the lake.

In **Lazise** is another **Castello Scaligero** (now incorporated into the garden of a privately owned villa); an arcaded 16th-century Venetian custom-house shows how important the place once was. South of here lie the delights of Gardaland (*see p213*) and its tacky imitators.

Castello Scaligero & Museo (Malcesine)
Via Castello, Malcesine (045 740 0837/045 657 0333). **Open** *Mid Mar-Oct* 9.30am-7pm daily. *Dec-mid Jan* 10am-5pm daily. *Mid Jan-mid Mar* 10am-5pm Sat-Sun. **Admission** €4; €3 concessions. **No credit cards**.

Castello Scaligero (Torri del Benaco)
Viale Fratelli Lavanda 2, Torri del Benaco (045 629 6111). **Open** *Late Apr-Oct* 9.30am-1pm, 4.30-7.30pm daily. *Dec-Mar* 2.30-5.30pm Sun. **Admission** €3; €1 concessions. **No credit cards**.

Where to stay & eat

The 34-room **Albergo Gardesana** in Torri del Benaco (piazza Calderini 20, 045 722 5411, www.hotel-gardesana.com, doubles €86-€144) has a fine lakeside location; such personalities as Winston Churchill and Kim Novak have stayed here.

In Garda, away from the lake, the **Stafolet** (via Poiano 9, 045 725 5427, closed Wed & Nov-mid Mar, average €25-€30) does good grilled dishes and pizza. On the lake, the best of the numerous restaurants is probably **Miralago** (lungolago Regina Adelaide 52, 045 725 5198, closed Mon, average €25), which offers reasonable fish dishes and pizza.

In Bardolino, stay at **Hotel Gardenia** (piazza Serenissima 12, 045 621 0882, doubles €65-€130). The hotel is open all year round and offers two swimming pools and views over the lake. The **Ristorante Ai Platani di San Severo** (piazza San Severo 1, 045 721 0038, closed Wed, average €15-€25) serves reliable local dishes and pizza.

Tourist information

APT Garda
Lungolago Regina Adelaide 13, 045 627 0384/ www.aptgardaveneto.com). **Open** *Apr-Oct* 9am-noon, 3-6.15pm Mon-Sat; 10am-noon Sun. *Nov-Mar* 8.30am-1.30pm, 3-6pm Tue, Thur, Fri; 8.30am-1.30pm Wed-Sat.

IAT Bardolino
Piazzale Aldo Moro 5 (045 721 0078). **Open** *Apr-Oct* 9am-1pm, 3-6pm Mon-Sat; 9am-1pm Sun. *Nov-Mar* 9am-1pm, 3-6pm Tue, Thur; 9am-1pm Wed, Fri, Sat.

Bergamo & Around

Head north-east from Milan and take a step back in time.

Cappella Colleoni. *See p222.*

The Milanese like to look down on their *bergamaschi* cousins. They're too stubborn, they say, too dull – too, well, provincial.

Often, they say these things as they drive off to Bergamo's valleys and lakes to the north-east of Milan. The Milanese will tell you they come to the province because the air is cleaner. They also come because the *bergamaschi* have managed to preserve much: the commerce and industry that made Bergamo wealthy, the mountains and small valley hamlets that give it its soul, as well as the often-unintelligible local dialect (*see p226* **Speaking in tongues**). Provincial or preservationist – either way, the real reason the Milanese come to Bergamo is that they find something Milan lost long ago.

Bergamo

Bergamo's **Città Alta** (Upper City) is more than just a walled medieval town on a hill: it's a reassuring reminder of the way things have always been, and presides stolidly over the banks and businesses of modern Bergamo (Città Bassa, or Lower City).

Though Bergamo dates back to pre-Roman times, the key date in its history is 1428, when it became part of the Venetian Republic, gaining protection against Milan's Viscontis (*see p11*), who had been ruling and attacking the city on and off for almost 200 years. The arrival of the Venetians did not guarantee peace straightaway (the fighting in Bergamo didn't stop until 1516), but it did mark the beginning of a 350-year relationship between Venice and its new, small border town.

Even before the Viscontis, Bergamo was a popular target, coveted by Goths, Huns, Vandals, Lombards and Franks, as well as the Spanish, the French and the Holy Roman Empire. Its geographic position made it a valuable prize: the city commands a good portion of the fertile plains of the Po river, as well as the entrance to two river valleys – the Serio and the Brembo. Bergamo still reflects the influences of Venice's commerce and industry. The massive *mura* (defensive walls) of the Città Alta were built by the Venetians, and St Mark's lion – the symbol of Venice – shows up throughout the city.

Lakes & Cities

Sightseeing

Città Alta

Viale Vittorio Emanuele II, Bergamo's principal thoroughfare up to Città Alta, passes through the city's defensive walls at Porta Sant'Agostino, built in 1575 by the Venetians and still featuring the lion of St Mark. The Venetians were not the first to build walls in Bergamo; there is evidence that the Etruscans had fortified sites on the hills, and there are remnants of 14th-century defensive systems, such as La Rocca and La Cittadella (for both *see p222*). The walls did provide the city with the protection it needed, but they were also the reason behind its limited growth. It was only in 1430, when the Venetians built a further stretch of wall (torn down in 1902), that merchant-class *bergamaschi* felt safe enough to move down from the hill, into Città Bassa.

Accessible from Porta Sant'Agostino, the viale Mura promenade – built in the 1880s – follows a good portion of the walls, passing by two more of Città Alta's four extant gates: San Giacomo and Sant'Alessandro. (The fourth gate – San Lorenzo, or Garibaldi – is off the tourist track at the end of via della Fara.) Besides a pleasant tree-lined stroll and views of Città Bassa, viale Mura offers an insight into just how tight space is in Città Alta.

Just inside the Porta Sant'Agostino, via Porta Dipinta leads up to the heart of Città Alta. The gate guarding the street is long gone, but one of its towers – called Sub Foppis – remains, a piece of the pre-Venetian defensive system. Further up the street to the left is the church of **San Michele al Pozzo Bianco**. Via Porta Dipinta is named after another gate into Città Alta, which sported pre-1500 frescoes. Unfortunately this 'painted gate' was torn down in 1815 in an ill-judged fit of urban development; a small plaque about halfway up the street marks the spot where it once stood.

At the top of via Porta Dipinta, which is lined with impressive palazzi built in the 16th and 17th centuries by successful *bergamaschi*, is piazza Mercato delle Scarpe, an important hub in Città Alta. On the southern side of the square is the *funicolare*, linking Città Bassa to Città Alta. Stretching to the north-west is via Gombito, Città Alta's main drag. A few steps into via Gombito, via Rocca (right) leads up to **La Rocca**.

Via Gombito was the main *decumanus* (north–south axis) of Roman Bergamo; today it's a narrow street lined with small shops and bars. At the intersection with via Lupo stands the **Torre Gombito** (not open to the public), which dates back to the Guelph–Ghibelline struggles of the 12th century (*see p11*). Across the street from the tower, are the picturesque houses of piazza Mercato del Fieno.

Via Gombito opens out into piazza Vecchia. Stunningly lovely, this square is also a very functional part of 21st-century Bergamo. The medieval buildings on its eastern side house the offices of the local university; the magnificent **Palazzo della Ragione** is used as an exhibition space; the neo-classical Palazzo Nuovo is home to the municipal archives and library; and the bells in the **Torre del Campanone** still toll 100 times each evening at 10pm, a reminder of the city's old curfew.

A passage through the loggia of the Palazzo della Ragione leads to piazza Duomo, which houses some of Bergamo's most important buildings: the **Duomo**, the basilica of **Santa Maria Maggiore** and the **Cappella Colleoni**. Behind Santa Maria Maggiore, via Arena leads to the **Museo Donizettiano**, dedicated to Bergamo-born composer Gaetano Donizetti.

Past piazza Vecchia, via Gombito becomes via Colleoni and leads to piazza Mascheroni, home to **La Cittadella**. Built in the 14th century to defend Città Alta from an attack from the west, the citadel was adapted to more peaceful uses by the Venetians. Beyond piazza Cittadella, historic Città Alta ends at Colle Aperto, an open space just inside the porta Sant'Alessandro, with views across to the foothills of the Alps.

A combined ticket for entry into six Bergamo sites, including the Museo Donizettiano, La Rocca and the Torre del Campanone, costs €3, and can be purchased at any of the participating sites.

Cappella Colleoni

Piazza Duomo (035 210 061). **Open** *Mar-Oct* 9am-12.30pm, 2-6.30pm Tue-Sun. *Nov-Feb* 9am-12.30pm, 2-4.30pm Tue-Sun. **Admission** free.
No one would accuse Bartolomeo Colleoni (*see below* **Soldier of fortune**) of being a modest man. Believing that the *bergamaschi* wanted nothing more than to venerate his body after he was gone, the Venetian general had the old sacristy in Santa Maria Maggiore demolished to make way for his mausoleum, which was finished in 1475, one year after his death. Colleoni's tomb – a late Gothic work – and that of his daughter Medea, whose serene-looking statue lies on top of the sarcophagus, grace the chapel, as do frescoes (1733) by Giambattista Tiepolo. On the gate outside the chapel, the Colleoni

Soldier of fortune

In the Middle Ages, mercenaries held the military power in Italy. City-states such as Genoa, Milan and Venice could not afford the costs of a standing army, but were still caught in a vicious circle of defending and enlarging their territories. Bands of mercenaries, known as *condotti*, were the preferred solution.

Of course, there were disadvantages to outsourcing armed forces. Indeed, it was common for the mercenaries to switch sides before, or even during, battles. As a *condottiere* (mercenary captain) in the Venetian army, Bartolomeo Colleoni (1400-75) was the man responsible for the defence of *bergamasco* territory. He was also a man known, on occasion, to change his allegiance from Venice to Milan (and back again). Nevertheless, the Venetians and *bergamaschi* chose to focus on his virtues rather than his perfidy, rewarding him with land and fame.

After the Peace of Lodi in 1454 put an end to the fighting with Milan, Venice somewhat forcefully retired Colleoni to the splendour of his court at the castle of Malpaga in Ghisalba (*see p229*). There he pursued a strikingly unhumble appreciation of the arts, having part of the basilica in Bergamo's Città Alta demolished to create space for his mausoleum (*see p222*).

He also left money in his will for an equestrian statue in Venice. Characteristically, he left instructions for the statue to be placed in piazza San Marco. The Venetian authorities, however, had no desire to place a reminder of the fact that their military might was based on hired help in such a prominent place. Creative will-reading eventually placed the statue (designed by Verrocchio, Leonardo da Vinci's influential teacher) in the courtyard of Scuola San Marco.

Drop by **Cavour** and drool over the delicious displays of chocolate. *See p227.*

coat of arms has been polished to a bright sheen by hands rubbing it for luck. The coat of arms, it should be noted, bears three testicles – as did Colleoni, according to legend; Italians, it should be noted, rub testicles where Anglo-Saxons touch wood.

Duomo
(Cattedrale di Sant'Alessandro)
Piazza Duomo (035 210 223). **Open** 7.30-noon, 3-6.30pm daily. **Admission** free.
Of the buildings in piazza Duomo, the least interesting is the Duomo itself. Building began on it – to a design by Il Filarete – in 1459, on a spot previously occupied by an early Christian church. The project passed through the hands of several architects before completion in 1886. In the first chapel on the left is a *Madonna e Santi* by Giovan Battista Moroni (1576), while among the mainly 18th-century works surrounding the main altar is Giambattista Tiepolo's *Martyrdom of St John the Bishop*. The 17th-century wooden choir is by Johann Karl Sanz. The statue of Pope John XXIII at the Duomo's entrance is a reminder of the importance of the *bergamasco* pope to the city.

Funicolare al Mercato delle Scarpe
Piazza Mercato delle Scarpe/viale Vittorio Emanuele II (035 364 211). **Open** *Mid Sept-mid June* 7am-midnight daily. *Mid June-mid Sept* 7am-1.30am daily. **Tickets** 95¢. **No credit cards**.
A crucial link between Città Alta and Città Bassa, the funicular inspires justifiable local pride. Built in 1887, it is a remarkable feat of Italian engineering, travelling 240m (800ft) at angles of up to 52 degrees.

Museo Donizettiano
Via Arena 9 (035 399 269). **Open** *Apr-Sept* 10am-1pm, 2.30-5pm Tue-Sun. *Oct-Mar* 10am-1pm Tue-Sun. **Admission** €3 combined ticket. **No credit cards**.
This one-room museum is dedicated to Gaetano Donizetti (1797-1848), composer of such operas as *Anna Bolena* and *Lucia di Lammermoor.*

Palazzo della Ragione
Piazza Vecchia (035 210 204). **Open** for exhibitions only. **Admission** prices vary. **No credit cards**.
Originally constructed in the 12th century, the Palazzo della Ragione has seen many changes. The covered staircase leading to the principal meeting room was added in 1453, and the street-level loggia dates from 1520. Inside, the fresco-covered *sala superiore* provides an impressive backdrop for temporary exhibitions. Also here are Donato Bramante's frescoes of *Tre Filosofi* (1477), which were removed from the Palazzo del Podestà on the north-west corner of the square.

La Rocca
Piazzale Brigata Legnano (035 224 700). **Open** *June-Sept* 9.30am-1pm, 2-5.30pm Tue-Fri; 9.30am-7pm Sat, Sun. *Oct-May* 9.30am-1pm, 2-5.30pm Tue-Sun. **Admission** *Grounds* free. *Museo Storico* €3 combined ticket. **No credit cards**.
Construction on La Rocca, part of Bergamo's pre-Venetian defences, began in 1331 on the site of the Roman capitol. It was finished under the Viscontis. The Venetians added the Sala dei Bombardieri; in the 19th century the Austrians turned it into a key fort. It has also been used as a barracks and a prison; these days it houses the Museo Storico and a public park.

Lakes & Cities

San Michele al Pozzo Bianco

Via Porta Dipinta (035 247 651). **Open** 8am-6pm Mon-Sat; noon-6pm Sun & holidays. **Admission** free.
Set off the street on a little square, this church dates back to the eighth century and has been revamped and rebuilt a number of times: the façade is less than a century old, though most of the interior is from the 1400s. Inside, the walls of the single-naved church are covered in magnificent frescoes, including scenes from the life of Mary by Lorenzo Lotto, in the chapel to the left of the high altar. In the crypt are more frescoes, some from the 13th century.

Santa Maria Maggiore

Piazza Duomo (035 223 327). **Open** *Apr-Oct* 9am-1pm, 3-6pm Mon-Sat; 9am-noon, 2.30-4.30pm Sun. *Nov-Mar* 9am-1pm, 3-6pm Mon-Sat; 9am-noon, 2.30-4.30pm Sun. **Admission** free.
Santa Maria Maggiore is piazza Duomo's most impressive edifice. Begun in 1157 on the site of an earlier church, construction did not end until 1521, when the Porta della Fontana was completed. Each period of construction offers something of beauty, from the presbytery (1187), to the prothyum (1350), to the new sacristy (late 15th century). The most

Lake placid

Lago d'Iseo is not as famous or as big as its other Lombard lacustrine brethren, but it boasts the same sterling panoramas and weekend recreation opportunities, not to mention two names (its other is Sebino). Nestled in the mountains of eastern Bergamo and western Brescia (it forms part of the boundary of the two provinces), the waters of the lake not only mirror majestic mountains and host determined fishermen and boaters; they also hold one of the jewels of Lombardy: Monte Isola, the largest lake island in Italy.

THE BERGAMO SHORE

Sarnico, at the south-western tip of the lake, has been inhabited since prehistoric times. These days, particularly in summer, 'occupied' might be a better word. The lake front gets crowded with campers in town for supplies and *gelato*, as well as weekend waterskiers, windsurfers and motor-boaters enjoying the lake. The winding streets of the medieval centre offer picturesque window-shopping.

At the northern end of the lake is **Lovere**. Strategically important because it guards the passage from the lake to the Valcamonica (*see p271*), this town traditionally played a big role in the trade and industry – particularly textiles – of the region. Today, its lake-front *piazze* offer outdoor cafés and people-watching opportunities in abundance. Fine palazzi along the shore bear witness to the prosperity Lovere has enjoyed over the centuries. Behind, the different levels of the medieval *borgo* (village) run along the hillside, connected by a series of stairs and alleys. On the first level is piazza Vittorio Emanuele. The tower in the square is a much-modified remnant of the old fortifications.

THE BRESCIA SHORE

Across from Lovere sits the small town of **Pisogne**, which owes its existence to its iron ore deposits, worked by the Romans, and the via Valeriana, the Roman road linking Brescia with the Valcamonica. The uncrowded lake-front piazza del Mercato contains the 13th-century torre del Vescovo. The relative lack of tourists in the small, melancholy medieval *borgo* behind the tower makes it easy to feel transported back in time.

From Marone, a narrow road (SP32) climbs through a series of hairpin turns to **Zone**, a small hamlet surrounded by mountain peaks and offering glimpses of the lake. In Zone's stunning aspect, however, is the series of wooden inlay works on the presbytery stalls. These exquisite 16th-century carvings, designed by Venetian artist Lorenzo Lotto, who emigrated to the city in 1513, tell stories from the Old Testament; they also contain detailed comments in the form of alchemic symbols.

Torre del Campanone
Piazza Vecchia (035 247 116). **Open** *Apr-Oct* 9.30am-7pm Tue-Sun. *Nov-Mar* 9.30am-4.30pm Tue-Fri (reservations necessary); 9.30am-4.30pm Sat, Sun. **Admission** €3 combined ticket. **No credit cards**.

The *Torre Civica*, or Torre del Campanone, was built by the Suardi family in the 12th century as a Ghibelline counterbalance to the Guelph Torre Gombito (*see p222*). Climb to the top for a different view of Città Alta.

Outside the walls

Historic Città Alta occupies the first of seven hills. On the other hills are woods with trails plus residential Città Alta, an Eden of villas, gardens and vineyards.

small nature reserve, erosion has left boulders stranded atop towering pinnacles called *piramidi di terra* (earth pyramids); trails around them allow visitors to get a closer look. At the entrance to the park, the isolated 15th-century church of San Giorgio nonchalantly offers a series of stunning frescoes on its walls.

Further south, **Iseo** is the lake's principal and most cosmopolitan town. But despite its focus on modern-day tourism, Iseo manages to retain its ancient air and to convey a peculiar timelessness, with a labyrinth of narrow streets and alleys, the 12th-century Pieve di Sant'Andrea church (open 7.30am-12.30pm, 3-6.30pm daily), and the 14th-century Castello Oldofredi, which is now the town library.

MONTE ISOLA
The ferry (*see below*) from Sulzano to **Peschiera Maraglio** on **Monte Isola** only takes a few minutes, but carries visitors to a very different world. There are no cars, and the paths up and down the mountain are filled with the most unfamiliar sounds of silence. Besides Peschiera Maraglio, the island is home to a number of other small villages. At **Sensole**, at the south-western corner of the island, the microclimate allows for olive-growing, while along the western coast, **Menzino**, **Sanchignano** and **Siviano** all keep at least one foot firmly planted in the past. And at the top of the mountain, the Madonna della Ceriola sanctuary (open access) offers unparalleled views of the lake.

Where to stay & eat

In Iseo, **Il Volto** does a wonderful blend of *haute cuisine* and lake comfort food (via Mirolte 33, 030 981 462, closed Wed & Thur

lunch, average €40). The **Relais Mirabella** (via Mirabella 34, Clusane sul Lago, Iseo, 030 989 8051, www.relaismirabella.it, closed Jan-Mar, doubles €130-€150) offers comfort, plus lake views.

Getting there

By car
From Bergamo, take the A4 towards Brescia; exit at Grumello del Monte and follow signs for Lago d'Iseo.

By bus
From Bergamo, SAB (035 289 011/www. sab-autoservizi.it) runs frequent services to Lovere and Sarnico.

By train
From Bergamo, take the Brescia train and change at Palazzolo; six trains a day run each way between Palazzolo and the Paratico line (summer only). Brescia–Iseo trains leave regularly from Brescia's Stazione Centrale.

Getting around

By boat
The ferry (035 971 483/www.navigazione laghi.it) from Sulzano to Peschiera Maraglio costs €2.50 round-trip; from Iseo to Peschiera costs €4.20 round-trip.

Tourist information

IAT Iseo
Lungolago Marconi 2c, Iseo (030 980 209/www.apt.brescia.it). **Open** *Easter-Sept* 9am-12.30pm, 3.30-6.30pm daily. *Oct-Easter* 9am-12.30pm, 3-6pm Mon-Fri; 9am-12.30pm Sat.

Lakes & Cities

Outside Porta Sant'Alessandro, via San Vigilio leads up to piazza San Vigilio and via Castello (for the less fit, there's the San Vigilio funicular). At the top is Il Castello, another part of the city's defences. Now a public park, it offers views of Città Alta and a swathe of the Apennines and Alps, including Monte Rosa, the second-highest mountain in Europe.

Città Bassa

There are more office buildings and apartment blocks than historic monuments in busy, hard-working Città Bassa, but this doesn't mean there's nothing to see. In piazza G Carrara, the **Pinacoteca Accademia Carrara**, with its collection stretching from Raphael to Rubens, is a case in point. From the piazza, via San Tomaso leads to via Pignolo, one of the old approaches to Città Alta. After 1430, when the Venetians constructed a wall for Città Bassa, Bergamo's merchants felt better protected. The result of their new-found security was this narrow street lined with substantial palazzi and churches, which adds a distinctly medieval touch to modern Bergamo.

Moving towards the Città Bassa's centre, via Tasso leads to Sentierone, a tree- and portico-lined avenue that was once Bergamo's fairground. Sentierone ends in Bergamo's modern centre, which owes its looks to architect Marcello Piacentini. Starting in 1914, he began the lengthy process of giving a homogenous appearance to the buildings and *piazze* of the centre. The faux-classical feel of his designs was to make him a darling of the fascist regime.

Via XX Settembre is Bergamo's high-fashion shopping strip, filled with hordes of Italy's well-maintained teenagers. Moving away from piazza Matteotti, it leads to piazza Pontida, the centre of medieval Città Bassa. From piazza Pontida, the ancient via Sant'Alessandro begins its ever-steeper ascent towards Città Alta. Along the final stretch stands a viaduct built on triumphal arches dating from the late 1500s.

Pinacoteca Accademia Carrara

Piazza G Carrara 82a (035 399 640/www.accademia carrara.bergamo.it). **Open** *Apr-Sept* 10am-12.45pm, 3-6.30pm Tue-Sun. *Oct-Mar* 9.30am-1pm, 2.30-5.30pm Tue-Sun. **Admission** €2.58; €1.55 concessions. Free to all Sun. **No credit cards**.

The Pinacoteca's permanent collection is concentrated on the second floor, with the tour starting in earnest with a couple of Botticellis – note the wonderfully smug contentment on the face of the portrait of Giuliano de' Medici in Sala II. The focus of the Accademia's collection is on Lombard painters, and while they may not be as famous as other Italian artists, this only adds to the joy of discovering the quality of their works: Vincenzo Foppa's *I tre crocifissi*, Moroni's *Ritratto di bambina di casa Redetti*, and Lorenzo Lotto's *Nozze mistiche di Santa Caterina* are world-class works. (French soldiers in the 1520s were so charmed with the view of Mount Sinai seen through a window in Lotto's work that they took it home with them – hence the painting's

Speaking in tongues

Around the province of Bergamo, you'd be forgiven for demanding a refund on your Italian lessons. Daily life here is still conducted in the *bergamasco* dialect to a remarkable extent.

As the old saying goes, 'a language is a dialect with an army', highlighting the point that there is no difference between 'language' and 'dialect' in linguistic terms: languages are simply dialects that have received special status. So the reason Italians speak Italian is that over time they have agreed to use the Tuscan dialect of Dante first as a common literary language and then as a unifying force.

But unifying is not something that has interested the *bergamaschi* all that much. Nor is communicating with a large swathe of fellow citizens – the main advantage a language offers. For them speaking with the other members of the village or, at most, the other villages of the valley, is enough.

How incomprehensible is *bergamasco*? Despite the cries of other Italians, *bergamasco* does have firm Latin roots and therefore belongs to the Gallo-Italic family, though it does have a strong Celtic undercurrent (the name Bergamo is itself derived from the Celtic word for mountain, 'berg'). It sounds so alien because so many of its words have been reduced to a monosyllable, often just a vowel. And *bergamasco* can do phonetic gymnastics with vowels: there are open vowels, closed vowels and umlauts. Coupled with changes in vocabulary, the results can be daunting – '*U, u if? A ó a öa. E u? A ó a ï*', translates as: '*Voi, dove andate? Vado a raccogliere l'uva. E voi? Io vado a bere il vino.*' (Both mean: 'Hey, where are you going? I'm going to harvest the grapes. And you? I'm going to drink some wine.')

Lakes & Cities

missing panel.) Lotto is Bergamo's favourite artist, so it's no surprise he's well represented in the collection. He spent 13 years here, starting in 1513, and became successful, fulfilling commissions for the newly energised merchant class. One portrait, of Lucina Brembatti, is a famous example of his symbolism and the way he challenged viewers to look again. A rebus at the upper left-hand corner of the painting reveals the sitter's name.

Where to eat & drink

Bergamasco cuisine is for hearty appetites. Starters focus on cold cuts, particularly homemade *salame* and *lardo*, creamy white slices of pork fat (it's better than it sounds). *Casoncelli*, Bergamo's contribution to the pasta canon, are meat-filled ravioli in a sage and butter sauce. Main courses tend towards roasts and braised dishes, invariably served with polenta. *Polenta taragna* is a speciality of the valleys and is made with the addition of buckwheat, rich cheese and occasionally cream.

Antica Trattoria la Colombina

Via Borgo Canale 12 (035 261 402). **Meals served** 12.15-2.15pm, 7.45-10.15pm Wed-Sun. Closed 3wks Jan, 3wks June-July. **Average** €30. **Credit** AmEx, DC, MC, V.
This welcoming, historic *trattoria* has impeccable food and a marvellous view from the terrace outside.

Bar Pizzeria Martiriggiano Teresa

Via Pignolo 92 (035 234 822). **Meals served** noon-2pm, 6.30-11.30pm Mon, Tue, Thur-Sun. Closed Aug. **Average** €15. **No credit cards.**
Not far from the Accademia Carrara (*see p226*) is this small pizzeria. The sign on the outside says 'Bar Genie' – a remnant of past ownership – and the inside is casual, bordering on funky. The pizzas are baked in a wood-fired oven and the *fritto misto* is far better than it has any right to be. There is also a bar, open 9.30am-midnight.

Borgo San Lazzaro

Via San Lazzaro 8 (035 242 452). **Meals served** noon-2.30pm, 7.30-11pm Mon-Sat. **Average** €22-€25. **Credit** DC, MC, V.
In a small *vicolo* (alley) off piazza Pontida, this restaurant offers stylish takes on *bergamaschi* stalwarts such as the cold-cut *antipasto* and *coniglio e polenta* (rabbit with polenta).

Cavour Pasticceria

Via Gombito 7a (035 243 418). **Open** 7.30am-midnight Mon, Tue, Thur-Sat; 8am-midnight Sun. Closed 3wks Aug. **Credit** MC, V.
There is nothing more civilised than a morning cappuccino and brioche in the slightly Austrian elegance of Cavour's dining room, and nothing more inviting than a hot chocolate there in the afternoon. The displays of chocolates alone can occupy the sweet-toothed for hours.

Cooperativa Città Alta

Vicolo Sant'Agata 19 (035 218 568). **Meals served** noon-2am, 8-10pm daily. **Average** €15 (€10 lunch). **Credit** MC, V.
Known to the locals as Il Circolino (the little circle), this rambunctious restaurant, bar and beer hall has a wide menu. Meals are available for most of the day.

Da Ornella

Via Gombito 15 (035 232 736). **Meals served** noon-3pm, 7-11pm Mon-Wed, Fri-Sun. **Average** €22-€25. **Credit** AmEx, DC, MC, V.
Large servings of traditional food are Ornella's mainstay. The main course of mixed grilled meats comes on a big platter made for sharing.

Pub St Orsola

Via San Orsola 2/4 (035 225 930). **Open** 4pm-2am Mon-Sat; 2.30pm-2am Sun. **No credit cards.**
Better known as the Canadian (it used to serve Labatt's beer) this is one of Bergamo's better bars.

Vineria Cozzi

Via B Colleoni 22 (035 238 836/www.vineriacozzi.it). **Meals served** 10.30am-2am Mon, Tue, Thur-Sun. Closed 1wk Jan, 1wk July. **Average** €25. **Credit** AmEx, MC, V.
The bar is open all day for a reviving coffee or glass of wine. At lunch and dinner, the back room fills with *bergamaschi* looking for a civilised repast, and Cozzi becomes one of the better restaurants in Bergamo. Food is served for most of the day.

Where to stay

In Città Alta, the reception area of the **Agnello d'Oro** (via Gombito 22, 035 249 883, www.agnellodoro.it, doubles €92) is a mind-boggling bazaar; the location is as central as it gets, the building dates back to the 16th century and the 20 rooms are small but comfortable. Across from the Cittadella, the **Albergo San Lorenzo** (piazza Mascheroni 9a, 035 237 383, doubles €160) has some of the few Roman ruins left in Bergamo (they were excavated while the hotel was building its parking lot).

In Città Bassa, the **Cappello d'Oro** (viale Papa Giovanni XXIII 12, 035 232 503, www.hotelcappellodoro.it, doubles €215) strives – with some success – to combine modern comforts with tradition. The recently constructed **Jolly Hotel** (via Paleocapa 6, 035 227 1811, www.jollyhotels.it, doubles €210) is conveniently located, close to the train station.

Essentials

Getting there

By car

Take the A4 autostrada from Milan east towards Venice; exit at Bergamo.

Enjoy the waters at **San Pellegrino Terme**.

By train
Services run from Milan's Stazione Centrale via
Treviglio and from Stazione Porta Garibaldi via
Carnate. The Carnate service is more regular and
crosses the Adda river over the dramatic Ponte di
Paderno (848 888 088). Journey time: about 1hr.

By bus
Autostradale buses (035 244 354) leave Milan's
Stazione Porta Garibaldi for Bergamo every
30mins. Journey time: about 1hr.

Getting around
Bergamo buses are operated by ATB (035 364 211).
Tickets, which cost 95¢, must be purchased before
boarding. They can be obtained at tobacconists and
some newsstands. Destinations outside the city are
served by SAB (035 289 011/www.sab-autoservizi.it).

Car hire

Avis
Central Parking, via Paleocapa 3 (035 271 290).
Open 8am-8pm Mon-Fri; 8am-12.30pm Sat.
Credit AmEx, DC, MC, V.

Tourist information

APT
*Viale Vittorio Emanuele 20, Città Bassa (035 210
204/www.apt.bergamo.it).* **Open** 9am-12.30pm,
2-5.30pm Mon-Fri.

IAT
*Vicolo Aquila Nera 2, Città Alta (035 242 226/
www.apt.bergamo.it).* **Open** 9am-12.30pm,
2-5.30pm daily.

Around Bergamo
The province of Bergamo offers a little of
everything. There are the valleys and mountains
of the Alpi Orobie, the plains between the Adda
and Oglio rivers, and the waters of Lake Iseo
(*see p224* **Lake placid**). Most of all, the province
offers a sense of timelessness. Not only in the
sense that history has been preserved – though
the medieval *borghi* (hamlets) and art collections
in obscure churches bear witness to that – but
also in the sense that things are much the same
as they always were. Notwithstanding satellite
dishes and BMWs, a twilight stroll will give
you the definite feeling that nothing – or at
least nothing important – has changed for
centuries. And, indeed, that nothing needs to.

The valleys
Bergamo gets its character from the valleys
and mountains that make up about two thirds
of the province. The principal valley is **Valle
Brembana** (formed by the Brembo river).
Narrow and lined with domineering crags,
it was isolated until the 16th century. Even
today, with a revamped highway (SS470)
designed to speed tourist euros from Milan
to the valley's upper reaches, it retains a
sense of aloofness.

San Pellegrino Terme is the valley's most
famous town. Though now synonymous with
bottled water, it has long been known for its
waters: it has been a spa since the 1700s, and
enjoyed a spell as a trendy destination in the
early 1900s. Today the abandoned and slightly
decrepit remains of the Grand Hotel hulk on
the far side of the Brembo, and the old casino
is used as a conference centre. But the baths
(via Taramelli 2, 0345 22 455, closed Oct-Apr)
still offer mud and hot-water treatments in
season, the many Liberty-style buildings (*see
p77*) continue to please the eye, and the main
viale Papa Giovanni XXIII still fills with
strollers on summer evenings.

Further up the valley, a small road on the
right just beyond the town of San Giovanni
Bianco brings you to **Camerata Cornello**, the
home of the Tasso (or Taxis) family, founders
of a medieval courier company that operated
throughout much of Europe (the plot of Thomas
Pynchon's *The Crying of Lot 49* hinged on the
firm). Today a few people continue to live in the
small village – accessible on foot only, about a

kilometre (half a mile) from the parking lot – which contains the ruins of the Tassos' ancestral home and some marvellous porticoed streets.

While not as important geographically as Valle Brembana, **Valle Imagna** still holds its charms. The town of **Almenno San Bartolomeo**, at the mouth of the valley, provides one of the jewels of the Bergamo province, **San Tomé** (via San Tomé, open Oct-Apr 2-4pm Sun, May-Sept 2-6pm Sat, Sun), an 11th-century Romanesque church. Circular and utterly simple, San Tomé continues to offer a sense of tranquillity today.

Where to eat

In San Pellegrino Terme, the **Ristorante Tirolese** (via de' Medici 3, 0345 22 267, closed Tue and 2wks June or Sept, average €20) offers honest takes on valley cuisine and, when the mood strikes, surprisingly good fish.

Valle Serina is another small, but important valley, adjacent to Valle Brembana. Once a main trade route, today its main claim to fame is **La Peta** in the town of Costa Serina (località Gazzo, via Peta 3, 034 597 955, closed Mon, Sun pm, average €40).

Getting there from Bergamo

By car
For Valle Brembana: the SS470 follows the valley. For Valle Imagna: take the SS471 and fork left at Almè for Valle Imagna.

By bus
Trains are useless for travel around Bergamo: if you're using public transport, opt for a bus. All destinations covered in this section can be reached by SAB buses (035 289 011/www.sab-autoservizi.it).

Tourist information

IAT San Pellegrino Terme
Viale Papa Giovanni XXIII 18 (0345 210 20). **Open** *June-Sept* 9.30am-12.30pm, 3-5pm daily. *Oct-May* 9.30am-12.30pm, 3-5pm Mon-Wed, Fri-Sun.

West of Bergamo

If it weren't for saintly Pope John XXIII, aka *il Papa buono* (the good Pope), the small farming community of **Sotto il Monte** would still be an obscure hamlet in the *bergamasco* foothills. Pilgrims flock, however, both to the **Casa Natale**, the house where Angelo Roncalli was born (via Colombera 5, 035 791 101, open 8.30am-5.30pm daily), and to **Cà Maitino**, his summer residence, which is now a museum (via Cà Maitino 12, 035 791 195, open Oct-Mar 8.30-11.30am, 2.30-5.30pm Tue-Sun, Apr-Sept 8.30-11.30am, 2.30-6.30pm Tue-Sun).

In the hills above Sotto il Monte, the beautiful **abbazia di Fontanella** (in frazione di Fontanella), with its Romanesque church and sarcophagus-filled courtyard, offers another reason to visit.

Getting there from Bergamo

By car
Take the SS342; at Ponte San Pietro, take the SP166 for Sotto il Monte.

Tourist information

Pro Loco Sotto il Monte
Via Privata Bernasconi 7 (035 790 902). **Open** 9.30am-12.30pm Mon-Fri.

South of Bergamo

The Middle Ages saw the development of an intricate defence system in the vast plains that stretch away from Bergamo towards the River Po far to the south. Fortified small towns were built at short distances, both to protect the people working the plains and to help look out for approaching threats. **Romano di Lombardia** boasts a rectangular castle built by the Viscontis, as well as piazza Roma – a marvellous square typical of the towns of the Po plains, with Renaissance porticoes and character in buckets, marred only by the hulking, out-of-place medieval Palazzo della Comunità. **Martinengo**, a town with Roman origins, offers a distinctive *centro storico* with porticoed streets and decorative frescoes. At **Ghisalba** is the **Castello di Malpaga**, the home and headquarters of Bartolomeo Colleoni (*see p222* **Soldier of fortune**). With its history of intrigue, lost corpses and hidden tunnels, the castle (open Feb-Nov 3-6.30pm Sun & public holidays, admission €4.13) is well worth touring.

Getting there from Bergamo

By car
Take SS 498 for Romano di Lombardia, Martinengo, and Ghisalba.

By bus
If you're using public transport, opt for a bus. All destinations covered in this section can be reached by SAB buses (035 289 011/www.sab-autoservizi.it).

Tourist information

APT
Viale Vittorio Emanuele 20, Bergamo (035 210 204/www.apt.bergamo.it). **Open** 9am-12.30pm, 2-5.30pm Mon-Fri.

Lakes & Cities

Brescia & Around

Wines and weapons are the mainstay of the Brescian economy, but the area also offers much artistic and natural beauty.

La Rotonda. *See p231.*

La Rotonda. *See p231.*

(see p10)

With a reputation as an industrial town, Brescia, the second-largest town in Lombardy, is not high on the list of Italy's tourist destinations. But for those who take the trouble to explore it, the city offers a number of significant treasures from almost every period of history since the Roman age. The town centre, apart from some unfortunate examples of fascist pomposity, is a fascinating mixture of medieval intimacy and Renaissance splendour, and contains several notable churches, many with paintings by such local artists as Moretto and Romanino. Well-enforced traffic restrictions make the centre a pleasant place to stroll.

The province of Brescia offers the natural attractions of Val Trompia and Val Sabbia, popular skiing and hiking areas, and the vinous delights of Franciacorta, a major wine-making area.

Brescia

The town was founded by a Gallic tribe in the fourth century BC and became the Roman colony of Brixia in 89 BC. It was soon an important trading and manufacturing centre and remained so as one of the 36 Lombard duchies between the sixth and eighth centuries. In the communal period, Brescia, a Guelph town, found itself under constant pressure from its Ghibelline neighbours, especially Bergamo and Cremona. In the 13th century, it joined the Lega Lombarda against the Holy Roman Emperor, Frederick Barbarossa (*see p10*). Throughout the 14th century Brescia continued to be squabbled over by more powerful neighbours and only achieved a certain stability when it was absorbed into the Venetian Republic in 1426; the winged lion remains prominent on many public buildings. The city was heavily bombed in World War II.

Lakes & Cities

Sightseeing

Roman Brixia extended in grid form around what is now via dei Musei (the *decumanus maximus*) and via Gallo (the *cardus*). At the junction of these two streets stood the forum, built AD 69-96. Buried until the early 19th century, the ruins of the **Tempio Capitolino** and **Teatro Romano** that surrounded the forum have since been brought to light: the towering columns of the temple give some idea of its former splendour. In piazzetta Labus, to the south of piazza del Foro, the building at No.3 has parts of the ancient *curia* (basilica) incorporated into its façade.

Towering above the forum on Colle Cidneo – site of Bronze Age settlements – the massive **Castello** (via del Castello, open 8am-8pm daily) is a mainly 16th-century construction containing elements from previous centuries. The view from here over Brescia and the surrounding countryside is striking. Inside the castle are a history museum and the **Civico Museo delle Armi Luigi Marzoli** (030 293 292, open Oct-May 9.30am-1pm, 2.30-5pm Tue-Sun, June-Sept 10am-5pm Tue-Sun, admission €3), which pays tribute to the area's prosperous arms industry with a collection of 1,000 weapons dating from the 15th to 18th centuries.

East of the forum, along the via dei Musei, the **Monastero San Salvatore** complex was begun in the eighth century. It now houses the splendid **Museo della Città**.

West from the forum, via dei Musei opens out into piazza Paolo VI (formerly piazza del Duomo and still referred to as such), a medieval square where all the symbols of religious and political power are concentrated. The **Broletto** has housed the town's council offices since its completion at the end of the 13th century. Next door, the **Duomo Vecchio**, aka **La Rotonda** – is an 11th-century structure built over a palaeo-Christian church; it stands well below the current piazza at the level of the Roman road that passed through here. The **Duomo Nuovo** is a 'recent' 17th-century addition.

Via Beccaria leads to piazza della Loggia, a magnificent example of Renaissance town planning dominated by **La Loggia** itself, a quintessentially Venetian structure built between 1492 and 1574. The Venetian influence is equally visible in the exterior of the **Monte di Pietà**, a two-part palazzo joined by an arch and constructed between 1484 (Monte Vecchio, on the right) and 1600 (Monte Nuovo, on the left). The collection of Roman epigraphs set into the façade of the Monte Vecchio in 1485 may have been Italy's first-ever municipal archaeological collection. Opposite La Loggia, the **Torre dell'Orologio** (clock tower) is a mid

16th-century structure with a clock dating from the same era. The memorial next to the fountain in front of the clock tower honours the victims of a terrorist bombing that took place here on 28 May 1974 (*see p232* **One day in May**).

The city expanded into the area north and west of piazza della Loggia in the late 12th century, when new walls were built to take into account the town's growing population. The **Torre di Palata** (1248) at the junction of via della Pace and corso Garibaldi was part of these fortifications.

Across via dei Musei from the piazza, the convent attached to the church of **San Giuseppe** (vicolo San Giuseppe, open 6-11am, 3-5.45pm Mon-Sat, 6-11am Sun) houses the small **Museo Diocesano e Museo di Tessuto Liturgico** (via Gasparo di Salò 13, 030 375 1064, open 10am-noon, 3-6pm daily, admission €3) with artefacts and vestments from churches around the city. Further west, **San Giovanni Evangelista** (contrada San Giovanni, open 7-11am, 4-6.30pm daily) is a 16th-century church built over a fourth-century one, with some Romanesque touches in its pretty cloister.

Moving south from piazza della Loggia to the piazza della Vittoria, the contrast couldn't be more striking. A swathe of ancient Brescia was razed to allow space for Marcello Piacentini, darling of the inter-war fascist regime, to let rip with this strong-but-sterile glorification of the Second Roman Empire that was believed to be at hand. The **Palazzo delle Poste** (main post office) is a veritable extravaganza.

In the mid 13th century, still greater population growth meant Brescia's walls had to be extended again; though the fortifications were torn down in 1875, the shape of the walls is clearly visible on a map (they follow via XX Settembre, via Fratelli Ugoni, via Leonardo da Vinci, via Pusterla, via Turati, and so on).

Piazza del Mercato, a 16th-century reconstruction, marked the southern extent of the earlier medieval walls; it is dominated by the baroque **Palazzo Martinengo Palatino**, now the main building of the University. To the south-west, on corso Martiri della Libertà, stands **Santa Maria dei Miracoli** (open 6-11.30am, 3-6pm Mon-Sat), with its richly decorated Renaissance façade. The interior is equally lavish in its decoration, the work of 16 Renaissance sculptors.

A detour to the right along vicolo San Nicola before reaching Santa Maria dei Miracoli leads to **San Francesco d'Assisi** (church open 7-11.30am, 3-6pm daily, large cloister open 8am-noon, 2.30-6.30pm Mon-Fri, 8am-noon, 3-7pm Sat), a splendid 13th-century Romanesque-Gothic church. Of the 13th- to 15th-century frescoes that once covered the whole church,

Lakes & Cities

only those on the right wall of the nave survive. On the high altar is a painting of an enthroned Madonna, by Romanino, in a richly carved and gilded frame. The smaller of the church's two cloisters has 13th-century frescoes.

Two streets beyond Santa Maria, turn left for the 15th-century church of **Santi Nazaro e Celso** (corso Matteotti, open 2-4pm daily or by appointment, phone 030 375 4387), where the *Averoldi Polyptych* (commissioned by a member of the Averoldi family, 1522), with the *Resurrection* and *Annunciation*, is by a young Titian; it greatly influenced the development of Brescian art.

Corso Zanardelli – Brescia's choicest shopping boulevard – runs east out of piazza del Mercato, changing its name to corso Magenta further along, and following the line of the first set of

medieval walls. Designer boutiques cluster beneath porticoes that were built in fits and starts up until the late 18th century. On corso Zanardelli, the plush **Teatro Grande** (box office and information: via Paganora 19a, 0302 979 333) was built in 1739, refitted by Luigi Canonica in 1811, and underwent further redecoration in 1862-63; it is home to an international piano festival held each spring.

South off corso Magenta, via Crispi leads to the **Pinacoteca Civica Tosio Martinengo**. At the eastern end of corso Magenta stands **Sant'Afra in Sant'Eufemia** (open 7-11am, 4-7pm Mon-Sat, 7.30am-1pm, 3.30-7pm Sun), where an 18th-century church conceals a 15th-century crypt. In the first chapel on the left are a *Martyrdom of St Afra* by Veronese and other works by Palma il Giovane.

One day in May

On 28 May 1974, after a long series of acts of intimidation carried out by right-wing groups in Brescia, a public demonstration was organised by the workers' unions in piazza della Loggia to denounce the situation. At 10am, after the rain had driven a number of the demonstrators under the cover of the arcades, a bomb hidden in a bin under one of these arcades exploded. Eight people were killed and several injured.

After the dead and wounded had been carried away, the first order of the police chief was that the square should be thoroughly cleaned; this was done before the investigating magistrates had had a chance to examine the scene of the crime. As a result, vital evidence was almost certainly eliminated.

This was just the first anomaly in an investigative process that has led many people to accuse the state of colluding in the slaughter. The explosion has been linked to a string of other right-wing atrocities carried out since 1969, when a bomb blew up the bank in piazza Fontana in Milan – the so-called 'mother of all massacres'.

A parliamentary committee (the disturbingly titled Commissione Stragi, 'slaughter commission') has been set up to look into the murky tangle of extremist politics, cover-ups and espionage behind these atrocities, but after over 30 years and innumerable trials (for piazza Fontana alone, eight trials have been held), little more than empty rhetoric has emerged. A number of shady figures on the far right have been investigated but

in the few cases where they have actually been convicted, the sentences have nearly always been overturned in appeal (the most recent example was in March 2004, when an Italian court absolved three men who had been sentenced to life in 2001 for the piazza Fontana bombings). Today all these crimes remain unsolved. Meanwhile, some figures whose names have been mentioned in association with the crimes have even been known to engage in parliamentary activities.

The main conclusion that can be drawn is that these atrocities formed part of what has been termed the 'strategy of tension', the purpose of which was to favour a dictatorial right-wing takeover, with the ultimate aim of eliminating any risk of a communist-led government. The strategy was elaborated with the active assistance of elements of the Italian secret services, and, according to conspiracy theorists, of the CIA.

There is no doubt that, in the 1970s, Italy ran the risk of undergoing a right-wing coup, similar to the one that took place in Greece. This risk was averted thanks to the persistence of certain investigating magistrates and some interfering journalists. In the eternal manner of Italian politics, however, many of the murky people associated with this whole period have managed to 'recycle' themselves. For example, one of the organisations connected with the strategy of tension was the masonic lodge P2, of which one member was the current prime minister, Silvio Berlusconi.

La Loggia.

Broletto

Piazza Paolo VI (030 2977 7300). **Open** 8.30am-
1.30pm Mon-Fri; 8.30am-12.15pm Sat. **Admission**
free.

The Broletto, a Romanesque-Gothic building, was
built in the 12th century as the seat of the local
government. There's a 17th-century fountain at
the centre of its pretty coat-of-arms-filled courtyard, while the 12th-century Torre del Popolo
towers above the building. Now the local records
office, it is possible for visitors to wander in
during business hours.

Duomo Nuovo

Piazza Paolo VI (030 42 714). **Open** 7.30am-noon,
4-7pm daily. **Admission** free.

The Duomo was built between the 17th and early
19th centuries on the site of a palaeo-Christian
basilica. The Greek-cross interior houses a very
Venetian-looking sarcophagus of saints Apollonio
and Filastrio (1510; third chapel on the right).

Duomo Vecchio – La Rotonda

Piazza Paolo VI (no phone). **Open** Apr-Oct 9am-
noon, 3-7pm Tue-Sun. Nov-Mar 9am-noon, 3-5pm
Tue-Sun. **Admission** free.

The Duomo Vecchio is an 11th-century structure
built over the sixth-century church of Santa Maria
Maggiore (it's built at the same level, well below
the modern road). Locals call it La Rotonda for
obvious reasons. In the vast, stark interior, stairs
lead up to a circular ambulatory, at the far end of
which is a sarcophagus in red Verona marble with
sculptures by *maestri campionesi* (see p26).

   Central sections of the ambulatory floor contain
mosaics from the sixth-century church. Also from
the ambulatory, more stairs lead down into the
ninth- to 11th-century crypt of San Filastrio, with

columns taken from Roman ruins, and some
remains of Byzantine frescoes. Over the high altar
is an *Assumption* (1526) by Moretto da Brescia.

La Loggia

Piazza della Loggia 1 (030 297 7300). **Open** 7am-
8pm Mon-Fri; 7am-1pm Sat. **Admission** free.

Begun in 1492 but not completed until 1574, the
imposing Loggia, with its ground-floor porticoes,
dominates the city centre. Many leading architects –
including Jacopo Sansovino and Andrea Palladio –
had a hand in the ever-changing blueprint, though
Lodovico Beretta was probably responsible for its
final shape. The ship's-hull-shaped cupola was added
in 1914 after the removal of an attic floor that had
been added in 1769 by Luigi Vanvitelli. The upper
octagonal room has a striking wooden ceiling. The
Loggia now houses the city's council offices.

Santa Giulia – Monastero San
Salvatore & Museo della Città

*Via dei Musei 81b (0302 977 834/www.comune.
brescia.it/www.asm.brescia.it/musei).* **Open** May-Sept
9am-7pm Tue-Sun. July-Sept 10am-6pm Tue-Sun.
Oct-Apr 9.30am-5.30pm Tue-Sun. **Admission** €8;
€4 concessions. **No credit cards**.

Queen Ansa, wife of Lombard king Desiderius,
began this huge Benedictine monastery complex in
753. Besides the monastery of San Salvatore itself,
the complex includes the churches of San Salvatore,
Santa Giulia and Santa Maria in Solario.

   The monastery proper houses the Museo della
Città, a superbly curated museum documenting
Brescia's history and prehistory from the Bronze
Age, through the Romans (digs in the Tempio
Capitolino, *see p234*, and forum area yielded up
many treasures) and the Lombards, to Venetian
rule. Among the Roman works, note the Winged

Victory, a first-century AD bronze statue that was originally gilded. In March 2003 the Roman section was extended to include the interior of two Roman houses, both with mosaic floors and painted walls; it's possible to observe the restoration work that is still under way. Of special interest is the so-called viridarium, an outdoor area immediately attached to these houses where a Roman garden is being carefully reproduced.

The museum also contains the basilica of San Salvatore, one of Lombardy's most stunning medieval churches. Built by Desiderius and overhauled in the ninth century, its three-naved interior contains columns dating from the sixth century and sections of ninth-century fresco in the central aisle. There are more frescoes – dating from the eighth and ninth centuries – in the exquisite crypt that was built in 762-63 to house the relics of St Julia and other martyrs.

The church of Santa Giulia, which is attached to San Salvatore, is used as an exhibition space. It contains the Nuns' Choir, with 16th-century frescoes, including a large *Crucifixion* by local artist Floriano Ferramola.

The church of Santa Maria in Solario – perhaps named after the pre-Christian altar to the sun god incorporated into the church's lower room – was built in the 12th century. The upstairs oratory is another riot of wall-to-wall 16th-century frescoes by Ferramola and his workshop. However, these take second place to the late eighth-century Cross of Desiderius, inlaid with gems and cameos, which is housed here, along with other pieces from the monastery's treasury.

Pinacoteca Civica Tosio Martinengo

Piazza Moretto 4 (030 377 4999). **Open** *June-Sept* 10am-5pm Tue-Sun. *Oct-May* 9.30am-1pm, 2.30-5pm Tue-Sun. **Admission** €3; €1 concessions. **No credit cards.**

Housed in a 15th-century palazzo, this art gallery contains works of the Renaissance and after. In Room II are a Christ (1505) and the head of an angel (1501) by Raphael. In Room IV is a *St George and the Dragon* by a Lombard artist of the late 15th century; the foppish armoured saint takes second place to his superbly adorned, prancing white horse. The central rooms of the museum are devoted to such local artists as Vincenzo Foppa, Moretto da Brescia and Romanino. Note the splendid *Nativity* by Romanino, with a kneeling Madonna swathed in a magnificent white cloak.

Tempio Capitolino & Teatro Romano

Via dei Musei 57a (030 297 7834). **Admission** free. The Capitoline temple was built under emperor Vespasian in AD 73 but was left to crumble and became gradually concealed by landslides from Colle Cidneo above. Digs began in 1835 to uncover the temple; some areas of the complex were dug out

and reconstructed – not entirely faithfully – in the 1930s. The steps and 11m (36ft) columns of the temple convey an idea of the area's former grandeur. To the left of the temple, the theatre has been excavated only in part. Much of it was incorporated into the Renaissance Palazzo Gambara, now semi-abandoned. The complex has been closed for excavations for some years now. The ruins are visible from outside and important works have been moved to the Museo della Città (*see p233*).

Where to eat

What the **Trattoria al Frate** (via dei Musei 25, 030 377 0550, closed Mon and 3wks Aug, Christmas-New Year, average €35) lacks in atmosphere, it makes up for with great renditions of local treats. The **Trattoria Mezzeria** (via Trieste 66, 030 40 306, closed Sun & July, average €30) serves great home cooking at fair prices. Simple but satisfying Brescian food can be found at the popular and very reasonable **Trattoria Due Stelle** (via San Faustino 48, 030 423 708, closed Mon), which offers a fixed-menu lunch for €9 and dinner for €13.

Where to stay

The five-star, art nouveau **Vittoria** (via X Giornate 20, 030 280 061, www.hotelvittoria. com, closed Aug, doubles €217) is the only top-notch hotel in the city centre. Located near the station, the **Jolly Hotel** (viale Stazione 15, 030 44 221, www.jollyhotels.it, doubles €132-€220) is anonymous but convenient; the **Hotel Cristallo** (viale Stazione 12a, 030 377 2468, closed 2wks Aug, doubles €85-€103) is a cheaper option in the same area. The cheapest hotel in the centre is probably the **Albergo Sirio** (via Capriolo 24, 030 375 0706, doubles €62), which offers the basic comforts and is clean and friendly.

Essentials

Getting there

By car

Take the A4 Milan–Venice motorway and exit at Brescia Ovest or Brescia Centro.

By train

Brescia is on the main Milan–Venice line (departures from Stazione Centrale, journey time 50mins). Fast Intercity and/or Eurostar trains run approximately once an hour.

By bus

SIA (030 44 061) runs three daily services to Brescia from Milan's piazza Castello (journey time 90mins).

Getting around

The centre of Brescia can be negotiated on foot.
Alternatively, Brescia Trasporti (030 355 3700) runs
an efficient bus service (tickets cost €1). Linea C
runs from the station to the central corso Zanardelli.
Alternatively grab one of the bicycles (*bici blu*)
provided free by the city council at car parks,
including the one near the station (viale Stazione).

Tourist information

APT
*Corso Zanardelli 34 (030 43 418/www.brescia
holiday.com).* **Open** 9am-12.30pm, 3-6pm Mon-Fri;
9am-12.30pm Sat.

Servizio Turismo Comune di Brescia
*Piazza della Loggia 6 (030 377 3773/www.
comune.brescia.it/musei).* **Open** *Apr-Sept* 9.30am-
6.30pm Mon-Sat. *Oct-Mar* 9.30am-12.30pm, 2-5pm
Mon-Fri; 9am-12.30pm Sat.

Around Brescia

North from Brescia

For Brescia province's most northerly area, the
Valcamonica, *see chapter* **The Mountains**. For
the area along the shores of Lake Iseo, *see p224*
Lake placid. For the area along the shores of
Lake Garda, *see chapter* **Lago di Garda**.

The area north of Brescia is a land of
contrasts, with glorious countryside and
soaring mountains alternating with ugly,
heavy industry. The locals have a reputation
for being hard-working folk, who can turn their
hand to traditional crafts, cheese-making, as
well as precision instrument manufacture.

In an area with a high average per-capita
income, the wealthy and not-so-wealthy share
a consuming passion for hunting, perhaps
connected to the area's traditional industry:

weaponry. Each weekend in the hunting season locals in their thousands converge on the **Val Trompia** to wreak carnage on the valley's fauna.

The town of **Gardone Valtrompia** has been famous for its weapons for over 500 years: the Beretta firm has its headquarters here. East of Gardone, **Lumezzane** puts its steel to more peaceful purposes: cutlery and saucepans.

Further still up the valley, the little resort town of **Bòvegno** is a great base for hiking; a relatively easy jaunt is to climb **Colle San Martino** for a look at the ruins of the castle and Romanesque-Gothic chapel (always open) at its summit. For more strenuous treks, try Monte Muffetto, Monte Ario or Colmo di Marcuolo. There's some skiing in Bòvegno, but even more at **Collio**, once an iron- and silver-mining town.

To the east of Val Trompia, **Val Sabbia** runs from Brescia to little Lake Idro and beyond. Marquetry was the traditional industry of this less bellicose area, as shown by the beautiful and intricate intarsia work in the little churches along the valley.

At 370 metres (1,233 feet) above sea level, **Lago di Idro** is one of Lombardy's highest bodies of water. Less well known than its larger counterparts, the lake has fewer tourist facilities and less pollution. The towns of **Idro** on the eastern and **Anfo** on the western shore are popular for sailing, windsurfing and swimming, if you can take the cold. Above Anfo looms the **Rocca d'Anfo** (closed to the public), a fortress built in 1450 and rebuilt on numerous occasions, including in 1796 by the French to keep the Austro-Hungarians on the other side of the border marked by the lake. North-west of the lake, the rural hamlet of **Bagolino** (altitude 800 metres/2,667 feet) is famous for its rambunctious carnival: on each Monday and Tuesday from 6 January to Ash Wednesday anyone dressed up as an elderly peasant can play tricks on anyone who isn't… and they do.

Getting there from Brescia

By car
The SS345 from Brescia runs the length of Val Trompia; the SS237 follows the Val Sabbia.

By bus
SIA (030 44 061) operates buses for Val Trompia and Val Sabbia every 30mins from via Stazione.

Tourist information

Pro Loco Idro
Via Trento 27 (0365 83 224/www.lagodidro.it). **Open** *June-Sept* 9.30am-12.30pm, 3-6pm Mon-Wed, Fri, Sat; 9.30am-12.30pm Sun. *Oct-May* 9am-12.30pm, 1.30-6pm Tue, Thur, Sat; 9am-12.30pm Fri.

Franciacorta

Between Brescia and Lago d'Iseo, the wealthy Franciacorta area is today famous for more than its artistic riches. In the 1960s the Berlucchi family shook up the region's lacklustre grape-growing sector, making a much-praised *spumante* (sparkling wine). Other producers rose to the challenge. In 1995 the Consorzio per la Tutela del Franciacorta (association for the protection of Franciacorta) gave its members strict production rules and obtained a DOCG Franciacorta appellation for its *spumanti*.

The Cluniac **Abbazia Olivetana di San Nicola** (via Brescia 83, 030 610 182, church always open, phone ahead for guided tours at weekends) on the outskirts of **Rodengo-Saiano** was recorded in documents in the 11th century, though its church was built in the late 15th century. The complex is constructed around three lovely cloisters, the oldest of which has Gothic capitals to its columns.

The winemaking centre of **Erbusco** is Franciacorta's capital. It has a quaint medieval sector along via Castello and a two-Michelin-starred restaurant, the modestly named **Gualtiero Marchesi** (via Vittorio Emanuele 11, 030 776 0562, closed Sun pm, Mon & Jan, average €90), where Mr Marchesi himself – guru of Italy's new gastronomic age – holds court, serving up his own takes on local specialities.

Pretty medieval **Capriolo** is home to the **Museo Agricolo e del Vino Ricci Curbastro**, which displays tools and equipment used in winemaking. There's another 11th-century Cluniac foundation, the monastery of **San Pietro in Lamosa** (via Monastero, 030 983 477), in **Provaglio d'Iseo**.

Museo Agricolo e del Vino Ricci Curbastro
Villa Evelina, via Adro 3, Capriolo (030 736 094/ 030 746 0558/www.riccicurbastro.com). **Open** 8am-noon, 2-6pm daily. **Admission** €5 (includes cellar visit and wine tasting). **Credit** AmEx, MC, V. The friendly Ricci Curbastro family also has seven apartments available for rent (from €48 per night).

Getting there

By car
Exit the A4 motorway Milan–Venice at either Palazzolo sull'Oglio, Rovato or Ospitaletto.

By bus
SIA (030 44 061) runs services approximately hourly between Brescia and Erbusco.

Tourist information
See p235.

Mantova & Around

Uncover the Gonzaga family legacy, relax in peaceful countryside and gorge yourself on pumpkin-filled pasta.

Hidden away in the south-eastern corner of Lombardy, Mantova (Mantua in English) today is an agricultural province, cultivating rice and pumpkins, and producing the only real Parmigiano Reggiano found outside the borders of Emilia Romagna, as well as the similar Grana Padano. In olden days, however, Mantova was an independent duchy and a fulcrum in the balance of power between Milan and Venice. For more than 300 years, the ruling Gonzaga family (*see p240* **The Gonzaga saga**) adeptly played in the currents of city-state intrigue, and turned their fortified capital into one of Italy's great Renaissance cities.

Mantova

Mantova enjoys the protection of water, built as it is on a promontory surrounded to the north by three lakes: Superiore, di Mezzo, and Inferiore (which are, in reality, wide spots in the Mincio river). The site was originally settled by the Etruscans; in Roman times it became a commercial centre and home to Virgil, author of the *Aeneid* and future tour guide to Dante in the latter's *Divine Comedy*. However, the city did not really begin to assert itself until the 12th century, when it started expanding beyond its original walls (basically the small corner of the promontory formed by piazza Sordello and the Palazzo Ducale). Things really got going in 1328, when Luigi Gonzaga took over, starting a dynasty that would not officially end until 1707.

Today, the historic centre reflects the influence of the Gonzagas, and their take on the Renaissance. The Gonzagas dictated every aspect of the city's life and growth, hiring the best artists and architects to mould Mantova into a showcase of urban planning and also – not coincidentally – Gonzaga strength. Patronage began in earnest under Gianfrancesco I (ruled 1404-44), who called Pisanello to paint chivalric frescoes inside Palazzo Ducale and educational theorist Vittorino da Feltre to set up a school in the city where ducal heirs would mix with the plebs. One of Vittorino's pupils was Ludovico III (1444-78); immersed in the new humanist culture, Ludovico invited artist Andrea Mantegna and architect Leon Battista Alberti to make Mantova a city worthy of a scholar-prince. His son, Gianfrancesco II, was more into war than art and left the latter to his wife Isabella d'Este, whose court sparkled with creativity. But by the early 16th century Gonzaga patronage had become more inward-looking, more of a family affair: nowhere was this more evident than in the decadent pleasure palace of Palazzo Te, designed and frescoed by mannerist painter Giulio Romano for Duke Federico II in 1524. Later dukes continued the tradition in a minor key. Claudio Monteverdi's *Orfeo*, the first modern opera, was composed for Vincenzo I in 1607.

Today the city has sprawled beyond the now-drained lake to the south, and parts of the centre – especially around the railway station – are blighted by post-war reconstruction. But the nucleus of the medieval and Renaissance city, which centres on the interlinked piazze delle Erbe and Sordello, remains gloriously intact. To see Mantova at its buzzing, cultural best, come here at the beginning of September, when the **Festivaletteratura** literary festival comes to town (for dates, visit www.festivaletteratura.it).

Sightseeing

Expanding out of the north-eastern corner of the promontory, Mantova's *centro storico* remains the city's civic, commercial and religious hub.

Mantova's two main shopping streets, via Roma and the arcaded corso Umberto I, converge on piazza Mantegna, dominated by the audacious triumphal arch façade of Leon Battista Alberti's basilica of **Sant'Andrea**. Around the corner to the right, charming piazza delle Erbe – site of a Thursday morning market – is surrounded on three sides by Gothic and Renaissance *logge*. The castellated 13th-century **Palazzo della Ragione** (0376 220 097, open only for exhibitions) on the east side culminates with the **Torre dell'Orologio** (1473), a tower crowned

by a little classical temple. The astrological clock on the façade was designed to tell not just the time, but whether the time was right. Below the tower stands the pretty Romanesque **Rotonda di San Lorenzo**, Mantova's oldest church.

The 15th-century **Palazzo del Podestà** (Governor's Palace, closed to the public) divides piazza delle Erbe from tiny piazza Broletto. Here, at the base of the **Torre Civica**, a covered passage leads into the palace's court of honour, dominated by an arcaded late-Gothic external staircase. On the north side of piazza Broletto, via Cavour and its eastward extension via Accademia mark the line of the moat that guarded the *civitas vetus* – the town's original nucleus.

Via Accademia offers a worthwhile diversion in the form of the pretty 18th-century interior of the **Teatro Accademico Bibiena**, near the end of the street on the right. From piazza Broletto, an archway leads into the vast cobbled expanse of piazza Sordello, the result of a huge clearance of the medieval town, carried out by the Gonzagas in the 13th and 14th centuries.

To the right is the forbidding castellated façade of **Palazzo Ducale**, where the Gonzagas slept, ate, partied and wove intricate diplomatic webs. Opposite, **Palazzo Castiglioni** (closed to the public) was probably built by the Gonzagas

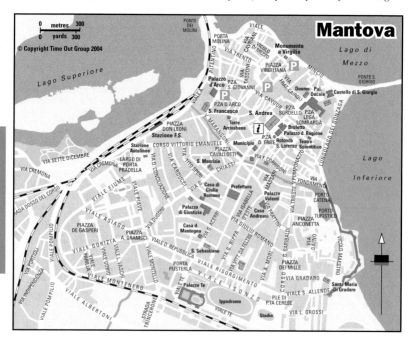

Lakes & Cities

Slaughter at Solferino

One of the main engagements in the war for Italian independence took place in the flatlands north of Mantova, at Solferino, on 24 June 1859. The Austrians – still, at that point, the masters of Lombardy and the Veneto – were commanded by the emperor, Francis Joseph I. On the other side, King Vittorio Emanuele II of Sardinia-Piedmont led his troops and the troops of his French ally, Napoleon III.

Neither the Franco-Italians nor the Austrians had anticipated a full-scale engagement, but disorganisation and a lack of clear information about the other side's movements turned what might have been a minor skirmish into one of the bloodiest battles fought anywhere in the world before World War I. Both sides were so evenly matched that a victory could only be secured through messy man-to-man combat, and by the end of the day, 38,000 men lay dead or severely wounded. Though the French and Italians had won the day – and secured Lombardy for the Kingdom of Savoy – they were too tired to pursue the retreating Austrians. Shocked by the extent of his losses, Napoleon III soon made peace with Austria, leaving Vittorio Emanuele to fight the rest of his battles alone.

Another man shocked by the bloodshed was Swiss humanitarian Henri Dunant, who happened to be in the nearby town of Castiglione dello Stiviere when the battle broke out. He worked alongside local people to treat the wounded, and the experience – narrated in his pamphlet *Un Souvenir de Solférino* – led in 1863 to his foundation of the world's first volunteer-based, non-aligned relief and medical agency: the International Red Cross. Dunant's work, and the courage

of the townspeople, is remembered at the **Museo Internazionale della Croce Rossa** in Castiglione dello Stiviere.

In Solferino itself, the **Museo Risorgimentale** – which contains material on the battle and the movement for Italian independence – is housed in the town's heavily restored 11th-century castle, Rocca Spia d'Italia. Behind the church of San Pietro is the *ossuario*, with its rather macabre accumulation of the skulls and bones of thousands of combatants.

To the north is the **Torre** of San Martino della Battaglia, a tower built in 1893 on the site of the battle. If the musty display of battle relics that punctuate the climb to the top doesn't do it for you, the view across Lake Garda (*see p212*) should compensate.

Museo Internazionale della Croce Rossa

Via Garibaldi 50, Castiglione dello Stiviere (0376 638 505/www.micr.it). **Open** Apr-Sept 9am-noon, 3-6pm Tue-Sun. Oct-Mar 9am-noon, 2-5pm Tue-Sun. **Admission** €2. **No credit cards**.

Museo Risorgimentale

Rocca Spia d'Italia, Solferino (0376 854 019). **Open** 16 Mar-14 Oct 9am-12.30pm, 2.30-7pm Tue-Sun. **Admission** €2. **No credit cards**.
Same times and entrance fee apply to the *ossuario*.

Torre

Via Torre 2, San Martino della Battaglia (030 991 0370). **Open** 6 Mar-14 Oct 9am-12.30pm, 2.30-7pm Tue-Sun. Nov & Feb 9am-noon, 2-5pm. **Admission** €2. **No credit cards**.

before their rise to power. The north end of the square is closed off by Mantova's fiddly baroque **Duomo**, officially known as the **Cattedrale di San Pietro**. On the corner of piazza Sordello with vicolo Gallo is a 15th-century house known as the **Casa del Rigoletto** (0376 368 917, open for exhibitions) – not because Verdi's hero was supposed to have lived here, but because it was once used as a backdrop for open-air performances of the opera.

The area to the west of piazza Sordello and piazza delle Erbe is full of medieval, Renaissance and baroque houses and palazzi, dotted among the more anonymous parts of the urban fabric.

From piazza Mantegna, arcaded via Verdi leads past the late 17th-century **Palazzo Canossa** (closed to the public) – home to the descendants of powerful medieval countess Matilde of Canossa – to piazza d'Arco. **Palazzo d'Arco**, which dominates the square, is worth a visit for the vivacious 16th-century frescoes in the Sala dello Zodiaco. The church of **San Francesco** (piazza San Francesco 5), just south of here, has some good (if fragmentary) frescoes by Tommaso di Modena from the 1370s.

Mantova's other sights lie in the 'third circle', south of the canal that once formed the boundary of the medieval city. The main

Lakes & Cities

The Gonzaga saga

At the beginning of the 14th century, the Corradi family lived the life of country gentry in the farmland south of Mantova, near the small town of Gonzaga. Luigi Corradi, though, wasn't happy with the way the Bonacolsi family was running things around Mantova, and one hot August night in 1328, he took matters into his own hands, overthrowing the Bonacolsis and starting a dynasty that would not officially end until 1707: the Gonzagas (named after their place of origin). As you'd expect of a man from a family that would become known for working both ends against the middle, Luigi made sure he had the support of the powerful Scaligeri family, rulers of Verona, before starting his coup.

Throughout the 15th and 16th centuries, the Gonzagas carefully negotiated their way around the Guelph/Ghibelline rivalry in Italy. Nominally aligned with the Ghibellines (the Gonzagas were named princes of the Holy Roman Empire as early as 1432), Mantova was careful to stay on the good side of the pope. At the same time, the province found itself between the two northern Italian heavyweights: Venice and Milan. Here, too, it was successful in finding the proper balance, and both the Venetians and the Milanese were convinced that an independent Mantova was in their interests (the Mantovans' strong reputations as military commanders didn't hurt).

The Gonzagas loved intrigue, and didn't hesitate about marrying into the ruling families of Renaissance Europe. In 1433, Gianfrancesco Gonzaga married one of Holy Roman Emperor Sigismondo's nieces, and another Gonzaga leader, Lodovico III, married a Hohenzollern princess in the mid-1400s. Another marriage – between Federico II and Margherita Paleologo, in 1531 – marked the height of Gonzaga power.

Strategic matrimony could not immortalise the Gonzaga dynasty, however, and by the 1580s things had decidedly declined. Vincenzo II, loaded down with debts, began selling off the family's art – including masterpieces by Titian and Mantegna. Adding insult to injury, Vincenzo died without an heir and Mantova passed to a French prince belonging to a junior branch of the family. Foreign rule chafed at Mantovan self-esteem and set in motion the fall of the Gonzagas.

The Spanish and the Austrians both set their sights on the small but strategic duchy, and the city was finally sacked by Habsburg troops in 1630. A succession of weak Gonzagas continued to hold nominal power over the depopulated, plague-ridden shadow of the former duchy until 1707, when the final Gonzaga, Ferdinando Carlo IV, fled to Venice after supporting France in a showdown with Spain. The 'traitor' died the next year, and Austria revoked any claim the Gonzaga family might have had over Mantova.

---

north–south axis is via Principe Amedeo and its continuation, via Acerbi, which ends in front of the extravagant and mannerist **Palazzo Te**.

Fun-loving artist Giulio Romano put heart and soul into the construction and decoration of this ducal love nest; but he also found time to build himself the house that can be seen at via Poma 18. Another, earlier artist's house stands near the Palazzo Te end of via Acerbi (No.47): the cube-shaped **Casa di Mantegna** (0376 360 506, open 10am-12.30pm, 3-6pm Tue-Fri) dates from 1496 and may or may not have been designed by Andrea Mantegna himself. Opposite is Leon Battista Alberti's often-overlooked second Mantovan church, **San Sebastiano**. Its façade was messed around with in 1925, when the two flights of stairs were added; but Alberti's penchant for classical mix-and-match is still evident in the clutter of doors that run the gamut of architectural history. The Greek cross interior is permanently closed.

Fans of the Romanesque style may want to trek out to the mid 13th-century church of **Santa Maria del Gradaro** (via Gradaro 40) in the south-eastern suburbs: a barn-shaped brick structure with a good rose window, it conserves traces of Byzantine frescoes, including a charming *Last Supper*.

Mantova no longer depends on the Mincio river for its commercial and defensive well-being, and busy roads separate the *centro storico* from the lakes. The waterside remains popular with *mantovani*, however, and the lake-front gardens are a good place to contemplate life and watch the droves of Sunday cyclists.

Duomo

Piazza Sordello (0376 320 220). **Open** 7am-noon, 3-7pm daily. **Admission** free.

Behind the rococo façade is an uncharacteristically austere interior designed by Giulio Romano in 1545. The five-nave plan harks back to Rome's early Christian basilicas. Off the left-hand nave is the Cappella dell'Incoronata, an ensemble of stonework and frescoes commissioned by Ludovico II Gonzaga in 1480.

Palazzo d'Arco

Piazza d'Arco 4 (0376 322 242). **Open** *Mar-Oct* 10am-12.30pm, 2.30-6pm Tue-Sun. *Nov-Feb* 10am-12.30pm, 2-5pm Sat, Sun & public hols. **Admission** €3. **No credit cards.**

The noble d'Arco family had this elegant neoclassical townhouse built in 1782-4. When the last descendant died in 1973, the house became a museum, offering a glimpse of a provincial aristocratic residence after two generations of minor art collecting and furniture rearrangement. The real treat comes right at the end, when the obligatory guided tour crosses the garden and climbs the stairs of a 15th-century building to enter the Sala dello Zodiaco, its walls covered in lively *trompe l'oeil* frescoes (1509) by Giovanni Maria Falconetto.

Palazzo Ducale

Piazza Sordello (0376 352 100/0412 411 897). **Open** 9am-6.30pm Tue-Sun. **Admission** €6.50; €3.25 concessions. **No credit cards.**

A city within the city, the vast, sprawling Gonzaga power base takes up two thirds of the area occupied by Roman and early medieval Mantova. When the Gonzagas took over from the Bonacolsi clan in 1328, they also inherited the fortified palazzo that the Bonacolsis had built on this site in the 1290s. This Corte Vecchia (old court) formed the nucleus of the Gonzagas' diplomatic and residential headquarters, which mushroomed over the next four centuries to include gardens, galleries, bedrooms, state rooms and private chapels.

Visitors follow a rigid one-way itinerary through around 100 of the palace's 500 rooms. The first big treat comes almost immediately, in the Sala del Pisanello. Long thought lost, Pisanello's frescoes, based on episodes from the courtly epic *Lancelot*, came to light in 1972. Though painted over 500 years ago, around 1442, when the first stirrings of the Renaissance were animating the Mantovan court, their style is deliberately retro-medieval.

A series of neo-classical rooms just beyond houses a collection of 16th-century Flemish tapestries based on Raphael's cartoons of the Acts of the Apostles. The rococo Sala dei Fiumi (river room) looks over a pretty, porticoed hanging garden; in the long, barrel-vaulted Sala degli Specchi (mirror room), composer Claudio Monteverdi organised musical soirées, including the very first opera performances. The Salone degli Arcieri (archer hall) has a pious family portrait (1605) by Rubens; Napoleon's kleptomaniac troops are to blame for its missing pieces. Gods and heroes spill over into the Sala di Troia (Troy room), frescoed by assistants of Giulio Romano in 1536-9.

Just as all this gilded pomp is beginning to drag, we enter the Gonzaga's austere fortress, the Castello di San Giorgio, erected between 1390 and 1406. A horse-friendly spiral ramp leads up to the first-floor

The Sala dello Zodiaco in **Palazzo d'Arco**.

star turn: Andrea Mantegna's frescoes in the Camera degli Sposi (bridal suite), painted some time between 1465 and 1474. The two frescoed walls show episodes that took place on 1 January 1462: Ludovico II receiving news of the illness of his ally, Francesco Sforza of Milan, then meeting his son Francesco, recently created cardinal, while hurrying to Milan to lend his aid.

Palazzo Te

Viale Te (0376 323 266). **Open** 1-6pm Mon; 9am-6pm Tue-Sun (ticket office closes at 5.30pm). **Admission** €8; €5.50 concessions. **No credit cards.**

Mannerism is Renaissance style gone decadent; and Palazzo Te is the apotheosis of mannerism. Of course, Giulio Romano's tumbling artistic excess is not unconnected with the function of this pleasure dome: it was, essentially, a love nest, built for Federico II's mistress, Isabella Boschetti, on a (then) rural site far away from the disapproving eyes of his mum, Isabella d'Este. The name apparently derives from *tejeto*, a place of reed huts; a more fanciful etymology has it punning on the two meanings of *te* in Italian: 'tea' and 'you'.

Romano was one of Raphael's most talented apprentices. In 1524 he relocated from Rome – where a series of erotic prints he'd created had almost landed him in jail – to Mantova, and a year later he secured this major commission, which would occupy the next ten years of his life. Both architect and artist, he based the whole project on the concepts of variety, change and instability. Gods, heroes and transformations are the subjects of the frescoes that decorate most of the rooms on the ground floor. Giulio really

Sant'Andrea.

Although a baroque dome was added in 1765, the bizarre triumphal arch entrance and the lofty, barrel-vaulted nave are pure Alberti. Wade through the rich, overladen decoration of the interior to find Andrea Mantegna's tomb, in the first chapel on the left, and the Mausoleo Strozzi (1529), in the left transept; its elegant caryatids were inspired by classical statues in the Gonzaga collection.

Teatro Accademico Bibiena

Via Accademia 47 (0376 327 653). **Open** 9.30am-12.30pm, 3-6pm Tue-Sun. **Admission** €2.07; €1.03 concessions. **No credit cards.**

An under-publicised jewel, the Teatro Accademico is one of Europe's most perfect late-baroque theatres. In the 18th century, three successive generations of the Bibiena family delighted the courts of Europe with their theatrical set designs, wedding pageants and festive tableaux. Some – such as Antonio Galli Bibiena – also designed more permanent structures, such as the present theatre (also known as the Teatro Scientifico), built in 1769. A cadenced curve of arched boxes undulates around the auditorium and continues in an arcade behind the stage. The 14-year-old Mozart played here in 1770, and was enchanted by the backdrop.

Where to eat & drink

Aquila Nigra

Vicolo Bonacolsi 4 (0376 327 180). **Meals served** Nov-Mar, June, July noon-2pm, 8-10pm Tue-Sat. Sept-Oct, Apr, May noon-2pm, 8-10pm Tue-Sat; noon-2pm Sun. Closed 3wks Aug. **Average** €65. **Credit** AmEx, DC, MC, V.

In a late-Gothic townhouse near the Palazzo Ducale, this is currently Mantova's best and most elegant restaurant. The cuisine – like the decor – combines respect for tradition with a light, creative touch. Game dishes, such as pigeon cooked in honey and balsamic vinegar, are a speciality. Try also the gnocchi with nettles and the risotto with frogs.

Bar Venezia

Piazza Marconi 9/10 (0376 363 499). **Open** 7am-9pm Mon-Sat. **Credit** AmEx, MC, V.

Mantova's most celebrated literary café dates from the end of the 18th century. The decor has changed a few times since then, but the place still takes its vocation seriously, with shelves of books available for browsing – though mind not to do this while indulging in the house speciality, *fondue du chocolat*. There are tables outside, and a good range of lunchtime snacks and pizzas on offer. The wine lists features more than 100 labels.

Due Cavallini

Via Salnitro 5 (0376 632 2084). **Meals served** noon-2pm, 8-10pm Wed-Mon. Closed mid July-mid Aug. **Average** €25. **Credit** MC, V.

This classic *trattoria* along the eastern edge of the *centro storico*, has been serving up down-home Mantovan cooking for 40-odd years. Once upon a

gets into his stride in the Sala di Psiche, with scenes of Bacchanalian revelry adapted from Apuleius's *The Golden Ass*. In the vertiginous Sala dei Giganti, a huddle of hammy Titans cowers from the wrath of Jupiter amid broken columns. Upstairs is a display of Mesopotamian and Egyptian antiquities. The Palazzo often organises temporary art exhibitions.

Rotonda di San Lorenzo

Piazza Erbe (no phone). **Open** 10am-1pm, 2-6pm Mon-Fri; 10am-6pm Sat, Sun. **Admission** free.

A surviving testimony of early medieval Mantova, the Rotonda is modelled on the Church of the Holy Sepulchre in Jerusalem. Built towards the end of the 11th century, it was later swallowed up by Mantova's Jewish ghetto. Inside, an ambulatory supports a *matroneum* (women's gallery); there are also traces of frescoes from the 11th to 13th centuries.

Sant'Andrea

Piazza Mantegna (0376 328 504). **Open** 7.30am-noon, 3-7pm daily. **Admission** free.

This mighty basilica, based on a design by Renaissance *wunderkind* Leon Battista Alberti, is closer to the heart of most *mantovani* than their official cathedral. In 1470 Ludovico II Gonzaga asked Alberti to design a temple for his family's number-one relic: a phial of Christ's blood. Alberti died two years into the project, and his plan, based on Vitruvius's drawing of an Etruscan temple, was watered down by his successor, Luca Fancelli.

Lakes & Cities

time, it dished up *tortelli alla zucca* (*see p243* **Tortelli addicts**) to workers toiling at the port. Mantova may no longer be a river trading centre, but the *tortelli* are as good as ever.

Ochina Bianca

Via Finzi 2 (0376 323 700). **Meals served** 12.30-2pm, 7.45-10.30pm Tue-Sun. Closed 1wk Jan, 3wks Aug. **Average** €20-€30. **Credit** AmEx, DC, MC, V.
The best of a new breed of Mantuan restaurants, this bright, modern *osteria* combines local specialities (including *asino* – donkey meat) with creative turns.

Where to stay

Broletto

Via Accademia 1 (0376 326 784/fax 0376 221 297). **Rates** €70 single; €115 double. *Breakfast* €6.50. **Credit** AmEx, MC, V.
Just off piazza Broletto, this small, neat two-star is a good budget option. All rooms have en suite bathrooms, air-conditioning and satellite TV.

Locanda dell'Opera

Via Bachelet 12, San Giorgio di Mantova (0376 371 414/www.operaghiotta.com). **Rates** €50 single; €75 double. **Credit** MC, V.
Located 3km (2 miles) from Mantova's centre, this hotel is surrounded by three luxuriant gardens. The rooms are pleasant enough, but the real reason to stay here is the hotel's association with the Italian-born Slow Food movement. The adjoining restaurant offers dinners cooked in traditional ways.

San Lorenzo

Piazza Concordia 14 (0376 220 500/fax 0376 327 194/www.hotelsanlorenzo.it). **Rates** €150 single; €175 double; €202 suite. **Credit** AmEx, DC, MC, V.
Mantova's best hotel is right in the centre. Rooms are mostly large and comfortable, and there's a terrace with views over piazza delle Erbe and San Lorenzo.

Villa Bogoni

Via Veneto 19a, Sorgà (045 737 0129/www. villabogoni.it). **Rates** €67-€77 single; €103-€118 double. **Credit** AmEx, DC, MC, V.
Sleep in a 16th-century Gonzaga villa decorated with frescoes by a follower of Giulio Romano. In the village of Sorgà, 18km (11 miles) east of Mantova, Villa Bogoni has bedrooms that bristle with antiques, including charming *baldacchino* canopy beds.

Essentials

Getting there

By car

From the A4 Milan–Venice motorway take the A22 and exit at Mantova Nord.

By train

Take the high-speed mainline train service from Milan's Stazione Centrale to Verona and change at

Tortelli addicts

Stuffed with pumpkin, crushed *amaretti* and *mostarda* (candied fruit flavoured with mustard oil) then covered with freshly grated parmesan, browned butter and sage, Mantova's famous *tortelli con zucca* fill your mouth with a sensation that is both sweet and savoury, a throwback to the medieval days when the tomato was still a gleam in Columbus's eye.

The *tortelli* also hark back to the days when pasta fillings were a leading indicator of economic status. These days, cutting-edge chefs see stuffed pastas as a testament to their creativity, and cookbooks think little of instructing you to spend three hours braising a stew for your ravioli. Once, though, the creativity came from making do: people put Sunday's stew into Monday's *tortelli* to ensure nothing went to waste; when there wasn't enough dosh for meat, they took vegetables from the family garden and turned them into something special.

In Mantova, pumpkin – or winter squash if you prefer, there's no firm distinction – is treated with a heady mixture of disdain and admiration. There is no doubt that it is *cibo povero* (peasant food), but with its ability to last through the winter, it also kept generations of *mantovani* from going hungry. Beyond *tortelli*, you'll also find pumpkin soup and pumpkin risotto; and occasionally more daring dishes pop up, such as roast pumpkin on the side, pumpkin jam, and even pumpkin sweets.

Verona for a *interregionale* (long-distance train with frequent stops) for Mantova.

Getting around

All the main sights are within easy walking distance. Local bus company APAM (freephone 800 821 194, www.apam.it) runs both city and country routes. The bus station is at via Mutilati e Caduti del Lavoro 4, five minutes south of the train station. Bus 1 runs between the station and the centre (tickets 90¢; daily pass €1.85).

Tourist information

APT

Piazza Mantegna 6 (0376 328 253/www.apt mantova.it). **Open** 8.30am-12.30pm, 3-6pm Mon-Sat; 9.30am-12.30pm Sun.

Caffè Liberty.

Around Mantova

Rice paddies, pumpkin and melon fields, and long lines of poplars – welcome to the province of Mantova. Though **Sabbioneta** – the short-lived ideal city of a Renaissance scholar-prince – is popular, the rest of the region is one of the least-visited rural areas in Italy. For those with time on their hands, and no particular place to go, provincial Mantova offers crumbling castles, rustic *trattorie* and lots of peace. However, this hasn't always been the case: in 1859 along the stretch of countryside around Solferino (*see p239* **Slaughter at Solferino**) more blood was shed than in any other battle prior to World War I.

Getting there & around

By train

Four rural train lines radiate from Mantova, one for every point of the compass. Few, however, stop anywhere useful to tourists.

By bus

APAM (freephone 800 821 194/www.apam.it) runs services to most towns and villages in the Mantova province, and also offers long-distance routes to Brescia, Parma and Peschiera sul Garda. Buses depart from and arrive at the bus station in via Mutilati e Caduti del Lavoro 4. Services to Sabbioneta run hourly (€3.25; journey time 45mins).

The Oglio Valley

The entire course of the River Oglio, which flows from Lago d'Iseo (*see p224* **Lake placid**) to the Po, is a regional park. Perhaps the best place to appreciate its lazy, reedy charm is from the garden of Dal Pescatore (*see p245*), just outside

Canneto sull'Oglio – one of the best restaurants in this, or indeed any, part of the world. There's little to see in Canneto itself; better to head north to **Asola**, for a long time a Venetian bulwark against the local Gonzaga hegemony. The Venetian influence is felt in the church of **Sant'Andrea** (open 7am-noon, 3-7pm daily), which has a remarkable cycle of paintings dating from 1525-36 by Il Romanino, and in **Caffè Liberty** (piazza XX Settembre, 0376 710 167), an incongruous art nouveau jewel in the middle of Mantova's combine-harvester belt.

Across the Oglio from Canneto, **Piadena** was the birthplace of Platina, the assumed name of Bartolomeo Sacchi (1421-81), Renaissance humanist, Vatican librarian and author of possibly the first printed cookery book, *De Honesta Voluptate*. However, Platina lifted most of his recipes from the *Libro de Arte Coquinaria*, a vernacular manuscript of recipes committed to paper by a certain Maestro Martino of Como.

Sabbioneta

When Vespasiano Gonzaga was born in 1531, his family – a cadet branch of the Gonzagas – had been ruling the medieval village of Sabbioneta for around 70 years. His predecessors had been content to build up the walls and collect the tithes, but cultured Vespasiano was determined to turn this sleepy Po valley community into the ideal city of a scholar-prince.

In less than 40 years, beginning in 1556, Vespasiano gave Sabbioneta most of the appendages of the Renaissance city-state: a castle (since demolished), a garden palace, an academy, a long gallery to display the requisite collection of classical statues, a theatre, a library, a mint and a printing press.

The leading artists and architects of the day were summoned to paint, sculpt and build; scholars – especially Jewish scholars – were drawn here by the climate of enlightened tolerance. But when Vespasiano died without an heir in 1591 (apparently of syphilis), so did his dream of a 'Little Athens'. The town reverted to the main Gonzaga line, its inhabitants went back to growing their pumpkins (they'd never really stopped, to tell the truth), and Sabbioneta became what it is today: a historical curiosity, frozen in time.

Palazzo del Giardino (*see below* **Tickets**), formerly Vespasiano Gonzaga's private residence, takes up most of the southern part of Sabbioneta's main piazza d'Armi (also referred to as piazza Castello). Its façade and much of the interior decoration have seen better days, but there is still plenty left to marvel at: the rooms are an intricate hive of fresco, stucco and grotesque, all on mythological and Arcadian themes. A pretty ivy-frescoed staircase leads into the Galleria degli Antichi. Truncated – like Sabbioneta itself – this ornate gallery displayed Vespasiano's collection of classical sculpture until it was filched by Maria Teresa of Austria in 1774.

The two other big sights lie north of via Gonzaga. Easily the most charming is Vincenzo Scamozzi's **Teatro Olimpico** (*see below* **Tickets**), designed in 1588 and opened for a single, brief season before the prince's demise brought an end to masques and revels. Scamozzi was a pupil of Palladio, and the latter's Teatro Olimpico in Vicenza is the obvious model. Just down the road in piazza Ducale (or piazza Garibaldi – most squares around here have at least two names) is Vespasiano's official seat, the imposing **Palazzo Ducale**, one of the few buildings finished in time for him to enjoy it. Traces of frescoes by Bernardino Campi and others remain inside, but the real treats are the polychrome wooden equestrian statues of the prince and four of his ancestors in the Sala delle Aquile; and the Galleria degli Antenati, with more ancestors – this time in stucco bas-relief.

Tickets

A combined ticket covering all Sabbioneta's main sights costs €8 (€3.50 for 7-18s) and can be bought from the Ufficio di Turismo del Comune (*see below*). It includes a guided tour (Italian only) lasting around 90mins. An adult ticket for a single sight costs €3; admission for everything is free for under-sixes.

Opening hours for all the sights are: 10am-1pm, 2.30-5.30pm Tue-Sat; 10am-1pm, 2.30-6pm Sun. The ticket office closes 30 minutes before the sights do.

Tourist information

Pro Loco di Sabbioneta

Via Vespasiano Gonzaga 27 (0375 52 039).
Open 10am-12.30pm Tue-Sat; 10am-12.30pm, 2.30-5.30pm Sun & hols.

Ufficio di Turismo del Comune

Piazza d'Armi 1, Sabbioneta (0375 221 044/ 0375 223 001/www.comune.sabbioneta.mn.it).
Open 10am-1pm; 2-5pm Mon-Fri; 10am-1pm, 2-5.30pm Sat, Sun.

Basso mantovano

The huge porticoed central square in the tiny village of **Pomponesco** – a gift of Giulio Cesare Gonzaga at the end of the 16th century – ends rather incongruously in one of the high banks that protect the area from flooding. Underneath the arches is the **Trattoria Saltini** (piazza XXIII Aprile 10, 0375 86 017, closed Mon & mid July-mid Aug, average €25), an excellent, cheap local hostelry that does good local pasta staples, such as *tagliatelle al sugo di anatra* (with duck sauce), to be washed down with a glass or two of Lambrusco. Covering one wall is a curious mock-Egyptian mural from the 1920s.

South-east of Mantova, just below the Po is **San Benedetto Po**, a dozy brick village that is dominated by the **Abbazia di Polirone** (0376 615 124, open 6.30am-12.30pm, 2.30-7.30pm daily), a Benedictine abbey founded in 1007. The rambling complex – its present form mostly dates from the 16th century – is worth a visit for the sacristy, an exuberant mannerist concerto with frescoes by the school of Giulio Romano, and the 12th-century Oratorio di Santa Maria, which harbours a medieval mosaic of a black St George taming a dragon. Look out also for the tomb of medieval power broker Matilde di Canossa.

Where to stay & eat

The only hotel worth considering in Sabbioneta itself is the three-star **Al Duca** (via della Stamperia 18, 0375 220021, doubles €60), a family-run place with a touch of class. The same hotel's restaurant is the best of the town's uninspiring eateries.

Dal Pescatore (località Runate 17, Canneto sull'Oglio, 0376 723 001, closed Mon, Tue, Wed lunch, 2wks Jan, Aug, average €130) is one of the temples – many gourmands would say *the* temple – of Italian high cooking. There is nothing forced about the cooking here; it's just spot-on modern Italian cooking and impeccable service in a country-house setting. It is essential to book ahead. *See also p189* **Lombard gourmands**.

Cremona, Crema & Lodi

The lowland towns offer some of Lombardy's best art, valuable violins and all the cheese you can eat.

Get high in Cremona by climbing the 110-metre **Torrazzo** next to the Duomo. *See p247.*

Despite the many attractive towns and villages with charming piazze and interesting churches, the *Bassa Pianura* (lowlands) has never quite made it on to the tourist map. This does not mean that the area is not worth visiting, just that visiting has to be done in a certain manner.

Trains from Milan reach only the key towns in the area, and buses are not a realistic option; a car is essential for visiting the towns around Cremona, many of which have something worth seeing, but usually only from the outside. However, visits to the interiors of many villas and castles can be arranged with suitable prior notice.

The other downside of visiting places that are not 'tourist' towns is that they make few concessions to those who come in what might be considered a holiday period. Not only do many of the restaurants close for holidays for part or all of August as well as the Christmas period, but so do some of the hotels. That said, if you do come during the holiday periods, you won't starve. You'll always find a pizzeria, providing better fare than you might imagine.

Cremona

Founded by the Romans in 218 BC, Cremona was a major fortress and staging post on the road that linked Genoa and Acquilea. From about AD 550, Cremona spent 50 years under Byzantine rule; at this point, it was the westernmost point of the Eastern empire.

That period came to an end in 603, when the Lombard king Agilulf marched in and ordered the city's destruction. Cremona regained its prominence in 1098 as a *libero comune* (free city), and was soon warring with Milan, Brescia and Piacenza. In 1334, it was taken by Azzone

Visconti, the ruler of Milan, and remained largely under that city's control until the creation of the Italian state in 1870.

During the Renaissance, Cremona acquired a considerable number of handsome brick buildings adorned with terracotta decorations. **Palazzo Fodri** is one example. At this time the city also had some outstanding painting talent, both local and from outside. Examples of the latter include Bonifacio Bembo from Brescia, and Boccaccio Boccaccino from Ferrara; the brothers Campi, Giulio (c1505-72), Antonio (1524-87) and Vincenzo (1536-91), were *cremonesi* born and bred.

In the age of the baroque, the city gave birth to at least one masterwork that would change the world: the violin, which emerged in its modern form in the workshop of Andrea Amati (*see p255* **Fiddling about**). During the same period, Cremona also produced the composer Claudio Monteverdi and the painter Sofonisba Anguissola.

Cremona's main square, **piazza del Comune**, is a premier example of the medieval public space, with the **Duomo** (the representation of clerical authority)

and the **Palazzo del Comune** (the seat of civil power) facing each other. The Duomo is flanked by Italy's highest medieval bell tower, the **Torrazzo** (0372 27 386, open 10am-1pm Tue-Sun, €4), a 110-metre (370-foot) campanile built between 1250 and 1267. The Gothic lantern was added between 1287 and 1300, while the astrological clock dates from 1583. The clock still works with the original mechanism, marking lunar and solar eclipses, as well as the time.

To the other side of the Duomo is the octagonal **Battistero** (0372 27 386, open 10am-12.30pm, 2.30-6pm Tue-Sun, €2, includes the Museo delle Pietre Romaniche). This dates from 1167, but was spruced up with marble in the 16th century. Facing it, the **Loggia dei Militi**, built in 1292, is one of the finest examples of Gothic Lombard civil architecture.

Leading north towards piazza Roma, the narrow medieval via Solferino is a good place to pick up local delicacies such as *torrone* (nougat confection) and *mostarda cremonese*, an extremely spicy fruit chutney to be eaten with roast meat or cheese. North of the well-kept patch of green in piazza Roma (the statue

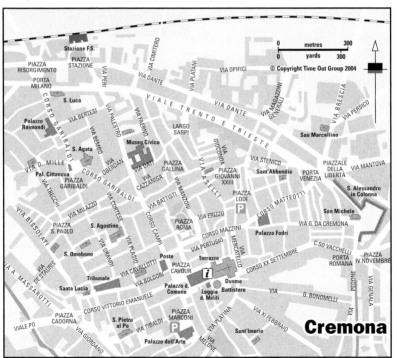

is of violin-maker Stradivarius, *see p255*
Fiddling about) are the **Museo Civico**
and the **Museo Stradivariano**.

A couple of streets west, in corso Garibaldi,
the pointed medieval arches of **Palazzo
Cittanova** (not open to the public) mark
what was once an alternative town centre
(hence Cittanova or new city). Built in the
11th century, this became the power base
of the *popolari*, who were at daggers drawn
with the Ghibelline faction (*see p11*) until 1344
when Azzone Visconti of Milan took control.

From piazza Garibaldi, via Trecchi leads
to the tiny church of **Santa Margherita**
(open 7.45am-6.30pm Mon-Sat, 7.45am-noon
Sun). Built in 1547, this is perhaps the best
example of the Cremonese mannerist style.
Giulio Campi and his brother Antonio were
responsible for the frescoes and terracotta
decorations inside.

Further on, via Trecchi becomes via
Grandi. If you take a left into via Breda,
you get to piazza **Sant'Agostino** where
the main attraction – in the church of the
same name – (open 8am-noon, 3.30-6pm
daily) is the *Madonna Enthroned with Saints*
(1494) by Perugino, one of many paintings
pilfered by Napoleonic troops, and one of the
few to come back. A portrait of Bianca Maria
Visconti and Francesco Sforza by Bonifacio
Bembo is also worth a look.

Come back through piazza del Duomo
and head towards corso Mazzini. Take the
left fork into corso Matteotti to get to the
elegant Renaissance **Palazzo Fodri** (No.17,
open 8.30am-12.30pm, 2-6.30pm Mon-Fri).
The façade features a terracotta frieze of
mythological figures and lifelike busts.
The courtyard is porticoed on three sides
and is decorated with terracotta friezes.

Retrace your steps and then take the
right fork into via Gerolamo da Cremona
to see Cremona's oldest church, **San
Michele** (open 7.30am-noon, 4-7.30pm
daily). Founded in the seventh century
and rebuilt after the earthquake in 1117,
it was restored in the 1800s.

In nearby via Lauretano is the church of
Sant'Abbondio (open 7am-noon, 3-7pm
daily). This is late-mannerist in style, and
features a stately cloister, as well as a 17th-
century replica of the Virgin Mary's 'home'.
The original *Santa Casa* was, apparently,
transported by angels from Nazareth and
deposited in Loreto – in the Marches region
of east-central Italy – in 1294.

Cremona's most spectacular church, **San
Sigismondo**, is two kilometres (1.5 miles)
down the road to Casalmaggiore and Parma
(bus 2 stops outside).

Caravaggio's **Saint Francis in Meditation**.

Duomo
Piazza del Comune (no phone). **Open** 7.30am-noon,
3.30-7pm Mon-Sat; 7.30am-1pm, 3.30-7pm Sun.
Admission free.
Started in 1107, the Duomo is a high point of the
Lombard Romanesque, with Gothic, Renaissance
and baroque elements tacked on over the centuries.
On the elaborately sculpted marble façade – begun
in the 13th century but not completed until well
into the 16th – are medieval peasants going about
their daily tasks, Byzantine-style prophets and
Madonnas from various periods. Inside, a fresco
cycle of the life of Christ and his mother starts with
Boccaccio Boccaccino's *Apparition of the Angel
to St Joachim* (1514; first left-hand arch of the central aisle) and ends with a *Crucifixion* by the mannerist painter Pordenone (facing the altar). The
inlaid choir stalls (1490) have views of Cremona;
the two pulpits were pieced together in 1813
from 15th-century fragments.

Museo Civico Ala Ponzone
*Palazzo Affaitati, via Ugolani Dati 4 (0372 31 222/
0372 407 770/www.comune.cremona.it).* **Open** 9am-
6pm Tue-Sat; 10am-6pm Sun. **Admission** €6; €3.50
concessions. **No credit cards.**
The art gallery contains works by the likes of the
brothers Campi and the Boccaccino family. It also
features *Saint Francis in Meditation* by Caravaggio,

whose treatment of light clearly influenced the Campis (for more on Caravaggio, *see p25*, **The dark side**). Cremonese noblewoman Sofonisba Anguissola (1532-1625), the first female Italian artist to win international recognition, contributes a family portrait. Portraiture of a different kind features in Carlo Francesco Nuvolone's *David with Goliath's Head*, while Arcimboldo's *The Vegetable Gardener* transforms into a bowl of salad if you stand on your head.

Museo Stradivariano
Via Ugolani Dati 4 (0372 31 222/0372 407 770/ www.comune.cremona.it). **Open** 9am-6pm Tue-Sat; 10am-6pm Sun. **Admission** €6; €3.50 concessions. **No credit cards.**
Many of Antonio Stradivari's models, forms and tools have now been brought back to his home town and are displayed here along with historic instruments. If you are interested in violins, also check out the Civica Raccolta di Violini in the Palazzo del Comune (*see below*), as well as Palazzo Fodri (*see p248*). *See also p255* **Fiddling about**.

Palazzo del Comune
Piazza del Comune 8 (0372 20 502/www.comune. cremona.it). **Open** 9am-6pm Tue-Sat; 10am-6pm Sun. **Admission** €6; €5 concessions. **No credit cards.**
Built between 1206 and 1246 as the seat of the city government, this building has been remodelled various times over the years. The last major overhaul was undertaken by Luigi Voghera between 1837 and 1847, when the large windows were added. On the first floor landing is a fine Renaissance doorway, while the council chamber (Sala della Giunta) boasts a 16th-century chimney piece. In the Saletta dei Violini are four examples of the world's most precious fiddles: a 1715 Stradivari called *Il Cremonese*, Niccolò Amati's 1658 *Hammerle*, Andrea Amati's *Charles IX of France* and a nameless 1734 piece by Giuseppe Guarnieri del Gesù. Some are played in the morning, Mon-Sat. To book a seat (allow at least 15 days' notice), call 00 39 0372 22 138 during office hours.
In the courtyard of the Palazzo del Comune is the bookshop (open 9am-6pm Tue-Sat, 10am-6pm Sun). Here you can buy a combined ticket (€10) for all of Cremona's paying attractions.

San Sigismondo
Largo Visconti (0372 437 357). **Open** *Apr-Oct* 9am-noon, 3-6pm daily. *Dec-Mar* by appointment. **Admission** free.
This church was commissioned in 1463 by Bianca Maria Visconti, and stands on the site of the chapel where her wedding to Francesco Sforza took place in 1441. A fine example of Lombard Renaissance architecture, it contains the work of many local artists such as Camillo Boccaccino Bernardino Gatti, and the brothers Campi. The mannerist frescoes offer food for thought. Especially unusual are those depicting various breeds of small dog.

Where to eat & drink

La Centrale della Birra
Viale Trento e Trieste 62a (0372 33 267). **Meals served** noon-3pm Tue; noon-3pm, 7.30pm-1am Wed-Thur; noon-3pm, 7.30pm-2am Fri; 7.30pm-2am Sat, Sun. Closed 1wk Sept. **Average** €18. **Credit** DC, MC, V.
This lively microbrewery with a capacious beer garden serves its own lager and pizzas cooked in a wood oven to a young clientele. It also does big salads (*insalatona*) and steaks.

Hosteria Settecento
Piazza Gallina 1 (0372 36 175).. **Meals served** 12.30-3pm Mon; 12.30-3pm, 8pm-midnight Wed-Sun. Closed Aug. **Credit** AmEx, DC, MC, V.
Located in an 18th-century palazzo, this recently opened restaurant is in the centre of town. House specialities include *marubini* (meat-filled ravioli) served either in broth or with melted butter and sage (*burro e salvia*). There's also the 'risotto 700', made with salami, rocket and scamorza cheese, and the 'torta 700': a layered sponge-cake topped with berries, and served with an orange-flavoured mascarpone sauce.

Martinelli
Palazzo Cattaneo, via degli Oscasali 3 (0372 30 350/www.ristorantemartinelli.it). **Meals served** noon-2.30pm, 8-10pm Mon, Tue, Thur-Sat. Closed 1wk Jan, 3wks Aug. **Average** €35. **Credit** Amex, MC, V.
In the neo-classical splendour of Palazzo Cattaneo, the Martinelli revisits regional favourites, its specialities being risotto and *marubini*. For antipasti try Cremonese salami, which is tender and features garlic. For dessert, try *torroncino*, a nougat mousse confection served with a delicate pistachio and chocolate sauce.

Ristorante Centrale
Via Pertusio 4 (0372 28 701). **Meals served** noon-2.30pm, 7.30-10pm Mon-Wed, Fri-Sun. Closed July. **Average** €25. **Credit** MC, V.
Unpretentious traditional fare in an unpretentious traditional atmosphere. The ideal place to try the Cremonese speciality *marubini in brodo*, meat-filled ravioli in a broth made from chicken and beef stock and flavoured with sausage. In the bar, the men cluster round the TV for crucial soccer matches.

La Sosta
Via Sicardo 9 (0372 456 656). **Meals served** noon-2.30pm, 7.30-10pm Tue-Sat; noon-3.30pm Sun. Closed 1wk Feb, 3wks Aug. **Average** €30-€35. **Credit** AmEx, DC, MC, V.
This restaurant's speciality is *gnocchi alla vecchia Cremona*. These are still prepared according to a 17th-century recipe: the potato-flour gnocchi are stuffed with a blend of local *salame*, honey, and garlic, and are then topped with sesame seeds, breadcrumbs and cheese, before being put in the oven.

Where to stay

The 62-room, four-star **Hotel Continental** (piazza della Libertà 26, 0372 434 141, www. hotelcontinentalcremona.it, doubles €110) has long been considered the best in the city.

For the Italian version of a boutique hotel, try the **DelleArti Design Hotel** (via Bonomelli 8, 0372 23 131, www.dellearti.com, doubles €132-€165, closed Aug), just 50 metres from the Duomo. Prices include use of the Turkish bath, sauna and hot tub.

Getting there

By car
Take the A1 motorway from Milan to Piacenza Sud; change to the A21 and exit at Cremona (1hr). The SS415 offers a more scenic route (1hr 30mins).

By train
Trains for Cremona leave from Milan's Stazione Centrale and Lambrate. There are four direct services (two from each station), which each take 1hr. Otherwise you have to go via Treviglio (2hrs).

By bus
There is no bus service linking Milan and Cremona.

Getting around

Cremona is small enough to be explored on foot. KM (0372 442 011) operates the city bus service. Tickets cost 90¢, and are valid for 1hr.

Tourist information

APT
Piazza del Comune 5 (0372 23 233/www.apt cremona.it). **Open** *Sept-July* 9am-12.30pm, 3-6pm daily. *Aug* 9am-12.30pm, 3-6pm Mon-Sat; 9am-12.30pm Sun.

South & east from Cremona

Mantova's Gonzaga dynasty (*see p240* **The Gonzaga saga**) imposed its style on what are now the eastern reaches of the Cremona province. The best example is **Isola Dovarese**, east of Cremona, where the extraordinary **piazza Matteotti** was remodelled between 1587 and 1590 by Giulio Cesare Gonzaga. The piazza's former garrison building is now a well-known ice-cream parlour, bar and restaurant (**Crepa**, 0375 396 161, closed Mon pm & Tue).

Casalmaggiore, stands scenically – and strategically – on the banks of the Po. Indeed, up to 1500 it was the main port on the river. The neo-classical **Duomo di Santo Stefano** (open for service 5-6pm Mon-Sat, and 8am-noon Sun. At other times, ring the bell at the priest's house

or call 0375 42 001) is in piazza Marini, aka piazza del Duomo. Also there is **Palazzo Mina Tentolini** (not open to the public), with its bas-relief-adorned façade. If you are into costume jewellery, head to the **Museo del Bijou** (via Porzio 9, 0375 43 682, www.museodelbijou.it).

Getting there

By car
From Cremona take the road for San Giovanni in Croce and then head south to Casalmaggiore (30mins).

By train
From Milan's Stazione Centrale head to Brescia or Parma and change on to one of the infrequent trains to Casalmaggiore. Journey time 1hr 10mins from Brescia; 30mins from Parma.

By bus
KM (0372 44 2011/0372 29 212) operates a Mon-Sat service to Casalmaggiore from Cremona (1hr 10mins).

Tourist information

Pro Loco Casalmaggiore
Piazza Garibaldi 6 (0375 40 039). **Open** 10am-noon, 4-7pm Mon-Fri; 10am-noon Sat, Sun.

Crema

Located in the flood plains between the rivers Adda and Oglio, and standing just 79 metres (265 feet) above sea level, Crema was originally a kind of island in a swamp.

Given by Matilde di Canossa (*see also p239*) to the bishop of Cremona in 1098, Crema later became a *libero comune* (free city), forging an alliance with Guelph Milan against the Ghibelline Cremona and Lodi, which supported the emperor. This proved catastrophic and, in 1160, the city was sacked and destroyed by several armies in the name of Frederick Barbarossa (*see p10*). Two years after the Peace of Konstanz (1183), the emperor authorised the rebuilding of the walls, and Crema was able to resume its existence as a settlement. In 1335, Crema came under the dominion of Milan, where it stayed until Francesco Sforza handed the city over to the Venetians in exchange for supporting his claim to the dukedom of Milan (1449).

Crema was part of the Venetian republic until 1797. The signs are still very evident: there's not just the lion of St Mark, the symbol of the *Serenissima*, strutting on façades all around piazza del Duomo, but also the white Istrian marble and the traces of architectural marvels conjured by Palladio and Scamozzi.

Interestingly, the **Duomo** (piazza del Duomo, 0373 256 218, open 7am-noon, 4-7pm Mon-Sat, 7am-1pm, 3.30-8pm Sun) itself pre-dates the

Lakes & Cities

Crema's **Palazzo Terni de Gregory** is a perfect example of Lombard baroque.

Venetians' arrival. Part of the original cathedral survived Barbarossa's rampage, but the main part was constructed between 1284 and 1341, modified over the centuries and then restored between 1952 and 1959. Appearances are deceptive: front-on, it looks tall; side-on, though, you can see the façade is just a windbreak and the bulk of the building is less imposing.

In the badly lit fourth niche on the right is *Saint Mark in Prison, Visited by The Redeemer*, the last (and unfinished) work of Guido Reni (1575-1642), the darling of the Victorian Grand Tourists. At the far end of the left nave is a wooden 14th-century crucifix.

Opposite the Duomo is the **Palazzo del Comune** (town hall). Built in 1525, it reflects the Venetian Renaissance style. The archway under the Comune leads to the main street, via XX Settembre. About halfway down is the baroque church of the **Santissima Trinità** (open 7am-noon, 4-7pm daily) – note the *Deposition* by Pompeo Batoni (1708-87). The street ends at Porta Ombriano. Staying inside the walls, go along via delle Grazie and you get to the church of **Santa Maria delle Grazie** (open 7am-noon, 4-7pm daily). The frescoes are by Gian Giacomo Barbelli, Crema's top 17th-century artist.

Barbelli was also responsible for all the frescoes in the church of **San Giovanni Battista** (via Matteotti, open 7am-noon, 4-7pm daily), which is south of the Duomo. On the corner of via del Ginnasio and via Dante Alighieri stands the early 18th-century

Palazzo Terni de Gregory (aka Terni Bodenti) with its statue-topped wavy baroque wall, one of the town's most striking noble residences (not open to the public). Opposite stands the 15th-century former **Convento di Sant'Agostino**. The building is now the **Museo della Città** (0373 257 161, open 2.30-6.30pm Mon, 9am-noon, 2.30-6.30pm Tue-Fri, 10am-noon, 4-7pm Sat, Sun), which houses local archaeological finds and some local art.

At the end of via Mazzini stands the city's eastern gate, the neo-classical **Porta Serio**. Pass through the gate, and then it's just one kilometre (half a mile) to Crema's architectural jewel, the Bramantesque basilica of **Santa Maria della Croce** (via Santa Maria della Croce 25, 0373 259 597, open 7.30am-noon, 2.30-7pm Mon-Sat, 7.30am-noon, 2-7pm Sun). In 1490, local noblewoman Caterina degli Uberti was attacked near here by her husband, Bartolomeo Contaglio, and left for dead. As the story goes, the Virgin Mary made sure a peasant family found her. They kept her alive and the next day she got to see her children for one last time. After this, miracles started to happen in the area, and the authorities decided to build a church there. Constructed between 1490 and 1500, the church has a circular exterior and an octagonal interior – a design originally laid out by Giovanni Battagio. It is richly decorated by Carlo Urbino, as well as Bernardino and Antonio Campi; beneath the altar, a tableau depicts Caterina degli Uberti with Mary.

Lakes & Cities

Say cheese

Italy is Europe's number-three cheese producer. The best-known is what is called parmesan in English and *grana* in Italian (because of its grainy texture). There are two types: grana padano and parmigiano reggiano. The former is produced in the Po Valley, while the latter comes from the area around Reggio Emilia, in the Emilia Romagna region. That said, parmigiano reggiano is also produced in the area south of Mantova, known as the Oltrepò Mantovano (*see p237*).

The Cistercian monks at the Chiaravalle abbey just on the outskirts of Milan were, apparently, the first to make *grana* in about the year 1000. For the last 500 years or so, Lodi has had its own version; called *grana lodigiano* or, locally, *granone*, it is very hard to find these days. Changes in fodder for dairy cattle have reduced the amount that can be made. This local *grana* is used for making the local speciality antipasto, *raspadura*.

There's more, though. The cream cheese par excellence – mascarpone – comes from the Lodi area. Traditionally eaten as a dessert with cocoa, sugar and a touch of liqueur, it is also the main ingredient in every Italian's favourite dessert, tiramisù.

Where to eat & drink

Il Ridottino (via A Fino 1, 0373 256 891, closed Sun pm, all Mon and 1wk Jan & 3wks Aug, average €50) is a lively place; the innovative cuisine includes lots of fish and poultry. **Mario** (via Stazione 118, 0373 204 708, closed Tue pm & Wed, average €30/37) is a spacious restaurant serving traditional fare in an ex-warehouse.

In a cellar with a vaulted ceiling near the Duomo, **Enoteca** (piazza Trento e Trieste 14, 0373 84 339, open 7.30pm-2am Wed-Sun, closed Mon & Tue, 2wks Aug, average €30) serves a huge range of wines and snacks.

Four kilometres (2.5 miles) north-west of Crema in Trescore Cremasco, the **Trattoria del Fulmine** (via Carioni 12, 0373 273 103, closed Tue pm, all Mon, Aug and 2 wks Jan, average €50) serves elegant takes on local staples.

Where to stay

Just outside Porta Serio – Crema's liveliest area – the 33-room **Ponte di Rialto** (via Cadorna 5/7, 0373 82 342, closed 3wks Aug, doubles €92)

has been a hotel since Venetian times. It has since been rebuilt almost out of recognition, but retains touches of character.

In Offanengo, four kilometres (2.5 miles) from Crema, on the road to Brescia, the **Albergo Ristorante Mantovani** (circonvallazione Sud 1, 0373 780 213, doubles €90) has an outdoor swimming pool and pretty garden.

Getting there

By car
From Milan, take the SS415 via Paullo to Crema. This road can be slow, so allow an hour.

By train
Take one of the hourly trains from Milan's Stazione Centrale to Treviglio and change. Journey time 1hr.

By bus
The Milan–Crema service is run by Autoguidovie (0373 204 524/freephone 800 110 310). Journey time 1hr.

Tourist information

Pro Loco
Via Racchetti 8 (0373 81 020/www.acrema.it/ proloco). **Open** 9.30am-12.30pm Tue-Fri; 9.30am-12.30pm, 3pm-6pm Sat; 10am-noon Sun.

Around Crema

To the east, on the banks of the River Oglio, lies **Soncino**, a rather small town (population 1,088) with a very rich history, quite a lot of it violent. Because it's a natural ford on the River Oglio, people have struggled long and hard to make it theirs. And once they had, they often razed it to the ground – Lombard king Lothar II, Frederick Barbarossa and then the Milanese all sacked it.

In 1329, after many years of domination by Cremona, Soncino came under the aegis of the Visconti of Milan, then the Venetians (1432-48) and finally the Sforzas, who were not going to take any risks. In 1473, Galeazzo Maria Sforza built the **Rocca** (fortress).

Attached to the church of **San Giacomo** (via IV Novembre, open 9-11.30am, 3-6pm daily) is a rare seven-sided tower. The lean is the consequence of an earthquake in 1802. Via IV Novembre leads to the town's southern gate, some ten minutes' walk from which, in via Fontane Sante, is the church of **Santa Maria delle Grazie** (open 10am-12.30pm, 2.30-6pm daily, ring the bell next door to be allowed in), a gem of Lombard decoration, with frescoes complementing terracotta and tempera. Giulio Campi is but one of the artists who contributed. Begun in 1492 for the Carmelite order, the church was consecrated in 1528 in the presence of Francesco II Sforza.

The **Museo della Stampa** commemorates an important 15th-century printing works once based here. Started in the late 1400s by the Nathan family who had fled to Italy from Germany, it produced the first Bible to be printed in Hebrew (1488). The museum includes incunabula and old printing presses. As was common practice with immigrants, the Nathans changed their name to that of their new home, in this case, Soncino. The Soncino Press still exists.

While countless places owe their destruction to Frederick Barbarossa, **Castelleone** (about 10 kilometres/6 miles south of Crema on the SS415, direction Cremona) owes its existence to him. When Barbarossa razed nearby Castel Manfredi, the *comune* and the bishop of Cremona decided to build a fortress here instead. All that remains of the fortifications is the 47-metre (157-foot) **Torre Isso**, which is also known as the Torre del Leone or Torrazzo. One kilometre north of town is the brick-built church of **Santa Maria di Bressanoro**. Constructed in the ninth century, and therefore one of the oldest in the area, it was redesigned in Renaissance style in 1461 at the behest of Bianca Maria Visconti. On the wall on your right as you enter, a fresco depicts a multicultural *Last Judgment*, with black Africans and white Italians being resurrected on their respective sides of the Mediterranean.

Twelve kilometres (7.5 miles) south of Castelleone, on the banks of the River Adda, is **Pizzighettone**. Its massive defence system only rivals that of Soncino in terms of bulk. In 1525, after his defeat at Pavia by Emperor Charles V, Francis I of France was imprisoned in the **Torre del Guado**, all that remains of a medieval castle. He was set free a year later and in recognition of the kindness shown him by the local priest, sent a number of gifts, including a cloak, a reliquary, and an altar covering. These can be seen in the 12th-century church of **San Bassiano**, which was rebuilt almost entirely in 1533 and its campanile erected in 1900. The *Crucifixion* fresco is by Bernardino Campi.

Museo della Stampa

Via Lanfranco 6, Soncino (0374 83 171). **Open** *Oct-Mar* 10am-noon Tue-Fri; 10am-noon, 2.30-5.30pm Sat, Sun. *Apr-Sept* 10am-noon Tue-Fri; 10am-12.30pm, 3-7pm Sat, Sun. **Admission** €2.60; €2 concessions. **No credit cards**.

Rocca

Largo Salvini, Soncino (0374 84 883). **Open** *Oct-Mar* 10am-noon Tue-Fri; 10am-noon, 2.30-5.30pm Sat, Sun. *Apr-Sept* 10am-noon Tue-Fri; 10am-noon, 3-7pm Sat, Sun. **Admission** €2.60; €2 concessions. **No credit cards**.

Where to eat & drink

In Soncino, the **Enoteca I Cinque Frati** (via de Baris 11, 0374 85 560, open 7.30pm-2am daily, closed Mon and 2wks Jan-Feb, average €20) is a wine bar with a roaring fire in winter. Nibbles are available to go with your wine.

Getting there & around

By car

Car is by far the best way to explore this region's well-kept byways. *See p283* for information on where to hire a vehicle.

By train

Two trains a day run direct to Pizzighettone from Milan, the 13.15 from Garibaldi, and the 14.20 from Stazione Centrale. Journey time 1hr 10mins. Two trains in the morning run from Cremona to Pizzighettone (20mins).

By bus

The Milan–Crema service run by Autoguidovie (freephone 800 110 310 or 0373 204 524) stops at Soncino. Journey time 1hr. The same company runs a Mon-Sat Crema-Soncino service (30mins).

Tourist information

Gruppo Volontari delle Mura Pizzighettone

Piazza d'Armi (0372 730 333/www.gvm pizzighettone.it). Two-hour guided tours (in Italian) of the walls, towers and dungeons take place at 3pm Sat and 2pm Sun and public holidays. In July and Aug there is also an evening walk (9.30pm). Cost €2.50.

Pro Loco Soncino

Via IV Novembre 14 (0374 84 883/0374 84 499/ www.prolocosoncino.it). **Open** 8.30am-12.30pm Tue-Sat.

Lodi

This small town, originally known as Laus, was a prime ally of the emperor in the wars that waged in medieval Italy. Its current location is actually its second: after it had been razed to the ground by the Milanese for the second time in less than 50 years, Emperor Frederick Barbarossa decided, in 1158, that a new position, rather than a new ally, was called for. Laus Nova was placed on the Colle Eghezzone, a slight slope on the right bank of the River Adda.

The town of Lodi and its province are overwhelmingly agricultural, the speciality being cheese (*see p252* **Say cheese**). Check out the local goodies at the morning market (Tue, Thur, Sat and Sun) in piazza Mercato,

Lakes & Cities

a square that also houses the sumptuous **Palazzo Vescovile** (bishop's palace, 1730), the location of the **Museo Diocesano**.

Piazza della Vittoria (aka piazza del Duomo) has a typically medieval layout, sharing space between the religious and the secular – the **Duomo** and the **Palazzo Comunale** (town hall) respectively.

From piazza della Vittoria, via Incoronata leads to the **Tempio dell'Incoronata**, Lodi's chief treasure; or take a right from the square into corso Umberto I for the **Museo Civico** and the imposing baroque church of **San Filippo** (open 9am-noon Mon-Sat, 9am-1pm Sun).

The continuation of corso Umberto I (corso Adda) leads to the church of **San Francesco**. Started in 1289, its façade provided a model that was later adopted throughout Lombardy. Corso Adda continues to the bridge over the River Adda, where, in 1796, Napoleon routed the Austrians to conquer Italy.

On the corner of via XX Settembre and via Volturno, **Palazzo Mozzanica**, aka Palazzo Mozzanica-Vignati and Palazzo Varesi, (not open to the public) has elaborate Renaissance terracotta decorations.

Napoleon and several monarchs stayed in the baroque **Palazzo Modignani** (not open to the public) on the corner with corso Roma. At the southern end of corso Roma is the church of **Santa Maria delle Grazie** (open 9am-noon, 3-6pm daily). Left incomplete, this church was given a neo-*barocchetto* façade in 1954, based on that of the aforementioned church of San Filippo. Note the funerary chapel of Maria Hadfield Cosway (1760-1838), artist, musician and educator, whose achievements included the creation of a school for girls (the Collegio delle Dame Inglesi) in 1830.

Further down via XX Settembre, turn into via Marsala for the 14th-century church of **Sant'Agnese** (open 8-11.30am daily), a fine example of Lombard Gothic. At the end of via Marsala, turn left into via Garibaldi for the church of **San Lorenzo** (open 9am-noon, 4-6pm daily), a 12th-century structure much revamped over the centuries. This is Lodi's second-oldest church and has some stucco, frescoes and a *St Catherine* by Callisto Piazza. At the end of the street is what remains of Lodi's castle – which is not a lot.

Duomo & Museo Diocesano
Piazza della Vittoria (Duomo 0371 511 341/Museo 0371 410 512). **Open** *Duomo* 7.30am-noon, 3.30-7.30pm daily. *Museo* 3-6pm Sun; by appointment at other times. **Admission** donation of at least €1.
The Duomo, which was begun in 1160, two years after the new city was founded, and finished a century later, is dedicated to Santa Maria Assunta. It underwent a controversial revamp in 1956, when

later accretions inside were hacked away and the building was 'restored' to the way the original Romanesque church may (or may not) have looked. The columns of the entrance porch rest on marble lions believed to come from Lodi Vecchio (*see p256*). The main entrance is 12th century and the rose window 16th century. The bell tower dates from the mid 1500s and is by Callisto Piazza (1500-62).

The Museo Diocesano (entrance from inside the Duomo) has a selection of art and artefacts from a number of churches in the diocese.

Museo Civico
Corso Umberto I 63 (0371 420 369). **Open** *Aug-mid June* 9.30am-12.30pm Sat; 3.30-6.30pm Sun. *End June-July* 9.30-12.30pm Sat; 9.30-12.30pm, 3.30-6.30pm Sun. Closed Aug. **Admission** free.
Of special interest at this museum is the ceramics collection. Lodi has been renowned for its ceramics for many centuries; the industry reached its zenith in the 18th century. See more Lodi ceramics in the Civiche Raccolte d'Arte Applicata in the Castello Sforzesco in Milan (*see p68*).
If you're interested in the origins of the Italian nation, you might want to visit the Risorgimento section, which traces the developments from 10 May 1796, when Napoleon defeated the Austrians at the nearby bridge over the Adda (*see above*), to the third war of Independence.

San Francesco
Piazza San Francesco (0371 420 019). **Open** 6.30am-noon, 4-6.30pm Mon-Sat; 7am-noon, 4-7pm Sun. **Admission** free.
Observing the flat, rectangular brick façade of this 13th-century Gothic church, you might be tempted to think that the builders stopped halfway; you would be right. Inside, the church preserves its original interior to a unique extent. In the third chapel on the left, the Fissiraga Chapel (named after the family who sponsored the construction of the church), are remarkable frescoes of the life of San Bernardino painted in 1477.

Tempio dell'Incoronata
Via dell'Incoronata (0371 56 055). **Open** 9-11.20am Mon, Sat, Sun; 9-11.20am, 3.30-6.30pm Tue-Fri. **Admission** free.
A masterpiece of the Lombard Renaissance, this ornate octagonal church was designed by Giovanni Battagio and built between 1468 and 1469. It contains frescoes by Giovanni and Matteo Dalla Chiesa of Pavia and the Piazza family; and four canvases by Ambrogio da Fossano (il Bergognone), including an *Annunciation* and *Christ Being Presented at The Temple*.

Where to eat

La Quinta
Viale Pavia 76 (0371 35041). **Meals served** noon-2.30pm, 7-10pm Tue-Sat; noon-2.30pm Sun. Closed Aug. **Average** €50. **Credit** AmEx, DC, MC, V.

Fiddling about

Around Lake Garda, they'll tell you that Gasparo da Salò (1540-1609) invented the violin (*see also p214*), while in Bologna they'll say it was a certain Antonio Brensio (1485-1561). But irrespective of where it originated, violin-making reached its apogee in Cremona, in the workshop of Andrea Amati (c1511-76). Both his sons Antonio and Girolamo (both c1550-1635) and his grandson Nicola – Girolamo's son – (1596-1684), carried on the tradition. Nicola's pupils included Andrea Guarnieri (who established a rival dynasty) and, possibly, the greatest violin-maker of them all, Antonio Stradivari (c1644-1737), who experimented with violin shapes in his search for the perfect pitch. The most famous of the Guarnieri dynasty was Giuseppe (1725-45), the grandson of Andrea. He was generally referred to as Giuseppe or Guarnieri del Gesù. This was because he used the monogram IHS, the first three Greek letters of the name Jesus.

There are several violin collections in Cremona. These are in the **Palazzo del Comune** (*see p247*) and in **Palazzo Fodri** (*see p247*); the **Museo Stradivariano** (*see p248*) is in via Dati. The Cremona tourist office (APT) (*see p250*) will provide a list of violin workshops.

The XI Violin-Making Competition is due to take place in Cremona in 2006, which gives you plenty of time to perfect your craft, if you are so inclined. For more details of this triennial event that, last year, included concerts on the original instruments, see www.entetriennale.com.

The dining-room of this somewhat stuffy sort of place is all exposed roofbeams and bare brick walls. The food is also pleasantly straightforward, with local specialities and fish on the menu. If you can find room for dessert, choose the mouth-watering *sabbiosa al mascarpone*.

Tre Gigli all'Incoronata
Piazza della Vittoria 47 (0371 421 404). **Meals served** 12.30-2pm, 8-9.45pm Tue-Sat; 12.30-2pm Sun. Closed Aug and 1 wk Dec-Jan. **Average** €50. **Credit** AmEx, MC, V.

Lodi's best restaurant has an excellent location in the main square and a relaxed family atmosphere. Great fish in the summer.

Volpi
Via Indipendenza 34, Nosadello (0373 90 100). **Meals served** noon-2pm, 8-11pm. Closed dinner Sun, all Mon, 2wks Jan & 2wks Aug. **Average** €30. **Credit** AmEx, MC, V.

Twelve kilometres (7.5 miles) north of Lodi, at Nosadello, is this simple family-run *trattoria* serving unpretentious local dishes.

Where to stay

Anelli (viale Vignati 7, 0371 421 354, www.albergoanelli.com, closed 3wks Aug, 2wks Dec-Jan, doubles €115) is a small, family-run hotel conveniently located within walking distance of the city centre. Borrow one of their bicycles to tour the city. Alternatively, stay at the three-star **Europa** (viale Piave 5, 0371 35 215, www.hoteleuropa-lodi.it, closed 3wks Aug, 2wks Dec-Jan, doubles €99).

Getting there

By car
From Milan, take the A1 motorway towards Bologna; exit at Lodi. Journey time 30mins.

By train
Trains to Lodi depart from Milan's Stazione Centrale Lambrate and Rogoredo stations. Journey time 40mins.

By bus
STAR (0371 51011, www.starlodi.it) operates some 20 services daily from Milan's San Donato metro station to Lodi. Journey time 50mins. The Crema–Lodi service is run by Line (0371 44 911, 0373 84 887, www.lineservizi.it).

Tourist information

APT del Lodigiano
Piazza Broletto 4 (0371 421 391/www.apt.lodi.it/ www.rassegnagastronomica.lodi.it). **Open** 9am-12.30pm, 3-6pm Mon-Fri; 9am-1pm Sat. During spring usually also 3-6pm Sat; 9am-1pm Sun.

Around Lodi

Small is beautiful, they say, and the towns around Lodi surely confirm this. **Maccastorna** boasts fewer than 100 inhabitants, but it does have a fortress with crenellated towers and a moat. That's because it is almost on the border with the province of Cremona, and was thus of major strategic importance in military terms for many centuries. These days, the castle is a private residence, and the main activity of the area is farming.

Traces of the area's violent past are all around. In addition to the castle at Sant'Angelo Lodigiano (*see below*), which is surely the largest in the region, there are plenty more fortified places to be glimpsed as you drive around, including the Trecchi castle at **Maleo** and the ones at **Castiglione d'Adda**, **Somaglia**, **Borghetto** and **Camairago**.

There are also plenty of abbeys and churches in the area. The late Romanesque **Abbazia del Cerreto** (0371 72 219, open by appointment) in

the hamlet of **Abbadia Cerreto**, just across the Adda from Lodi, stands in flatlands drained by the Cistercian monks, who took over from the Benedictines in 1135. Also by appointment, one can visit the abbey at **Ospedaletto Lodigiano**, the church of **San Biagio** at **Codogno** – which has paintings by Marco d'Oggiono, Callisto Piazza and Camillo Procaccini – the church of the **Madonna dei Cappuccini** at **Casalpusterlengo**, as well as the sanctuaries of the **Madonna della Costa** at **Cavenago d'Adda** and the **Mater Amabilis** at **Ossago**.

With so many small towns, and so few monuments open to the public, a car is the only viable way of touring this area.

With just 6,000 inhabitants to modern-day Lodi's 42,000, **Lodi Vecchio** is worth seeing just 'for old times' sake'. The **Basilica of San Bassiano** was apparently founded in the fourth century by Bassiano himself, who was the local bishop at the time. The church was rebuilt in Gothic style between 1320 and 1323 and restored in 1960. See the animals and stylised vegetation on the 11th-century capitals.

Sant'Angelo Lodigiano is 13 kilometres (eight miles) south-west of Lodi, on the banks of the river Lambro. As with Soncino (*see p252*), its strategic location means fortifications. However, in this case, **Castello Bolognini** (0371 211 140, www.castellobolognini.it, 8.30am-12.30pm, 2-6pm Tue-Sun) was built in 1224 not to defend Lodi, but to make it easier for the Milanese, long-time foes of Lodi, to attack it.

If you're all 'towned out', you might enjoy a visit to the **Parco Regionale Adda Sud**, a regional park set up in the 1980s with the aim of protecting the river environment, the few remaining stretches of undrained wetlands and the unique flora and fauna (over 200 species of bird have been counted here).

Parco Regionale Adda Sud
Via A Grandi 6, Lodi (0371 45 081/www.parco addasud.lombardia.it). **Open** *Office* 9am-12.30pm, 2pm-5pm Mon; 9am-12.30pm, 2-4pm Tue-Fri.

Where to stay

Cascina Fraccina (località Spino d'Adda, 0373 965 166, www.fraccina.it, closed Jan, Feb & Aug, apartments €180 per weekend) is an *agriturismo* in a 16th-century farmhouse. It is a good base for exploring the Parco Adda Sud.

Getting there and around

By bus
For Sant'Angelo Lodigiano, take the STAR (0371 51011, www.starlodi.it) Lodi–Pavia service. Line (0371 44 911, www.lineservizi.it) operates services to Lodi Vecchio (Mon-Sat).

Pavia & Around

A big-name past, a near-perfect piazza and a plethora of paddy fields.

Unassuming, understated Pavia is a pretty important place that has attracted a number of important people over the years. The Lombards made it their capital in AD 572, then Charlemagne was crowned in the cathedral in 774, as was Frederick Barbarossa (*see p10*) in 1155. Saint Augustine (the one who wrote the *Confessions*) came here in AD 722, though truth be told he had little say in the matter – it was his remains that were transported here from Hippo (modern-day Annaba, in Algeria), where he'd died in AD 430, to be interred in the church of San Pietro in Ciel d'Oro (*see p258*). Boethius, the Roman poet, statesman, and philosopher, was executed in Pavia for treason in AD 524.

Some of these folks treated the town less than ceremoniously. Charlemagne took it by storm; marauding Hungarians destroyed no fewer than 43 of its churches; and two German emperors sacked it to within an inch of its life. Napoleon also pillaged Pavia and, because resistance from locals had put his nose out of joint, was minded to destroy it completely, leaving just a column to commemorate the fact. He did not, however – which was very nice of him, and very nice for us, because Pavia is well worth visiting.

Pavia

Pavia is laid out as a typical Roman *castra* (settlement), which it was from about 220 BC when it was known as Ticinum. The layout consists of two axes: the *decumanus*, which ran east–west (today's via Cavour and corso Mazzini), and the *cardus* (north–south, the Strada Nuova). The two intersect at piazza della Vittoria, where you will find the 12th-century town hall, or **Broletto** (closed to the public), which was reconstructed in the 19th century and is the largest in Lombardy. Also here is the **Duomo** (open 7.30am-noon, 3-7pm daily). Started in 1488, and involving the efforts of Cristoforo Rocchi and local boy Giovanni Antonio Amadeo, as well as Bramante and perhaps Leonardo da Vinci, it remains unfinished to this day. The octagonal cupola was added in 1884, and the façade is from 1933. In 1989, the **Torre Civica**, an 11th-century structure remodelled in 1583 as the bell tower for the Duomo, collapsed without warning, killing five people. A pile of masonry to the left of the Duomo marks the spot.

Between the Duomo and the river is the medieval heart of the city, with narrow cobbled streets and ancient buildings. The brick-built

Lakes & Cities

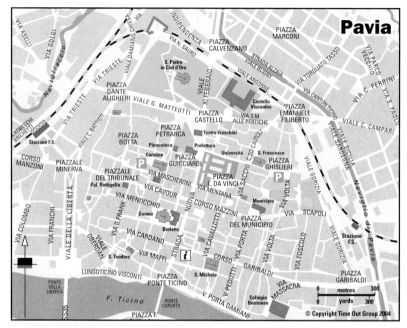

12th-century Romanesque basilica of **San Teodoro** (piazza San Teodoro, 0382 538 110, open 7.30am-noon, 3-7pm daily) has an octagonal cupola-tower. On the west wall are highly detailed frescoes, by Bernardino Lanzani, of the town as it was in 1522. Though only five survive, they help you see why Pavia was known as the 'city of the hundred towers'. The frescoes also show the **Ponte Coperto**. Built in the early 1350s, the bridge was covered in 1583. The one that now crosses the Ticino is not the original, and isn't even in the same place; the original collapsed in 1947 and was rebuilt further downstream.

On the other side of the river the fishing village of **Borgo Ticino** is a pretty place to stop for lunch at a riverside *osteria*.

Back on the north side of the bridge, at the end of via Capsoni stands the basilica of **San Michele Maggiore** (piazza San Michele, 0382 26 063, open 7.30am-noon, 3-7pm daily). Founded in AD 661, it was rebuilt in the 12th century after it was either struck by lightning or damaged in an earthquake (there is no consensus). It was here that Charlemagne celebrated his defeat of the Lombards and assumed the crown of Italy. Unfortunately, the soft sandstone that gives San Michele its lovely honey colour also means that the creatures that adorn its façade have been somewhat eroded.

Further north along the Strada Nuova stands the **Università di Pavia**. Established in 1361, it is one of the oldest European schools of law and medicine. The cloistered courtyards (open 7am-8pm daily) are lined with busts and statues of the institute's alumni. Among these is Alessandro Volta, inventor of the battery (*see p204*) and the man after whom the volt is named.

At the northern end of the Strada Nuova is the **Castello Visconteo**, which houses the **Museo Civico**. This was built by Galeazzo II Visconti (1320-78) between 1360 and 1365, as both a fortified house and an elegant residence. The frescoes in the Sala Azzurra testify to the owner's taste and wealth – note the extensive use of gold leaf and lapis lazuli. A patron of the arts, Galeazzo II also founded the university, as well as laid the foundations for the library or **Libreria Viscontea**. His son Gian Galeazzo Visconti succeeded him and built the Certosa di Pavia.

East of the castle, in the pedestrianised zone, stands the lovely basilica of **San Pietro in Ciel d'Oro** (piazza San Pietro in Ciel d'Oro 2, 0382 303 036, open 7.30am-noon, 3-7pm daily). 'St Peter in the golden sky' was founded in the first half of the seventh century and rebuilt in 1132 in its present glory (though without the gilded vault from which it takes its name). The mortal remains of three unlikely bedfellows rest here. First is St Augustine (345-430). The beautiful marble structure over the main altar is known as the Arca di Sant'Agostino and was executed in 1362 by the *maestri campionesi*, stonemasons working in the style of the Pisan artist Giovanni di Balduccio. Second is the Lombard king Liutprand, the man responsible for transporting Augustine's bones to Pavia in 722. The third is another would-be unifier: Boethius, who played matchmaker between the Goths and Romans but was ultimately imprisoned and murdered by king Theodoric in 524. While in prison in Pavia he wrote his famous work *De Consolatione Philosophiae*.

The magnificent **Certosa di Pavia** is located nine kilometres (5.5 miles) north of the city centre, on the SS35 (take the Binasco exit off the A7 motorway). In 1393, Gian Galeazzo Visconti started donating land to the Certosini of Siena and, one year later, he nominated Bernardo da Venezia as *ingegnierius generalis*. Progress was less than swift, but this turned out to be no bad thing – at the time innovations from the south were challenging traditional northern architectural styles. Thus the Certosa di Pavia became a record – in stone and fresco-work – of the stylistic shift from Gothic to the Renaissance and on to mannerism.

The monastic complex itself, parts of which are included in the guided tour, is of a standard design, with individual monks' cells laid out around a great cloister. The entrance vestibule contains frescoes of saints by Bernardino Luini. Note also the inscription 'Gra-Car' (*Gratiarium Charusia* or Charterhouse of Grace), which is repeated all over the complex.

Beyond lies the great courtyard and the church's façade, a masterpiece of Lombard Renaissance art completed in the 16th century. The lowest, earliest decorations date from 1473 and were designed by Guiniforte Solari; the portal by Benedetto Briosco dates from 1501.

The second chapel of the left aisle features a polyptych by Perugino (1499), while Bergognone's *St Ambrose with Four Saints* (1490) is in the sixth chapel on the left. Also by Bergognone is the *Crucifixion* (1490) in the fourth chapel of the right aisle. The funerary statues of Ludovico il Moro (*see p261* **The Moor of Vigevano**) and Beatrice d'Este by Cristoforo Solari stand in the transept. The charming small cloister (c1462) with its lively terracotta decorations around columns with elaborate capitals may have been designed by Guiniforte Solari.

Castello Visconteo & Museo Civico
Piazza Castello (0382 33 853/304 816). **Open** *Feb-June* 10am-5.45pm Tue-Sun. *July-Aug* 9am-1.30pm Tue-Sun. *Sept-Nov* 10am-5.45pm Tue-Sun. *Dec-Jan* 9am-1.30pm Tue-Sun. **Admission** €6; free under-18s or over-65s. **No credit cards**.

Natural oasis

Set in the grounds of one of the oldest, most forbidding castles in Europe, the **Oasi di Sant'Alessio** provides a privileged habitat for many of the rarest species of birds of the Po Valley. Among the many species that can be observed here are herons, glossy ibises, hermit ibises, cormorants and storks. In addition to wilderness areas, the Oasi also includes sensitively designed observation sites that let visitors view the birds without disturbing them.

The remit of the Oasi di Sant'Alessio also includes raising endangered species and releasing them back into nature. Among these are flamingoes, avocets, peregrine falcons, and storks. Indeed, it has recently been estimated that all the storks in southern Lombardy and south-eastern Piedmont are direct descendants of those raised at the Oasi di Sant'Alessio in the late 1970s.

Castello di Sant'Alessio
Sant'Alessio con Vialone (0382 94 139/ www.oasisantalessio.com). **Open** *Mid Mar-June, Sept-Oct* 10am-6pm Tue-Sun. *July-Aug* 10am-6pm daily. **Admission** €9; €6 concessions. **No credit cards**.

Getting there
From Pavia, take the *strada provinciale* for Lardirago/Landriano. After about 7km (4.5 miles), look for signs for Sant'Alessio. From the Certosa di Pavia (*see p259*), follow signs to Sant'Alessio (10km/7 miles). From Milan (25km/ 15 miles), take the Tangenziale Ovest and exit at Pavia Val Tidone; at Lardirago take a left to Sant'Alessio.

The archeological and medieval sculpture sections contain artefacts from Gallic, Roman and Lombard Pavia, while the picture gallery has the memorable *Portrait of a Man* by Antonello da Messina, as well as works by Lombard and Venetian masters, including Correggio, Giovanni Bellini, Vincenzo Foppa and Giambattista Tiepolo.

Certosa di Pavia
Via del Monumento 5, Pavia (0382 925 613). **Open** 9-11.30am, 2.30-5pm Tue-Sun. **Admission** free (you can give a donation to the monk taking your guided tour). Buses for the Certosa depart about every 20mins from Pavia bus station (www.asm.pv.it).

Where to eat & drink

Antica Osteria del Previ
Via Milazzo 65 (0382 26 203). **Meals served** 12.30-2pm, 8-11pm Mon-Sat. Closed 2wks Jan, 3wks Aug. **Average** €40. **Credit** MC, V.
Three generations of family recipes ensure that every plate here is tied to tradition. Ingredients are seasonal and local, and the dining room is warm and inviting.

Bar Bordoni
Via Bordoni, at via Mentana 26 (0382 21 652).
Open 7am-7.30pm Mon-Sat. **No credit cards**.
If you speak fluent Italian, come and talk philosophy with the university students who hang out here.

Caffè Janko
Via Riboldi 48 (0382 21 365). **Open** 3.30-7pm Mon; 8am-12.30pm, 3.30-7pm Tue-Sat. Closed 3wks Aug. **No credit cards**.
The golden ceiling here reflects that of San Pietro in Ciel d'Oro (*see p258*) pre-1132. Enjoy a coffee or pick up a bag of chocs. The aromas alone are to die for.

Locanda Vecchia Pavia al Molino
Via al Monumento 5 (0382 925 894). **Meals served** 7.45-10.30pm Mon; 12.30-2.30pm, 7.45-10.30pm Tue-Sat. Closed 2wks Aug, 2wks Jan. **Average** €50. **Credit** AmEx, DC, MC, V.
Originally the mill serving the monastery, this eaterie is part of the Certosa di Pavia complex. It offers delicious local favourites, the speciality being *risotto alla Certosina* (with sturgeon eggs, frogs' legs and river shrimp). Book ahead.

Osteria della Madonna da Peo
Via Cardano 63, at via dei Liguri (0382 302 833).
Meals served 12.30-2pm, 7.45-10pm Mon-Sat. Closed 2wks Aug, 26 Dec-6 Jan. **Average** €20-€30. **Credit** AmEx, DC, MC, V.
Located in a 16th-century wine cellar in the medieval neighbourhood between San Teodoro and the Duomo, this warm, cosy restaurant offers regional specialities such as *risotto con l'osso buco* (marrowbone), as well as home-made pasta. Veggies beware: the menu here leans heavily towards meat dishes.

Where to stay

The Ritz (via dei Longobardi 3, San Genesio ed Uniti, 0382 580 280, www.hotelritzpavia. com, doubles €91) offers more facilities than you would expect for the price. This 70-room hotel is in the village of San Genesio ed Uniti, three kilometres (two miles) from Pavia.

The **Excelsior** (piazzale Stazione 25, 0382 28 596, www.excelsiorpavia.com, doubles €73, excl breakfast) has 35 rooms, and is right across from the station. It's nothing to write home about, but the rooms are pleasant and clean.

Getting there

By car
From Milan, take the A7 motorway southbound; exit at Bereguardo-Gropello.

By train
Many trains on the mainline service to Genova from Milan's Stazione Centrale stop in Pavia (journey time 25mins). The town's main railway station is on piazza Stazione, on the west of the city.

By bus
SILA (02 8954 6132) runs buses every 15 minutes between Milan's Famagosta metro station and Pavia, (6.45am-7.45pm Mon-Sat; very reduced service Sun). The one at 15 and 45 minutes past the hour travels on the motorway (journey time 30mins). The bus stop is adjacent to Pavia's main train station, in via Trieste. The one on the hour or the half-hour makes more stops and heads to the Certosa di Pavia (journey time 1hr).

Getting around

Pavia is best covered on foot. The tourist office (APT) (*see below*) provides a comprehensive list of walking tours around town.

Tourist information

APT del Pavese
Via Filzi 2 (0382 22 156/www.apt.pavia.it/ www.comune.pavia.it). **Open** 8.30am-12.30pm, 2-6pm Mon-Thu; 8.30am-12.30pm, 2-5pm Fri; 8.30am-12.30pm Sat.

Certosa di Pavia.
See p259.

The Moor of Vigevano

As if being the Duke of Milan, creating a brilliant court whose members included Bramante and Leonardo da Vinci, and being involved in a mind-boggling number of military and political intrigues were not enough, Ludovico Sforza – known as il Moro (the Moor) – also found time and energy to dedicate to his birthplace: Vigevano.

The town had been the summer home of the Milan court since the early 1300s, when Luchino Visconti (an antecedent of the film director) started work on turning its castle into a handsome summer residence. Ludovico completed the task, drafting in Bramante to design a number of enhancements. The castle's original purpose had been defeated, anyway, and around its walls a *borgo*, or shanty town, had developed. It consisted of the homes and shops of all kinds of traders and suppliers to the inhabitants inside the *castello*. Ludovico had the *borgo* swept away, and in its place, he put Piazza Ducale, arguably the most beautiful Renaissance piazza of all – 84 columns creating a perfect

symmetry of porticoed arcades. If you want an incomparably romantic place to have a drink at dusk, this is it. Ironic that it should have been provided by one whose CV features murder and mayhem in industrial quantities.

Ludovico's third major achievement in Vigevano lies three kilometres (two miles) south-east of the town. Commissioned in 1486, this is La Sforzesca, a template farm designed by Bramante and built by Guglielmo da Camino, the ducal *ingegnere*. Irrigation schemes were provided by Leonardo da Vinci, who had come to Milan at Ludovico's behest. The farmhouse itself, built around a courtyard with towers at each corner, set the pattern for the typical Lombard *cascina*. To the estate, and later to the area as a whole, Ludovico introduced mulberry trees and the critters that thrive on their fruit – silkworms. Since silk-production is what ultimately provided the wealth that led to Italy's industrialisation and Lombardy's pre-eminence in this field, we can say it's likely Ludovico accomplished more than he ever imagined.

La Lomellina

Named after the town of Lomello (*see p262*), once an ancient Lombard capital, the Lomellina area lies north-east of Pavia, and is bound to the west by the River Sesia, to the south by the River Po and to the east by the River Ticino. Given all this water, it's not surprising that, to the Italians, the Lomellina is synonymous with rice-growing. In spring, the rice fields shimmer as the *arborio, rosa marcheti, ribe* and *carnaroli* varieties grow quietly beneath the surface. It's not all that romantic, though. Watch Giuseppe De Santis' *Riso Amaro* (*Bitter Rice*, 1948), to get some insight into the exploitation of the women who harvested the rice (*le mondine*).

These days the top town in the Lomellina area is **Vigevano**, a place rendered memorable by the Sforza family (*see above* **The Moor of Vigevano**). The **Piazza Ducale**, in particular, is a marvel not to be missed. If it was Ludovico who commissioned additions to the **Castello** – such as the tower (**Torre del Bramante**), the falconery and the stables – it was his son, Francesco II, who made sure they were completed. In 1530, he managed to get pope Clement VII (the one who would not give Henry VIII a divorce) to upgrade Vigevano

to city status, and the church to a cathedral. Two years later, Francesco commissioned Antonio da Lonate to design the **Duomo** (piazza Ducale, open 8am-noon, 3-7pm daily). The death of Francesco II Sforza in 1535 delayed the work, and the Duomo, dedicated to Sant'Ambrogio (Milan's patron saint, *see p7* **St Misbehavin'**), was not completed until 1606. The elliptical baroque façade was added in 1684. The small **museum** (0381 690 370, open 3-6pm Sun, or by appointment, closed Aug, mid Dec-mid Jan, admission €2.30) consists mainly of gifts given by Francesco II Sforza, including Flemish and local tapestries, as well as illuminated codexes.

Thirteen kilometres south-west of Vigevano, is **Mortara**. The **Collegiata di San Lorenzo** (via San Lorenzo, 0384 99 772, open 8am-noon, 3.30-6.30pm daily) is a Gothic construction (1375) with a Romanesque bell tower, all heavily reworked in the 19th century by Alfredo D'Andrade. Inside, the *Madonna del Rosario, Santi e Devoti* by Bernardino Lanino (1578) is worth seeing. More Lanino, as well as a *Saint Michael* by Moncalvo, can be admired in the church of **Santa Croce** (piazza Vittorio Emanuele 5, 0384 98 161). Mortara is also known for its *salame d'oca*, or goose salami, as well as other goose-based products. If you

Vigevano's **Piazza Ducale**. *See p261.*

are interested, check out **La Corte dell'Oca**, a well-stocked deli in via Francesco Sforza 27 (0384 98 397, closed Sun).

Sartirana Lomellina is home to the area's largest **castello** (0384 800 804, open 11am-6pm Sat, Sun, or by appointment). Probably built in the late 14th century and then extended in about 1462, the castle was given by Francesco Sforza to Cicco Simonetta. He had entered the service of the Sforza family in about 1420, but was executed in 1480 by Ludovico il Moro, who was determined to become duke of Milan in place of Gian Galeazzo Sforza, then a minor for whom Simonetta was acting as regent. The castle now houses collections of contemporary silver and gold objects, textiles and graphic art.

In Roman times, **Lomello** was a *mansio*, or staging post, on the road that led from Pavia to Gaul, and from Genoa to the Sempione Pass. Everyone who was anyone had to go through here, and Lomello was fitted out with lodgings to suit all tastes. In Lombard times, Lomello was a local capital on a par with Vigevano (*see p261*); Queen Theodolinda married her second husband Agilulf, the duke of Turin, here in 590.

There are some lovely buildings in the town, including the **castle** (piazza Castello 1, 0381 690 370, open Apr-Oct 2.30-6.30 Sat, Sun), which was rebuilt by Gian Galeazzo Visconti in 1381. Two of the rooms feature 16th-century frescoes, along with some Roman mosaics. Also look at the basilica of **Santa Maria Maggiore**, first built in 1025 over the site of a paleo-Christian chapel, and the fifth- to seventh-century **Battistero di San Giovanni ad Fontes** (via Castrovecchio, 0384 85 542, open Apr-Oct 2.30-6.30 Sat, Sun), which lay buried for centuries below street level and has an oversized full-immersion font. The town's other Romanesque church, **San Michele** (via Cavour 5, 0381 690 370, open 8am-12.30pm, 2.30-7pm daily), houses a chip from the True Cross.

Castello
Piazza Ducale, Vigevano (0381 691 636). **Open** *Winter* 8.30am-6pm Mon-Fri; 8.30am-7pm Sat, Sun. *Summer* 8.30am-7pm Mon-Fri; 8.30am-8pm Sat, Sun. **Admission** free.

Santa Maria Maggiore
Via Castrovecchio, Lomello (0384 85 542). **Open** *Easter-Oct* 9am-noon, 3pm-sunset daily. *Nov-Easter* by appointment. **Admission** free.

Torre del Bramante
Piazza Ducale, Vigevano (0381 691 636). **Open** 11am-noon, 3-4pm Tue-Fri; 10am-12.30pm, 2.30-5.30pm Sun. **Admission** €1.50. **No credit cards**.

Where to eat

In Vigevano, the **Ristorante Marmonti** (via del Popolo 13, 0381 690 968, closed Mon, Aug & 1wk Jan, average €30) excels at both traditional dishes and daring modern interpretations. The restaurant also features an excellent wine list.

In Piazza Ducale, head for **Caffè La Piazza** (0381 691 261, closed Thur). The novelist Italo Calvino apparently did whenever he was in town. A fixed-price menu (€10) is served noon-3pm Mon-Fri; at other times there are sandwiches.

Delectable home-made pastries can be found at **Pasticceria Dante** (via Dante 6, 0381 83 776, and via Madonna Sette Dolori 11, 0381 73 800, both closed Tue and Aug). At the latter location you can also sample delicious ice-creams and lunchtime snacks (average €6).

Getting there & around

By car
The SS494 Milano–Vigevano–Casale Monferrato passes through Mortara.

By train
Trains to Vigevano and Mortara depart from Milan's Porta Genova station. Change at Pavia for Lomello.

By bus

All buses from Pavia to surrounding towns depart from the via Trieste bus station. The STAV company (0381 23 725) runs services from Vigevano to Pavia and Mortara. Cuzzoni Gilona (0382 84 025) operates between Pavia and Lomello.

Tourist information

IAT Pro Loco Vigevano

Corso Vittorio Emanuele 29 (0381 312 624). **Open** 10am-noon, 4-7pm Mon-Fri; 10am-noon, 4-6pm Sat.

Oltrepò Pavese

Situated, as its name says, *oltre il Po*, or beyond the River Po, this area of rolling hills is, if you use a bit of imagination, shaped somewhat like a bunch of grapes. This is fitting, given that it is home to around 500 producers of some very drinkable wine (*see p118* **Vinous delights**).

The fact that you can see hills at all between Milan and the Pianura Padana (or Po Valley) is quite something. And indeed, this is the only part of the Apennine in Lombardy. From these hills, on a clear day, you can see right the way over to Maritime Alps in Piedmont to the west, Monte Cevedale (3,769 metres/12,365 feet) in the Stelvio National Park (*see p270*) to the north and the Apuan Alps (in Tuscany) to the south-west.

The area's main town is **Voghera**, another crossroads, this time on the Milan–Genova and Turin–Piacenza routes. Piazza del Duomo provides the scene for the **Collegiata di San Lorenzo** (0383 43 532, open 8am-noon, 3.30-6.30pm daily). This was built in 1605 by Antonio Maria Corbetta on original 10th-century foundations, but was not completed until 1881. The fresco of the *Madonna del Soccorso* (Our Lady of Succour) dates from 1496 and is the most valuable work of art in the place. The brick church of **Sant'Ilario** (via Tempio Sacrario della Cavalleria, 0383 212 278, open by appointment) – aka Chiesa Rossa, or red church – is a pretty Romanesque structure with a shrine to the Italian cavalry.

South of Voghera, **Salice Terme** (willow-tree spa) has been offering health treatments since Roman times. Indeed, even Julius Caesar checked in here on at least one occasion to recharge his batteries. The scene today is slightly different, consisting of serious water-takers at hospital-like hotels, with the emphasis more on medical treatment than pampering.

At Ponte Nizza, a road forks east towards the village of **Pizzocorno**. Just beyond the village is the abbey of **Sant'Alberto di Butrio** (no phone, eremo.sant.alberto@libero.it, open 7am-noon, 3-7pm daily), a medieval gem built by the noble Malaspina family as thanks to the local cave-dwelling hermit, Alberto, who cured their mute son. Alberto died in 1073 and was canonised six years later. The complex consists of three interconnected churches – Sant'Antonio, Santa Maria Genitrice and Sant'Alberto – the latter containing relics of the saint as well as traces of 15th-century frescoes.

The main road swings east towards **Varzi**, with its low-hanging medieval porticoes, narrow, twisting alleys and looming towers. The **Chiesa dei Cappuccini** (via Cappuccini, 0383 545 221, open 6am-9pm daily) stands guard at the entrance to the village. A Romanesque facelift hides its true age: the church dates from AD 448, when it was dedicated to St Germain. Capuchin monks were its longest-standing tenants, hence the church's name. But, in 1802, it was deconsecrated and rented out to local families as a barn. Fortunately, in 1971 it was restored to its former Romanesque beauty.

Where to shop

The *salame* made in Varzi is a delicacy. Buy some at the **Salumeria Vecchio Varzi** (via Catelleletto 11, 0383 52 283, closed Sat, Sun, Aug).

For sweeter options, try the **Pasticceria Zuffada** (via Lombardia 68, 0383 52 227, closed Mon, 1wk Jul, 1wk Sept). Its speciality is almond cake.

Getting there & around

By car

The SS35 leads from Milan to Pavia and on to Casteggio from where minor roads fan out.

By train

Trains run from Pavia to Voghera every 20mins. There is a direct service from Milan's Stazione Centrale to Voghera; some trains to Genova also stop there.

By bus

The SAPO company (0383 41 268) runs services from Voghera to Salice Terme and Varzi. The STUMP company (0383 365 111) operates a Milan–Pavia–Salice–Ponte Nizza–Stradella–Broni route.

Tourist information

Visit www.oltreweb.it/turismo (Italian only) for itineraries, and ideas on where to eat and where to stay in the Oltrepò Pavese.

IAT Pro Loco Salice Terme

Via Marconi 8 (0383 91 207). **Open** 9am-12.30pm, 2.30-6pm Mon-Sat.

IAT Pro Loco Varzi

Piazza della Fiera (0383 545/www.varziviva.net). **Open** *Apr-Sept* 8am-noon, 4-6pm daily. *Oct-May* 9am-noon daily.

The Mountains

History, art and ski slopes: these Alpine areas are doing it for themselves.

Mountain lovers in Italy usually head for the chic resorts of the Valle d'Aosta, or the spiky peaks of the Dolomites, giving Lombardy's Alpine valleys (Valtellina, Valchiavenna and Valcamonica) short shrift. But adventurous types who venture up here won't regret it. While the mountains in this centre-north region might not be the highest (only one, Pizzo Bernina, is over 4,000 metres/13,000 feet), the area is home to Italy's most difficult ski run (at Madesimo, Valchiavenna), the country's two largest glaciers (*see p267* **End of an ice age?**) and a top-class ski resort (Bormio, which will host the Alpine World Ski Championships in 2005). But you don't have to be a sports fanatic to enjoy the valleys' unrivalled scenery, unique art and architecture – more or less intact, despite some unfortunate resort developments – and hearty mountain fare (*see p268* **Mountain goodies**).

For information on all public transport to and between the locations covered in this chapter, consult the website www.infopoint.it.

Valchiavenna

Valchiavenna's proximity to **Lake Como** (*see p200*) makes it warmer and wetter than its sister valleys. The first part of the valley flanks the River Mera; where the Mera and the Adda river (from neighbouring Valtellina) plunge into the lake lies the **Riserva Naturale del Pian di Spagna e del Lago di Mezzola** (www.parks.it), a protected wetland zone.

From here, the SS36 continues to **Chiavenna**, one of the loveliest towns in the Italian Alps. The earliest road in these parts was built by the canny Romans, who were the first to appreciate the valley's strategic position. Over the following centuries, the coming and going of merchants, pilgrims and travellers gave Chiavenna an international touch that remains today. The town's most important monument is the **Collegiata di San Lorenzo**, a fifth-century complex whose church, baptistery, cloisters and tower were largely rebuilt between 1537 and 1719. Its most jealously guarded artwork, a jewel-studded gold gospel cover known as *La Pace* ('the peace', *see p274* **Hidden treasure**), is housed in the adjoining **Museo del Tesoro di San Lorenzo**. San Lorenzo's other major work –

a Romanesque font sculpted from a single chunk of *pietra ollare* (soapstone) – is tucked away in the baptistery. Carved around this 850-year-old monolith are figures taking part in a baptismal ceremony, including an incense-swinging altar boy, a horseman clutching a falcon and a blacksmith busily bashing away at his anvil.

The locally crafted, grey-green *pietra ollare* stonework on doorways, portals and fountains along via Pedretti and via Dolzino testifies to the large number of stonemasons in previous centuries, but it's a tradition that is dying out.

At Chiavenna, the SS37 forks east from the SS36 towards **Prosto di Piuro** and the hamlet of **Cortinaccio**, where the noble **Palazzo Vertemate Franchi** was the only building to survive the landslide that buried this wealthy area and its 1,000 inhabitants in 1618. The 16th-century interior contains some of the region's best Renaissance frescoes, including those in the Salone dello Zodiaco inspired by Ovid's *Metamorphoses*, and two 17th-century paintings showing what Piuro looked like before and after the landslide. The garden has orchards, chestnut trees and a vineyard.

North from Chiavenna, the SS36 winds up through some wild, steep mountainside to the ski resort of **Madesimo** (*see p272* **Sloping off**) and the **Spluga Pass** (2,113m/7,050ft) to Switzerland.

Collegiata di San Lorenzo
Piazza Bormetti 3, Chiavenna (0343 37 152). **Open** 7.30-11.45am, 2-6pm daily. *Baptistery* times vary. **Admission** free.

Museo del Tesoro di San Lorenzo
Piazza Bormetti 3, Chiavenna (0343 37 152). **Open** *Mar-Oct* 3-6pm Tue-Fri, Sun; 10am-noon, 3-6pm Sat. *Nov-Feb* 2-4pm Tue-Fri; 10am-noon, 2-4pm Sat; 2-5pm Sun. **Admission** €3.10. **No credit cards**.

Palazzo Vertemate Franchi
Località Prosto-Cortinaccio (0343 36 384). **Open** 10am-noon, 2.30-5.30pm Mon, Tue, Thur-Sun. Closed Nov-Feb. **Admission** €5, €3 concessions (includes guided tour). **No credit cards**.

Where to stay, eat & shop

Chiavenna is best known for its *crotti* – cavities formed during ancient landslides with a steady air flow that makes them perfect larders. Over time, many have morphed into gastronomic treasure troves, complete with a shop and *osteria*. Among the best to visit is **Crotto Crotasc** (via Don Lucchinetti 63, 0343 41 003, closed Mon & Tue, 2wks June, average €30), in Mese, two kilometres (1.25 miles) outside Chiavenna.

If you are celebrating a special occasion, head along the SS37 to Villa di Chiavenna, where **Lanterna Verde** (via San Barnaba 7, 0343 38 588, closed lunch Wed & Thur, 2wks June, 2wks Nov, average €40) is the only restaurant in the Sondrio province with a Michelin star.

Back in Chiavenna, stay at the recently opened **Palazzo Salis** (piazza Castello, 0343 32 283, closed Jan & Feb, doubles €100), a centrally located 17th-century villa housing one of Italy's most glamorous B&Bs.

The valley's ancient *pietra ollare* stone-carving tradition rests exclusively in the hands of artisan **Roberto Lucchinetti** in Prosto di Piuro (via alla Chiesa 5, 0343 35 905, call for appointment). Lucchinetti's traditional stone cooking pans (*laveggi*) are coveted by chefs everywhere. His wife sells hand-grown and woven linen in the workshop next door.

Valtellina: how do you like them apples?

Getting there

By car
From piazzale Lagosta, in the north of Milan, head out along viale Zara. This road eventually becomes the SS36. Follow signs for the superstrada Ai Laghi, then Lago di Como. Continue along the eastern shore of Lake Como and on to Chiavenna (journey time around 1hr 40mins).

By train
Local services run from Milan's Stazione Centrale to Colico, Sondrio or Tirano; change at Colico for Chiavenna. Journey time to Chiavenna is 2hrs 40mins.

Getting around

By car
The main road links in Valchiavenna are the SS36 and the SS37, which passes through Piuro.

By train & bus
Although it's easier to get around by car, trains can be much quicker in heavily trafficked periods (Sun evenings, holidays). Trains go no further north than Chiavenna. The Società Trasporto Pubblico Sondrio (STPS) (0343 33 442) runs buses from Chiavenna to Madesimo, Samolaco, Villa di Chiavenna and Sondrio.

Tourist information

APT Chiavenna
Corso Vittorio Emanuele II 2 (0343 36 384/www. valtellinaonline.com). **Open** *July-Aug* 9am-12.30pm, 3-6.30pm Mon-Sat; 9am-12.30pm Sun. *Sept-June* 9am-12.30pm, 2.30-6pm Mon-Sat; 9am-12.30pm Sun.

APT Madesimo
Via alle Scuole (0343 57 039/www.madesimo.com). **Open** *May-mid June, Sept-Nov* 9am-12.30pm, 2.30-6pm Mon-Sat; 9.30am-12.30pm Sun. *Mid June-Aug* 9am-12.30pm, 3-7pm Mon-Sat; 9am-12.30pm, 4-6pm Sun. *Dec-Apr* 9am-12.30pm, 3-6.30pm Mon-Sat; 9am-12.30pm, 4-6pm Sun.

Valtellina

'The Valtellina,' wrote Leonardo da Vinci in the 1480s, 'is a valley surrounded by lofty and terrible mountains; it produces a great quantity of strong wine, and has so great a stock of cattle that the peasants say that it produces more milk than wine.'

While the valley bottom, dominated by the River Adda, is now splattered with patches of ugly development, Leonardo's description still holds true for the upper reaches of Valtellina. Its east–west direction has created two contrasting microclimates: the south-facing Alpi Retiche are covered with vineyards and apple orchards and dotted with ancient stone villages, churches and castles. The north-facing Orobie chain is wilder – snow sticks around for longer here, and there are forests and pastures where small herds of Alpine dairy cattle graze. The **Parco Regionale delle Orobie Valtellinesi** (0342 211 236) protects the slopes above 1,000 metres (3,500 feet).

Valtellina's strategic position explains its chequered history. Celts, Romans, Lombards, Franks, Milan's Visconti and Sforza families,

Swiss Grigioni, French, Spaniards and Austrians have all held sway here, each leaving their mark in historical structures. Because of its proximity to Switzerland, Valtellina also has a long history of Protestant/Catholic struggles.

Getting there

By car

From piazzale Lagosta, in the north of Milan, head out along viale Zara. This road eventually becomes the SS36. Follow signs for the superstrada Ai Laghi, then Lago di Como and Lecco. Keep on the eastern shore of Lake Como; after Colico take the SS38, which runs the length of the Valtellina and over the Stelvio Pass (open May-Nov, snow permitting). Journey time to Morbegno is 1hr 20mins.

By train

Trains run from Milan's Stazione Centrale to Sondrio or Tirano every couple of hours. Journey time to Sondrio is 2hrs; to Tirano, 2hrs 30mins.

Getting around

By car

A car is the best way of exploring the Valtellina. The main route is the two-lane SS38, but the panoramic drives from Monastero to Sondrio, and from Sondrio to Tirano are a slower, pleasurable alternative. For routes that wind between the vineyards, see www.valtellinavini.com.

By train

FS (state railway) trains go as far as Tirano. From here, a small scenic railway, the Bernina Express (0342 701 353), winds its way into Switzerland and St Moritz, with views of the Morteratsch Glacier and the Bernina chain. Journey time 2hrs 20mins.

By bus

Buses meet trains to link Tirano to Bormio and Livigno. An extensive, if somewhat irregular, network connects most towns in the valley.

Bassa Valtellina

Morbegno (alt 248m/814ft) is a bustling place with a sprawling modern zone. Impressive churches and palazzi in the old centre reflect this strategically placed town's former importance. Sadly, many of these buildings are now much the worse for wear. The **Palazzo Malacrida** (via Malacrida 6, 0342 606 211 or 601 140, open by appointment) is the valley's best example of 18th-century rococo, with frescoes by Valtellinese artist Cesare Ligari (1716-70). On via Garibaldi, baroque palazzi with wrought-iron balconies and frescoes now house alternative boutiques, antique and food shops, and cafés.

From Morbegno, the SS405 heads south along **Valgerola**, one of Valtellina's most unspoilt valleys, where *bitto* cheese (*see p268*

Mountain goodies) is made. In the village of **Sacco**, the mythical *uomo selvatico* (wild man) – a hairy, bearded figure wielding a vicious-looking club – is portrayed in a rare 15th-century fresco in the **Museo dell'Homo Salvadego** (località Sacco, 0342 617 028, open by appointment). Also at Sacco is the **Museo Vanseraf** (località Rasura, 0342 610 460/www. museovanseraf.com, open by appointment), a small museum of peasant culture in a working flour mill. But this tiny hamlet's main claim to fame is being the birthplace of 15th-century female goatherd-turned-mercenary Bona Lombarda. Inside the church is a peeling 17th-century portrait of the feisty lady (ask Signor Vaninetti, the Homo Salvadego museum guide, to let you in).

East of Morbegno, on the SS38, is the turn-off for Valmasino and Valle di Mello. These two valleys are a paradise for mountain climbers, containing the Pizzo Badile (3,308m/11,026ft), Pizzo Cengalo (3,367m/11,223ft) and Monte Disgrazia (3,678m/12,260ft).

Where to stay, eat & shop

Morbegno's best restaurant is the **Vecchio Ristorante Fiume** (contrada di Cima alle Case 1, 0342 610 248, average €35), though locals also recommend the **Antica Osteria Rapella** (via Margna 36, 0342 610 377, average €24).

The **Hotel Trieste** is located in a converted stable block in the centre (via San Rocco 3/5, 0342 610 259, doubles €56).

In Morbegno, visit the fabulous **Fratelli Ciapponi** gourmet store (piazza 3 Novembre 23, 0342 610 223, closed lunch Mon, all Sun), where most of Valgerola's *bitto* cheese ends up. Don't miss the 500-year-old cheese cellars beneath the main shop.

Tourist information

Consorzio Turistico Porte di Valtellina

Piazza Bossi 7/8, Morbegno (0342 601 140/www. portedivaltellina.it). Open Sept-July 9am-12.30pm, 2-6pm Mon-Fri; 9am-noon Sat. Aug 9am-12.30pm, 2-6pm Mon-Fri; 9am-noon Sat, Sun.

Media Valtellina

Sondrio (alt 307m/1,023ft) is Italy's second-least-populated provincial capital; its territories encompass Valchiavenna and Valtellina. The town's main square, piazza Garibaldi, is dominated by a statue of the seemingly ubiquitous Italian hero (yes, he spent the night here too, at via del Gesù 7). The 16th-century **Palazzo Pretorio** (closed to the public) is in

End of an ice age?

Valtellina and Valcamonica may be home to Italy's two largest glacial complexes – but if the experts are right, these several-thousand-year-old snow deposits could disappear soon.

The biggest of all is the Adamello complex, a massive glacier plus offshoots at the northern tip of Valcamonica, whose surface measures more than 18 square kilometres (seven square miles). Equally dramatic is the 13-square-kilometre (five-square-mile) block known, inappropriately, as Dei Forni (from the ovens), which runs along the semi-circular Ortlès-Cevedale range that marks the end of Valtellina.

If you're keen to see them, you may have to get a move on. Alpine glaciers have lost an average of 14 metres (46 feet) of ice since the 1960s, including more than three metres (10 feet) in the hot summer of 2003. The glaciers of Valtellina and Valcamonica are no exception: the Dei Forni glacier has retreated over two kilometres (1.25 miles) in the past 150 years. If the melt-down continues at current rates, the WWF says the glaciers could become giant puddles within a matter of decades.

A network of *rifugi* (remote Alpine hostels, usually providing accommodation in shared dormitories) makes the Dei Forni complex easy to visit. Among the most dramatic is the **Rifugio Branca** (Valle dei Forni, Valfurva, 0342 935 501/0342 935 350, closed Oct-mid March & mid May-June, from 36 per person), right at the glacier's foot. The Rifugio is an hour's uphill hike from the **Rifugio Ghiacciaio dei Forni** (Località Forni, Valfurva, 0342 935 365/0343 901 916/www.forni 2000.com, closed Nov-mid March, from 34 per person), which is situated six kilometres from Santa Caterina Valfurva on the road to Valle dei Forni. At times, this road is closed to traffic; jeeps run a shuttle service up and down it for a small fee. If you want to walk on the glacier, take proper equipment and a guide (ask at the Rifugio before you go).

If exercise isn't your thing, take the Bernina train from Tirano to St Moritz and admire the Morteratsch glacier (in Switzerland, but a hop, skip and a jump from the Italian border) from the comfort of your carriage. Those who feel up to it can get off at the Morteratsch stop, and follow a gentle pathway that shows the glacier's retreat over the past decades.

piazza Campello. In the same square is Sondrio's main church, the **Collegiata dei Santi Gervasio e Protasio**, based on 18th-century plans by Pietro Ligari, but completed by Swiss architect Pietro Taglioretti after Ligari fell out with the powers that be. Close by is the **Museo Valtellinese di Storia e Arte**, with works by the Ligari family. The museum also has some interesting pieces by female artists, including sketches by Pietro Ligari's daughter, Vittoria, and a portrait attributed to the Swiss artist Angelika Kaufmann. Sondrio's central shopping streets – the pedestrian-only via Dante and via Beccaria – are lined with some great little fashion, food and flower shops.

The road to **Valmalenco** leads north from Sondrio. Most people head up this valley to admire, walk, hike, ski (*see p272* **Sloping off**) or climb on the spectacular Bernina group, capped by Valtellina's highest peak, Pizzo Bernina (4,049m/13,496ft). Rock freaks can admire some of the 261 types of mineral from the valley in the church of **Santi Giacomo e Filippo** attached to the Museo della Valmalenco, in the hamlet of **Chiesa in Valmalenco** (for information, call APT Chiesa in Valmalenco; *see p269*).

From Sondrio, the SS38 continues east to Tirano. Running more or less parallel is the aptly named Strada Panoramica, a more winding alternative, passing vineyards and orchards. Pick up this road (signposted to Montagna) before Sondrio hospital, east of the town centre.

At **Montagna** (alt 567m/1,890ft), the ruined 14th-century **Castel Grumello** has been recently restored by the FAI (Italy's equivalent of the National Trust).

Ponte in Valtellina (alt 485m/1,616ft) is one of the best-preserved medieval/Renaissance towns in the Alps. Its principal monument is the church of **San Maurizio** in piazza Luini (0342 482 158, open by appointment), a combination of Romanesque, Gothic and Renaissance styles, and containing a 16th-century fresco, *Madonna and Child with San Maurizio*, by Bernardino Luini.

Teglio (alt 851m/2,837ft) is home to **Palazzo Besta** (1433), Valtellina's most important Renaissance residence. Its courtyard contains frescoes of scenes from Virgil's *Aeneid*.

At Tresenda is the turn-off (SS39) for **Aprica** (alt 1,172m/3,907ft) and the pass to Valcamonica. Hurriedly constructed in the 1960s, '70s and '80s, Aprica is not the classiest of the valley's resorts (*see p272* **Sloping off**),

Mountain goodies

Like most Italian regions, Valtellina has a gourmet tradition all of its own. A typical meal may begin with a platter of sliced **bresaola** – the locally produced salt-dried beef – and end with a chunk of **bitto**, a prestigious cheese made from 90 per cent cow's milk and ten per cent goat's milk in the pristine ValGerola, perhaps served with a wedge of rye bread and some rare rhododendron honey.

In between, you may be offered **pizzoccheri** (buckwheat noodles served with potatoes, greens, melted *casera* cheese and lashings of melted butter) or **sciatt** (deep-fried buckwheat batter cheeseballs).

Connoisseurs wash this down with the valley's red wine (the best-known cellar is Nino Negri, *see p269*) and a final swill of **braulio**, a medicinal-tasting, alcoholic *amaro* (after-dinner drink), made from mountain herbs, roots and berries in Bormio (*see p269*).

but its splendid position – wedged on a sunny pass between Valtellina and Valcamonica – makes it a good base for sporty types and walkers. The **Osservatorio Eco-Faunistico Alpino** (0342 746 113, admission €10) offers the opportunity for some wildlife spotting.

The SS38 continues to the market town of **Tirano** (alt 441m/1,470ft), home to one of the valley's most successful baroque constructions, the **Basilica della Madonna di Tirano** (piazza Basilica, opening times vary, call the UIT Tirano for information, *see p269*). The highlight is its 17th-century hand-carved organ sound box, festooned with flowers, fruit and religious scenes, and containing 2,200 pipes, played during 11am mass each Sunday. Nearby is the **Museo Etnografico Tiranese**, with well-organised displays of rural tools.

Just before **Grosio** (alt 653m/2,177ft) on the SS38 is an entrance to the **Parco delle Incisioni Rupestri** (guided tours 0342 847 454), containing the **Rupe Magna**, the most engraved rock in the Alps, with over 5,500 prehistoric carvings. Also in the park are the ruins of two medieval castles, the newly restored **Castello Vecchio** and the **Castello Nuovo**, both of which you can wander round.

Castel Grumello
Località Montagna (0342 380 994). **Open** 10am-6pm daily. Closed Jan, 3wks June/July. **Admission** €1.50 (voluntary contribution). **No credit cards.**

Collegiata dei Santi Gervasio e Protasio
Piazza Campello, Sondrio (0342 514 510). **Open** 7am-noon, 3-7pm daily. **Admission** free.

Museo Etnografico Tiranese
Piazza Basilica 30, Tirano (0342 701 181). **Open** *June-Sept* 10am-noon, 3.30-6.30pm Tue-Sun. *Oct-May* 10am-noon, 2.30-5.30pm Sat; or by appointment. **Admission** €2. **No credit cards.**

Museo Valtellinese di Storia e Arte
Palazzo Sassi de' Lavizzari, via Quadrio 27, Sondrio (0342 526 269). **Open** *June-mid Sept* 10am-noon, 3-6pm Tue-Sat. *Mid Sept-May* 9am-noon, 3-5pm Tue-Sat. **Admission** €4. **No credit cards.**

Palazzo Besta
Via Besta 7, Teglio (0342 781 208). **Open** *May-Sept* 9am-noon, 2-5pm Tue-Sat; 8am-2pm 1st, 3rd & 5th Sun of mth, 2nd, 4th Mon of mth. *Oct-Apr* 8am-2pm Tue-Sat, 1st & 3rd Sun of mth, 2nd & 4th Mon of mth. **Admission** €2. **No credit cards.**

Where to eat & drink

In Sondrio, the **Terra di Mezzo** serves no-frills pizzas and pasta dishes to a young crowd (via Bonfadini 14/16, 0342 212 902, closed Wed, average €12).

As befits a route that winds through vineyards, the Strada Panoramica (*see p267*) offers plentiful opportunities to eat and drink. At Montagna is the **Ristoro Castel Grumello** (0342 380 994, closed dinner Sun, all Mon, 3wks Jan & 3wks June-July, average €30), a stylish restaurant at the foot of the ruined castle, serving freshly prepared, unusual dishes. At Tresivio is the not-to-be-missed **Jom-Bar** (via Chioso 42, 0342 430 609, closed lunchtimes and Mon), an old stone house with quirky furnishings, a 3,000-strong cocktail list, 250 wine labels and jazz. From 6pm until 9pm, the bar is laden with free snacks, and cocktails are half price (€5).

At Ponte in Valtellina, the **Ristorante Cerere** (via Guicciardi 7, 0342 482 294, closed Wed, 2wks Jan & 3wks July, average €30) serves local dishes in a refined, traditional interior, while the rougher-and-readier **Osteria Sole** (via Sant'Ignazio 11, 0342 565 298, closed dinner Mon, all Tue, 1wk Mar, 1wk July & 2wks Sept, average €17) dishes up platters of steaming *pizzoccheri* and *sciatt* (*see above* **Mountain goodies**).

Where to shop

In Sondrio, **Vel: La Libreria del Viaggiatore** (via Angelo Custode 3, 0342 218 952/www. vel.it, closed Mon, Sun) offers a vast array of informative travel books in English and Italian.

At Lanzada in Valmalenco, Valtellina's most respected bee-keeper, **Walter Nana** (via Spini 316, 0342 453 053), sells his delicious honey, liqueurs and own-brand cosmetics. At Ponte in Valtellina is **Pezzotti della Valtellina** (via Nazionale 2, 0342 482 232), which sells Valtellina's traditional, multicoloured rag rugs (*pezzotti*), while further along the SS38, at Chiuro, is the ski and knitwear factory outlet **Samas** (*see p272* **Sloping off**). Also at Chiuro is Valtellina's most prestigious vineyard, **Nino Negri** (via Ghibellini 3, 0342 485 211, closed Sat, Sun), where you can buy directly from the cellar's store. In Tirano, the **Erboristeria Helleboro** (viale Italia 77, 0342 701 067) sells beauty products and natural remedies made from Alpine and other herbs.

On a winding track off the SS39 just west of Aprica, local character Luigi della Moretta makes fresh goat's cheese at **Li Spondi** (via Sponde, 338 565 6112 mobile). Get there after 5pm; Luigi doubles as the village bus driver.

Where to stay

Sondrio's poshest hotel is the 165-year-old **Hotel della Posta** (piazza Garibaldi 19, 0342 510 404, doubles €110). It also has a well-known restaurant (closed Sun, 3wks Jul-Aug, average €25).

In the old centre of Tirano is the friendly **Casa Mia** (via Arcari 6, 0342 705 300, doubles €40-€62), a B&B offering three clean rooms and abundant breakfasts.

Tourist information

APT Valtellina
Via Trieste 12, Sondrio (0342 512 500/www.apt valtellina.it/www.valtellinaonline.com). **Open** 9am-12.30pm, 2.30-6pm Mon-Fri.

APT Aprica
Corso Roma 150 (0342 746 113/www.apricaonline. com). **Open** *Apr-June, Sept-Nov* 9am-12.30pm, 2.30-6pm Mon-Sat; 9.30am-12.30pm Sun. *July, Aug* 9am-12.30pm, 3-7pm Mon-Sat; 9am-12.30pm, 4-6pm Sun. *Dec-Mar* 9am-12.30pm, 3-6.30pm Mon-Sat; 9am-12.30pm, 4-6pm Sun.

APT Chiesa in Valmalenco
Piazza San Giacomo e Filippo (0342 451 150/www. valmalenco.it). **Open** *Apr-June, mid Sept-Nov* 9am-12.30pm, 2.30-6pm Mon-Sat; 9am-12.30pm Sun. *July-mid Sept* 9am-12.30pm, 3-7pm Mon-Sat; 9am-12.30pm, 4-6pm Sun. *Dec-Apr* 9am-12.30pm, 3-6.30pm daily.

UIT Tirano
Piazza Stazione (0342 706 066/www.prolocotirano. it). **Open** *Mid June-mid Sept* 9am-6pm Mon-Sat; 9am-1pm, 2-5pm Sun. *Mid Sept-mid June* 9.30am-12.30pm, 2-5pm Mon-Sat; 10am-12.30pm Sun.

Alta Valtellina

Bormio (alt 1,225m/4,083ft) has it all. One of the oldest settlements in the valley, it boasts a well-preserved centre and an impossibly scenic position at the foot of the Ortlès-Cevedale range. Bursting with hotels, restaurants and sporting facilities – not to mention a Roman spa – it is fast becoming a favourite haunt for Milan's fashion set, though this doesn't mean ordinary mortals can't join in the fun too. The 2005 Alpine World Skiing Championships are expected to give this buzzing town a further boost.

Bagni Vecchi Bormio. *See p270.*

Bormio's most imposing church is the baroque **Santi Gervasio e Protasio** (piazza Cavour, open 8am-noon, 3-6pm daily), with its candy-pink striped spire. Across the piazza from the church is the squat **Kuèrc**, a 14th-century building with a slate-tiled roof and cut-away walls, that served as a court of justice. Just off the via Buon Consiglio is the **Museo Civico**, where highlights include ancient wooden skis and reconstructions of a carpenter's and a cobbler's workshop.

Across the bridge at the end of via Morcelli is the rustic **Combo** neighbourhood. At via Sant'Antonio 3 is **Casa Settomini**, Bormio's most photographed house with roof-props and beams carved like twisted ropes. Nearby, the house at via Zuccola 5 has an external 15th-century fresco of the Madonna and Child attended by angels. The heart of Combo is the church of **Santo Crocefisso** (piazza del Crocefisso, open 8am-noon, 2-6pm daily), which contains a gruesome 16th-century crucifix, said to have healing and miraculous powers.

The recently restored **Bagni Vecchi Bormio** (0342 910 131, admission €30-€32) is three kilometres (two miles) north of town on the SS38. This Roman spa complex has waters flowing from nine hot springs at temperatures of 36°C-43°C; it includes a long, hot-water tunnel carved from a cave, hot waterfalls, a natural steam bath and an outdoor thermal pool with spectacular views of the surrounding Alps, and offers around a dozen beauty and relaxation treatments. A second five-star hotel opened in the spa complex in December 2003, adding new attractions – including a more modern Turkish bath, waterfalls and a pool. Both spas are open to non-hotel guests.

The SS38 continues to the Stelvio Pass and the **Parco Nazionale dello Stelvio** (0342 910 100, www.stelviopark.it), one of Italy's largest protected natural areas, covering 1,340 square kilometres (517 square miles) in the Lombardy and Trentino-Alto Adige regions. The park contains the entire Ortlès-Cevedale massif, one of Italy's largest glacial complexes (*see p267* **End of an ice age?**), as well as countless plant species and a huge variety of mammals and birds. A visitors' centre (via Roma 26, Bormio, 0342 910 100, www.stelviopark.it) dispenses information and maps.

The SS301 branches off the SS38 just north of Bormio, and leads to Livigno (alt 1,816m/6,053ft). Until 1951, when its access road first became open all year round, **Livigno** was completely cut off for nine months of the year and going there still feels like driving to the edge of the world. To compensate, the town was granted duty-free status in the 16th

century, a privilege it still enjoys. These days people head here to ski, or shop. Bargain-hunters can pick up designer clothes, perfume and ski equipment at discounted prices.

Museo Civico di Bormio

Via Buon Consiglio 25, Bormio (0342 912 216). **Open** *Jan-Easter* 3-7pm Mon-Sat. *Mid June-mid Sept* 3-7pm Mon; 10am-12.30pm, 3-7pm Tue-Thur, Sat, Sun; 10am-12.30pm, 3-7pm, 9-11pm Fri. *Easter-mid June, mid Sept-mid Dec* 3.30-6.30pm Tue, Thur, Sat.

Where to stay, eat & shop

The recently opened **Grand Hotel Bagni Nuovi** (via Bagni Nuovi 4, Bagni di Bormio, 0342 901 890, www.bagnidibormio.it, doubles €160-€270, min stay 2 nights) is housed in a 19th-century structure three kilometres (two miles) from town in Bormio's spa resort complex and park (*see above*). A less pricey alternative is **Hotel Bagni Vecchi** (strada Statale dello Stelvio, Bagni di Bormio, 0342 910 131, doubles €125-€175, min stay 2 nights), an old-fashioned hotel attached to the Roman baths. At both hotels, prices include breakfast, lunch and entry to the spa.

For Valtellinese dishes with a twist, try **Bormio's Al Filò** (via Dante 6, 0342 901 732, closed lunch Tue, all Mon, 2wks May & 2wks Nov, average €25), housed in a 17th-century stable. Also in Bormio, the **Vecchia Combo** (via Sant'Antonio 4, 0342 901 568, closed Sun, average €25) serves traditional food in an ancient building.

At the **Bar Braulio** (via Roma 27, 0342 902 726, closed Wed), customers pick at snacks in a contemporary stone-and-wood salon. The bar is owned by the makers of Bormio's famous herbal post-prandial *amaro*; pick up a bottle of the stuff while you're here, or book a tour around the company's cellars (Tue & Fri, Dec-Easter & Jul-Aug, admission €3).

Further down the street is **Grizzly** (via Roma 36, 0342 904 772, closed May, Sun & Mon Oct & Nov), a tiny, Bormio-based fashion label selling some surprisingly funky knits and linens.

Tourist information

APT Bormio

Via Roma 131b (0342 903 300/www.valtellinaonline. com). **Open** *Apr-June, Oct-Nov* 9am-12.30pm, 2.30-6pm Mon-Sat; 9.30am-12.30pm Sun. *July-Sept* 9am-12.30pm, 3-7pm daily. *Dec-Apr* 9am-12.30pm, 3-6.30pm daily.

APT Livigno

Via dala Gesa 407a (0342 996 379/www.aptlivigno. it). **Open** 9am-12.30pm, 2.30-6.30pm daily.

Good as new: **Hotel Bagni Nuovi**. *See p270.*

Valcamonica

Situated in the province of Brescia (*see p230*), Valcamonica is very different from the neighbouring Valtellina, and the two valleys have a long tradition of rivalry. The Camuni will proudly tell you that they have one of Europe's longest-documented histories, thanks to over 300,000 pictorial rock carvings dating back 10,000 years. Valcamonica also enjoyed a long period of stability as part of the Venetian Republic (1428-1796), while Valtellina was being ravaged by war. Their economies differ, too: Valcamonica's is primarily industrial and the 80-kilometre (50-mile) valley bottom is pervaded by factories producing textiles, lingerie and steel. But head up any of the mountains or minor valleys and you'll find undisturbed historic and natural treasures.

The SS39 swirls down the mountainside from Aprica, past the **Riserva Naturale delle Valli di Sant'Antonio**, a popular area for walks and picnics. At **Edolo** (alt 699m/2,230ft), a pleasant market town with some attractive rustic dwellings, the SS42 heads north to Ponte di Legno, or south to Darfo Boario Terme, running the length of the valley.

Getting there

By car
From Milan, take the A4 motorway east; exit at Seriate and follow the SS42 through Lovere to Darfo Boario Terme. Journey time to Darfo is around 1hr 40mins.

From Valtellina, take the SS38 to Tresenda, then the SS39 to the Aprica Pass. At Aprica, continue east to Edolo. Alternatively, the Passo di Gavia road (open June-Oct, snow permitting) goes from Bormio to northern Valcamonica.

By train
Railway links are slow and irregular. Take a mainline train from Milan's Stazione Centrale to Brescia. From here a branch line winds its way through spectacular countryside up the valley to Edolo.

By bus
SAB (035 289 000/www.sab-autoservizi.it) runs services from Stazione Garibaldi in Milan to Ponte di Legno via Edolo. Journey time 4hrs. There are irregular services from Aprica to Edolo.

Tourist information

Ufficio Turistico IAT Edolo
Piazza Martiri di Libertà 2 (0364 71 065). **Open** *Mid June-mid Sept* 9am-12.30pm, 3.30-6.30pm Tue-Sat; 9am-12.30pm Sun. *Mid Sept-mid June* 9am-12.30pm, 3.30-6.30pm Tue-Sat.

North from Edolo

Valcamonica's northern reaches are much more spectacular than the southern stretches. Factories give way to mountain slopes, pine forests and the occasional *baita* (farm buildings traditionally used during summer grazing).

At **Temù** (alt 1,144m/3,813ft) is the **Museo della Guerra Bianca**, with photographs, documents and artefacts from the dramatic 'White War' fought between the Austrians and Italians on the nearby mountains during World War I.

Ponte di Legno (alt 1,257m/4,190ft) is best known as a ski resort (*see p272* **Sloping off**) but is also a good departure point for summer hiking and mountain biking in the nearby Stelvio (*see p270*) and Adamello (*see below*) parks. The town centre – razed during World War I and rebuilt in the early 20th century – is blissfully closed to traffic, making it a pleasant place to stroll.

Just outside the village is the **Scuola Italiana Sleddog** (case Sparse 10, 0364 92 231/www.scuolaitalianasleddog.it), which organises courses for wannabe mushers (mostly children) (Dec-Easter, €62 for 2hr beginner course), as well as husky trekking (Apr-Sept, €32 per hr).

The 510-square-kilometre (197-square-mile) **Parco Naturale dell'Adamello** runs along the eastern side of Valcamonica from Breno to Ponte di Legno, where it borders with the Parco dello Stelvio. Within its confines are the Lombardy slopes of the Adamello group, which

Lakes & Cities

Sloping off

Aprica

See p267.
The ideal spot for families and beginners, with also enough for more competent skiers. **Vital stats** 40km (25 miles) of pistes; 2 black runs, 9 red runs, 6 blue runs; 2 cableways, 5 chairlifts, 8 ski lifts; 8.5km (5 miles) of cross-country tracks, outdoor ice rink. A third cableway and new pistes should open in 2005.

Ski hire

Larino
Corso Roma 127 (0342 745 434). **Rates** *Skis & boots* €13 per day. **Open** 8.30am-1pm, 2.30-8pm daily. Closed Mon Apr-June. **Credit** AmEx, MC, V.

Ski school

Scuola Sci e Snowboard Aprica
Piazza Palabione (0342 745 108). **Rates** €26-€30 per hr. **Credit** AmEx, DC, MC, V. **Open** *Dec-Easter* Lessons 8am-5pm. Office 8am-6.30pm. **Credit** AmEx, DC, MC, V.

Bormio

See p269.
Valtellina's classiest ski resort, Bormio lets you punctuate your skiing with history and culture, as well as test your stamina on the 3.5km (2-mile) World Cup Pista Stelvio run. **Vital stats** 50km (31 miles) of pistes; 2 black runs, 5 red runs, 4 blue runs; 3 cableways, 7 chairlifts, 7 ski lifts; 12km (4.5 miles) of cross-country tracks, indoor ice rink.

Ski hire

Celso Sport
Via Vallecetta 5 (0342 901 459). **Rates** *Skis &* boots €15-€31 per day. **Open** 8am-12.30pm, 3-7.30pm daily. **Credit** AmEx, DC, MC, V.

Ski school

Scuola Nazionale Sci Bormio
Via Funivia 16 (0342 901 553/www.scuola scinazionale.bormio.it). **Open** *Dec-Easter* 9am-5pm. **Rates** €35 per hr. **Credit** AmEx, DC, MC, V.

Chiesa in Valmalenco

See p267.
Rustic buildings nestle among Chiesa's more modern constructions, but no one comes here for the architecture. The town's ski slopes overlook the spectacular Bernina range, including Pizzo Bernina, Valtellina's highest peak. The resort's Thoeni black run drops 2,700m (8,858ft) from Alpe Motta. **Vital stats** 35km (22 miles) of pistes; 3 black runs, 7 red runs, 6 blue runs; 1 cableway, 5 chairlifts, 4 ski lifts; snowboard park, 37km (23 miles) of cross-country tracks, 2 outdoor ice rinks.

Ski hire

Pircher Sport
Via Roma 150 (0342 451 301). **Rates** *Skis & boots* €10-€20 per day. **Open** 9am-7.30pm daily. **Credit** AmEx, DC, MC, V.

Ski school

Scuola Italiana Sci Valmalenco
Alpe Palù (0342 451 409). **Open** *Dec-Apr* 9am-5pm. **Rates** €27 ski, €29 snowboard. **No credit cards**.

Livigno

See p270.
Sunny Livigno's extensive network of pistes runs down six different mountain slopes in Valtellina. The town's altitude means it often has snow for longer than rival resorts; there's also a lively, youthful atmosphere. **Vital stats** 115km (94 miles) of pistes; 10 black runs, 36 red runs, 28 blue runs; 3 cableways, 15 chairlifts, 14 ski lifts; 2 snowboard parks, 40km (25 miles) of cross-country tracks, outdoor ice rink, snow go-carts and quad bikes.

Ski hire & school

Scuola Italiana Sci Livigno
Via Saroch 634 (0342 970 300/www.sisl.it). **Open** *Shop* 9am-12.30pm, 2.30-7.30pm daily. *Lessons* 8am-7pm daily. **Rates** *Skis & boots* €20 per day. *Lessons* €30-€32 per hr. **Credit** AmEx, DC, MC, V.

Madesimo

See p264.
This modern resort has gorgeous surroundings and is close to the delights of Chiavenna (*see p264*). Its 2,750m (9,022ft) long Canalone run is said to be Italy's most difficult.
Vital stats 50km (31 miles) of pistes; 4 black runs, 11 red runs, 10 blue runs; 2 cableways, 1 funicular railway, 11 chairlifts; 1 ski lift; snowboard park; 25.5km (16 miles) of cross-country tracks; outdoor ice-skating.

Ski hire

Olympic Sport
Via dei Giacomi 3 (0343 54 330). **Open** 8.30am-12.30pm, 2.30-7.30pm daily.
Rates *Skis & boots* €15.50 per day.
Credit AmEx, DC, MC, V.

Ski school

Scuola Italiana Sci Madesimo Valle Spluga
Via alle Fonti 4 (0343 53 049). **Open** *Dec-Easter* 8.30am-6.30pm daily. **Rates** €28 per hour. **Credit** AmEx, DC, MC, V.

Passo dello Stelvio

See p270.
At 2,758m (9,193ft), Valtellina's Passo dello Stelvio is Europe's largest summer ski area, in full swing from May until October.
Vital stats 20-25km (12-16 miles) of pistes; 2 cableways, 8 ski lifts; 2 cross-country tracks.

Ski hire & school

Pirovano
Corso Vittorio Veneto 7, Sondrio (summer 0342 904 421/winter 0342 210 040). **Open** 9am-5pm daily. **Rates** *Skis & boots* €20 per day. *Lessons* €30 per hr. **Credit** AmEx, DC, MC, V.

Ponte di Legno & Tonale

See p271.
Not so much one ski resort as a whole stack of them. Ponte di Legno is a modern resort, while higher up are the Tonale pass (1,800m/

6,000ft) and the Presena glacier (3,100m/ 10,330ft), where you can ski all year round.
Vital stats 80km (50 miles) of pistes; 4 black runs, 17 red runs, 7 blue runs; 1 cable car, 14 chairlifts, 10 ski lifts; 1 sledgeway; 16.5km (10 miles) of cross-country tracks; 2 outdoor ice rinks, sledge dog school and motor-sledge circuit at Tonale. Tonale also has a ski play area for kids aged 4-9, plus a babysitting zone.

Ski hire

Le Ski Lab
Via Corno d'Aula 21 (0364 900 393). **Open** *Dec-Apr* 8am-7pm. **Rates** *Skis & boots* €17 per day. **No credit cards**.

Ski school

Scuola di Sci Ponte di Legno–Tonale
Corso Milano 6 (0364 91 301); Via Case Sparse del Tonale (0364 903 943). **Open** *Dec-Easter* Lessons 8am-6pm. Office 4.30-7.30pm. **Rates** €29 per hr. **Credit** AmEx, MC, V.

Weather & emergencies

The Swiss site www.meteosvizzera.ch has reliable weather reports in English. Call 118 for Soccorso Alpino (Alpine Rescue).

Getting into gear

For discounted ski gear, head to the **Samas** factory outlet on the SS38 (via Nazionale, Località Giardini, Chiuro, 0342 485 011, closed Tue, credit AmEx, DC, MC, V). For factory-priced cross-country equipment, try **Skitrab** (via Tirano 6, Bormio, 0342 901 650, closed Sun, credit AmEx, MC, V).

Lakes & Cities

includes Italy's largest glacier and one of the last habitats of the Alpine brown bear. A visitor's centre at **Vezza d'Oglio** (via Nazionale 132, 0364 76 165, www.parco adamello.it, opening times vary), provides information about this beautiful region.

Museo della Guerra Bianca

Via Adamello, Temù (0364 94 617/www.museo guerrabianca.it). **Open** *Mid June-mid Sept* 5-7.30pm daily. *Mid Sept-mid June* by appointment.

Tourist information

Ufficio Turistico IAT Ponte di Legno

Corso Milano 41 (0364 91 122/www.pontedilegno. it). **Open** *Sept-June* 9am-12.30pm, 3.30-7pm Mon-Sat; 9.30am-12.30pm Sun. *July, Aug* 9am-12.30pm, 3-7pm daily.

South from Edolo

Valcamonica's most visited town is **Capo di Ponte**, home to the **Parco Nazionale delle Incisioni Rupestri**, a UNESCO World Heritage site. This park contains over 100 rocks with carvings dating back 10,000 years, depicting everything from antler-headed deer-gods to primitive carts. Two isolated mountains – Monte Concarena (2,549m/8,496ft) and Pizzo Badile Camuno (2,435m/8,116ft) – tower over this sacred site. The **Centro Camuno di Studi Preistorici** (0364 42 091) organises archaeological summer courses.

Capo di Ponte also boasts two atmospheric Romanesque churches. To reach the 11th-century monastery church of **San Salvatore** (0364 42 080, open by appointment), follow the signs from the SS42 just north of the town. This privately owned church, with its octagonal dome, sits in a little park where the only sounds are the trickle of water and the occasional peacock screech. The simple, austere interior has pillars carved with eagles, imaginary beasts and mermaids. The floor laid in the church 1,000 years ago is still there, while the first pillar on the left has a base that rests on bare rock, as, indeed, does the church itself. To visit the 11th-century **Pieve di San Siro** (at Cemmo, near Capo di Ponte) leave a document with the Pro Loco at Capo di Ponte (*see p275*) in exchange for the keys. The church's exterior has an arched doorway, while the stone portal is carved with mythical fauna, enhanced with well-preserved scales, feathers and fur. The no-frills interior has a baptismal font carved from a single block of stone, a huge stone altar platform, some 15th-century frescoes and a crypt partly carved from the rock below the church.

At **Cerveno** (alt 500m/1,667ft) is one of the valley's most surprising works of art. Attached to the church of **San Martino** (0364 434 014/434 012, open Oct-May 8am-noon, 2.30-5pm daily; June-Sept 8am-noon, 2.30-6pm daily) is the Via Crucis (Stations of the Cross), a closed-in flight of steps lined with 14 chapels containing 198 life-size 18th-century

Hidden treasure

Tired of hiking up mountains? Take a half-day out to gaze at **La Pace**, a stunning jewel-encrusted gospel cover tucked away in Chiavenna's Museo del Tesoro (*see p264*) – said to be among the best examples of medieval goldsmithery in the world.

The origins of *La Pace* (the peace) are shrouded in mystery: legend has it that it was a gift from a bishop who accompanied Frederick Barbarossa (*see p10*) to the town in 1176. But experts will only hazard that it was probably created in the 11th or 12th century, possibly in Milan. What seems certain is that *La Pace* is a patchwork of whatever precious bits and pieces the artist – or artists – had to hand. Mounted on a walnut-wood tablet, it contains gold laminates of the apostles, colourful enamelled panels, a central gold cross and assorted jewels. Many of the 94 pearls and

97 gems have tiny perforations, indicating they had previous lives as part of various jewellery collections. A remote-control-operated magnifying glass (ask to have it switched on at the entrance) reveals that some of the stones have tiny engravings, including an inscription in Arabic, translated for the first time just a couple of years ago, and leading to speculation that some – or all of the pieces – may have been gathered during the Crusades. Other imagination-tickling peculiarities include the signatures beside the apostles – 'EVG', and in one case 'VEG' – indicating that whoever made them may have been illiterate. There's also an inscription: 'Those who have made or had made a work like this live in Christ and obtain by their work His reign' – which begs the question of who commissioned this mysterious work of art?

narrow, cobbled streets with arches, towers and frescoed palazzi at every turn. There is also a working flour mill, the **Mulino Museo** (via Glere, 0364 300 307, open 8.30-11.30am Mon-Sat, admission free). Further down the road, at **Darfo Boario Terme** (alt 218m/726ft) the **Terme di Boario** (viale Igea 3, 0364 5391, www.termediboario.it, closed mid Dec-mid Jan) is a thermal spa with water reputed to do great things for those with liver complaints. For the hale and hearty, there are also saunas and Turkish baths.

Just north of Darfo Boario Terme on the SS42 is the **Archeopark**, which has reconstructions of a prehistoric farm (complete with wild boars), an artisans' village and traditional Camuni houses on stilts around a lake.

Archeopark

Località Gattaro (0364 529 552/www.archeo park.com). **Open** *Mar-Nov* 9am-5.30pm daily. **Admission** €8. **No credit cards**.

Parco Nazionale delle Incisioni Rupestri

Località Naquane (0364 42 140). **Open** *Mar-Oct* 8.30am-7pm Tue-Sun. *Nov-Feb* 8.30am-2pm Tue-Sun. **Admission** €4. **No credit cards**.

Where to stay, eat & shop

In the beautiful medieval village of Pescarzo, **I Camuni** (via S Rocco, 0364 42 367, doubles from €50) offers bed and breakfast in a newly restored hotel.

If you run out of clean knickers, call in at the **Cotonella** factory outlet in Malonno (via Nazionale 135, 0364 759 311, closed Mon am, all Sun), which sells underwear at discounts of around 30 per cent.

At Ponte di Legno **La Cantina** (corso Trieste 55, 349 602 9580 mobile, closed Mon off-season) serves wine and snacks at large wooden tables. Also at Ponte di Legno, you'll find **Antonio e Pietro Sandrini** (via Nino Bixio 27, 0364 92 526), a father-and-son wood-carving team, who fashion exquisite little frogs, grasshoppers and snails.

Tourist information

Pro Loco Capo di Ponte

Via Briscioli 42 (0364 42 080). **Open** 9am-noon Mon, Sun; 9am-noon, 2.30-4.30pm Tue-Sat.

Ufficio Turistico IAT Darfo Boario Terme

Piazza Einaudi 2 (0364 531 609). **Open** *Mid Sept-mid July* 9am-12.30pm, 3-6pm Mon-Fri; 9am-12.30pm Sat. *Mid July-mid Sept* 9am-12.30pm, 3-6pm Mon-Fri; 9am-12.30pm Sat, Sun.

Ponte di Legno. *See p271.*

sculptures. To find it, walk through the church and unbolt the main door. The best of these lifelike tableaux (chapels I-VII, XI-XIII) are by the Brescian sculptor Beniamino Simoni (1720-1800), and show the agony of Christ before, during and after the crucifixion. The sculptor's skill can be seen in the faces of the men who torture Jesus along the way, and the women who look on with pity.

Just before Bienno is **Cividate Camuno**, a tiny town that was once the main Roman centre in the valley. A newly excavated archaeological park containing the remains of a theatre and amphitheatre opened in 2003 (0364 344 301, visits by appointment). The **Museo Archeologico Nazionale della Valcamonica** (via Mosé Tovini, 0364 344 301, www.civitascamunnorum.com, open 8.30am-2pm Tue-Sun) houses the area's most important Roman finds.

Bienno's (alt 445m/1,483ft) well-preserved medieval/Renaissance centre has a network of

Lakes & Cities

What Londoners take when they go out.

SAVE ME! GIVE ME Your
mpty Shopping Bags, PLEASE
SAUVEZ-MOI, DONNEZ MOI
OS SACS VIDES, S.V.P.
1i-Salvi ! Mi-DiA
Suoi Sacchetti vuoti, grazie

Directory

Getting Around	278
Resources A-Z	284
Vocabulary	295
Further Reference	296

Features

Travel advice	285
Telephone codes	293
Weather	294

Directory

Getting Around

Aeroporto di Malpensa

02 7485 2200/www.sea-aeroporti milano.it. **Map** p306 (Greater Milan). Milan's main airport is 50km (30 miles) from the centre. Malpensa has two terminals: Terminal 1 is for domestic, international and intercontinental flights; Terminal 2 is mostly for charter flights, although it's also used by a few international services.

Aeroporto di Linate

02 7485 2200/www.sea-aeroporti milano.it. **Map** p306 (Greater Milan). Milan's national airport is in Segrate, about 7km (4.5 miles) from the centre of town. It handles domestic and continental flights.

Aeroporto di Orio al Serio

035 326 323/flight information 035 326 111/www.orioaeroporto.it. Bergamo's airport is about 45km (28 miles) from Milan and 5km (3 miles) from Bergamo. It handles national, continental, intercontinental and charter flights. When Milan's airports are fog-bound, flights are often re-routed here.

On from Malpensa

By train (Malpensa Express)

02 20 222 (7am-8pm)/recorded info in English 02 27 763/www.ferrovie nord.it. **Tickets** €12 return; €9 single; €4.50 4-12s; free under-4s. The Ferrovie Nord's Malpensa Express runs every 30mins 6am-8pm (to 9.30pm Sun) between Terminal 1 and Cadorna metro station (journey time 40mins), stopping at Bovisa/Politecnico, Busto Arsizio and Saronno. Buy tickets at the Ferrovie Nord (FN) desks in the airport, all FN stations and at stations where the Malpensa Express stops. There's a hefty surcharge for buying tickets on the train. Remember to stamp your ticket in one of the yellow machines on the platform before boarding.

Between 8pm and midnight, the train is replaced by a bus service (journey time 50mins). A free shuttle bus runs at 15-min intervals between Malpensa's terminals 1 and 2.

By bus

Two main bus services link Malpensa to Milan. The **Malpensa Bus Express** departs every 20mins (6.30am-11.50pm Malpensa Terminal 1 to Stazione Centrale; 5.10am-10.30pm from Stazione Centrale to Malpensa) and takes approximately 1hr 10mins. The service to the airport also stops at Milano Fiera and on request at Terminal 2; the service to Milan stops at Terminal 2 and on request at Milano Fiera.

Tickets are available in the arrivals halls at the airport, at the Società Air Pullman (SAP) office at piazza Luigi di Savoia, to the side of the Stazione Centrale, and at the APT office (*see p280*) near the Duomo. You can also buy tickets on the bus. After 8pm, when the bus acts as a substitute for the Malpensa Express train, the arrival station is Cadorna.

Malpensa Shuttle services leave every 20mins (6.20am-12.15am from Malpensa; 5am-10.30pm from Stazione Centrale) and take approximately 50mins. Buses stop at Fiera and Terminal 2 on request. Tickets can be purchased in the airport arrivals halls; at the SAP office at piazza Luigi di Savoia, near the Stazione Centrale; on the bus itself; or at the Colombo and Salerno newsstands (both at the Stazione Centrale).

Malpensa Shuttle also runs 11 shuttle bus services a day each way between Malpensa and Linate, with request stops at Terminal 2 (journey time 1hr 10 mins). Tickets, which can be bought on the bus, cost €8, or €4 for children 2-12 years.

Malpensa Bus Express *(02 9619 2301/www.ferrovienord.it).* **Open** 8am-12.20pm, 2-6pm Mon-Fri. **Tickets** €5.50; €2.25 4-12s; free under-3s.
Malpensa Shuttle *(02 5858 3185/ www.malpensashuttle.it).* **Tickets** €4.50; €2.25 2-12s; free under-2s.

By taxi

See also p281.
A taxi from Malpensa to Milan costs approximately €75. Journey time is around 45 minutes. Beware of rush-hour traffic, which can lengthen the trip substantially (and increase your fare). Use only white or yellow taxis lined up at the ranks and avoid all drivers who solicit business as you exit the terminal.

On from Linate

By bus

There is no train service into Milan from Linate, but the excellent ATM bus 73 departs every 10mins from Linate Airport and San Babila metro station. Travel time is around 25mins (40mins at rush hour). A €1 city bus ticket is valid for the airport service.

By taxi

See also p281.
A taxi from Linate will cost €18-€25, depending on what part of town you are travelling to.

On from Orio

By train

Trains depart hourly from Bergamo's train station for Milan's Stazione Centrale (tickets €3.85); less regularly for Milan's Porta Garibaldi (tickets €3.30). Travelling time is about 1hr. **Autoservizi Zani** (035 678 611/www.zaniviaggi.it) runs buses every 20mins 5.30am-midnight between Bergamo railway station and the airport and vice versa. A ticket costs €1.05. Journey time is about 10mins. If you get a taxi to take you to the station, be sure to ask for 'Stazione di Bergamo', not just 'Stazione', or the taxi driver might assume you want Centrale in Milan, which costs a lot more. Taxis from Orio to Bergamo station charge a fixed fee of €15.

By bus

Autoservizi Zani (035 678 611/www. zaniviaggi.it) runs a service between Orio al Serio and Milan Lambrate (piazza Bottini); coaches run 8am-11.45pm from Orio and 5.15am-8.45pm from Milan. The trip costs €6 (€3 concessions) and takes 50mins.

Autostradale (02 637 901/www. autostradale.it) runs buses daily 4.45am-9.15pm between the air terminal at Milan's Stazione Centrale and Orio al Serio and 8.30am-12.30am in the other direction. Tickets can be bought on board and cost €6.70 (€3.35 3-12s). Autostradale also has half-hourly bus links between Bergamo bus terminus and Milan's Garibaldi Station. When fog closes Milan's airports, airlines provide buses to take stranded passengers to and from Orio al Serio.

Airlines

Alitalia

*24hr domestic flight information
& ticket sales 848 865 641/24hr
international flight information
& ticket sales 848 865 642/www.
alitalia.it.* **Credit** AmEx, DC, MC, V.
*Via Albricci 5, Centre (02 2499
2700). Metro Duomo/bus 54, 65/
tram 12, 23, 27.* **Open** 9am-6pm
Mon-Fri. **Map** p311 A1/p312 B2.
*Piazzale Cadorna 14, West (02 2499
2500). Metro Cadorna/bus 50, 58, 94/
tram 1, 27.* **Open** *For tickets, check-in
and connection to Malpensa Express
train service (see p278)* 7am-7pm
Mon-Fri; 7am-6pm Sat. *For frequent-
flyer ticket pick-up and assistance*
9am-6pm Mon-Fri; 9.30am-5pm Sat.
Map p310 A2/p312 A1.
*Malpensa Airport Terminal 1, 2nd
floor (848 865 643).* **Open** 5.30am-
11pm daily. **Map** p306.

British Airways

*Flight information & ticket sales 848
812 266 (open 8am-8pm Mon-Fri;
9am-5pm Sat)/www.britishairways.
com/italy.* **Credit** AmEx, DC, MC, V.
*Corso Italia 8, South (02 724 161).
Metro Missori/bus 65/tram 4, 23, 24.*
Open 9am-5pm Mon-Fri. **Map** p310
A2, B2.
*Malpensa Airport Terminal 1,
2nd floor (02 7486 6596).*
Open 9am-5.30pm daily. **Map** p306.

Ryanair

899 899 844/www.ryanair.com.

Arriving by bus

The long-distance bus
companies that serve Milan use
Porta Garibaldi (02 637 901) as
a terminus (map p308 B2).

Arriving by train

Long-distance, international
and Eurostar (Italy's fast train,
not to be confused with the
Channel tunnel service) trains
arrive at and depart from
Milan's Stazione Centrale. If
you arrive late at night, take
a taxi to your destination;
the metro stops shortly after
midnight (*see p280*). For
information on buying train
tickets, *see p281*. Milan's
Stazione Centrale is a
pickpocket's paradise, so
watch your wallet and
luggage carefully.

Public transport

See also transport map, p316.
The services operated by the
Azienda Trasporti Milanesi
(ATM) (www.atm-mi.it) are the
mainstay of Milan's transport
system, handling both the
inner-city *rete urbana* (urban
network) and the Greater
Milan area. ATM manages a
public transport network of
three metropolitan railway
lines and 120 tram, trolleybus
and bus lines, covering nearly
1,400km (870 miles) and
reaching 86 municipalities.

Public transport in Milan is
fairly safe, even at night, but
do watch out for pickpockets
in packed buses and subways.
There was a major overhaul
of the bus and tram system in
December 2003; the citywide
ATM transport map printed on
page 316 includes details of the
changes. For more information,
head to the ATM points in the
metro stations at Duomo,
Centrale FS, Cadorna, Loreto
and Romolo (7.45am-8.15pm),
or by ringing freephone 800
808 181 (7.30am-7.30pm).

Most ATM buses, trams
and metro trains are orange,
though you will see the
occasional green one, such as
the new supertram or an early
20th-century service tram.

The transport system is
easy to use once you get the
hang of it. There are three
metro lines (1/red, 2/green,
3/yellow) that connect to **buses**
and **trams** throughout the
city. The city centre is circled
by three concentric ring roads,
each of which is covered by
public transport. Buses 50,
58, 61 and 94 travel along
(portions of) the inner circular
route, which passes close to
the centre. Trams 29 and 30
circle the city along the middle
circular route, while buses
90, 91 and 92 travel the outer
circular route. Many trams
cut across the city, connecting
ring roads and continuing into
suburban areas. One such tram

is 2, which travels from the
north to the south of Milan
(and vice versa), taking in
areas such as via Manzoni,
piazza della Scala, via Torino,
corso Genova, corso Colombo
and Ripa Ticinese.

The **Passante Ferroviario**
is a train service connecting
piazza Dateo, Porta Venezia,
Repubblica, Garibaldi (FS),
Lancetti, Bovisa (FN) and
Certosa (FS) metro and train
stations. It runs overground
outside Milan and
underground in the city.

Metro trains run every 4-
5mins 6am-9pm daily; after
that, services run only every
10-12mins. All ATM bus and
tram services – except night
services (*see p280*) – also run
6am-midnight daily, departing
every 5-20mins, depending on
the route and time of day.

The doors for boarding are
clearly marked *entrata*; those
for alighting are marked *uscita*.
Some new buses require you to
push a button to open the
doors. When you want to alight
from a bus, push the red button
before your stop to alert the
driver. Drivers will drive past
stops if there's no request and
they see no passengers waiting.

At each bus stop, a sign
shows all stops made along the
route and includes a timetable.
Major changes are made to the
timetables in the summer
when Milan empties.

Radiobus (02 4803 4803) is
a request-only bus service run
by ATM that operates mainly
within the city centre and also
in the trendy Navigli area. Call
to communicate your route and
the time you want to travel,
and a minibus will pick you
up at the nearest bus stop (see
the specially signed Radiobus
stops). You can book several
days in advance, but you can
also make bookings up to half
an hour before you want to
travel. The service is rarely
busy, so you'll find yourself
riding in a luxury minibus
possibly with others, but more

Directory

likely alone. To travel on a Radiobus, you'll need a regular single ticket (or season ticket) for the urban network (*see below* **Tickets & fares**) in addition to a Radiobus ticket. Radiobus tickets are sold at all ATM sale points (€1.50) and on the bus (€2). If you board the bus without a ticket or season ticket, your fare will be €3.

Transport information

Bus and tram routes and numbers change with some regularity. If you plan to use public transport while in Milan, consult www.atm-mi.it, ring the freephone information line on 800 808 181 or pick up a copy of *City*, a free daily available in any metro station. It has a full page of ATM transport updates, areas under construction or renovation and route changes. Maps of the metro system are usually available at any hotel (ask your concierge), but if you're planning on using buses and trams, it might be worth buying a detailed map of all transport options. This is available from ATM points (*see below*) and at most newsstands for €2.

The main ATM information desk is at the **Duomo** metro station (open 7.45am-8.15pm Mon-Sat). It has English-speaking staff, although its phone line (freephone 800 808 181; 7.30am-7.30pm daily) is Italian only. ATM points are also found at mezzanine levels at the following metro stations: **Duomo Cadorna, Loreto, Romolo, Centrale FS**. All are open 7.45am-7.45pm Mon-Sat.

Night services

The three metro lines operate until 12.30am; buses then ply the same routes until about 1.30am. There are also 55 night bus and tram routes, which run 12.30-2.30am. There is no public transport between 2.30am and 6am.

Tourist services

See also p53 **Guided tours**.
The hop-on hop-off Ciao Milano tourist tram run by Air Pullman (02 7200 2584/www.airpullman.com/ciao/ciaoe.htm) departs from piazza Castello. Tickets are €20 and are valid for 24hrs; passengers can get off to investigate sights en route and then pick up a later tram.

Tickets & fares

Buy your ticket before boarding. ATM tickets can be bought at all metro stations (6am-8pm at staffed desks; from ticket machines at other times), ATM points (*see above* **Transport information**), tobacconists (look for a big 'T'), most newsstands and cafés, as well as Lampugnano, Bisceglie and Famagosta station car parks.

The same tickets are valid on all ATM bus, tram and metro lines operating within the inner-city *rete urbana* (urban network). Travel to and through other zones requires appropriate tickets.

When you board a tram or a bus, stamp your ticket in the machines by the rear and/or front doors. If travelling without paying looks an easy option, bear in mind there are ticket inspectors around: if you are caught you will be fined €100 on the spot. When travelling on the metro, only stamp your ticket the first time you use it at the turnstiles. There is no need to feed it through the machines on your way out.

Children less than one metre in height travel free of charge. Students, pensioners and the disabled pay lower rates for monthly and yearly tickets.

Biglietto singolo (€1)

Valid for 75mins after it is stamped for use on unlimited ATM trams and buses on the inner-city network, plus one trip on the metro. You need to keep an eye on how long you've been travelling, though there is some leeway. This ticket is also valid on the Passante Ferroviario and on the urban sections of the Ferrovie Nord and Ferrovie dello Stato mainline railways.

Carnet (€9.20)

A book of ten tickets. This may be shared by several people.

Biglietto integrato per quattro viaggi (€4)

Normally valid for 75mins. However, if stamped before 1pm on Sundays and holidays (for example, at 10am), it is valid until 1pm. If stamped after 8pm on ordinary days, it is valid until the end of the service.

Biglietto giornaliero (€3)

Valid 24hrs from the time of stamping for unlimited use on all transport in the inner-city area.

Abbonamento due giorni (€5.50)

Valid 48hrs from the time of stamping for unlimited use on all transport in the inner-city area.

Abbonamento settimanale

Valid seven days for unlimited use of all transport in the inner-city area. €16.75 for the first week (this includes an ID card, for which you will need a passport-sized photo) and €9 to renew it.

Abbonamento mensile

Valid one calendar month for unlimited use of all transport within the inner-city area. €37.75 for the first month (this includes a photo ID card, as above) and €30 to renew it.

Greater Milan services

ATM manages a Greater Milan fare system called SITAM (Milan Area Integrated Transport System). Many transport operators with routes running into the city from outside participate in this system. Beyond the urban network, the area is divided into concentric outer zones; fares depend on the number of these zones you travel through.

For information on travel to Greater Milan destinations, ask at the ATM point in the Duomo metro (*see above* **Transport information**).

TICKETS

To travel from what the Milanese call *l'hinterland* (the suburbs) into the city, or from one town to another in the suburbs, *biglietti interurbani* (inter-urban tickets) and *biglietti cumulativi* (combined tickets) are available. The former are for use exclusively on routes outside the urban network; the latter can be used both in the suburbs and on the urban network.

Abbonamento un giorno cumulativo area grande (€7.40)

Valid 24hrs on all ATM routes and most inter-urban SITAM routes.

Rail services

Milan's metropolitan rail network is reliable and heavily used. Regular bus/tram/metro tickets are valid on trains as far as the stations marked *limite tariffe urbane*.

For train travel in Lombardy, see individual destinations in the **Lakes & Cities** section of this guide (*see p188-275*).

Mainline train services are operated by the Ferrovie dello Stato (FS; aka Trenitalia).

TIMETABLES AND TICKETS

Train timetables can be bought at any newsstand. The easiest to read is *Nuovo Grippaudo Orario*, which includes all Milan suburban train timetables, as well as boat schedules for Lake Maggiore (*see p193*).

Train tickets can be bought at stations or travel agents with an FS sign, by credit card over the phone on 892 021 (only from landlines)/199 166 177 (24-hour service) or on the FS website (www.trenitalia.com). The site is well organised and available in English, though making reservations and paying online are still challenges. Children under 12 pay half fare; children under four travel free. There are also special deals for family bookings (if two adults travel with one child, the child travels free) and group bookings (if six people book together, they get a 20 per cent discount – ten per cent on Eurostar). For information on taking wheelchairs on trains, *see p285*.

Train fares in Italy are much cheaper than in the UK but be aware: *diretti*, *espressi*, *regionali* and *interregionali* can be tortuously slow, stopping at every little station. It's usually worth paying the extra money to take the InterCity (IC), EuroCity (EC) or Eurostar (ES), Italy's fast-train service), which make fewer stops.

Advance reservation is automatic and free when you buy your ticket for an ES train. It is not compulsory but if you jump on a train without a ticket, you may not get a seat and will have to pay €8 extra; you will also have to sort this out with the guard straight away.

Booking a seat on IC and internal EC routes costs €3 and is worth it to avoid standing at peak times. What's more, if you have a seat booking and your ES, IC or EC train arrives more than 30 minutes late, you can claim a non-transferable reimbursement of 50 per cent

(30 per cent for IC trains) of the ticket price. To apply for this, put your ticket into the specific envelope (get it at the station on arrival) and hand it in to the ticket office immediately.

Larger stations and ticket machines accept all major credit cards. Most travel agents accept them for train tickets too.

Stamp your train ticket – and any supplements you have – in the yellow machines by each platform before boarding the train: failure to do so can lead to a hefty fine. Being foreign and looking forlorn can sometimes get you off the hook. Eurostar train tickets do not have to be stamped as their booking information is on them and they are valid for that journey only.

Milan's main stations are listed below. For which station to use for other destinations in Lombardy, *see p283*.

FS Informa
892 021 (landlines only; 7am-9pm daily)/199 166 177 (24hrs daily).
FS Customer Assistance
02 6371 2016. **Open** 7am-9pm daily.
FS Disabled Passengers
02 6707 0958. **Open** 7am-9pm daily.
FS Lost and Found office
02 6371 2667. **Open** 6am-1am daily.

Stazione Centrale

Piazzale Duca D'Aosta, North.
Map p309 B2. Connects with metro lines 2 and 3.

Stazione di Cadorna (Milano Nord)

Piazzale Cadorna, West. **Map** p308 C2. Connects with metro lines 1 and 2.

Stazione Porta Garibaldi

Piazza Freud, North. **Map** p309 B1. Connects with metro line 2, the Passante Ferroviario and Milan's bus station.

Taxis

Licensed taxis are white and meter-operated. If anyone comes up to you at Stazione Centrale or any of the major tourist magnets muttering 'Taxi?',

always refuse – they are likely to charge you up to 400 per cent more than the normal rate.

Most of Milan's taxi drivers are honest; if, however, you suspect you're being ripped off, make a note of the driver's name and number from the metal plaque inside the car's rear door. The more ostentatiously you do this, the more likely you are to find the fare returning to its proper level. Report complaints to the drivers' co-operative (the number is on the outside of each car) or, in serious cases, the police.

Fares & surcharges

When you pick up a taxi at a rank or hail one in the street, the meter should read zero. As you set off, it will indicate the minimum fare – €3 at time of writing – for the first 200 metres, after which the charge goes up according to time and distance. Minimum fare on Sundays, public holidays and at night (9pm-6am) is €5.

Taxi ranks

Ranks are indicated by a white sign with 'Taxi' written in black. In the city centre there are ranks at piazza Duomo, piazza della Scala, piazza San Babila, piazza Fontana, piazza Diaz, piazza Beltrade, largo Cairoli, piazza Cavour, largo Carrobbio, via Manzoni, largo Augusto, piazza Cadorna and largo Greppi.

Phone cabs

To phone for a taxi, look under 'Taxi' in the phone book or dial any of the companies listed below. When your call is answered, name the street and number, or the name and location of a bar, club or restaurant where you wish to be picked up. You will be given the taxi code name (always a location and a number) and a time – for example, '*Havana 69, in tre minuti*' (Havana 69, in three minutes). The meter will start from the moment the taxi sets off to pick you up.

If you intend to use a taxi at rush hour, during a major event, or in bad weather, order it well in advance.
Taxi Blue 02 4040.
Radio Taxi 02 8585.
Taxi Subito 848 814 781 (use this number if you don't know where the nearest rank is. A recorded message in Italian will read a list of nearby ranks and ask you to digit the corresponding number to call for a cab).

Directory

Driving

Short-term visitors should have no trouble driving with their home licences, although if they are written in different scripts or less common languages, an international licence can be useful. Driving licences issued in other EU states are valid in Italy and there is no legal obligation to convert them. Other international licences must be converted after the owner has been resident in Italy for one year. Full details can be found on the Automobile Club of Italy's website (www.aci.it).

Italy's new system of points (*punti*) brings the country's road legislation in line with the rest of Europe. Traffic cops will detract a certain number of points for infringements such as speeding, jumping red lights and so on. The important thing to remember is that if you have 20 points deducted in one year you'll be banned from driving for two years.

USEFUL TIPS:

● You are required by law to wear a seat-belt at all times, and to carry a warning triangle in your car.
● If you are thinking of driving in winter, especially in the mountains, keep a set of snow chains in the boot. If you drive on snow, it's advisable to fit them and if you see a sign saying '*obbligo di catene*' or showing a wheel with chains on it, you have to fit them by law from that point on.
● You are required by law to keep your driving licence, insurance papers, vehicle registration and photo ID documents on you at all times.
● Do not leave anything of value (including a car radio) in your car.
● Flashing your lights means that you intend to pass the driver in front of you, so you want him to pull over into the supposedly slower right lane. It doesn't mean that you will slow down (contrary to British practice).
● On motorways Italians flash their hazard warning lights when approaching a traffic jam.
● If traffic lights flash amber, stop and give way to the right.
● Green men are few and far between, so pedestrians assume right of way when the traffic lights show green – be careful when turning right at crossroads.

● Watch out for death-defying mopeds and pedestrians. Pedestrians usually assume they have right of way in the older, quieter streets without clearly designated pavements.
● Italian drivers are not in the habit of stopping for pedestrians at zebra crossings – be aware that the car in front of you won't necessarily stop.
● Mobile phones can only be used with earphones or on speaker.

Restricted areas

Large sections of the city centre are closed to non-resident traffic during business hours, and sometimes in the evening. You may be fined if you are caught trying to get in, and your car may be wheel-clamped if you manage to slip in and park – you'll have to pay a fine and a charge to have the clamp removed. If you are in a hired car or have foreign plates and are stopped, mention the name of your hotel, and you will likely be waved on.

Occasional Sundays are designated no-car days. These are heavily advertised beforehand, which is just as well as they are rigidly enforced in the city centre. There are, however, exceptions for moving around outside the inner ring road.

The *corsie veloci* (fast lanes) that form the central parts of the ring roads are strictly for buses and taxis.

Breakdown services

It is advisable to join a national motoring organisation, such as the AA or RAC in Britain or the AAA in the US, before taking a car to Italy. These organisations have reciprocal arrangements with the Automobile Club d'Italia (ACI) (www.aci.it).

If you require extensive repairs and do not know a mechanic, pay a bit more and go to a manufacturer's official dealer, as reliable service at many garages depends on having built up a good client-mechanic relationship over several years. Dealers are listed in the *Pagine Gialle* (Yellow Pages) under '*auto*', along with specialist repairers, such as *gommista* (tyre repairs), *marmitte* (exhaust repairs) and *carrozzerie* (bodywork and windscreen repairs). The English-language *Yellow Pages*, available from most English bookshops (*see p133*), has a list of garages where English is spoken.

Automobile Club d'Italia (ACI)

Corso Venezia 43, East (02 77 451/ 24hr emergencies 803 116/traffic info 166 664 477, 8am-8pm daily/ www.acimi.it). Metro Palestro. **Open** 8.30am-12.45pm, 2.15-5pm Mon-Fri. **Map** p309 C1.

The ACI has English-speaking staff. Members of associated organisations are entitled to free basic repairs, and to other services at preferential rates. This is still the best place to call in the event of a breakdown, even if you are a non-member. You will be charged, but prices are generally reasonable.

Europ Assistance

803 803/freephone 800 830 044 (both 24hrs)/www.europassistance.it. Piazza Trento 6, South (02 5838 4275). Metro Lodi/bus 90, 91. **Open** 9am-1pm, 2-6pm Mon-Fri. **Credit** AmEx, DC, MC, V. **Map** p311 C1. *Via Albricci 2, Centre (02 5824 2424). Metro Missori/bus 54, 65/ tram 12, 20, 27.* **Open** 9am-6pm Mon-Fri. **Credit** AmEx, DC, MC, V. **Map** p311 A1/p312 B2.

Europ Assistance, which operates in 24 countries, has been offering a 24hr breakdown service since 1963. Prices are reasonable and the staff speak good English.

Parking

Parking is a nightmare in Milan: the best solution is to leave your car in one of the 20-odd guarded car parks (*see below*) in the downtown area. Alternatively, use the Sosta Milano parking system: parking areas are marked on the road with blue lines. Those with yellow lines are strictly for residents only. Parking is generally free after 7pm except where indicated (in this case €2 will get you five hours). Buy tickets (€1.50 for an hour) at newsstands, *tabaccherie* (*see p292*) or from some parking attendants, and scratch them to indicate the day and time. Leave the ticket visible on the dashboard. Cars with disabled signs can park free within blue stripes.

Watch out for signs by entrances saying '*Passo carrabile*' (access at all times), '*Sosta vietata*' (no parking) and road signs denoting spaces for handicapped drivers. The sign '*Zona rimozione*' (tow-away area) means no parking and is valid for the length of the street, or until you come to a tow-away sign with a red line through it. If a street or square has no cars parked in it, you can safely assume it's a seriously enforced no-parking zone. In some areas, self-appointed *parcheggiatori* will look after your car for a small fee; although this practice is illegal, it's worth coughing up to ensure your tyres remain intact.

Autosilo Diaz

Piazza Diaz, Centre (02 8646 0077). Metro Duomo/bus 54/tram 15. **Open** 7am-2am daily. **Rates** €2.50 per hr; €28.50 24hrs. **Credit** AmEx, DC, MC, V. **Map** p311 A1/p312 B2.

Garage Meravigli
Via Camperio 4, North (02 8646 1784). Metro Cairoli/bus 54, 58/ tram 1, 19, 24. **Open** 7am-8pm daily. **Rates** €4 per hr; €24.80 24hrs. **No credit cards. Map** p308 C2.

Rinascente
Via Agnello, Centre (02 885 2419). Metro Duomo. **Open** 7.30am-1.30am daily. **Rates** €9 3hrs; €11 4hrs; €1 each subsequent hr. **Credit** AmEx, DC, MC, V. **Map** p311 A1/p312 B1.

Car pounds
If you can't find your car, chances are it has been towed away. There is an information office in via Beccaria 19; ring it on 02 7727 0280/1 quoting your number plate to find out to which car pound it has been taken. There is a hefty charge for recovering your car.

Petrol
Petrol stations sell regular petrol (*benzina*), unleaded petrol (*senza piombo* or *verde*) and diesel (*gasolio*). Liquid propane gas is GPL. Most stations offer full service on weekdays, but are often closed at lunchtimes. At night and on Sundays many stations have self-service pumps that accept €5, €10 or €20 notes in good condition. Note that few petrol stations accept credit cards.

Car hire
To hire a car you must be over 21 – in some cases 23 – and have held a licence for at least a year. You will be required to leave a credit card as security. It's advisable to take out collision damage waiver (CDW) and personal accident insurance (PAI) on top of basic third party insurance. Companies that do not offer CDW are best avoided.

Avis
National booking line *02 7541 9761.* **Credit** AmEx, DC, MC, V. **Open** 24hrs daily.
Linate airport (02 715 123). **Open** 7.30am-midnight daily.
Malpensa airport (02 585 8481). **Open** 7am-midnight daily.
Stazione Centrale, North (02 669 0280). **Open** 8am-8pm Mon-Fri; 8am-4pm Sat. **Map** p309 B2.
Piazza Diaz, Centre (02 8901 0645). Metro Duomo/bus 54. **Open** 8am-7pm Mon-Fri. **Map** p311 A1/p312 B2.

Hertz
Linate airport (02 7020 0256/0297). **Open** 7.30am-12.30am daily.
Malpensa airport (02 5858 1312/ 1081). **Open** 7.30am-midnight daily.

Piazza Duca d'Aosta 9, Stazione Centrale, North (02 6698 5151/ 6153). **Open** 8am-8pm Mon-Fri; 8am-2pm Sat-Sun. **Map** p309 B2.
Via Alcuino 16, West (02 3360 3073). Metro Lotto/bus 48, 78. **Open** 8am-7.30pm Mon-Fri; 8am-1pm Sat. **Map** p308 B2, C2. **Credit** AmEx, DC, MC, V.

Bicycles & motorbikes
Aggressive drivers, numerous tram tracks and cobbled streets mean Milan is less than kind to bikes or bikers. The number of cycle paths is growing, though, especially around the grounds of the Milano Fiera (*see p97*), Parco Sempione (*see p67*) and along the Navigli (*see p86*).

The Ciclobby club (02 6931 1624/www.associazioni.milano. it/ciclobby) organises bike tours in cultural and environmentally interesting areas every Sunday for members and non-members.

Bike hire
To hire a scooter or moped (*motorino*) you'll need a credit card, an identity document and a cash deposit. Helmets are required on all kinds of scooters, motorbikes or mopeds; the police are very strict about enforcing this.

For bicycles, it is normally enough to leave an identity document. For mopeds up to 50cc you need to be over 14; a driver's licence is required for anything over 50cc.

AWS Bicimotor
Via Ponte Seveso 33, North (02 6707 2145). Metro Centrale FS or Sondrio/bus 90, 91, 92/tram 2. **Open** 9am-1pm, 3-7pm Tue-Sat. **Credit** MC, V. **Map** p309 A2.
City and mountain bike rental.

Biancoblu
Via Gallarate 33, West (02 308 2430/ www.biancoblu.com). Tram 14, 19, 33. **Open** 9am-12.30pm, 2.30-7pm Mon-Fri; 9am-12.30pm Sat; 8-10am, 6-8pm Sat, Sun for pre-booked bikes. **Credit** AmEx, DC, MC, V. **Map** off p308 A1.
Bikes and electric bikes for rent.

Motorcycle Tours & Rentals
Via del Ricordo 31, East (02 2720 1556/www.mototouring.com). Metro Crescenzago then bus 53. **Open** 9am-6pm Mon-Sat. **Credit** AmEx, DC, MC, V. **Map** off p309 A2.
Bikes, motorbikes and scooters.

Getting around Lombardy
For public transport in the Greater Milan area, *see p280*. For general train information, *see p280*. For travel between Milan and the other destinations covered in this guide, see the **Lakes & Cities** section (*pp188-265*). There are over 100 national bus services that pass through Milan, 41 of which pass through Stazione Garibaldi.

The Lombardy regional council's website (www.info point.it) has a handy journey-planner for the area, but this is only available in Italian.

Regional rail services
Regional train services start at Milan's numerous stations (*see p281*). The fastest trains leave from Stazione Centrale; regional and inter-regional trains from other stations:
● **Cadorna**
for commuter trains to northern suburbs: Meda–Canzo–Asso; Saronno–Varese–Laveno Monbello; Saronno–Como.
● **Porta Garibaldi**
for Rho, Novara, Vercelli, Chivasso.
● **Lambrate**
for Pavia, Tortona, Treviglio, Brescia, Desenzano and Sirmione.
● **Lambrate & Rogoredo**
for Lodi.

Driving
For general driving information, *see p282*.
Once you have negotiated Milan's Tangenziale ring road and exited the city, you can opt to travel on the excellent *autostrade* (motorways), which will whisk you efficiently (though at a cost) from A to B, but may be short on scenery. Alternatively, there is a far-reaching and, on the whole, well-maintained network of *strade statali* (SS; state highways), which provide a more picturesque view of the region. *Strade provinciali* (SP; provincial roads) are not always in tip-top condition, and don't necessarily take the most straightforward route from A to B, but will undoubtedly provide some memorable Lombard driving moments.

Directory

Resources A-Z

Accommodation

It's wise to have a reservation before arriving in Milan. If you don't, the following booking agencies will help you.

Associazione Provinciale Albergatori di Milano

Malpensa 02 5858 0230/Linate 02 7020 0443/Fiera di Milano 02 4997 7610. **Open** 9am-6pm Mon-Fri.

Centro Prenotazione Hotel Italia

Freephone 800 015 772/02 2940 4616/www.hotelme.it. **Open** 9am-8pm Mon-Fri; 9-5pm Sat.

Hotel Central Booking

02 805 4242/www.hotelbooking.com. **Open** 9am-6pm Mon-Fri.

Traveleurope

www.traveleurope.it. **Credit** AmEx, MC, V.

Age restrictions

Cigarettes and alcohol cannot legally be sold to under-16s. Beer and wine can be bought at bars from the age of 16, spirits from 18. Anyone aged 14 or over can ride a moped or scooter of 50cc; no licence is needed. You must be over 18 to drive and over 21 to hire a car. The age of consent is 14 for both heterosexuals and homosexuals.

Business

If you're doing business in Milan, a call or visit to the commercial section of your embassy or consulate (*see below*) is a good first move. As ever in Italy, any personal recommendations will smooth your way immensely: use them shamelessly and mercilessly.

American Chamber of Commerce

Via Cantù 1, Centre (02 869 0661/ www.amcham.it). Metro Duomo or Cordusio/bus 50/tram 19, 20, 24, 27. **Open** 9am-12.30pm, 2-5.30pm Mon-Fri. **Map** p310 A2/p312 B2.

British Chamber of Commerce

Via Dante 12, North (02 877 798/ www.britchamitaly.com). Metro Cairoli/bus 43, 70/tram 1, 20, 24, 27. **Open** 9am-1pm, 2-5pm Mon-Fri. **Map** p310 A2/p312 A1.

Business centres

Conservatorio 22 Business Centre

Via Conservatorio 22, East (freephone 800 895 562/02 77 291/www.cogesta. it). Metro San Babila/bus 54, 61. **Map** p311 A1.

Executive Service Network

Via V Monti 8, West (freephone 800 938 373/02 467 121/www.executive network.it). Metro Cadorna or Conciliazione/bus 61, 68/tram 1, 19, 27. **Open** 8.30am-6pm Mon-Fri. **Map** p310 A1.

Tiempo Group

Via Giovanni da Udine 34, North (freephone 800 246 868/02 3809 3456/www.tiemponord.it). Bus 40, 69/ tram 14, 19, 33. **Map** off p308 B1.

Conference organisers

Milan offers excellent conference facilities of all kinds and locations. The city moves and shakes with over 900 conventions held each year at the Fiera di Milano (*see p97*).

Company conferences can be held in magnificent historic buildings such as the Milan Chamber of Commerce's very central Palazzo Affari Ai Giureconsulti (piazza Mercanti 2, Centre, 02 8515 5873) or in the very modern Magna Pars (via Tortona 15, South, 02 8940 1384), situated near the fashionable Navigli district (*see p86* **Canals plus**). Alternatively, most of the major hotels can cater for events (*see chapter* **Where to Stay**).

If you don't wish to handle the details yourself, a number of agencies will smooth the way for you. First, there's the Milan Conference Bureau (02 227 6000, www.milanconference. com); then there's the AIM Group, (via Ripamonti 129, 02 566 011), which has 40 years experience in the business. Based in Rome, Italcongressi (www.italcongressi. com) has a lot of useful information on regional conference organisers and interpreters.

Couriers (international)

There are many courier services in Milan and pick-up at your doorstep is reliable. Make sure the driver provides you with a company envelope or box – if you send courier documents in a plain envelope to the US, the receiver will be charged customs duty when they arrive. DHL 199 199 345/02 8247 0288 from abroad/www.dhl.it. **Federal Express** freephone 800 123 800/www.fedex.com. **TNT** 803 868/www.tntitaly.it. **UPS** freephone 800 877 877/ www.ups.com.

Couriers (local)

There are two local courier services that deliver extremely quickly. If you're planning a lengthy stay, get a subscription to either. **Pony Express** 02 8441/www.pony.it **Rinaldi L'Espresso** 02 760 311/ www.rinaldilespresso.it.

Interpreters

International Association of Conference Interpreters (AIIC)

www.aiic.net.

Communication Trend Italia

Via Palestrina 31, East (02 669 1338/www.cti-communication.it). Metro Caiazzo or Loreto/bus 90, 91, 92/tram 1. **Open** 9am-1pm, 2-6pm Mon-Fri. **Map** p309 B2.

Executive Service Network

Via V Monti 8, West (freephone 800 938 373/02 467 121/www.executive network.it). Metro Cadorna or Conciliazione/bus 61, 68/tram 1, 19, 27. **Open** 8.30am-6pm Mon-Fri. **Map** p310 A1.

Consulates & embassies

Listed below are the Milan consulates of the main English-speaking countries. A full list is found under *Consolati* in the phone book.

Australia
*Via Borgogna 2, Centre (02 777 041).
Metro San Babila/bus 54, 60, 61, 73.*
Open 9am-noon, 2-4pm Mon-Thur;
9am-noon Fri. **Map** p309 C1/p312 C1.

South Africa
*Vicolo San Giovanni sul Muro 4,
Centre (02 809 036). Metro Cairoli/
tram 1, 16.* **Open** 8.30am-4.30pm
Mon-Fri. **Map** p310 A2/p312 A1.

UK
*Via San Paolo 7, Centre (02 723
001). Metro Duomo or San Babila/
bus 15, 60, 73.* **Open** 9.15am-
12.15pm, 2.30-4.30pm Mon-Fri.
Map p309 C1/p312 B1.

US
*Via Principe Amedeo 2/10, North
(02 290 351). Metro Turati/tram 1,
2, 94.* **Open** 8.30am-4.30pm Mon-Fri.
Map p309 C1.

Embassies in Rome

Australia 06 852 721/
www.australian-embassy.it.
Canada 06 445 981/www.canada.it.
Ireland 06 697 9121.
New Zealand 06 441 7171/
www.tradenz.govt.nz.
South Africa 06 852 541.
UK 06 4220 0001/
www.britishembassy.gov.uk.
US 06 46 741/www.usembassy.it.

Customs

As long as they arrive from
another EU country, EU
citizens do not have to declare
goods imported into or
exported out of Italy for
their personal use up to
the following limits: 800

cigarettes; 200 cigars; ten
litres of spirits; 90 litres of
wine; up to €12,500 in cash.
  For non-EU citizens, the
following limits apply: 200
cigarettes or 100 small cigars
or 50 cigars or 250g (8.8oz) of
tobacco; one litre of spirits
(over 22 per cent alcohol) or
two litres of wine; 50g (1.76oz)
of perfume; 500g (17.6oz) of
coffee and 100g (3.52oz) of tea.
There are no restrictions on the
import of cameras, watches or
electrical goods, but proof of
purchase may be requested.
Visitors are also allowed to
carry up to €12,500 in cash.

Disabled travellers

Information

The best source of information for
the disabled is AIAS (Associazione
Italiana Assistenza Spastici). Most
literature is in Italian, but the website
(*see below*) has up-to-date information
on Milan and Lombardy in English.
Or you can send a specific request
to aiasmi.vacanze@tiscalinet.it to
receive information in English.
  The city council also runs a *sportello
disabili* (disabled desk), where helpful
information is dispensed, in Italian
only (02 6765 4740, sportello_disabili
@regione.lombardia.it).
  The website www.asphi.it/english
provides information in English on
hearing and visual impairment,
Down's Syndrome, autism,
specialised teachers and therapists,
aids and prostheses, sport and leisure
time, alternative communication and
related associations.

AIAS Milano Onlus
*Via Cittadini 3, North (02 6765 4740/
www.milanopertutti.it). Bus 40/tram
12, 19.* **Open** 9am-6.30pm Tue, Thur;
9am-1.30pm Sat. **Map** off p308 A1.

Sportello disabili
*Via Fabio Filzi 22, North (02 6765
4740). Metro Centrale FS, Gioia or
Repubblica/tram 2, 9, 20, 33.* **Open**
9am-5pm Mon-Thur; 9am-3pm Fri;
9am-1.30pm Sat. **Map** p309 A1.

Sightseeing

Pavements in Milan's centre are
narrow, and negotiating cobbled
streets is a challenge. On the upside,
most street corners have pram/
wheelchair ramps, and well-designed
ramps and lifts and disabled toilets
have been installed in many museums.
Visit the AIAS website (*see p285*) for
up-to-date details.

Toilets

While the law requires all public
facilities to have bathrooms for
the disabled, many of those in old
buildings haven't yet faced the
music. The more modern-looking the
bar, restaurant, convention facility or
museum, the more likely it is to have
renovated and appropriately adapted
all of its public facilities.

Transport

Some city transport lines are equipped
for the disabled. The newer yellow
metro line is fully accessible with
elevators, while the older red and
green lines were being brought up
to scratch as this guide went to
press. See www.atm-mi.it for a full
listing in English, or visit the ATM
information points (see *p280*). AIAS
(*see above*) provides up-to-the-minute
bus, tram and metro information.
  The Ferrovie dello Stato (FS, state
railway) is phasing in easy-access
carriages, slowly. Trains with
wheelchair facilities are indicated by
a wheelchair symbol on timetables.
The CAD Centro Assistenza Disabili
(disabled assistance; 02 6707 0958) at
Centrale, Cadorna or Garibaldi stations
will arrange help for boarding
or alighting from trains. Call 24
hours prior to departure to organise
assistance. For the principal stations
of the 14 main Italian cities (Torino,
Milano, Verona, Venezia, Trieste,
Bologna, Genova, Firenze, Roma
Termini, Ancona, Bari, Napoli,
Reggio Calabria, and Messina)
the request can be made three
hours in advance. For assistance
on international trains, the request
must be made three days in advance.

Travel advice

For up-to-date information on travel to a specific country –
including the latest news on safety and security, health
issues, local laws and customs – contact your home
country government's department of foreign affairs.
Most have websites packed with useful advice for
would-be travellers.

Australia	**Republic of Ireland**
www.dfat.gov.au/travel	www.irlgov.ie/iveagh
Canada	**UK**
www.voyage.gc.ca	www.fco.gov.uk/travel
New Zealand	**USA**
www.mft.govt.nz/travel	www.state.gov/travel

Directory

Transport to both Linate (bus 73) and Malpensa (Malpensa Express) airports (*see p278*) is wheelchair-accessible. Inform your airline when you book that you will require assistance.

Book taxis in advance, specifying if you need a car large enough to cope with a wheelchair (*carozzella*). Alternatively, the following services use small vans and seating for up to eight; book at least 48 hours ahead. **CTA** 02 355 9360/02 357 4768 **Missione Handicap** 02 453 1236 (both open 7.30am-6pm Mon-Fri).

Where to stay & eat

AIAS (*see p285*) keeps an updated list of wheelchair-accessible hotels: see the website for listings. See also pp38-50 for details of hotels with disabled facilities.

Few restaurants or bars are fully accessible, though staff will be more than willing to help you overcome barriers in most of them. The situation improves in the summer, when tables are placed outside. AIAS has listings of accessible bars and restaurants in all zones of Milan – see under *cerca locale* on its website.

Wheelchair hire

Farmacie (pharmacies, *see p287*) either rent wheelchairs or can direct you to specialised wheelchair rental services.

Drugs

If you are caught in possession of drugs of any type, you will be taken before a magistrate. If you can prove that what you were carrying was for personal use, you will be let off with a fine or ordered to leave Italy. Recent calls for stricter laws and the city's drive to clean up Milan's parks have meant that the police are even more on the alert. Habitual offenders will be offered rehab. Anything more than a tiny amount will push you into the criminal category: couriering or dealing can land you in prison for up to 20 years. It is an offence to buy, sell or even give drugs away. Sniffer dogs are a fixture at most ports of entry into Italy and customs police take a dim view of visitors entering with even the smallest quantities of narcotics; they are nearly always refused entry.

Electricity

Most wiring systems work on 220v, which is compatible with British-bought appliances. With US 110v equipment you need a current transformer. A few systems in old buildings are 125v. Two-pin adaptor plugs (*adattatori*) can be bought at any electrical shop (*elettricità*).

Emergencies

See also below **Health**; *p289* **Money**; *p290* **Police**; *p291* **Safety & security**.

Thefts or losses should be reported immediately at the nearest police station (*see p290*). You should report the loss of your passport to your embassy or consulate (*see p284*). Report the loss of a credit card or travellers' cheques immediately to your credit card company (*see p290*).

National emergency numbers

Ambulance Ambulanza 118.
Fire service Vigili del Fuoco 115.
Police Carabinieri (English helpline) 112; Polizia di Stato 113.

Car breakdown (*see also p282*) Automobile Club d'Italia (ACI) 800 3000; Europ Assistance freephone 800 830 044.

Domestic emergencies

If you need to report a malfunction, these emergency lines are open 24 hours a day.
Electricity AEM 02 2521; Enel freephone 800 900 800.
Gas Italgas freephone 800 900 777; AEM 02 5255.
Telephone Telecom Italia 187.
Water 02 412 0910.

Health

Emergency health care is available for all travellers through the Italian national health system. By law, hospital accident-and-emergency departments (*see below*) must treat all emergency cases free.

Before travelling to Milan, EU citizens should obtain an E111 form (available in the UK from health centres, post offices and social security offices). This allows them to consult a national health service doctor free of charge. *See also p287* **Insurance**.

Accident & emergency

Should you be in need of urgent medical care, head to the *Pronto Soccorso* (casualty department) of one of the hospitals listed below, all of which offer 24hr casualty services. If your child needs emergency treatment, go to the casualty department of the Ospedale dei Bambini Vittore Buzzi.

Ospedale dei Bambini Vittore Buzzi

Via Castelvetro 32, North (02 5799 5363). Bus 43, 57/tram 12, 14. **Map** p308 B1.
Obstetric as well as paediatric casualty departments.

Ospedale Fatebenefratelli

Corso Porta Nuova 23, North (02 63 631). Metro Turati/bus 43, 41. **Map** p309 B1, C1.

Ospedale Maggiore di Milano

Via F Sforza 28/35, South (02 5503 3209/switchboard 02 55 031). Metro Crocetta or Missori/bus 77, 94/tram 4, 12, 24. **Map** p311 A1.

Ospedale Mangiagalli

Via della Commenda 12, South (02 57 991/sexual violence casualty department 02 5799 2489). Metro Crocetta/bus 77/tram 4. **Map** p311 B1.

Ospedale Niguarda

Piazza Ospedale Maggiore 3, North (02 64 441/poison centre 02 6610 1029/burns centre 02 6444 2381/www.ospedale-niguarda.it). Bus 5, 40, 51, 83/tram 4. **Map** off p308 A2.
The Niguarda is renowned all over the country for its departments for severe burns and poisoning.

Complementary medicine

A wide range of homeopathic remedies is available from most chemist's shops (*see p287*).

Contraception & abortion

Condoms are on sale near checkouts in supermarkets, or over the counter in pharmacies (*see below*). The contraceptive pill is available on prescription. The morning-after pill can be obtained at hospital casualty departments (*see p286*) – the doctor on duty will write a prescription that you take to a pharmacy.

Abortion is available on financial hardship or health grounds, and legal only when performed in public hospitals.

Each district has a family-planning clinic (*consultorio familiare*), run by the local health authority, and EU citizens with an E111 form are entitled to use them, paying the same charges for services as locals. They also give advice and help on contraception, abortion and gynaecological problems. They are listed in the phone book under *Consultorio Familiare*; or visit www.asl.milano.it/DipAssi/consultorio.asp.

Gynaecological advice can also be had at the following women's clinic, or at the international health centres listed further below.

AIED

Via Vitruvio 43, East (02 6671 4156). Metro Lima/bus 60/tram 5, 20, 33. **Open** 9.30am-7pm Mon-Fri. **Map** p309 B2.

Dentists

Most dentists (*see Dentisti* in the *Pagine Gialle*) in Italy work privately. You may wait for months for a dental appointment in a public hospital. Dental treatment in Italy is not cheap and may not be covered by your health insurance. For serious dental emergencies, make for the hospital casualty departments listed on p286. Check with your consulate for international health clinics where English-speaking dentists can help you. The English *Yellow Pages* lists English-speaking dentists.

Doctors

EU nationals with an E111 form can consult a national health service doctor free of charge. Drugs that he or she prescribes can be bought from chemists at prices set by the Health Ministry. If you need tests or specialist outpatient treatment, this too will be charged at fixed rates (*il ticket*).

Non-EU nationals who need to consult health service doctors will be charged a small fee at the doctor's discretion.

Pharmacists (*see below*) are generally useful sources of information: they will recommend local doctors and provide you with addresses of laboratories to have tests done.

Milan's long-established international health clinics have highly qualified medical staff, will do tests, and deal with emergency situations.

American International Medical Center (AIMC)

Via Mercalli 11, South (02 5831 9808/www.iht.it/aimc). Metro Missori/bus 94/tram 15. **Open** 9am-6pm Mon-Fri. **Map** p311 B1.

International Health Centre

Galleria Strasburgo 3 or via Durini 17, Centre (02 7634 0720). Metro Duomo or San Babila/bus 61. **Open** 9am-7pm Mon-Fri. **Map** p309 C1/p312 C2.

The Milan Clinic

Via Cerva 25, Centre (02 7601 6047). Metro San Babila/bus 60, 65, 73. **Open** 9am-6pm Mon-Thur; 9am-5pm Fri. **Map** p311 A1/p312 C2.

Helplines & agencies

See also p286 **Ospedale Mangiagalli**.

ALA

02 8951 6464. **Open** 9.30am-1.30pm Mon-Fri.
STD, HIV and AIDS helpline.

CADMI

02 5501 5519. **Open** 10am-1pm, 2.30-6pm Mon-Thur.
Sexual violence and rape helpline. There is normally an English-speaking volunteer available.

Hospitals

Milan's public hospitals (*see p286* **Accident & emergency**) offer good to excellent treatment for most ills.

Opticians

See p150 **Opticians**.

Pharmacies & prescriptions

See also p145 **Pharmacies**.
Pharmacies (*farmacie*, identified by a green cross) give informal medical advice for straightforward ailments, as well as make up doctor's prescriptions. Most pharmacies also sell homeopathic and veterinary medicines, and all will check your height/weight/blood pressure on

request. Over-the-counter drugs such as aspirin are considerably more expensive in Italy than in the UK or US. Anyone who requires regular medication should bring adequate supplies of their drugs with them. Also, take care to know the generic name of any medicines you need, since they may be available in Italy under different names.

Normal opening hours are 8.30am-12.30pm and 3.30-7.30pm Mon-Sat. Outside of normal hours, a duty rota system operates. Night service typically operates 9pm-8am. A list by the door of any pharmacy indicates the nearest open ones; this is also published in the local paper. At duty pharmacies there is a surcharge of €3.87 per client (not per item) when the main shop is shut.

The following pharmacies have night services.

Carlo Erba

Piazza del Duomo 21, Centre (02 7202 3120). Metro Duomo. **Open** 24hrs daily. **Map** p311 A1/p312 B2.

Formaggia

Corso Buenos Aires 4, North (02 2951 3320). Metro Porta Venezia. **Open** 24hrs daily. **Map** p309 B2.

Stazione Centrale

First Floor Galleria, Stazione Centrale, North (02 669 0935). Metro Centrale FS. **Open** 24hrs daily. **Map** p309 B2.

ID

You are required by law to carry photo ID with you at all times. You will be asked to produce it if you are stopped by traffic police (who will demand your driving licence, which you must have on you whenever you are in charge of a motor vehicle). You will also need ID when you check into a hotel.

Insurance

See also p286 **Health** *and p290* **Police**.
EU nationals are entitled to reciprocal medical care in Italy, provided they have an E111 form (*see p286*). This will cover you for emergencies, but using it involves having to deal with the intricacies of the Italian state health system. For short-term visitors it's better to take out health cover under

private travel insurance. Private
insurance allows you to choose
your health-care provider.

Non-EU citizens should take
out private medical insurance
for all eventualities before
setting out from home.

If you rent a vehicle,
motorcycle or moped, pay the
extra charge for full insurance
cover. Sign the collision
damage waiver when hiring a
car. *See also p283* **Car hire**.

Internet & email

Most hotels – even budget ones
– will allow you to plug your
modem into their phone system;
more up-market establishments
should have PC points in
bedrooms. Italian providers
offering free internet access
include: **Caltanet** (www.calta
net.it), **Libero** (www.libero.it),
Tiscali (www.tiscali.it) and
Kataweb (www.kataweb.it).

Checking email or surfing
the net is no problem in Milan –
there are many internet cafés.

Gr@zia Internet Café
*Piazza Duca d'Aosta 14, North
(02 6700 543). Metro Centrale
FS/bus 60/tram 5, 20, 33.* **Open**
8am-2am daily. **Rates** €4/hr.
Map p309 B1, B2.

Thenetgate
*Via Aselli 23, East (02 7000
6248). Bus 93/tram 5.* **Open**
10am-1pm, 3-8pm Mon-Sat.
Rates €4.70/hr; €3.90/hr
students. **Map** off p309 B2.

Left luggage

Most hotels will look after
your luggage for you, even
after you have checked out.
The left-luggage depot at
Stazione Centrale (02 6371
2667) operates 6am-1am
daily; at Malpensa airport
Terminal 1 (02 5858 0069) 6am-
10pm daily; Linate airport (02
7012 4451) 7am-9.30pm daily
(if you find it closed during
these hours, ring the bell and
someone will turn up, though
it may take ten minutes).

Legal help

The first stop if you find
yourself in need of legal
help should always be your
consulate; *see p284.* You may
be directed to local law firms
with English-speaking staff.
Milan is also home to many
associates of English and
American law firms.

Libraries

Milan has some 40 libraries
with public access, the most
useful and central of which
are listed below. Visit www.
comune.milano.it/biblioteche
for a full list. It is always
useful to take an identity
document with you.

Biblioteca del
Conservatorio G Verdi
*Via Conservatorio 12, East (02 762
1101/www.conservatorio-milano.it).
Metro San Babila/bus 54, 61.* **Open**
8am-7.30pm Mon-Fri; 8am-1pm Sat.
Map p311 A1, A2.
Attached to Milan's conservatory,
this library has a huge collection of
music-related books and manuscripts.
Requests for books must be made
9am-noon, 2.30-6pm weekdays and
9am-noon Saturday.

Biblioteca Nazionale
Braidense
*Via Brera 28, North (02 8646
0907/www.braidense.it). Metro
Lanza or Montenapoleone/bus 61,
94/tram 1, 2, 3, 4, 12, 27.*
Open 8.30am-6.15pm Mon-Fri;
9am-1.45pm Sat.* **Map** p308 C2.
The Braidense contains over a
million books, plus manuscripts,
periodicals, 19th-century prints
and antique books, microfilms and
CDs. Consultation is free, but only
Lombardy residents can borrow.

Biblioteca Sormani
*Corso di Porta Vittoria 6, South
(freephone 800 880 066/02 8846
3397). Metro Missori or San Babila/
bus 54, 60, 65, 73, 84, 94/tram 12,
23, 27.* **Open** 9-7.30pm Mon-Sat.
Map p311 A1, A2.
Milan's central public library has over
600,000 works, including Stendhal's
library, a great collection of dailies,
and a range of audio recordings.
Entrance is free, but limited to over-
14s only. Only Milan and provincial
residents can borrow. Visit www.
comune.milano.it/biblioteche for
more information.

Civico Archivio
Fotografico
*Castello Sforzesco, Piazza Castello 1,
North (02 8846 3664). Metro
Cairoli/bus 57, 70, 94/tram 1, 4, 7,
20 27.* **Open** 9am-2pm Mon-Fri.
Map p308 C2/p312 A1.
A great collection of over 600,000
images and photographs dating back
to the 19th century. They are mainly
of Milan and Italy, but there are also
noteworthy shots of the Crimean
war. You can get prints made up
too. Consultation by appointment.

English-language
libraries

CSSU (Centro di Studi
sugli Stati Uniti)
*Piazza Sant'Alessandro 1, Centre
(02 5031 3563/http://users.unimi.it/
cssu). Metro Missori/bus 15/tram 2,
3, 14.* **Open** 10am-5pm Mon-Thur.
Map p310 A2/p312 B2.
Housed in Milan University, this
library hosts a collection of over
10,000 English-language volumes,
focusing on US literature, history
and social and political issues.

Università Cattolica
del Sacro Cuore
*Largo Gemelli 1, West (freephone
800 209 902/02 72 341/Bibliopoint
02 7234 3849). Metro Sant'Ambrogio/
bus 50, 58, 94.* **Open** 9am-8pm Mon-
Fri; 9am-1pm Sat. **Map** p310 A2.
A well-stocked university library
of over one million books, many in
English. A free three-day ticket is
free from Bibliopoint, the office on
the ground floor of the university's
Gregorianum building)

Lost property

Ufficio Oggetti
Rinvenuti
*Via Friuli 30, South (02 8845 3900/
08/09). Bus 62, 90, 92/tram 4.* **Open**
8.30am-4pm Mon-Fri. **Map** p311 B2.
Milan city council's lost property
office lists everything found the
previous week on its website
(www.comune.milano.it) –
look under *Oggetti Rinvenuti*.

Ufficio Oggetti
Smarriti Ferrovie
dello Stato
*Stazione Centrale, Galleria delle
Partenze (in the left-luggage office),
North (02 6371 2667). Metro
Centrale FS/bus 53/tram 2.* **Open**
6am-1am daily. **Map** p309 A2.
Anything lost on trains should
end up here.

Directory

Media

See also chapter **Media
Central**.

Magazines

With the naked, glistening female
form emblazoned across their
covers most weeks, Italy's serious
news magazines are not always
immediately distinguishable from
the large selection of soft porn on
newsstands. But *Panorama* and
L'Espresso provide a generally
high-standard round-up of the
week's news; *Sette* and *Venerdì* –
colour supplements of *Corriere
della Sera* (Thur) and *La Repubblica*
(Fri) – have nice photos, though the
text often leaves much to be desired.
Instead try the *Corriere della Sera*'s
Io Donna supplement (Sat), which
has more meat to it… and isn't
just for women. For tabloid-style
scandal, try *Gente* and *Oggi*, or the
execrable *Eva 3000, Novella 2000*
and *Cronaca Vera*.

The biggest-selling title of them,
however, all is *Famiglia Cristiana* –
available from newsstands or most
churches – which alternates Vatican
line-toeing with Vatican-baiting,
depending on relations between
the Holy See and the idiosyncratic
Paoline monks who produce it.

National dailies

Italian newspapers can be a
frustrating read. Long, indigestible
political stories with very little
background explanation
predominate. On the plus side, Italian
papers are delightfully unsnobbish
and happily blend serious news,
leaders by internationally known
commentators, and well-written,
often surreal, crime and human-
interest stories. Sports coverage
in the dailies is extensive and
thorough, but if you're not sated
there are the mass-circulation
sports papers *Corriere dello
Sport, Gazzetta dello Sport* and
Tuttosport. Milan's businessmen
are major purchasers of the three
big financial dailies, *Il Sole 24 Ore,
Italia Oggi* and *MilanoFinanza*.

Corriere della Sera

www.corriere.it
To the centre of centre-left, the
Milan-based *Corriere della Sera*
is good on crime and foreign news.
It includes a daily Milan section,
which is useful for information on
films and cultural events, not to
mention strikes, roadworks etc.
Its *ViviMilano* supplement (Wed)
has weekly listings.

La Repubblica

www.repubblica.it
This left-ish daily is good on the mafia
and the Vatican, and comes up with
the occasional major scoop on its
business pages. It has a Milan
section and Friday listings.

La Stampa

www.lastampa.it
Part of the massive empire of Turin's
Agnelli family, *La Stampa* has good
(though inevitably pro-Agnelli)
business reporting.

Local dailies

See also *Corriere della Sera* and
La Repubblica above. A rash of
free newspapers is currently being
distributed on the underground. The
best is *City*, owned by *Corriere della
Sera*, which has public transport
updates and useful addresses.

Il Giorno

www.ilgiorno.it
Owned by Silvio Berlusconi's family,
Il Giorno is understandably pro-
government… often to a nauseating
(when not risible) extent.

Foreign press

The *Financial Times, International
Herald Tribune* (with *Italy Daily*
supplement), *Wall Street Journal*,
USA Today, and most British and
European dailies can be found on the
day of issue at central newsstands;
some US dailies appear a day late.

Listings & small ads

Easy Milano

www.easymilano.it
Free bimonthly classified-ad mag for
the English-speaking community,
distributed at consulates and expat
hangouts in Milan.

Hello Milano

www.hellomilano.it
A free monthly in English with event
and exhibition listings, distributed at
the APT office (*see p294*).

The Informer

www.informer.it
Although not specifically Milanese,
this has been going strong for 17 years
and has extremely useful advice on
dealing with red tape and a good
small-ads section. Worth reading if
you are thinking of moving to Italy.

Secondamano

www.secondamano.it
The mother of all classifieds (though
in Italian). Includes ads for car,

household and other second-hand
sales, plus flat rents and shares.
Just the place to advertise English
lessons if you're thinking of staying.
Available daily at newsstands.

Radio

The three state-owned stations (RAI
1, 89.7FM, 1332AM; RAI 2, 91.7FM,
846AM; RAI 3, 93.7FM, 1107AM)
play classical and light music, and
also feature endless chat shows and
regular, excellent news bulletins. If
you can't stand babbling DJs, try
LifeGate Radio 105.1FM (*see p172*
Power stations); for world events
as seen through the eyes of the
Catholic Church in English and
Italian, listen to **Radio Vatican**'s
(1260AM) news bulletins at 8.30am,
11am, 4pm and 6.15pm daily.

For UK and US chart hits, mixed
with home-grown offerings, try these:
GammaRadio 97.1FM
Radio DeeJay 106.9FM
Radio Lombardia 100.3FM
Radio Monte Carlo 105.5FM
Radio 105 105FM
Radio Reporter 103.7FM

Television

Italy has six major networks (three
owned by state broadcaster RAI and
three belonging to Mediaset, owned
by prime minister Silvio Berlusconi,
who, as head of the government, also
indirectly owns RAI). Many smaller,
local stations provide hours of
compulsively awful channel-zapping
fun. The standard of television news
and current affairs programmes
varies; most, however, offer a breadth
of coverage that makes British TV
news look like a parish magazine.

Money

Italy's currency is the euro.
There are euro banknotes of
€5, €10, €20, €100, €200 and
€500, and coins worth €1 and
€2 as well as 1, 2, 5, 10, 20 and
50 cents. Euros from any Euro-
zone country are valid in Italy.

ATMs

Most banks have 24-hour cashpoint
(*Bancomat*) machines, and the vast
majority accept cards with the
Maestro and Cirrus symbols.

Banking hours

Most banks are open 8.30am-1.30pm
and 2.45-3.45pm, Mon-Fri. Banks are
closed on public holidays.

Bureaux de change

Commission rates vary considerably. Banks usually offer better exchange rates than private bureaux de change (*uffici di cambio*). Watch out for 'No Commission' signs, as the rate of exchange will almost certainly be bad. Main post offices (*see below*) also have exchange bureaux, though they don't accept travellers' cheques. Many city centre bank branches have automatic cash-exchange machines, which accept notes in most major currencies (in good condition). Take a passport or other identity document whenever you're dealing with money, particularly to change travellers' cheques or withdraw money on a credit card.

American Express
Via Larga 4, Centre (02 7210 4010). Metro Missori/bus 54/tram 12, 15, 20, 27. **Open** 9am-5.30pm Mon-Fri. **Map** p308 C2/p312 B2.

Traverex
Malpensa Airport Terminal 1 (02 7486 7162). **Open** 6.30am-10.30pm daily.
Via Dante 8, North (02 8909 6459). Metro Cairoli or Cordusio/tram 1, 24, 27. **Open** 9.30am-6.30pm Mon-Fri; 9.30am-12.30pm Sat. **Map** p310 A2/p312 A1.

Credit cards

Italians have a fondness for cash, but persuading them to take plastic has become a lot easier in the last few years. Nearly all hotels of two stars and above now accept at least some of the major credit cards. If you lose a credit card, phone one of the freephone emergency numbers listed below. All lines have English-speaking staff and are open 24 hours a day.

American Express
800 131 141 (*see also above*).
Diners' Club 800 864 064.
MasterCard Global Service Centre 800 870 866.
Visa and MasterCard 800 018 548.
Visa International Assistance Centre 800 819 014.

Police

Polizia locale, the city police (or what might be called traffic wardens), deal with traffic and minor problems that upset the smooth running of the city. They have a headquarters in via Beccaria 19 (Centre, 02 77

271, map p311 A1, p312 B2). Milan's main Polizia di Stato station, the Questura Centrale, is at via Fatebenefratelli 11 (North). The addresses of others, and of the Carabinieri's *commissariati* (police stations), are listed in phone books under *Polizia* and *Carabinieri* respectively. Incidents can be reported to either force.

Postal services

For couriers, *see p284* **Business**.

Italy's equivalent to first-class post, *posta prioritaria*, generally works very well: it promises delivery within 24 hours in Italy, three days for EU countries and four or five for the rest of the world. More often than not, it succeeds (62¢ minimum cost).

Stamps for all letters are sold at post offices and *tabaccherie* (*see p292*) only. Most post boxes are red and have two slots, one marked *Per la città* (for Milan) and the other *Per tutte le altre destinazioni* (for everywhere else).

The CAI-Postacelere service (available only at main post offices) costs somewhat more than *posta prioritaria* and delivers at the same speed, the only advantage being that you can track the progress of your letter on its website (www.poste.it) or by phone (info line 803 160, service operates 8am-8pm Mon-Sat). Registered mail (*raccomandata*) costs €2.35 on top of the normal rate to EU countries.

Local post offices usually open 8am-2pm Mon-Fri, and 8.30am-noon on Sat and any day preceding a public holiday. They close two hours earlier than normal on the last day of each month. Main post offices have longer opening hours and additional services, including fax.

For postal information of any kind, phone the central information office (803 160).

Posta Centrale
Via Cordusio 4, Centre (02 7248 2126). Metro Cordusio/tram 2, 3, 4, 12, 14, 24, 27. **Open** 8am-7pm Mon-Sat. **Map** p310 A2.

Ufficio Posta – Stazione Centrale
Stazione Centrale, North (02 673 95). Metro Centrale FS/bus 90, 91, 92/tram 1, 5, 33. **Open** 8am-7pm Mon-Fri; 8.30am-noon Sat. **Map** p309 A2.

Queuing

Most Milanese wait their turn in line courteously, grumbling their displeasure loudly if they're there too long. Queue-jumpers are given short shrift.

Religion

Anglican
All Saint's Church, via Solferino 17, North (02 655 2258). Metro Moscova/bus 43, 94. **Service** usually 7.15pm Wed; 10.30am Sun. **Map** p308 B2, C2.

Catholic
San Carlo, piazza Santa Maria del Carmine 2, North (02 8646 3365). Metro Lanza/bus 61/tram 3, 4, 12, 20. **Service** in English 10.30am Sun. **Map** p308 C2.

Jewish
Lower Ground Floor, via Guastalla 19, East (02 551 2301). Bus 60, 77. **Service** times vary, call for details. **Map** p311 A1.

Russian Orthodox
San Nicola, via San Gregorio 5, East (02 204 6996). Metro Lima or Repubblica/tram 1, 5. **Service** 10am Sun. **Map** p309 B2.

Zen Buddhist
Via Agnesi 18, South (02 5830 6763). Metro Porta Romana/bus 62/tram 9, 29, 30. **Service** call for details (6-8pm Mon-Sat). **Map** p311 B1.

Relocation

Anyone relocating to Italy is obliged to procure a series of forms and permits. EU citizens should have no problem in getting documentation once they are in Italy, but non-EU citizens are strongly advised to enquire at their local Italian embassy or consulate before travelling. There are agencies that specialise in obtaining documents for you – for a price, of course (see *Pratiche e certificati – Agenzie* in the *Yellow Pages*). An important address for all these tasks is the town hall (*municipio*).

Milan town hall
Via Larga 12, Centre (02 8846 2062). Metro Missori/bus 54/tram 12, 15, 20. **Open** 8.30am-1pm, 2.30-6pm Mon-Fri. **Map** p308 C2/p312 B2.

Paperwork

Permit to stay
EU citizens need a *permesso di soggiorno* if they're staying in Italy for over three months; non-EU citizens should (but usually don't) apply for one within eight days of their arrival in Italy. To get one, take four passport photographs, a *marca da bollo* (an official stamp available from *tabaccai*; see *p292*) worth €10.33, your passport, and proof that you have some means of supporting yourself and reason to be in Italy (such as a letter from an employer or certificate of registration at a school or university) to the Ufficio Stranieri for Milan at the Questura (via Montebello 26, North, 02 622 61); otherwise see *Polizia di Stato* in the phone book.

Residency certificate
If you plan to stay in Milan for over three months you will need a residency certificate (*certificato di residenza*). This is your registered address in Italy, and you'll need it to buy a car, get customs clearance on goods brought from abroad, and many other transactions. In order to obtain this, you need a *permesso di soggiorno* (permit to stay, original plus a photocopy) and your passport (plus a photocopy). Take these to the Ufficio Stranieri (foreigners office) at the town hall, which will then send someone round to check you are telling the truth.

Once armed with your residency certificate, you can request a *carta d'identità* (identity card), although a passport will suffice if you can't be bothered with the red tape. For this you need three passport photos and your *permesso di soggiorno*. Take this to the town hall or any local branch of the Central Records Office (www.comune.milano.it).

Scheda Professionale
This has replaced the old *libretto di lavoro* work permit and in theory, all non-Italian citizens employed in Italy

need one. Application forms can be obtained from the local Ispettorato di Lavoro (via Macchi 9, East, 02 679 21). The form must be signed by your employer; you then need to take it with your *permesso di soggiorno* and a photocopy back to the Ispettorato. Don't rush into getting one, however: often the requirement is waived, or employers arrange it for you.

Tax code & VAT number
Anyone living or working in Italy needs a *codice fiscale* (tax code). It is essential for opening a bank account or setting up utilities contracts. Take your passport and *permesso di soggiorno* to your local tax office (see *below*), fill in a form and return a few days later to pick up the card. You can also have it posted to you.

The self-employed or anyone doing business in Italy may also need a *partita IVA* (VAT number). It is free to open, but Italian bureaucracy is such that it is best to get an accountant to deal with the practicalities. Take your passport and *codice fiscale* to your nearest tax office (see *below*). Make sure you cancel your VAT number when you no longer need it: failure to do so may result in a visit from tax inspectors years later.

Addresses of tax offices can be found under *Agenzia delle Entrate* in the phone book or by looking them up at www.agenziaentrate.it/indirizzi/agenzia/uffici_locali. Call the Ministry of Economy and Finance's information line (freephone 848 800 333) or consult www.agenziaentrate.it for further information.

Bank accounts
To open an account you'll need a valid *permesso di soggiorno* or *certificato di residenza*, your *codice fiscale* (see *above*), proof of regular income from an employer (or a fairly substantial sum to deposit) and your passport.

Work
Casual employment can be hard to come by, especially for non-EU citizens, as document requirements are more complicated. English-language schools often look for mother-tongue teachers; the best of these will demand qualifications and/or experience. Expat periodicals (see *p289*) have help-wanted ads, as does *Secondamano*. The Friday edition of *Corriere della Sera* has a jobs supplement, where many larger companies and headhunters place ads. Temporary agencies offer call centre and secretarial jobs.

Adecco
Corso di Porta Romana 19, South (02 7200 2121). Metro Missori/tram 4, 24. **Open** 9am-1pm, 2-7pm Mon-Fri. **Map** p311 A1, B1.

Randstad
Corso Gasparrotto 1, North (02 6764 261/02 6703 170/www.randstad.it). Metro Centrale FS/bus 40, 43, 90, 91/tram 2, 9, 20, 33. **Open** 9am-6.30pm Mon-Fri. **Map** off p309 A2.

Accommodation
House-hunting in Milan is a challenge. Walk the neighbourhoods that appeal to you and look out for *affittasi* (to let) notices on buildings. Check classifieds in *Secondamano* (see *p289*) or *Trovo Casa*, the Wednesday supplement to the *Corriere della Sera*. The weekly *Più Case* magazine is on newsstands on Friday afternoon. Expat periodicals (see *p289*) also carry rental and sale notices. Estate agents are everywhere, but are not cheap – you will probably have to pay the equivalent of two months' rent in commission.

When you move into an apartment, it's normal to pay three months' rent in advance plus another two to three months' deposit, which should be refunded when you move out, although some landlords make this problematic. By law, you have a right to a four-year (plus four more years) renewable) contract, registered within 20 days at the *Ufficio del Registro* in the *Agenzia delle Entrate* (see *above* **Tax code & VAT number**). It's not unusual for owners to demand that your company sign the contract. The mushrooming of estate agents means it pays to shop around.

Safety & security
Milan is, by and large, fairly safe. However, as in any large city, petty crime is a fact of life, so take the usual precautions with your personal belongings. Tourists who stand out as such are most susceptible to small-time theft and pickpocketing. Pickpockets often work in pairs or groups and target tourist areas and public transport routes, and the international arrival area of Malpensa airport. Everyone – and lone females especially – should be careful in the Stazione Centrale, parklands and Arco della Pace areas in the evenings.

Directory

A few basic precautions will greatly reduce a street thief's chances:

● Don't carry wallets in back pockets, particularly on buses. If you have a bag or camera with a long strap, wear it across your chest and not dangling from one shoulder.

● Keep bags closed, with your hand on them. Whenever you sit down, do not leave bags or coats on the ground or the back of a chair where you cannot keep an eye on them.

● When walking down a street, remember to hold cameras and bags on the side of you towards the wall, so you're less likely to become the prey of drive-by motorcycle thieves.

● If you see groups of ragged children brandishing pieces of cardboard, avoid them or walk by quickly, keeping tight hold on your valuables. They will wave the cardboard to confuse you while their accomplices pick pockets or bags.

If you are the victim of a crime, call the police helpline (*see p286*) or go to the nearest police station and say you want to report a *furto* (theft). A *denuncia* (written statement) of the incident will be made for you. You will need the *denuncia* to make an insurance claim.

Smoking

Smoking is not permitted in public offices (including post offices and police stations) or on public transport. Though public transport is a smoke-free zone, the rule tends to be applied laxly elsewhere. Smoking in restaurants and bars is at the discretion of the owner, but the anti-smoking lobby is gaining ground. For where to buy cigarettes, *see below* **Tabaccherie**.

Study

See also p288 **Libraries**. Milan has two state universities, a highly regarded language institute and two private universities, including the prestigious Bocconi. Most of these offer international programmes and have agreements with foreign universities. Consult university websites to see what's on offer.

EU citizens have the same right to study at Italian universities as Italian nationals. However, you will need to have your school diplomas translated and authenticated at the Italian consulate in your own country before presenting them to the *Ufficio Studenti Stranieri* (foreign students' department) of any university.

There are also universities in Bergamo (www.unibg.it), Brescia (www.unibs.it) and Pavia (www.unipv.it).

The Open University also offers degree-level study programmes with tutors throughout Italy. Contact Jane Pollardat on www.open.ac.uk or on 02 813 8048.

Libera Università di Lingue e Comunicazione IULM www.iulm.it

Politecnico di Milano www.polimi.it/english

Universita' Cattolica del Sacro Cuore www.unicatt.it/ucsc_EV.asp

Università Commerciale Luigi Bocconi www.uni-bocconi.it

Università degli Studi di Milano www.unimi.it/engl

Language schools

Consult *Scuole di Lingua* in the *Yellow Pages*. The Società Dante Alighieri (02 669 2816) and Linguedue (02 2951 9972) are highly recommended for foreigners learning Italian.

Tabaccherie

Tabaccherie or *tabaccai* (identified by signs with a white T on a black or blue background) are the only places to buy tobacco products of any kind legally. They also sell stamps (including the ones you need for official documents called *marche da bollo*), phone cards, tickets for public transport, lottery tickets and the stationery required for Italian bureaucracy. Most *tabaccherie* keep proper shop hours; many, however, are attached to bars or have external vending machines so can satisfy your nicotine cravings well into the night.

Tax

See also p290 **Relocation**. For VAT rebates on goods purchased in Italy, *see p132*. Sales tax (IVA) is charged at varying rates on most goods and services, and is almost invariably quoted as an integral part of prices, though there are a few top-end hotels that will quote prices without IVA. Some tradespeople will also offer you rates without IVA. The implication is that if you are willing to hand over cash and not demand a receipt in return, you'll be paying around 20 per cent (ie the amount you would have spent on IVA) less than the real fee – but note that both you and the tradesperson risk hefty fines should you fall prey to a policeman demanding to see your receipt. Also remember you legally have to keep a receipt from any purchase and you may be required to show it to the Guardia di Finanza.

Telephones

Dialling & codes

All normal Milan numbers begin with the area code 02, and this must be used whether you call from within or outside the city. Phone numbers within Milan generally have seven or eight digits, although some numbers (such as the central operator of a large firm) may have six or fewer. If you have difficulties, check the directory or ring enquiries (412).

All numbers beginning with 800 are freephone lines (until recently, these began 176 or 167: you will still find old-style numbers listed; replace the prefix with 800). For numbers beginning 840 and 848 (147 and 148 until recently) you will be charged one unit only, regardless of where you're calling from or the length of the call. These numbers can be called from within Italy only; some only function within one phone district.

Rates

The biggest Italian telephone company (Telecom Italia) is very expensive, especially for international calls. Keep costs down by phoning off-peak (6.30pm-

8am Mon-Sat, all day Sun and holidays), buying any of the many cheap-rate international phone cards at a *tabaccheria* (see *p292*) and making use of one of the many cheap telephoning shops around the city. Avoid using phones in hotels, which charge extortionate rates.

Public phones

Milan has no shortage of public phone boxes and many bars have payphones. Most public phones only accept phone cards (*schede telefoniche*); a few also accept major credit cards. Telephone cards are available from *tabaccherie* (see *p292*), some newsstands and some bars. Beware: phone cards have expiry dates (usually 31 Dec or 30 June) and don't forget to tear off the corner.

International calls

To make an international call from Italy, dial 00, then the country code: Australia 61; Canada 1; Irish Republic 353; New Zealand 64; UK 44; US 1. Then dial the area code (for calls to the UK, omit the initial zero of the area code) and then the number. To phone Milan from abroad, dial the international code (00 in the UK), then 39 for Italy and 02 for Milan, followed by the number.

Operator services

To make a reverse charge (collect) call, dial 170 for the international operator in Italy. Alternatively, to be connected to the operator in the country you want to call, dial 172 followed by a four-digit code for the country and telephone company you want to use (for the UK and Ireland this is the same as the country code above; check the phone book for other countries).
International Operator 170.
International Directory Enquiries 4176.
Operator and Italian Directory Enquiries 412.
Wake-up calls 4114; an automatic message will ask you to dial in the time you want your call – in four figures, using the 24hr clock – followed by your phone number.

Mobile phones

Italian cellphone numbers begin with 3. GSM phones operate on both 900 and 1800 bands. British, Australian and New Zealand mobiles work just fine, but US mobiles cannot be used. Mobile phones can be rented from:

Easy Line/Global Phone Network
Via Fratelli Bronzetti 1, East (02 7012 0181). Bus 60, 62/tram 12, 27. **Open** 9am-1pm, 2-6pm Mon-Sat. **Credit** AmEx, DC, MC, V. **Map** p311 A2.

Future Service
Corso Lodi 83, South (02 5681 5129). Metro Brenta. **Open** 9am-1pm, 3-7.30pm Mon-Sat. **Credit** AmEx, DC, MC, V. **Map** p311 B1, B2.

Fax

Faxes can be sent from most large post offices (see *p290*), which will charge you according to the number of pages you send, starting from around €1.20. Note that only certain countries (and the UK is not one of them) can be reached with this service. Otherwise try telephone shops, some *cartolibrerie* (stationers) or photocopying outlets, but be aware that the cost will be higher.

Telegrams & telexes

These can be sent from main post offices. The telegraph office at the Posta Centrale (see *p290*) is open 9am-7pm Mon-Sat. Or you can dictate telegrams over the phone. Dial 186 from a private phone and a message in Italian will tell you to dial the number of the phone you're phoning from. A telephonist will then take your message.

Time

Italy is one hour ahead of London, six ahead of New York, eight behind Sydney. Clocks are moved forward by one hour in early spring and back in late autumn, in line with other EU countries.

Tipping

Foreigners are expected to tip more than Italians; ten per cent is generous even for the richest-looking tourist. Most locals leave 5¢ or 10¢ on the counter when buying drinks at the bar and, depending on the standard of the service, €1-€5 for the waiter. In restaurants, check to see if a service charge (*servizio*) is already included, as well as the amount of the cover charge (*coperto*), and calculate your tip based on any amounts already added and the quality of service.

Many of the larger restaurants now include a 10-15 per cent service charge. Tips are not expected in family-run restaurants, though a euro or two is appreciated. Taxi drivers will be happy if you round the fare up to the nearest whole euro.

Toilets

By law, Italian bars are obliged to let anyone use their toilets. Buying something will ensure the loo isn't 'out of order'. Don't expect a bar's toilets to be clean or have toilet paper. There are modern toilets at or near most major tourist sites, in some metro stations and at the Cadorna railway station; most have attendants and you'll have to pay a small fee. Fast-food joints and department stores also come in handy.

Telephone codes

Most fixed-line prefixes in Lombardy begin 03.
The following is a selection of local fixed-line prefixes.

Bergamo 035	Brescia 030
Como 031	Crema 0373
Cremona 0372	Lecco 0341
Lodi 0371	Monza 039
Pavia 0382	Sondrio 0342
Varese 0332	Vigevano 0381

Directory

Weather

Month	Average temperature		Average rain	
	C°	F°	mm	in
January	3.5	38.3	65	2.6
February	5	41	50	2
March	9	48.2	75	3
April	13.5	56.3	95	3.7
May	18.5	65.3	120	4.7
June	22	71.6	85	3.4
July	24.5	76.1	75	3
August	24	75.2	85	3.4
September	19	66.2	100	4
October	14	57.2	115	4.5
November	9	48.2	85	3.4
December	4.5	40.1	60	2.4

Tourist information

Friendly smiles, patience and printed information are rather thin on the ground in Milan's main APT office by the Duomo. Their Welcome Card (€8) will get you discounts on selected sites and tours. *Hello Milano*, a free English publication available at the APT and consulates, includes a useful map, heaps of information on the city and details of events.

APT

Via Marconi 1, Centre (02 7252 4301/www.milanoinfotourist.com). Metro Duomo/tram 2, 3, 4, 12, 14, 24, 27. **Open** 9am-1pm, 2-6pm Mon-Sat; 9am-1pm, 2-6pm Sun & public hols. **Map** p311 A1/p312 B2.

Ufficio Informazioni Turistiche

First Floor, Stazione Centrale, North (02 725 241/www.milano infotourist.com). **Open** 9am-1pm, 2-6pm Mon-Sat; 9am-5pm Sun & public hols. **Map** p309 B2.

Tours

See p53 **Guided tours**.

Visas

EU nationals and citizens of the US, Canada, Australia and New Zealand don't need visas for stays in Italy of up to three months. For EU citizens, a passport or identity card valid for travel abroad is sufficient; all non-EU citizens must have full passports. All visitors should declare their presence to the police within eight days of arrival. If you're staying in a hotel, this will be done for you. If not, contact the Questura Centrale (main police station, *see p290*) for advice.

Water & drinking

There are public drinking fountains throughout Italy and in most cases the water is perfectly acceptable to drink. If you have any doubts, opt for bottled water. In bars, specify that you want *acqua minerale naturale* (still) or *gassata* (fizzy).

When to go

See also chapter **Festivals & Events**.

Public holidays

On public holidays (*giorni festivi*) virtually all shops, banks and businesses are closed, although (with the exception of May Day, 15 August and Christmas Day) bars and restaurants tend to stay open. Public transport is practically non-existent on 1 May and Christmas afternoon. Holidays falling on a Saturday or Sunday are not celebrated the following Monday; however, if a holiday falls on a Thursday or a Tuesday, many people will take the Friday/Monday off as well, a practice known as *fare il ponte* (doing a bridge).

Public holidays are as follows: New Year's Day (*Capodanno*), 1 January; Epiphany (*Epifania*), 6 January; Easter Monday (*Pasquetta*); Liberation Day, 25 April; May Day, 1 May; Republic Day, 2 June; Feast of the Assumption (*Ferragosto*), 15 August; All Saints' (*Tutti Santi*), 1 November; Feast of Sant'Ambrogio, 7 December; Immaculate Conception (*Festa dell'Immacolata*), 8 December; Christmas Day (*Natale*); Boxing Day (*Santo Stefano*).

Weather

The low-lying Po Valley is bound on the north by the Alps and the south-west by the Pennines, which keeps all that moisture firmly where it is. Hence the notoriously thick fog that can bring traffic in and around Milan to a halt. Winter in Lombardy can be bitter, with winds zipping down from the Alps. Spring brings warmer temperatures and blossoming trees, while autumn offers changing colours and balmy days, though rain may intrude in late October and November. Summer tends to be muggy and mosquito-ridden.

Women

Foreign women will be the object of attention in Italy, no matter where they go. Most Italian men are attentive, interested and mostly courteous. You are unlikely to encounter any aggressive behaviour. Having said that, take the usual precautions. Avoid outlying areas and don't wander by yourself at night except in lively central zones. There are prostitutes and pushers in the area around Stazione Centrale after dark. They are unlikely to hassle you, but will make your late-night movements less than picturesque. A taxi (*see p281*) is a good idea if you're crossing the city late at night.

Vocabulary

Italians always appreciate attempts to speak their language, however incompetent those attempts may be.

Note that there are two forms of address in the second person singular (you) in Italian: the formal *lei*, which should be used with strangers and older people; and the informal *tu*. The personal pronoun is usually omitted.

Italian is pronounced as it is spelled.

Pronunciation

a – as in **a**sk.
e – like a in **a**ge (closed e) or e in s**e**ll.
i – like ea in **ea**st.
o – as in h**o**tel (closed o) or in h**o**t.
u – as in b**oo**t.

In front of e and i, c and g sound like **ch**eck and **gi**raffe respectively. A c before a, o and u sounds as in **c**at; g before a, o and u sounds as in **g**et. An h after any consonant makes it hard. Before a vowel, the h is silent. gl sounds like lli in mi**lli**on. gn sounds like ny in can**y**on. qu sounds as in **qui**ck. r is always rolled. s has two sounds, as in **s**oap or ro**s**e. sc sounds like sh in **sh**ame. sch sounds like sc in **sc**out. z can be sounded ts or dz.

Useful phrases

hello/goodbye (informal) – ciao
good morning – buon giorno
good evening – buona sera
good night – buona notte
please – per favore, per piacere
thank you – grazie
you're welcome – prego
excuse me, sorry – mi scusi (formal), scusa (informal)
I'm sorry, but... – mi dispiace, ma...
I don't speak Italian (very well) – non parlo (molto bene) l'italiano
I don't/didn't understand – non capisco/ho capito
where's the toilet? – dov'è la toilette?
open – aperto
closed – chiuso
entrance – entrata/ingresso
exit – uscita
help! – aiuto!
there's a fire! – c'è un incendio!
I want a doctor/policeman – Voglio un dottore/poliziotto
Leave me alone, please – Lasciami in pace

Times & timetables

could you tell me the time, please? – mi sa (formal)/sai (informal) dire l'ora, per favore?
it's – o'clock – sono le (...)
it's half past – sono le (...) e mezza
when does it open? – a che ora apre?

Directions

(turn) left – (giri a) sinistra
(it's on the) right – è a destra
straight on – sempre diritto
where is...? – dov'è...?
could you show me the way to the Duomo? – mi potrebbe indicare la strada per il Duomo?
is it near/far? – è vicino/lontano?

Transport

car – macchina
bus – autobus
underground/subway – metro(politana)
coach – pullman
taxi – tassi, taxi
train – treno
tram – tram
plane – aereo
bus stop – fermata (d'autobus)
station – stazione
platform – binario
ticket/s – biglietto/biglietti
one way – solo andata
return – andata e ritorno
(I'd like) a ticket for – (vorrei) un biglietto per...
fine – multa
I'm sorry, I didn't know I had to stamp it – mi dispiace, non sapevo che lo dovevo timbrare

Communications

phone – telefono
stamp – francobollo
how much is a stamp for England/Australia/the United States? – quanto viene un francobollo per l'Inghilterra/l'Australia/ gli Stati Uniti?
can I send a fax? – posso mandare un fax?
can I make a phone call? – posso fare una telefonata?
postcard – cartolina
courier – corriere, pony

Shopping

I'd like to try the blue sandals/black shoes/brown boots – vorrei provare i sandali blu/le scarpe nere/gli stivali marroni
do you have it/them in other colours? – ce l'ha in altri colori?
I take (shoe) size... – porto il numero...
I take (dress) size... – porto la taglia...
it's too loose/too tight/just right – mi sta largo/stretto/bene
can you give me a little more/less? – mi dia un po' di più/meno
100 grams of... – un etto di...
300 grams of... – tre etti di...
one kilo of... – un kilo/chilo di...
five kilos of... – cinque chili di...
a litre/two litres of... – un litro/due litri di...

Accommodation

a reservation – una prenotazione
I'd like to book a single/twin/double room – vorrei prenotare una camera singola/doppia/matrimoniale
I'd prefer a room with a bath/shower/window over the courtyard – preferirei una camera con vasca da bagno/doccia/finestra sul cortile
can you bring me breakfast in bed? – mi può portare la colazione a letto?

Eating & drinking

I'd like to book a table for four at 8pm – vorrei prenotare un tavolo per quattro alle otto
I don't eat meat; what do you recommend? – non mangio carne; cosa mi consiglia?
this is lukewarm; can you heat it up? – è tiepido; lo può riscaldare?
this wine is corked; could you bring me another bottle? – questo vino sa di tappo; mi può portare un'altra bottiglia, per favore?
that was poor/good/(really) delicious – era mediocre/buono/(davvero) ottimo
the bill – il conto
is service included? – è incluso il servizio?
I think there's a mistake in this bill – credo che il conto sia sbagliato
See also p115 What's on the Menu.

Days & nights

Monday – lunedì; **Tuesday** – martedì; **Wednesday** – mercoledì; **Thursday** – giovedì; **Friday** – venerdì; **Saturday** – sabato; **Sunday** – domenica; **yesterday** – ieri; **today** – oggi; **tomorrow** – domani; **morning** – mattina; **afternoon** – pomeriggio; **evening** – sera; **night** – notte; **weekend** – fine settimana or, more usually, weekend; **have a good weekend!** – buona domenica!

Numbers & money

0 zero; 1 uno; 2 due; 3 tre; 4 quattro; 5 cinque; 6 sei; 7 sette; 8 otto; 9 nove; 10 dieci; 11 undici; 12 dodici; 13 tredici; 14 quattordici; 15 quindici; 16 sedici; 17 diciasette; 18 diciotto; 19 diciannove; 20 venti; 30 trenta; 40 quaranta; 50 cinquanta; 60 sessanta; 70 settanta; 80 ottanta; 90 novanta; 100 cento; 200 duecento; 1,000 mille.
how much is it? – quanto costa?
do you take credit cards? – accettate carte di credito?
can I pay in pounds/dollars, with traveller's cheques? – posso pagare in sterline/dollari/con i traveller's cheques?

Further Reference

Books

Classics

Catullus *Poems* Uncannily modern musings from Lake Garda's most famous Roman.

Pliny the Elder *Natural History* Observations of an antique Como native.

Fiction

D'Annunzio, Gabriele *The Child of Pleasure* Autobiographical novel by a *bon viveur* and *grand poseur* (see p215).

Eco, Umberto *Foucault's Pendulum* Milan takes on a sinister air in this esoteric novel by the renowned Italian professor.

Fo, Dario *Accidental Death of an Anarchist* Darkly hilarious take on the fatal 'tumble' of an anarchist from a Milanese police HQ window during an interrogation.

Hemingway, Ernest *A Farewell to Arms* Part of this love 'n' war epic is set in Milan.

Manzoni, Alessandro *I promessi sposi* (*The Betrothed*) The seminal Lombard novel (see p64), so ubiquitous you begin to wonder whether it isn't the only Lombard novel.

Non-fiction & travel

Burnett, Stanton H and Mantovani, Luca *The Italian Guillotine: Operation Clean Hands and the Overthrow of Italy's First Republic* A fine account of *Tangentopoli*, the scandal that brought Milan to its knees in the early 1990s, and its consequences.

Foot, John *Milan Since the Miracle: City, Culture and Identity* Intriguing study of the city's recent history and culture.

Grundy, Isobel *Lady Mary Wortley Montagu* This 18th-century English traveller spent many years in and around Lovere on Lake Garda.

Lawrence, DH *Twilight in Italy* Contains wonderful descriptions of Lake Garda.

Wharton, Edith *Italian Backgrounds* A clever, spirited refutation of the 'there's nothing to see in Milan' argument.

Film

Bitter Rice (*Riso Amaro*, Giuseppe De Santis, 1948) Passion and exploitation among Lombardy's rice-paddy workers.

Incantesimo Napoletano (Paolo Genovese & Luca Miniero, 1999) A Neapolitan girl rejects her local heritage and embraces all things Milanese.

Miracle in Milan (*Miracolo a Milano*, Vittorio De Sica, 1950) A magical neo-realist tale about a young orphan who brings light to Milan's beggars.

A Month by the Lake (John Irvin, 1994) The beauty of Lake Como compensates for the turgid tug-of-love in the plot.

1900 (Bernardo Bertolucci, 1976) This two-part epic on the conflict between fascism and communism was shot around Cremona.

Piso Pisello (Peter Del Monte, 1982) A Milanese teenager becomes a father and decides to raise the child alone in this oddball comedy.

Rocco and his Brothers (*Rocco e i suoi fratelli*, Luchino Visconti, 1960) Five Sicilian brothers and their mother struggle to earn a living in industrial Milan.

Salò, or the 120 Days of Sodom (*Salò o le 120 giornate di Sodoma*, Pier Paolo Pasolini, 1975) A nasty S&M allegory of Mussolini's last stand.

The Tree of the Wooden Clogs (*L'albero degli zoccoli*, Ermanno Olmi, 1978) This film about substinence farming at the turn of the century was made with non-professional actors speaking in the *bergamasco* dialect (*see p226* **Speaking in tongues**).

Music

Verdi, Giuseppe (1813-1901) Lombard *per eccellenza*, Verdi gave many of his operas local themes or settings: *The Lombards at the First Crusade* (1843), *The Battle of Legnano* (1849) and *Rigoletto* (1851; set in Mantova). Many more reflect the tribulations of nations oppressed by foreign rulers, a sore point in Milan in Verdi's time.

Websites

www.beniculturali.it The Cultural Heritage ministry's site (Italian only) lists all state-owned museums, galleries, and provides details on temporary exhibitions and initiatives such as the Settimana dei Beni Culturali (*see p152*).

www.hellomilano.it Comprehensive English-language city guide.

www.infopoint.it Local transport information site (Italian only): type in departure point and destination and it will provide timetables.

www.milanotonight.it Italian-only site offering reader reviews of restaurants, bars and the like, all divided by area. Also has a small gay section.

www.provincia.milano.it/cultura/oltremilano/index.htm and **www.cultura.regione.lombardia.it** Information (Italian only) on every point of cultural interest in the Milan province and Lombardy region respectively.

Index

Page numbers in **bold**
indicate the main reference
to a topic. Page numbers in
italics refer to illustrations.

a

Abatantuono, Diego, 159, *159*
Abbazia di Viboldone
106-107, *107*
Abbiategrasso 107
abortion 287
accessories 135-138
accommodation **38-50**, **291**
  agencies 284
  alpine hostels 267
  by price
    budget 45-49
    expensive 39-42, *41*, *42*,
    43, 43-45, 46, **47**, 49-50
    moderate 42-43, *45*, 45,
    46, 49, 50, *50*
  camping 100
  out of town *see specific
  area*
  vocabulary 295
  wheelchair-accessible 286
  youth hostels 45-46
  *see also p302
  accommodation index*
Adda, River 102
Adelaide 9
Affari, piazza & around
63-65
age restrictions 284
Agliate 100
Agnesi, Maria Gaetana 15
AIDS/HIV helpline 287
airlines 279
airports 278
  disabled travellers 286
  left luggage 288
Alberti, Leon Battista
237, 238, 240, 242
Albertini, Gabriele 21
Alemagna, Emilio 70
Alessi, Galeazzo 61
Alessi Outlet Store **192**
Almenno San Bartolomeo 229
Alta Valtellina 269-270
alternative medicine 145, 286
Amaretto & museum 104
Amati, Andrea & Nicolò
247, 249, 255
Ambrogio, Sant' (St Ambrose)
7, 25, 59, 84, 95
  church 91, *91*, **94-95**
  feast day 61
Amedeo, Giovanni Antonio 74
Anfo 236
Angera 199
Anguissola, Sofonisba 247
Annunciata 83
antiques:
  fair 153
  markets 142
  shops 132
Antonio, Pietro 80
Aprica 267, 272
APT offices
  see tourist information
aquarium 67
Arata, Giulio Ulisse 77
archaeology 92, 94, 96, 104,
  106, 194, 195, 199, 275

archaeology courses 274
Archeopark 275
architecture:
  bio-architectural
  design 49
  Duomo 54-59
  fascist style 65, 67, 82, 226
  Liberty style 74, **77**, 228
  neo-Palladian 78
Arco della Pace 67, *67*, 291
Arcore 100
Arena Civica 70
Arese 103
Aregno 207
Armani, Giorgio
  35, *35*, 126, 133, 136
Arona 193
art **24-28**
  avant-garde movements
  28
  in cafés and bars
  126, 128, **130**
  galleries 81, *161*, **161-164**
  photography **163**
  hotels for art lovers
  41-42, 45
  The Last Supper **92-93**,
  93
  libraries 65, 164
  open-air art exhibition 152
  supplies 132-133
  see also museums and
  galleries
Artò 192
Ascona, Switzerland 197
Asola 244
ATM transport company
  22, **279**
Auditorium di Milano 174
Augustine, Saint 257
Augustus, Emperor 7
Averlino, Antonio 68

b

babysitting 157
Bagolino 236
bakeries 53
di Balduccio, Giovanni 26
banks 289, 291
Barbarossa, Frederick
  10, 101, 253, 274
Barbelli, Gian Giacomo 251
Bardolino 219
Barnaba, San (Saint) 7
bars *see* cafés & bars
  gay bars & clubs
  128, 129, 166
Basilica di San Babila 77, **79**
Bassa Pianura lowlands 246
Bassa Valtellina 266
Battaglio, Giovanni 80, 251
Baveno 194
beauticians &
  beauty treatments
  144-145, 168, 180
  see also spas
Belgirate 193
Bellagio 211
Beltrami, Luca 68
Bembo, Bonifacio 26, 247, 248
Beretta headquarters 236
Bergamo & around **220-229**
  restaurants 189
  university 292

Bergognone, Bernardino
  27, 259
Berlucchi, Guido 35
Berlusconi, Silvio 21, 22, *29*,
  29-31, 100, 167, 232
Berri Meregalli family 77
Biassono 100
Biblioteca Ambrosiana
  63-65
Biblioteca del Conservatorio
  G Verdi 288
Biblioteca Nazionale
  Braidense 288
Biblioteca Sormani 288
Bienno 275
Binasco 107
birds & birdwatching **259**
  see also nature reserves
  & regional parks
boat tours, canals 87
Boccaccino, Boccaccio
  247, 248
Bogliaco 216
Boito, Camillo 98
Boleto 192
Bollate 103
Boltraffio, Giovanni 27
Bonaparte, Napoleon 54, 63,
  81, 91, 96, 194, 254, 257
books & bookshops 133-135
  children's 157
  gay & lesbian 168-169
  on Milan & Lombardy 296
Bormio 269-270, 272
Borromeo family 28, 100,
  105, 194
Borromeo, Cardinal Federico
  11, 63, **105**
Borromeo, Cardinal
  (San Carlo) 11, 17, 57, 59,
  78, 94, 96, **105**
  statue 193, 196
Borsa (stock exchange)
  see Palazzo della Borsa
Boscoincittà 156
Bossi, Giovanni Battista 77
Bossi, Umberto 10, 33
botanical gardens 71, 215
Bòvegno 236
Bovisa 74
Bramante, Donato
  27, 65, 74, 94, 95, 97, 261
Bramantino 84
bread riots 77
Brera district 66, **70-73**
da Brescia, Moretto 233
Brescia & around **230-236**
  restaurants 189
  university 292
  see also Valcamonica
Brianza district 99-102
Brissago, Switzerland 197
Broletto, Brescia, 233
Broletto Nuovo, piazza del 65
bureaux de change 290
buses 279-280
  long-distance 279
  tours 53
business & business services
  150, **284**
  conference organisers
  & facilities 284
Fiera di Milano, 97, **98**
tax code & VAT number
  291

c

cabaret 183, *183*
Cadenabbia 208
cafés & bars **125-130**
  bar/restaurants
  114, 117, *117*, 123
  gay & lesbian 128, 129
  happy hour 130
  late-night bars 176
  live jazz 126, 127, 174
  *see also p302 cafés
  & bars index*
Cagnola, Luigi 70
Ca' Grande 82, **83**, *84*
Calderara, Antonio 191
Camerata Cornello 228-229
Campi brothers
  28, 247, 248, 249, 251
camping 100
da Campione, Bonino 26
Camun people 6, 271
canals 54
  see also Navigli, the
Cannero Riviera 194
Cannobio 194
Canonica, Luigi 70, 184
Capo di Ponte 274
Cappella Colleoni,
  Bergamo **220**, 222-223
Capriolo 236
Carate Brianza 100
Caravaggio **25**, 248
  *Saint Francis in
  Meditation* 248, *248*
  Supper at Emmaus 24
Caravaggio, Fermo,
  Stella da 192
car hire & breakdown
  services 282-283
  see also driving
Carnevale celebrations 154
Carrà, Carlo 28
Carroccio **101**
Casa Fontana Silvestri 77, *78*
Casa Galimberti 77
Casa Guazzoni 77
Casa del Manzoni 60
Casa degli Omenoni 60, *61* .
Casa di Riposo
  per Musicisti 98
Casa Rossi 96
cashpoints 289
Castelleone 253
Castello Sforzesco
  53, 66, **68-69**
  with children 156
  museums 69
Castiglione Olona 106
Catullus 215
Cavour, piazza 75-76
Celentano, Adriano 171
central Milan *see*
  Duomo & Central Milan
Centro di Ricerca per Teatro
  see CRT Teatro dell'Arte
Cerano, Il 28
Cernobbio 207
Certosa di Garegnano 67
Certosa di Pavia
  15, *15*, 259, 260
Ceruti, Giovanni 81
Cerveno 274-275
Chambers of Commerce 284
Charlemagne 9

Charles V,
  Holy Roman Emperor 16
cheeses **252**
chemists *see* pharmacies
Chiaristi 28
Chiavenna 264-265, 274
Chiesa in Valmalenco 267, 272
children **155-157**
  bookshops 135
  Carnevale 154
  child-friendly hotels 46
  clothes 148, 149
  hospitals 286
  museums 156
  on public transport
    280, 281
  skiing 272-273
  theme parks 213
  tours for 53
Christianity,
  development of 7, 9
  churches, convents
    & monasteries 52
  art in **24-28**
  etiquette 52
  worship 290
  see also by name
Cimitero Monumentale *73*, **74**
cinemas *see* film
Cinque Giornate
  15, *16*, **16-17**
Citterio, Antonio 133
Civiche Raccolte
  Archeologiche e
  Numismatiche 69
Civiche Raccolte d'Arte
  Antica 68-69
Civiche Raccolte d'Arte
  Applicata 69
Civici Musei del Castello
  68-69
Civico Acquario e Stazione
  Idrobiologica (Aquarium)
  67
Civico Museo
  Archeologico 96
Civico Museo di Storia
  Naturale 81
Cividate Camuno 275
Clean Hands investigations
  (*Mani Pulite*) 31
climate 294
clothes shops 131, **135-141**
  accessories 135-138
  boutiques 138-139
  designer boutiques
    139, **136-137**, 139-141
  fashion: mid-range 141
  for children 157
  leatherwear 141
  lingerie 141
  markets 142
  outlet malls 149
  second-hand & vintage
    144, 148-149
  stock houses 148
Colico 209
Colleoni, Bartolomeo
  222, 229
Collio 236
Cologno Monzese 29
colonne, the 85, 90
Colorado Café 183, *183*
comedy 184
Como **204-207**
Il Corriere della Sera 31
comuni, age of the 10, 12
confectionery 143
conference organisers &
  facilities 284
Conservatorio di Musica
  'Giuseppe Verdi' 79, **80**,
  174

consulates 284-285
contraception 287
Corrente 28
corruption **19**, 35
Cortili Aperti 153
Cortinaccio 264
cosmetics 145, *145*
couriers 284
craft fair 154
Craxi, Bettino 29, 31
credit cards 290
Crema & around
  250-253
Cremona **246-250**
Crespi, Daniele
  11, 28, 67, 95, 100
Crespi, Giovanni Battista 28
crime, safety & security
  291-292
CRT Teatro dell'Arte 183
Cultural Heritage Week
  53, **152**
customs restrictions 285
cycling 179, **283**
  bicycle hire 283
Brianza parks 102

d

dance companies,
  venues & tickets
  182-183
D'Annunzio, Gabriele
  214, 215-216, 217
Dante, via 53, **66**
D'Anzi, Giuseppe 56
Darsena 85, 86, 87
de' Grassi,
  Giovannino 26
dentists 287
department stores 135
Desenzano 212
disabled travellers
  285-286
doctors 287
Domaso 208
Dongo 208
driving **282-283**
  breakdown services 282
  car hire 283
  insurance 288
  around Lombardy 283
  mountain driving 282
  parking 38, **282-283**
  Sunday car bans 52
drugs & the law 286
dry-cleaning 147
Dunant, Henri 239
Duomo 53, **54-59**
  with children 155-156
Duomo & Central Milan
  54-65
  accommodation *39*, 39-43,
    42, *43*, *45*, *47*, **47**
  cafés & bars 125-126
  nightclubs 176
  piazza del Duomo 54, 55
  restaurants 113-114, 114
Duomo, Como 204, **205-206**
Duomo, Cremona
  246, 247, **248**
Duomo, Mantova
  239, **240-241**
Duomo, Monza 100-101
Duomo Vecchio, Brescia
  230, 231, **233**

e

eastern Milan *see*
  San Babila & Eastern
  Milan
economy 20-22, **33-36**

Edolo 271-275
electricity 286
Elio e le Storie Tese 170, *170*
email & internet
  135, 158, **288**
embassies 284-285
emergency numbers 286
  alpine rescue 273
English language:
  libraries 288
  listings & small ads 289
  newspapers 289
Environmental Fund,
  Italian 52
environmental projects 49
Erbusco 236
d'Este, Beatrice 15
etiquette:
  in churches 52
  queuing 290
euro, the 22, 289
exports 35

f

fabric shops 147
FAI (Fondo per l'Ambiente
  Italiano) 52
fascism, World War II 19
fashion industry:
  cafés & bars
    126, 127-128, 129
  Fashion Week 154
  Men's Fashion Week
    153, 154
  shopping *see* clothes
fax services 150, 293
Ferrari, Gaudenzio 28
Ferrario, Rosina 15
Festival del Cinema
  Africano a Milano 160
Festival Internazionale di
  Cinema Gaylesbico 160
festivals & events **152**
  dance 183
  film 160
  jazz 197
  literature 238
  poetry 185
Fiera di Milano 97, **98**
Filaforum 171
Il Filarete 83
film **158-160**
  cinemas 158-160, *160*
  gay films festivals
    160, 166
  Milan & Lombardy
  in the movies 296
  museum 81
  videos & DVDs 135, 150
Film Festival Internazionale
  di Milano 160
financial district 63-65
flower fair 152
Il Foglio 29
Fondazione Nicola
  Trussardi 164
Fondazione Prada 164
food & drink **111-113**
  Amaretto di Saronno 104
  cheese **252**
  fairs 154
  fast food 122
  happy hour 130
  kosher food 143
  markets 142
  menus 111, **115**
  mountain food **268**
  museums 104
  organic 143
  in hotels 49
  pumpkin 243
  shops 141-144

tortelli **243**
  tours & courses 53
  vocabulary 295
  see also restaurants; wine
football **20-21**, **179-180**
  Museo Inter e Milan 179
  players hangouts
    129, **177**
Foppa, Vincenzo 27
della Francesca, Piero
  26-27, 71-72
Franciacorta 236
Frankish rule 9, 12
funfairs 156
furniture
  see household goods
  fair 152
Futurists, the 28

g

Gaber, Giorgio 170
Galleria d'Arte Moderna 8
Galleria Vittorio Emanuele II
  53, **54**, *55*, **59**
galleries
  81, *161*, **161-164**
Garda 219
Gardaland 213
gardens *see*
  parks & gardens
Gardone Riviera 215
Gardone di Sopra 215
Gardone Valtrompia 236
Gargnano 216, 218
gay & lesbian **165-169**
  bars 128, 129, **166**
  discos 166-168
  film festival 160
gelati see ice cream
general strike of 1898 *6*, 19
Gervasio, San (Saint)
Ghibelline party 11
Giacomo, Gian 78
Giardini Botanici Hruska,
  Gardone Riviera 215
Giardini Pubblici 81
Giardini della Villa
  Comunale 82
Giardino della Guastalla 82
Il Giornale 29
Giornata FAI di Primavera
  152
Giovane, Palma 232
glaciers 267
golf 53, **180**
Gonzaga family 14, 16, 237,
  238, 239, **240**, 241, 242,
  250
  Vespasiano 244-245
Grand Prix, Monza 100
Grattacielo Pirelli 73-74
Gravedona 208
Grosio 268
Grotte di Catullo,
  Sirmione 213, *217*
Guarnieri family 255
Gucci 136
Guelph party 11
gyms 144, 168, **180-181**
gay 168

h

hairdressers 147-150
Hayez, Francesco 28
The Kiss 27
health & beauty
  144-145, **286-287**
  accident & emergency 286
  all-night pharmacy 145
  alternative medicine
    145, 286

health food 143
  in hotels 49
  restaurants 119, 121, 172
  shops 143
insurance 286, 287-288
helplines 287
hiking *see* walking and hiking
history **6-19**
  economy 33-36
  key events **12**
  Lake Como 202-203
  Milan & Lombardy
   today 20-23
  military **101, 239**
  navigli 86-87
HIV helpline 287
holidays, public 294
hospitals 287
hostels, alpine 267
hotels **38-50**
  bars 128
  best 38
  with children 46
  wheelchair-accessible 186
  see also accommodation
   and *p302 accommodation
   index*
household goods 131, **133**,
  133, **145-147**, 192
Salone Internazionale del
  Mobile (furniture fair) 152

i

ice-cream
  shops & cafés 143
ice-skating 156, 272-273
ID 287
Idro 236
Idropark Fila 156
Idroscalo Park 153
immigrants **23**, 36
inflation 22
infrastructure 36
Insubre people 7
insurance, health,
  286, 287-288
internet & email
  135, 158, **288**
interpreters 284
Intra 194
I promessi sposi
  (*The Betrothed*) 16, **64**, 77
Iseo 225
Isola area 73-74
Isola Comacina 207-208
Isola del Garda 215
Isola Inferiore/Bella 194
Isola Madre 194, *196*
Isola San Giulio **191**
Isola Superiore/
  dei Pescatori 194
Isola Virginia 106
Isole Borromee 194
IVA sales tax 39, 132, 292
  partita IVA (VAT
   number) 291

j

jazz *173*, **173-174**, 185
  in cafés and bars 126, 127,
   174
  festivals & events 153, 197
jewellery shops 135-138
Julius, St (San Giulio) 191

l

Laglio 207
Lainate 103
lakes, introduction
  188-189

Lago di Como & around
  200, **200-211**, *205*
  restaurants 189
Lago di Garda & around
  212-219
Lago di Idro 236
Lago d'Iseo (Sebino) 224
Lago Maggiore & around
  193-199
Lago d'Orta & around
  190-192, *191*
language
  bergamasco dialect 226
  original-language films
   158, 159
  schools 292
  see also vocabulary
Last Supper, The
  see Vinci, Leonardo da
late-night Milan
  cafés & bars 116
  pharmacies 145, **287**
  public transport 280
  restaurants 41, 117
  see also nightlife
Latin American festival 154
launderette 147
Laveno 199
Lazise 219
lazzaretto 11
League of Cambrai 14
Lecco & around 211
left luggage 288
legal help & law 288
Lega Nord
  see Northern League
legends, foundation 65
Legnano 104
  battle of 10, **101**
Lenno 208
Leonardo da Vinci
  see Vinci, Leonardo da
Leoni, Leone 60
lesbian Milan 169
Liberty style
  see architecture
libraries 63-65, **288**
  art 65, 164
  music, classical 80, 288
Ligurian tribes 6, 7
Limone sul Garda 216
lingerie shops 141
literature 64
  festival 238
Livigno 270, 272
locanda/s 38
Locarno, Switzerland 197
Locati, Sebastiano 67
Lodi & around **253-256**
Lodi Vecchio 256
La Loggia, Brescia 233, *233*
Loggia degli Osii 63
Lombard invasions 9, 12
Lombardy League 10
Lombardy
  history 10, 12, 16-19, 33-36
  lakes & cities of 188
  mountains & valleys of
   264-275
  parks & reserves **188**
  restaurants, best in **189**
  tours 53
  transport 283
La Lomellina 261
Lomello 262
lost property 288
Lotto, Lorenzo 226-227
Lovere 224
Luini, Bernardino 27, 68, 89,
  90, 93, 96, 104, 206
Luino 199
Lumezzane 236

m

Maccastorna 256
Machiachini, Carlo 72, 74
Madesimo 264, 272, 273
Madonnina, la
  56-57, *57*
maestri campionesi
  26, 92, 233, 259
magazines 289
Magenta corso 96
Malcesine 218
Malpensa airport 278
Mandello del Lario 210
Mantegna, Andrea
  237, 240, 241, 242
Mantova & around
  237-245
  restaurants 189
Manzoni, Alessandro
  16, 60, 61, **64**, *64*, 77,
  193, 195
  birthplace 211
Manzoni, via 75-76
Marathon, Milan *153*, **154**
Marinetti, Filippo
  Tommaso 28
markets **142**
Martinengo 229
massage 144
Mazda Palace 171-172
Mazzucotelli,
  Alessandro 28
media **29-32**, **289**
Media Valtellina 266-269
Mediaset 29, 31
Mediolanum *see* Roman
  Milan & Lombardy
Meina 193
Menaggio 208
Menabuoi, Giusto de' 26
Mengoni, Giuseppe 59
Mercanti, piazza dei
Mercato dei Fiori 152
Merisi, Michelangelo
  (Caravaggio) **25**
metro trains 279
Mezzanotte, Paolo 65
Milano Film Festival
  (MFF) 160
Mirasole 107
money 289-290
Monforte, corso 79-81
Montagna 267
Monte Isola 225
Montenapoleone, via 76
Monte Stella 98
Monteverdi, Claudio
  237, 247
da Montofarno, Donato 27
Monza 99-102
  Grand Prix 100
Mora, Giangiacomo 11
Il Morazzone 28
Morbegno 266
Moro, Ludovico il
  11, *13*, **14**, 15, 86, 94,
  95, 97, **261**
motorcycles & mopeds 283
  insurance 288
  museum 210
motor racing, Monza **100**, 101
mountains & valleys of
  Lombardy **264-275**
  mountain driving 282
  see also lakes
Museo Bagatti Valsecchi 76
Museo del Cinema 81, **160**
Museo del Collezionista
  d'Arte Fondazione
  Goffredo Matthaes 67
Museo Diocesano
  53, **85-89**

Museo del Duomo
  53, 54, **59**
Museo di Fotografia
  Contemporanea 163
Museo del Giocattolo e
  del Bambino 156
Museo Inter e Milan 179
Museo di Milano e Storia
  Contemporanea 76
Museo Nazionale della
  Scienza e della Tecnologia
  'Leonardo da Vinci' 92,
  93-94
Museo Poldi Pezzoli
  53, 75, **78**
Museo del Presente 74
Museo del Risorgimento
  17
Museo Storico Alfa Romeo
  103, **104**
Museo degli Strumenti
  Musicali 69
Museo del Teatro 53,
  61-63
museums and galleries
  free entry during
   Settimana
  dei Beni Culturali 152
  opening times & tickets
   52-53
  specialist museums:
   archaeology &
    prehistory 69, 96
   art 59, 63-65, 68-69, 71,
    76
   art fakes 67
   art, modern 81, 161-164
   see also art &
    art galleries
   art, religious
    68-69, 85-89
   arts, decorative
    & applied 69
   cars & motor 103, **104**
   for/with children 156
   film 81, 160
   food and drink 104
   football 179
   history 76
   miscellaneous
    collections 76, 78
   musical instruments
    66, 69, 80
   see also violins
   natural history 81
   photography 163
   science & technology
    92, **93-94**
   theatre 63
music **170-174**
  Conservatorio di Musica
   'Giuseppe Verdi' 80
  instruments museum
   66, 69, 80
  jazz *173*, **173-174**, 185
   in cafés & bars
    126, 127, 174
   festival & events
    153, 197
  library 80, 288
  Milan & Lombardy
   in music 296
  opera & classical **174**
   in cafés & bars 125, 126
   festivals & events 153
  rock & pop **170-173**
music & instruments
  shops 135, 147, *147*
Mussolini, Benito
  18, 19, 76, 208,
  214, 215, **218**
Muzio, Giovanni
  67, 76, 96

Index

n

nature reserves
& regional parks **188**
around Milan 107
Cremona, Lodi
& around 256
Lago Maggiore &
around 194, 195, 198
Lago d'Orta
& around 190
Mantova & around 244
the mountains 264, 265,
270, 271-274
Navigli, the & around
82-90, **86-87**, *86, 87*
festivals & events 153
shops 144
Naviglio Martesana
86, 99, 102, 179
newspapers 29, **31, 289**
press agencies 76
nightlife **175-178**
gay & lesbian **166-168**
see also late-night Milan
Northern League 19, 33, 36
Novecento group & style 28

o

O'Donnell, Heinrich Graf 16
Oglio valley & river 244
Oh Bej! Oh Bej! 154
Oltrepò Pavese 263
open-air party venues 178
opening hours:
banks 289
restaurants 113
shops 131-132
opera **174**
cafés 125
opticians 150
Orio al Serio airport 278
Orrido di Bellano *208,* 209
Orrido di Sant'Anna 194
Orta San Giulio **190-191**
Orto Botanico di Brera 71
Otto, I, II & III 9, 10
outlet stores **192**

p

PAC Padiglione d'Arte
Contemporanea 81, **164**
La Pace 27
Palazzo/palazzi,
Milan &Around,
Open Weekend 52
d'Arco, Mantova **241,** *241*
Arese Litta *95,* 96
dell'Arte (Triennale) 67-70
via Barozzi 1, 77
Belgioioso 60
Borromeo 194, 195
della Borsa 63, **65**
via Cappuccini 8 77
Carmagnola 66
Castiglioni 78
Clerici 60, *61*
Cusani 70
Dugnani 81
Estense, Varese *103,* 104
dei Giureconsulti 63
di Giustizia 82
dell'Informazione 76
Marino 60, **61**
Morando Attendolo
Bolognini 76
via Mozart 21, 77
della Permanente 71
(Museo) Poldi Pezzoli
75, **78**
della Ragione 63, **65**

in Bergamo 222, 223
Reale 16, 53, **59**
Resta-Pallavicino 79
Rocca Saporiti 78
delle Scuole Palatine 63
Serbelloni 78
Sormani 82
Stampa 85
delle Stelline 96
Terni de Gregory, Crema
251, *251*
see also Berri Meregalli
family
Pallanza 194
Parco Sempione 67, **70**
Parco del Tranno 98
parks & gardens **156**
of the Brianza 100, **102**
for/with children 156
Como & around **202-203**
of Lombardy **188**
Maggiore & around
194, 195
safety 291
see also nature reserves
& regional parks
Passione, via della 79
Passo dello Stelvio 270, 273
pasticcerie (pastry shops) 125
Pavia & around **257-263**
university 292
pedestrians 52, 282, 292
pensione/s 38
Perego, Giovanni 78
permits 291
Peschiera 213
pet services 150
Peterzano, Simone 28
pharmacies & medicines
145, **287**
photocopy services 150
photographic services 150
photography **163**
in cafés and bars 126, **130**
galleries & museums
161-164, **163**
libraries 288
shops 150
Piacentini, Marcello 226, 231
Piadena 244
Pianura lowlands 246
piazza
see under specific name
Piazza, Guglielmo 11
Piccolo Teatro 66
picnic areas 156
Piedmont region **193-197**
piercing 145
Piermarini, Giuseppe
59, 60, 61, 70, 79, 81, 103
di Pietro, Antonio 19, *19*
Pinacoteca Ambrosiana **63**
Pinacoteca di Brera
17, 53, *70,* **71-72**
Pinacoteca Civica Tosia
Marinengo, Brescia 234
Pirelli, Giovanni Battista 33
Pirelli skyscraper 73-74
Pisogne 224
Pisanello 237, 241
Pizzala, Andrea 47
pizzerie see restaurants
plague 1630 11
Planetario Ulrico Hoepli 81
Platina
(Bartolomeo Sacchi) 244
play centres *155,* 157
poetry 126, 184
festival 185
Poldi Pezzoli
museum 75, **78**
polenta 110
restaurant menu **115**

police 286, 290
reporting thefts 292
politics 21, 31
'strategy of tension' 232
Ponte di Legno 271, 273, *275*
Ponte in Valtellina 267
Porta Garibaldi 73-74
Porta Nuova 75-76
Porta Romana 82-85, *83*
Porta Romana
& Southern Milan **82-90**
accommodation 49
cafés & bars **128-129,**
128-129
nightclubs 178
restaurants 121-124
Porta Ticinese 85-90
Porta Ticinese,
corso di 85, **144**
Porta Venezia 79
postal services 290
pottery, make your own 157
Prada Foundation 164
Procaccini, Giulio Cesare 28
Prodi, Romano 22
Progetto Chiesa Rossa, Dan
Flavin, *Untitled* 1996 164
Prosto di Piuro 264
public holidays 294
public transport
22, **279-280,** 283
regional transport 283
puppet theatre 157
Pusterla di Sant'Ambrogio 92

q

Quadrilatero della Moda 76
queuing 290

r

Raccolte d'Arte Antica 68-69
racism 23
Radetzky, Count Joseph
16, **18,** 81
radio 172, **289**
RAI 31
rail travel
see trains & rail travel
religion 7, 16, 198, **290**
festivals 154
relocation 290-291
Reni, Guido 251
residency certificate 291
restaurants **110-124**
best in Lombardy **189**
best in Milan **111**
for/with children 156-157
courses 111
by cuisine:
African 121
French 114
Indian 118
Italian *110, 114,* 113-
117, 118-124
Calabrian 122
Milanese 119, 123
Roman 122
rustic 114, 123
Tuscan 117
Japanese 117, 123, *123*
Latin-American 123
Mediterranean 117
Sri Lankan 118
fast food 122
health food 172
menu **115**
opening hours 113
late-opening 41, 117
pizza & snacks 121, 124
seafood 121, 124, 126
tipping 113

vegetarian **113,** 119, 121,
147, 172
with views *110,* 113, 121
vocabulary 295
out of town *see specific
area chapters*
*see also p302
restaurants index*
Ricchini, Francesco
Maria 72, 78
Ricci, Sebastiano 28
riots 1848 *16,* **16-17**
Risorgimento, the 10, **18**
Riva del Garda 216
rock art, prehistoric
25, 268, 271
Roman Milan & Lombardy
7, 12, 94, 202, 257
monuments & remains
Milan 25, 85
Bergamo 220, 222
Brescia 230-231, 233, 234
Desenzano 212-213
Maderno 216
Sirmione 213, 215
spa 263
Romano, Giulio
240, 241-242
Romano di Lombardia 229
Roncalli, Angelo Giuseppe
229
Rosmini, Antonio 194, **198**
La Rotonda, Brescia
230, 231
Rotonda della Besana 79
Roveda, Marco 172
Ruggeri, Giovanni 70
running
Marathon *153,* **154**
Stramilano 152

s

Sabbioneta 244-245
Sacchi, Bartolomeo
see Platina
Sacco 266
safety & security 291-292
sales tax *see IVA*
Salò 214
da Salò, Gasparo 214, **255**
Salone Internazionale del
Mobile (furniture fair) 152
Sammartini, via 165, **166**
San Babila & Eastern Milan
75-81
accommodation 46-49
cafés & bars 127-128
church 77, **79**
designer stores
136-137, *137*
nightclubs 177-178
piazza 77
restaurants 118-121
San Bernardino alle Ossa
82, **83-84**
San Calimero 84
San Carlo al Corso
77, **79**
San Cristoforo 87, 88
San Fedele 60, **61**
San Francesco di Paola 76
San Giorgio al Palazzo 89
San Giuseppe 70, **72**
San Gottardo al Corso 85
San Lorenzo Maggiore
(alle Colonne) 85, **89,** *90*
San Marco 71, **72**
San Maurizio 96
San Nazaro Maggiore 84
San Nicola 11
San Pellegrino Terme
228, *228,* 229

San Pietro in Gessate 79, **80**
San Sebastiano 63, **65**
San Sepolcro 63, **65**
San Simpliciano 71, **72**
San Siro **97-98**
  Stadio Giuseppe Meazza 98, 171, **172**, **179**, *181*
San Vincenzo in Prato 85, **90**
San Vittore al Corpo 92-93, **95**
Santa Maria alla Fontana 74
Santa Maria del Carmine 70, **72**
Santa Maria delle Grazie, piazza & around **96-97**
  church 15, 53, **96**, *97*
Santa Maria Incoronata 73, **74**
Santa Maria dei Miracoli & San Celso 85, *86*, **90**
Santa Maria della Passione 79, **80-81**
Santa Maria presso San Satiro 63, **65**
Santa Maria della Vittoria 92, **94**
Sant'Ambrogio & Western Milan **91-98**
  accommodation 49-50
  cafés & bars 129-130
  church 91, *91*, **94-95**
  restaurants 124
Sant'Andrea, Mantova **242**, *242*
Sant'Angelo 71, **73**
Sant'Eustorgio 53, 85, **89-90**
Santo Stefano Maggiore 82, **84-85**
Sarnico 224
Saronno 104
Sartirana Lomellina 262
Sassi, Luisa Battistotti 15
Sassu, Aligi 28
saunas, gay *166*, 168
La Scala
  (theatre) **61-63**, 170, **174**
  piazza & around 54, **59-60**
Scapigliatura school 28
sculpture 56-57, 59, 60, 63
seafood 111, 121, 124, 126
Seminario Arcivescovile 78
Settimana dei Beni Culturali 15, **152**
sex club 168
Sforza, the, & dynastic rule 12, **13-16**, 16, 74, 83, 85, 248, 252
  Ludovico il Moro 11, *13*, **14**, 15, 86, 94, 95, 97, **261**
Sforzesco & Northern Milan **66-74**
  accommodation 43-46, *50*
  cafés & bars *125*, 126-127, *127*
  nightclubs *175*, *176*, 176-177
  restaurants 114-118
shoe shops 138
shops & services **131-150**
  for children 157
  gay & lesbian 168-169
  opening hours 131-132
  vocabulary 295
sights, major 53
sightseeing tours *see* tours
Sirmione 213, *214*, 215
Sironi, Mario 28

skiing 194, 236, **272-273**
  ski shops 273
  2005 Alpine World Skiing Championships 269
  see also mountains & valleys
sled dog rides 271, 273
slimming centres 179
'SME affair' 31
smoking 292
soccer *see* football
Società Umanitaria 28
Solari, Guiniforte 74, 80, 97
Solferino, Battle of **239**
Soncino 252, 253
Sondrio 266
Sòrico 208-209
Sotto il Monte 229
Southern Milan *see* Porta Romana & Southern Milan
spas 180, 228, *228*, 229, 263, 269, 269-270, 275
della Spiga, via 75, **76**
sport & fitness **179-181**
  media coverage 31
Sport Movies & TV International Festival 160
sports bars 126
squash 181
Stadio Giuseppe Meazza (San Siro) 98, *98*, 171, **172**, **179**, *181*
Stampa, Massimiliano 85
stationery shops 132-133
Stazione di Cardona (Milano Nord) 281
Stazione Centrale & around 74, 281, 291
Stazione Porta Garibaldi 281
Stile Liberty (stile floreale) see architecture: Liberty Style
Stock Exchange (borsa) 65
Stradivari, Antonio 249, **255**
Stramilano 152
Stresa 193-194, 198
studying in Milan 292
supermarkets 143
swimming
  lakes *see* lakes of Lombardy
  pools 181
  pool-side bars 130
Switzerland 197-198
  outlet malls 149

Tangentopoli investigation 19, *19*
tattooists 145
tax code 291
tax, sales *see* IVA
taxis 281
  disabled travellers 286
  to and from airport 278
Teatridithalia Elfo 183
Teatro Dal Verme 174
Teatro degli Arcimboldi 174
Teatro Arsenale 183-184
Teatro dell'Arte 183
Teatro del Buratto al Pime 157
Teatro Carcano 184
Teatro Ciak 185
Teatro Franco Parenti 185
Teatro Grassi 66
Teatro Litta 185
Teatro Manzoni 185
Teatro Nuovo 185
Teatro Out Off 185
Teatro alla Scala **61-63**, 170, **174**

Teatro Smeraldo 185
Teatro Strehler (Nuovo Piccolo) 66, **185**
Teatro Studio 66
technology fair 154
Teglio 267
telegrams 293
telephones **292-293**
  faults 286
  mobile phones in cars 282
television 21, **31-32**, **289**
Tempio Capitolino & Teatro Romano, Brescia 231, **234**
Temù 271
Teresa of Austria, Empress Maria *14*, 18
theatre companies, venues & tickets **182-185**
theme parks 213
Theodolinda, Queen 9, 15, 100, 103, 262
  crown 26
Tibaldi, Pellegrino 61, 65, 207
ticket agencies 150
  concerts 170
  theatre 182-183
Tiepolo, Giambattista 28
time 293
Tintoretto 28, 89
tipping 293
  in restaurants 113
Tirano 268
Titian 28, 232
toilets 293
  for the disabled 285
Tonale 273
Torino, via 85-90
Torre Velasca 83
Toscolano-Maderno 216
tourist information **294**
  accommodation 39
  out of town *see specific area chapter*
tours **53**
  bus 53
  canal 87
  for children 53
  cycling 283
  guided **53**
  tram 53, 155, 280
  wine 53
trains & rail travel 278, 279
  disabled travellers 285
  lost property 288
  regional rail services 283
  timetable & tickets 280-281
trams 20, **279**
  Ciao Milano
  Tourist Tram 53, 155, 280
transport information 280
  vocabulary 295
travel agencies 150
Treccani, Ernesto 28
Tremezzo 208
Trussardi Foundation 164
Turkish baths 181

Unification, Italian 18-19
Università Cattolica del Sacro Cuore 92, **95-96**
Università di Milano 79
Università degli Studi di Milano 82, **83**, *84*

Valcamonica 267, 271-274
Valchiavenna 264-265
Valle dell'Adda 102-103

Valle Brembana 228
Valle Imagna 229
Valmalenco 267
Valtellina 265, 265-266, 267
Val Trompia 236
Varenna 209, *210*
Varese & around **104-106**
Varzi 263
VAT *see* IVA
VAT rebates 292
veline **32**, *32*
Venezia, corso 17, **77-79**
Verbania 194
Verdi, Giuseppe 10, 18, 47, 208, 239, 296
  burial place 98
Versace, Gianni 35
Vetra, piazza 85
via see under individual street name
Viafarini 164
Viboldone 106
videos & DVDs 135, 150
viewpoints &
panoramas 53, 56
  Lake Garda 239
  restaurants & café 113, *113*, 121
Vigevano 261, 262
Villa Reale *80*, **81**
Villa Reale, Monza *52*, **100**, **101**
Vimercate 101
Vinci, Leonardo da 27, 50, 74, 86, **92-93**, 179, 210, 261, 265
  Codex Atlanticus 63
  The Last Supper 52, 53, **92-93**, *93*
violins 247, 248, **255**
Virgin and Child with Saints 72, *72*
visas 294
Visconti, the & dynastic rule 11, 12, 13, 26, 211, 258, 259
  & art in Milan 26-27
  Caterina 13
  Gian Galeazzo *10*, 13, 26
  shields 63
Vittoriale degli Italiani 215
Vittorio Emanuele II 59
Vittorio Emanuele II, corso 76-77
vocabulary **295**
  menus **115**
Voghera 263
da Volpedo, Pelizza 28
Volta, Alessandro 204, 258

walking & hiking,
  Milan & around 52, 102
  around Brescia 236
  Lago di Como &
  around 204-205, 208, 210
  Lago Maggiore &
  around 194
  mountains 267, 268
watch repairs 135
water, drinking 294
watersports 156, 212
weather & climate 294
weather reports 273
websites,
  information 296
wedding organiser 190
Western Milan *see*
  Sant'Ambrogio &
  Western Milan
wheelchair hire 286
windsurfing 212

Index

wine & wines
  35, 113, **118**, 208, 268
in bars 126
of Franciacorta 236
in restaurants 113
shops 141, *143*, 143-144
spumante 236
tasting 126, 144
tours 53, 102
women
  in history 15
  lesbian Milan 169
  sexual violence &
  rape helpline 287
  travellers 294
  veline **32**, *32*
working in Italy 291
World War I 271
World War II 35, 191, 216
worship 290

youth hostels 45-46

Zanuso, Marco 66
Zelig **184**
Zone 224-225

Where to stay
Antares Hotel Rubens 49-50
Antica Locanda Leonardo 50
Antica Locanda
  dei Mercanti 42, *45*
Antica Locanda
  Solferino 45, *50*

Ariosto 50
Ariston 49
Aspromonte 46
Etrusco 46
Four Seasons 41
Grand Hotel
  et de Milan 41, **47**, *47*
The Gray 41
Gritti 42-43
King 50
Liberty 49
London 45
Manzoni 43
Marconi 45
Mazzini 46
Mercure Milano
  Corso Genova 49
Minerva 49
Nettuno 46-49
Ostello Piero Rotta 45-46
Palazzo delle Stelline 50
Park Hyatt Milan 41, *42*
San Francisco 49
Sheraton Diana Majestic 46
Del Sole 46
Spadari al Duomo 41-42
STRAF 42, *43*
UNA Hotel Century 43-45
Vecchia Milano 43
De La Ville 40-41

Cafés & Bars
Art Deco Café 127-128
ATM *125*, 126
Baci e Abbracci 129
Bar Basso 128
Bar Magenta 129
Bhangrabar 126

Le Biciclette 128
Biffi 129
Caffè Letterario 126
Caffè Louisiana Bistro 126
Caffè Miani (aka Zucca)
  125
Caffè della Pusterla 128
Caffè Verdi 125
Da Claudio
  Pescheria dei Milanesi 126
Colonial Fashion Café 129
Cuore *128-129*, 129
Diana Garden 128
Dynamo 126
L'Elephante 128
Fresco Art 129
Good Fellas 126-127
Jamaica 127
Lounge Paradise 130
Morgan's 130
Nordest Caffè 127
Radetzky 127
Ragno d'Oro 129
Roialto 127
10 Corso Como 126, *127*
Victoria Café 125-126

Restaurants
Da Abele 119
Ai Sabbioni 121
Al Merluzzo Felice 121
Anema e Cozze 114-117
L'Ape Piera 121
Armani/Nobu 117, *119*
Be Bop 124
Bistrot Duomo
  110, 113-114

Bottiglieria
  Da Pino 118
Café Real 114
Compagnia Generale dei
  Viaggiatori Naviganti e
  Sognatori 123, *123*
Dongiò 122
Emilia & Carlo *114*, 117
Emporio Armani Café 117
Feijào Com Arroz 123-124
Da Giacomo 119
Giulio Pane e Ojo 122
Innocenti Evasioni 117
Jacaranda 124
Joia 119
Just Cavalli Café 117
La Latteria 117
Da Leo 124
Il Luogo di Aimo e Nadia
  124
Masuelli San Marco 119
Osteria delle Vigne 122
Osteria Grand Hotel 121
Pastarito/Pizzaria 114
Pizzeria 40 121
Premiata Pizzeria 124
Serendib 118
Shambala 124
Super Pizza 124
Sushi-Kôboo 124
Tara 118
10 Corso Como Caffè 117
Da Teresa 121
La Terrazza
  di via Palestro 121
La Topaia 123
Trattoria Madonnina 123
Tuberi Americani 123
Warsa 121

Advertisers' Index

Please refer to the relevant sections for contact details

Western Union   **IFC**

In Context
travelpan.it   **4**
RefrigiWear   **8**
Hilton Milan   **30**
Energie   **34**

Where to Stay
HotelConnect   **40**
International Homes   **44**
Grand Hotel et de Milan   **48**

Sightseeing
Downtown Palestre   **58**
Bluecar   **62**

Restaurants
Exploit/Living   **112**

Shops & Services
Urushi   **134**
Il Bisonte   **140**
Energie   **146**

Lakes & Cities
Time Out City Guides

National border	– – –
Province border	– –
Motorway (*autostrade*)	═══
Main road	········
Lake/River/Canal	▨
Place of interest	▨
Church	✚
Park	▨
Hospital/university	▨
Pedestrianised area	▨
Car park	**P**
Tourist information	***i***
Metro station	**M**

Maps

Lombardy	**304**
Greater Milan	**306**
Milan Overview	**307**
Street Maps	**308**
Street Index	**313**
Milan Metro	**316**

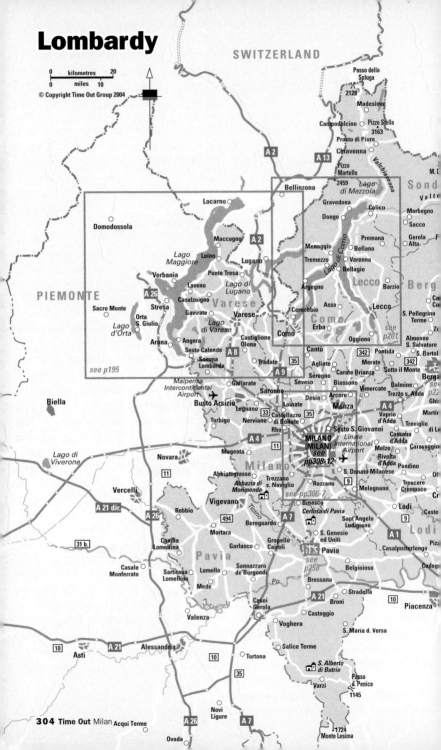

Lombardy

kilometres 20
miles 10

SWITZERLAND

PIEMONTE

Domodossola

Biella

Lago di
Viverone

Vercelli

Novara

Robbio

Mortara

Candia
Lomellina

Casale
Monferrato

Sartirana
Lomellina

Lomello

Mede

Valenza

Asti

Alessandria

Tortona

Novi
Ligure

Ovada

Acqui Terme

Pavia

Po

Locarno

Lago
Maggiore

Luino

Maccagno

Verbania

Laveno

Stresa

Sacro Monte

Lago
d'Orta

Orta
S. Giulio

Arona

Angera

Gavirate

Casalzuigno

Ponte Tresa

Lugano

Lago di
Lugano

Varese

Lago
di Varese

Castiglione
Olona

Sesto Calende

Somma
Lombarda

Gallarate

Tradate

Malpensa
Intercontinental
Airport

Busto Arsizio

Legnano

Turbigo

Nerviano

Castellazzo
di Bollate

Rho

Magenta

Saronno

Lainate

Desio

Seregno

Seveso

Agliate

Carate Brianza

Biassono

Arcore

Monza

Vimercate

Sesto S. Giovanni

MILANO
(MILAN)
see
pp308-12

Linate
International
Airport

S. Donato Milanese

Melzo

Rivolta
d'Adda

Pandino

Trezzano
s. Naviglio

Rozzano

Abbiategrasso

Abbazia di
Morimondo

Vigevano

Ticino

Bereguardo

Binasco

Certosa di Pavia

Sant'Angelo
Lodigiano

S. Genesio
ed Uniti

Gropello
Cairoli

Garlasco

Sannazzaro
de' Burgondi

Casei
Gerola

Casteggio

Voghera

Salice Terme

Varzi

Bellinzona

Lago
di Mezzola

Gravedona

Colico

Dongo

Menaggio

Tremezzo

Argegno

Cernobbio

Como

Erba

Cantù

Oggiono

Merate

Sotto il Monte

Trezzo s. Adda

Vaprio
d'Adda

Treviglio

Cassano
d'Adda

Caravaggio

Lago di Como

Varenna

Bellagio

Bellano

Premana

Lecco

Asso

Barzio

S. Pellegrino
Terme

Almenno
S. Salvatore

S. Bartol

Pontida

Morbegno

Sacco

Gerola
Alta

Passo dello
Spluga
2128

Madesimo

Campodolcino

Pizzo Stella
3163

Prosto di Piuro

Chiavenna

Pizzo
Martello
2459

Valchiavenna

Sond

Valte

Berg

Lodi

Caste

Melegnano

Trescore
Cremasco

Of

Cr

Casalpusterlengo

Codog

Belgioioso

Bressana

Stradella

Broni

S. Maria d. Versa

Piacenza

S. Alberto
di Butrio

Passo
d. Penice
1145

Monte Lesima
1724

Valenza

Mortara

Pavia
see
p258

Milano

Milano

see
pp306-7

Lodi

Varese

Como

Lecco

Berg

see p201

see p195

see
p22

A 2

A 13

A 2

A 26

A 8

A 9

A 4

A 26

A 21 dir.

A 4

A 21

A 21

A 7

A 7

A 26

A 1

342

342

35

11

33

35

9

9

494

11

31 b.

10

10

10

35

10

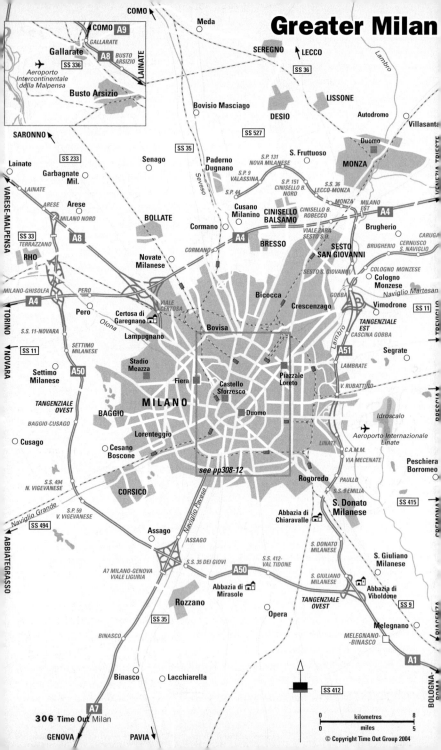

Greater Milan

see pp308-12

© Copyright Time Out Group 2004

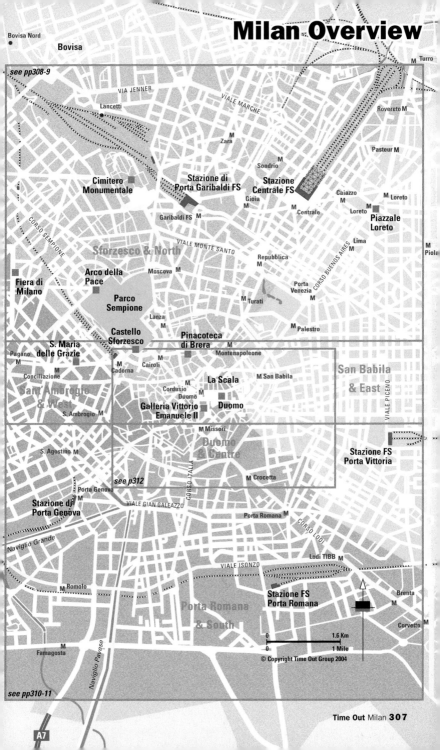

1

PIAZZALE LUGANO

VIA DEGLI IMBRIANI

VIA BODIO

PIAZZALE NIGRA

Ospedale A. Bassi

VIA BUTTI

VIA JENNER

PIAZZALE MACIACHINI

VIA RESEGONE

VIA E. PORRO

VIALE E. PORRO

PIAZZA PASOLINI

VIA CANTONI

VIA V. TORELLI

VIA CALABRIA

VIA TEGLIO

VIA LANCETTI

VIA BERNINA

VIALE

VIA VALTELLINA

Isola

VIA MENABREA

VIA GENERALE GOVONE

VIA AOSTA

VIA STILICONE

VIA MALOJA

APRICA

VIA G. PIAZZI

STELVIO

PIAZZA SPOTORNO

A

VIA AMMIRAGLIO CARACCIOLO

VIA CESENA

VIA GENERALE GOVONE

VIA ITALO CALVINO

VIA G. FERRARIS

Scalo Farini F.S.

VIA VALTELLINA

VIA CUSIO S. MARIA A. FONTANA

Santa Maria alla Fontana

VIA TELLINI

VIA MAC MAHON

VIA EUGENIO

VIA PRINCIPE

VIA CUCCHIARI

VIA GRAN SAN BERNARDO

VIA MESSINA

PIAZZA G. PEREGO

VIA BORSIERI

Dogana

VIA PORRO

VIA UGO BASSI

VIA TOCE

CARLO

FARINI

VIA M. ROSSO

MONTANO

VIA ALSERIO

VIA BOLTRAFFIO

PIAZZA LAMBERTENGHI FIDIA

PIAZZA ANGELO D. PERGOLA

CHERUBINO

STRADONE

PIAZZA CANEVA

VIA CENISIO

PIAZZA DIOCLEZIANO

PIAZZA CENISIO

PIAZZA CORIOLANO

Cimitero Monumentale

VIA L. NONO

VIA COLA

VIA ARCHINTI

VIA J. DAL VERME

Bullona

VIA KORISTKA

VIA GARANCETTI

VIA MARUSSIG

VIA CASTELVETRO

VIA FRATELLI INDUNO

VIA G. SOLDATI

VIA M. ASELONE

PIAZZALE CIMITERO MONUMENTALE

VIA CARLO FARINI

VIA PASTRENGO

VIA G. FERRARI

Stazione di Porta Garibaldi F.S.

BUSSA

VIA CAMPOBASSO

B. FAUCHE

PIAZZA GERUSALEMME

PAOLO

VIA MONVISO

TARTAGLIA

VIA PROCACCINI

VIA CERESIO

VIA M. QUADRIO

VIA TITO SPERI

VIA TAZZOLI

CAVALCAVIA

Garibaldi

VIA PIERO DELLA FRANCESCA

VIA SAVONAROLA

CORSO SEMPIONE

VIA AGUDIO

VIA CHIZZOLINI

VIA SARONNO

VIA MANTEGNA

BERTINI

VIA ALEARDI

MESSINA

FIORAVANTI

VIA A. DEL CAMBIO

SARPI

PIAZZALE BAIAMONTI

VIA G. BONNET

VIA DI TOCQUEVILLE

CORSO COMO

VIA DOMODOSSOLA

VIA TREBAZIO

VIA FILELFO

PIAZZA A. GRAMSCI

VIA PROCACCINI

VIA G.

LARGO C.E. GADDA

PAOLO

VIA G. BRUNO

VIA ARNOLFO DI CAMBIO

G. B. BRUSCO

VIA GIOR. PEPE

VIALE CRISPI

PIAZZA XXV APRILE

B

VIA GIOVANNI DA PROCIDA

VIA F. FERRUCCI

VIA MUSSI

VIA SABATELLI

VIA ALBERTINI

VIA LOMBARDO

VIA FLONDONO

MANFREDINI

PRINA

CORSO SEMPIONE

VIA MOSCATI

VIA L. CANONICA

VIA ALFIERI

VIA VERGA

PIAZZA S.S. TRINITÀ

BRAMANTE

BASTIONI DI PORTA VOLTA

VIA VOLTA

Santa Maria Incoronata

GARIBALDI

VIA MARSALA

Moscova

VIA MILAZZO

Sforzesco & North

VIA PONTIDA

VIA A. VOLTA

Moscova

VIALE SEVERINO BOEZIO

VIA G. PRATI

VIA LINNEO

VIA PIRELLI VILLASANTA

VIA MASSENA

VIA MELZI D'ERIL

VIA D. CIRILLO

PIAZZA ALFIERI MORSELLI

PIAZZA GIANNONE

VIA P. PINAMONTE

VIA VARESE

MOSCOVA

PIAZZA VI FEBBRAIO

VIA COMERIO

VIA PANGRAZI

VIA PUCCI

PIAZZA CANONICA

VIA CESARIANO

PIAZZALE BIANCAMANO

PORTA TENAGLIA

LARGO LA FOPPA

VIA MAROSTATO

VIA STATUTO

VIA ROTONDI

VIA F. NIEVO

TONOLI

VIA EUPILI

SANGIORGIO

VIA BERTANI

VIA C.M. MAGGI

VIA PORTA LEGA LOMBARDA

VIA VASTO

VIA TOMMASO DA CAZZANIGA

LARGO TREVES

VIA DEI PRAGA

VIA LEONE

VIA UGO FOSCOLO XIII

PIAZZA GIOVANNI XXIII

VIA SANGIORGIO

VIA GUERRAZZI

Arco della Pace

PIAZZA SEMPIONE

VIA BERTANI

VIALE BYRON

ELVEZIA

VIA LEGNANO

VIA SOLERA MANTEGAZZA

VIA PALERMO

DEI CHIOSTRI

VIA ANCONA

P

VIA VINCENZO MONTI

VIA N. MACHIAVELLI

VIA PIERMARINI

PIAZZA SEMPIONE

Parco Sempione

VIALE CERVANTES

VIALE GADIO

Arena

VIALE ELVEZIA

VIALE ANFITEATRO

San Simpliciano

VIA CAVALIERI DEL SANTO SEPOLCRO

VIA

LARGO CAMUS

VIA REGGIMENTO SAVOIA CAVALLERIA

Corpus Domini

VIALE ALEMAGNA

VIALE GIORGIO

VIALE MALTA

VIALE CONS. LOMBARDO

PIAZZA VISCONTI DI MODRONE

Teatro Strehler

VIA S. MARC

VIA ROSSETTI

VIA ORIANI

VIA PALLAVICINO

VIA PAGANO

VIALE MARIO PAGANO

VIALE MILTON

VIALE CAMOENS

VIALE IBSEN

BEAUHARNAIS

VIALE CONC.

MARENGO

PIAZZA DEL FORO

LARGO A. GREPPI

PONTACCIO

VIA FIORI CHIARI

Pinacoteca di Brera

VIA PANZINI

VIA MASCHERONI

VIA A. TASSO

VIA G. LEOPARDI

Palazzo dell'Arte

VIALE MOLIÈRE

VIALE SHAKESPEARE

PIAZZA CASTELLO

Palazzo Cusani

C

VIA GIUSSANO

VIA LODOVICO ARIOSTO

PETRARCA

VIALE

CHERIE

VIA CANOVA

Castello Sforzesco

CASTELLO

VIA SELLA

VIA ERBE

VIA LANDOLFO CARMINE

Santa Maria del Carmine

PIAZZA DEL CARMINE

Palazzo Citterio

VIA GIUDO D'AREZZO

VIA BAZZONI

PIAZZA TOMMASEO

VIA XX SETTEMBRE

VIA SEBETO

VIA SAFFI

VIA G. GIOBERTI

PIAZZA VIRGILIO

VIA MINGHETTI

VIA CUSANI

LARGO CAIROLI

Cairoli

VIA BROLETTO

VIA DELL'ORSO

VIA MARIO D'AREZZO

VIA RASORI

VIA SCARPA

PIAZZA CONCILIAZIONE

PIAZZA GIOVINE ITALIA

BOCCACCIO

Stazione Ferrovie Nord

PIAZZALE L. CADORNA

FORO BUONAPARTE

Palazzo Arese Litta

VIA PUCCINI

VIA DANTE

Palazzo Clerici

Pagano

CORSO VERCELLI

Conciliazione

Cenacolo Vinciano

S. Maria delle Grazie

PIAZZA SANTA MARIA DELLE GRAZIE

CORSO

MAGENTA

See p310

CORSO MAGENTA

MERAVIGLI

Cordusio

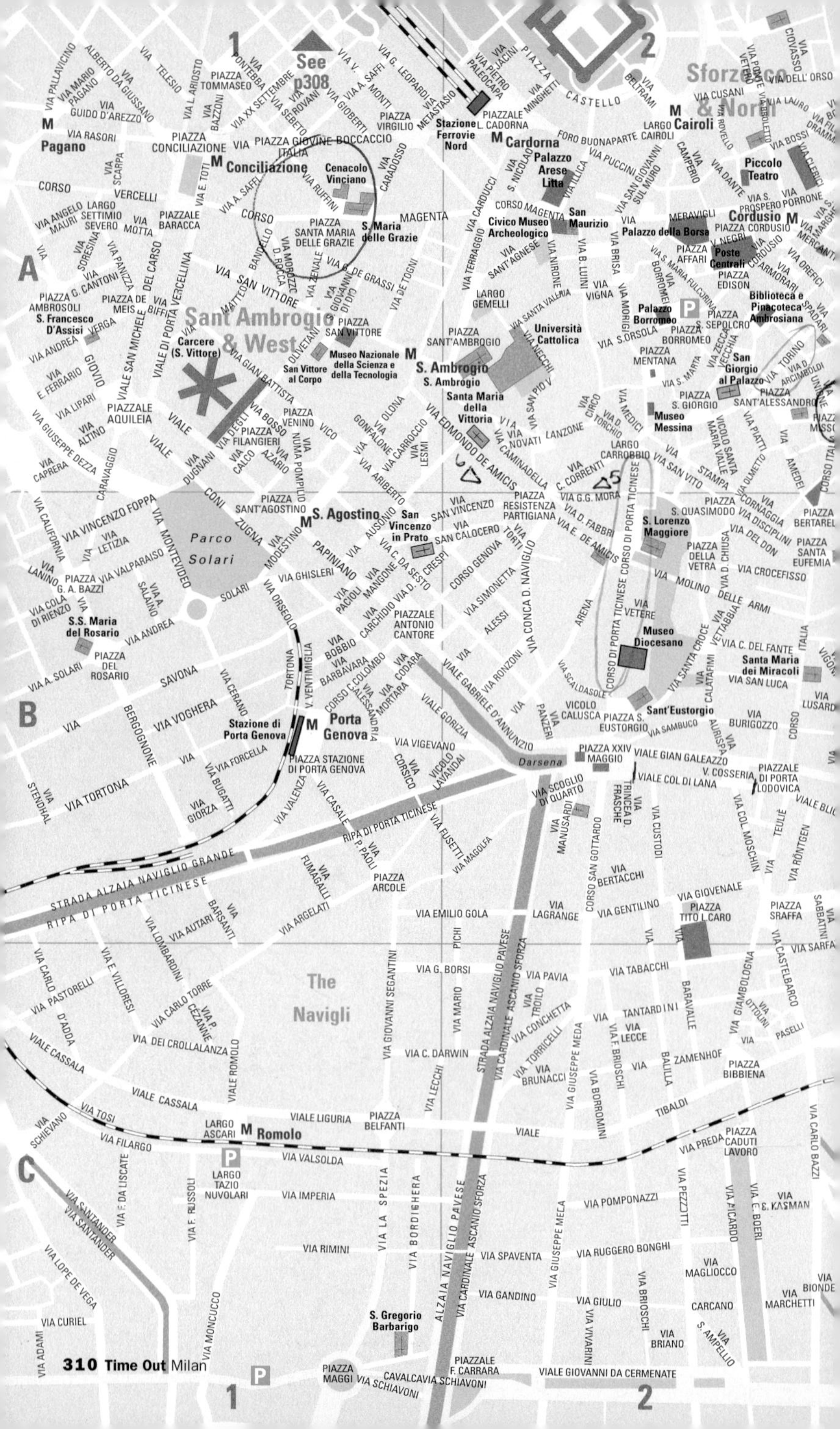
1
2
A
B
C
See p308
Sforzesco & North
Sant'Ambrogio & West
The Navigli
Parco Solari
Darsena
M Pagano
M Conciliazione
M Cardorna
M Cairoli
M Cordusio
M S. Ambrogio
M S. Agostino
M Porta Genova
M Romolo
Stazione Ferrovie Nord
Stazione di Porta Genova
Cenacolo Vinciano
S. Maria delle Grazie
Palazzo Arese Litta
Civico Museo Archeologico
San Maurizio
Palazzo della Borsa
Piccolo Teatro
Poste Centrali
Biblioteca e Pinacoteca Ambrosiana
Palazzo Borromeo
Università Cattolica
San Giorgio al Palazzo
Museo Messina
Carcere (S. Vittore)
S. Francesco D'Assisi
San Vittore al Corpo
Museo Nazionale della Scienza e della Tecnologia
S. Ambrogio
Santa Maria della Vittoria
San Vincenzo in Prato
S. Lorenzo Maggiore
Museo Diocesano
Sant'Eustorgio
Santa Maria dei Miracoli
S.S. Maria del Rosario
S. Gregorio Barbarigo
PIAZZA TOMMASEO
PIAZZA CONCILIAZIONE
PIAZZA GIOVINE ITALIA
PIAZZA VIRGILIO
PIAZZALE L. CADORNA
PIAZZA CASTELLO
LARGO CAIROLI
FORO BUONAPARTE
CORSO VERCELLI
CORSO MAGENTA
PIAZZA SANTA MARIA DELLE GRAZIE
LARGO SETTIMIO SEVERO
PIAZZALE BARACCA
PIAZZA AMBROSOLI
PIAZZA DE MEIS
PIAZZA SAN VITTORE
PIAZZA SANT'AMBROGIO
LARGO GEMELLI
PIAZZA AFFARI
PIAZZA CORDUSIO
PIAZZA EDISON
PIAZZA S. SEPOLCRO
PIAZZA BORROMEO
PIAZZA MENTANA
PIAZZA S. GIORGIO
PIAZZA SANT'ALESSANDRO
PIAZZALE AQUILEIA
PIAZZA VENINO
PIAZZA FILANGIERI
PIAZZA SANT'AGOSTINO
PIAZZA RESISTENZA PARTIGIANA
LARGO CARROBBIO
PIAZZA S. QUASIMODO
PIAZZA BERTARELLI
PIAZZA SANTA EUFEMIA
PIAZZA DELLA VETRA
PIAZZA G. A. BAZZI
PIAZZA DEL ROSARIO
PIAZZALE ANTONIO CANTORE
VICOLO CALUSCA
PIAZZA S. EUSTORGIO
PIAZZA XXIV MAGGIO
PIAZZALE DI PORTA LODOVICA
PIAZZA STAZIONE DI PORTA GENOVA
PIAZZA ARCOLE
PIAZZA TITO L. CARO
PIAZZA SRAFFA
PIAZZA BIBBIENA
PIAZZA BELFANTI
LARGO ASCARI
LARGO TAZIO NUVOLARI
PIAZZA CADUTI LAVORO
PIAZZA MAGGI
PIAZZALE F. CARRARA
CAVALCAVIA SCHIAVONI
VIA SCHIAVONI
VIALE GIOVANNI DA CERMENATE
STRADA ALZAIA NAVIGLIO GRANDE
RIPA DI PORTA TICINESE
ALZAIA NAVIGLIO PAVESE
VIA CARDINALE ASCANIO SFORZA
VIALE DI PORTA VERCELLINA
VIALE SAN MICHELE DEL CARSO
VIA SAN VITTORE
VIA EDMONDO DE AMICIS
CORSO DI PORTA TICINESE
CORSO GENOVA
VIA CONCA D. NAVIGLIO
VIALE GABRIELE D'ANNUNZIO
VIALE GORIZIA
VIA VIGEVANO
VIA TORTONA
VIA SAVONA
VIA VOGHERA
VIA BERGOGNONE
VIA SOLARI
VIALE CASSALA
VIALE LIGURIA
VIA VALSOLDA
VIA IMPERIA
VIA RIMINI
VIA SPAVENTA
VIA GANDINO
VIA GIULIO
VIA CURIEL
VIA SANTANDER
VIA LOPE DE VEGA
VIA FILARGO
VIA TOSI
VIA SCHIEVANO
VIA RUGGERO BONGHI
VIA POMPONAZZI
VIA TABACCHI
VIA PAVIA
VIA G. BORSI
VIA EMILIO GOLA
VIA C. DARWIN
VIA GIOVANNI SEGANTINI
VIA LA SPEZIA
VIA BORDIGHERA
VIA GIUSEPPE MEDA
VIA BORROMINI
VIA BRIOSCHI
VIA VIVARINI
VIA E. BOERI
VIA RICARDO
VIA CARLO BAZZI
VIA GENTILINO
VIA GIOVENALE
VIA BERTACCHI
VIA LAGRANGE
CORSO SAN GOTTARDO
VIALE COL DI LANA
VIALE GIAN GALEAZZO
VIA CROCEFISSO
VIA MOLINO DELLE ARMI
VIA SAN VITO
VIA TORINO
VIA DANTE
VIA MERAVIGLI
VIA OREFICI
VIA ROVELLO
VIA CUSANI
VIA CLERICI
VIA BOSSI
VIA LUINI
VIA NIRONE
VIA BRISA
VIA S. ORSOLA
VIA CARDUCCI
VIA TERRAGGIO
VIA S. NICOLAO
VIA PUCCINI
VIA SAN GIOVANNI SUL MURO
VIA CALATAFIMI
VIA SANTA CROCE
VIA LUSARDI
VIA BURIGOZZO
VIA SAMBUCO
VIA ARENA
VIA VETERE
VIA SCALDASOLE
VIA RONZONI
VIA ALESSI
VIA SIMONETTA
VIA TORTI
VIA PAPINIANO
VIA ORSEOLO
VIA MODESTINO
VIA COLOMBO
VIA MORTARA
VIA CODARA
VIA CASALE
VIA VALENZA
VIA FUSETTI
VIA MAGOLFA
VIA ARGELATI
VIA FUMAGALLI
VIA BARSANTI
VIA AUTARI
VIA LOMBARDINI
VIA E. VILLORESI
VIA CARLO D'ADDA
VIA PASTORELLI
VIA CARLO TORRE
VIA P. CEZANNE
VIA DEI CROLLALANZA
VIALE ROMOLO
VIA LECCHI
VIA MARIO PICHI
VIA TROILO
VIA CONCHETTA
VIA TORRICELLI
VIA BRUNACCI
VIA F. BRIOSCHI
VIA BALILLA
VIA ZAMENHOF
VIA TANTARDINI
VIA BARAVALLE
VIA GIAMBOLOGNA
VIA OTTOLINI
VIA PASELLI
VIA CASTELBARCO
VIA SABBATINI
VIA TEULIÉ
VIA RÖNTGEN
VIA COL. MOSCHIN
VIA CUSTODI
VIA TRINCEA D. FRASCHE
VIA SCOGLIO DI QUARTO
VIA MANUSARDI
VIA PREDA
VIA TIBALDI
VIA MAGLIOCCO
VIA CARCANO
VIA S. AMPELLIO
VIA BRIANO
VIA MARCHETTI
VIA BIONDE
VIA E. KASMAN
VIA PEZZOTTI
VIA F. RUSSOLI
VIA F. DA LISCATE
VIA MONCUCCO
VIA ADAMI
VIA CALIFORNIA
VIA VINCENZO FOPPA
VIA MONTEVIDEO
VIA VALPARAISO
VIA LETIZIA
VIA LANINO
VIA COLA DI RIENZO
VIA ANDREA
VIA A. SOLARI
VIA STENDHAL
VIA GIORZA
VIA BUGATTI
VIA FORCELLA
VIA CERANO
VIA TORTONA
VIA V. VENTIMIGLIA
VIA BOBBIO
VIA BARBAVARA
VIA GHISLERI
VIA CARCHIDIO
VIA PACIOLI
VIA MANGONE
VIA C. DA SESTO
VIA D. CRESPI
VIA SAN CALOCERO
VIA SAN VINCENZO
VIA AUSONIO
VIA ARIBERTO
VIA CARROCCIO
VIA LESMI
VIA GONFALONE
VIA OLONA
VIA NUMA POMPILIO
VIA AZARIO
VIA CALCO
VIA DUGNANI
VIA BOSSO
VIA DEGLI
VIA GIAN BATTISTA
VIA CORI ZUGNA
VIA CARAVAGGIO
VIA CAPRERA
VIA GIUSEPPE DEZZA
VIA ALTINO
VIA LIPARI
VIA E. FERRARIO
VIA GIOVIO
VIA ANDREA VERGA
VIA G. CANTONI
VIA PANIZZA
VIA SORESINA
VIA MOTTA
VIA ANGELO MAURI
VIA BIFFI
VIA MATTEO BANDELLO
VIA MOROZZO D. ROCCA
VIA ZENALE
VIA GIOVANNI DA DIO
VIA G. DE GRASSI
VIA DE TOGNI
VIA OLIVETANI
VIA RUFFINI
VIA CARADOSSO
VIA A. SAFFI
VIA E. TOTI
VIA SCARPA
VIA RASORI
VIA GUIDO D'AREZZO
VIA MARIO PAGANO
VIA PALLAVICINO
ALBERTO DA GIUSSANO
VIA TELESIO
VIA L. ARIOSTO
VIA BAZZONI
VIA PONTEBBA
VIA XX SETTEMBRE
VIA SEBETO
VIA ROVANI
VIA V. MONTI
VIA GIOBERTI
VIA G. LEOPARDI
VIA METASTASIO
VIA PIETRO PALEOCAPA
VIA JACINI
VIA MINGHETTI
VIA BELTRAMI
VIA CIOVASSO
VIA DELL'ORSO
VIA PONTE VETERO
VIA BROLETTO
VIA LAURO
VIA CAMPERIO
VIA S. PROSPERO
VIA PORRONE
VIA ARMORARI
VIA MERCANTI
VIA SPADARI
VIA ZECCA VECCHIA
VIA S. MARTA
VIA ARCIMBOLDI
VIA UNIONE
VIA AMEDEI
VIA OLMETTO
VIA PIATTI
VIA CORNAGGIA
VIA DISCIPLINI
VIA DEL DON
VICOLO SANTA MARIA VALLE
VIA STAMPA
VIA MEDICI
VIA TORCHIO
VIA CIRCO
VIA LANZONE
VIA CAMINADELLA
VIA NOVATI
VIA SAN PIO V
VIA NECCHI
VIA SANTA VALERIA
VIA VIGNA
VIA MORIGI
VIA BORROMEI
VIA S. MARIA FULCORINA
VIA SANT'AGNESE
VIA CHIUSA
VIA C. CORRENTI
VIA G.G. MORA
VIA D. FABBRI
VIA E. DE AMICIS
VIA VETTABBIA
VIA C. DEL FANTE
VIA SAN LUCA
VIA AURISPA
VIA PANZERI
VIA ITALIA
VIA VIGONI
VIA SARFATTI
VIALE BLIGNY
V. COSSERIA
VICOLO LAVANDAI
VIA CORSICO
VIA P. PAOLI
VIALE RIPA DI PORTA TICINESE

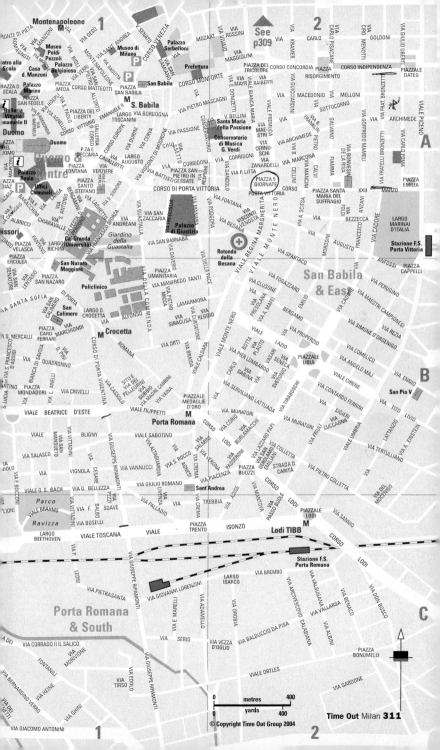

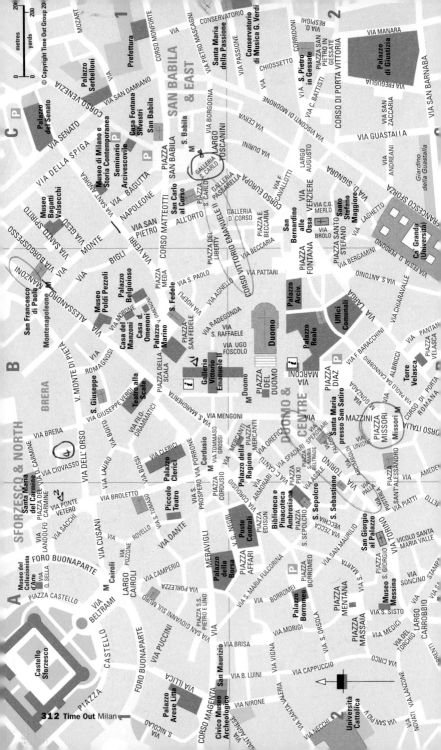

& Max Mara

Street Index

VI Febbraio piazza p308 B1
VIII Novembre 1917 piazza p309 C2
XX Settembre via p308 C1
XXII Marzo corso p311 A2
XXIV Maggio piazza p310 B2
XXV Aprile piazza p308 B2
Abruzzi viale p309 B2
Adamello via p311 C1
Adami via p310 C1
Adda via p309 B1
Adige via p311 BC2
Affari piazza p310 A2/p312 A2
Agnello via p311 A1/p312 B1
Agnesi via p311 B1
Agudio via p308 B1
Aicardo via p310 C2
Albertini via p308 B1
Alberto da Giussano via p308 C1
Albini via p311 C2
Albricci via p311 A1/p312 B2
Alemagna E viale p308 C1/2
Alessandria via p310 B1
Alessi via p310 B2
Alfieri via p308 B2
Altino via p310 A1
Ambrosoli piazza p310 A1
Amedei via p310 A2/p312 B2
Ancona via p308 C2
Andreani via p311 A1/p312 C2
Anelli L via p311 B1
Anfiteatro via p308 C2
Annunciata dell' via p309 C1
Antonini Giacomo via p311 C1
Anzani Francesco via p311 A2
Aosta via p308 A1
Appiani Andrea via p309 B1
Appio Claudio piazza p309 A1
Aprica via p308 A2
Aprile F via p309 B1
Aquileia piazzale p310 A1
Archimede via p311 A2
Arcimboldi via p312 B2
Arco via p308 C2
Arcole piazza p310 B1
Arena via p310 B2
Arese via p309 A1
Argelati via p310 B1
Argentina piazza p309 B2
Ariosto Lodovico via p308 C1
Armorari via p310 A2/p312 B2
Arnolfo da Cambio via p308 B2
Ascari piazza p310 C1
Asole via p312 B2
Asolone M via p308 AB1
Augusto largo p311 A1/p312 C2
Ausonio via p310 B1
Autari via p310 B1
Azario via p310 A1
Bagutta via p309 C1/p312 C1
Balbo Cesare via p311 B1
Baldissera via p309 C2
Balduccio da Pisa via p311 C2
Balestrieri via p308 B2
Bandello Matteo via p310 A1
Baracchini F via p311 A1/p312 B2
Barbarigo via p309 C2
Barbaro viale p308 C2
Barinetti via p308 B1
Barsanti via p308 B1
Bassi Ugo via p308 A2
Bastioni di Porta Nuova p309 B1
Battaglia Natale via p309 A2
Battisti Cesare via p312 C2
Battisti via p311 A1
Beatrice d'Este viale p311 B1

Beauharnais viale p308 C2
Beccaria E piazza p312 C2/p311 A1
Beccaria via p312 C2
Beethoven largo p311 C1
Belfanti piazza p310 C1
Belgirate via p309 A1/2
Bellani via p309 B1
Bellini V via p309 C2
Belotti via p309 C2
Beltrami via p308 C2/p312 A1
Benaco via p311 C2
Bergamini via p311 A1/p312 B2
Bergamo via p311 B2
Bergognone via p310 B1
Bergonzoli via p309 A2
Bernina via p308 A2
Bertani via p308 B1/2
Bertarelli piazza p310 B2
Bertini G via p308 B1
Besana via p311 A2
Bezzecca via p311 A2
Bianca di Savoia via p311 B1
Bianca Maria viale p309 C2
Biancamano piazzale p308 B2
Bibbiena piazza p310 C2
Biffi via p310 A1
Bigli via p309 C1/p312 B1
Biondelli via p310 C2
Bixio Nino via p309 C2
Bligny viale p310 B2/p311 B1
Bobbio via p310 B1
Boccaccio via p308 C1
Bocconi F via p311 BC1
Bodio via p308 A1
Boeri G via p310 C2
Bognetti dei via p311 C1
Boito A via p308 C2/p312 B1
Bonnet via p308 B2
Bonomelli piazza p311 C2
Bordighera via p310 C1
Bordoni via p308 B1
Borgese via p308 A1
Borghetto via p309 C2
Borgogna via p309 C1/p312 C1
Borgonuovo via p309 C2
Borgospesso via p309 C1/p312 BC1
Borromei via p310 A2/p312 A2
Borromeo piazza p310 A2/p312 A2
Borromini via p310 C2
Borsi G via p310 C1/2
Borsieri via p309 A1
Boschetti F via p309 A1
Boselli via p311 C1
Bossi via p308 C2/p312 B1
Bosso via p310 A1
Bracciano via p309 A1
Brahms viale p311 C1
Bramante via p311 B2
Brembo via p311 C2
Brera via p308 C2/p312 B1
Briano via p310 C2
Brianza viale p309 AB2
Brioschi via p310 C2
Brisa via p310 A2/p312 A2
Broggi via p309 B2
Broletto via p308 C2/p312 A1
Brolo via p312 C2
Bronzetti Fratelli via p311 A2
Brunacci via p310 C2
Buenos Aires corso p309 B2
Bugatti via p310 B1
Bullona via p308 B1
Buozzi piazza p311 B2
Byron via p308 BC2
Cadore via p311 B2
Cadorna L piazzale p308 C2
Caduti del Lavoro piazza p310 C2
Cagnola L via p308 B1

Caiazzo piazza p309 B2
Cairoli largo p308 C2/p312 A1
Calabria via p308 A1
Calatafimi via p310 B2
Caldara via p311 B1/2
Calvi Pietro via p311 A2
Calvino Italo via p308 A1
Caminadella via p310 A2
Camoens viale p308 C1
Campanini via p309 B1
Camperio via p308 C2/p312 A1
Campobasso via p308 B1
Camus largo p308 C1
Canonica L via p308 B1/2
Canova via p308 C1
Cantoni G via p310 A1
Cantore A piazzale p310 B1
Cantù Cesare via p312 B2
Cappelli piazza p311 AB2
Cappellini via p309 B1
Cappuccini dei via p309 C1/2
Caprera via p310 A1
Caradosso via p308 C1
Caravaggio via p310 A/B1
Carbonari piazza p309 A1
Carcano Giulio via p310 C2
Cardano via p309 B1
Cardinale Ferrari piazza p311 B1
Cardinale Sforza A via p310 BC2
Carducci G via p308 C2
Carità della strada p311 B2
Carmagnola via p308 AB2
Carmine del piazza p308 C2/p312 A1
Carmine del via p312 B1
Caro Tito Livio piazza p310 B2
Carrara F piazzale p310 C2
Carrobbio largo p310 A2/p312 A2
Carroccio via p310 A1
Cartesio via p309 B1
Casale via p310 B1
Casanova via p309 B1
Casati Felice via p309 B1/2
Cassala viale p310 C1
Cassolo via p311 B1
Castaldi Panfilo via p309 BC1/4
Castel Morrone via p309 C2
Castelbarco via p310 BC2
Castelfidardo via p309 B1
Castello piazza p308 C2/p312 A1
Castelvetro via p308 B1
Castiglioni via p311 C1
Cavalieri del Santo Sepolcro via p308 C2
Cavallotti F via p312 C2/p311 A1
Cavour piazza p309 C1
Cellini B via p311 A2
Cenisio via p308 A1
Cerano via p310 B1
Cernaia via p309 C1
Cernuschi via p311 A2
Cerva via p311 A1/p312 C2
Cervantes viale p308 C2
Cesariano via p308 B2
Chiaravalle via p311 A1/p312 B2
Chiostri dei via p308 C2
Chiusa della via p310 B2
Cimitero Monumentale piazzale p308 B2
Cinque Giornate piazza p311 A2
Ciovasso via p312 B1
Circo via p310 A2/p312 A2
Cirillo D via p308 B1
Clerici via p308 C2/p312 B1

Clusone via p311 B2
Codara via p310 B1
Col di Lana via p310 B2
Col Moschin via p310 B2
Cola di Rienzo via p310 B1
Colombo C corso p310 B1
Comizi di Lione viale p308 BC2
Commenda della via p311 B1
Como corso p308 B2
Conca del Naviglio via p310 B2
Conciliazione piazza p308 C1
Concordia corso p309 C2
Confalonieri F via p309 B1
Conservatorio via p311 A1/p312 C1/2
Copernico via p309 A1/2
Cordusio piazza p310 A2/p312 AB1
Cordusio via p310 A2/p312 A2
Corio via p311 B2
Coriolano via p308 A1/2
Cornaggia via p310 B2
Cornalia via p309 B1
Corrado Il Salico via p311 C1
Correnti C via p310 A2
Correnti Cesare via p312 A2
Corridoni via p311 A1/2/p312 C2
Corsico via p310 B1
Cossa via p309 C2
Crespi D via p310 B1
Crispi viale p308 B2
Crivelli via p311 B1
Crocefisso via p310 B2
Crocetta della Largo p311 B1
Cuccagna via p311 B2
Curie via p308 C1
Curiel via p310 C1
Curtatone via p311 B1
Cusani via p308 C2/p312 A1
Cusio via p308 A2
Custodi P via p310 B2
Da Sesto Cesare via p310 B1
D'Adda Carlo via p310 C1
Dal Verme Jacopo via p308 A2
Dandolo via p311 A2
D'Annunzio Gabriele viale p310 B2
Dante via p310 A2/p312 A1
D'Arezzo Guido via p308 C1
Darwin C via p310 C1/2
Dateo piazzale p309 C2
D'Azeglio via p308 B2
De Amicis Edmondo via p310 A2
De Bernardi via p309 C2
De Castillia via p309 B1
De Cristoforis via p309 B1
De Filippi via p309 B/C2
De Grassi G via p310 A1
De Marchi Marco via p309 C1
De Meis piazza p310 A1
De Togni via p310 A1
Del Fante Cosimo via p310 B2
Del Grillo Borromeo via p309 B1
Deledda G via p309 AB2
Della Francesca Piero via p308 B1
Dell'Orso via p312 B1
Diaz piazza p311 A1/p312 B2
Diocleziano piazza p308 A1
Disciplini via p310 B2
Domodossola via p308 B1
Don Bosco via p311 C2
Donegani Largo p309 C1
Donizetti G via p309 C2
Doria Andrea viale p309 B2
Duca d'Aosta piazza p309 B1/2
Dugnani via p310 A1
Duomo del piazza p311 A1/p312 B2

Durini via   p311 A1/p312 C2
Duse piazza   p309 C2
Edison piazza
      p310 A2/p312 A2
Einaudi piazza   p309 B1
Einstein A via   p311 B2
Elvezia viale   p308 B2
Emila piazza   p311 A2
Erbe via   p308 C2
Europa corso p311 A1/p312 C2
Eustachi Bartolomeo via
      p309 BC2
Fabbri D via   p310 B2
Farini C via   p308 B2
Farneti via   p309 B2
Fatebenefratelli via   p309 C1
Fauché B via   p308 B1
Ferdinando di Savoia viale
      p309 B1
Ferrini Contardo via   p311 B2
Ferruccio F via   p308 B1
Festa Del Perdono via
      p312 C2/p311 A1
Filarete via   p308 BC1
Filargo via   p310 C1
Filippetti via   p311 B1
Filodrammatici via
      p308 C2/p312 B1
Filzi Fabio via   p309 B1
Fioravanti via   p308 B2
Fiori Chiari via   p308 C2
Fiori Oscuri via   p309 C1
Fogazzaro via   p311 B2
Fontana piazza
      p311 A1/p312 B2
Fontana via   p311 A2
Fontanili dei via   p311 C1
Foppa Vincenzo via   p310 B1
Forcella via   p310 B1
Formentini via   p308 C2
Foro Bonaparte
      p308 C2/p312 A1
Fortis L via   p309 A1
Foscolo Ugo via   p312 B2
Fratelli Bandiera
      piazza   p309 C2
Freud S piazza   p309 B1
Frignani via   p309 A1
Friuli via   p311 B2
Fumagalli via   p310 B1
Gadda CE largo   p308 B1
Gadio via   p308 C2
Galdino S via   p308 AB1
Galilei G via   p309 B1
Galleria del Corso
      p311 A1/p312 C2
Galleria Passarella p312 C1/2
Galleria S Carlo   p312 C1
Galvani via   p309 B1
Gandino via   p310 C2
Gardone via   p311 C2
Garibaldi corso   p308 BC2
Garigliano via   p309 A1
Gasparo da Salò via   p309 B1
Gemelli largo   p310 A2
Genova corso   p310 B2
Gentilino via   p310 B2
Gerusalemme piazza p308 B1
Gesù via   p309 C1/p312 C1
Gherardini via   p308 B1
Ghini via   p311 C1
Ghisleri via   p310 B1
Giambologna via   p310 C2
Gian Galeazzo viale   p310 B2
Giannone P via   p308 B2
Giardini dei via   p309 C1
Gioberti via   p308 C1
Giordano Bruno via   p308 B2
Giorgone via   p308 B2
Giovanni XXIII piazza p308 C1
Giovenale via   p310 B2
Giovine Italia piazza   p308 C1
Giovio via   p310 A1
Giusti G via   p308 B2
Giustiniano via   p309 C2
Goethe viale   p308 C2
Gola Emilio via   p310 B1/2
Goldoni Carlo via   p309 C2
Gomes via   p309 B2
Gonfalone via   p310 A1

Gonzaga M via
      p311 A1/p312 B2
Gorizia viale   p310 B1/2
Gramsci piazza   p308 B1
Gran San Bernardo via
      p308 A1
Grancini via   p308 C1
Greppi A largo   p308 C2
Grossi Tommaso via p312 B1
Guastalla via p311 A1/p312 C2
Gubbio via   p311 B1
Guerrazzi via   p308 BC1
Guicciardini via   p309 C2
Heine via   p311 C1
Hoepli via p311 A1/p312 B1
Illica via   p310 A2/p312 A1
Imperia via   p310 C1
Indipendenza corso   p309 C2
Isarco largo   p311 C2
Isonzo viale   p311 C1/2
Italia corso p310 AB2/p312 B2
Jacopo dal Verme via p308 A2
Jan Giorgio via   p309 B2
La Foppa largo   p308 B2
Laghetto via p311 A1/p312 C2
Lagosta piazzale   p309 A1
Lagrange via   p310 B2
Lambro via   p309 C2
Lancetti via   p308 A2
Lanciano via   p309 A1
Landolfo via p308 C2/p312 A1
Lanino via   p310 B1
Lanza G via   p308 C2
Lanzone via p310 A2/p312 A2
Larga via p311 A1/p312 B2
Lario via   p309 A1
Lattanzio via   p311 B2
Lauro via   p308 C2/p312 B1
Lavandai vicolo   p310 B1/2
Lazio viale   p311 B2
Lazzaretto via   p309 B1
Lazzaroni via   p309 B1
Lecce via   p310 C2
Lecchi via   p310 A2
Lecco via   p309 B2
Lega Lombarda piazza p308 B2
Legione Lombarda via p308 C2
Leone XIII via   p308 C1
Leoni P via   p311 C1
Leopardi via   p308 C1
Lesa via   p309 A2
Liberazione della via p309 B1
Liberty del piazza
      p309 C1/p312 BC1
Liguria viale   p310 C1
Lima piazza   p309 B2
Lipari via   p310 A1
Litta P via   p311 A2
Lodi corso   p311 B1/2
Lodi piazzale   p311 C2
Lombardini via   p310 BC1
Lope de la Vega via   p310 C1
Lorenzini Giovanni via p311 C1
Loreto piazzale   p309 B2
Lugano piazzale   p308 A1
Luigi di Savoia piazza p309 B1
Luini Bernardino via   p312 A2
Luini via   p310 A2
Lunigiana viale   p309 A1/2
Lusardi via   p310 B2
Macchi Mauro via p309 A/B2
Macchiavelli N via   p308 C1
Maciachini piazzale   p308 A2
Maestri Campioneni via
      p311 B2
Maestri via   p311 A2
Maffei A via   p311 B2
Magenta corso
      p308 C1/2/p312 A1
Maggi CM via   p308 B2
Maggi piazza   p310 C1
Mahler largo   p310 B2
Maiocchi Achille via p309 C2
Maj Angelo via   p311 B2
Majno Luigi viale   p309 C2
Malpighi via   p309 C2
Malta viale   p308 C2
Mameli Goffredo via p311 A2
Manara via p311 A1/p312 C2
Mancini via   p311 A2

Manfredini via   p308 B1
Manin via   p309 C1
Mantegna via   p308 B1
Mantova via   p311 BC2
Manzoni A via
      p309 C1/p312 B1
Marche viale   p309 A1
Marchetti via   p310 C2
Marco Polo via   p309 B1
Marcona via   p311 A2
Marconi via p311 A1/p312 B2
Marelli E via   p311 C1
Marengo piazza   p308 C2
Maria Adelaide Di
      Savoia piazza   p309 C2
Marinai d'Italia largo p311 A2
Marinella via   p309 A2
Maroncelli via   p308 B2
Marsala via   p308 B2
Martignoni via   p309 A1
Martiri Oscuri via   p309 A2
Mascagni Pietro via
      p309 C1/2/p312 C1
Mascheroni via   p308 C1
Massaia piazza   p312 B1
Massari piazzale   p309 A1
Massena via   p308 B1
Matteotti corso
      p309 C1/p312 BC1
Mazzini via p310 A2/p312 B2
Meda Giuseppe via   p310 C2
Meda piazza p309 C1/p312 B1
Medaglie d'Oro
      piazzale   p311 B1
Medici via   p310 A2/p312 A2
Melchiorre Gioia via
      p309 AB1/2
Melegnano via   p310 B2
Melzi d'Eril via   p308 B1
Melzo via   p309 C2
Menabrea via   p308 A2
Mengoni via
      p310 A2/p312 B1/2
Menotti Ciro via   p309 C2
Mentana piazza
      310 A2/p312 A2
Meravigli via p308 C2/p312 A1
Mercadante via   p309 B2
Mercalli G via   p311 B1
Mercanti piazza   p312 B2
Mercanti via p310 A2/p312 B2
Mercato via   p308 C2
Merlo Carlo Giuseppe via
      p312 C2
Messina via   p308 B1/2
Metastasio via   p308 C1/2
Micca Pietro via   p311 B1
Milazzo via   p308 B2
Mille dei viale   p309 C2
Minghetti Marco via
      p312 A1/p308 C2
Minniti piazza   p309 B1
Mirabello piazza   p309 C1
Missori piazza
      p310 A2/p312 B2
Mocenigo del via   p311 BC2
Modena G via   p309 C2
Molière viale   p308 C2
Molino delle Armi via p310 B2
Moncucco via   p310 C1
Mondadori piazza   p311 B1
Monforte corso
      p309 C1/2/p312 C1
Monte Cristallo via   p309 A1
Monte di Pietà via
      p309 C1/p312 B1
Monte Grappa via   p309 B1
Montenapoleone via
      p309 C1/p312 BC1
Monte Nero viale   p311 AB2
Monte Santo viale   p309 B1
Montebello via   p309 C1
Montepulciano via   p309 B2
Monteverdi via   p309 B2
Montevideo via   p310 B1
Monti Vincenzo via   p308 C1
Monviso via   p308 B1
Mora G via   p310 AB2
Morandi piazzale   p309 C1
Morbegno piazza   p309 A2

Morelli G via   p309 C2
Morgagni GB via   p309 B2
Morone via p311 A1/p312 B1
Morosini Emilio via p311 AB2
Morselli via   p308 B1/2
Mortara via   p310 B1
Moscati via   p308 B1
Moscova della via   p308 B2
Motta via   p310 A1
Mozart via p309 C1/2/p312 C1
Murat via   p309 A1
Muratori via   p311 B2
Muzlo vla   p309 A1
Nava F via   p309 A1
Naviglio Grande Alzaia
      strada   p310 B1
Naviglio Pavese Alzaia
      strada   p310 BC2
Necchi via   p312 A2
Negri Gaetano via p312 A1/2
Negri via   p310 A2
Niccolini GB via   p308 B2
Nievo Ippolito via   p308 C1
Nigra piazzale   p308 A1
Nirone via   p310 A2/p312 A2
Nono L via   p308 AB2
Novati via   p312 A2
Numa Pompilio via   p310 A1
Oberdan piazza   p309 C2
Olivetani degli via   p310 A1
Olmetto via p310 AB2/p312 A2
Olona via   p310 A1
Omenoni via   p312 B1
Orefici via p310 A2/p312 B2
Orobia via   p311 C2
Orseolo via   p310 B1
Orso dell' via   p308 C2
Orti via   p311 B1
Ortles viale   p311 C1
Ottolini via   p310 C2
Pace della via   p311 AB1
Pacioli via   p310 B1
Paganini via   p309 B2
Pagano via   p308 C1
Palazzi L via   p309 B2
Paleocapa Pietro via p308 C2
Palermo via   p308 C2
Palestro via   p309 C1
Palla via   p312 AB2
Palladio via   p311 B1
Pallavicino via   p308 C1
Pancaldo via   p309 BC2
Pancrazi via   p308 B1
Panizza via   p310 A1
Pantano via p311 A1/p312 B2
Panzini via   p308 C1
Paoli A via   p309 B1
Paoli P via   p310 B1
Paolo da Cannobbio via
      p312 B2
Papi Lazzaro via   p311 B2
Papiniano viale   p310 AB1
Parini via   p309 B1
Pasolini via   p308 A2
Passeroni via   p311 B2
Passione via p311 A1/p312 C2
Pastorelli via   p310 C1
Pastrengo via   p308 B2
Pasubio viale   p308 B2
Pavia via   p310 C2
Perego G piazza   p308 A1
Pergolesi via   p309 B2
Perugino via   p311 B2
Peschiera via   p308 B1
Petrarca via   p308 C1
Petrella via   p309 B2
Pezzi via   p311 BC1
Pezzotti Giovanni via p310 C2
Piacenza via   p311 B1/2
Piatti via   p310 A2/p312 A2
Piazzi via   p308A2
Piave viale   p309 C2
Piccinini via   p309 B2
Piceno viale   p311 A2
Pier Lombardo via   p311 B2
Pier Luigi da Palestrina via
      p309 AB2
Piero della Francesca via
      p308 B1
Piermarini via   p308 C1

Pietrasanta via p311 C1
Pini G via p311 B1
Pio XI piazza p312 AB2
Pirelli via p309 B1
Pisacane Carlo via p309 C2
Pisoni via p309 C1
Plauto via p311 B2
Plinio via p309 B2
Poerio via p309 C2
Pola via p309 A1
Poliziano via p308 B1
Pollaiolo via p308 A2
Poma Carlo via p311 A2
Ponchielli Amilcare via p309 B2
Pontaccio via p308 C2
Ponte Seveso via p309 A2
Ponte Vetero via p309 C1/p312 A1
Pontida via p308 B2
Porrone B via p310 A2/p312 B1
Stazione di Porta Genova piazza p310 B1
Porta Nuova Bastioni di p309 B1
Porta Nuova di corso p309 BC1
Porta Romana corso p311 AB1/p312 B2
Porta Ticinese di corso p310 AB2
Porta Ticinese di Ripa p310 B1
Porta Venezia di Bastioni p309 BC1
Porta Vittoria p311 A1/2/p312 C2
Porta Volta di Bastioni p308 B2
Prati G via p308 B1
Preda via p310 C2
Prina via p308 B1
Principe Amedeo via p309 C1
Principe Eugenio via p308 A1
Procaccini via p308 B1/2
Procida Da via p308 B1
Progresso del via p309 A2
Pucci via p308 B2
Puccini via p308 C2/p312 A1
Puskin viale p308 C2
Pusterla via p312 A2
Quasimodo S piazza p310 A/B2
Quattro Novembre piazza p309 B1
Raiberti via p309 C2
Rasori via p308 C1
Redi via p309 B2
Reggio via p311 B1/2
Regina Giovanna viale p309 C2
Regina Margherita viale p311 AB2
Repubblica Cisalpina viale p308 C2
Repubblica della piazza p309 B1
Resistenza Partigiana piazza p310 AB2
Respighi O via p311 A1/2/p312 C2
Ressi via p309 A2
Revere via p308 C1
Ricasoli via p308 B2
Richini largo p311 A1/p312 B2
Ripamonti Giuseppe via p311 BC1
Risorgimento piazza p309 C2
Ristori via p309 C2
Rivoli via p 308 C2
Romano Giulio via p311 B1
Romolo viale p310 C1
Rosario del piazza p310 B1
Rosellini I via p309 A1
Rosmini via p308 B2
Rossetti via p308 C1
Rossini via p309 C2
Rosso M via p308 A2
Rotondi via p308 C1
Rovani via p308 C1
Rovello via p308 C2/p312 A1
Ruffini via p308 C1
SS Pietro e Lino piazza p312 A1

Sabatelli via p308 B1
Sabaudia via p309 B2
Sabbatini via p310 B2
Sabina via p311 B2
Sabotino viale p311 B1
Sacchi via p312 A1/p308 C2
Saffi A via p310 A1
Salvini via p309 C1/2
Sammartini GB via p309 A2
San Babila piazza p309 C1/p312 C1
San Barnaba via p311 A1/p312 C2
San Calimero via p311 B1
San Carlo piazza p312 C1
San Dalmazio via p308 C2
San Damiano via p312 C1
San Fedele piazza p310 A2/p312 B1
San Francesco d'Assisi via p311 B1
San Gioachino piazza p309 B1
San Giorgio piazza p310 A2/p312 A2
San Giovanni di Dio via p310 A1
San Giovanni sul Muro via p308 C2/p312 A1
San Gottardo corso p310 B2
San Gregorio via p309 B2
San Luca via p310 B2
San Mansueto via p311 B1
San Marco piazza p308 C2
San Marco via p308 BC2
San Martino via p311 B1
San Maurilio via p312 A2
San Michele del Carso viale p310 A1
San Nazaro piazza p311 B1
San Nicolao via p308 C2/p312 A1
San Paolo via p309 C1/p312 B1
San Pietro all'Orto via p309 C1/p312 C1
San Pietro In Gessate piazza p312 C2
San Pietro In Gessate via p311 A1
San Pio V via p310 A2/p312 A2
San Prospero via p312 A2
San Raffaele via p311 A1/p312 B1/2
San Rocco via p311 B1
San Sepolcro piazza p310 A2/p312 A2
San Simpliciano via p308 C2
San Tomaso via p312 A1
San Vincenzo via p310 B1/2
San Vittore piazza/via p310 A1
Sangiorgio via p308 C1
Sannio via p311 C2
Sant'Agnese via p310 A2/p312 A2
Sant'Agostino piazza p310 B1
Sant'Alessandro piazza p310 A2/p312 AB2
Sant'Ambrogio piazza p310 A2
Sant'Andrea via p309/C1/p312 C1
Sant'Angelo piazza p309 BC1
Sant'Antonio via p311 A1/p312 B2
Sant'Eustorgio piazza p310 B2
Sant'Orsola via p310 A2/p312 A2
Santa Croce via p310 B2
Santa Eufemia piazza p310 B2
Santa Giovanna d'Arco via p309 B2
Santa Lucia via p311 B1
Santa Margherita via p310 A2/p312 B1
Santa Maria alla Fontana via p308 A2
Santa Maria Beltrade piazza p312 B2
Santa Maria del Suffragio piazza p311 A2

Santa Maria delle Grazie piazza p308 C1
Santa Maria Valle vicolo p310 A2/p312 A2
Santa Marta via p310 A2/p312 A2
Santa Radegonda via p311 A1/p312 B1/2
Santa Sofia via p311 B1
Santa Valeria via p310 A2/p312 A2
Santander via p310 C1
Santissima Trinità piazza p308 B2
Santo Spirito via p309 C1/p312 BC1
Santo Stefano piazza p311 A1/p312 C2
Saronno via p308 B1
Sarpi Paolo via p308 B1/2
Sauro Nazario via p309 A1
Savona via p310 B1
Savonarola via p308 B1
Scala della piazza p311 A1/p312 B1
Scaldasole via p310 B2
Scarlatti Domenico via p309 B2
Scarpa via p308 C1
Schiapparelli via p309 A2
Schuster largo p312 B2
Scipioni degli via p309 C2
Secchi via p309 B2
Segantini Giovani via p310 C1
Segrino piazza p309 A1
Sella Q via p308 C2/p312 A1
Sempione corso p308 B1
Sempione piazza p308 B2
Senato via p309 C1/p312 C1
Seneca via p311 B2
Serbelloni via p309 C1
Serio via p311 C1
Settembrini Luigi via p309 B2
Sforza Francesco via p311 A1/p312 C2
Signorelli via p308 B1
Simone d'Orsenigo via p311 B2
Simonetta via p310 B2
Siracusa via p311 B1
Solari Andrea via p310 B1
Soldati G via p308 B1
Solferino via p308 BC2
Sondrio via p309 A1
Soresina via p310 A1
Sottocorno via p309 C2
Spadari via p310 A2/p312 B2
Spalato via p309 A1
Spallanzani via p309 B2
Spaventa via p310 C2
Speronari via p312 B2
Spezia La via p310 C1
Spiga della via p309 C1/p312 C1
Spluga via p308 C1
Spontini via p309 B2
Spotorno piazza p308 A2
Stampa via p310 A2/p312 A2
Statuto via p308 BC2
Stelvio via p308 A2
Stendhal via p310 B1
Stoppani A via p309 C2
Stradella via p309 B2
Stradivari via p309 B2
Stresa via p309 A1/2
Sturzo Luigi via p309 B1
Tabacchi via p310 C2
Tadino Alessandro via p309 B2
Tamagno via p309 B2
Tamburini via p308 C1
Tarchetti via p309 B1
Tarra via p309 AB1
Tartaglia via p308 B1
Tasso T via p308 C1
Tazzoli via p308 B2
Teglio via p308 A2
Tenca via p308 A1
Tertulliano via p311 B2
Thon di Revel via p309 A1
Tibaldi viale p310 C1

Tiraboschi via p311 B2
Tito Livio via p311 B2
Tito Speri via p308 B2
Tivoli via p308 C2
Toce via p308 A2
Tocqueville via p308 B2
Tommaseo piazza p308 C1
Tommaso da Cazzaniga via p308 B2
Tonale via p309 A1/2
Toniolo via p311 B1
Tonoli via p308 C1
Torchio del via p312 A2
Torelli via p308 A1
Torino via p310 A2/p312 A2
Torre Carlo via p310 C1
Torriani Mapo via p309 B2
Torricelli via p310 C2
Tortona via p310 B1
Toscana viale p311 C1
Toscanini largo p311 A1/p312 C1
Tosi via p310 C1
Toti E via p308 C1
Trebbia via p311 C1/2
Trento piazza p311 C1
Treves largo p308 C2
Tricolore del piazza p309 C2
Trincea delle Frasche via p310 B2
Troilo via p310 C2
Tunisia viale p309 B1/2
Turati F via p309 BC1
Uberti Giulio via p309 C2
Uguccione da Pisa via p308 C1
Umbria viale p311 B2
Unione via p312 B2
Valenza via p310 B1
Valparaiso via p310 B1
Valsugana via p311 C2
Valtellina via p308 A2
Vannucci via p311 B1
Varese via p308 B2
Vasari via p311 B2
Velasca piazza p311 A1/p312 B2
Venezia corso p309 C1/p312 C1
Ventimiglia via p310 B1
Vercelli corso p308 C1
Verdi G via p309 C1/p312 B1
Verga A via p310 A1
Verga G via p308 B2
Verona via p311 B1/2
Verri via p309 C1/p312 C1
Verro Bernardino via p311 C1
Verziere via p311 A1/p312 C2
Vespucci via p309 B1
Vetere via p310 B2
Vetra della piazza p310 B2
Vezza d'Oglio via p311 C2
Vico Gianbattista via p310 A1
Viganò via p309 B1
Vigna via p310 A2/p312 A2
Vignola via p311 B1
Villoresi E via p310 BC1
Virgilio piazza p308 C1
Visconti di Modrone via p311 A1/p312 C2
Visconti Venosta via p311 A2
Visconti via p308 C2
Vitali via p309 C2
Vitruvio via p309 B2
Vittor Pisani via p309 B1
Vittorio Emanuele II corso p311 A1/p312 BC1/2
Vittorio Veneto viale p309 BC1/2
Vivaio via p309 C2
Viviani via p309 B1
Voghera via p310 B1
Volta A via p308 B2
Zambeletti via p309 BC2
Zanardelli via p311 A2
Zara viale p309 A1
Zecca Vecchia via p310 A2/p312 A2
Zuccoli via p309 A2
Zuretti G via p309 A2

Rete metropolitana e tratte ferroviarie urbane / Underground network and urban railway system

AGGIORNAMENTO: APRILE 2004
UPDATE: APRIL 2004

LEGENDA / LEGEND

METROPOLITANA LINEA 1
UNDERGROUND LINE 1

METROPOLITANA LINEA 2
UNDERGROUND LINE 2

METROPOLITANA LINEA 3
UNDERGROUND LINE 3

TRATTA IN COSTRUZIONE
TRACK SECTION UNDER CONSTRUCTION

COLLEGAMENTO CON OSPEDALE S. RAFFAELE
CONNECTION WITH S. RAFFAELE HOSPITAL

PASSANTE FERROVIARIO MILANESE
URBAN RAILWAY

TRATTA IN COSTRUZIONE
TRACK SECTION UNDER CONSTRUCTION

TRATTE FERROVIARIE URBANE
URBAN RAILWAY LINES

RETE FERROVIARIA REGIONALE
REGIONAL RAILWAY SYSTEM

COLLEGAMENTO FERROVIARIO CON MALPENSA
RAIL CONNECTION TO MALPENSA AIRPORT

COLLEGAMENTO AUTOMOBILISTICO CON MALPENSA, LINATE, ORIO AL SERIO
BUS INTERCONNECTION WITH MALPENSA, LINATE, ORIO AL SERIO AIRPORTS

AUTOBUS 73 PER LINATE
BUS 73 TO LINATE AIRPORT

INTERSCAMBIO CON RETE FERROVIARIA
INTERCONNECTION WITH RAILWAY SYSTEM

CAPOLINEA BUS EXTRAURBANI
INTERURBAN BUS TERMINAL

PARCHEGGIO ATM DI CORRISPONDENZA
ATM INTERCHANGE PARKINGS

OSPEDALE
HOSPITAL

LIMITE TARIFFA URBANA
URBAN FARE LIMIT

ATM POINT: INFORMAZIONI E ABBONAMENTI ATM
ATM POINT: INFORMATIONS AND ATM SUBSCRIPTIONS

GESSATE
CASCINA ANTONIETTA
GORGONZOLA
VILLA POMPEA
BUSSERO
CASSINA DE PECCHI
VILLA FIORITA
CERNUSCO S.N.
CASSINA BURRONA
VIMODRONE
OSPEDALE S. RAFFAELE
CRESCENZAGO
CIMIANO
UDINE
LAMBRATE FS

COLOGNO NORD
COLOGNO CENTRO
COLOGNO SUD
GOBBA

TREVIGLIO
BERGAMO
BRESCIA
VENEZIA
CREMONA
MANTOVA

LECCO
COMO
SONDRIO
CARNATE
SEREGNO
SESTO 1° MAGGIO FS
SESTO RONDÒ
SESTO MARELLI
VILLA SAN GIOVANNI
PRECOTTO
GORLA
TURRO

ROVERETO
PASTEUR
LORETO
PIOLA
LIMA
CAIAZZO
P.TA VENEZIA
REPUBBLICA
GIOIA
TURATI
PALESTRO
S. BABILA
DUOMO
DATEO
P.TA VITTORIA
P.TA VENEZIA

LODI
PIACENZA
BOLOGNA

S. DONATO
ROGOREDO FS
ROGOREDO
PORTO DI MARE

PAVIA
GENOVA

CORVETTO
BRENTA
LODI TIBB
P.TA ROMANA
CROCETTA
MISSORI
CORDUSIO
CAIROLI
S. AMBROGIO
S. AGOSTINO
P.TA GENOVA FS
ROMOLO
FAMAGOSTA
ABBIATEGRASSO

MACIACHINI
ZARA
CENTRALE FS
LANZA
P.TA GARIBALDI FS
MONTENAPOLEONE
MOSCOVA
Piccolo Teatro
Brera
CADORNA FNM
Triennale

S. CRISTOFORO FS

ALESSANDRIA
MORTARA

SEVESO

ASSO
SEVESO

SARONNO

VARESE
LAVENO
COMO
NOVARA
SARONNO
MALPENSA
QUARTO OGGIARO FNM

AFFORI FNM
BRUZZANO FNM
GRECO FS
BOVISA FNM
VILLAPIZZONE FS

DOMODOSSOLA FNM
CONCILIAZIONE
PAGANO
BUONARROTI
WAGNER
DE ANGELI
GAMBARA
BANDE NERE
PRIMATICCIO
INGANNI
BISCEGLIE

CERTOSA FS

RHO

DOMODOSSOLA
GALLARATE

TORINO
NOVARA

NOVARA

GALLARATE

RHO Fiera
MOLINO DORINO
S. LEONARDO
BONOLA
URUGUAY
LAMPUGNANO
LOTTO Fiera 2
QT8
AMENDOLA Fiera
QT8

Limite tariffa urbana

ATM

316 Time Out Milan